Methodology in TESOL

A Book of Readings

Michael H. Long
Jack C. Richards
EDITORS

University of Hawaii at Manoa

HEINLE & HEINLE PUBLISHERS

A Division of Wadsworth, Inc.
Boston, Massachusetts 02116

Text Design Adaptation and Cover Design: Sally Carson
Text Art: Carol Ann Gaffney
Production: Kewal K. Sharma
Compositor: ComCom Division of Haddon Craftsmen, Inc.
Printer and Binder: R. R. Donnelley & Sons Company

Methodology in TESOL: A Book of Readings

Library of Congress Cataloging in Publication Data

Methodology in TESOL.

Includes index.

1. English language—Study and teaching—Foreign speakers.   I. Long, Michael H. II. Richards, Jack C.
PE1128.A2M47   1987   428.6′4   86-25004

Printed in the U.S.A.
63 23687
ISBN 0-8384-2695-6

First printing: April 1987
10

Contents

94056

Preface

Teaching English to speakers of other languages, whether in a second or foreign language context, has become one of the major growth industries of the twentieth century. English is spoken natively by millions of the world's inhabitants and as an additional language by millions more.

The dramatic rise in the numbers of would-be users of English has meant an increased need for teachers of English and for specialized teacher education courses. Much of this training takes place at the graduate level in programs leading to a diploma or certificate in teaching English as a second or foreign language, applied linguistics or linguistics, and language teaching. It is for the introductory teaching methodology course in such programs that this book is intended.

The aim of the book is to make accessible in one place a selection of representative papers on the topics usually covered in basic methodology courses. All of the papers have appeared before, although a few have been updated or slightly amended for this volume. They were written by a wide range of authors working in different parts of the world at different levels: some in ESL settings and some in EFL, some with adults and some with children. Although we have used all of the papers in our own methodology course in the MA in ESL program at the University of Hawaii, we know that several of the articles are not as well known as we think they should be, usually because they first appeared in journals with regional rather than international circulation.

The articles represent a variety of viewpoints on central topics in the teaching of English. We have chosen for each section papers which, taken together, review broad issues and deal with practical pedagogical matters. The reader will be informed of important differences in opinion and alternative options throughout the volume in three ways. First, we have provided brief introductory notes for each section that give an overview of the issues and practices. Second, we have included a set of discussion questions on each topic, some of which are designed to raise issues or viewpoints other than those presented by the authors. And third, we have provided some suggestions for further reading on each topic. These last references, together with those in the articles themselves, will give readers a strong foundation to pursue in greater depth some of the topics introduced here.

Michael H. Long
Jack C. Richards

Acknowledgments

The editors and publisher are grateful to the authors and copyright holders of the following articles for permission to reprint the articles included here.

Judd, Elliot L. 1981. Language policy, curriculum development, and TESOL instruction: A search for compatibility. *TESOL Quarterly* 15, 1:59–66.

Strevens, Peter D. 1978. The Nature of Language Teaching. In Jack C. Richards (ed.), *Understanding Second and Foreign Language Learning.* Rowley, MA: Newbury House Publishers, pp. 179–203.

Krashen, Stephen D. 1983. Applications of psycholinguistic research to the classroom. In Charles J. James (ed.), *Practical Applications of Research in Foreign Language Teaching.* Skokie, Ill.: National Textbook Co., pp. 51–66.

Taylor, Barry P. 1983. Teaching ESL: Incorporating a communicative, student-centered component. *TESOL Quarterly* 17, 1:69–89.

Swain, Merrill. 1979. Bilingual education: Research and its implications. In Carlos Yorio, Kyle Perkins, and Jacqueline Schacter (eds.), Washington D.C. *On TESOL '79.* pp. 23–33.

van Ek, J. A. 1975. *The Threshold Level.* Strasbourg: Council of Europe, pp. 103–115.

Chamot, Anna Uhl. 1983. Toward a functional ESL curriculum in the elementary school. *TESOL Quarterly* 17, 3:459–471.

Widdowson, H. G. 1981. ESP: Criteria for course design. In *English for Academic and Technical Purposes: Studies in Honor of Louis Trimble.* Rowley, MA: Newbury House Publishers, pp. 1–11.

Phillips, M. K., and C. C. Shettlesworth. 1978. How to arm your students: A consideration of two approaches to providing materials for ESP. In ELT Documents, *English for Specific Purposes.* London: British Council Teaching Info. Centre, pp. 23–35.

Richards, Jack C., and Ted Rodgers. 1982. Method: Approach, design, and procedure. *TESOL Quarterly* 16, 2:153–168.

Crawford-Lange, Linda M. 1982. Curricular alternatives for second language learning. In Theodore V. Higgs (ed.), *Curriculum, Competence, and the Foreign Language Teacher.* Skokie, Ill.: National Textbook Co., pp. 81–113.

Richards, Jack C. 1983. Listening comprehension: Approach, design, procedure. *TESOL Quarterly* 17, 2:219–239.

Porter, Don, and Jon Roberts. 1981. Authentic listening activities. *ELT Journal* 36, 1:37–47.

Carruthers, Rod. 1983. Teaching pronunciation. Reprinted from TESL TALK, Vol. 14, Nos. 1 & 2 (Winter/Spring 1983) with permission of the Ministry of Citizenship and Culture, Ontario, Canada.

Bassano, Sharron Kay, and Mary Ann Christison. 1981. Developing successful conversation groups. *CATESOL Occasional Papers.*

Scarcella, Robin C. 1978. Socio-drama for social interaction. *TESOL Quarterly* 12, 1:41–46.

Carrell, Patricia L., and Joan C. Eisterhold. 1983. Schema theory and ESL reading pedagogy. *TESOL Quarterly* 17, 4:553–573.

Clarke, Mark A., and Sandra Silberstein. 1977. Toward a realization of psycholinguistic principles in the ESL reading class. *Lang Learning* 27, 1:48–65.

Mackay, Ronald. 1974. Teaching the information-gathering skills. *RELC Journal* 4, 2:79–90.

White, Ronald V. 1981. Approaches to writing. *Guidelines* 6:1–11.

Zamel, Vivian. 1982. Writing: The process of discovering meaning. *TESOL Quarterly* 16, 2:195–209.

Eisenstein, Miriam R. 1980. Grammatical explanations in ESL: Teach the student, not the method. *TESL Talk* 11, 4:3–13.

Richards, Jack C. 1979. Introducing the perfect: An exercise in pedagogic grammar. *TESOL Quarterly* 13, 4:495–499.

White, Ronald V. 1978. Teaching the passive. *ELT Journal* XXXII, 3:188–194.

Fox, Len. 1979. On acquiring an adequate second language vocabulary. *Journal of Basic Writing* 2, 3:68–75.

Honeyfield, John G. 1977. Word frequency and the importance of context in vocabulary learning. *RELC Journal* 8, 2:35–42.

Kruse, Anna Fisher. 1979. Vocabulary in context. *ELT Journal* XXXIII, 3:207–213.

Gaies, Stephen J. 1983. The investigation of language classroom processes. *TESOL Quarterly* 17, 2:205–217.

Long, Michael H. 1983. Native speaker/non-native speaker conversation in the second language classroom. *On TESOL '82* pp. 207–225.

Hendrickson, J. M. 1978. Error correction in foreign language teaching: Recent theory, research, and practice. *Modern Language Journal* 67, 1:41–55.

Wesche, M. Bingham. 1983. Communicative testing in a second language. *Modern Language Journal* 67, 1:41–55.

Keitges, David J. 1982. Language proficiency interview testing: An overview. *JALT Journal* 4:17–45.

Hinofotis, Frances Butler. 1980. Cloze testing: An overview. *CATESOL Occ. Papers* 6:51–55.

THE CONTEXT
OF LANGUAGE
TEACHING

INTRODUCTION

The papers in this section provide an introduction to the scope of language teaching and describe some of the elements that can affect the planning and implementation of a language teaching program. Language teaching takes place in a context which includes societal, educational, instructional, and individual factors. These factors determine the policies and goals that have been established for second and foreign languages at the national level; the delivery system by which these goals are implemented in terms of objectives, syllabuses, and teaching procedures; and the learning outcomes that result from particular methodological options or instructional systems.

Societal factors include the role of English within society and how this affects the need for English in particular kinds of educational and occupational settings. As Judd points out, the range of possible contexts for the teaching of English varies from country to country. This is reflected in the terms that have been proposed to distinguish different settings and circumstances for the use of English, such as English as a Second Language, English as Foreign Language, or English as an International Language. Educational factors include the kinds of objectives that have been established for English teaching programs and the type of curriculum and syllabus that has been developed. Instructional factors include the amount of time devoted to English instruction, the type and quality of instruction, the role and nature of materials and tests, as well as the degree of teaching skill and language proficiency of teachers. Individual factors include learner attitudes, learner motivation, and learning styles.

Both papers in this section stress that language teaching should be viewed from a broad perspective, and that successful language teaching depends on the coordination of many interrelated elements. Strevens discusses these in terms of the

Community, the Language Teaching Profession, Teachers, and Learners, and shows how each can contribute to the success or failure of the language teaching enterprise.

DISCUSSION QUESTIONS

1. How do you use the terms TESL and TEFL? How does the way these terms are customarily used relate to the distinctions Judd makes among English as a Second Language, English as an Additional Language, English as a Language of Wider Communication, and English as a Foreign Language?

2. How are differences between a TESL and a TEFL situation (or among an ESL, EAL, ELWC, and EFL situation) likely to affect (a) goals of English teaching, (b) learner attitudes and motivation, and (c) classroom procedures and methodology?

3. What do you think is the relationship between theoretical disciplines (such as linguistics and psycholinguistics) and language teaching? If, as Strevens suggests, language teaching is an independent field of activity, what kinds of theoretical bases does it draw on?

4. List as many factors as you can that are likely to influence the success of an ESL program. Then rank the factors on your list in terms of importance. What kinds of research might be appropriate to confirm or disconfirm the importance of the factors you ranked highly?

5. Discuss and compare your own experience as a foreign language learner. Examine Strevens' discussion of constraints on the effectiveness of teaching and learning. To what degree is Strevens' discussion confirmed by your own experience?

6. List what you consider to be the essential skills of a language teacher. Then suggest how a teacher might acquire these skills in an applied linguistics or TESL/TEFL teacher training program. What would the ideal curriculum be for such a course, in your opinion?

FURTHER READING

1. J. C. Richards. 1985. The context of language teaching. In J. C. Richards, *The Context of Language Teaching.* New York: Cambridge University Press, 1–15.
2. H. H. Stern. 1983. Talking about language teaching. In H. H. Stern, *Fundamental Concepts of Language Teaching.* Oxford: Oxford University Press, 9–22.
3. G. R. Tucker. 1978. The implementation of language teaching programs. In J. C. Richards (ed.), *Understanding Second and Foreign Language Teaching.* Rowley, MA: Newbury House Publishers, 204–217.

CHAPTER 1

Language Policy, Curriculum Development, and TESOL Instruction: A Search for Compatibility

Elliot L. Judd

This author and several other writers have previously argued that language policy has a direct impact on TESOL instruction and therefore should be considered as a crucial factor in planning ESOL programs (Judd, 1978; Richards, 1978; Tucker, 1977; Kachru, 1976; Noss, 1971; Bowen, 1971). Each of these writers takes a slightly different perspective; yet underlying all of the articles is the basic premise that the socio-political environment in which English language instruction occurs has a direct impact on the shape of ESOL instruction. Failure to consider these socio-political factors can lead to dire consequences for all those involved.

At present English has been shown to be the major world language (Conrad and Fishman, 1977). It is the native language of many throughout the world but for an even greater number English is learned as a second language. Those of us currently concerned with TESOL find ourselves flooded with terminology and acronyms to describe the theory and process of teaching English to non-native English speakers. The two most widely used terms are TESL, the Teaching of English as a Second Language, and TEFL, the Teaching of English as a Foreign Language. More recent terms are TEIL, the Teaching of English as an International Language; TEAL, the Teaching of English as an Auxiliary Language (both used by Richards, 1978); TEIAL, the teaching of English as an International-Auxiliary Language (Smith, 1976); and TELWC, the Teaching of English as a Language of Wider Communication (adapted from Fishman et al., 1977).

As both a researcher and a teacher trainer, I see this plethora of terms as both a blessing and a curse. On the positive side they show that the process of teaching English to non-native speakers is multidimensional and complex. On the negative side my students, colleagues, and I have spent a lot of time ostensibly discussing the heart of the matter only to realize that we had been using either different terms to mean the

3

same thing or the same term to mean different things.

Therefore, one major aim of this paper is to offer a redefinition of terms based on the examination of the socio-political context in which English functions. Once this is accomplished the terminology will be discussed in terms of its practical impact on ESOL curriculum design and instruction.

A CLASSIFICATION OF ENGLISH LANGUAGE USE

Basic Framework

When I was a graduate student the classical terms used were TESL and TEFL. The basic differences between these have to do with the language environment in which the non-native speakers were learning English. In a TESL situation, the dominant environment is English and the non-native speakers are learning the language of the majority of the population. For example, a non-English speaker coming to the United States or Great Britain would be studying ESL or English as a Second Language. On the other hand, a non-native English speaker who studies English in an environment where the dominant population speaks a language other than English is studying EFL or English as a Foreign Language, as in the case of a Costa Rican student learning English in Costa Rica or a Japanese student studying English in Japan.

Several questions arise from this simple dichotomy: Exactly what is a dominant or non-dominant English-speaking environment? For example, if a non-English speaker goes to Montreal, is it an EFL or an ESL situation? One could answer that it must be ESL since Canada is a dominant English-speaking country. However, since the province of Quebec is dominant French-speaking and French is one of the official languages of the country, then studying English there must be EFL. Of course, one could counter this point by noting that in certain neighborhoods in Montreal English dominates, thus rendering it ESL. But other neighborhoods are French dominant and thus we are back to EFL.

The two terms may also be considered ambiguous in certain multilingual countries where English is officially recognized as one of the principal languages. For example, in Nigeria or India are we teaching ESL or EFL? Certainly, English is an official language in both places and dominates in certain socio-linguistic contexts, especially among the educated. Yet despite this official recognition English may only be used by a small minority of the total population and in very limited situations, and for most people English is a foreign language (see Prator, 1968, and Kachru's, 1976 response). The same ESL/EFL debate has occurred with respect to the Commonwealth of Puerto Rico.

A final point of controversy revolves around the term *foreign language* in EFL. Is a foreign language used in an English conversation between:

1. Two non-native English speakers who each speak different primary languages, or
2. Two non-native English speakers who speak the same primary language, or
3. One native and one non-native speaker of English?

Perhaps it includes all of the above situations. The question becomes even more complex when *foreign language* is used by some to mean English conversations between non-native English speakers from different countries and by others to mean English conversations between non-native speakers in the same country.

Because of these difficulties with ESL and EFL, people have resorted to some or all of the other terms mentioned earlier in the paper. Rather than criticizing these terms or proposing completely new ones, which further adds to the confusion, I propose a redefinition of some of the existing terms. The classifications to be presented have in fact already proven useful in both socio-linguistics and TESOL courses that I have taught.

English as a Second Language

An ESL situation can be redefined as a situation in which non-native English speakers spend a vast majority of their time communicating in English. More precisely, the speakers will be using English to express basically all of their ideas and feelings, with the possible exception of intimate conversations with close friends and family. In an ESL context all four skills—listening, speaking, reading, and writing—will be used, and the English language will be employed in a variety of registers ranging from the very informal to the highly formal. Of course, the exact proportion for each of the language skills and registers will vary from person to person and situation to situation, but in an ESL situation nothing can definitely be ruled out. It should also be remembered that the non-native speaker will be communicating primarily with native speakers of English. Here again though, depending on the specific case, there is the possibility that there will be communication with other non-native English speakers in English.

Examples of an ESL situation can be seen in the United States, Great Britain, English-speaking Canada, Australia, and New Zealand. One might also include certain nations like Jamaica, Barbados, or Trinidad if dialect questions are ignored.

English as an Additional Language

An EAL situation can be defined as one in which speakers learn English after they learn another primary language and use it for the purposes of communicating with others who have different primary languages. Such situations are found in countries that are multilingual and recognize English as the language for intra-country communication. EAL corresponds to Richards' description of English for Intergroup Functions (1978), or Smith's English as an Auxiliary Language (1976).

The key difference between EAL and ESL concerns socio-linguistic contexts. Since students already speak a language that fulfills a variety of communicative needs beyond the intimate levels, English is used in more limited ways than in an ESL situation. The registers where English is used tend to be of a much more formal nature and are limited to certain areas such as national governmental affairs, intra-country commerce, and mass media. In addition, the proportion of the population in an EAL context who actually use English is much less than in an ESL situation and those who use it tend to be of a high social, political, and economic level. As in an ESL context, in an EAL situation all four language skills will be employed, although percentages will vary from country to country. The other important socio-linguistic characteristic of many EAL situations is that a localized version of English has probably emerged (Kachru, 1976).

Many of the countries that fall into the EAL category are former British or American territories such as Nigeria, Fiji, Liberia, Botswana, and Ghana, to name a few. Other countries in the EAL category are countries where English is one of several co-official languages such as in French-speaking Canada, Afrikaans-speaking South Africa, India, and Puerto Rico.

English as a Language of Wider Communication

ELWC refers to an environment in which English serves no intra-country uses and instead is used for international communicative purposes (Richards, 1978; Conrad and Fishman, 1977; Smith, 1976; Bowen, 1971). Since English has become the major lingua franca of the world, many people need to use English for scientific, technical, and commercial purposes.

An ELWC situation is characterized by the fact that the register range in English is often quite limited and quite formal and the lexical and topical repertoire is quite narrow. Furthermore, the skills to be mastered are also quite limited. In many ELWC contexts reading is the primary form of English information and face-to-face contact with people who use English in any form is rare. Writing is also limited because the need to encode information in English is much rarer than the need to decode. In an ELWC situation some will need to use oral skills: those people, for instance, who must deal with visiting English-speaking colleagues or those who might occasionally travel to an English-speaking country for business or lecturing. Yet even in these cases the percentage of time spent yearly in oral language use is quite small. In most ELWC cases one or more native languages serve intra-country daily communicative needs and, as in an EAL situation, only a small highly educated elite need and use English. Examples of countries that clearly fall into this category are Japan, Taiwan, Indonesia, Tanzania, and Germany. There are many more.

It should be noted in passing that many countries that are in the EAL situation are moving or have already moved to an ELWC situation, as indigenous languages become more standardized and gain more prestige (Conrad and Fishman, 1977; Rubin and Shuy, 1973; Rubin and Jernudd, 1971; Bowen, 1971; and Fishman, Ferguson, and Das Gupta, 1968).

English as a Foreign Language

The last major category is the EFL context. In these situations English is studied as one of many foreign languages and serves little communicative function for students once they finish the actual course. Communicative use is limited and may focus on literature and high culture. Translation may also be stressed. The use of English for any purpose outside the classroom is minimal and of short duration. At most it might serve, according to J. A. van Ek, "in temporary contacts with foreign language speakers in everyday situations, whether as visitors to the foreign country or with visitors to their own country, and to establish and maintain social contacts" (van Ek, 1976: 24–25). For many even such temporary usage might never occur. Thus, in an EFL situation very few people other than those in the teaching profession use English on a regular, long-term basis. In short, English has no special status or use over any other foreign language.

Some General Comments on the Categories

The four classifications present a continuum of English language use. In terms of both the percentage of time spent using English and the number of registers employed when speaking English, they can be ranked from high to low as follows: ESL, EAL, ELWC, and EFL. As with all typologies, not every country or every educational situation falls neatly into any one of the categories. Some countries may currently be in the process of switching between categories (for example Malaysia) and certain groups of students may need English for two categories: ESL when they study at an American university, and later EAL or ELWC when they return home. Yet despite these weaknesses the four categories offer the ESOL professional some useful perspectives in developing instructional materials and teaching strategies.

APPLICATIONS TO ESOL INSTRUCTION

The four categories have a practical value in the development of ESOL programs which correspond to the realities of English use. Instructional programs that are compatible with the socio-political situations in which they are located are more likely to succeed, while those that are in conflict with the English language policy of a given country run a greater chance of failure (Judd, 1978).

In an English-as-a-Second-Language situation, programs need to stress all four language skills. Students must also be exposed to a variety of registers in English and must develop an ability to interact with a variety of native speakers in a variety of different circumstances. Curricula that stress pattern drills and rote memorization of vocabulary, dialogues, and gramatical paradigms will fail to prepare the students to deal with the realities of the ESL situation. Since greater English use is required of a student in an ESL context, emphasis must be placed on linguistic creativity and innovation and both academic and non-academic topics have to be introduced. In addition, teachers should be native speakers who have a complete understanding of the varieties of roles that English plays in an ESL context.

In an English-as-an-Additional-Language situation, the curricula and methods of ESOL instruction change. Again, all four skills need to be emphasized, but materials can focus on the more formal registers of English with less emphasis on the informal ones. Since English is used on fewer occasions than in an ESL situation, those studying in an EAL context can be introduced to a narrower range of topics and the lexical items chosen can reflect the situational demands which students will encounter. Again, it is still important to stress the need for linguistic creativity, since those in an EAL situation will still be expected to respond to a variety of linguistic situations. The need for native-English-speaking teachers is not imperative in an EAL situation; teachers who are fluent English users are more important. Fluency here is defined as the ability to engage in all communicative functions in which the students themselves will need to function.

In an English-as-a-Language-of-Wider-Communication context, the curriculum can place less emphasis on all four skill areas but instead emphasize reading. Within the reading component formal registers associated with the language of journals, reports, and business correspondences should be studied. It is within the ELWC context that English for Special Purposes (ESP) or English for Science and Technology (EST) find their greatest application because of the narrowness of topics and the limited use of English language registers. A notional-functional approach, such as the one suggested by Findley and Nathan (1980) or Wilkins (1976), might provide a good method of organizing and presenting the English language. If the students need to write, speak, or listen to English in the future, it should be remembered that the amount of time will be of short duration and have very limited focus and register domain in the ELWC context. Materials that assume too wide a focus or emphasize equally all four skills run the risk of not preparing the students for real situations and can cause resentment. The teachers in such ELWC situations need not have the oral proficiency of native speakers but they should have full fluency in the written medium, which obviously allows the recruitment of non-native English speakers. Tapes or other materials which provide native language speech models should suffice for the limited amount of oral work that may be necessary. Another criterion in the selection of instructors for an ELWC program is that they possess some technical knowledge of the subject areas to which the students are being exposed.

In an English as a Foreign Language situation the fluency and registers of English are limited. Therefore, fluency among teachers is less of a prerequisite than in the other three contexts and there is no need to recruit native English speakers. In an EFL program controlled materials such as a classical audiolingual or even a grammar-translation approach may be employed since students will probably have little future need for English. As mentioned earlier, for some students there may be occasions for short-term contacts with English speakers. If such situations were apt to occur, then the notional-functional approach with its "minimal competencies" (see van Ek, 1976, or Findley and Nathan, 1980) may prove quite useful. Such a presentation of language should appeal to students' interest, whether or not they will have any direct contact with English speakers. Whatever teaching method is employed and whatever manner is used to organize materials, topics should be chosen for immediate student interest without the need to focus on long-range, long-term goals.

CONCLUSION

This paper has emphasized the need to consider the role of English in the overall language policy context in any given country. Such knowledge can aid those who are interested in both language policy and the teaching of English to speakers of other languages. Analysis of the role of English around the world makes it easier to reach sound curricular and instructional decisions. By attempting to develop an instructional approach which relates to the various needs for, and uses of, English, all involved in the teaching and learning process are more likely to succeed. Because English language instruction will fit the needs of the students, motivation will be higher. The long-range impact will also be greater because speakers will develop a knowledge of real English for real communication roles. In conclusion, it is crucial that we realize that the role of English varies around the world. No single ESOL curriculum or instructional strategy will suit all circumstances. As G. Richard Tucker says, "Educational or national policy serve to define the parameters within which language problems can be developed" (1977:16), and only through an understanding of the English language policy of a given country can we help devise the proper curricular and teaching approach for the particular educational environment.

REFERENCES

Bowen, J. Donald. 1971. Trends in English abroad. ERIC Document ED 052 651. Paper presented at the Fifth Annual TESOL Convention, New Orleans.

Conrad, Andrew W., and Joshua A. Fishman. 1977. English as a world language: The evidence. In *The Spread of English.* Joshua A. Fishman, Robert L. Cooper and Andrew W. Conrad (eds.). Rowley, MA: Newbury House Publishers.

Findley, Charles A., and Lynn A. Nathan. 1980.

Functional language objectives in a competency based ESL curriculum. *TESOL Quarterly 14,* 2:-221–231.

Fishman, Joshua A., Robert L. Cooper, and Andrew W. Conrad (eds.). 1977. *The Spread of English.* Rowley, MA: Newbury House Publishers.

Fishman, Joshua A., Charles A. Ferguson, and Jyotirindra Das Gupta (eds.). 1968. *Language Problems of Developing Nations.* New York: John Wiley and Son.

Judd, Elliot L. 1978. Language policy and TESOL: Socio-political factors and their influence on the profession. In *On TESOL '78: EFL Policies, Programs, Practices.* Charles H. Blatchford and Jacquelyn Schachter (eds.). Washington, D.C.: TESOL.

Kachru, Braj B. 1976. Models of English for the third world: White man's linguistic burden or language pragmatics? *TESOL Quarterly 10,* 2:221–239.

Noss, Richard B. 1971. Politics and language policy in Southeast Asia. *Language Sciences 16:* 25–32.

Prator, Clifford H. 1968. The British heresy in TESL. In *Language Problems of Developing Nations.* Joshua A. Fishman, Charles A. Ferguson and Jyotirindra Das Gupta (eds.). New York: John Wiley and Son.

Richards, Jack C. 1978. The dynamics of English as an international, foreign, second and auxiliary language. ERIC Document ED 161 269. Paper presented at the Conference on English as an International Auxiliary Language, Honolulu, East-West Center.

Rubin, Joan, and Bjorn H. Jernudd. 1971. *Can Language Be Planned?: Sociolinguistic Theory and Practice for Developing Nations.* Honolulu: University of Hawaii Press.

Rubin, Joan, and Roger W. Shuy. 1973. *Language Planning: Current Issues and Research.* Washington, D.C.: Georgetown University Press.

Smith, Larry E. 1976. English as an international auxiliary language. *RELC Journal 7,* 2: 38–53.

Tucker, G. Richard. 1977. Can a second language be taught? In *On TESOL '77: Teaching and Learning English as a Second Language.* H. Douglas Brown, Carlos A. Yorio, and Ruth H. Crymes (eds.). Washington, D.C.: TESOL.

van Ek, J. A. 1976. *The Threshold Level for Modern Language Learning in Schools.* London: Longman.

Wilkins, D. A. 1976. *Notional Syllabuses.* London: Oxford University Press.

CHAPTER 2

The Nature of Language Teaching

Peter D. Strevens

INTRODUCTION

Acquisition: Learning/Teaching

This paper is concerned with the nature of institutionalized foreign language learning—the process which takes place when a learner sets out to learn a language other than his primary language (mother tongue or native language), given the mediation of a teacher and within a deliberately organized framework of instruction. The rather cumbersome definition used above is necessary in order to distinguish the language learning/teaching process (LL/LT) from "picking up a language" without formal instruction, whether during the acquisition of the primary language or while subsequently achieving some command of a foreign language by informal and unorganized means.[1]

Is Language Teaching Simply Applied Psycholinguistics?

Discussion of the effectiveness of language teaching and of ways to improve the achievement of learners has been inhibited in recent years by two hidden assumptions about the applicability to foreign language learning and teaching of psycholinguistic research into first language acquisition and the unstructured picking up of a foreign language. These assumptions are, first, that psycholinguistic research *is* directly relevant to language teaching, and second, that this research is not only relevant but uniquely so: that it is the *most* relevant research and by implication that no other area of knowledge or understanding—certainly not the rather low-valued craft of teaching—is of significance for language teaching. It is no part of the intention of this paper to criticize or to diminish the importance, in their own field, of the principal findings of language acquisition research. A great deal of valuable understanding has been gained through this research. What this paper will attempt to do, however, is to suggest that the language learning/teaching process is a highly complex set of events in which many elements coexist and interact which have no counterpart in psycholinguistic models of first language acquisition, and that current psycholinguistic theory applies to only a small area of the total field of foreign language learning/teaching. The conclusion will be drawn that perhaps the most relevant and helpful intellectual contribution that can be made to language teaching is the development of models of LL/LT considered *in its own terms.* To rephrase the distinction, first language acquisition and LL/LT belong in different universes of discourse which overlap in only limited ways. To see language teaching as simply applied psycholinguistics is to misunderstand the relationships between a predominantly intellectual activity and a predominantly practical one, and to ignore the immense and subtle complexity of education, methodology, and teaching. Language teaching, too, needs an intellectual basis, but the simple importation of a theory developed in a quite different area does not meet this need.

Can Teaching Affect Learning?

Having stated the stance of this paper to be that the study of the LL/LT process is *sui generis* and not subject to any single external discipline, it is further necessary to state that the basic philosophy of the paper is interventionist, accepting as rational and realistic the proposition that teaching *can* affect learning. There are those who deny this, and who regard the effects of teaching as being either negligible, counterproductive, or uncontrollable; and who in consequence conceive the function of a teacher as being limited to a combination of language informant, attention-getter and pupil-minder. There is indeed a great deal of low-grade language teaching throughout the world, to which these limitations may apply to varying degrees. Many institutionalized programs produce average levels of achievement so low as to invite the criticism that simple contact with speakers of the language might at least do no worse. But the undoubted existence of *inferior* language teaching in no way obscures the existence—equally real, but often overlooked—of *superior* language teaching, in which learners achieve high levels of command of languages in direct re-

sponse to deliberate schemes of learning and teaching.[2]

The Temptation to Oversimplify

If it is the case that psycholinguistic research fosters the belief that certain universal human characteristics of first language acquisition are the sole or principal determinants of success in LL/LT, it is also true that the language-teaching profession has similarly regarded its own practices and activities (usually labeled "method" or "methodology") as the principal determinant. From either standpoint, the argument has seemed to lie between a preference for the one or the other, for the intellectual rigor of psycholinguistics, or the humane art of teaching; and this polarization of views has virtually ignored the possibility not only that *both* these features may be important, but that others too may be crucial. Yet close study shows that the process as a whole is complex, not simple, that a number of elements, of very different kinds, have to be taken into account, and that in some cases a shortcoming in one or more of these elements can be largely compensated by unusual excellence in others.

The Value of Identifying Fundamentals

The purpose of identifying elements of the language learning/teaching process is to provide organizing principles for simplifying our thinking about a highly complex event. The test of whether the elements are well chosen is a pragmatic one: Do they account for everything that happens in language teaching? Can we allocate to some place in the total scheme of elements all those features of learning and teaching languages that have a bearing on the effectiveness of the process? Does the analysis into elements help us to understand why levels of achievement may be higher in one set of circumstances and lower in another? Will it enable us to identify the major impediments to success and to specify what has to be altered in order to bring about major improvements in language learning/teaching achievements? The main section of this paper attempts to offer a contribution toward these aims by considering four principal elements in the language learning/teaching process. These are The Community, The Language Teaching Profession, The Teacher, and The Learner.[3]

The Four Components of the Model

The Community. The organized learning and teaching of languages is essentially social in character. The great majority of teachers are public servants, engaged in the implementation of the public will that tuition in such and such languages shall be made available; they are typically paid by the community, trained at the expense of the community, administered, supported, and brigaded by the mediation of a branch of central or local government. Language teaching, in short, is an integral part of a community's total educational provision.

This much is obvious: Is it not also banal and trivial? It is a major contention of this paper that beneath the surface banality of the way in which a community organizes its education, including (among many other subjects) foreign language teaching, lie a number of hidden but critical choices, influences, exclusions, preferences, or prejudices.

In order to understand the underlying importance of The Community for language learning it is necessary to distinguish two separate elements within this component:

1. The public will
2. Administration and organization

The first of these, the public will, consists of the current consensus at any time that particular languages should be learned within the community; the second, administration and organization, senses the public will and interprets it by allocating funds, training teachers, providing buildings, and so forth. Looked at in different terms, one aspect of the community's contribution to the overall language learning/teaching process is the expression of an intention that particular languages should be learned (and therefore taught); the other is to sanction the entire *system* of learning and teaching which brings the learner and the teacher together and encourages or constrains the learner's achievement.

The public will, then, determines in large part which foreign languages are available to learners. Its influence is usually quiescent: it is noticed principally at times of change. When Malaysia, as an act of policy, deliberately adopts Bahasa Malaysia as its national language, the consequences for the learning and teaching of languages in that country are profound and far-reaching. When the people of Quebec elect a pro-French government and understandably seek to redress the anti-French balance in legislation and administration, the consequences for the learning and teaching of languages in the Province turn out to go far beyond the simple promotion of French and to arouse the hostility not only of the English-speaking minority but also the indigenous Indian and Eskimo population, as well as the large communities of European immigrants, for all of whom future prosperity has been equated with learning English, not French. When the European community considers the principal barriers to easy communication and circulation among its members, the consequences for language teaching go beyond the simple favoring of neighboring European languages in existing schools and extend to deliberate, large-scale schemes of systems development in language learning and teaching (Trim, 1973, 1974; van Ek, 1975).

But equally important as a consequence of the public will is the creation of general levels of expectation, within a community, for the achievement in language learning of its citizens. It is possible to argue that the generally high level of achievement in learning English in Sweden results more from the fulfillment of high public expectations than from a general level of outstandingly good language teaching. (There *are* outstanding teachers, but even in Sweden they are the exception rather than the rule.) People learn English rather well because above all, it can be argued, they take it for granted that they will do so.

Here can be seen at work an interconnection between The Community and The Learner. As we shall see in a later section, the learner's expectations about his own possibilities of achievement form part of the profile of his individuality as a learner, which in turn influences his performance. This feature is frequently lumped together under the catchall heading of *motivation:* the learner's willingness to learn a language, his reasons for giving time and effort to the learning task, his perception of the benefit he will gain from doing so—all these are affected in a fundamental way by the attitudes, prejudices, fashions, and intentions which make up the sociolinguistic situation in the community to which he belongs: i.e., the public will.

The existence of the second subcategory, administration and organization, is a recognition of the fact that language teaching, like the provision for tuition in any other subject, is totally dependent upon a "ministry of education" or its equivalent. Yet this is a double-edged blessing. On the one hand the bureaucratic structure for employing teachers and organizing schools and classes puts education onto a footing of large-scale organization, while the provision of training facilities and the development of a career-long progression of events and stages attracts suitable people to teaching and retains them once they have been inducted. To that extent this element of administration provides the almost indispensable framework of organization within which learners and teachers come into contact with each other. Yet, on the other hand, some aspects of the very system which creates opportunities for learning and teaching may make it difficult or impossible for either learning, teaching, or both, to take place at all—or at least to do so effectively.

Examples of this paradoxical situation are easy to find. They include overcrowded classes, low standards of teacher recruitment, lack of provision of books and materials, the creation of "examination neurosis" under the guise of achievement testing, and many more.

Earlier in this paper we mentioned the existence of inferior as well as superior language learning and teaching. It is unfortunately the case that the differences between the two extremes very often rest on features of administration and organization: in the inferior case, adequate teaching and learning are frustrated by faults in the system; in the superior case, merely adequate teaching and learning are enhanced by a high-quality system.

It seems to be the situation in many parts of the world that the great progress in language-teaching professionalism which has taken place in recent years has not been assimilated into the administrative and organizational framework of general education within which language teaching exists as one "subject" among many.[4] Thus language teaching is offered as if all that the teachers know about carrying it out with maximum effectiveness is what their predecessors knew, 70 or 100 years ago, when the subject was first incorporated into organized education. In other words, there is frequently insufficient interaction between the administrative element of The Community and the next component to which we shall turn, The Language Teaching Profession.

The Language Teaching Profession

The term "profession" is here used in two distinct but complementary ways. First, it relates to those disciplines, in the academic or quasi-academic sense, which contribute to our understanding of the nature of language learning and teaching—i.e., linguistics, psychology, educational theory, social theory, scientific method, principles of educational technology, etc.—and which are "available," so to speak, in broadly similar ways throughout the world by way of universities, research institutes, and similar centers of intellectual activity. But second, the term profession also relates to those principles by which teachers of language organize themselves, select the succeeding generations of their fellows, set entry standards (e.g., of age, personal education, character, etc.), insist upon special training for entrants to the profession, support their colleagues throughout their careers, study continually to raise the level of effectiveness of that which they do, and above all, maintain the ethic of social responsibility and devotion to the interests of their pupils (Strevens, 1978).

It is essential to realize that we are discussing a profession—an *industry* might almost be a more appropriate term—of truly immense size. Millions of language teachers teach scores of millions of language learners, distributed the world over. Within this occupational community of some millions of teachers there exists a large subset comprising those who are responsible for standards of teacher training, for awareness of relevant developments in other disciplines and other places, for the promotion of research, for the continued drive toward greater effectiveness—in short, for the intellectual basis and the evolutionary drive of the profession.

Of course, all members of this subset are not located in one place or one country. They are found spread among the staff of many training colleges, university departments, research centers and specialized institutes, in many countries. They have their own networks of information, cross-fertilization, visits, exchanges, publications, etc. Their function, essentially, is to mediate between the contributory disciplines on the one hand, and the practical tasks and problems of the language teaching classroom on the other.

Two observations are required here: in the first place, the contributory disciplines, necessary though they are for the profession in its broadest sense, do not in themselves provide a sufficient basis for ensuring the effective learning and teaching of languages. It is perfectly possible for an individual teacher to be exceptionally successful in encouraging optimum learning in his or her pupils without ever having heard of linguistics or even psychology, let alone having studied these subjects. For the learner, an awareness of the disciplines is even less directly relevant to his progress in learning a foreign language. What *is* essential, however, is that the profession as a whole should possess, distributed in an appropriate way through its various levels, a sufficient number of members with interest in and understanding of the *why* of their profession, not just the *what* and *how*.

The second observation is that there is a distinction to be made between *professionalism* and *instructional techniques*. Of course techniques are a part of being professional, but they are not the whole of it. It is possible to discern three different stages of language teaching activity (Strevens, 1978). The first is that of the *instructor,* who is able to manipulate the techniques of language instruction, who knows the coursebooks and materials in use for his particular pupils, and who presents the foreign language material with adequate competence to his or her students. The second is that of the *teacher,* who is a good instructor and more. The good teacher cherishes his pupils, knows them, understands their individuality as learners, recognizes their learning preferences and their difficulties, and sees their language learning progress on a timescale greater than simply that of the class, the week, the semester, or the year. The third is that of the *educator,* who is a good teacher, but whose perspective is wider, who thinks of the students in relation to the whole of their needs for tuition and training, and who is aware of the interrelations between the techniques of language teaching, the contributory disciplines, and the needs of society.

It is a feature of the tremendous rise in professionalism in the past 15 years that language teaching now provides suitable training and encouragement for all its members to become competent as instructors, for the majority to become competent and caring as teachers, and for a sufficient proportion to become language educators, capable of maintaining and extending the intellectual basis and the practical effectiveness of language teaching, and of meeting new needs for language learning with innovative, appropriate, principled, acceptable, and successful responses.

The Teacher

Each of the two main components already touched upon, The Community and The Profession, are reductions from great complexity to a single mnemonic label. So it is, too, with The Teacher. It is here that nearly all aspects of teaching, as a deliberate activity, will be included, so that under the heading "The Teacher" it becomes necessary to consider at least the following elements:

1. the teacher
   minimum qualities of a teacher
   teacher training (see also 2.)
   upkeep of command of the foreign language and upgrading of professionalism
2. teacher training
   criteria for selection
   components of *skills, information, theory*
   initial training, further training, "higher echelon" training (including applied linguistics)

3. teaching
   approach: particular philosophies or ideologies or myths of language-learning/teaching
   methodology: the full range of techniques for promoting effective learning
   syllabus design: principles for deciding what to teach, in which sequence, and how organized
   materials production: principles for creating suitable ancillaries
   testing
   selection of teaching type
4. constraints on teaching/learning effectiveness
   physical impediments: fatigue, extremes of temperature, overcrowding, distraction
   organizational impediments: insufficient total time for instruction, too much time, insufficient intensity, lack of premises, materials, and staff, absenteeism
   psychological impediments: negative social attitudes, examination neuroses, intimidating teacher-pupil relationships

It will be obvious that this component of our analysis is extremely complex, and each of the four elements within it merits a chapter—indeed, a book—to itself.[5] Here we shall confine ourselves to a brief explanatory comment on each element of the component labeled The Teacher, which incorporates not only the characteristics of the teacher but also the training and preparation for the task, the whole gamut of instructional procedures, and those features which diminish the effectiveness of learning and teaching.

The Teacher. Again we must notice an ambiguity. In the widest sense, the teacher is the human agency responsible for presenting foreign language material to a learner. He or she may be either physically present (as in the conventional case of a teacher working with a class or group), or, in the case of self-study courses, embodied within the handbook and possibly in accompanying recordings, or, in computer-assisted instruction, known to the learner only through instructions he receives as to his optimum learning procedures. Many other manifestations of the teacher are possible in this metaphorical use of the term, referring to the progenitor and/or presenter of learning material. The other sense of the word "teacher" is the technical and professional one which distinguishes between individuals whose capabilities merit the label and those who do not. In this sense, a teacher is identified by the possession of certain characteristics which affect his ability to perform as a language teacher.

Cutting through the great range of possible specialized abilities, an absolute minimum statement of the requirements of an adequate language teacher might be the following (see also Perren, 1968, and Strevens, 1974, 1977b):

a nondiscouraging personality

adequate classroom command of the language being taught

adequate presentational skills as a teacher

In addition to these minimum requirements for any given individual teacher, the sound continuation of the profession requires that the majority of teachers should also possess and display dedication to learning in general and to language learning in particular. This entails two parallel and continuous lines of concern: first, a high degree of awareness of the learners as individuals, of their progress and difficulties, and of the best means at any time of promoting their continued learning; and second, a high degree of self-awareness as a teacher, including conscious efforts to improve his or her command of the foreign language (or at the very least, taking steps to counter the gradual attrition in one's foreign language ability that normally occurs with the passage of time), and seeking always to extend and improve the grasp and understand-

ing of the profession by keeping in touch with changing ideas and techniques.

Teacher Training. Teachers being, by definition, among the educated rather than the uneducated members of society, the selection and training of language teachers necessarily includes attention to the individual teacher's personal education, as well as his or her professional training, and ideally should include a measure of temperamental suitability and of a sense of vocation, difficult though these criteria are to identify.

The vocational and professional aspects of teacher training must depend for the detail of their design upon who the trainees are and in what circumstances they will be employed. But a few general principles can be adduced. First, there is a difference in kind between *initial training,* in which the aspirant is first introduced to the nature of the profession, and all *further training.*

Second, within initial training there are two main streams of content: (1) general training as a teacher, irrespective of any particular subject specialty, and (2) special training as a teacher of a specified foreign language. These are usually combined in a single multifaceted course, but both are normally present.

Third, initial training will deal with an appropriate mixture—appropriate, that is, to the prior education of the trainee, the level and type of educational establishment the trainee expects to be employed in, the duration and intensity of the training course, and the available competencies within the training staff—of the three basic components of vocational training: a component of *practical skills,* a component of relevant *information,* and a component of *principle and theory.* Achieving the best mixture in a given training institution is a difficult task. But the difficulty generally centers around the ratio of *skills* to *theory.* Too little theory, and a teaching force is created which can perform well in the classroom but lacks the understanding to change with the times and to cope with new conditions. Too much theory, and the teaching force may become separated from the practical demands of the learners, or prove to follow pseudointellectual fashions.

A fourth general principle of teacher training provides a possible solution to the difficulty of getting the mixture right: ideally, all teachers should receive the chance of *further* training, either in the form of "in-service" training, or by being withdrawn from teaching in order to be given additional full-time training, not just once but at suitable intervals throughout their careers. If such opportunities are available, additional training in principle and theory can be provided for those whose professional work especially requires it, and for those whose personal abilities can best assimilate and utilize it, while at the same time *all* teachers can keep up with new ideas, share their experience, consider the future, and in general give a professional dynamism to language teaching.

It is interesting to observe that in recent years the teaching of English as a foreign language has gone further than the teaching of French, German, or most other languages, both in the nature of its provision of further training and in the numbers of teachers who are enabled and encouraged to take advantage of this provision. In Britain, for example, each year since about 1970 roughly 150 qualified, graduate teachers, each with about five years of teaching experience, have taken one-year higher degree courses of further training, described as "M.A. in Applied Linguistics," "M.A. in English and Linguistics," "M.A. in TEFL," or some equivalent label. These are the individuals who become language advisers, inspectors, syllabus designers, team leaders—they constitute a high and growing proportion of the upper echelon of the profession.

But more than numbers is involved. The crucial feature of these courses has been their content, and above all the high intellectual level at which much of the content is offered. Typically,

these courses of further training assume the prior possession of sound initial training together with solid practical experience of teaching. They then offer a range of subjects, including advanced work in methodology and practical aspects of language learning and teaching, but also including the opportunity of becoming familiar with relevant work in linguistics, psycholinguistics, sociolinguistics, educational theory, experimental design, test construction—in short, the contributory disciplines referred to during our discussion of The Profession. It is this amalgam of relevant work in all the contributory disciplines that is usually referred to, in Britain, as *applied linguistics* (Allen and Corder, 1973; Strevens, 1977b; Corder and Roulet, 1973; Wilkins, 1976).[6]

The point at issue here concerns the importance within teacher training of further training, and especially of provision for sufficient language teachers to receive training for the higher echelons of the profession. In the teaching of English as a foreign language such provision has existed for over a decade: the teaching of other foreign languages tends to suffer by comparison, and will continue to do so until additional advanced further training can be provided for teachers of those languages, too.

Teaching. This is the element which has received the greatest amount of attention in the past. As was noted earlier, teachers have been inclined to assume that it was exclusively, or at least principally, those variables which they controlled that had the greatest influence upon learners' achievement. It is not the intention of this paper to suggest that teaching is unimportant, but rather to point out that its importance is not unique, and that teachers need to be aware of many other factors in the total language learning/teaching process.

Since so much attention has been paid to this area, we shall confine ourselves here to a brief justification of the subdivisions it seems necessary to make.

1. Approach   Beginning with the most general consideration, language teaching from time to time throws up sets of integrated, interrelated ideas, philosophies, techniques, and possibly also materials. Examples are: direct method, audiolingual method, cognitive code teaching. An ideological set of concepts of this kind can be called an "approach." (It must be stressed that the effective learning and teaching of languages is not dependent upon adherence to any approach, still less to one particular approach rather than any other.) The principal effect of an approach is to concentrate enthusiasm and energy: it is concerned with polemics, propaganda, and politics, rather than with pedagogy *tout pur.*

The next two elements within this component of The Teacher require a word of prior explanation. Until recently the single term "method" (e.g., Mackey, 1965) has been used to refer simultaneously to criteria for organizing the content of teaching courses and the teaching techniques for presenting them. However, so much intellectual effort has been applied to the first of these in recent years, with such far-reaching results, that it has become essential to recognize "syllabus" as an essential category in its own right, distinct from "methodology."

2. Syllabus   One stage closer to the learner than approach then, is the syllabus. More accurately, it is *principles of syllabus design* that we are concerned with. Ever since it became the accepted doctrine among language teachers that the effectiveness of learning can be significantly improved by manipulating the *content* and the *sequence* of what is taught, there have been devised a series of refinements and of additional sets of criteria. From *linguistic* to *situational* to *notional/functional to communicative* syllabuses, the sophistication has lately increased dramatically (Wilkins, 1976). This is an area in which the relevant disciplines, especially through the synthesis of applied linguistics, have recently made and continue to make important contributions. It is also the area in which the general trend in education toward learner-centered instruction has the greatest impact, particularly in the form of "special-purpose" language teaching (Strevens, 1977c) and various types of individualization.

3. Methodology   Within this main component of the total process, methodology or method has usually seemed to be the most obviously central element, embracing as it does the whole range of presentational techniques, learning/teaching tactics and instructional procedures. It is worth noting, however, that two distinct though related types of activity are included under the heading of methodology. One of these consists of the techniques, procedures, tactics, etc., for deliberately promoting learning; the other concerns relationships between learner and teacher, and especially those activities on the part of the teacher which are calculated to influence and improve the learner's attitudes toward learning and toward the teacher. It is a feature of recent developments in language teaching that the importance of the learner's attitudes toward his task and toward his teacher has been given greater recognition, and that teaching methods have been devised which concentrate upon the establishment of helpful learning attitudes. This aspect of methodology is the principal feature of The Silent Way, Community Language Learning, and even Suggestopedia.

4. Materials   The function of this subdivision of The Teacher is difficult to assess, not only because of the sheer diversity of course books, readers, workbooks, reference works, flashcards, wallcharts, recordings, films, filmstrips, videotapes, etc., but also because in any given teaching/learning situation it is the relation and interaction between the materials actually used, the syllabus being followed, and the professional ability of the teachers which is important. In some circumstances, materials can have a teacher-training function in addition

to their contribution to the teaching task; in other situations they may enable highly trained teachers to present courses of great sophistication; or they may simply be pedagogical extras chosen almost casually from the great range of the publishers' lists. Whatever their function in a particular case, there is no doubt that "materials" constitutes an important element of The Teacher.

5. Testing   Any process that is being deliberately carried out requires a continual supply of information about how far the process has gone, how effectively it is being achieved, what deficiencies it may contain. In the case of language learning and teaching, this information is supplied through testing, both formal and informal. At the extreme of informality, testing is barely distinguishable as a separate element of teaching, since a great many exercises and techniques of instruction incorporate ways for the teacher (and the learner) to check whether that which was taught has been learned, or that which was learned has been accurately and adequately assimilated. At the extreme of formality, as a device for measuring achievement or progress, testing becomes in addition—or instead—a piece of social administration, identifying the learner as having "passed" or "failed," as meriting (or not meriting) promotion or acceptance for some purpose quite distinct from that of language learning. Between these extremes there exists a growing array of techniques for testing the whole range of language activities. Against the convenience and advantage of the new availability of tests of various kinds must be set the very real danger that teachers may confuse testing with teaching, may use simple testing techniques as if they were equally effective in teaching, and may spend so much time on testing that teaching (and, more important, learning) flies out the window.

6. Selection of Teaching Type   Teachers of languages often fail to recognize that different teaching takes place according to certain dimen-sions or variables. The kind of difference that occurs is sometimes methodological, sometimes out of pace and intensity, sometimes a question of entire pedagogical outlook. These variables are:

Pupil age: different teaching is appropriate to *young children, adolescents,* and *adults*

Level of proficiency: different teaching is appropriate for *beginners, intermediate* level, and *advanced* level learners

Educational framework: different teaching is required in a context of *general education,* or *acquiring a practical command,* "culture-free," and of *special-purpose* learning, e.g., vocational or educational ends

Learner volition: different teaching may sometimes be appropriate, depending on whether the learner is a *volunteer* or a *non-volunteer*

Language of instruction: different teaching is required if the foreign language instruction is carried out in the *mother tongue,* or in the *target language* itself, or in some *other foreign language*

Target language status: different teaching is indicated depending on whether the language being learned has the status, in the situation where it is being learned, of a *second language* or a *foreign language*

The expression "teaching type" is used here in order to suggest that these six variables each have different values in particular situations, and that therefore the most appropriate teaching for any given situation is indicated by a profile along these six variables (Strevens, 1977b).

7. Constraints on Teaching/Learning Effectiveness   Accompanying all organized language learning is the potentiality for the effectiveness of the process to be constrained or restricted by impediments, which may be of three kinds: *physical, organizational* or *psychological.* Physical impediments include the obvi-

ous ones of fatigue and extremes of heat or cold; it is necessary also to guard against the constant distractions that sometimes occur in schools and against overcrowding, which not only reduces the available share of teacher-attention per pupil, but also frequently produces real physical discomforts and distractions.

Organizational impediments—frequently imposed by educational administrators many years ago and subsequently accepted as if they were unchallengeable facts of life—relate above all to the quantity and intensity of tuition. There is a good deal of shared experience in the language teaching profession to suggest that within broad limits the rate of learning per hour of instruction improves with greater intensity; and also that while it is obviously true that enough total time of instruction has to be provided in order for the learner to reach any particular goal, it may well be the case that some school language courses spend too many years on too little content, thereby virtually ensuring low standards of achievement. Other organizational impediments include the lack of premises, books or equipment, or suitable staff; absenteeism of students or staff is yet another way in which faults in organization can reduce the effectiveness of teaching.

This concludes the summary of the four elements which make up this major component, The Teacher. We now come to the last, yet in some ways the most important component, The Learner. In it we shall consider what contribution the learner brings to the learning/teaching process. We shall also deal with the psychological makeup of the learner and the fact that sometimes there are impediments of a psychological nature that reflect negative social attitudes (for example, learners do not find it easy to learn, and teachers find it difficult to teach a language which is unpopular in the community). Or a teacher and a learner may develop strong likes or dislikes for each other that get in the way of learning. Or anxieties about examinations may have a similar effect.

The Learner

The essence of this component is the fact that every learner of a foreign language is an individual, with his own profile of characteristics that mark him as different from all other learners, even though he obviously also shares the universal characteristics of all humans. Research in psycholinguistics has tended to concentrate (though with notable exceptions: see especially Tucker, 1976, and Schumann, 1978) upon the universals. What the teacher notices and, indeed, what the teacher has to work with when teaching is the individuality.

Learners differ in a large number of ways (Strevens, 1977b) which can be loosely divided into two groups.

Group 1
Age; *willingness* to give time and effort to learning; *special language abilities* (a "good ear," superior talent at mimicry, a good verbal memory, etc.); *learning stamina* over a long period; *previous linguistic experience,* (a) in the mother tongue (e.g., whether literate or not, what command of different varieties, etc.), (b) in other foreign languages including the extent to which these are cognate with the language currently being learned; *general educational experience.*

Group 2
Personal optimum learning rate; preferred learning styles or strategies; *minimum success-need; self-view as a language learner,* including level of expectations of success; *relations with teachers.*

Group 1 contains, on the whole, "givens" with which the teacher must come to terms; Group 2, on the other hand, contains qualities within which the management of learning (another name for teaching) can be manipulated by a skilled teacher to produce the best possible result. Indeed, it is a partial definition of a good teacher that he or she is capable of identifying the profile of qualities of each learner, and of so conducting the management of learning that each individual achieves as nearly as possible his own optimum rate of language learning.

We have now completed a brief outline of the four fundamental components of the language learning/teaching process. In the remaining section of the paper we shall consider commonly occurring reasons for failure in learning languages, as well as common conditions for success, and we shall relate them to the four-component model already described.

FAILURE AND SUCCESS IN LEARNING AND TEACHING LANGUAGES

Variability of Achievement

The terms "failure" and "success" are relative: they make sense only in relation to the degree of achievement of particular aims and goals. The important point, however, is that teachers and learners alike observe the existence of variability in achievement, while the teachers' experience goes a stage further and recognizes a number of factors to be commonly associated with greater or less achievement, respectively.[7]

1. Factors commonly associated with below-average achievement:
   a. unwilling learners
   b. low expectations of success
   c. unattainable aims and objectives
   d. unsuitable syllabus (or no syllabus)
   e. confusion between language learning and the study of literature (or, more recently, linguistics)
   f. physical, organizational and psychological shortcomings
   g. insufficient or excessive time or intensity of tuition
   h. poor materials not compensated by good teachers
   i. inadequate teacher training
   j. incompetent class teaching and lack of interest in learners
2. Factors commonly associated with above-average achievement:
   a. willing learners
   b. high expectations of success
   c. realistic and attainable aims
   d. suitable syllabus

   e. competent organization of teaching/learning situation
   f. sufficient time, not excessive, at reasonably high rate of intensity
   g. helpful materials
   h. teachers adequately trained
   i. teachers display professionalism and devotion to learners

Analysis of Failure and Success

We should now recall the four basic components of our theoretical model of the process and consider the origins of below-average achievement.

C   The Community
P   The Profession
T   The Teacher
L   The Learner

Origins of "Failure"

1. Unwilling learners. Poor learning (or even no learning at all) takes place when the learner is unwilling to give time, effort, and attention to the task. In the first instance, then, the responsibility for low achievement lies with the learner. Sometimes the reasons for unwillingness are trivial, and can be partly or wholly countered by tactful cajoling on the part of the teacher. Sometimes the unwillingness stems from social atti-

tudes which defy the teacher's best efforts.

L

2. Low expectations of success. This obstacle to learning is very often personal to the learner, who may have persuaded himself or been persuaded by family or friends that he will not do well. But sometimes there is a national myth, shared by the community that, for example, "The English can't learn foreign languages." The skillful teacher can do a good deal to overcome these low expectations, for instance by simple demonstrations of personal success in learning.

C

3. Unattainable aims and objectives. In some countries, the officially promulgated syllabus or program supposes the imparting of skill in the spoken language, to a high standard by the end of 10 or 12 years, whereas in fact the majority of teachers lack the command of the spoken language necessary for the achievement of these aims, and everyone accepts a very low terminal standard of achievement. Responsibility for this rests principally with the community, in that the public will is being incompetently put into practice. But as the sophistication of the profession and of individual teachers increases, so it becomes more and more a part of their duty to recognize where the defect lies and to press for the necessary changes to be brought in.

P

4. Confusion of aims. Where learners are taught what is basically a course in literary texts or in linguistic theory, in the expectation that they will thereby acquire adequate command of the foreign language, it is basically the profession that is at fault, for having misled the community's administration of education, though the same reservation about the growing responsibility of the teachers also applies here.

C

5. Physical, organization, and psychological shortcomings. In the majority of cases, these obstacles are squarely the responsibility of the community—that is to say, of the administration and organization of education.

C

6. Insufficient or excessive time or intensity. Again, it is almost always the community's administrators of education who lay down procedures for allocating tuition time to particular subjects. Yet even here, as more teachers are trained for the higher echelons, their responsibility grows for pointing out ways of improving the situation.

T

7. Poor materials not compensated by good teachers. This stems chiefly from inadequate standards of teacher training, though the profession can play a part in encouraging the community's administrators to initiate action on both fronts: the preparation of better materials and the improvement of teacher training.

C

8. Inadequate teacher training. Usually this is due to the community's servants not being able to obtain enough money to improve matters. Taking a worldwide view, enough understanding and experience now exist, within the profession and among individual teachers at the advanced level, to be able to specify immediate action that would produce drastic improvements.

T

9. Incompetent class teaching and lack of interest in the learners. Here the teachers are squarely at fault; the community and the profession between them need to organize for change.

Conditions for "Success"

We are now in a position to use the four-component model of the nature of the learning process to suggest how possibilities of high achievement can be maximized.

But success cannot be absolutely *predicted,* any more than failure can, by the simple presence of one factor or group of factors. Almost the only absolute statements that one can make are, first, that unwilling learners are unlikely to learn while, conversely, willing learners are likely to learn well; and second, that enough learning time must be provided. In most other respects excellence in one area can compensate for inadequacy in another, while major hindrances in one area can largely nullify excellence elsewhere.

Where then can we confidently expect to find success? Each of our components need to be included, since the overall process involves them all, in suitable interaction.

The Community
The community needs to have positive attitudes toward a particular language (or the society and culture of those who use it); in addition, it needs to be served by an administration which encourages, in a professionally understanding way, the creation of a helpful learning/teaching system, free from gross impediments.

The Profession
The language teaching profession needs to provide its teachers with support of all kinds: information, access to the contributory disciplines, a network of centers of excellence, etc.

The Teacher
The teacher needs adequate training (including a sufficiently large higher echelon), suitable syllabuses and materials, helpful testing arrangements, and above all to display devotion toward his or her pupils.

The Learner
The learner needs to be a *willing* learner, and to give the necessary time, effort, and social collaboration to the task.

Willing learners, devoted and well-prepared teachers, support from the profession and from the community. These would seem to be the fundamental ingredients to success. Many teachers will comment that there is nothing surprising in that. But the intention of this paper has been to show, first, that behind and beyond the obvious truths lies a set of interrelationships of great complexity, and second, that teachers and the profession now understand a great deal about the total process, and therefore we now bear a new responsibility for ensuring that changes are made, improvements are sought, and failure (where it habitually occurs) is no longer tolerated but is replaced by success.

NOTES

1. In an important paper, Lamendella (1977) points out the need for distinguishing between ": . . *primary language acquisition* and two distinct types of *nonprimary language acquisition: secondary language acquisition* and *foreign language learning.* " Lamendella's arguments are adduced from general principles of neurofunctional organization.

2. Lamendella's 1977 article cited in Note 1 equates *Foreign Language Learning* with " . . . a tedious process . . ." whose end-product is the possession of ". . . only rudimentary communicative abilities in real-world situations." The existence of high-grade learning /teaching is nowhere mentioned.

3. In a previous paper (Strevens 1977a) I have referred to only three elements: learner, teacher, system. But using the label "system" obscures a crucial distinction between that part of the total circumstances which depends upon society and that part which depends upon the worldwide profession of language teaching. Hence my preference here for a four-part analysis.

4. It is one of the great achievements of the Culture Learning Institute of the East-West Center, in Hawaii, that they have offered for several years courses designed specifically for educational administrators responsible for English-language education in South-East Asia, Japan, and the South Pacific. See also Beeby (1966).

5. Mackey (1965) is a pioneer work in analyzing the great range and complexity of language teaching in its modern forms. See also the important contributions of Rivers (1964 and 1968) and of Tucker (1976).

6. It is interesting to observe that when theoretical concerns become central, direct relevance to language teaching diminishes. The possession of a Ph.D. in *theoretical* linguistics, for example, important though it may be for linguistics, is but rarely capable of making a useful contribution to advanced work in the learning and teaching of languages. Too much linguistics is too much, in this context; and linguistics alone is not enough. Hence the observable value of "applied linguistics," which brings together selected (relevant) portions of *all* the disciplines concerned.

7. These considerations are discussed in greater detail in Strevens (1977a); they also form a central theme in this author's book, *Conditions for Success in Language Teaching,* Oxford University Press, 1979.

REFERENCES

Allen, J. P. B., and S. P. Corder, eds. *The Edinburgh Course in Applied Linguistics,* 4 Vols. London: Oxford University Press, 1973–1977.

Beeby, C. E. *The Quality of Education in Developing Countries.* Cambridge, MA: Harvard University Press. 1966.

Corder, S. P. *Introducing Applied Linguistics.* London: Penguin, 1973.

Corder, S. P., and E. Roulet, eds. *Linguistic Insights in Applied Linguistics.* Brussells, AIMAV, and Paris, Didier, 1973.

Lamendella, John T. General principles of neurofunctional organization and their manifestation in primary and nonprimary language acquisition. *Language Learning,* 1977, *27,* 155–196.

Larsen-Freeman, D., and V. Strom. The construction of a second language acquisition index of development. *Language Learning,* 1977, *1,* 123–134.

Mackey, William F. *Language Teaching Analysis.* London: Longman, 1965.

Perren, G. E., ed. *Teachers of English as a Second Language: their Training and Preparation.* Cambridge University Press, 1968.

Rivers, W. M. *The Psychologist and the Foreign Language Teacher.* University of Chicago Press, 1964.

————. *Teaching Foreign Language Skills.* University of Chicago Press, 1968.

Schumann, J. Affective factors and the problem of age in second language acquisition. *Language Learning,* 1975, *25,* 209–235.

Strevens, Peter. Some basic principles of teacher training. *ELT Journal, XXIX,* No. 1, 1974. London: Oxford University Press, 19–27.

————. A theoretical model of the language learning/teaching process. *Working Papers in Bilingualism, N. 11.* Toronto: O.I.S.E., 1976, 129–152. (A revised version of this paper appears in Strevens, 1977b.)

————. Causes of failure and conditions for success in the learning and teaching of languages. In D. Brown, ed., *On TESOL 77.* TESOL, Washington, D.C., 1977a.

————. *New Orientations in the Teaching of English.* London: Oxford University Press, 1977b.

————. Special-purpose language learning: A perspective. *Language Teaching and Linguistics: Abstracts.* 10, No. 3, 1977c, 145–163.

————. From the classroom to the world; from student to citizen, from teacher to educator, *Foreign Language Annals,* 1978.

Trim, J. L. *Draft Outline for a European Unit/Credit*

System for Modern Language Learning by Adults. Strasbourg: Council of Europe, 1973.

———. A unit/credit system for adult language learning. In G. Perren, ed., *Teaching Languages to Adults for Special Purposes.* CILT Reports and Papers No. 11, London, 1974.

Tucker, G. R. *Cross Disciplinary Perspectives in Bilingual Education: A Linguistic Review Paper.* Arlington, VA: Center for Applied Linguistics, 1976.

van Ek, J. *The Threshold Level.* Strasbourg: Council of Europe, 1975.

Wilkins, D. A. *Notional Syllabuses.* London: Oxford University Press, 1976.

SECOND LANGUAGE ACQUISITION AND BILINGUALISM

INTRODUCTION

A lot of trees have given their lives in the service of writers of prescriptive pieces on language teaching. One way of cutting down on the need for so much paper in the future is for methodologists to take account of theory and research in second language acquisition (SLA). We should aim, that is, to place language teaching on as sound a scientific footing as the current state of knowledge allows, and SLA theory and research is a more likely source of sound ideas than convention and intuition. (Teachers' intuitions differ alarmingly.) SLA researchers, after all, are working hard to understand how languages are learned and taught, both in and out of classrooms. They do not have all the answers, but they can help in two ways.

First, their findings have discredited some erroneous beliefs about language learning and teaching. For example, from work on contrastive, error, and performance analysis, we now know, among many other things, that learning a new language is not simply a matter of acquiring a (new) set of habits; that areas of similarity between L1 and L2 cause students problems, not just areas of great difference; that many of the errors learners make are the same, regardless of the L1 involved; and that students pass through fundamentally the same stages in acquiring grammatical constructions, no matter what teachers and textbook writers may do. From carefully designed teaching experiments, we know that students learn what they are psycholinguistically ready to learn, not whatever teachers attempt to teach them, and that teaching itself has many positive effects, for example, speeding up learning and, it seems, producing higher ultimate levels of SL proficiency. SLA research, that is, has shown the learner to be a mentally active participant in the SL classroom, not an empty vessel into which the teacher drills the SL as he or she chooses.

Second, where research findings give out, *theories* of SLA provide potentially true interim explanations of how students learn and thereby offer rational bases for selecting coherently from among the remaining options in methodology, syllabus design, materials and the like. We do not know, of course, that the theories are right. After all, if we knew exactly how students learned second languages, we wouldn't need theories. All but one *must* be wrong, and perhaps no existing theory is right. That does not matter. Until we have a proven understanding of the SLA process, theoretically motivated language teaching gives us a *chance* of being correct today.

Programs lacking any coherent theoretical underpinnings, on the other hand, obviously must be ill founded, just as eclectically based methodologies must be. Eclecticism, after all, assumes that we know which are the best parts of different theories (or "methods"), and that as teachers we will unerringly pick just those from among all the others. In fact, there is just as much chance that we will accidentally pick the wrong parts. In any case, classroom practices based on *different* underlying theories are guaranteed to be wrong, at least in part, for the simple reason, again, that at least one (and perhaps all) of the theories that generate them are wrong.

One of the most articulate advocates of theory-based language teaching has been Stephen Krashen. He has done a lot to make "theory" a respectable word among informed language teachers at a time when theoretically and empirically *un*supported "quick fix" methods abound. In the first article in this section, Krashen outlines his own theory of SLA, Monitor Theory, along with some of its implications for language teaching. It might well be that Monitor Theory and the Natural Approach (Krashen and Terrell, 1983), the language teaching method most closely associated with it, have some serious flaws. (For some recent critiques, see, e.g., Gregg, 1984; Long, 1985; and Pienemann, 1985.) Nevertheless, Krashen's (theory-based) *approach* to improving language teaching is arguably the correct one, and Monitor Theory raises enough important questions about traditional language teaching methodology to justify the informed language teacher being familiar with its basic claims. Further, whatever one's views of the particular position Krashen espouses, his ideas have had such an impact on modern language teaching programs for children and adults in many parts of the world that again it behooves the modern professional to be acquainted with those ideas.*

The second article, by Taylor, takes several developments in SLA theory and research, including Krashen's ideas, and relates them to various aspects of classroom practice. Taylor is especially interested in the implications of research findings for "communicative language teaching." He discusses a number of characteristics of a learner-centered, communicative classroom, with special emphasis

---

*The paper by Krashen was first published in 1980. For more recent statements and elaborations of Krashen's position, see:
S. D. Krashen. 1982. *Principles and Practice in Second Language Acquisition.* New York: Pergamon Press.
S. D. Krashen. 1985. *The Input Hypothesis: Issues and Implications.* New York: Longman.

on the role of the teacher (as guide, not God), Curran's Counseling Learning/ Community Language Learning, task-oriented materials design, the use of group work, and a revised concept of the role of grammar instruction.

As with Krashen's ideas, Taylor's recommendations for classroom practice were not intended to be the final word on the implications of work in SLA for language teaching. Indeed, even among researchers with broadly similar views about how second languages are learned there is often sharp disagreement about what their findings say to the teacher. (See Hyltenstam and Pienemann, 1985, and Lightbown, 1985, for some alternative views.) The articles by Krashen and Taylor, however, serve to introduce some recent thinking on the matter and to stimulate further reading.

Another area in which work on SLA has had a major impact is in the field of bilingual and immersion education. For millions of people in the world, English has long been not simply a second language, but also the medium through which they obtain their school or university education. This is the situation in many parts of Africa and Asia, and increasingly in English-speaking countries that have non-English or limited-English-speaking children in their education systems. In addition to the problems this last group of children faces in trying to compete with age-peers who are native speakers of English, language minority children are often from poor, socially disadvantaged backgrounds, the sons and daughters of refugees, migrant workers, and the like.

The societies that receive them vary greatly in the extent to which they are willing to accommodate to their linguistic and educational needs. Thus, in some parts of the world, they are thrown into English-medium classrooms with monolingual English classmates, and left to do as well as they can. This is known as *submersion,* or the "sink-or-swim" approach, the cost of which to the children's language and educational development has been well documented.

In societies with a sense of social responsibility for *all* their members, not just those of the majority culture, various educational options have been used for minority children. *Immersion* programs involve setting up special classes in which English (or some other SL) is the medium of instruction from the outset, with the teacher focusing on subject matter, not the language, but (crucially different from *submersion*) where *all* the children are *non*-native speakers of approximately equivalent SL proficiency. This enables the teacher to concentrate on presenting the content material in appropriately adjusted language the children will be able to understand without having simultaneously to cater to native speakers of that language in the same class. Considerable success has been reported for *immersion* in cases, such as French immersion for Anglophone children in Canada, where the SL is an additional language for children from the dominant linguistic and cultural group whose first language is maintained by out-of-school contact and who rarely come from socially disadvantaged homes. Variants of this approach, sometimes known as "structured immersion," are currently being tried in some parts of the United States for language *minority* children, a practice which may prove to be an unjustified extension of the immersion model.

Another approach popular in the United States and elsewhere is *bilingual education.* Bilingual education programs vary greatly in such areas as the age and ethnic group membership of the children involved, the amount of class time in L1 or L2, the subject matter taught through native language and English, the length of time the native language is used (about three years in "early-exit" and about six years in "late-exit" programs), and most fundamentally in the *goals* of the program: are they *transitional* programs, designed to move the children from their first language to English as quickly as possible, or *maintenance* programs, designed to maintain the L1 and to produce children bilingual and bicultural in English and their mother tongue?

Bilingual education programs have been heavily criticized in recent years. They are expensive, difficult to staff adequately, and difficult to provide instructional materials for. In addition, the current sparsity of *evidence that they work* is currently in danger of being used successfully by opponents as *evidence that they do not work,* an unwarranted but politically attractive inference in some quarters.

Swain's article reviews many of these issues, as well as some of the studies that have attempted to evaluate bilingual programs. She points out several of the contextual factors that distinguish Canadian immersion and American bilingual education programs, and she attempts to identify factors commonly associated with success in programs of both types.

The last alternative (considered here) is that of *ESL,* either in the form of an initial full-time, intensive program, at the end of which children are exited to the mainstream classroom, or on a *pull-out* basis, so many hours a day, taken concurrently with regular classes on a *submersion* basis. Within either model, the full range of options in TESL curricula and methodology is potentially open to teachers and administrators. In the past, unfortunately, the teachers in such public school programs have generally been untrained in TESL and the programs' administrators have been ignorant of developments in ESL in the past decade, with the result that a very limited traditional set of outdated, inappropriate practices have been inflicted on the children. ESL, in turn, has often lost favor with bilingual educators, who have seen only its "dark" side, and who often also perceive it, wrongly, as a threat to bilingualism in that it does nothing to foster L1 maintenance. This is a shame because there is nothing inherently incompatible between using the best of ESL methodology in the relevant *parts* of a true bilingual education program, while recognizing that much more is needed if minority languages and cultures are to be maintained—a goal, incidentally, which many, probably the majority of, ESL professionals strongly support.

DISCUSSION QUESTIONS

1. Some language teaching methodologists disparage theory and research and urge language teachers to base their classroom practice on "what they know works for them in their teaching situation." Compare this view with Krashen's,

and evaluate them. Can you propose alternatives of your own, or do you think the two positions embody the basic choice confronting the teacher?

2. Krashen claims that the provision of comprehensible input to learners with low affective filters is necessary and sufficient for successful classroom language learning. Can you think of three (or more) traditional classroom activities that would be ruled out if Krashen is correct, and three (or more) practices that would be supported by his claim?

3. Krashen attacks structurally based language teaching, or the teaching of isolated grammatical forms. His ideas imply that the teacher should focus on meaning, or real communication, at all times, thereby providing comprehensible input. Can you think of any defensible intermediate positions, or are these the only two choices open to teachers?

4. Suppose that you believed Krashen (or some other theorist) was right, but had students who wanted to be taught in some other way than the theory you ascribed to would support. What would you do?

5. Notice that, although Krashen does not list CL/CLL as a method that comes close to meeting the requirements of a successful program according to Monitor Theory, Taylor (who agrees with much of what Krashen says) finds Curran's ideas attractive for other reasons. Which aspects (if any) of CL/CLL, as described by Taylor, are consistent with Krashen's views, and which (if any) are not?

6. If you have access to a classroom, observe how another teacher teaches grammar, or tape-record yourself doing so. Alternatively, or in addition, look at how grammar is taught in one or more EFL/ESL textbooks. In light of Krashen's and Taylor's views on the topic, and of your observations, how useful do you consider that formal grammar instruction? Would your opinion be the same if the students concerned were young (elementary school) children, secondary school children, or adults?

7. Swain cites subtractive bilingualism as one factor associated with failure in some bilingual education programs. What is the difference between additive and subtractive bilingualism, and what could be involved in practice in converting subtractive to additive bilingual programs, as she suggests?

8. If you were a school administrator faced with an increasing minority language enrollment, which of the educational alternatives discussed in this section would you introduce in your school, and why? If you were a language minority child, what would you like the school administrator to do?

9. What, if anything, do you think is the role of the ESL teacher in a bilingual education program? In what ways could your goals as a teacher of ESL appear threatening to a teacher who believes in bilingual education, and how could the apparent differences be reconciled?

10. How do children learn English in societies, such as Hong Kong, Malaysia, Nigeria, and the Philippines, in which ESL is sometimes used as a medium of instruction in school or at university? What implications does this have, if any, for the education of minority language children in English-speaking countries?

FURTHER READING

1. K. Baker, and A. de Kanter. 1983. *Bilingual Education: A Re-appraisal of Federal Policy.* Lexington, MA: Lexington Books.
2. S. Churchill. 1984. *The Education of Linguistic and Cultural Minorities in the OECD Countries.* Clevedon, Avon: Multilingual Matters.
3. R. Ellis. 1985. *Understanding Second Language Acquisition.* Oxford: Oxford University Press.
4. K. Gregg. 1984. Krashen's monitor and Occam's razor. *Applied Linguistics* 5, 2, 79–100.
5. K. Hyltenstam, and M. Pienemann (eds.). 1985. *Modelling and Assessing Second Language Acquisition.* Clevedon, Avon: Multilingual Matters.
6. S. D. Krashen, and T. D. Terrell. 1983. *The Natural Approach. Language Acquisition in the Classroom.* New York: Pergamon Press.
7. P. M. Lightbown. 1985. Great expectations: Second language acquisition research and classroom teaching. *Applied Linguistics* 6, 2, 173–189.
8. M. H. Long. In press. Instructed interlanguage development. To appear in L. Beebe (ed.), *Issues in Second Language Acquisition: Multiple Perspectives.* Cambridge, MA: Newbury House Publishers.
9. B. A. Mohan. 1986. *Language and Content.* Reading, MA: Addison-Wesley.
10. M. Pienemann. 1985. Learnability and syllabus construction. In K. Hyltenstam and M. Pienemann (eds.), *Modelling and Assessing Second Language Acquisition.* Clevedon, Avon: Multilingual Matters, 23–75.
11. L. A. Schinke-Llano. 1983. Foreigner talk in content classrooms. In H. W. Seliger and M. H. Long (eds.), *Classroom-Oriented Research in Second Language Acquisition.* Rowley, MA: Newbury House Publishers, 146–164.
12. *Studies on Immersion Education: A Collection for United States Educators.* 1984. Sacramento: California State Department of Education.

CHAPTER 3

Applications of Psycholinguistic Research to the Classroom

Stephen D. Krashen

RESEARCH AND PRACTICE

The purpose of this paper is to discuss what our research priorities in second language acquisition should be. It will be helpful, however, before discussing these priorities, to discuss what research is for in second language acquisition, and how it can serve the teaching profession.

Our goal in foreign language education, at all times, is to improve teaching practice, and research must always serve this goal. It can do this in two ways. First, research can serve as confirming and counter-evidence to theories of second language acquisition, which can be extremely practical tools in improving practice. We will refer to research that has this goal as "theoretical" research. Second, research can be neutral to theory, and seek only to determine what works and does not work in the second and foreign language classroom. We will refer to this kind of research as "applied" research. In this section, we will take some time to briefly describe these two kinds of research and how they relate to practice. In the sections that follow, I will present what appears to be the state

of the art (or science) in both these areas, discuss some gaps in our research efforts, and suggest some directions for the future.

Theoretical Research

Theoretical research has as its goal the development of theory. A theory is simply a set of interrelated hypotheses that are supported by empirical evidence. It is thus an attempt to account for a number of phenomena in terms of a set of generalizations. It is important to point out that theoretical hypotheses can be supported by empirical data, but cannot be "proven." The existence or discovery of just one genuine counter-example is enough to "disprove" a theory, no matter how many confirming cases are found. For illustration, let us assume that a formal linguist proposes the following universal: All languages have pronouns. He presents us with a list of 547 languages, all of which contain pronouns. Can he claim that his universal is "proven?" All he can really claim is that his hypothesis finds support. The critic can always remain "unconvinced" and ask for more data, suggesting that some unknown, unstudied, long-dead, or yet to be developed language lacks pronouns. Science is, thus, a dangerous game, easy to lose!

Theoretical hypotheses remain our, or someone's, best guess as to how nature works. They are not objects of faith, and not truth. When scientists state their "position," they are not stating what they "believe," but which hypotheses they feel are supported by the evidence and which are worthy of further testing.

In section two of this paper, I will state my position in second language acquisition theory, a set of hypotheses which are consistent with and account for many of the phenomena and experimental results in second language acquisition and foreign language education. They are supported by evidence, but are not "proven." What is very important is that they are testable, that it is possible to find evidence counter to each of them and thus to the theory as a whole, and this makes progress possible.

Applied Research

Applied research seeks to determine which methods, techniques, and/or procedures are more efficient, which ones work, and which ones do not. This kind of research can be, and has been, conducted completely independently of theory, or it may be done in such a way that theory is affected and instructed by its results as well. Applied research may attempt to determine, for example, which of two teaching methods produces better gain scores on tests, whether older students learn faster than younger students, whether visuals help students in foreign language classes.

There is a growing body of applied research in foreign language education, and I will attempt to summarize some of it in the third section, pointing out what its main conclusions

have been, and how it relates to the theory discussed in section two.

Research and Practice

It seems logical to assume that both theoretical and applied research should have some impact on language teaching practice. My impression, however, is that neither form of research has much effect on how languages are taught today. To understand this, it is necessary to look into the past.

At one time, theoretical research was the main source of knowledge for many language teachers. They assumed, as we did, that those in the university knew best, and methodologies based on theory were widely used. The problem, however, was that these methodologies did not work very well. Our assumption, from the university, was that the fault was not with the theories but with the teachers, who clearly did not understand the true nature of our insights into language and language acquisition.

This has happened twice in recent years, with very different kinds of theories. One was audiolingualism, a method based on behaviorism, a theory of learning with serious limitations and of limited relevance (we know now) to language acquisition. The second time this occurred was when transformational grammar assumed dominance in formal linguistics. Many of us thought that this new system for describing the competence of the adult native speaker should form the basis for syllabi in language teaching. This also did not work, but many of us blamed its failure on teachers' inadequate grasp of *Aspects of the Theory of Syntax,* rather than our failure to understand that a theory of grammatical structure and language universals is not necessarily the same as a theory of language acquisition.

Because of the university's inability to provide the answers, teachers have turned away from theory and research of any sort, theoretical and applied, and have turned to a third source of inspiration and guidance: their own ideas and experience. A look at the programs of conferences and workshops shows us that this is true: we no longer see papers and presentations on topics such as "An analysis of the verb system in German," or "Pattern drilling techniques." We see, instead, teachers informing other teachers what has worked for them in the classroom. And what has worked for them is the use of language for real communication (see, for example, the 1980 ACTFL program, with such titles as "Food for thought: teaching French and German language and culture through cookery;" "Inkblots, Norman Rockwell and New Yorker Ads—Let's talk!" "Techniques for active language use at the intermediate and advanced levels").

Perhaps unknown to teachers, theoretical and applied research are now reaching similar conclusions, conclusions consistent with what teachers are coming up with on their own. Our goal for the future should thus be to restore some balance, to allow all three sources, theory, applied research, and teachers' ideas, to contribute to practice and to enrich each other.

THEORETICAL RESEARCH AND SECOND LANGUAGE ACQUISITION THEORY

I will attempt to summarize the theoretical research that has gone on in the last decade by stating five hypotheses about second language acquisition. Following this, we will look at the implications of these five hypotheses for other theoretical work in second language acquisition, and then see what this theory has to say, or predict, about second and foreign language teaching. There will be discussion of the gaps in the research literature, places where more support or testing of hypotheses is called for.

FIVE HYPOTHESES ABOUT SECOND LANGUAGE ACQUISITION

I. The Acquisition/Learning Hypothesis

This hypothesis states that we have two different and independent ways of developing ability in second languages. We can *acquire* and we can *learn*. *Acquisition* is defined as the process children use to acquire first language. It is subconscious in two different ways. First, the process is subconscious; we are usually not aware that we are acquiring while we are acquiring. Rather, we have the impression that we are doing something else, such as having an interesting conversation or reading an interesting book. We are also not always aware that we have acquired something; the knowledge itself is subconscious. This is illustrated by the fact that native speakers do not always "know" (consciously) the rules of their language. It is the purpose of current formal linguistics (transformational-generative grammar) to describe these subconscious intuitions about language, the native speaker's "tacit" knowledge.

Learning is conscious, or explicit knowledge about language. Learning is developed, it is thought, by explicit, or formal instruction, and is thought to be aided by the practice of error correction. Error correction, supposedly, helps the learner come to the correct mental representation of a rule. In everyday language, acquisition is "picking up" a language, while learning is "grammar," or "rules."

It is difficult to test the acquisition/learning hypothesis directly, but it plays an important role in all the other hypotheses, so evidence in favor of them serves as evidence supporting the acquisition/learning hypothesis. The issue of error correction has been investigated directly, and we will return to the possibilities in a later section, once the relationship between acquisition and learning is stated.

II. The Natural Order Hypothesis

This hypothesis states that we acquire (not learn) grammatical structures in a predictable order, that is, certain structures tend to be acquired early, and others tend to be acquired late. This order can be altered by first language influence (see below), but cannot be altered by the effects of instruction.

Much of the research supporting the Natural Order hypothesis comes from English. Brown, for example, reported that children acquiring English as a first language tend to acquire certain morphemes early (plural /s/ and progressive *ing*) and others late (third person singular ending /s/ and the possessive *'s*) (Brown, 1973). Similar claims were made for child second language acquisition initially by Dulay and Burt and subsequently by others (Dulay and Burt, 1974), and for adult second language acquisition, beginning with Bailey, Madden, and Krashen (1974). The second language order is not identical to the first language order, but there are some similarities (Krashen, 1981a).

Related to the Natural Order hypothesis is the phenomenon of transitional forms. It appears to be the case that second language learners pass through predictable stages on their way to acquiring the correct form for many, if not all, structures. For example, in the acquisition of English negation, both first and second language acquirers often pass through a stage in which the negative marker is placed outside the sentence, as in

No like it now (Ravem, 1975).

A second stage consists of placing the negative marker between the subject and verb, as in

This no have calendar (Schumann, 1978).

Finally, in the third stage, which not all acquirers reach, the correct form is acquired.

There are many areas of research and unanswered questions regarding the natural order hypothesis. A major one, of course, is why an order exists. What determines the order? Why are some structures early and others late? There has been considerable research and speculation on this topic. See, for example, Clark and Clark, 1977; Hatch and Wagner-Gough, 1976; Dulay and Burt, 1977; and Larsen-Freeman, 1976. While this is a theoretically interesting question, it may not be crucial to second language teaching practice. We need to know that an order exists to understand why students make the errors they do and to alter our expectations accordingly, but it is not yet clear that we need to know the determinants of the order.

Another possible priority is to expand our knowledge of what the order is for as many languages and as many structures as possible. We have enough evidence to state the hypothesis, but our data is limited to a few well studied languages and a handful of structures. Such additional confirming evidence is desirable in order to support the hypothesis, or to disconfirm it, but it may not be crucial for language teachers. As I will point out later, in discussing the Input hypothesis (hypothesis IV), the major implication of the Natural Order hypothesis is *not* that we teach along the Natural Order, beginning with those structures shown to be acquired early. In fact, the available evidence strongly suggests that we should not use a grammatical syllabus at all, no matter what it is based on!

A very important question is when the order appears and when it does not, that is, what conditions are necessary to show that a Natural

Order is indeed present. This is discussed as part of the next hypothesis.

III. The Monitor Hypothesis

The acquisition/learning hypothesis stated that two separate processes exist for developing ability in a second language. The Monitor hypothesis describes their interrelationship and how each is utilized by the second language performer. The Monitor hypothesis claims that acquisition, not learning, is responsible for our fluency in second language performance, for our ability to use second languages easily and comfortably. Conscious learning does not contribute to fluency, but has only one function: it can be used as an editor, or Monitor. We use conscious learning to make corrections, to change the form of the output of the acquired system before we write or speak, or sometimes after (self-correction).

This hypothesis regulates learning to a less than starring role in second language performance. Research over the last few years suggests strongly that the use of conscious learning is very limited. Not only is it restricted to the Monitor function, but it is not easy to use the Monitor effectively. I have posited that three conditions need to be met in order to use the Monitor, conditions that are necessary, but not sufficient:

1. *Time*   In normal conversation, there is rarely enough time to consult and utilize conscious rules, although some performers claim to be able to do this very well.
2. *Focus on Form*   Just having time is not enough. Even when acquirers have plenty of time, they do not always think about grammatical correctness. Dulay and Burt have pointed out that a second condition is necessary: the acquirer must be focused on form, or correctness.
3. *Know the Rule*   This is a formidable condition, considering how incomplete our knowledge of formal grammar is. Linguists concede that they have described only fragments of natural languages, and teachers and students have access only to a portion of these descriptions.

Research support for this hypothesis comes originally from studies of the natural order phenomenon. It has been found that second language performers show "natural orders" (in this case, a difficulty order similar to the longitudinal order of acquisition) in what can be considered "Monitor-free" situations, in which use of the conscious grammar is precluded, when there is little time or focusing on form. When the conditions for Monitor use are met, the natural order does not appear, which represents the intrusion of the conscious grammar.

It is interesting to note just how the natural order is disturbed by the Monitor. What we see is a rise in rank of late acquired items that are "easy" to learn. In English as a second language, for example, accuracy on items such as the third person singular morpheme will rise in rank and accuracy when students are given time and are focused on form. I would expect that similar increases would occur on similar items in other languages, items that are late acquired but are "learnable" and taught early. The simple *de + le = du* rule in French is a good example, as are case endings in German. Our students are often able to perform well on these items on pencil and paper grammar tests, but are much less accurate in free conversation.

Another very interesting point is our current hypothesis that for most students anything short of a discrete-point grammar test will not invoke the conscious grammar to any great degree. We see only mild, if any, Monitor use in composition, and in other situations in which students are asked to "be careful." Only a grammar test seems to meet all three conditions.

A great many questions can be asked with respect to this hypothesis. Most obviously, since most of the data in support of this hypothesis comes from English as a second language, we need to confirm its validity for foreign language situations. This work has been begun by some students at the University of Southern California. We also need to gather more data on when the Monitor is used and when it is not: what situations bring out the grammar? Is it true that extensive grammar use is only possible on grammar tests?

The question of individual variation is another important one. I have suggested that we find basically three types of performers: Monitor over-users, who Monitor all the time, to the detriment of their fluency; Monitor under-users, those who fail to consult the conscious grammar at all; and optional users, performers who use the grammar when they can, but only if such use does not interfere with communication (Krashen, 1981a). Optimal users typically are able to use grammar rules in writing; for example, but may not always use them in speaking. This individual variation schema was developed from a consideration of case histories, and has found some support in other studies (So, 1980; Stafford and Covitt, 1978). It needs not only further confirmation, but investigation of what sorts of programs might be optimal for different types of learners.

IV. The Input Hypothesis

This hypothesis deals with the important question of how we acquire. It consists of three interrelated parts:

1. We acquire by understanding input containing structures that are a bit beyond our current competence. In terms of the Natural Order hypothesis we move from our current level i to the next level $i + 1$ by understanding input containing $i + 1$.

We acquire, the hypothesis states, by going for meaning, by focusing on what is said rather than how it is said. We are aided in this process by extralinguistic context, and our knowledge of the world. We do *not* acquire by first learning about the structure of the language. We try to understand the message, and structure is thereby acquired.

2. Speaking "emerges." We do not teach speaking but give acquirers comprehensible input. Speech will come on its own, when the acquirer feels ready. Early speech is not grammatically accurate, but accuracy develops as the acquirer obtains more comprehensible input.

3. The best input is *not* grammatically sequenced. Rather, if the acquirer understands the input presented, and enough of it is made available, $i + 1$, the structures the acquirer needs for further development, will be automatically provided. Thus, the best input is not grammatically sequenced. Not only is it not necessary, but it may be harmful, when the goal is acquisition (this is not the case when the goal is conscious learning). The acquirers will receive comprehensible input containing structures just beyond them if they are in situations involving genuine communication, and these structures will be constantly provided and automatically reviewed. They need not worry about missing a class and thereby missing the past tense forever (or at least until next year). With natural, comprehensible input the hypothesis predicts that they will hear the past tense again and again.

In other words, part (3) of the Input hypothesis claims that input for acquisition need not focus only on $i + 1$, it just needs to contain it. $i + 1$ will be supplied, and naturally reviewed, when the acquirers obtain enough comprehensive input.

Evidence for the Input hypothesis is given in some detail in other publications (Krashen, 1981a, 1981b), but it is useful to briefly mention two phenomena in second language acquisition that relate to and are consistent with the Input hypothesis. The first is the presence of the silent period, a period of time before the acquirer actually starts to speak. The silent period is very noticeable in child second language acquisition; young children in a new country facing a new language may say nothing (except for some memorized sentences and phrases) for several months. According to the Input hypothesis, this is a time during which they are building up competence via input, by listening and understanding. When they are ready, they start to talk.

We generally do not allow our students to have a silent period. We insist on production, and accurate production, right away. When adults have to talk too early, before they have had a chance to acquire much of the second language, they have only one choice, and that is to fall back on their first language, an idea first proposed by Newmark (1966). They "think" in the first language, supply lexical items from the second language, and use the conscious grammar as best they can to make repairs. According to this view, first language interference is not interference at all, but is the result of using old knowledge. Its cure is acquisition, or more comprehensible input.

A great deal of research related to this central hypothesis needs to be done. Most important, we can ask whether acquirers who have had a chance to get more comprehensible input actually do better than those who do not. Also, does comprehensible input with imperfections, that is, the speech of other acquirers, help or hurt? The "first language interference" hypothesis is also quite testable (Krashen, 1981a).

The input hypothesis is perhaps the most crucial of all, since if it is correct, it will revolutionize our methodology in second language teaching (see Asher, 1979; Nord, 1980; Postovsky, 1974; Terrell, 1977; and Winitz and Reed, 1973).

V. The Affective Filter Hypothesis

This hypothesis deals with the role of affective variables. Briefly, the research literature in second language acquisition tells us that the fol-

lowing affective variables are related to success in second language acquisition:

1. *Anxiety* The lower the level of anxiety, the better the language acquisition. In Stevick's terms, the student should be "off the defensive" (1976).
2. *Motivation* Certainly, higher motivation predicts better second language acquisition. Certain types of motivation are more effective in certain situations, "integrative" motivation helping most in long-term, and "luxury" second language acquisition and "instrumental" helping for short-term acquisition where there is a practical need for the language (Gardner and Lambert, 1972).
3. *Self-confidence* The acquirer with more self-esteem and self-confidence tends to do better in second language acquisition (Heyde, 1977).

I have hypothesized that these affective factors relate more directly to subconscious language acquisition than to conscious learning, since we see stronger relationships between these affective variables and attainment in second languages when communicative-type tests are used, and when we test students who have had a chance to *acquire* the language (and not just learn it). Dulay and Burt (1977) have made this relationship more explicit and clear by positing the presence of an "Affective Filter."

According to the Affective Filter hypothesis, acquirers in a less than optimal affective state will have a filter, or mental block, preventing them from utilizing input fully for further language acquisition. If they are anxious, on the defensive, or not motivated, they may understand the input, but the input will not enter the "language acquisition device."

According to this hypothesis, given performers with identical comprehensible input, there may still be variation in rate of acquisition and ultimate attainment in acquisition. The one with the "lower filter" will go faster and farther.

As with the other hypotheses, there is much

work left to do. The generalizations concerning affective variables and subconscious acquisition were made *post hoc,* on the basis of previously reported studies. This relationship needs to be experimentally verified. (I have similarly claimed that what we call *aptitude* in second language acquisition is closely tied to conscious learning, also on the basis of a *post hoc* analysis of previously done experiments and reports.) Also, the Filter hypothesis itself is indirectly testable. Will we find that acquirers with similar input progress at different rates, and are these differences traceable to affective factors? What other affective factors contribute to the filter, and will we find different factors prevalent in different situations? (Krashen, 1981a; Schumann, 1975).

The Causative Variable in Second Language Acquisition

We can summarize the five hypotheses with a single claim: People acquire second languages when they obtain comprehensible input, and when their Affective Filters are low enough to allow the input "in." Thus, comprehensible input is the true and only causative variable in second language acquisition. This predicts that other variables posited to be related to success in second language acquisition are actually intervening variables for comprehensive input. This is quite testable, and, of course, quite exciting.

The first testable component of this hypothesis is that *instruction* itself is an intervening variable, that it helps second language acquisition only when it provides comprehensible input. The little data that is available supports this, but

it is truly shocking how little data is available. In short, the research done to date suggests that instruction helps only when it is the main source of comprehensible input, when the acquirer has no other source. It helps, for example, for beginners, even those in second language situations (who are not yet competent enough to understand the language outside the class), but does not seem to help intermediate students who have another rich source of comprehensible input. This makes sense. It suggests that the goal of instruction is not to produce advanced native-like speakers but to bring students to the point where they can begin to take advantage of the natural input available to them outside of class.

Similarly, studies probing the effect of *exposure* and *reported use* of second languages come to similar conclusions. They predict attainment in second language when they genuinely reflect real use of the language, interaction, comprehensible input. Again only a handful of studies speak to this question, and my conclusions are again *post hoc.* This is thus a wide-open area for research.

It can even be hypothesized that *age* is an intervening variable. The literature tells us that older acquirers are faster acquirers, for early stages. Younger acquirers, however, are superior in terms of ultimate attainment (Krashen, Long, and Scarcella, 1979). The older acquirers' advantage in rate may be due to their ability to obtain comprehensible input (Scarcella and Higa, 1982), while the younger acquirers' superiority in eventual attainment has been hypothesized to be due to the strengthening of the affective filter. As Scarcella and Higa have demonstrated, these are very testable hypotheses.

IMPLICATIONS FOR TEACHING

The theory makes definite predictions for second and foreign language teaching, all of

which are testable, and some of which have been tested to some extent in applied research experiments. Briefly, the theory predicts that successful second language teaching programs will have these characteristics:

1. They will supply a great deal of comprehensible input that is interesting and relevant to the students. The goal of this input will not be to provide practice on specific points of grammar, but will be to transmit messages of interest.
2. They will not force students to speak before they are ready and will be tolerant of errors in early speech.
3. They will put grammar in its proper place. Some adults (and very few children) are able to use conscious rules to increase the grammatical accuracy of their output, and even for these people, very strict conditions need to be met before the conscious grammar can be applied.

Several methods come close to meeting these requirements, including Asher's Total Physical Response method, Terrell's Natural Approach, Lozanov's Suggestopedia, and recent materials developed by Harris Winitz. In addition, several nonmethods meet these requirements nicely. Successful *conversation* with a speaker of the language you are trying to acquire may be the best lesson of all, as long as the speaker succeeds in making the speech comprehensible to you. According to the theory, acquirers profit not from what they say, but from what the native speaker says. Output thus makes an indirect but powerful contribution to acquisition by inviting comprehensible input! Also, *pleasure reading* has the potential for supplying comprehensible input helpful for acquisition.

Of course, the claim that a method is successful is quite testable, as we shall see in the next section. In addition, the hypothesis that conversationalists and pleasure readers acquire (but not necessarily learn) more is also testable, but has not, to my knowledge, been tested directly in theoretical research.

A prediction that the theory makes that has

been extensively tested is that subject matter teaching can help language acquisition. The research is quite extensive for children, coming from the very well studied immersion programs (Lambert and Tucker, 1972), but the possibility that adults may also benefit remains a theoretical prediction.

Applied Research

We will focus on just one aspect of applied research here, that of method comparison studies, the attempt to determine which of two methods is better by direct comparison. While this sort of research looks to be straightforward, it is loaded with difficulties and confounds. Nevertheless, a substantial number of studies have been done, and, since they involve fairly large numbers of students in many different settings, and they give remarkably consistent results, they are worth examining.

The studies can be divided historically into two time periods. First came what can be termed "traditional" method comparison studies, studies comparing the more common methods, such as audiolingual, cognitive-code, and grammar-translation. We can summarize the results of these studies (Chastain, 1970; Mueller, 1971; van Elek and Oskarsson, 1976):

1. There is little difference between audiolingual-type teaching and grammar-based approaches (grammar-translation and cognitive-code style) for adolescents.

2. For adults, cognitive type methods are a little better. Cognitive students outperform audiolingual students, but the differences are quite small. This result had two different kinds of reactions in the field. Stevick noted the implicit contradiction, asking how methods based on totally different theories of language acquisition could produce such similar results (Stevick, 1976). Many methodologists and teachers, however, simply assumed that the answer was to be eclectic, to choose parts of each system in the

belief that the answer must be somewhere in the middle. As fair-minded as this sounds, it often resulted in teachers choosing the worst from each, the parts least likely to cause acquisition: drill from audiolingual and extensive grammar explanation from grammar-translation and cognitive code!

There is an explanation. Neither approach provided much in the way of comprehensible input, and neither met the requirements outlined above for successful language teaching methods. This predicts that methods that do not meet these requirements should do much better, and there is some indication that they do. Asher has provided the profession with an extensive series of studies demonstrating the efficacy of Total Physical Response teaching, showing that TPR is not just a little better, but is much better than audiolingual teaching. In one study, in fact, his TPR students acquired *five times faster* than controls (Asher, 1972). Swaffar and Woodruff also confirm that methods focusing on comprehensible input and that keep grammar in its place do much better than the older alternatives (Swaffar and Woodruff, 1978).

These kinds of results are very encouraging. They support the theory, even though they were done without this particular theory in mind, and point to exciting new directions.

What remains to be done? A great deal. We need, despite their flaws, more comparisons, more program development research, using the model of Swaffar and Woodruff. This includes more direct tests of newer methods. Also useful would be case histories of students in these methods, a means of getting at their reactions and problems.

Experimentation I would be particularly in-terested in involves a new direction for the language laboratory. Up to now, the lab has been a place where students can come to exercise their output and have it corrected. A far easier and technologically simpler use for the lab is as a supplementary source of comprehensible input. Here are some possibilities: taped stories, with pictures to aid comprehension and add to the enjoyment (as currently being developed by Harris Winitz), radio programs, commercials on tape, a "cheap" library, for casual pleasure reading, filled with books that the lab is not afraid of losing. And perhaps most important, a native speaker, willing to chat with whomever comes in! The theory predicts that such a lab would do great things for language acquisition, and this prediction is certainly testable.

The question of materials can also be considered an (applied) research priority. The predictions made for methods also can be applied to materials. Simply, the best materials will be those that supply comprehensible input, that do not force overuse of grammar, and that keep the student off the defensive. This predicts that specialized readers, readers on topics that truly interest students, aids to comprehension in the classroom (e.g., visuals), and materials that aid Monitor use without creating over-users will succeed. This is quite testable, and calls for a new tradition of field testing. In the past, for example, we assumed our readers were acceptable if they contained certain structures and avoided others. The theory predicts now that successful readers are simply those that are comprehensible and interesting. If these requirements are met, the structural requirements (that $i + 1$ be present) will automatically be met.

CONCLUSION

We have touched on a few places where more research needs to be done. In all cases, the gaps I have identified are related to current hypothe-ses. Of course, new hypotheses will be developed, but this is unpredictable. What is predictable is that if we continue our thinking and research, research designed to test old hypotheses, new ideas will come, deeper generalizations to account for anomalies.

What is most important is the realization that both theoretical and applied research can contribute to progress in foreign language education, and that accepting research as a determinant of practice does not necessarily mean rejecting teachers' experiences and intuitions. But language teaching should not be based entirely on fashion, and matters of methodology should not be settled by committee and vote. Our top priority should be to form a real partnership between theoretical researcher, applied researcher, and language teacher, so we can work together toward a common goal.

REFERENCES

Asher, James J. *Learning Another Language Through Actions.* Los Gatos, CA: Sky Oaks Productions, 1979.

————. Children's first language as a model for second language learning. *Modern Language Journal* 53(1972):133–39.

Bailey, Nathalie, Carolyn Madden, and Stephen D. Krashen. Is there a 'natural sequence' in adult second learning? *Language Learning* 24(1974):235–43.

Brown, Roger. *A First Language.* Cambridge, MA: Harvard University Press, 1973.

Chastain, Kenneth. A methodological study comparing the audio-lingual habit theory and the cognitive-code learning theory. *Modern Language Journal* 54(1970):257–66.

Clark, Herbert H., and Eve V. Clark. *Psychology and Language.* New York: Harcourt Brace Jovanovich, 1977.

Dulay, Heidi C., and Marina K. Burt. Natural sequences in child and adult second language acquisition. *Language Learning* 24(1974):37–53.

Dulay, Heidi, and Marina Burt. Remarks on creativity in language acquisition, 95–126. In Marina Burt, Heidi Dulay, and Mary Finocchiaro, eds. *Viewpoints on English as a Second Language.* New York: Regents Publishers, 1977.

Gardner, Robert C., and Wallace E. Lambert. *Attitude and Motivation in Second Language Learning.* Rowley, MA: Newbury House Publishers, 1972.

Hatch, Evelyn, and Judy Wagner-Gough. Explaining sequence and variation in second language acquisition. *Language Learning Special Issue* 4(1976):39–57.

Heyde, Adelaide W. The relationship between self-esteem and the oral production of a second language, 226–40. In H. Douglas Brown, Carlos Alfredo Yorio, and Ruth H. Crymes, eds. *On TESOL '77. Teaching and Learning English as a Second Language: Trends in Research and Practice.* Washington, D.C.: Teachers of English to Speakers of Other Languages, 1977.

Krashen, Stephen D. *Second Language Acquisition and Second Language Learning.* New York: Pergamon Press, 1981a.

————. The input hypothesis. In James Alatis, ed. *Georgetown Roundtable on Language and Linguistics.* Washington, D.C.: Georgetown University Press, 1981b.

Krashen, Stephen D., Michael H. Long, and Robin C. Scarcella. Age, rate, and eventual attainment in second language acquisition. *TESOL Quarterly* 13(1979):573–82.

Lambert, Wallace E., and G. Richard Tucker. *The Bilingual Education of Children.* Rowley, MA: Newbury House Publishers, 1972.

Larsen-Freeman, Diane. An explanation for the morpheme acquisition order of second language learners. *Language Learning* 26(1976):125–34.

Mueller, Theodore. The effectiveness of two learning models: The audio-lingual theory and the cognitive code learning. In Paul Pimsleur and Terence Quinn, eds. *The Psychology of Second Language Learning.* Cambridge: Cambridge University Press, 1971.

Newmark, Leonard. How not to interfere with language learning. *International Review of American Linguistics* 40(1966):77–83.

Nord, James R. Developing listening fluency before speaking: An alternative paradigm. *System* 8(1980):1–22.

Postovsky, Valerian A. Effects of delay in oral practice at the beginning of second language learning. *Modern Language Journal* 58(1974): 229–39.

Ravem, Roar. The development of wh-questions in first and second language learners. 153–75. In John H. Schumann and Nancy Stenson, eds. *New Frontiers in Second Language Learning.* Rowley, MA: Newbury House Publishers, 1975.

Schumann, John H. Affective factors and the problem of age in second language acquisition. *Language Learning* 25(1975):209–35.

———. *The Pidginization Process.* Rowley, MA: Newbury House Publishers, 1978.

So, W. Y. Toward a more effective method in ESL writing. Paper presented at the 1980 TESOL Convention, San Francisco.

Stafford, C., and G. Covitt. Monitor use in adult second language production. *ITL: Review of Applied Linguistics* 39–40(1978):103–25.

Stevick, Earl. *Memory, Meaning, and Method.* Rowley, MA: Newbury House Publishers, 1976.

Swaffar, Janet King, and Margaret S. Woodruff. Language for comprehension: Focus on reading. *Modern Language Journal* 62(1978):27–32.

Terrell, Tracy. A natural approach to second language acquisition and learning. *Modern Language Journal* 61(1977):325–37.

van Elek, Tibor, and Mats Oskarsson. *Teaching Foreign Language Grammar to Adults.* Stockholm: Almqvist & Wiksell, 1976.

Winitz, Harris, and James Reed. Rapid acquisition of a foreign language (German) by the avoidance of speaking. *IRAL* 11(1973):295–317.

Scarcella, Robin, and C. Higa. Input and age differences in second language acquisition. In Stephen D. Krashen, Robin Scarcella, and Michael Long, eds. *Child-Adult Differences in Second Language Acquisition.* Rowley, MA: Newbury House Publishers, 1982.

CHAPTER 4

Teaching ESL: Incorporating a Communicative, Student-Centered Component

Barry P. Taylor

Recent writings in second language acquisition and classroom methodology have raised important questions about language learning and teaching. The observation that many students fail to acquire communicative competence in the target language despite years of language instruction has prompted researchers, theoreticians, and teachers to question the effectiveness of our current approaches: traditional, grammar-based instruction has been widely criticized as being ineffective, and recent notional/functional syllabuses, although proposed as potentially more viable curricular alternatives, are not without their critics. Evaluations of both of these approaches to curriculum design have been discussed widely (see Taylor, 1982, for a representative summary).

In response to the perceived weaknesses of both structural and notional/functional syllabuses in producing communicatively competent speakers, the current literature stresses the importance of providing language learners with more opportunities to interact directly with the target language—to acquire it by using it rather than to learn it by studying it. It has been suggested that when language classrooms focus on task-oriented activities which give students experience in functioning in extended, realistic discourse in the target language, those students are able to learn not only appropriate language use, but real communicative processes as well.

But a teaching approach which focuses on real communication also requires a classroom atmosphere in which communication can take place comfortably. Our roles as teachers and our students' roles as learners therefore become significant considerations. Our particular students' needs and the dynamics of our particular classes become major factors in deciding what to teach and how to teach it. This article will begin exploring these issues by first offering a brief summary of some recent research.

BACKGROUND RESEARCH

One of the most frequently repeated suggestions in the current literature on language learning and teaching is that, for most learners, acquisition of a second language will take place only to the extent that those learners are exposed to and engaged in contextually rich, genuine, meaningful communication in that language (see Taylor, 1982). An examination of the relevant literature reveals two major arguments to support this claim:

1. First, findings from research in second language acquisition indicate that although some adult learners are successful at learning grammar rules which they have been taught and then using those rules productively and communicatively, most learners cannot utilize their intellectual understanding of the grammar of the language in real communication (Johnson, 1981a; d'Anglejan, 1978; Long, et al. 1976). Krashen (1977, 1979) and others have argued that communicative competence, for most learners, can only be achieved by subconsciously acquiring the language through active participation in real communication that is of interest to those learners—such as in conversation—in a process similar to the way children acquire their first language. Although this claim is based only on research findings relating to the learning of explicit grammar rules, it seems reasonable to conclude that it would apply equally to cases involving the learning of any explicit language rules, including those which are functional (see Johnson, 1979, for his discussion of "analytic" vs. "synthetic" teaching).

2. The second argument in favor of providing students with real communicative experiences in the target language is supported by investigations into communicative curriculum design. It has been argued that the ability to be grammatical and formally correct is important —and it is—but formal correctness is only part of communicative competence (Johnson, 1981a; Allwright, 1979; Brumfit, 1981; Scott, 1981). If we expect our students to learn how to use language to fulfill real communicative functions, they must have opportunities to do so in a full range of real situations and social settings. Widdowson (1978) has pointed out that classroom presentations and contrived simulations that focus on language and language forms are inadequate; because such presentations are artificial and often incomplete, they do not provide enough examples of the different kinds of authentic discourse data which students will need in order to learn.

Taken together, these two arguments appear to suggest that for most students language is best acquired when it is not studied in a direct or explicit way; it is acquired most effectively when it is used as a vehicle for doing something else (Saegert et al., 1974; Upshur, 1968; Tucker, 1977)—when learners are directly involved in accomplishing something via the language and therefore have a personal interest in the outcome of what they are using the language to do.

Warshawsky's finding (1978:472) that "grammatical structure appears to develop in the learner's speech in response to communicational need" provides further evidence for this claim. Her research supports the hypothesis that when the transmission of essential information is at stake and there is a compelling communicative need, learners will be motivated to continue to try to communicate. These attempts to communicate can, in turn, facilitate acquisition as students work to meet that need (see Taylor, 1982, for a fuller discussion).

Most of us have undoubtedly observed situations that support this hypothesis. How often have those of us who work in domestic pre-university ESL programs, for example, wondered why students did not improve appreciably despite months of language study, and then later marveled at how much their proficiency had increased—but only after they had left our classes and had actually had to struggle with academic courses taught in English? One conclusion which can be drawn is that students are not as likely to involve themselves as fully in our classroom activities, which are often contrived and uncompelling, as they are when they have a real stake in the outcome of their endeavors. This example illustrates, and there are research findings and observations (for example, Gardner and Lambert, 1972; Lukmani, 1972; Schumann, 1978; Stevick, 1976, 1980; and Taylor, 1973) to suggest, that although many adult second language learners may stop learning when they feel that their proficiency is adequate for their purposes (Selinker, 1972), "when there is a pressing need, and the motivation is high, . . . the acquisition process seems to continue" (Taylor and Wolfson, 1978:32).

In sum, then, it appears that second language acquisition depends upon the extent to which learners are exposed to and involved in genuine communication in the target language. Although some students do appear to be able to transfer their intellectual understanding of the structure of the target language (either of the syntax or of notions and functions) into real communicative situations, most cannot do so successfully. But even if they could, neither a grammatical focus nor a notional/functional focus without a real communicative component would be sufficient; neither approach alone provides students with enough examples of how language is used in real communication and with adequate opportunities for them to actually use it.

In the classroom our goal as language teachers is, therefore, to maximize opportunities for language acquisition to take place. While language teaching need not always be entirely communicative (Yorio, 1982; also see section, "The role of explicit grammar," in this article), the research which we have considered highlights the need to include a strong communicative component in our teaching and suggests that classroom instruction incorporate the following features:

1. Opportunities for students to be exposed to real communication
2. Opportunities for students to engage in using real communication
3. Activities which are meaningful to students and which will motivate them to become committed to sustaining that communication to accomplish a specific goal, such as solving a problem or completing a task

DESIGNING A COMMUNICATIVE COMPONENT

In devising ways to make these features operational in the language classroom, we must first consider what is involved in designing a strong communicative component. It has been proposed (Johnson, 1981a) that an effective communicative approach must include at least two independent factors.

The first is the selection of appropriate linguistic information to be taught. Johnson (1979) and Morrow (1981) have both suggested that information about the language should be chosen to be taught not simply because it exists, but rather on the basis of what contribution it can be presumed to make to the acquisition of skills or to the performance of specific tasks which are both communicatively useful and relevant to the students' own particular language needs.

But a fuller specification of what to teach, whether it be grammar or linguistic categories of meaning and use (notions and functions), is not enough. The second major factor to consider in implementing a communicative approach is the methodology that will be used to impart that information. Syllabuses, either grammatical or functional, are, in the end, only lists of forms to be taught. The way in which they are taught can make the difference between an approach which is communicative and one that is not (Brumfit, 1981; Morrow, 1981; Johnson, 1981a). A coherent, principled methodology that will help students to acquire the linguistic skills and abilities which we want them to learn, and then use them productively and communicatively, is required. As Johnson (1981a:10) notes,

> we may begin our teaching operation with a semantic syllabus carefully and scientifically drawn up to cover the student's communicative needs, yet utterly fail to teach him how to communicate. If, in other words, we are to meet our communicative aims, we must give attention to questions of methodology as well as syllabus design.

Recent explorations into communication-based language teaching have begun to identify some of the features of real communication which can have direct applicability to the development of a communicative methodology. Let us briefly consider five:

1. Morrow (1981) has pointed out that in order to engage in real communication participants must be able to deal with stretches of spontaneous language above the sentence level. Since the ability to manipulate the formal features of language in isolation does not necessarily imply the larger ability to be communicatively competent, a communicative teaching approach will need to provide students with the opportunity to engage in extended discourse in a real context.

2. Johnson (1979) and Morrow (1981) have proposed that one of the major purposes of communication is to bridge an information gap. If the speaker and hearer are both in possession of the same information prior to beginning their communication, communication cannot, technically, be said to take place. Therefore, a communicative methodology will need to create situations in which students share information not previously known by all participants in the communication.

3. Morrow (1981) has observed that real communication always allows speakers choices to decide not only what they will say but also how they will say it. In similar fashion, since there is always uncertainty about what a speaker will say, the hearer remains in doubt and must maintain a state of readiness (Johnson, 1979; Morrow, 1981). A communicative methodology, therefore, will need to provide learners with opportunities to engage in unrehearsed communication and thereby experience doubt and uncertainty, and learn to make appropriate content and linguistic choices accordingly.

4. Morrow (1981) has noted that most participants in real communication keep a goal in mind while they are speaking. That goal is usually the successful completion of some kind of real task. What speakers decide to say to each other and how they evaluate what is said to them are both determined by that goal. That is, what one speaker says to a second speaker is shaped not only by what the second speaker has just said, but also by what the first speaker wants to get out of the conversation (also see Johnson, 1979). A communicative methodology, therefore, will need to provide learners with opportunities to negotiate conversations on topics which are goal-oriented and in which the learners have a vested interest.

5. Johnson (1979) has suggested that real communication requires that both the speaker and hearer attend to many factors quickly and at the same time. A communicative methodology, therefore, will need to provide students with opportunities to engage in extended discourse on real topics, using real language and, most importantly, in real time.

Johnson (1981a:11) elaborates on some of these features of communication when he writes that

> apart from being grammatical, the utterance must also be appropriate on many levels at the same time; it must conform to the

speaker's aim, to the role relationship between the interactants, to the setting, topic, linguistic context, etc. The speaker must also produce his utterance within severe constraints; he does not know in advance what will be said to him (and hence what his utterance will be in response to) yet, if the conversation is not to flag, he must respond extremely quickly. The rapid formulation of utterances which are simultaneously "right" on several levels is central to the (spoken) communicative skill.

This view of some of the processes involved in real communication prompts a reconsideration of many of our current teaching practices and highlights the need for students to be communicatively active in class. In fact, Johnson (1979) proposed that

> these processes . . . can only really be practiced in a language teaching which is "task-oriented" (199) . . . [one which focuses] on tasks to be mediated through language, and where success or failure is seen to be judged in terms of whether or not these tasks are performed (200).

Such a teaching approach requires "an environment where doing things is possible" (Morrow, 1981:64). Concerns for curriculum and syllabus design, methodology, and, ultimately, the classroom atmosphere in which that teaching approach takes place all become relevant.

THE CLASSROOM

In adopting a communicative approach, therefore, it does not appear possible to separate issues of curriculum and methodology from issues of classroom interaction and environment. Real communication is a shared activity which requires the active involvement of its participants, who must all exercise what we can call "communicating initiative" in guiding that communication. If it is our intention to provide opportunities for students to communicate realistically in class, we have a responsibility to create an atmosphere in which communication is possible, one in which students can feel free to take communicating initiative and are motivated to do so. Making classes "student-centered" (see Bodman, 1979) can contribute to creating such an atmosphere.

But creating a supportive, student-centered environment, while important, is not enough. True communication to which students are committed will only take place if we also have engaging content that will involve the participants and in which those participants have a stake.

We can find such content by basing our in-struction on task-oriented activities in the target language which focus on issues that are relevant and meaningful to students. When these activities are undertaken in an atmosphere conducive to active participation, they can be intrinsically motivating and can engage learners directly. In this environment students can feel comfortable exercising the communicating initiative necessary to complete the tasks. When they have a personal stake in what they are communicating and in the outcome of that communication, teaching can then be most profitably addressed to those learners' immediate language needs (be they grammatical or functional) as they emerge in the course of their communicative attempts (see Taylor, 1982).

D'Anglejan's summary (1978:231) of Corder's observations on the teaching/learning process is significant here. She writes that the teacher and the learner must function as

> equal partners in a cooperative enterprise. The learner must seek out the linguistic data and process it when he needs it and can assimilate it. It must be the learner and not the teacher

who sets the pace. The role of the teacher is that of responding to the developing communicative needs of the learner by making the appropriate linguistic data available "on request." If the focus of the second language classroom is to be on developing the learner's ability to get the message across, then the teacher's feedback must be related to the communicative appropriateness and not the linguistic form of the students' utterances.

In this way, "communicative functions arise naturally from the activity itself" (Maley, 1980:-11), and students are able to determine for themselves how successful they have been at getting their meaning across. An evaluation by the teacher becomes unnecessary.

Much of what has been said here is not new. Over the last few years there has been a strong movement away from highly structured, teacher-centered, grammar-based teaching in favor of task-oriented, communicatively based, learner-centered teaching, often including the use of certain so-called "humanistic" approaches. Some of these newer approaches, however, have been misunderstood and have caused considerable anxiety and confusion among both ESL teachers and their students (Stevick, 1980, Clarke, 1980).

Let us now examine some of these issues more closely by addressing two significant concerns: 1) the role of classroom atmosphere in communicatively based, student-centered language classes, and 2) the selection and use of communicative teaching materials.

Classroom Atmosphere. Student-centered teaching does not require that the teacher abdicate authority in the classroom. To do so would create chaos. Teachers are invested with a responsibility which only they have the right to assume. According to Allwright (1979), that responsibility includes providing samples of the target language, providing guidance concerning the nature of the target language (which includes rules, cues, and feedback on success or failure), and providing classroom management. These issues are not in question. What is significant in student-centered teaching, however, is the manner in which teachers assume this responsibility and how much of it they share (see Bodman, 1979; Stevick, 1980).

For many of us, there appears to be an assumed incompatibility between learner-centered teaching and the teacher's authority to direct the class. Stevick (1980) addresses this point directly by making a distinction between what he calls teacher "control" and student "initiative." Control, Stevick suggests, consists of two elements: the structuring of classroom activities and the providing of constructive feedback on performance. He proposes that at the beginning stages of any course both aspects of control should reside entirely with the teacher in order to create a secure, stable environment for the students; in time, these responsibilities can be shared with the students but only as long as those students feel secure in knowing that this shift in responsibility is part of the teacher's overall plan, and there is no serious disruption of the effectiveness of the activity. Stevick warns that it can be dangerous to turn these responsibilities over to the students prematurely.

Stevick contrasts control with initiative, which, he says (1980:19), "refers to decisions about who says what, to whom, and when . . . and consist[s] of choices among a narrow or a very broad range of possibilities which are provided by whoever is exercising 'control.'" He argues that control and initiative must be kept distinct and can be adjusted independently of each other; in the name of "taking control," teachers must be careful not to monopolize initiative. As he explains (1980:20),

> in exercising "control," then, the teacher is giving some kind of order, or structure, to the learning space of the student. In encouraging him to take "initiative," she is allowing him to

work, and to grow, within that space. The trick, for the teacher, is not only to preserve this distinction; it is also to provide just the right *amount* of learning space. If there is too little, the learner will be stifled. If there is too much, the student will feel that the teacher has abandoned him" (for further discussion of these and related issues, see Stevick, 1980, Chapter 2).

This kind of teaching approach places some serious responsibilities on teachers and requires that they adopt a point of view toward their teaching which can be significantly different from that which they may be most accustomed to. The teacher's attitude and the resultant relationship created between the teacher and the students is the single most important variable in successfully executing student-centered teaching. Within this framework, the teacher does not function as a drill leader or an authority figure, no matter how benevolent, but rather as a "facilitator" (Rardin, 1977) who responds to the students' emerging language needs.

One current teaching approach which has attempted to incorporate these ideas in an explicit way is Counseling-Learning/Community Language Learning (C-L/CLL), founded by Charles Curran (1961, 1972, 1976). In brief, C-L/CLL represents a philosophy of education which draws heavily on the field of counseling psychology, and especially "client-centered therapy" (Rogers, 1965). When Curran, who was himself a psychologist and not a language teacher, began to notice that many language students exhibited the same kinds of anxieties and fears as clients in psychotherapy, he began to experiment with applying counseling techniques to language teaching. Curran felt that competition, fear of failure or rejection, and a host of other personal conflicts and hostilities which students bring to the language learning situation could create serious blocks to intellectual learning and needed to be dealt with productively if successful, non-defensive language

learning and language use were to take place (Rardin, 1976).

Curran (1976) envisioned a low-pressure language class in which students could feel secure and could cooperate, rather than compete, in a community learning environment. In this environment the teacher and the students supported and accepted each other and worked together as a group. The teacher, in this setting, did not function as an authority or strong presence, but rather as an understanding, supportive, non-judgmental counselor who had the knowledge that the students were there to learn and who was able to see the learners and their fears and needs from their perspective. The teacher's responsibility was to relate to the learners as "whole persons" and to structure opportunities for those learners to draw knowledge from him/her, as they felt ready to do so.

In formulating the C-L/CLL approach, Curran (1976) stressed the importance of this kind of supportive atmosphere to encourage students to exercise what we have called communicating initiative. But a primary focus of Curran's work was to highlight what we can call "learning initiative."

From Curran's perspective, students would be truly receptive to learning only if they assumed some of the responsibility for directing that learning and played a role in determining both the content and manner of their instruction. He envisioned a nurturing learning environment taught by a teacher who provided structure and direction without placing demands on the students. The teacher's function was to be sincerely responsive to student needs and input and encouraging of student initiative. This responsibility included taking into consideration what the students wanted to learn and how they wanted to learn it as long as the general goals and objectives which the teacher had established for the course were being met (Bodman, 1979). A brief description of a technique which practitioners of C-L/CLL call the "human computer" can serve as a good illustration of one way that C-L/CLL accomplishes this goal.

The "human computer" is used in C-L/CLL classes to practice both pronunciation and what C-L/CLL teachers call "creative sentence building." As a teaching technique, it is consistent with Stevick's (1980) distinction between control and initiative; that is, it enables the teacher to maintain full control of the activity, while at the same time it allows students to play a role in directing their own learning by offering them the possibility of taking as much initiative as they wish. The key element is that students are permitted options within the teacher's structure. As in all C-L/CLL techniques, the atmosphere is secure and supportive.

The "human computer" is a simple procedure. When it is used to practice "creative sentence building," for example, students take turns orally constructing their own original sentences. They are entirely free either to draw on grammar and vocabulary that they already know and feel confident of, or to explore and test out structures that they are unsure of. There are no teacher-imposed expectations on how complicated or adventuresome those sentences need to be, and the students can feel secure in knowing that they can take as much or as little risk as they feel comfortable with. The teacher, standing at the back of the room facing in the same direction as the students, offers feedback after each sentence by repeating the full sentence (in corrected form, if necessary) back to the students, without comment, to give the students themselves the opportunity and the responsibility to recognize and correct whatever mistakes they may have made. The teacher does not judge or make evaluative remarks, and the students are free to try their sentences as many times as they wish, or, if they prefer, they can experiment with different sentences. Individual students take their turns in an orderly fashion, without being called on by the teacher, and are free to participate, or not participate, as they see fit.

This kind of non-threatening teaching technique can serve as a clear example of one way that student motivation and initiative can be maximized at the same time that the teacher is able to maintain full control of the activity. Because the atmosphere is supportive, students are able to take risks and actively participate, at their own pace, without feeling pressured to keep up with an imposed learning agenda. As they become increasingly involved in the activity, their self-investment can be an even greater motivating force than any teacher's demands (see Curran, 1976).

Communicative Teaching Materials.   Earlier in this article we outlined several features of real communication which could have applicability both to our teaching and to communicative curriculum design. In examining these characteristics from the point of view of the classroom, we noted (Johnson, 1979) that these kinds of communicative skills could be most effectively practiced only in a classroom environment in which it was possible to engage in task-oriented activities mediated through language, but not focusing on it. We highlighted the importance of creating a structured, yet supportive, non-judgmental atmosphere in order to allow the students to feel free to take the risks inherent in these kinds of activities and stressed that performance should be evaluated not in terms of language, but rather in terms of success or failure in completing the task.

Creating opportunities for students to exercise their own communicating and learning initiative and play a role in directing their own learning, while at the same time maintaining teacher control, does not necessarily require adopting any kind of special curriculum or following any of the so-called "humanistic" methodologies. "Humanism," if it can be defined at all, is more of a philosophy or an attitude than a method or a technique (Clarke, 1980). Even C-L/CLL, although it does have some specific techniques which have become associated with it, does not prescribe what should happen in class; it is only an approach, not an explicit syllabus (Taylor, 1979). Within this general learner-centered approach, instructors are free to structure their classes as they see fit; the teacher always has that right. This approach can be applied to the teaching of any of the language skills, using any curriculum, and the proponents of C-L/CLL have repeatedly stressed that there is considerable variation in the way different teachers use C-L/CLL (Rardin, personal communication).

For teachers who are able to create some of their own teaching materials or adapt existing ones, there are numerous ways to structure their classes to provide opportunities for students to be actively engaged in real communication and to thereby learn communicative skills in the classroom. For example, such activities might include involving students in goal- or task-oriented group projects which interest or affect them (see Allwright, 1979; Geddes, 1981; Johnson, 1981b; White, 1981; Wright, 1981), in logical problem-solving activities which are conceptually worth solving (see Huckin, 1980; Maley, 1980, 1981; Long, 1975; Widdowson, 1981), in information-gathering activities (see d'Anglejan, 1978), or in task-oriented communication with invited native-speaker "guests" (see Gunterman, 1980) (e.g., public opinion surveys or interviews). These activities can be undertaken not only in class, but out of class as well and can be designed to incorporate practice in any of the language skills. The students and the teacher can get ideas for topics and activities from a variety of sources, such as books, magazines, newspapers, radio, television, students' interests, experiences, feelings, or reactions.

The setting up of an information gap in the classroom is one particularly valuable tool to use to create a real communicative situation. Activities which require the bridging of information gaps provide students with opportunities to learn how to deal with extended discourse above the sentence level, to cope with receiving information which is new and unexpected, to exercise both linguistic and informational choices in forming their responses, and to do so at a natural pace.

Two pedagogical techniques which have been developed to create information gaps in the classroom are the "jigsaw" (Geddes and Sturtridge, 1979) and "task dependency" (Johnson, 1981b) principles. The jigsaw principle is used primarily in group activities which are of a task-oriented or problem-solving nature. When activities are structured according to this principle, key information required to complete the task is given only to some of the students, but withheld from others. Because a pooling of information is then required to successfully complete the task, this kind of information gap creates a real need for students to communicate with each other.

The task dependency principle is often used in conjunction with the jigsaw principle. When activities are structured according to the task dependency principle, students must first successfully complete certain sub-tasks before they are able to complete the major task which they have been assigned. For example (adapted from Geddes, 1981), if students in a class are planning to take an automobile trip of some kind, the major task of selecting the best route for them to take might be set up to require that they first complete several sub-tasks, such as extracting the pertinent information they will need from a number of real informational sources. These sources might include taped discussions of road conditions in a specific region, road maps, recorded weather reports, weather maps, and recorded traffic reports. The jigsaw principle could also be employed here by structuring the activity so that different students engage in different sub-tasks. All students would then need to pool their information before they would be able to jointly complete the major task of selecting the best route.

An activity of this kind provides opportunities for students to practice a variety of communicative skills. The major task of selecting the best route creates real reasons for students to undertake the sub-tasks and offers an opportunity for them to practice evaluating a body of information against a real goal, extracting the relevant, rejecting the irrelevant. The jigsaw principle creates an information gap that enables the students to practice serving as both giver and receiver of new information. Bridging this information gap makes individual students accountable to the whole group and allows them to experience the unexpectedness which is characteristic of spontaneous communication. Throughout this communication they remain in a state of uncertainty regarding what they will hear, and they therefore expreience the freedom to choose what they consider to be the most appropriate response. Negotiating the final solution to the major task of selecting the best route gives them practice in engaging in extended discourse in real time.

Students can be given considerable latitude in how they engage in these kinds of activities. The teacher's role is to assume the responsibility for setting up the conditions for communication to take place (Scott, 1981) by structuring and outlining the activity. Rather than taking an active role, however, teachers are advised to maintain a "low profile," perhaps asking only "attention-directing" questions (Allwright, 1979), allowing the students to pursue the task largely on their own. In C-L/CLL, for example, the teacher often divides the class into small groups, allowing each group to work on the task in its own way. Alternatively, different groups can each be given the responsibility to decide which aspect of a larger class project they wish to pursue. Or, the teacher may decide to set up several alternative activities, incorporating student suggestions, and allow students to choose which activity they would like to participate in; small groups are created accordingly. Each small group has the responsibility to carry out its own activity, calling upon the teacher, as needed.

It does not matter, ultimately, how successful students actually are in accomplishing the tasks that they undertake. The real language experience is what is most important, and this kind of approach can be particularly successful because students are directly involved. They are interested in what they are doing because they have a say in selecting their own tasks and activities and in deciding how they will carry them out. They develop confidence in their ability to cope with the language for some useful purpose (Allwright, 1979). They are self-invested and their motivation is likely to be greater. In these kinds of activities students get real, meaningful practice in authentic communication with their minds directly on communication, rather than on language. As they plan and execute their projects, or discuss their tasks, they are engaging in purposeful communication that focuses on content and real issues. While it may not always be possible to devise activities that are real in an absolute sense, it has been suggested that activities of this kind, even when they are simulated, can "foster 'natural,' 'creative,' 'authentic' language behavior on the part of learners once the framework of rules and conventions has been firmly established" (Maley, 1981:137).

THE ROLE OF EXPLICIT GRAMMAR

In the light of these comments, it is now appropriate to question where explicit grammar teaching fits into this general framework. If, as has been suggested, students need to be actively engaged in real communication with the focus of their attention on content rather than on grammar, should grammar be taught at all? And if so, how, when, and in what sequence?

Although long-standing traditions have supported an explicit, sequential grammar component in language teaching, recent research in second language acquisition has questioned its value. Consider the following four observations:

1. Most learners are unable to successfully transfer their mechanical control of grammatical patterns to real communicative situations (d'Anglejan, 1978; Long et al., 1976).
2. The acquisition of syntax appears to be a natural developmental process in learners and may have its own timetable (Krashen, 1979).
3. The order of acquisition of grammar rules may be determined more by communicative need than by the teaching order (Kessler et al., 1979; Taylor, 1981).
4. There is considerable variation among learners in the manner in which they acquire grammatical forms: some can profit from rules, some cannot; some can use forms quickly—almost immediately after they are presented, others need more time; many students need to see how the form is used in a number of different contexts—approached from a number of different directions—before they can use it, some do not (Krashen, 1977; Bodman, 1979; Taylor, 1982).

Taken together, these observations suggest that since it is unlikely that all of our students will be at the same learning stage at the same time, a sequenced presentation of grammar may not meet their needs. Just because an item is next on the syllabus does not imply that the students are ready to receive that information. So, while we may feel the need to "cover" a certain amount of material in class, what is actually acquired may well be beyond our control.

There are few linguistically compelling reasons to support sequencing grammar teaching in any particular way. While it is clear that some of the more complex linguistic structures require a prior control of some of the simpler structures, the order in which those structures is learned need not be fixed. Why, for example, is it necessary for students to learn the simple present tense before the past? Or the progressive before the imperative? Or questions before modal auxiliaries? If we take a communicative point of view, in fact, it would be fair to say that students who are studying in the target culture need all of the structures simultaneously if they are going to be able to meet the real communicative needs which they face every day. When, in their daily encounters, they find that they are required to ask for information, or give directions, or talk about something that happened to them yesterday, it will not help them to know that the necessary linguistic forms are on the syllabus, but will not be taught for another month. Students will simply make do with whatever linguistic resources are at their disposal to get their point across (Selinker, 1972; Taylor, 1974), and what has been suggested throughout this article is that this kind of real communicative need provides a more reasonable starting-off point for language instruction than a pre-determined teaching order.

When an explanation of a new linguistic form is offered at a time when it can be perceived to fulfill a real or present communicative need, learners are able to focus on active, communicatively based, self-invested learning. The psychological impact of recognizing the immediate communicative utility of a new form is greater than that which exists when language forms are presented in an arbitrary order and then practiced through contrived activities designed to create the illusion of reality. Not only does this approach demonstrate to students quite clearly that what they are learning can enable them to successfully communicate in a realistic way on issues that matter to them, it also provides real language input for processing and rules for those students who can use them. This is a very different situation from one in which we make the decisions about when to teach new structures to our students, since it is entirely likely that those new linguistic forms will only be stored away as just more information about the language, their functional value as yet undemonstrated (Taylor, 1982).

It is important to recognize that this article is not proposing that there is no need for explicit grammar instruction. It is simply being suggested that we reconsider the long-standing assumption that that instruction needs to follow a prescribed sequence. Widdowson (1981) has pointed out, for example, that the major weakness of grammar-based instruction is not that the focus of attention is on structure, but rather that, in teaching, structures are often not represented as a resource to communicate meaning. Taught within a communicative, needs-based context, however, explicit grammar instruction can meet four significant needs:

1. Since it has been shown that some students are able to profit from direct instruction in grammar (Krashen, 1977), that instruction should be offered as a supplement to, but not instead of, real communicative experiences for those students who can profit from it. "Mastery," however, should not be required—nor should participation.
2. Since our classes, no matter how communicatively based, may not provide enough real language input for students to be able to acquire forms on their own (Krashen, 1980), grammar can be offered as an optional supplement for those students who can make use of explanations, clarification, and rules.
3. Because the language used in presenting, explaining, and discussing grammar is real, communicative language, students can profit from this additional exposure to language even if they cannot profit directly from the grammatical information being discussed (Krashen, 1980).
4. Students typically expect, want, and demand instruction in explicit grammar. To ignore what they consider to be important or necessary, regardless of our point of view, is to invite resistance, either overt or covert, to our teaching (Stevick, 1980). It seems more reasonable to try to expand and broaden their expectations than to try to change them. This may well involve our spending a limited amount of time on activities which we might otherwise prefer to avoid.

C-L/CLL deals with explicit grammar instruction in much the way it has been discussed here. While there is a strong grammatical component incorporated within the approach, grammar rules are typically taught in the order in which they are needed by the students. The teacher rarely engages in long, elaborate explanations, but rather concentrates on the specific need as it arises. The teacher offers the grammar as an aid to students and does not require mastery or force students to participate.

What is significant is that the students motivate themselves to learn the rules. Because of the strong emphasis in C-L/CLL on group work and on students' assuming responsibility for their own learning, the pressure to learn comes directly from the students. Students become motivated to learn because they do not want to let their group down, or because they feel a pressing need to acquire what has been taught. The teacher is therefore relieved of having to impose that pressure.

The extent to which students are able to assume this responsibility comes out most clearly in small group work. In groups, students are occasionally given flexibility, within the general structure established by the teacher, to select for themselves what they want to practice and how they want to practice it, whether it be grammar, or vocabulary, or idioms. Different groups select different points and practice them in different ways. The better learners help the slower learners. The language forms which have been most recently presented or discussed are left on the blackboard or on large sheets of newsprint posted on the wall in full view of the class. The teacher is always there to answer any questions that the students may have, but only if called on. It is apparent, in observing these groups, that a lot of learning is going on. Students are practicing, puzzling out points, experimenting, testing hypotheses, and drawing conclusions. They are relying on each other and learning from each other. And, most importantly, they are communicating. As Krashen points out (1976:165), even during times when students may choose to discuss grammar, or vocabulary, or idioms, "to the extent that the target language is used realistically, to that extent will acquisition occur."

There will be times, of course, when the teacher may want to take the lead—to offer forms, to introduce a new pattern, to explain a structure, to provide vocabulary, or to identify an error. This is not inconsistent with the approach which has been presented here if it is done subtly, sparingly, and in the spirit of learner-centeredness. That is, when trust between the students and the teacher is established, teachers can assume this kind of role as long as students understand that what is being offered is optional, and that the teacher is not requiring "mastery." For students who, for whatever reason, would not be able to acquire the form being taught in such a direct way, demands for immediate learning can be threatening and demoralizing. It can take a long time for teachers to acquire this kind of judgment (Stevick, 1980; Bodman, 1979).

CONCLUSION

What has been suggested throughout this article is that we take the students' communicative attempts in the target language as the starting-off point for our instruction, rather than the rules or the structure of the language. The basic approach, as outlined here, requires a commitment on the part of the teacher to reverse many of the teaching practices which have become traditional in language teaching methodology over the years. It involves looking at students, not as students per se, but as whole people with needs, and fears, and goals, and commitments and then capitalizing on those students' ability to invest themselves in accomplishing their goals and objectives. It stresses the close interrelationship which exists between the issues of classroom interaction and curriculum, content and atmosphere, and focuses on the need for students to feel secure, unthreatened, and nondefensive. It highlights the need for instructors to avoid adopting a teacher-centered, authoritarian posture.

When such an atmosphere is achieved, students can then feel free to exercise their own initiative in communicating and in directing their own learning. This approach recognizes that the need to accomplish something can be a compelling factor in language learning and can foster "self-investment"—a whole-person commitment to accomplishing a goal. When a class provides opportunities for students to participate in guiding their own learning, selecting their own activities, and deciding what they want to practice, those students have a stake in the outcome of their endeavors, their interest and motivation are likely to be higher, and they become more receptive to instruction if that instruction will help them meet that goal—whether it is to understand a syntactic pattern, or to solve a problem, or to complete a task. This approach highlights the importance that initiative plays in promoting real communication. This communication provides opportunities for students to be exposed to language and to use it. The need to accomplish something through that language keeps the communication going.

When students are committed to accomplishing something which depends upon their further mastery of the target language, instruction can then be provided to meet those emerging language needs. This kind of situation can create the sort of classroom atmosphere in which teaching can be most profitably received. This approach stresses the need to teach what is needed when it is needed—to give learners the flexibility to learn in their own way, at their own pace, rather than to follow a pre-determined syllabus. It emphasizes the need to provide learners with the space they need to receive the instruction without feeling compelled to master it immediately. It points out the need to maintain a non-authoritarian presence throughout this process so that students can continue to feel secure and non-defensive—to enable them to learn not because the teacher demands it of them, but because they need to in order to accomplish their own goals.

And finally, this approach stresses that sharing the responsibility for structuring learning with the students does not require that teachers abdicate their fundamental authority to guide and structure their classes. It highlights the need for teachers to be sensitive to what is happening in the classroom and to respond to the dynamics of the class. This approach may not work equally well for all teachers and all students. Nevertheless, for those who are able to use it, classes which incorporate these ideas can be exciting, exhilarating, and satisfying. This approach has been called "student-centered," but the responsibility for accomplishing it resides with us.

REFERENCES

Allwright, Richard. 1979. Language learning through communicative practice. In C. J. Brumfit and K. Johnson (eds.), *The Communicative Approach to Language Teaching.* Oxford, England: Oxford University Press, 167–182.

Bodman, Jean W. 1979. Student-centering education: The gentle revolution in ESL teaching. In Diana E. Bartley (ed.), *The Adult Basic Education TESOL Handbook.* New York: Collier-Macmillan International, 19–31.

Brumfit, Christopher. 1981. Teaching the 'general student.' In Keith Johnson and Keith Morrow (eds.). *Communication in the Classroom.* Essex, England: Longman Group Ltd., 46–51.

Clarke, Mark A. 1980. The tyranny of "humanism." Unpublished paper.

Curran, Charles A. 1961. Counseling skills adapted to the learning of foreign languages. *Bulletin of the Menninger Clinic 25,* 78–93.

Curran, Charles A. 1972. *Counseling-Learning: A Whole-Person Model for Education.* New York: Grune and Stratton.

Curran, Charles A. 1976. *Counseling-Learning in Second Languages.* Apple River, IL: Apple River Press.

d'Anglejan, Alison. 1978. Language learning in and out of classrooms. In Jack C. Richards (ed.), *Understanding Second and Foreign Language Learning.* Rowley, MA: Newbury House Publishers, 218–236.

Gardner, Robert C., and W. E. Lambert. 1972. *Attitudes and Motivation in Second-Language Learning.* Rowley, MA: Newbury House Publishers.

Geddes, Marion. 1981. Listening. In Keith Johnson and Keith Morrow (eds.), *Communication in the Classroom.* Essex, England: Longman Group Ltd., 78–86.

Geddes, Marion, and Gill Sturtridge. 1979. *Listening Links.* London, England: Heinemann Educational Books Ltd.

Gunterman, Gail. 1980. Factors in targeting proficiency levels and an approach to "real" and "realistic" practice. *Studies in Second Language Acquisition 3.* 1:34–41.

Huckin, Thomas N. 1980. Review of Henry G. Widdowson, *Teaching language as communication. Language Learning 30,* 1:209–227.

Johnson, Keith. 1979. Communicative approaches and communicative processes. In C. J. Brumfit and K. Johnson (eds.). *The Communicative Approach to Language Teaching.* Oxford, England: Oxford University Press, 192–205.

Johnson, Keith. 1981a. Introduction: Some background, some key terms and some definitions. In

Keith Johnson and Keith Morrow (eds.), *Communication in the Classroom*. Essex, England: Longman Group Ltd., 1–12.

Johnson, Keith. 1981b. Writing. In Keith Johnson and Keith Morrow (eds.), *Communication in the Classroom*. Essex, England: Longman Group Ltd., 93–107.

Kessler, Carolyn, David C. Harrison, and Curtis W. Hayes. 1979. Teacher input—learner intake: Aspects of discourse analysis. Paper presented at the 13th Annual TESOL Convention, Boston, February 28–March 4, 1979.

Krashen, Stephen D. 1976. Formal and informal linguistic environments in language acquisition and language learning. *TESOL Quarterly 10*, 2:157–168.

Krashen, Stephen D. 1977. The monitor model for adult second language performance. In Marina Burt, Heidi Dulay, and Mary Finocchiaro (eds.), *Viewpoints on English as a Second Language*. New York: Regents Publishing Company, 152–161.

Krashen, Stephen D. 1979. The input hypothesis. Paper presented at the Georgetown University Roundtable on Languages and Linguistics, Washington, D.C.

Krashen, Stephen D. 1980. The theoretical and practical relevance of simple codes in second language acquisition. In Robin C. Scarcella and Stephen D. Krashen (eds.), *Research in Second Language Acquisition*. Rowley, MA: Newbury House Publishers, 7–18.

Long, Michael H. 1975. Group work and communicative competence in the ESOL classroom. In Marina Burt and Heidi Dulay (eds.), *On TESOL '75*. Washington, D.C.: TESOL, 211–223.

Long, Michael H., L. Adams, M. McLean, and F. Castaños. 1976. Doing things with words—verbal interaction in lockstep and small group classroom situations. In John Fanselow and Ruth H. Crymes (eds.), *On TESOL '76*. Washington, D.C.: TESOL, 137–153.

Lukmani, Yasmeen M. 1972. Motivation to learn and learning proficiency. *Language Learning 22*, 2:261–273.

Maley, Alan. 1980. Teaching for communicative competence: Reality and illusion. *Studies in Second Language Acquisition 3*, 1:10–16.

Maley, Alan. 1981. Games and problem solving. In Keith Johnson and Keith Morrow (eds.), *Communication in the Classroom*. Essex, England: Longman Group Ltd., 137–148.

Morrow, Keith. 1981. Introduction: Principles of communicative methodology. In Keith Johnson and Keith Morrow (eds.), *Communication in the Classroom*. Essex, England: Longman Group Ltd., 59–66.

Rardin, Jennybelle. 1976. A model for second language learning. In Charles A. Curran, *Counseling-Learning in Second Languages*. Apple River, IL: Apple River Press.

Rardin, Jennybelle. 1977. The language teacher as facilitator. *TESOL Quarterly 11*, 4:383–387.

Rogers, Carl A. 1965. *Client-Centered Therapy: Its Current Practice, Implications, and Theory*. Boston: Houghton-Mifflin Co.

Saegert, Joel, M. Scott, J. Perkins, and G. Tucker. 1974. A note on the relationship between English proficiency, years of language study and medium of instruction. *Language Learning 24*, 1:99–104.

Schumann, John H. 1978. *The Pidginization Process*. Rowley, MA: Newbury House Publishers.

Scott, Roger. 1981. Speaking. In Keith Johnson and Keith Morrow (eds.), *Communication in the Classroom*. Essex, England: Longman Group Ltd., 70–77.

Selinker, Larry. 1972. Interlanguage. *International Review of Applied Linguistics 10*, 209–231.

Stevick, Earl W. 1976. *Memory, Meaning and Method*. Rowley, MA: Newbury House Publishers.

Stevick, Earl W. 1980. *Teaching Languages: A Way and Ways*. Rowley, MA: Newbury House Publishers.

Taylor, Barry P. 1973. Review of Robert C. Gardner and Wallace E. Lambert, *Attitudes and motivation in second-language learning*. *Language Learning 23*, 1:145–149.

Taylor, Barry P. 1974. Toward a theory of language acquisition. *Language Learning 24*, 1:23–35.

Taylor, Barry P. 1979. Exploring community language learning. In Carlos A. Yorio, Kyle Perkins, and Jacquelyn Schachter (eds.), *On TESOL '79*. Washington, D.C.: TESOL, 80–84.

Taylor, Barry P. 1981. Content and written form: A two-way street. *TESOL Quarterly 15*, 1:5–13.

Taylor, Barry P. 1982. In search of real reality. *TESOL Quarterly 16*, 1:29–42.

Taylor, Barry P., and Nessa Wolfson. 1978. Breaking down the free conversation myth. *TESOL Quarterly 12,* 1:31–39.

Tucker, G. Richard. 1977. Can a second language be taught? In H. Douglas Brown, Carlos A. Yorio, and Ruth H. Crymes (eds.), *On TESOL '77.* Washington, D.C.: TESOL, 14–30.

Upshur, John A. 1968. Four experiments on the relation between foreign language teaching and learning. *Language Learning 18,* 1:111–124.

Warshawsky, Diane R. 1978. The acquisition of four English morphemes by Spanish-speaking children. Abstract in Evelyn Hatch (ed.), *Second Language Acquisition.* Rowley, MA: Newbury House Publishers, 472.

White, Ronald V. 1981. Reading. In Keith Johnson and Keith Morrow (eds.), *Communication in the classroom.* Essex, England: Longman Group Ltd., 87–92.

Widdowson, Henry G. 1978. *Teaching Language as Communication.* Oxford, England: Oxford University Press.

Widdowson, Henry G. 1981. Course design and discourse process in English for specific purposes. Paper presented at the 8th Annual MEXTESOL National Convention, Guadalajara, Mexico, October 2–5, 1981.

Wright, Andrew. 1981. Visuals. In Keith Johnson and Keith Morrow (eds.), *Communication in the Classroom.* Essex. England: Longman Group Ltd., 117–125.

Yorio, Carlos A. 1982. Communicative language teaching: Why and what? Paper presented at the 2nd Annual Penn TESOL-East Fall Conference, Philadelphia, November 6, 1982.

CHAPTER
5

Bilingual Education:
Research and its Implications

Merrill Swain

Bilingual education has different meanings to different people. By bilingual education I mean the use of two languages as mediums of instruction at some stage in a student's educational career. This allows for wide variation with respect to when the languages are used within any grade level or across grade levels. Thus, included as bilingual educational, are programs such as French immersion programs where English-speaking unilingual students are initially instructed in French and do not receive instruction in, or about, their first language until the third or fourth year of schooling, as well as programs for unilingual Chinese students who are taught initially in their mother tongue and introduced to instruction in, or about, English simultaneously or at later grade levels. Bilingual education does not, and should not, exclude the teaching of either language as language per se, but it necessarily involves using both languages as vehicles of instruction.

The sheer volume of words that have been devoted to the topic of bilingual education is, to say the least, overwhelming. One can read about bilingual education from a linguistic perspective, an educational perspective, a philosophi-

cal, psychological, sociological, political, historical, or a legal perspective (see, for example Spolsky and Cooper, 1977; Centre for Applied Linguistics, 1977). One can find discussions and descriptions of bilingual education in multilingual societies in both developed and developing countries, of bilingual education for immigrant groups, for indigenous populations, for minority language groups, as well as for majority language groups (see, for example, Lord and T'sou, 1976; Spolsky, 1972; Swain and Bruck, 1976). And one can read about research and evaluation studies associated with bilingual education (see, for example Lambert and Tucker, 1972; Cohen, 1976; Mackey, 1972).

However, attempting to come to grips with all the literature, and the contradictory conclusions reached in the various research and evaluation studies, quite simply, boggles the mind! Consider some of the research evidence, for example. On the one hand, evidence has been presented which suggests that bilingual education leads to enhanced cognitive development, high levels of achievement in content learning, high levels of proficiency in second language skills, enrichment of first language skills, increased feelings of self-worth, as well as more positive attitudes toward schooling and toward other ethnic groups. On the other hand, evidence which supports virtually the opposite conclusions has also been presented.

Can these differences be reconciled? I believe they can. Furthermore I think they must be, if our concern is with the provision of educational programs which maximize a child's opportunity for learning and personal growth. What I want to do, then, is to try to provide a basis for understanding the contradictory conclusions associated with bilingual education. In order to do this we will need to consider differences in programs, differences in the children attending the programs, differences in the communities in which the programs operate, and differences in the research strategies employed in the studies themselves.

As one outcome of this exercise, several underlying concepts which in part account for the contradictory results emerge. And it is with a brief discussion of these concepts that I will conclude.

So let me turn now to examine some contradictory evidence. In doing so, it is relevant to note that although studies which have examined the effects of bilingual education have measured a variety of student outcomes, they have all been concerned with at least two questions, and these are the questions we will consider here: First, how do students in a bilingual program perform academically relative to similar students who are not participating in the program? Second, how do the linguistic skills of students in a bilingual education program compare with those who are not participating in the program?

The results that I will refer to come mainly from two different sources: the Canadian data on early total French immersion education and the American data gathered by the American Institutes for Research (Danoff, et al., 1978). The Canadian data have been collected by a number of researchers over the last decade or so, each working in their own local area (see Swain, 1976, for a bibliography). The American Institutes for Research (AIR) study, a study commissioned by the US Office of Planning, Budgeting and Evaluation, examined the impact on Title VII students in Spanish-English programs. To do this a large nationwide representative sample of Title VII projects was selected and compared to similar students in non-Title VII programs. The major part of the study was conducted in the 1975–76 school year and included students from grades 2 to 6.[1] The programs from which the students were selected were in their fourth or fifth year of operation.

With respect to the first question, how do students in a bilingual program perform academically relative to students not participating in the program, studies of French immersion programs in Canada show that students in the French immersion program obtain scores equivalent to their English-educated counterparts on standardized tests of Science and Mathematics, typically scoring at or above their expected grade level in relation to national norms. On the other hand, the AIR study showed that Title VII students either performed similarly or not as well as non-Title VII students, and both groups scored below their expected grade level in relation to national norms in Mathematics. The expectation, of course, was that the Title VII students would do better than non-Title VII students.

With respect to the second question, how do the linguistic skills of students in a bilingual program compare with those who are not participating in the program, studies of French immersion students in Canada show that in relation to their first language, there is an initial lag in English language skills on the immersion students relative to their English-educated counterparts. However differences between the groups disappear by no later than grade four. In later grades, immersion students in some cases out-perform their English educated counterparts in various aspects of English language skills, and tend to stand at or above their expected grade level in terms of national norms. It is interesting—and we will return to this point later—that little attempt has been made to measure first language proficiency in the U.S. programs. However, in the AIR evaluation of Title VII programs just mentioned, Spanish reading was measured, and no differences were found between the scores of the students in the Title VII programs and similar students not participating in Title VII programs. The expectation was of course, that students in the bilingual program would do better.

In relation to second language skills, the Canadian French immersion results show that in reading and listening native-like levels are attained, but not in speaking and writing. On a French achievement test standardized on a Quebec francophone population, immersion students score around or below the 50th percentile; whereas the AIR results showed that on a standardized test of English reading and vocabulary knowledge the Title VII students score around the 20th percentile in grades 2 through 6.

I have taken extremes to illustrate how different the results can be. There are, indeed, other studies which show equally positive or negative results. The issue being raised here, however, is what possible factors might account for the differences in results. How, in fact, can these differences be reconciled?

First, there is the issue of how the data are interpreted with respect to expectations. Second, there are important differences in the strategies employed in carrying out the studies themselves that may account for the different results. And third, there are a variety of background, student and program variables that may also account for the differences. These will be examined in turn.

First, it is important to note that the goals of the two programs are different. In the French immersion program, the goal is to learn a second language without a decrease in native language skills or academic performance. In the

Title VII programs, the goal is to learn a second language and increase academic performance. The role of the mother tongue is seen as a bridge so that students are not prevented from learning content material while the second language is being learned. Thus, the results just mentioned are interpreted as positive in the case of the Canadian programs because the goals have been attained. However, in the U.S. the results are interpreted negatively because the expectations have not been met. However it is important to note, as Zappert and Cruz (1977) have done, and I quote them:

> a non-significant effect is not a negative finding with respect to bilingual education. A non-significant effect, that students in bilingual education classes are learning at the same rate as students in monolingual classes, demonstrates the fact that learning in two languages does not interfere with a student's academic and cognitive performance. Students in bilingual classes have the added advantage of learning a second language and culture without impeding their educational progress. Under these circumstances, a non-significant finding can be interpreted as a positive effect of bilingual education.

Let us consider next the nature of the differences between the two sets of studies. Although the AIR study evaluated student performance from grades two to six, it did so by looking at each grade level independently and examined achievement gains over approximately a six-month period within each grade level.[2] Although most of us may claim to be optimistic about the effects of education, even the most optimistic amongst us may consider that six months is a rather short period of time to expect significant changes to occur in one group relative to another, especially when one considers that the six-month period is not the only "input" time.[3] That is to say, gains may have already been made by the students during previous years in the program, and these previous gains would not be evident in a comparison of gains over a six-month period.

In this respect, the studies on immersion education have been considerably different. The studies have followed students for considerably longer periods of time, in most cases from kindergarten year to their current grade level, thus allowing for the cumulative effect of the program to be determined.

The problem of looking for significant differences in gains over short periods of time in the AIR study is compounded by the fact that very little was known about the previous educational experiences of the students, or their linguistic or attitudinal characteristics at the onset of their experience with bilingual education. We might ask in what ways were the Title VII students different from those who did not enter a bilingual education program? Presumably they were having difficulties with English, yet the results show that by grade 5 they were making gains equivalent to non-Title VII students, and were in fact scoring comparably on standardized tests of English.

Many of the students in the study had been placed into the bilingual program part way through their elementary education. For example, the average number of years previously spent in a bilingual education program for the grade 6 students in the AIR study at the time of testing was approximately three. What was the effect of the switch? Perhaps their parents did not want them in a bilingual education program because they feared their child might not learn English in a bilingual class? Perhaps switching was perceived by the child as a sign of failure in school? Perhaps the Spanish taught and used in class was not their own dialect of Spanish only to reinforce already existing feelings of inferiority?[4]

And what about the students who were in a bilingual education program in previous years and have since moved to non-Title VII programs because they have been judged to have sufficient knowledge of English to cope with instruction in English? Aside from the fact that their absence would have the effect of lowering the English scores attained by Title VII students, shouldn't they also have been studied as part of the impact of Title VII?[5]

In the Canadian immersion studies, on the other hand, the initial characteristics of the students are known. They are unilingual English-speaking children. They come from middle to upper-middle class homes, and their parents have chosen to enroll them in the program. Students do not leave the program when they have sufficient knowledge of the second language, but rather they remain in the program continuing to study in both their first and second languages. There is, however, attrition, and although it has not been studied systematically yet, it is an important question to ask why some students leave the program. In some cases it may be because the program was perceived by their parents or teachers to be too difficult for them, although recent data from Alberta suggests that moving was the main source of attrition. However, just as the "drop-outs" of Title VII programs might perhaps be viewed as a sign of the success of the program, perhaps the "drop-outs" of French immersion programs might be viewed as a sign of its failure.

The point being made here is that without knowing what the initial characteristics of the students were, and the cumulative effects of the program on the students, it is impossible to conclude that the results are either negative or positive. Interpretation of the results as either positive or negative is dependent on knowing what the children were like at the beginning of the program, and observing the effects over time of the program (see also, Cummins, 1979a).

Another difference between the AIR and Canadian studies is that of lumping together the results across different program variations. This simply has not been done in Canada. Comparison of results across different program variations have been made on an ad hoc basis (Swain, 1978), and generalizations from similar programs ongoing in different communities have been drawn (Swain, 1979). The AIR study has taken the opposite tact, and averaged results across communities and program formats. Given also the heterogeneity among students in terms of their abilities in each language, their language use patterns, their attitudes toward school and the use of each language from program to program, as well as within programs, the results are basically useless in providing information that would be helpful to program planners. Much more useful would have been to analyze results according to known differences in student and community characteristics and program treatment, examining the individual results to determine if any generalizations could be drawn, even if tentative.

In effect the AIR study violates the very common sense point that to determine what kinds of programs work best with what kinds of children under what circumstances, one needs to look at the effects of individual programs and community variables as they interact with initial student characteristics over a long enough period that cumulative effects of the program can be observed. Most likely some of the programs were effective at achieving their aims, and some were not. What would be interesting and useful to do is determine the characteristics of the successful and unsuccessful programs.[6]

Finally in terms of research methodology it is worth mentioning a problem that plagues both sets of studies: the instruments used to assess student language abilities and achievement levels. Here, the best that can be said at the moment is that we need to develop much more sophisticated tools for the assessment of linguistic abilities. We must address the issue, too, of language for what purpose?—for communication? as an instrument of thought? for self-reflection? for artistic and literary purposes? for what?

What do current language tests measure? Most of the tests used measure vocabulary knowledge, reading and grammatical knowl-

edge. Grammatical knowledge would appear to be a necessary although not sufficient condition for communicative performance, but clearly, tests of grammatical knowledge cannot substitute for tests of communicative performance. Then we must address the issue of what constitutes minimal levels of communicative performance if that is to define limited English (French, Spanish) speaking abilities. And if it is to define the necessary minimal level, then it is essential to consider the relationships between this minimum level of communicative performance and the psycholinguistic concept of threshold level as proposed by Cummins (1978; 1979a) and which will be discussed shortly.

As well as differences in approaches to the evaluation of programs, there are many differences both in the characteristics of the students involved in the Title VII programs and those of the students involved in immersion education. Many of these have already been mentioned in the preceding discussion, but it is important to note the considerable heterogeneity both across and within programs of student characteristics in the U.S. programs, especially as relates to their first and second language abilities at the onset of the program, and the students' perception of their participation in the program. The common characteristic among students participating in the Title VII programs as stipulated by the previous legislation was that they were from lower class families. The immersion students, on the other hand, form a much more homogenous group and for the most part, come from middle to upper-middle class homes.

Similarly there are differences in communities—in community attitudes toward the use of the languages involved and toward the program format. Where immersion programs exist, it is usually because the community has fought for it, often against administrator resistance. In effect, the programs have been tailored to meet the community demands. For example, in Ottawa and Montreal where the need for French is perceived as greater than in, for example,

Vancouver, more instructional time in French has been demanded. In the U.S. programs, it has often been the case that program formats have also been developed to meet community demands. However, it has also been the case that in some communities the programs have been imposed by legal mandates on communities which are more concerned with having their children learn English than maintain their mother tongue. To them it is anti-intuitional that bilingual education can provide both.

And finally there are program differences. The typical format of a French immersion program is that all instruction is given in French, the second language, until grade 2 or 3. Only then is English Language Arts introduced and taught in English for approximately an hour a day. With each successive year thereafter a larger proportion of the curriculum is taught in English until an approximately equal balance is reached between the time devoted to instruction in the mother tongue and the second language.

The first French immersion program in the public sector began in the Montreal area some 14 years ago. Since then other communities have pushed for an immersion program to be established, due in large part to the reported success of the original program. Each program has begun at the kindergarten level and each year added a successive grade. Thus, the growth both within programs and across Canada, has been slow and steady. Millions of dollars have been spent on the development of curriculum materials, and on evaluations of individual programs by a variety of researchers. The data collected have been fed back to the program developers, leading at times to changes in instructional emphasis and instructional techniques.

The programs in the U.S. are as different as are the students who enter them and the communities they are housed in. The extent to which each language is used, by whom, for what purposes, to teach what, vary from program to program. In addition many programs were implemented before materials were prepared or teachers were trained.

As I have already mentioned, there are differences in the goals of the programs. Title VII is trying to accomplish several things at once: to increase the level of academic achievement, to strengthen self-image and culture identity, and to develop second language skills. In the immersion program, the main aim is to develop second language skills without a decrease in academic achievement or mother tongue development. In the immersion program, no one is concerned with improving the child's self-image or cultural identity; it is not judged to be low in the first place.

Let us consider for a moment a common goal—that of learning a second language. Here I think the Canadian research has an important message to offer and that is, that in spite of the fact that immersion students have "everything going for them"—that is, they come from middle to upper-middle class homes, they have parents who are involved in their education and motivated to have their children learn French, they have native French-speaking teachers and so on—they still have not mastered the spoken and written codes with anything like native proficiency. In spite of their lack of native-like proficiency in speaking and writing, the immersion students have developed sufficient levels of understanding and reading to be able to deal effectively with the material presented to them in the second language. This suggests that limiting the definition of those who need English to profit from instruction in that language to speaking abilities only is perhaps misguided. In light of this, it is a significant step that has been taken by the U.S. Federal legislation to open the Title VII program to those with limited English proficiency in all four skills—understanding, speaking, reading, and writing. As I have already mentioned this means that considerable efforts will be necessary to establish what is to be meant by minimal levels of proficiency.

Cummins (1978; 1979a) has referred to the level which must be attained in a language in order to profit from instruction in that language as the threshold level. Cummins has also suggested that the development of second language competence[7] is a function of the level of the child's first language competence at the time when intensive exposure to the second language begins. This implies that because the level of competence in the second language is dependent on the level attained in the first language, it is important to ensure that the threshold level is also attained in the first language. There is evidence to support this notion from several studies where initial teaching in the mother tongue plus second language classes has led to higher levels of linguistic performance in both the first and second languages relative to those students receiving initial instruction only in the second language. The studies include Finnish immigrants in Sweden (Skutnabb-Kangas and Toukomaa, 1979), francophone minority groups in Manitoba (Hébert et al., 1976) and Alberta (Cummins, 1979b), and Navajo children in Rock Point (Rosier and Farella, 1976). This points to the critical importance of determining the linguistic proficiency of the students in their first language, something which has rarely been done in the U.S. programs because the goals have been oriented to second language learning. But if the potential level to be developed in the second language is dependent on the level attained in the first language, then information about the first language abilities of the children will be important in determining appropriate forms of educational intervention.

The differences in results, then, can be attributed to a number of factors. They are rather nicely summed up by the notions of subtractive and additive bilingualism as proposed by Wallace Lambert (1975). Subtractive bilingualism refers to situations where the learning of the second language reflects the loss, or "poor" learning of the first language. Additive bilingualism refers to situations where the learning of

a second language occurs with no loss to the first language.

For example, in the French immersion program, the children are members of the dominant linguistic and cultural group. Learning the second language does not portend the gradual replacement of the first language and the loss of cultural identity associated with that language. Furthermore the second language being learned is a socially relevant, nationally and internationally recognized language, through which individual economic advantages may accrue to the learner. This situation, that is, where the first language is maintained while a second language is being learned, is an "additive" form of bilingualism. This is in contrast to the situation faced by many immigrant groups, minority groups and indigenous populations who perceive knowledge of the majority school language to be the gateway to social and economic gains, and the home language to be of little consequence except in enabling them to communicate with their friends and relatives, and preserve ethnic identity. The overwhelming use of the dominant language in school and in the wider community often results in a "subtractive" form of bilingualism where the learning of the second language may reflect some degree of loss of the first language and culture.

Combining the ideas of Lambert and Cummins, that is, that the potential for linguistic development in the second language is dependent on the level attained in the first language, and that subtractive bilingualism may indicate lower levels of attainment in the first language —suggests a major implication for education. The implication is that if optimal development of minority language children's academic and linguistic potential is a goal, then the school program must aim to promote an additive form of bilingualism. Attainment of this goal will necessarily involve a home-school language switch at some stage in the educational process, but when, and how much, must be determined in relation to the linguistic and socio-economic characteristics of the learner and of the learning environment. Specifically when the home language is different from the school language and the home language tends to be denigrated by others and selves, and where the children come from socio-economically deprived homes, it would appear appropriate to begin initial instruction in the child's first language with the second language being introduced as a subject of instruction. At a later stage instruction in the second language would then be introduced. On the other hand, where the home language is a majority language valued by the community, and where literacy is encouraged in the home, then the most efficient means of promoting an additive form of bilingualism is to provide initial instruction in the second language (Swain and Cummins, 1979).

These are general statements which now need to be refined by examining specific research hypotheses. Specific hypotheses can be generated which take into account the level of first and second language competence of the learner at the onset of the program, the particular socio-cultural-political characteristics of the environment, and the characteristics of the program itself in determining linguistic, academic and psychological outcomes.

Research has much to offer if we take as our starting point the question: which kinds of children are going to do best in which kind of program in what kinds of communities? Asking the question this way recognizes that there are many possible formats of bilingual education, that communities may differ radically, and that children vary considerably in the characteristics they bring with them to school. Student outcomes must be seen as resulting from community and program variables as they interact with student characteristics.

In summary, the following are the points that I have tried to make:

1. Different formats of bilingual education are appropriate for different students. The program will interact in important ways with, among other things, the linguistic characteristics the children bring with them to school and community attitudes towards the languages. Research must direct itself to the isolation of other key variables.

2. Negative results related to bilingual education tend to be associated with situations fostering subtractive forms of bilingualism. The challenge facing educators is how to turn subtractive forms of bilingualism into additive ones. This has been done in some instances, for example, with Finnish immigrants in Sweden, minority francophone groups in Alberta and Manitoba, and indigenous populations in the U.S.

3. Slow, steady growth of programs, with well-planned curriculum and strong community and administrative support is bound to lead to more effective results than "shot-gun" implementation.

4. In trying to interpret the results of research associated with bilingual education, ask yourself the following questions:
   a. What were the characteristics, especially linguistic, academic, and attitudinal, of the students before they entered the program?
   b. What are the attitudinal and linguistic characteristics of the community in relation to the program?
   c. What is the nature of the educational treatment especially with regard to the use of the two languages, both as taught and as used as mediums of instruction?
   d. For how long were the students followed? Are cumulative effects of the program being demonstrated?
   e. How is the child experiencing the program, regardless of the program goals?
   f. What was the nature of the tests used? What were they measuring? In what languages were they given, the child's first or second language, the child's dominant or weaker language?

5. And finally, in relation to the issue of tests, it is obvious that considerable effort is going to be needed to determine what constitutes minimal levels of language proficiency, per-

haps most productively pursued by asking what are the threshold levels, that is what does the student need to know linguistically in relation to reading, writing, speaking and understanding in order to be able to profit from instruction in that language?

In conclusion, there is one other point I would like to make. Although I have focused on outlining some of the reasons why we might find different results in different studies of bilingual education, it is important to note that there is evidence which demonstrates that some bilingual programs have accomplished their aims (see Troike, 1978, for example). It is unlikely that it will ever be possible to determine whether or not the fact that the program is bilingual is the only reason for its success. However, the fact that it has been demonstrated that through bilingual education it is possible to learn a second language and enhance learning at no expense to the mother tongue for minority, immigrant, and indigenous populations is extremely important. It means it can be done! It is possible through the efforts of dedicated teachers and committed communities to change subtractive bilingualism into an additive form of bilingualism. If we are committed to developing to its fullest potential the linguistic, academic and personal growth of the child through education, then bilingual education can provide the means to do so.

NOTES

1. In the fall of 1976, a sample of classrooms from the grades 2 and 3 cohorts was tested again when the students were in grades 3 and 4.

2. It should be noted that there was a full year between testings of the grades 2 and 3 cohorts mentioned in footnote 1, with approximately similar results.

3. For the 1975–76 sample, about 75% of the students in grades 2 to 6 had two or more years of bilingual education, and 50% of the students in grades 3 to 6 had three or more years.

4. D. Reynolds has since pointed out to me "that these speculations are not backed up by any evidence that the students were indeed switching into and out of the Title VII project classrooms for the reasons you suggest. If we are to conjecture about reasons for sixth graders being in the program for fewer than six years, we might suggest that the students came in late because they recently moved into a district with a Title VII program, because they recently arrived in the United States, or because slots in the classroom opened up when the students originally enrolled moved out of the school district. (There is a very high mobility among the student populations in most of the districts with Title VII programs) (personal communication, May 11, 1979). I see no disagreement between the reasons she suggests for why the children were switched, and what I am suggesting—the possible psychological effect of the switch.

5. It should be noted, however, that "AIR found almost no programs consciously moving students out of the bilingual classrooms once they had learned English. No exit criteria were in effect, and 85% of the projects studied considered themselves native language maintenance programs" (D. Reynolds, personal communication, May 11, 1979).

6. It is the case that in the AIR study, relationships were examined between student achievement and educational processes (e.g., extent of grouping versus individualized instruction, hours devoted to ESL and SSL instruction, use of languages in class), teacher

and teacher aide characteristics (e.g., level of education, teaching credentials, years teaching, training in bilingual education), and contextual variables (e.g., proportion of Hispanic students in class, home, and neighborhood language use of English) for a subsample of the programs. Although several interesting overall patterns emerge, the problem remains that the analyses lumped together all the programs rather than analyzing individual programs that were successful or unsuccessful and relating these outcomes to the above mentioned variables. And, unfortunately, the analyses used partialled out the effect of several of the factors which are being suggested here as key factors, e.g., preference for English versus Spanish, and the use of Spanish and English. But indeed, the authors are to be commended for collecting and analyzing such significant data. The major suggestion is that further analyses on a class-by-class basis would be more revealing if the aim is to understand what types of educational treatments are most successful for students of different linguistic and attitudinal characteristics in communities of different linguistic and attitudinal characteristics, given the program goals. In all fairness to the AIR study, however, it must be stated that its aim was not to evaluate any specific approach to bilingual education, but rather to evaluate the overall impact of the Title VII program.

7. For Cummins, language competence means "the ability to make effective use of the cognitive functions of language; that is to use language effectively as an instrument of thought and represent cognitive operations by means of language" (Cummins, 1978, footnote 21).

REFERENCES

Center for Applied Linguistics. 1977. *Bilingual education: Current perspectives.* Vols. 1–5. Arlington, VA: Center for Applied Linguistics.

Cohen, Andrew D. 1976. *A Sociolinguistic Approach to Bilingual Education.* Rowley, MA: Newbury House Publishers.

Cummins, J. 1978. Educational implications of mother tongue maintenance in minority-language groups. *The Canadian Modern Language Review, 34:*395–416.

Cummins, J. 1979a. Linguistic interdependence and the educational development of bilingual children. *Review of Educational Research 49:*222–251.

Cummins, J. 1979b. Bilingual and educational development in anglophone and minority francophone groups in Canada. *Interchange 9:*40–51.

Danoff, M., G. Coles, D. McLaughlin, and D. Reynolds. 1978. *Evaluation of the Impact of ESEA Title VII Spanish/English Bilingual Education Programs, Volume III.* Palo Alto, CA: American Institutes for Research.

Hébert, R. et al. 1976. Rendement academique et langue d'enseignement chez les elevesnent franco-manitobains. Saint-Boniface, Manitoba: Centre de recherches du College Universitaire de Saint-Boniface.

Lambert, W. E. 1975. Culture and language as factors in learning and education. *Education of Immigrants.* A. Wolfgang (ed.). Toronto: The Ontario Institute for Studies in Education, 55–83.

Lambert, W. E., and G. Richard Tucker. 1972. *Bilingual Education for Children.* Rowley, MA: Newbury House Publishers.

Lord, R. and B. T'sou (eds.). 1976. *Studies in Bilingual Education: Selected Papers from the 1976 International Symposium on Bilingual Education, Hong Kong.* Hong Kong: Lammar Offset Printing.

Mackey, William F. 1972. *Bilingual Education in a Binational School.* Rowley, MA: Newbury House Publishers.

Rosier, P., and M. Farella. 1976. Bilingual education at Rock Point: Some early results. *TESOL Quarterly 10, 4:*379–388.

Skutnabb-Kangas, T., and P. Toukomaa. 1979. Semilingualism and middle class bias: A reply to Cora

Brent-Palmer. *Working Papers on Bilingualism 19.*

Spolsky, Bernard (ed.). 1972. *The Language Education of Minority Children.* Rowley, MA: Newbury House Publishers.

Spolsky, Bernard, and Robert Cooper (eds.). 1977. *Frontiers of Bilingual Education.* Rowley, MA: Newbury House Publishers.

Swain, Merrill. 1976. Bibliography: Research on immersion education for the majority child. *The Canadian Modern Language Review 32,* 592–596.

Swain, Merrill. 1978. Bilingual education for the English-Canadian. *Georgetown University Round Table on Languages and Linguistics 1978.* J. W. Alatis (ed.), Washington, D.C.: Georgetown University, 141–154.

Swain, Merrill. 1979. Target language use in the wider environment as a factor in its acquisition. Paper presented at the 13th annual TESOL Convention, March, 1979.

Swain, M., and M. Bruck. 1976. Proceedings of the research conference on immersion education for the majority child. *The Canadian Modern Language Review.* Special issue 32, entire no. 5.

Swain, Merrill, and J. Cummins. 1979. Bilingualism, cognitive functioning and education. *Language Teaching and Linguistics: Abstracts,* 4–18.

Troike, R. 1978. *Research Evidence for the Effectiveness of Bilingual Education.* Los Angeles: National Dissemination and Assessment Center, California State University.

Zappert, L., and B. R. Cruz. 1977. *Bilingual Education: An Appraisal of Empirical Research.* Berkeley: Bay Area Bilingual Education League/Lau Center, Berkeley Unified School District.

SYLLABUS AND COURSE DESIGN

INTRODUCTION

We now consider issues in syllabus and course design in language teaching. A syllabus (sometimes also known as a *curriculum*) is a specification of the content of a course of instruction and the order in which the content will be presented. Different approaches to syllabus and course design in language teaching reflect different theories of the nature of language and language learning because a syllabus is usually a specification of what are considered to be the basic units of learning in the language. Syllabus design does not take place in a vacuum, however. It is generally one stage within a broader sequence of curriculum development processes. These include *needs analysis,* or assessment of the kind of communicative needs and language proficiency the learners need; setting goals or *objectives* that specify the planned outcomes of the language program; *syllabus design,* in which the content to be covered is determined; *methodology,* which refers to the instructional procedures to be used; and *evaluation,* in which the effectiveness and efficiency of the program as a whole is assessed.

In the first paper, van Ek describes an approach which was used by the European organization the Council of Europe to develop program goals, objectives, and a syllabus suitable for foreign language programs destined for European learners. Van Ek and others associated with this project developed a syllabus known as the Threshold Level, which specifies the components of communicative competence that should be known by learners reaching a "threshold level" of foreign language proficiency, that is, a level in which the learners could use a foreign language for everyday oral communication in basic social survival situations. The Threshold Level is said to be an example of a "communicative syllabus" because it specifies units of communication as the organizing principles of the syllabus. In this extract from the Threshold Level syllabus, the settings in which the learners will use English are specified, as well as the topics they will be expected to talk about and the functions they should be able to understand and express. In the Theshold Level syllabus, objectives, grammar, notions (i.e., *concepts*), and vocabulary are also specified. This and other attempts to develop communicative syllabuses reflect a dissatisfaction with conventional approaches to syllabus design in which only grammar and vocabulary are listed. Such syllabuses typically identify neither the communicative goals the learners should attain nor the means by which they should attain communicative competence, and hence provide only a partial specification of what should be taught.

Chamot discusses an approach to ESL development for minority children at the elementary level where the main concern is to provide language instruction that is *relevant* to these children's needs in the broader school context. Chamot is particularly interested in ensuring that ESL instruction equip students with what, following Cummins, she calls cognitive and academic language skills, and not just with social communicative skills. Her proposal is to integrate a notional-functional ESL syllabus with a language learning model based on cognitive developmental stages, on the one hand, and development in the relevant content areas of the elementary school curriculum, on the other.

The next two papers discuss an approach to curriculum design generally referred to as English for specific purposes. Beginning in the late 1960s and early 1970s, increasing attention began to be given to designing programs for learners with specific, often quite specialized, needs in English. After detailed analyses of how students would eventually use English in their chosen occupation, vocational training, or field of study, courses were written for such groups as airline stewardesses, medical students, artificial inseminators, firemen, aircraft mechanics, and diplomats. Although *all* good syllabus design should start with learner needs identification, the kinds of programs designed with this emphasis became known as programs in English for specific purposes (ESP).

The rationale for this degree of specialization was and is that, while requiring an additional initial outlay in preparation time and money, ESP programs are far more cost effective once they exist. Their obvious relevance in satisfying students' needs should also make them more motivating than *general* English courses, sometimes referred to by ESP advocates as ENP—English for nebulous purposes —programs.

General programs are less useful than ESP programs in two ways. First, they may waste the learners' time with work on skills they will never use, with vocabulary they will never need, and so on. For example, if a group of Chilean medical students only need to know how to read textbooks and journal articles in their field of specialization, why devote equal amounts of class time to all four skills? Second, general courses may *not* provide help with aspects of the language and its uses that some learners *do* need, precisely because, while essential for one particular group, they are too unusual to include in a general course for a heterogeneous class of students. For instance, the kind of technical prose the Chilean medical students need to deal with is far too specialized for most EFL or ESL reading courses.

The obvious utilitarian nature of ESP offends some people, who argue that language teaching should introduce learners to a new culture, not just equip them with the language they need to take a vocational training course or to secure a job. The response by ESP practitioners has been that these specialized programs satisfy adult learners' needs as quickly as possible, but do not preclude subsequent study to achieve other goals. The typical refugee, for example, is more concerned about obtaining work than reading the classics. Shakespeare can come later.

ESP programs usually cater to adults, who tend to have more clearly definable communicative needs, specification of which underlies ESP program design. In the first article in this section, however, Widdowson argues *against* specifying syllabus content for EAP (English for academic purposes) programs, at least, in this way—the *goal-oriented* approach, as he refers to it. Instead, he favors a *process-oriented* definition of needs, where a syllabus is specified in terms of the *means* by which a learner will obtain the desired target communicative competence, not in terms of the *ends,* or target competence, itself. The claim is that, rather than teach a fixed set of target-like skills and abilities, learners should be equipped with the strategies they need in order to learn how to deal with their target communicative needs, and that their learning continues in this way after the ESP course is over. Widdowson goes on to discuss how such a process-oriented syllabus might cater to individual differences in students' cognitive styles and learning strategies.

While endorsing the priority given by ESP programs to student needs identification and the provision of *relevant* coursework, Phillips and Shettlesworth, like Widdowson, challenge a traditional assumption of such programs, namely, the feasibility of providing tailor-made materials for each new group of students. They suggest instead the use of authentic resource materials (ARMS) from the students' own discipline in the case of EAP programs, with appropriate adjustments to the way such materials have traditionally been used and to classroom goals in their use. For example, they suggest that full student comprehension of the texts may be not only unrealistic but actually counter-productive: it can take too long, and it can reduce a lesson to explanations of trivial vocabulary and grammar items. The kind of classroom discourse and language use opportunities for students that this kind of work engenders, Phillips and Shettlesworth point out, is likely to be as *irrelevant* to the learners' future language needs as the grammar-oriented approaches that communicatively oriented ESP programs were originally designed to replace.

DISCUSSION QUESTIONS

1. Van Ek suggests that in order to develop objectives for a language program, we must first try to determine what the learners need to use the language for. Select a situation you are familiar with, such as an ESL program for immigrants or a vocational ESL program. What needs analysis procedures could be used to determine the communicative needs of the learners destined for such a program? Suggest a variety of different ways of gathering data on learners' needs and compare the advantages and limitations of each procedure.

2. Examine a transcript of a short conversation, or if this is unavailable, an

extended dialog or a series of dialogs from an ESL text. Then look at the list of functions given in van Ek's article on page 86. To what extent can the conversation or dialogs be described with this list of functions? What aspects of the conversation are unaccounted for?

3. Chamot says that some school subjects, such as art, math, music, and physical education, make fewer linguistic demands on limited-English-proficient children, chiefly because they involve more listening comprehension and less reading and writing than such subjects as social studies, science, and language arts. She therefore suggests concentrating on these easier areas first. Outline how you might teach a lesson at the elementary school level designed to teach both a mathematical procedure, such as addition or multiplication, and the English involved in the procedure you choose. What of the language you plan to teach do you think would transfer usefully to other subject areas?

4. Students in ESP programs sometimes complain that the courses designed for them are boring because they are *too* relevant. They say that they prefer learning English through materials that do *not* deal with the subject matter they have to work with in other classes, as this gives them greater variety. How would you react to such complaints? How can a skillful teacher or course designer satisfy such students wishes and their future language needs?

5. Skeptics argue that the features said to characterize ESP programs, such as careful needs identification and a goal of teaching communicative competence in English, are not unique and should be present in *all* language courses. Do you think their skepticism is justified (a) in theory and (b) in practice?

6. Some so-called ESP materials are little more than relexified structural drills and exercises, where "This is a spanner" replaces "This is a book." What else is involved in (a) the theory of ESP course design and (b) a commercially published ESP course with which you are familiar?

FURTHER READING

1. K. Hyltenstam, and M. Pienemann (eds.). 1985. *Modelling and Assessing Second Language Acquisition.* Clevedon, Avon: Multilingual Matters.
2. R. K. Johnson. 1982. *Communicative Syllabus Design and Methodology.* Oxford: Pergamon.
3. R. Mackay, and A. Mountford (eds.). 1978. *English for Specific Purposes.* London: Longman.
4. R. Mackay, and J. D. Palmer (eds.). 1986. *Languages for Specific Purposes.* Program design and evaluation. Rowley, MA: Newbury House Publishers.
5. J. L. Munby. 1978. *Communicative Syllabus Design.* Cambridge: Cambridge University Press.
6. P. Robinson. 1980. *ESP (English for Specific Purposes).* New York: Pergamon.
7. J. C. Richards. 1984. Language curriculum development. *RELC Journal,* June, 1–29.

8. L. Selinker, E. Tarone, and V. Hanzeli (eds.). 1981. *English for Academic Purposes.* Rowley, MA: Newbury House Publishers.

9. A. M. Shaw. 1977. Foreign-language syllabus development: Some recent approaches. *Language Teaching and Linguistics: Abstracts* 10, 4, 217–233.

10. J. A. van Ek, and L. G. Alexander. 1980. *Threshold Level English.* Oxford: Pergamon.

11. D. A. Wilkins. 1976. *Notional Syllabuses.* Oxford: Oxford University Press.

12. J. Yalden. 1983. *The Communicative Syllabus: Evolution, Design and Implementation.* Oxford: Pergamon.

CHAPTER
6

The Threshold Level

J. A. van Ek

LANGUAGE-LEARNING OBJECTIVES

Language-learning objectives, like other learning-objectives, are defined in terms of *behavior*. The aim of learning is always to enable the learner to *do* something which he could not do at the beginning of the learning-process. This applies to physical ability, such as the ability to ride a bicycle, as well as to less directly observable abilities, such as the ability to appreciate the difference between a burgundy and a claret, or the ability to understand some scientific theory.

Moreover, learning-objectives must be geared toward learners' needs. This means that before defining an objective we must define the group of learners whose needs we wish to cater for, the target-group.

Once the target-group has been defined we try to determine as exactly as possible what they will need to do with, in our case, a foreign language.

It is not sufficient—not exact enough—to say that they "want to speak the foreign language." In the first place there is not much point, usually, in being able to *speak* a language if one cannot *understand* it as well. Moreover, when can one be said to "speak a language"? When one can discuss the weather with casual ac-

quaintances, or when one can address a formal meeting? It would seem that much depends on the kind of situations in which the learner may be expected to need the ability to use the foreign language. Will it be in the situation of an interpreter in a law court or in that of a casual tourist?

In order to define the learning-objective for a target-group we first have to specify the *situations* in which they will need the foreign language. Specifying a situation means stating the *roles* a language-user has to play, the *settings* in which he will have to play these roles, and the *topics* he will have to deal with. More technically: by situation we mean the complex of extra-linguistic conditions which determines the nature of a language-act.

Once we have determined the situations in which the members of the target-group will want to use the foreign language we can try to specify just what they will have to be able to *do* in those situations.

First we specify the *language activities* the learner will be likely to engage in. These may be as comparatively "simple" as understanding the weather forecast on the radio or as complex as summarizing orally in a foreign language a report written in one's native language. The traditional division of language-activities into four skills—speaking, listening, writing, reading—is not always fully adequate, as reflection on the last example will show.

Having determined the nature of the language activities we try to specify for what general purposes the learner will have to use the foreign language, what *language functions* he will have to fulfill. For instance, he may have to give information about facts, he may wish to express certainty or uncertainty, whether he considers something right or wrong, he may wish to express gratitude, he may wish to apologize.

But the learner will have to do more than fulfill such general language functions. He will not only have to give information in the abstract, but he will want to give information about *something;* he will wish to express certainty or uncertainty with respect to *something;* he will want to apologize for *something.* In other words, he will need the ability to refer to things, to people, to events etc., and to talk about them. In order to do all this he will have to be able to handle a large number of *notions* in the foreign language. What notions he will need depends to a large extent on the topics he will deal with. If he is dealing with the topic "weather," he will have to handle notions such as *fair, sunshine, to rain,* etc., when dealing with a menu the notions *meat, ice cream,* and *coffee* may be required. We can draw up lists of such notions for each topic if we ask ourselves just what the learners will want to be able to do with respect to each topic and what notions he will need in order to do this. There are also notions which are so general that they may be needed in any situation, when dealing with any topic. These are notions such as existence/non-existence, past/present, before/after, etc. Since such notions are not specifically related to any particular topic there is not much point in trying to derive them from a consideration of individual topics. Instead, they can be derived from a con-

sideration of what, in general, people deal with by means of language. We may say, again in general, that people deal with:

1. Entities (objects, persons, ideas, states, actions, events, etc.),
2. Properties and qualities of entities,
3. Relations between entities.

The entities themselves will be largely determined by the topics, whereas notions of properties and qualities, and those of relations, tend to be used more generally. In order to compose lists of these general notions we can set up a system of logically derived categories and subsequently determine what notions are likely to be used in each category.

When the specification of a language-learning objective has been completed up to this point we can determine what actual *language forms* (structures, words, and phrases) the learner will have to be able to use in order to do all that has been specified. These forms are determined by considering each of the language-functions and the notions separately and establishing how they are realized in a particular language, in other words by establishing their *exponents.*

The final component of a language-learning objective is a statement about the *degree of skill* with which a successful learner will be expected to be able to do all that has been specified, in other words *how well* he will have to be able to do it. It is fairly easy to make such a statement in general terms, but very difficult, if possible at all, to do it with anything approaching the degree of exactness we can achieve for the other components of the definition.

To sum up: Our model for the definition of language-learning objectives specifies the following components:

1. The situations in which the foreign language will be used, including the topics which will be dealt with;
2. The language activities in which the learner will engage;

3. The language functions which the learner will fulfill;
4. What the learner will be able to do with respect to each topic;
5. The general notions which the learner will be able to handle;
6. The specific (topic-related) notions which the learner will be able to handle;
7. The language forms which the learner will be able to use;
8. The degree of skill with which the learner will be able to perform.

THE DEFINITION OF THE THRESHOLD LEVEL

Specification of Situations

By *situation* we mean the complex of extra-linguistic conditions which determines the nature of a language-act. Properly speaking, situations are strictly personal and unique. One of the conditions is always the individual language-user himself with his unique background (the sum total of his experiences). For our purposes, however—the definition of a level of general language-ability will be an objective for a very large and heterogeneous population—we must ignore strictly individual conditions and we may concentrate on four components of situations, which, together, provide a sufficient basis for the further steps in our procedure. We shall, henceforward, distinguish four components of situations:

1. The *social roles* which the learner will be able to play;
2. The *psychological roles* which the learner will be able to play;
3. The *settings* in which the learner will be able to use the foreign language;
4. The *topics* which the learner will be able to deal with in the foreign language.

Social Roles

The principal social roles for which T-level learners have to be prepared are:

1. *stranger/stranger*
2. *friend/friend*

This selection is made from a study by Richterich[1]; on the basis of the characteristics of the target-group. Various other roles are subsumed under 1, e.g.:

> *private person/official*
> *patient/doctor, nurse, dentist*

A role such as

> *asker/giver*

may be subsumed under both 1 and 2.

The inclusion of role 2 *(friend/friend)* has important consequences for the definition of the T-level. It raises this level above that required for purely physical survival in a foreign-language environment. It will prepare the learner for the establishment and maintenance of social relationships with foreign-language speakers. Only when this need is fulfilled can our level be called "threshold level" in a meaningful way: it will enable the learner to cross the threshold into the foreign-language community.

Psychological Roles

On the basis of the characteristics of the target-group we select from Richterich[2] the following roles:

1. Neutrality
2. Equality
3. Sympathy
4. Antipathy

These roles are the more "neutral" roles and they are appropriate in a large variety of types of linguistic interaction.

Settings

On the basis of the characteristics of the tar-get-group, we may draw up a long list of settings in which the learners may want to use the for-eign language. The settings have been selected from lists provided by Richterich (op. cit.) and by Peck (private communication). In spite of its size this list is not to be considered exhaustive. It is assumed, however, that it is sufficiently comprehensive to produce—together with the other components of situation—specifications of language-ability which will enable the learn-ers to behave adequately also in various settings which have not been listed (transfer).

1. Geographical location
   a. foreign country where foreign language is native language
   b. foreign country where foreign language is not native language
   c. own country
2. Place
   2.1 Outdoors:
      a. street
      b. square
      c. park, garden
      d. terrace
      e. countryside
      f. beach
      g. lake, sea
      h. mountains
      i. sports field
      j. open air swimming pool
      k. camping site
      l. bus stop
      m. taxi stand
      n. sights
      o. marketplace
      p. car-park
   2.2 Indoors:
      2.2.1 *Private life:*
         a. house
         b. apartment
         c. room
         d. kitchen

2.2.2 *Public life:*
   2.2.2.1 *Purchases:*
      a. shop
      b. supermarket
      c. multiple stores
      d. indoor market
   2.2.2.2 *Eating and drinking:*
      a. restaurant
      b. café
      c. snack bar
      d. bar
      e. canteen
   2.2.2.3 *Accommodation:*
      a. hotel room reception
      b. camping site
      c. holiday camp
      d. hostel
      e. boarding house
      f. farm house
   2.2.2.4 *Transport:*
      a. railway station
      b. bus station
      c. airport
      d. ferry terminal
      e. ticket office
      f. travel bureau
      g. information office
      h. lost property office
      i. customs and immigra-tion
      j. garage
      k. petrol station
      l. indoor car-park
   2.2.2.5 *Religion:*
      a. church
   2.2.2.6 *Physical services:*
      a. hospital
      b. doctor's/dentist's waiting-room
      c. surgery
      d. chemist
      e. public lavatory
      f. sauna
      g. hairdresser
   2.2.2.7 *Learning:*
      a. school
      b. language institute
      c. classroom
      d. library

2.2.2.8 *Displays*:
  a. museum
  b. art gallery
  c. exhibition
2.2.2.9 *Entertainment*:
  a. theater
  b. cinema
  c. concert hall/opera
  d. nightclub
2.2.2.10 *Communication*:
  a. post office
  b. telephone booth
2.2.2.11 *Finance*:
  a. bank
  b. money exchange office
2.2.2.12 *Work*:
  a. office
  b. workshop
  c. factory
2.2.2.13 *Means of transport*:
  a. bus
  b. tram
  c. train
  d. underground railway
  e. boat/ferry
  f. aeroplane
  g. taxi
  h. private car
  i. bicycle
3. Surroundings (human)
  a. family
  b. friends
  c. acquaintances
  d. strangers

Topics

On the basis of the characteristics of the target-group, the following list of topics has been drawn up. A similar list provided by Peck has been used as the main source. In the composition of the list the social roles we have selected have been used as criteria for inclusion. With respect to this list the same remark applies which was made a propos of the list of settings: a certain measure of arbitrariness in the classification does not affect the value of the list as long as all the more important topics are included somewhere. Even this claim, however, cannot be upheld. No matter how carefully a list of this kind is composed, it is bound to be far from complete. However, this weakness is—to a certain extent—offset by the transfer-potential of linguistic ability. It may be assumed that a learner who is competent to deal with the topics listed will also be able to deal with several other topics for which he has not necessarily been prepared.

1. Personal identification
  a. name
  b. address
  c. telephone number
  d. date and place of birth
  e. age
  f. sex
  g. marital status
  h. nationality
  i. origin
  j. profession, occupation
  k. employer
  l. family
  m. religion
  n. likes and dislikes
  o. character, temperament, disposition
2. House and home
  a. types of accommodation
  b. accommodation, rooms
  c. furniture, bedclothes
  d. rent
  e. services
  f. amenities
  g. region
  h. flora and fauna
3. Trade, profession, occupation
  a. trades, professions, occupations
  b. place of work
  c. conditions of work
  d. income
  e. training
  f. prospects
4. Free time, entertainment
  a. hobbies
  b. interests

c. radio, TV, etc.
d. cinema, theater, opera, concerts, etc.
e. sports
f. intellectual pursuits
g. artistic pursuits
h. museums, galleries, exhibitions
i. press
5. Travel
   a. travel to work, evening class, etc.
   b. holidays
   c. countries and places
   d. public transport
   e. private transport
   f. entering and leaving a country
   g. nationalities
   h. languages
   i. hotel, camping site, etc.
   j. travel documents
   k. fares
   l. tickets
   m. luggage
   n. traffic
6. Relations with other people
   a. friendship/aversion
   b. invitations
   c. correspondence
   d. club membership
   e. political and social views
7. Health and welfare
   a. parts of the body
   b. positions of the body
   c. ailments/accidents
   d. personal comfort
   e. sensory perception
   f. hygiene
   g. insurance

h. medical services
i. emergency services
8. Education
   a. schooling
   b. subjects
   c. qualifications
9. Shopping
   a. shopping facilities
   b. foodstuffs
   c. clothes, fashion
   d. smoking
   e. household articles
   f. medicine
   g. prices
   h. weights and measurements
10. Food and drink
    a. types of food and drink
    b. eating and drinking out
11. Services
    a. post
    b. telephone
    c. telegraph
    d. bank
    e. police
    f. hospital, surgery, etc.
    g. repairs
    h. garage
    i. gas station
12. Places
13. Foreign language
    a. ability
    b. understanding
    c. correctness
14. Weather
    a. climate
    b. weather conditions

LANGUAGE FUNCTIONS

Here we shall list the various functions the learners will be able to fulfill at T-level, whatever language—here limited to those spoken in the member countries of the Council of Europe —they have studied.

In setting up our list of language functions we have distinguished six main categories of verbal communication:

1. Imparting and seeking factual information;
2. Expressing and finding out intellectual attitudes;
3. Expressing and finding out emotional attitudes;
4. Expressing and finding out moral attitudes;

5. Getting things done (suasion);
6. Socializing

Each of these six main categories, and, indeed, each of the functions, may be realised separately in language-acts. Often, however, two or more of them will be combined in a single language-act. Thus, one may seek factual information while at the same time expressing surprise (emotional attitude). Yet, it is convenient to deal with each function separately and to specify just what each function involves by way of language-content.

The list of functions is far from exhaustive. In the first place it is unlikely that it is possible at all to draw up a complete list. Secondly, the list represents a deliberate selection for T-level. At higher levels more functions would be added.

It should be emphasized that the lists presented here are not to be regarded as final or definitive. They will—it is hoped—provide a sufficiently solid basis for practical applications of an experimental nature. The feedback from this experimental work will undoubtedly lead to numerous modifications in the lists.

Language Functions for T-Level

I. Imparting and seeking factual information
   a. identifying
   b. reporting (including describing and narrating)
   c. correcting
   d. asking
2. Expressing and finding out intellectual attitudes
   a. expressing agreement and disagreement
   b. inquiring about agreement or disagreement
   c. denying something
   d. accepting an offer or invitation
   e. declining an offer or invitation
   f. inquiring whether offer or invitation is accepted or declined
   g. offering to do something
   h. stating whether one remembers or has forgotten something or someone
   i. inquiring whether someone remembers or has forgotten something or someone
   j. expressing whether something is considered possible or impossible
   k. inquiring whether something is considered possible or impossible
   l. expressing capability and incapability
   m. inquiring about capability or incapability
   n. expressing whether something is considered a logical conclusion (deduction)
   o. inquiring whether something is considered a logical conclusion (deduction)
   p. expressing how certain/uncertain one is of something
   q. inquiring how certain/uncertain others are of something
   r. expressing one is/is not obliged to do something
   s. inquiring whether one is obliged to do something
   t. expressing others are/are not obliged to do something
   u. inquiring whether others are obliged to do something
   v. giving and seeking permission to do something
   w. inquiring whether others have permission to do something
   x. stating that permission is withheld
3. Expressing and finding out emotional attitudes
   a. expressing pleasure, liking
   b. expressing displeasure, dislike
   c. inquiring about pleasure, liking, displeasure, dislike
   d. expressing surprise
   e. expressing hope
   f. expressing satisfaction
   g. expressing dissatisfaction
   h. inquiring about satisfaction or dissatisfaction
   i. expressing disappointment
   j. expressing fear or worry

k. inquiring about fear or worry
l. expressing preference
m. inquiring about preference
n. expressing gratitude
o. expressing sympathy
p. expressing intention
q. inquiring about intention
r. expressing want, desire
s. inquiring about want, desire

4. Expressing and finding out moral attitudes
    a. apologizing
    b. granting forgiveness
    c. expressing approval
    d. expressing disapproval
    e. inquiring about approval or disapproval
    f. expressing appreciation
    g. expressing regret
    h. expressing indifference

5. Getting things done (suasion)
    a. suggesting a course of action (including the speaker)
    b. requesting others to do something
    c. inviting others to do something
    d. advising others to do something
    e. warning others to take care or to refrain from doing something
    f. instructing or directing others to do something

6. Socializing
    a. to greet people
    b. when meeting people
    c. when introducing people and when being introduced
    d. when taking leave
    e. to attract attention
    f. to propose a toast
    g. when beginning a meal

NOTES

Extracts from *The Threshold Level in a European Unit/Credit System for Modern Language Learning by Adults.* Council for Cultural Co-operation of the Council of Europe, Strasbourg, 1975.

1. R. Richterich, 1972. A model for the definition of language needs of adults learning a modern language. *CCC/EES* 72 (49), Strasbourg.
2. *Ibid.*

CHAPTER 7

Toward a Functional
ESL Curriculum
in the Elementary School

Anna Uhl Chamot

A functional ESL curriculum in the elementary school should provide children with the language functions and notions needed to study school subjects in English. For language minority children in the United States, a functional ESL curriculum must go beyond the threshold level of social communicative skills and provide instruction and development in the cognitive and academic language skills needed in the classroom.

A language learning model based on cognitive developmental stages is discussed, and types of ESL learning activities corresponding to the different levels of the model are identified. Guidelines for developing an ESL curriculum that is congruent with the regular elementary school curriculum are proposed, and a process for setting up a scope and sequence of English language functions and skills in content areas is described. Finally, needs for further research in ESL curriculum development are suggested.

A functional ESL curriculum in the elementary school is one that provides children with

the language functions and notions needed to study school subjects in English. The specific language functions and notions that are needed at different grade levels and in different subjects need to be clearly described and systematically incorporated into ESL curricula.

The theoretical basis for such a curriculum can be found in the notional/functional syllabus designed by the Council of Europe (van Ek, 1977) and in the language proficiency model developed by Cummins (1980a, 1980b, 1982a). The notional/functional syllabus represents a radical departure from the grammatical/structural approach to second language curriculum design because it looks at language from a pragmatic rather than a descriptive point of view. Language is seen as a skill that allows one to get things done. The things that can be done through language are described as functions, such as: giving and receiving factual information; expressing and finding out opinions, likes, and dislikes; socializing. Notions are presented in general semantic categories such as existential, spatial, and temporal, and in specific notions such as personal identification, house and home, relations with other people, travel, education, and so forth.

By combining functions with notions, we can produce practical language objectives, such as giving information about who we are, finding out someone's opinion about school, and introducing two people to each other. Such objectives focus on what language does rather than on how it works grammatically. A single language function can usually be expressed with more than one grammatical structure or set of vocabulary items, and for that reason it is possible to use simpler structures and limited vocabulary for a given function at the beginning stages of second language instruction, saving more complex structures and vocabulary for more advanced levels. Each function, therefore, can be recycled throughout the second language curriculum with an increasing expansion of structures, vocabulary, and register.

The notional/functional syllabus was designed in Europe for adult foreign language instruction. Van Ek (1977) has adapted it for foreign language instruction in schools, but the differences between the two are minor. The developers of this syllabus looked first at the linguistic needs of the majority of foreign language learners in different European countries and matched these with what could realistically be accomplished by most learners in a limited period of time. Thus, the concentration is on oral communicative skills needed to survive in a foreign country. The syllabus adapted for schools adds the objective of reading and writing informal letters because school children are expected to have more opportunities to correspond with other children in a foreign language than to travel to the country where the language is spoken. The degree of language proficiency needed for these survival objectives is termed the *threshold level.*

Can the notional/functional syllabus be used as an ESL curriculum in elementary schools in the United States? Yes and no. Perhaps the most valuable contributions of the notional/func-

tional syllabus are that its objectives are specified according to what the learner will actually have to do with the language and that its emphasis is on content and language use rather than on language description and structure. However, in order to be successful in English-medium instruction, the limited English proficient child in the United States needs more than just the language skills which are specified for the threshold level. A needs assessment process was undertaken prior to the development of the notional/functional syllabus, and a similar process could usefully identify and describe the actual functions and notions required to communicate effectively in elementary classrooms in the United States.

Classroom language needs vary significantly from language needed outside the classroom; the language used for instruction is different from the language used for socialization. This distinction has most persuasively been argued by Cummins (1980a), who postulates two aspects of language proficiency. One is the language of social communication, which is *context-embedded, face-to-face communicative proficiency,* and the other is the language of instruction, which is *context-reduced, academic communicative proficiency* (Cummins 1982b). Context-embedded communicative proficiency refers to the ability to use language to interact socially and affectively with others and, as such, is crucial to a child's adjustment to a new language and culture. This social communicative proficiency closely follows the specification of the notions and functions at the threshold level. Research in Canada has found that immigrant children develop this type of communicative proficiency within about two years of exposure to the second language environment (Cummins, 1982b). But important though this social communicative proficiency is to a child's adjustment and relations with English-speaking peers and adults, in itself it is not enough to lead to success in the academic focus of school.

Although context-embedded language is certainly present and needed in the classroom, the type of language used in academic instruction, content subjects, and achievement tests is substantially different (Fillmore, 1982). Context-reduced, academic language proficiency is related to cognition, to concepts, and to the more formal language used to refer to such concepts. Face-to-face communicative language is embedded in a social context that includes people, objects, gestures, intonation, and other paralinguistic aids to comprehension. Context-reduced academic language, on the other hand, is much freer from physical referents. It exists in books and lectures, and learners must glean meaning from words and phrases through their understanding of the concepts they express. Cummins' (1980a, 1982a) research indicates that bilingual individuals have a single underlying linguistic/cognitive proficiency which can be expressed through two modes—their two languages. This means that what a child has learned about any subject in the first language, whether it is mathematics, reading, writing, grammar, or social studies, can be transferred to the second language as soon as the appropriate notions and functions needed to express such concepts have been acquired in the second language. The ESL teacher can and should facilitate this process.

SECOND LANGUAGE LEARNING MODEL

The model in Table 7.1 (adapted from Chamot, 1981) is a taxonomic representation of the cognitive aspects of second language learning. The basic structure is patterned on Bloom's taxonomy (Bloom and Krathwohl, 1977), which describes six cognitive levels, each successive one building on the concepts and skills acquired at the lower ones. Because Bloom's taxonomy identifies internal mental processes, verbs have been added to describe the linguistic process that appears to take place at each level.

Knowledge, the lowest cognitive level, refers in a linguistic context to memorization and recall of language chunks. *Comprehension,* at the second level, requires the ability to recombine previously learned elements in new ways. Here the *creative construction process* (Dulay and Burt, 1975; Ventriglia, 1982) begins to operate. *Application* in a language context means the functional use of language for communicative purposes. At the fourth level, that of *analysis,* language is used to receive and give information, to identify main ideas, and to engage in other analytical tasks. At the *synthesis* level, language goes beyond facts to find reasons, to make comparisons, to relate ideas, and to make inferences. Finally, at the highest cognitive level, *evaluation,* the language proficiency developed in the first five levels is used to understand, make, and express decisions and judgments.

The line of asterisks in Table 7.1 represents a threshold level of proficiency that separates the purely communicative, survival language skills from the more academic, literacy-related language used for instructional purposes. The next two columns describe the kinds of specific linguistic activities that the child engages in at each level. The receptive skills of listening and reading are grouped in one column, and the productive skills of speaking and writing performance in the other. We can expect children to be at a higher level in *internal language skills* (receptive skills) than in the corresponding *external* ones (productive skills) at any given time. For instance, children will be able to understand much more than they can produce verbally, and after the initial process of learning to read, they will be able to read higher level material than they can write.

The first three levels of the model describe many of the activities that take place in an ele-

Table 7.1 SECOND LANGUAGE LEARNING MODEL

Cognitive Domain Taxonomy	Linguistic Process	Internal Language Skills	External Language Skills
1 Knowledge	Recalling	Discrimination of and response to sounds, words, and unanalyzed chunks in listening. Identification of labels, letters, phrases in reading.	Production of single words and formulas; imitation of models. Handwriting, spelling, writing of known elements from dictation.
2 Comprehension	Recombining	Recognition of and response to new combinations of known words and phrases in listening and oral reading. Internal translation to and from L_1.	Emergence of interlanguage/telegraphic speech; code-switching and L_1 transfer. Writing from guidelines and recombination dictation.
3 Application	Communicating	**Social Interaction** Understanding meaning of what is listened to in informal situations. Emergence of silent reading for basic comprehension.	Communication of meaning, feelings, and intentions in social and highly contextualized situations. Emergence of expository and creative writing.

* *

Cognitive Domain Taxonomy	Linguistic Process	Internal Language Skills	External Language Skills
4 Analysis	Informing	Acquisition of factual information from listening and reading in decontextualized situations.	Application of factual information acquired to formal, academic speaking and writing activities.
5 Synthesis	Generalizing	Use of information acquired through reading and listening to find relationships, make inferences, draw conclusions.	Explanation of relationships, inferences, and conclusions through formal speech and writing.
6 Evaluation	Judging	Evaluation of accuracy, value, and applicability of ideas acquired through reading and listening.	Expression of judgments through speech and writing, use of rhetorical conventions.

mentary school ESL class. By the time children can operate successfully at the third level and are communicatively competent, the ESL teacher has every right to feel happy and proud. But the three higher levels reflect the typical kinds of language activities that take place in the regular elementary classroom into which the ESL child will be mainstreamed. Will the ESL child be successful at these higher levels? A great deal depends, of course, on factors such as the child's age, achievement in first language content areas, motivation, and ability.

Recent Canadian research (Cummins, 1982b) indicates that whereas most young children reach native speaker ability in context-embedded, face-to-face communicative proficiency (which corresponds to the first three levels of the model) after about two years of exposure in an English-speaking environment, it takes most children from five to seven years to reach a context-reduced, academic proficiency level in English comparable to that of a native speaker of the same age.

This gap might be shortened by teaching more of the academic language skills within the ESL curriculum. For the child who has developed academic skills in a first language before coming to the United States, or who is fortunate enough to be enrolled in a bilingual program that develops these skills in the first language, the time needed to transfer successfully to English-medium instruction will be considerably shortened for, as we have seen, these skills are related to concepts and subject matter and as such are readily transferable from the first language to the second.

This second language learning model can serve as a developmental guide for the cognitive and linguistic stages that children go through as they master a new language. It is restricted in two ways, however. First, it does not take into account the affective factors involved in second language acquisition. These are crucial to the degree of success a child experiences in the learning process, and a parallel affective model needs to be integrated into this purely cognitive one. This article concentrates on the cognitive aspects, not because the affective ones are not critically important, but because it is the cognitive skills that receive the most emphasis in the classroom and in the assessment of children's academic achievement.

The second restriction to this model is that the activities described relate only to the language areas of the curriculum. It needs to be expanded to include the language skills needed in all content areas of the curriculum.

GUIDELINES FOR AN ESL CURRICULUM

Several tasks need to be undertaken to plan an ESL curriculum that helps children learn the language functions and notions that are part of the decontextualized language proficiency they will need when they are mainstreamed into the regular curriculum.

Thorough familiarity with the regular curriculum is an essential beginning. Knowing the instructional objectives, the scope and sequence of concepts and skills, the textbooks and other instructional materials that are used, specific achievement and other types of tests which are administered, and the minimum competencies in basic skills that have been established for promotion will provide a reasonably accurate picture of the performance expected of language minority children exiting from the ESL or bilingual program.

A next step is the careful comparison of the regular curriculum with the ESL curriculum in current use. Obviously, many things taught in the regular curriculum are absent from the ESL one. Some relate purely to content, whereas others involve language functions and skills. For instance, which language functions are needed in the mathematics class? Children need to receive factual information about and explanation of math concepts, usually through the mode of listening. They need to read the language of story (or word) problems so that they can understand which operations are needed to find the answer. Most speaking will involve functions such as requesting clarification, expressing comprehension, and explaining a process. Virtually all writing is numerical rather than verbal. In addition to isolating the language functions for a given subject, the basic vocabulary in English of the discipline needs to be learned. These language functions and principal notions can then be incorporated into the ESL curriculum. The ESL teacher does not thereby become a math teacher, but rather a teacher of the language that is needed in order to learn math. By pulling out the language functions and content-specific notions for each subject area at each grade level and by incorporating as many as feasible into the ESL curriculum, children in ESL classes can begin to develop the specific academic language skills they will later need.

Because academic language skills and content knowledge are transferable from L1 to L2, it is important to assess children's language and content achievement in their first language. If children already know how to add and subtract, and the vocabulary needed for these operations in L1, then the ESL teacher's task is considerably simplified, for the transfer to English becomes a matter of attaching new labels to known concepts and vocabulary.

Limited English proficient children also need to have their English ability assessed as they enter the ESL program, and ideally this assessment should focus on classroom language functions rather than exclusively on communicative skills. Certainly the communicative skills are important in a child's social adjustment, but, as we have seen, they are not sufficient to lead to success with the more formal and decontextualized language used as a medium of instruction.

A good ESL curriculum, like any good curriculum, should allow for individualized instruction. Even children who are in the same

grade and know no English at all will have had different previous experiences, will have developed a somewhat different set of concepts, and will be more or less predisposed to acquire English as a second language. By diagnosing what children need to learn both in concepts and in English, it becomes possible to prepare individual learning plans and to organize homogeneous groups for different types of ESL learning activities. As children reveal their different language learning styles and strategies (see Ventriglia, 1982), a variety of approaches and techniques needs to be utilized so that preferred learning styles can be capitalized upon.

A curriculum is a master plan. By stating instructional objectives, teachers can plan for a specific group of children. Textbooks can be selected that present the language functions that correspond to those in the regular curriculum, and instructional materials from this curriculum can be linguistically adapted and simplified for ESL instruction.

The following suggestions can help teachers plan learning activities within a functional ESL curriculum:

1. Use the vocabulary and concepts from content areas at appropriate grade levels as you devise ESL drills and exercises.

2. When planning activities that practice different language skills, keep the realities of the regular classroom in mind. First grade children, whether ESL or native-English speaking, spend a great deal of classroom time in listening and speaking activities, but they are also beginning to learn how to read and write. If the ESL child has already learned how to read and write in L1, then transfer of the processes involved in these initial skills becomes possible. As children in the regular curriculum progress through the grades, literacy becomes increasingly important in acquiring and communicating information. Therefore, older ESL children need increasing amounts of instruction in reading and writing skills.

3. Content area instruction can be initiated in English in linguistically less demanding areas

such as art, math, music, and physical education. In these areas little is required in reading and writing skills, but listening comprehension assumes paramount importance, for children need to be able to understand directions and explanations.

4. Because in the regular curriculum information is acquired more and more through reading in subjects such as social studies, science, and language arts, comprehension should be the priority in teaching ESL reading. Oral reading can be seen primarily as pronunciation practice, whereas silent reading focuses on comprehension. Whether a child can pronounce a word or not is of far less importance than his or her ability to recognize the meaning of that word within a written context.

5. To develop classroom speaking skills, children need opportunities to participate in small group discussions, to present oral reports, and to respond adequately to teacher questioning, for these are the speaking skills needed for successful participation in the academic activities of the regular classroom.

6. ESL writing activities can also parallel the types of writing assignments required in the regular classroom. Creative writing will be the most difficult for ESL children because they have limited vocabulary and expressive modes in English, and the bulk of their conceptual knowledge will have been acquired through their first language. However, simple expository writing is less demanding linguistically and will be an extremely useful skill in the regular classroom.

7. Teach test wiseness in your ESL class. Language minority children often have great difficulty in understanding the directions and procedures for standardized tests (McPhail, 1981), whereas native English speakers are usually exposed to such test formats from their first encounters with school and develop test-taking strategies that help them achieve higher scores. As long as such tests are used to classify children's achievement, it is only fair to give limited English proficient children equal opportunities to learn how to do their best on them (see Murphy, 1980).

SCOPE AND SEQUENCE OF ENGLISH LANGUAGE FUNCTIONS IN CONTENT AREAS

Table 7.2 is a sample scope and sequence chart for English language functions and skills required in the content areas. It describes not only the language functions needed in each subject area by grade, but also the relative emphasis given in each subject and at each level to the four language skills of listening, reading, speaking, and writing. This scope and sequence model illustrates a way of describing language functions in the regular elementary curriculum that could be incorporated to some degree into the ESL curriculum.

Scope and sequence charts and instructional materials for each content subject were examined, and the basic *strands* (or components) identified for each subject were classified under the broad headings listed within each subject

area. Then, the language skills (L = listening, R = reading, S = speaking, W = writing) most *emphasized* in each subject and at each level were marked with a zero. This model of a possible scope and sequence would need to be adapted to the regular curriculum of a particular school district in order to work effectively in the planning of a compatible ESL curriculum.

Reading, spelling, grammar, and composition have all been listed in the single category of Reading/Language Arts because these are the subjects in which language is the content as well as the function. Most first and second grade reading books devote considerable time to teaching phonics as an initial word-decoding skill, but subsequent work in this area tends to

Table 7.2 SCOPE AND SEQUENCE OF ENGLISH LANGUAGE FUNCTIONS IN CONTENT AREAS

Language and Content Concepts/Skills	Grade 1				Grade 2				Grade 3				Grade 4				Grade 5				Grade 6			
	L	R	S	W	L	R	S	W	L	R	S	W	L	R	S	W	L	R	S	W	L	R	S	W
Reading/Language Arts																								
1. Phonics	o	o	o				o																	
2. Grammar/Usage	o	o	o		o	o	o		o	o	o	o	o	o	o	o			o	o			o	o
3. Vocabulary/Spelling	o	o	o		o	o	o	o	o	o	o	o	o	o	o	o	o	o	o	o	o	o	o	o
4. Comprehension	o	o			o	o			o	o	o	o	o	o	o	o	o	o	o	o	o	o	o	o
5. Study Skills[a]	o				o		o			o	o		o	o	o	o	o	o	o	o	o	o	o	o
6. Composition	o		o	o			o	o			o	o			o	o								
7. Literary Skills	o		o		o		o		o		o		o				o				o			
Social Studies																								
1. Vocabulary/Concepts	o				o				o	o			o				o				o			
2. Comprehension	o				o				o	o			o				o				o			
3. Map Skills	o				o				o	o			o	o			o	o			o	o		
4. Study Skills[a]	o				o				o	o	o		o	o	o		o	o	o		o	o	o	
5. Decision Making Skills	o				o				o				o	o			o	o			o	o	o	
6. Attitude/Appreciation	o				o				o				o				o		o		o		o	
Mathematics																								
1. Vocabulary/Concepts	o				o				o				o				o				o			
2. Comprehension	o				o				o				o				o	o			o	o		
3. Operations	o		o		o		o		o		o		o		o		o		o		o		o	
4. Study Skills[a]	o				o				o				o		o		o		o		o		o	
Science/Health																								
1. Vocabulary/Concepts	o				o				o				o				o				o			
2. Comprehension	o				o				o				o	o			o	o			o	o		
3. Experimenting	o				o		o		o		o		o		o		o		o		o		o	
4. Study Skills[a]	o				o		o		o		o		o		o		o		o		o		o	
5. Decision Making Skills	o				o		o		o		o		o		o		o		o		o		o	
Art, Music, and Physical Education																								
1. Vocabulary/Concepts	o				o				o				o				o				o			
2. Comprehension	o				o				o				o				o				o			

[a]Study Skills includes activities such as: following and giving directions, discussion of concepts, oral and written reports, classification, dictionary skills, library skills, research, outlining, graphs, and charts.

93

diminish and can be found mainly in spelling books. Grammar and usage are taught throughout, but the oral emphasis grows less and correct written English gains in importance each year. Vocabulary development and spelling also gradually shift from the oral to the written mode. Some listening comprehension is formally taught in the early grades, but after that the emphasis is on reading comprehension, probably on the assumption that by the middle grades children can understand all of a teacher's instructions and explanations. Study skills also become more concerned with reading and writing, and composition and literary skills, by their very nature, soon have few oral components.

In other subject areas, the relegation of formal instruction in oral skills (particularly speaking skills) to a less important place becomes even more pronounced as children move up through the grades. This unfortunate lack of specific instruction in academic listening and speaking skills in the middle and upper grades of the English-medium curriculum cannot only cause difficulties for native speakers of English, but can have even more serious consequences for limited English proficient children. ESL teachers can help children develop academic oral language skills through listening activities that focus on oral subject matter presentations and through practice in whatever formal speaking tasks will be required in the English-medium curriculum.

Each subject area has a central core of vocabulary and concepts related to the specific discipline, and each calls for listening comprehension of the teacher's presentations, explanations, directions, and corrections. Reading comprehension and expository writing skills are needed particularly in social studies and science, but less so in mathematics. For art, music, and physical education, they are virtually unnecessary.

Other language functions needed in subject areas are more specific to the discipline involved, and here the list might be somewhat different in different school settings. Some of the learning activities which require language that can be at least partially taught in the ESL class are map reading skills, explanation of mathematical operations, written and oral descriptions of science experiments, and development of an appreciation for other cultures.

The purpose of this sample scope and sequence chart is to illustrate a process, not to describe the precise linking of language functions to content areas in the English-medium curriculum. To do this, we need more information that can be gathered through research.

RESEARCH NEEDS

The research needs for ESL curriculum development are many. As a baseline, we need information about the language functions that exist in English-medium elementary classrooms and their relationship to the concepts and content that are at the heart of instruction. In other words, we need a detailed description of what context-reduced academic language is. Ethnographic research in a variety of instructional settings is beginning to provide us with the parameters of such functional language use (see Fillmore, 1982), but the details remain to be specified.

Follow-up studies of the achievement of ESL children who are mainstreamed need to be carried out longitudinally if we are ever to be able to diagnose how much ESL and bilingual support is necessary for most children. How do these children fare in the regular classroom after they are exited from special programs? This information would be helpful in increasing both the quality and the quantity of current language support programs.

The practicability and the results of teaching ESL through structured content needs to be explored further, even though research to date in this area is promising. Significant increases in both English language skills and content area achievement have been reported for limited English proficient children participating in science curricula using an inquiry approach and discovery learning (see Rodriguez, 1981, and De Avila, Duncan, and Cohen, 1981). In such programs two instructional objectives are accomplished with a single instructional tool. Approaches that make learning more efficient need to be identified and verified through additional research with other content subjects.

Finally, we need research on the effects of different models of ESL curricula and methodological approaches. What different results are obtained from structural and functional curricula? How effective are methodologies developed for adults in promoting the language skills children need to compete successfully in school with native English speakers?

We need to have these answers soon, for a whole generation of language minority, limited English proficient children is growing up in the United States and their numbers are increasing. They depend on us to provide something better than a hit or miss approach to language education.

REFERENCES

Bloom, Benjamin S., and David R. Krathwohl. 1977. *Taxonomy of Educational Objectives: Handbook I: Cognitive Domain.* New York: Longman.

Chamot, Anna Uhl. 1981. *Applications of Second Language Acquisition Research to the Bilingual Classroom. Focus* 8. Rosslyn, VA: National Clearinghouse for Bilingual Education.

Cummins, James. 1980a. The construct of language proficiency in bilingual education. In *Current Issues in Bilingual Education,* James E. Alatis (ed.), 81–103. Washington, D.C.: Georgetown University Press.

Cummins, James. 1980b. The entry and exit fallacy in bilingual education. *NABE Journal* IV (3):25–29.

Cummins, James. 1982a. *Interdependence and Bicultural Ambivalence.* Rosslyn, VA: National Clearinghouse for Bilingual Education.

Cummins, James. 1982b. *Tests, Achievement, and Bilingual Students. Focus* 9. Rosslyn, VA: National Clearinghouse for Bilingual Education.

De Avila, Edward A., Sharon E. Duncan, and Elizabeth G. Cohen. 1981. Improving cognition: a multicultural approach. Final Report, MCIS Project: Multi-cultural improvement of cognitive abilities. In *Bilingual Programs, Language Assessment, and Cognitive Functioning Among Minority Language Students.* Microfiche Special Collection 1. Rosslyn, VA: National Clearinghouse for Bilingual Education.

Dulay, Heidi C., and Marina K. Burt. 1975. Creative construction in second language learning and teaching. In *On TESOL '75,* Marina K. Burt and Heidi C. Dulay (eds.), 21–32. Washington, D.C.: TESOL.

Fillmore, Lily Wong. 1982. Language minority students and school participation: What kind of English is needed? *Journal of Education* 164 (2): 143–156. Boston University.

Murphy, Barbara. 1980. Second language reading and testing in bilingual education. *TESOL Quarterly* 14 (2):189–197.

McPhail, Irving P. 1981. Why teach test wiseness? *Journal of Reading* 25 (1):32–38.

Rodriguez, Imelda Z. 1981. An inquiry approach to science/language teaching and the development of classification and oral communication skills of Mexican-American bilingual children in the third grade. Ph.D. dissertation, The University of Texas at Austin.

van Ek, Jan A. 1977. *The Threshold Level for Modern Language Learning in Schools.* The Council of Europe. London: Longman.

Ventriglia, Linda. 1982. *Conversations of Miguel and Maria: How Children Learn a Second Language.* Reading, MA: Addison-Wesley.

CHAPTER
8

English for Specific Purposes:
Criteria for Course Design

H. G. Widdowson

The work that has been done to date on the teaching of English for Special or Specific Purposes (ESP) has generally been predicated on the following assumption: If a group of learners' needs for the language can be accurately specified, then this specification can be used to determine the content of a language program that will meet these needs. Thus, if, for example, we can specify what students of economics need to be able to do with English by analyzing their textbooks or what waiters need to be able to do with English by analyzing their interaction with patrons, we can devise custom-made courses of English that incorporate the results of the analysis.

This assumption of the necessary determination of course content by the learner's requirement for the language seems to underlie remarks in Halliday, McIntosh, and Strevens (1964), where mention is made here of "English for civil servants; for policemen; for officials of the law; for dispensers and nurses; for specialists in agriculture; for engineers and fitters." The authors go on to say: "Every one of these specialized needs requires, before it can be met by appropriate teaching materials, detailed studies of restricted languages and special registers carried out on the basis of large samples of the language used by the particular persons concerned. It is perfectly possible to find out just what English is used in the operation of power stations in India: once this has been observed, recorded and analyzed, a teaching course to impart such language behavior can at last be devised with confidence and certainty" (Halliday et al., 1964:190).

A more recent expression of this assumption, illustrated by a detailed demonstration of how it might be put into practice in ESP course design, appears in Munby (1978). The epilogue to that work contains the following statement: "This book has been concerned with language syllabus design. More specifically, the contention has been that, when the purpose for which the target language is required can be identified, the *syllabus specification is directly derivable from the prior identification of the communication needs* of that particular participant or participant stereotype" (Munby, 1978:218 [italics added]).

It seems reasonable enough to assume that a specification of language needs should define the language content of a course designed to meet such needs. My purpose in this chapter, however, is to argue that such an assumption is mistaken, at least as far as English for Academic Purposes (EAP) is concerned, and to suggest alternative criteria for course design.

The first point to be noted, perhaps, is that the expression "learner needs" is open to two interpretations. On the one hand it can refer to what the learner needs to do with the language once he or she has learned it. This is a *goal-oriented* definition of needs and relates to terminal behavior, the ends of learning. On the other hand, the expression can refer to what the learner needs to do to actually acquire the language. This is a *process-oriented* definition of needs and relates to transitional behavior, the means of learning. It is the first of these interpretations which is favored in current ESP work. The basic belief is that which seems to be expressed in the quotation from Halliday et al. just cited: Once the language the learners will have to deal with is described, then teaching courses can be devised (with confidence and certainty) by directly applying this description. Thus it is the ends that determine course design. The means, apparently, must shift for themselves.

This goal-oriented approach follows a well-established tradition. Its most familiar manifestation is in the early work on vocabulary selection that served as the basis for the structural syllabus. Here the basic procedure was to delimit the content of the syllabus in terms of linguistic items by reference to primary criteria like frequency, range, and coverage, all of which served to define what it was supposed the learner ultimately ought to acquire as terminal behavior. Factors like learnability and teachability, which relate to means, were only adduced as contingent considerations for making minor modifications to the basic course design. This procedure has been subject to much critical discussion (e.g., Mackay, 1965; Widdowson, 1968) and more recently Wilkins has pointed out their limitations as a preliminary to his own proposals for what he claims to be a radically

different approach. The approach he proposes however is, with respect to the two kinds of orientation I have mentioned, not really different at all. It is important for my argument here to demonstrate why not.

Having given an outline of the principles of vocabulary control, Wilkins reports, with approval, an observation made in Reibel (1969) to the effect that "what is happening here is that we are taking the language behaviour and the language knowledge that we aim to produce in our learners, we are analyzing the linguistic components of the desired performance and isolating its units. We are then teaching the units piece by piece so as to get back to the very position from which we started" (Wilkins, 1976:5).

Now it emerges from subsequent discussion that Wilkins's objection to this procedure is not that it allows goal-oriented needs to determine course design but that the kind of linguistic components that are specified represent only a part of the language knowledge and behavior that the learner needs to acquire eventually. His criticism of these criteria for defining course content is essentially that they operate on the wrong kind of unit: They isolate forms rather than functions and so develop grammatical rather than communicative competence. But the principle of allowing goal-oriented needs to determine the content of a course is retained as fundamental to the approach. This principle is stated quite explicitly in the following passage:

> The process of deciding what to teach is based on considerations of what the learners should most usefully be able to communicate in the foreign language. When this is established, we can decide what are the most appropriate forms for each type of communication. The labelling for the learning units is not primarily semantic, although there is no reason why the structural realization should not also be indicated. A general langue course will concern itself with those concepts and functions that

are likely to be of widest value. In the same way, in the provision of a course for a more specialized language learner, the limitation is on the types of content that he needs to express and not on the number of structures he needs to know or the situations in which he will find himself. In short, the linguistic content is planned according to the semantic demands of the learner (Wilkins, 1976:19).

The innovation here lies in the redefinition of learning units as "concepts and functions" rather than as structures, but the units themselves are still seen as derivable from desired terminal behavior. It is still assumed that syllabus content must be determined by the goals rather than the process of learning.[1] Wilkins's reference to specialized language learners returns us to the main theme of ESP. The point he makes here is much the same as that made by Halliday et al.: With ESP one can be more precise than one can be with "general" language courses in the specification of what language the learner will eventually have to cope with. The difference again lies in how this language is to be characterized. Halliday et al. think in terms of *what* English is used and speak of "restricted languages" and "special registers." Their attention, therefore, is focused on linguistic forms whose incidence can serve to identify different varieties of English usage. Wilkins, on the other hand, thinks in terms of *how* English is used for the expression of concepts and the performance of functions whose incidence can serve to identify different varieties of English *use.* With reference to distinctions I have suggested elsewhere (e.g., Widdowson, 1977) the view taken by Halliday et al. (and those of similar persuasion, like Crystal and Davy, 1969) leads to a description of language variety as *text* defined as the way a particular language is manifested when it is put to particular purposes. Thus statements about the frequency of the passive or certain modal verbs in written scientific English are statements about text. The view taken by Wil-

kins, (and those of similar persuasion) leads to a description of language variety as *textualization* defined as the way a particular language realizes the concepts and functions of a particular type of discourse. Thus statements about how the passive or certain modal verbs in English are used to conduct scientific analysis and exposition are statements about the textualization in English of scientific discourse.

There are, then, two ways of describing a particular variety of English identified as the terminal goal of a particular group of learners. One way is to describe it as register: This involves making statements about its formal properties as a type of English text. The other way is to describe it as rhetoric: This involves making statements about the English textualization of a type of discourse, of a mode of communicating. It is in adopting this second mode of description that Louis Trimble and his associates have made their very considerable contribution (e.g., Lackstrom, Selinker, and Trimble, 1970; 1972; see also Swales, 1974, chap. 4) and there seems little doubt that this is the more profitable line to take, accounting as it does for the communicative functioning of language. Furthermore, such a description can be used to adduce aspects of the methodology of academic subjects and so can be made relevant to a process-oriented approach. More of this later. For the present, the point I wish to make is that whether we describe text or textualization, register or rhetoric, if we assume that our language description must directly *determine* course content then in both cases we adopt a goal-oriented approach to course design and focus attention on ends rather than means. I have said that this is a mistaken thing to do. It is time to give some substance to this assertion.

If one allows the description of the language-to-be-acquired to determine course content, whether this is done in terms of linguistic forms or communicative functions, then one assumes an equation between teaching and learning. By this I mean that one assumes that what is to be learned must be expressly and explicitly taught. Yet we all know that learners have an irritating tendency towards independent action and will frequently follow their own patterns of learning behavior in spite of the teaching patterns imposed upon them. These expressions of self assertion are commonly characterized as errors. The term itself indicates that we interpret these expressions as evidence that learners learn *less* than they are taught, and our usual reaction is to try to restore the equation by more teaching. But of course we can equally well take these expressions as evidence that learners learn *more* than they are taught. As is now widely recognized, although these peculiarities of learner language may indicate a failure in teaching in that they deviate from the present norm, they are also evidence of the learner's capacity for developing creative learning processes of his or her own.

It seems to me that the pedagogic equation, upon which the goal-oriented approach to syllabus design depends, must be wrong because the two sides of the equation are essentially different in kind. The teaching side can be expressed as a kind of product, a collection of formal or functional units to be stored away in the mind as knowledge. The learning side can be expressed as a kind of process, a set of strategies for making sense. In the classroom what commonly happens is that the teacher busily tries to change the learner's process into a product and the learner busily tries to change the teacher's product into a process. The teacher attempts to get the learner to put the language data in store and the learner keeps on converting it into energy to drive his or her own acquisition strategies.

Thus a fundamental conflict is created between what the learner needs to do in learning on the one hand and what the learner needs to have acquired after learning on the other. A goal-oriented approach focuses on the latter and makes what I believe to be the mistaken assumption that what the learner has to acquire necessarily has to be taught directly. The irony of the situation is that in trying to place his or her product the teacher inhibits the very process that would enable the learner to eventually acquire it. What, then, is the alternative? I want now to consider what I have called a process-oriented approach, one concerned with transitional behavior and the means of learning.

To begin with, such an approach rejects the pedagogic equation and accepts from the outset that the language data given to the learner will not be preserved in store intact but will be used as grist to the mental mill. Hence the language content of the course is selected not because it is representative of what the learner will have to deal with after the course is over but because it is likely to activate strategies for learning while the course is in progress. In principle, therefore, it is possible to conceive of an ESP course containing very little of the language associated with the special purpose so long as the language that it *does* contain is effective in developing the ability to achieve the special purpose after the teaching is over. In practice, of course, this facilitating language will often correspond quite closely in some respects to that of the special purpose because of the likely correspondence between what the learners need the language for and the ways in which they will acquire it. This point is closely related to the observation I made earlier about the potential relevance of a rhetorical description of language variety. I shall return to it presently. For the moment it is enough to note that if one avoids presenting *The Grapes of Wrath* and *The Mayor of Casterbridge* to students whose goal is to read engineering textbooks it is not because these novels are unrepresentative of engineering English but because we judge that they are not likely to engage the interest and to activate the learning strategies of such students and so would not have the necessary facilitating function.

Whereas the goal-oriented approach, then, focuses on the selection of language by reference to the ends of learning, allowing the means to be devised ad hoc, the process-oriented approach focuses on the presentation of language by reference to the means of learning and allows the ends to be achieved by the learner by exercising the ability he or she has acquired. The first approach assumes that the completion of a course of instruction marks the completion of learning and that all that is left for the student to do is to apply this ready-made knowledge. The second approach assumes that learning will continue beyond the completion of instruction since the aim of such instruction precisely is to develop a capacity to learn: It does not itself realize any special purpose but provides the learner with the potential for its realization.

If one follows a goal-oriented approach one needs to take one's bearing from models of linguistic description since these will define the units of course content. A process-oriented approach, on the other hand, can only be pursued by reference to some idea about how people learn. There is, of course, a vast literature on this subject and this is not the place to review it, even if I felt competent to do so. What I would like to do, however, is to direct attention to certain recent work on different cognitive styles that, tentative though it is, promises to have some relevance to ESP course design.[2]

I want to consider first a distinction made in Pask and Scott (1972) between two types of learners: the serialist and the holist. The strategy adopted by the first of these is to follow a direct route, proceeding step by step, and avoiding digression and irrelevance. The holist's strategy, on the other hand, is to advance on a broad front allowing access to all manner of information that might help him or her to find the way. Pask and Scott express the difference in rather more technical terms: "Serialists learn, remember and recapitulate a body of information in terms of string-like cognitive structures where items are related by simple data links: formally, by 'low order relations.' Since serialists habitually assimilate lengthy sequences of data, they are intolerant of irrelevant information unless, as individuals, they are equipped

with an unusually large memory capacity. Holists, on the other hand, learn, remember and recapitulate as a whole: formally, in terms of 'high order relations' " (Pask and Scott, 1972: 218).

One might suppose that the terms *serialist* and *holist* could refer to alternative learning strategies within an individual's repertoire that are freely selected as appropriate to a particular learning task. But this is apparently not the case: Pask and Scott produce experimental evidence that indicates that there is a distinct difference in individual ability to deal with holist and serialist tasks. We are led to the conclusion that what we have here are two different kinds of competence. The pedagogic significance of this seems clear. If a teacher uses serialist methods he or she will inhibit the learning of holist pupils and vice versa. One might suppose that a solution to this dilemma would be to develop a methodology that combines serialist and holist procedures, thereby providing pupils with an equal opportunity to learn according to their natural cognitive tendencies. The difficulty with such a proposal is that one thereby imposes an unnatural program on the teacher since he or she will be inclined to teach according to his or her particular cognitive style and the lessons are unlikely to be very effective if forced to do otherwise.

We appear to have arrived at an impasse. I have said, approvingly, that a process-oriented approach to course design uses language data as a means of activating learning strategies. Clearly this activation can only occur if the manner in which the language is presented is in accord with the cognitive style of the learners. But how can it be in accord with different cognitive styles, which may indeed be mutually incompatible? As far as I can see, there are only two ways round this problem. One is to design language programs that will in some way provide for parallel development corresponding to the different styles. Here one runs up against the problem of the teacher's style, which I referred to earlier. The alternative is to separate the holists from the serialists and provide them with different programs altogether. This latter looks to be a hopelessly impracticable proposition particularly if it turns out (as seems likely on the face of it) that a much more delicate distinction between styles will be needed. However, in the ESP context, especially where the purposes refer to academic study, it may be that this is a natural and necessary course to take.

The grounds for this belief lie in the likelihood of different types of learners separating of their own accord to follow distinct lines of academic inquiry. There is some evidence to suggest that this does indeed happen and that there is a correspondence between disciplines and cognitive styles. Such evidence is to be found, for example, in the research recorded in Hudson (1967). Hudson also makes a broad distinction between two types of learner: He calls them convergers and divergers, and he defines them with reference to types of intelligence test. A typical question in a conventional intelligence test requires the subject to select from a restricted range of alternatives. Hudson gives the following example:

Brick is to house as plank is to . . . orange, grass, egg,
    boat, ostrich.

And he comments: "The victim knows that there is one solution which is correct, and his task is to ferret it out. His reasoning is said to *converge* on to the right answer."

Instead of restricting the subject to a choice from a closed system, however, one can set an open-ended task and so invite a "creative" response, as in the following example:

How many uses can you think of for a brick?

Hudson comments: "Here, the individual is invited to *diverge,* to think fluently and tangentially, without examining any one line of reasoning in detail" (Hudson, 1967:50).

Now it seems to be the case that, as with the case of serialist and holist strategies, these two modes of mental operation are not equally accessible to all individuals. Some perform well on conventional tests and badly on creative tests and are naturally convergent in cognitive style, while others do the opposite and are naturally divergent.

What is of particular significance for the present discussion, however, is that convergers and divergers appear not to be evenly distributed throughout the student population but tend to cluster according to subject. Floyd, in an admirably clear exposition of research on cognitive styles, summarizes the findings of Hudson's work with open-ended tests as follows:

> . . . Hudson had hoped that these open-ended tests would cut across the arts/science distinction and give some reflection of the boys' brightness. In fact, the opposite occurred. Scores on open-ended tests provided a very good measure of the arts/science split. Arts specialists tended to be divergers weaker on intelligence tests than open-ended tests, whilst the scientists went the other way. In Hudson's sample between three and four divergers went into history, English literature and modern languages for every one that went into physical science; and between three and four convergers did mathematics, physics, and chemistry for every one that studied arts subjects. Classics appeared to belong with physical science, while biology, geography, economics, and general arts were studied by convergers and divergers in roughly equal proportions. (Floyd 1976:46)

It is not clear how far the cognitive styles distinguished by Pask and Scott can be set into correspondence with those of Hudson. It does seem however that serialists and convergers are alike in preferring precision and rational control and in their inclination towards the exact sciences, whereas holists and divergers share a common preference for wider networks of association and for imaginative excursion and incline towards the arts and the social sciences. At all events, the possibility emerges that the methodologies of different disciplines can themselves be characterized in terms of cognitive styles, being formalizations of different ways of resolving problems and of conceptualizing and controlling reality. If this is so, then it becomes feasible in principle to design programs of English for academic study to accord with the learners' cognitive bias because the learners have already grouped themselves by the process of a kind of natural selection in their choice of subject specialization. Thus, a process-oriented approach to the teaching of English to, let us say, physical science students would adopt predominantly serialist/convergent type procedures of presentation. A course for social science students, on the other hand, would adopt procedures of a predominantly holist/divergent kind. All this sounds plausible enough. But how, the opposition might ask, does one set about discovering such procedures? For it must be recognized, (and is recognized by the scholars I have referred to) that a good deal of research has yet to be done before different cognitive styles can be isolated and defined with confidence. And it would seem unlikely that such definite distinctions between serialists/holists and convergers/divergers can be maintained. In these circumstances the best one can do, I think, is to design EAP programs by direct reference to the methodologies of subjects concerned on the grounds that these must of their nature incorporate the cognitive styles associated with their particular areas of inquiry.

Returning to the observation I made earlier, we can now see why it is that in respect to English for academic study what the learners need the language for may closely correspond to the ways in which they will acquire it. Both relate to the particular combination of cognitive styles that define the methodology of the subject of their specialization. So if one allows this methodology to determine the methodology of the language teaching, then one will necessarily be developing strategies in learning that will be applicable to later study. One can also see, I think, why it is that a description of the language to be learned as textualization is to be preferred to one that characterizes that language as text. It is because the discourse that is textualized must, as a particular mode of communicating, also correspond to the cognitive styles that characterize the subject. The difference between a goal-oriented and process-oriented approach lies in the way such a rhetorical description is used. The former uses it directly as a determinant of course content, an area of language to be selected and expressly taught. The latter uses it as evidence of ways of thinking that might indicate how language is to be presented so as to engage the appropriate cognitive styles. Of course, it may turn out in particular cases that the content of a course draws quite extensively on the description but with process orientation it will do so not because it represents the language to be learned but because it is effective in activating the process of learning.

There is, I think, some reason to suppose that a process-oriented approach based on the principles I have tried to outline here would, by satisfying the cognitive needs of the learners, guarantee the eventual attainment of the desired terminal behavior. The means imply the ends and transitional and terminal behavior are simply different points on the same learning continuum. Whereas, as I have suggested, a goal-oriented approach creates a conflict between what the learner needs to do in learning and what he or she needs to have acquired *after* learning, a process-oriented approach based on subject methodologies contains no such conflict because these needs converge in the learning process itself.

All this may sound reasonable enough, but of course no problem has been solved. Things are never as neat as a turn of phrase can make them seem to be. For one thing we clearly need to know more about varieties of cognition: On the one hand, pedagogy, and indeed the very possibility of social life, depends on establishing styles of thinking across individual differences: On the other hand, people are unlikely to fall into neat binary divisions. We need to know more, too, about the cognitive style constitution of different methodologies and to investigate particular ways in which they can be exploited by language teaching procedures. All I wish to suggest here is that we should consider academic purposes in terms of learning processes reflected in specific methodologies rather than as static goals defined as language knowledge. To do this is not to solve an old problem but to restate it in different terms so that it can be approached from another direction.

NOTES

1. It could be argued (a point made by Devon Woods) that the structural syllabus in fact focuses on process rather than goal since its proponents did not really suppose that the language presented constituted terminal behavior but only the basis for its ultimate acquisition. I am not so sure about that. Why, if this is so, did frequency, range, and coverage figure so prominently as criteria for course content? And why was success generally assessed by reference to achievement as a measure of knowledge rather than by reference to proficiency as a measure of ability? The truth of the matter is, I think, that the structuralists never really got their criteria clear and so their kind of syllabus contains a basic contradiction (discussed in Widdowson, 1968): It was designed by reference to goals but is essentially only justified by reference to process. In both structural and notional syllabuses, at any rate, the assumption is that whatever later learning might take place after the course, it can do so automatically from accumulated knowledge, either of structures or notions.

2. My attention was first directed to this work by Althea Ryan, who is currently conducting research in the Department of Linguistics, University of Edinburgh, on the relevance of cognitive styles to language teaching. This work is supported by the Hornby Trust and Oxford University Press.

REFERENCES

Crystal, D., and D. Davy. 1969. *Investigating English Style.* London: Longmans.

Floyd, A. 1976. *Cognitive Styles: Personality and Learning, Block 5.* Milton Keynes: The Open University Press.

Halliday, M. A. K., A. McIntosh, and P. Strevens. 1964. *The Linguistic Sciences and Language Teaching.* London: Longmans.

Hudson, L. 1967. *Contrary Imaginations.* Middlesex: Penguin.

Lackstrom, J. E., L. Selinker, and L. Trimble. 1970. Grammar and technical English: English as a second language. In *Current Issues,* ed. R. C. Lug-ton, pp. 101–33. Philadelphia: Center for Curriculum Development.

———. 1972. Technical rhetorical principles and grammatical choice. *TESOL Quarterly* 7.127–36.

Mackay, W. F. 1965. *Language Teaching Analysis.* London: Longmans.

Munby, J. 1978. *Communicative Syllabus Design.* Cambridge: Cambridge Univ. Press.

Pask, G., and B. C. E. Scott. 1972. Learning strategies and individual competence. *International Journal of Man-Machine Studies* 4, 217–53.

Reibel, D. A. 1969. Language learning analysis. *IRAL* 7.283–94.

Swales, J. 1974. The function of one type of particle in a chemistry textbook. In *English for Academic and Technical Purposes,* ed. L. Selinker, E. Tarone, and V. Hanzeli, pp. 40–52. Rowley, MA: Newbury House, 1981.

Widdowson, H. G. 1968. The teaching of English through science. In *Language in Education,* ed. J. Dakin, B. Tiffen, and H. G. Widdowson, pp. 115–75. Oxford: Oxford Univ. Press.

———. 1977. Description du langage scientifique. *Le Francais Dans le Monde,* no. 129.15–21.

Wilkins, D. 1976. *Notional Syllabuses.* Oxford: Oxford Univ. Press.

CHAPTER 9

How to Arm Your Students: A Consideration of Two Approaches to Providing Materials for ESP

M. K. Phillips
C. C. Shettlesworth

TEACHING MATERIALS AND CLASSROOM DISCOURSE

Criticism of ESP materials is, in general, restricted to the adequacy with which they meet certain theoretical postulates and to discussion of the postulates themselves. To our knowledge, relatively little has been done in the way of surveying the output, so to speak, of the materials, that is, the kind and relevance of the language practice they engender in the classroom. This is perhaps the more surprising since the ultimate touchstone of any materials must be the pragmatic one of the amount and quality of the learning they stimulate.

The specialized nature of classroom discourse is becoming well documented.[1] McTear, for example, suggests that language in the EFL classroom operates on three levels: metalinguistically, as the means of instruction; pedagogically, as the content of instruction; communicatively, as a general means of communication.[2] Other observers have made similar distinctions.

This implies that the gap between classroom discourse (in any normal classroom) and the target discourse of the learning objective is perhaps surprisingly wide. We confirmed this hypothesis in our own case through a short study based on transcripts of classes in EST and which revealed that not only did the kind of discourse generated bear little obvious relation to communicative uses or language in scientific situations but even arguably differed from the teacher's perceptions of the kind of discourse that was generated.[3] ESP materials are designed as teaching materials and their centrality in the teaching situation consequently tends to reinforce the peculiarities of classroom discourse.

This is not necessarily an insuperable criticism: it entails the necessity of creating the conditions for activities which encourage the student to transfer the language taught in the classroom to use in communicative situations.

PROBLEMS IN ESP MATERIALS DESIGN

The philosophy of materials designed for teaching purposes, however, inhibits the development of such activities. One typical illustration of this is the control of syntax and lexis that is exercised over specially written reading passages. It is difficult any longer to accept such simplification as an adequate basic for control of written discourse; it is only one element and arguably not the most important. The current concern with the rhetoric of written discourse has clarified linguistic features peculiar to texts such as the devices used to secure cohesion on the one hand and the organization of the information content, the management of coherence, on the other. Unless these aspects of text are accorded at least equal attention in the process of writing teaching texts to that given to the traditional criteria, the information structure of the text is correspondingly distorted and thus (i) the adapted texts cannot be viewed as a helpful stage toward dealing with authentic materials and (ii) this distortion renders the adapted text potentially more rather than less difficult to comprehend. It is clear, however, that achieving a simplification procedure which allows for these considerations is less than straightforward as Mountford[4] has pointed out.

A further problematic area is whether the material provided by the course can be exploited in the way a specialist would use authentic materials; whether, for example, the operations performed by the student on text and diagrams correspond to the use a scientist would make of them. This is one aspect of the wider problem of providing students with an adequate introduction to the language skills involved in studying in English. It has become clear that in the teaching of language for academic purposes, it is insufficient to develop materials which aim to introduce the student only to the linguistic features which are salient in a particular field of discourse without paying attention to the strategies required by the student which justify the study of those features in the first place. It has rarely been the case hitherto that teaching materials attach sufficient importance to the behavioral aspect of specialist language.

Related to this point is the disparity that can arise in ESP between the demands of materials designed with a pedagogic objective and the requirements of the subject matter. The original purpose of the materials, which is to equip the students to deal with authentic examples of specialist discourse, can be negated if, in the process, fidelity to the subject matter is not maintained. The result of such inaccuracy or over simplification is often highly counter-productive; the credibility gap yawns.

A final point regarding the use of specially written materials is that of the techniques employed for student assessment. Given the powerful structuring provided by such materials, testing is normally conducted within the terms of the course. Such assessment is thus open to precisely the same criticisms as the course design; it tells us less about the student's communicative ability than about the extent to which the student has assimilated and can reproduce the course content.

AUTHENTIC MATERIALS

It is with such considerations in mind that we approach the specification of ESP courses at the Centre for English Studies and in particular pre-sessional EAP courses. These generally raise the problem of catering for groups of mixed and very specific interests and varying levels of attainment. Moreover, the time available for finding a solution is more often than not, strictly limited. These factors lead us to question the practicability of preparing specialized teaching material to a high standard when one is dealing with a diversified demand often on a "one-off" basis at very short notice. In ESP situations where such a solution is attempted experience has shown that either the time and manpower involved can quickly become costly out of all proportion to the economic viability of the course or the quality of the materials suffers. Yet in an effort to avoid the latter, institutions continue to suppose that the first alternative is the only solution.[5] Even were it always possible to adopt this solution, however, and it is of course very unrepresentative of the average ESP situation which is the need to meet an immediate demand with existing resources, it is, as we have seen, questionable whether the expenditure of time, effort, and finance is justified by the end product.

We see one possible solution to the problem of providing specialist materials in different disciplines in a manner which is both practical and which avoids most of the theoretical criticisms levelled at specially prepared materials in the exploitation of authentic documents from the student's field of study. The absence of conventional selection and grading naturally entails a fresh look at the ways in which materials and the organization of the classroom are structured. Nevertheless, there are two fairly obvious ways in which a degree of control over the content of authentic materials can be exercised. Firstly, they can be graded in terms of *accessibility*. One would want to take into account the absolute length of the passage, the density of new information and the presence of supportive graphic features (see Appendix Ex. 1). In addition it is not difficult to establish a cline of accessibility depending upon the sophistication of the information content, although caution needs to be exercised in accepting the relative simplicity of the popularised account, for example, which is frequently achieved at the expense of introducing an unrepresentative register of discourse.

Secondly, it is possible to remove the forms of control from the materials themselves to the task complexity demanded of the student and for which the material acts as a stimulus. It does not always follow that because an authentic written text is being exploited that the objective of all lessons is necessarily reading comprehension. Indeed, it must be accepted that total comprehension has often to be abandoned as a lesson aim. Moreover, the traditional classroom approach aimed at predicting the language the student needs to learn and allowing him the smallest possible margin of error in its acquisition is unlikely to hold good when using authentic materials, which, for the student, represent very much of a confrontation with the language. Consequently an approach which accepts the inevitability of error and aims at its progressive elimination as successively more accurate hypotheses are tested out against the evidence of the materials seems to be more appropriate.

TWO METHODOLOGIES FOR ARMS (AUTHENTIC RESOURCE MATERIALS)

There seem to be two major ways of approaching an authentic text for use in the classroom. On the one hand it can be viewed as a repository of natural language use and on the other hand it can be seen as the stimulus for a variety of communication skills. The former is concerned with explicating the text, the latter with developing skill transfers of the type involved in, for example, note-taking. The former deals with information extraction, the latter with its application; both approaches therefore are relevant.

Natural Language Use

Authentic materials lend themselves admirably to procedures involving the induction of grammatical rules which can be tested against other occurrences in the text and generalized to create new formations. The criterion for selection of the text is thus (a) the relevance of the subject matter and (b) the importance of the language points exemplified and their frequency of occurrence. This is illustrated by Example 2 which has been used by us for practice in the interpretation and production of complex noun phrases. The passage serves the usual purpose of specially constructed texts in that it exemplifies a particular language point with high frequency but has the marked advantage consequent upon its being a sample of discourse in that its authenticity is a considerable motivational factor and the linguistic point occurs in a natural context.

A less rigidly structured approach to the use of authentic materials for the teaching of grammar would be to adopt the cloze technique. There is no reason why the technique should not be applied to authentic discourse, indeed, it is arguably most appropriately applied to natural samples of language use. The rich context that is thereby provided furnishes a maximum of contextual clues to interpretation. Such an approach, illustrated in Example 3, has two distinct advantages. Firstly, it provides practice in inductive techniques for the interpretation of authentic discourse which are of vital importance for the student to acquire if he is to achieve autonomy in handling the language and in his own language learning. Secondly, the representative sample of language points covered by cloze procedure will ensure that problems of real difficulty to the student will be identified; the cloze passage can act diagnostically and provide the input to straightforward language improvement sessions. In effect the student selects his own personalised syllabus, a technique which is virtually impossible when using specially written pedagogic materials since they tend to be based upon a predicted item selection and sequence.

There always remains the possibility, however, that the unrestricted nature of the linguistic content will lead to immediate difficulties in the classroom. There is no reason why this eventuality should prove disruptive; there are several options open to the teacher. The simplest is to ignore the problem accepting, as mentioned earlier, that total comprehension is an unrealistic initial objective. We have found that our students are prepared to accept this limitation provided it is explained to them. The converse is to teach the point in question; although this may have the disadvantage of deviating from the teacher's preconceptions regarding his lesson, it is acceptable in an approach based upon the progressive elimination of error through a syllabus determined by the student himself. Finally, the difficulty can be positively exploited as an exercise in linguistic problem solving.

There is a more serious difficulty, however, to be faced. The adoption of a grammatical focus in this manner, whilst it is significantly different in technique from traditional approaches, has no implications for the authenticity of the discourse generated in the classroom. In other words, this use of ARMS may not overcome the problems mentioned at the beginning of this paper as inherent to the discourse generated by materials developed solely for teaching purposes. Authentic materials can only stimulate more realistic classroom discourse if a task-oriented methodology is adopted; this brings us to the second approach to the exploitation of ARMS, their use as a stimulus for the acquisition of language skills.

Language Skills

It could well prove that the major difference between traditional approaches to language learning and the approach loosely characterised as ESP in so far as the latter does represent an identifiable unified approach, lies less in the attitude to language that the two techniques represent than in the essential difference in methodology characterizable as the predicted language item syllabus—whether this is expressed in structural or notional terms—as opposed to task orientated learning. The former, through having no specified task relevance, has to rely upon inventing teaching techniques which are extrinsically motivating as a result of the entertainment value of the devices used. The latter, by definition has no such problem; it is difficult, for example, to conceive of an EAP course which is not centered on study skills in English.

Authentic texts can be used as stimulus for discrete skills of the type involving different modes of information transfer. The information contained in the text as reading of listening passage can be transferred to the written mode as in report-writing or to the oral mode in "lecturettes" through the mediation of note-taking. In order to successfully stimulate the art of taking notes in the lecture situation it is precisely the redundancy and richness of textual rhetorical clues provided by authentic discourse that is the point of the exercise. One kind of practice material we have devised is illustrated in Example 4. It has also proved possible to use authentic texts to provide the content of sessions intended to practice seminar strategies. Obviously the presentation of lecturettes based upon the subject matter of the text will give students the opportunity to practice such techniques as in-

terrupting, time-gaining, floor-keeping, clarifying, etc. By dividing the class into groups and giving them different texts or different parts of the same text upon which to work with the instruction that they will have orally to convey the "gist" of the passage to the other members of the class, a situation is created in which there is a real communicative need for these verbal strategies. Any passage in which the information is itemised can prove suitable for this purpose, each group having to communicate the content of one or more sections to the other members of the class (see Example 5). It is also possible to manipulate the access different groups of students have to the information contained in a series of texts in order to set up a problem-solving situation based upon the sharing of relevant knowledge.

Such techniques approach a full study skills simulation where students are given either individual research projects or a cooperative case study integrating different disciplines. In either case, the full range of study skills will be required. The task of the teacher will be to monitor the efficiency or the skill techniques, to identify language problems as they arise and to prescribe remedial work where necessary. It is difficult to see how such task-oriented activities could be successfully encouraged by anything other than authentic materials and as a result a greater degree of authenticity in classroom discourse is to be expected.

CLASSROOM ORGANIZATION

It is clear, however, that one consequence of the use of authentic materials in this manner is that the teacher is no longer the undisputed authority on the text and must acknowledge the student's expertise in the subject. As a result, the teacher must adjust his role to meet the changed relations obtaining between teacher, student and text. Even in the case of a lesson

oriented toward structural learning and where the teacher's role will most closely resemble the orthodox one, it is quite possible, as mentioned earlier, that it will be the students rather than the teacher who set the objective for the lesson. In classes devoted to a direct attack on the comprehension of a text the responsibility will be more evenly shared between teacher and student; the teachers' role will be an advisory one, that of, in effect, a linguistic consultant called in by the students to elucidate difficult points. We are thus suggesting that the emphasis has to be placed on student-centered situations where the focus is upon *learning* strategies rather than *teaching* technique and ultimately the student is responsible, and rightly so, for his own progress.

The student, for his part, must appreciate that the teacher is dependent upon him for the evaluation of difficulties and must be prepared to participate in a higher level of cooperative activity than is normally the case. Such an acceptance of his own responsibility is essential if he is ever to settle into further study in this country but by no means easy for students whose experience derives from several years of authoritarian classroom methodologies. Indeed, one objective of the majority of our EAP courses is to achieve precisely this readjustment. If the burden of elicitation is thrown upon the students, then one of our tasks is to equip the students with the appropriate strategies to facilitate this role. We have often found that this is most effectively done in the context of fieldwork (see example 6).

Group work also clearly has an important function. It allows for differential pacing within a class which can be vital when authentic materials are used. It permits the differential handling of language problems; it obliges the students to discuss their problems and then fosters a high level of cooperative activity in their approach to a text: this turns the lack of homogeneity in terms of linguistic level to advantage and permits the integration of students or widely differing achievement. At the same time, grouping within the class allows for different selections of material for different groups both to stimulate communication and to increase the degree of specialization.

A PARTING SHOT IN THE ARM; OR RESOURCES FOR COURSES

We have argued that ARMS represent a more practical alternative—certainly they are readily and cheaply available in all subjects at different levels—to the expense and time involved in creating specially written materials which tend to suffer from the defects discussed in the first part of this paper and in any case are an unrealistic solution when faced with an immediate but short-term need. The course materials could then become less an ESP textbook in the accepted sense rather than a set of resource material together with procedural guidelines for their exploitation. These we are building up as a teachers report in note form on the manner in which they have used authentic texts (see Example 7). Most ESP materials are an attempt to insert a specific subject content into an EFL framework. This attempt, we suggest, has doubtful validity. We attempt to tackle the problem from the opposite viewpoint, that of accepting the subject matter and the modes of behavior appropriate to it and adapting or developing our exploitation or techniques.

NOTES

1. For example: Long, M. H. 1975. Group work and communicative competence in the ESOL classroom. In M. Burt and H. Dulay (eds.) *On TESOL '75.* Washington, D.C.: TESOL, pp. 211–233.

2. McTear, M. 1975. Potential sources of confusion in the foreign language lesson. *Proceedings of the 4th International Congress of Applied Linguistics,* Stuttgart.

3. Phillips, M. K., and Shettlesworth, C. C. 1975. Questions in the design and use of courses in ESP. *Proceedings of the 4th International Congress of Applied Linguistics,* Stuttgart.

4. Mountford, A. 1975. The notion of simplification and its relevance to materials preparation for EST. In *Teaching English for Science and Technology.* Selected Papers from the RELC Seminar in the Teaching and Learning of English for Scientific and Technological Purposes in SE Asia. Singapore, April 21–25.

5. See, for example, Newsletter 1 of Universidad de los Andes, Bogota, Colombia.

APPENDIX:
EXAMPLES OF ARMS EXPLOITED
FOR TEACHING PURPOSES

Example 1

Ingot Casting. Ingots are a convenient form in which to handle steel, and the molten steel is released through the base of a ladle into moulds. When the metal has solidified, the mould is removed. Each ingot is of carefully pre-arranged dimensions and weights from which which articles of required size can be rolled or forged.

(from "Making Steel," British Steel Corporation)

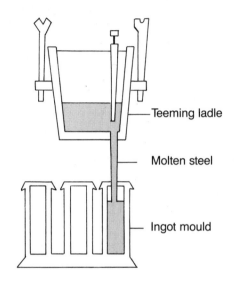

Teeming ladle

Molten steel

Ingot mould

Example 2

From November 25th to November 27th, officers of the *Milton Keynes Development Corporation* will be at the Post House Hotel, West Drayton, (Heathrow) between 10:30 am and 7:00 pm.

They'll be there to explain the very considerable advantages of moving a business to Milton Keynes.

As the map shows, Milton Keynes is an ideal location for most kinds of *manufacturing industry* and *distributive and service trades.* 60% of the country's population is within a *55-mile radius* of the city, housing is guaranteed to all *company staff* moving, and *factory sites* and *office space* are available to suit individual needs.

It could be well worth your while to come along to find out why. Especially since you'll be saving yourself a *55-mile journey* up the M1.

Milton Keynes
The logical place
for your business

(from advertisement in *The Guardian*)

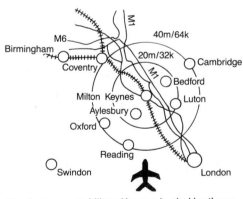

The best way to Milton Keynes is via Heathrow.

Example 3

In distinguishing its work from that of the trade associations, the CBI describes its work as "horizontal" rather than "vertical." The CBI sees itself as being concerned not only with national questions which concern all or several industrial sectors but also with those which cut across industries and affect groups of firms (or all firms) which have certain interests in common; such as being close companies, overseas investors, _____ users or taxpayers. The CBI points out _____, only in matters of detail which are _____ prime importance to a particular sector can _____ Trade Association gain the ear of the _____; even in such circumstances, the CBI is _____ to take up the cudgels on behalf _____ in support of the sector concerned, probably _____ greater effect than the Association itself can _____.

(from "Business" Open University)

Example 4

Transport in Britain

Transport and transport planning are regarded by the British Government as an essential part of the management of the environment how we get to work how we carry our goods and passengers from one part of the country to another in particular, in and out of the conurbations can no longer be regarded as a relatively simple matter of building roads or providing trains transport today is an integral part of land-use planning of local authority finance of pollution and of regional development.

(from "The Human Environment: The British View," HMSO)

Example 5

Some Basic Guidelines and Rules for Group Operation

When first operating in a group it is important and of real value to set down some of the factors which could cause friction among members.

The following Rules and Guidelines should be considered by all groups.

1. How is the purchase price divided? This can be divided by acreage, tonnage, gallonage, or hourly use. It is advantageous to make all members of the group liable for the group's debts.

2. How are the running costs and other expenses divided? It is desirable for the group to appoint one member as a secretary who should keep the account books, machine maintenance records and, if necessary, a minute book of all meetings. The group should ensure, if they are borrowing money, that a bank account is opened in the group's name.

3. How is the work pattern organized? This can only be . . . . etc.

(from Group Operations in Farm Management HMSO)

Example 6

Project—Oxford Planning Department

Remember:

Excuse me _____

(Can you tell me _____

(Could you tell me _____

Could you explain _____

(I'd like to know _____

(I've heard about _____

In your talk/lecture/description, you said

1. Public participation in planning?
2. Current major planning schemes?
3. Extend pedestrian precincts?

—etc.—

Example 7

Center for English studies

MATERIALS EXPLOITATION

Date _____	Group _____	Teacher _____

Skill:	Note-taking/Listening Comprehension
Materials used:	Transport and Road Research Laboratory: tree diagram of organizational structure: TRRL booklet, p. 5.
Duration:	25 minutes
Procedure:	1. SS draw tree—lines
	2. Teacher 'reads' out information, with *some* redundancy features (recapitulation mainly).
	3. Simultaneously SS write information on to the diagram, thus completing it.
	4. Vocabulary written up, to avoid spelling mistakes. It is not a spelling exercise.
	5. Language used by teacher: *is divided into; is organized into; to sum up.*
Evaluation:	The group were able to write down all information correctly without section headings (see attached sheet) having to be said more than once. The temptation to repeat and repeat has to be avoided.
	A useful exercise in highly guided listening for information, and showing comprehension by completing a given frame.

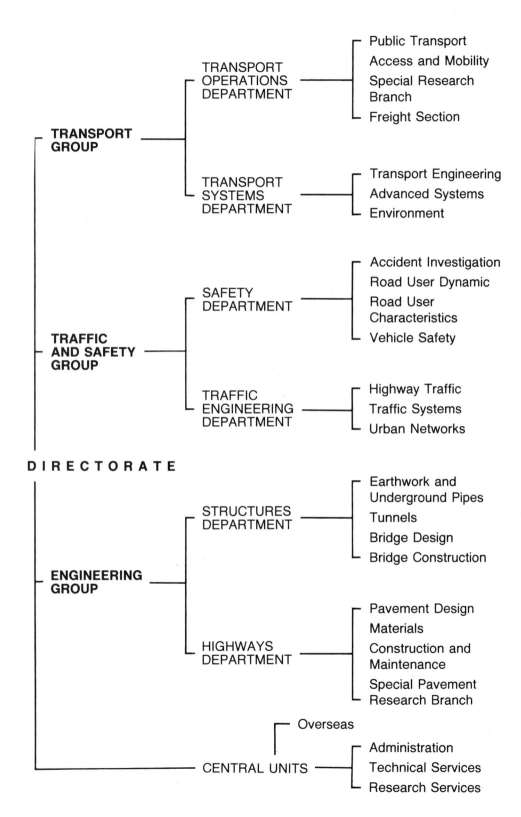

TRANSPORT
GROUP

TRANSPORT
OPERATIONS
DEPARTMENT
- Public Transport
- Access and Mobility
- Special Research Branch
- Freight Section

TRANSPORT
SYSTEMS
DEPARTMENT
- Transport Engineering
- Advanced Systems
- Environment

TRAFFIC
AND SAFETY
GROUP

SAFETY
DEPARTMENT
- Accident Investigation
- Road User Dynamic
- Road User Characteristics
- Vehicle Safety

TRAFFIC
ENGINEERING
DEPARTMENT
- Highway Traffic
- Traffic Systems
- Urban Networks

DIRECTORATE

ENGINEERING
GROUP

STRUCTURES
DEPARTMENT
- Earthwork and Underground Pipes
- Tunnels
- Bridge Design
- Bridge Construction

HIGHWAYS
DEPARTMENT
- Pavement Design
- Materials
- Construction and Maintenance
- Special Pavement Research Branch

CENTRAL UNITS
- Overseas
- Administration
- Technical Services
- Research Services

115

Section Four

METHODS AND METHODOLOGY

INTRODUCTION

The papers in this section examine curriculum, program, and method alternatives in language teaching, considering options available for the design and structuring of language programs. The nature of methods is also examined by considering a model for the description, analysis, and comparison of different methods of language teaching.

Crawford-Lange advocates a flexible approach to selecting a suitable design for a language program, summarizing and evaluating some of the possibilities currently available. Decisions about suitable program options must be made by considering the broader context of teaching and learning because any particular approach makes specific assumptions about program goals and learning outcomes, learner needs, teacher proficiency and skill, learning and teaching styles, instructional content, and methods of evaluation. She notes that a number of curriculum variables can be adjusted in an attempt to promote more effective learning, including timing, the way objectives are stated, choice of instructional strategies and materials, and evaluation procedures. Under *Curricular Alternatives* she considers the advantages and limitations of a systems-behavioral design approach and problem-posing education. Under *Content Alternatives* she examines the implications of adopting a Functional-Notional approach to syllabus design as well as the use of syllabuses that reflect content from outside the English curriculum. Under *Instructional Alternatives* she discusses the assumptions and techniques behind a number of current method options in language teaching (Suggestopedia, Counseling Learning, and Silent Way).

The paper by Richards and Rodgers examines the nature of methods in more detail and proposes a framework for their systematic description and analysis. A method is defined in terms of three interrelated levels: *approach, design, and procedure.* Approach refers to the theory of language and language learning underlying a method. Design refers to the objectives, syllabus, and roles of teacher, learners, and materials in a method. Procedure is concerned with the techniques and instructional practices in a method. The way these different levels of conceptualization, organization, and implementation are realized in different methodological proposals is illustrated from an examination of a number of current options. Methods (and those who propose or write about methods) are seen to differ not only in the solutions they adopt to questions of approach, design, and procedure, but also in the degree to which they make explicit their underlying assumptions.

DISCUSSION QUESTIONS

1. Discuss the advantages and disadvantages of an ESL/EFL program that meets intensively over a short period of time (e.g., 60 hours of instruction spread over two weeks) as compared to one in which the same amount of instruction is distributed over a longer time period.

2. Crawford-Lange discusses a number of alternatives for second-language education and classifies them as "alternative curricular designs," "content alternatives," and "instructional alternatives." Into which of the three categories would you place the following?

Behavioral objectives

Competency based instruction

Pattern practice

Role play

Bilingual education

Structural syllabus

English for Specific Purposes

3. To what extent is either a systems-behavioral design or individualized instruction compatible with the educational philosophy of teaching methods or approaches that you are familiar with?

4. Following the example cited by Crawford-Lange of the use of procedures derived from Problem-Posing Education in language teaching, suggest an exercise of this kind that could be useful in clarifying cross-cultural differences between the target culture and the student's native culture.

5. Examine a method you are familiar with and develop a profile of it in terms of approach, design, and procedure.

6. If possible, observe classes taught by teachers who are teaching according to two or more different methods. Find classes of a similar proficiency level. If possible, tape-record a sample of the lesson. To what extent were the teachers conforming to the principles of the method? Compare the observations from the two classes. What major similarities and differences can you observe?

FURTHER READING

1. R. W. Blair (ed.). 1982. *Innovative Approaches to Language Teaching.* Rowley, MA: Newbury House Publishers.
2. C. J. Brumfit, and K. Johnson (eds.). 1979. *The Communicative Approach to Language Teaching.* Oxford: Oxford University Press.
3. T. Higgs (ed.). 1982. *Curriculum, Competence, and the Foreign Language Teacher.* Skokie, IL: National Textbook Company.
4. T. Higgs (ed.). 1984. *Teaching for Proficiency, the Organizing Principle.* Skokie, IL: National Textbook Company.
5. W. Littlewood. 1981. *Communicative Language Teaching.* Cambridge: Cambridge University Press.
6. J. Oller, Jr., and P. A. Richard-Amato (eds.). 1983. *Methods that Work.* Rowley, MA, Newbury House Publishers.
7. J. C. Richards, and T. Rodgers. 1986. *Approaches and Methods in Language Teaching.* New York: Cambridge University Press.

10

Curricular Alternatives for Second-Language Learning

Linda M. Crawford-Lange

INTRODUCTION

The term *alternatives* has become securely incorporated into our educational vocabulary. That alternatives are present even within traditional situations has earned widespread acceptance and has grown out of several necessities. First, a need exists to apply new knowledge and understanding of human learning that comes from the psychology and sociology of learning; such application calls for a continual reformation of teaching techniques. Second, teachers are experiencing demands to provide variations for individual learners who are entering a society characterized by requirements for worldwide communication and a rapidly expanding technology. Third, the profession must address issues and problems for which current practices are inadequate.

Second language teachers have participated with educators in other fields in implementing alternatives such as programmed learning, computer-assisted instruction, and individualized instruction. Variables such as time for learning and group size have been manipulated to account for specific learning and instructional

needs. However, these alternatives do not account for all that is known about the nature of language and how it is learned; neither do they accommodate all the problems confronting today's classroom language teacher.

Despite recent attention at the federal level (Lange, 1980; Simon, 1980; *Strength through Wisdom,* 1979; U.S. Congress, 1980), language programs must fight for survival at the state and local levels. While a strong program actively supported by parents is more likely to earn administrative support, budget cutbacks and generally declining enrollments are largely out of teachers' hands. Within this larger framework, however, there exist considerations of enrollment and content that teachers can indeed address through curricular avenues.

Registration for foreign language courses drops off at all levels as competition for students with other departments increases. A weak junior high language program may deter students from enrolling in senior high language classes; on the other hand, junior high programs may "use up" senior high enrollments because students feel that they have "had all that." Enrollment problems evolve into scheduling problems. Multilevel classes are now common. Low registration means that only one section of some courses can be offered, opening the way to increased schedule conflicts, which further prevent students from taking a specific language course. Elementary and junior high programs in particular operate under abbreviated schedules, with short periods or lack of daily contact.

In addition to these technical problems, the content of courses may not meet student needs. For example, the daily culture of the speakers of the target language may be inadequately treated. Courses are generally not designed to meet specific career needs. Students, especially at beginning levels, want to speak the language quickly and become frustrated when they cannot. At the college level, there is often a lack of concentration on skill development and an inordinate focus on remediation. A college student,

for example, may be taught the full grammar of the target language each year, yet receive little exposure to stylistics and few opportunities to increase oral proficiency.

The purpose of this chapter is to provide teachers with a broad range of alternatives from which to select; these suggestions may be adapted in order to confront instructional challenges as well as problems such as those already mentioned. Although practical, this chapter is not a "how-to" manual. Rather, in an effort to supply teachers with the information they need in order to choose effectively and intelligently among the options, an overview of each alternative is presented with suggestions for implementation. A structure for constructing alternatives is defined in terms of those variables that can be manipulated. Specific curricular alternatives are then described in the areas of design, content definition, or instructional strategy.

A STRUCTURE FOR ALTERNATIVES

Individualized instruction provides students with the learning program most suited to their unique requirements. However, for a number of reasons including teacher time limitations, lack of materials, and insufficient research into learning styles and how to accommodate them, individualized instruction has been implemented so widely that it has virtually become its definition.

Defined short of its potential, individualized instruction may benefit from a renewed perspective. This perspective substitutes the term "personalized" for "individualized," thus reducing the isolationist tone, and interprets learning in a social context with the possibility of manipulating a number of variables. This slightly altered conception, contained in but not realized by the original ideal of individualized instruction, conforms well to the nature of language. The social nature of language must be recog-

nized within the process used for language learning. Although progressing through a set of learning materials alone may be an appropriate technique for skill-building or remediation, a social setting is essential if language is to be learned for communication.

While individualized instruction has focused largely on varying the element of time, allowing students to work at their own pace, personalized instruction reminds us of the full complement of variables to be considered in structuring curricular alternatives. A survey of these instructional variables including some examples of their application forms a framework for discussing curricular alternatives for second language teaching. Classroom teachers can use this framework to construct alternatives most appropriate to their situations. The variables treated are time, goals, learning strategies and materials, and evaluation strategies.

Time

Time can be manipulated in at least two ways, in terms of pace and in terms of course structure. Continuous progress learning (Logan, 1973) represents the variation of pace. Here, the student takes as much time as necessary to learn the course material. Variation of course structure by time involves either the utilization of time periods of various lengths and intervals for particular instructional needs or the devotion of considerable and concentrated periods of time to language learning. The differentiated use of time may be exemplified by the once popular modular-flexible schedule (Grittner and LaLeike, 1973; Saville, 1973). A second language course in a "mod-flex" schedule may meet for short periods twice a week for presentations and explanations, a long period every other week for a major lecture, guest speaker, or movie, and according to need for work in the language laboratory. The concentrated use of time may be either intensive or immersive. Intensive language-learning programs (Conner, 1977; Galt, 1980; Schulz and Benseler, 1979; Wattenmaker, 1979), those wherein the learner concentrates on the study of language for large periods of time each day over an extended period of time, can form the time structure for summer study or for a semester of study with language emphasis. Immersion language programs (Genesee, 1979; Hawkins, 1981; Hornby, 1980; Stern and Cummins, 1981) surround the learner continuously with the language over an extended period of time. Language camps and structured visits to a foreign country where the language is spoken are examples of immersion experiences.

Goals

As a variable, goals can be subdivided into course purpose and instructional objectives. A personalized program may identify and respond to the various purposes that the students have for taking a course. In the heterogenous public school classroom we typically find students who subscribe to language study for ethnic, career, social, scheduling, and intellectual reasons. These varying purposes may be accommodated by encouraging students to develop similar linguistic skills through different topics. As an alternative to adjusting one course to meet several purposes, the developer could design separate topics, each directed toward a specific purpose, such as reading for research, cultural exploration, or language for medical or business careers.

The second perspective from which course goals serve as a structural variable is that of instructional objectives. Three methods of varying objectives are proposed. First, objectives can be varied so that not all students are required to reach the same level of achievement, perhaps by establishing a range of acceptable achievement, by tailoring the expected achievement level to the student, or by posing a challenge beyond a standard achievement level. Second, the content of objectives (i.e., the material to be learned) can differ among students. Students could explore a single topic from different points of view, thus gaining a range of expertise to be shared during general discussion. The content of skill objectives can also vary. Because of diverse student interests and needs, one student may concentrate on listening comprehension while another focuses on grammatical accuracy in the written mode. Third, different kinds of objectives can fulfill alternate functions. Behavioral objectives (Mager, 1962), which delineate content quite carefully and set definite mastery levels for observable behavior, suit basic skill learning and development. Gronlund (1970) advances a format for behavioral objectives that lists sample behaviors which give evidence of the attainment of a general learning outcome. Objectives stated in this manner are quite appropriate for addressing language fluency, creativity, and communicative competence. Experiential objectives

(Charles, 1976), which describe an experience in which the student is to participate, relate well to cultural and situational learning. These three types of objectives can be combined within a course to provide a balanced and inclusive learning experience.

Learning Strategies and Materials

While the possibilities for varying learning strategies and materials are theoretically limitless, three elements define them within the structure of personalized language programs: group size, medium of instruction, and source. The size of the learning group should match instructional intent: large or medium groups for grammar presentations and explanations, skits, and discussions of literature; small groups for oral drills and conversations; and an individual setting for research, remedial work, and writing. These suggestions are not prescriptive but are simply a reminder that the effectiveness and efficiency of instruction depends in part on appropriate group sizes. With thought, group sizes can be adjusted even within the traditional classroom structure. A class session could open with a large group review. Then one section of the class could receive a grammar explanation while the remainder worked individually on writing tasks or with tape machines. The teacher might then have the first class section work together in pairs and divide the second half of the class into small groups for oral drill and conversation.

All forms of audio-visual devices come to mind at the word "medium of instruction." These include overhead projectors, pocket charts, slides, and posters. The technical meaning can be broadened to include activities through which students can learn: listening, discussing, writing, constructing, reading, drawing, painting, telling, viewing, visiting, teaching, illustrating, game playing, making, role playing, and manipulating. Each medium may be commercially produced, teacher-produced, or student-produced. Several of the alternatives discussed later in this chapter stimulate student production of materials. Personalized programs integrate sources, media, and group sizes for the most effective composite of learning strategies and materials.

Evaluation Strategies

Evaluation strategies can also be considered in terms of group size, medium, and source. Individually written tests, taped listening-comprehension tests, and oral interview procedures comprise commonly used approaches to formal evaluation. However, evaluation can also take place in a small group conversational setting where the teacher scores students on the situationally correct use of grammar, vocabulary, and style, or through the production of a group project. While such techniques are often applied for formative evaluation, or ongoing feedback, they are also useful for summative evaluation (i.e., the measurement of course outcomes).

The development of an alternative program involves not only a decision as to which approach best represents the teacher's philosophy of education and pedagogical theory, but also a respect for management and organizational problems and the students' needs, level of maturity, and flexibility. Teachers may select alternatives according to their beliefs about education and methods of instruction as well as identified learner needs. However, in order to prepare for proper management of the program and to anticipate the students' readiness for it, teachers are urged to ask questions of its structure:

Which variables—time, goals, learning strategies and materials, and evaluation strategies—are emphasized by this alternative?

How are the variables manipulated?

Does the manner in which they are manipulated serve the needs identified?

Can my students handle this set of variations? If not, how can I teach them to handle it?

Do I need to modify the alternative to deemphasize or stress one or more variables?

What management problems do I anticipate? What techniques can deal with them effectively?

Thorough understanding of the structure of an alternative leads to thorough preparation for its implementation and often determines the success or failure of a program.

CURRICULAR ALTERNATIVES

Ten curricular alternatives for second-language education are treated below under the headings *alternative curricular designs, content alternatives,* and *instructional alternatives.* At the level of curriculum design, that is, the level at which the pattern accepted for selecting, planning, and implementing educational experiences is defined (Saylor, Alexander, and Lewis, 1981), two very different designs—systems-behavioral and problem-posing—offer distinct options for approaching the teaching of second languages and cultures. Other alternatives affect primarily the content of the program: functional-notional syllabuses, cross-disciplinary approaches, career education, and global education. The central focus of this paper is not instructional methodology, but in a presentation of curricular options, instructional alternatives such as counseling-learning, the Silent Way, and cooperative learning cannot be overlooked.

Alternative Curriculum Designs

Systems-Behavioral Design. Skinner (1971, 1953, 1954) is recognized as the father of behaviorism. Based on the theory of operant conditioning (Skinner, 1968), behaviorism advocates a stimulus-response methodology for learning a carefully analyzed sequence of knowledge. Learning is measured by a change in observable behavior. For educational purposes, behaviorism has found a framework in the systems structure. A systems organization requires 1) the setting of specific objectives, 2) the determination of activities to enable learners to attain the objectives, and 3) the construction of measurement devices to determine if and how well learners have met the objectives. Usually, there is also provision for recycling through the learning activities if this proves to be necessary.

The pedagogical philosophy that evolves out of a systems-behavioral design stresses two concepts: incremental learning and mastery learning. The concept of incremental learning calls for an initial analysis of the subject matter into discrete learning units. For second languages, the structure of the target language is first analyzed into discrete learning units. These are ordered, respecting any sequences inherent in the structure itself. This ordering may ensure that subject pronouns are learned before object pronouns or that simple sentences are introduced before embedded sentences.

Since one assumption of incremental learning is that an earlier step is prerequisite for a subsequent step, acceptable performance on each step is required before progressing to the next stage in the sequence. The acceptable level of performance is usually stated in terms of a percent of correct items. It is assumed that, given appropriate learning activities, all students can achieve mastery if they have enough time. This assumption results in the practice of continuous-progress learning, where students proceed at their own pace, taking as much time as necessary to meet the learning objectives.

The systems-behavioral design for second language teaching has been most widely adapted in the familiar individualized instruction programs and in programmed learning (Altman and Politzer, 1971; Gougher, 1972; Grittner and LaLeike, 1973; Logan, 1973). The student with an analytical learning style may profit considerably from this approach. The identification of specific learning units and objectives makes this design particularly suitable to remediation of an individual student's weaknesses as well as to building and strengthening basic language skills. With its focus on ordering, the systems-behavioral design prompts the profession to rethink its traditional sequence for presenting the grammar of a language: Must all subject pronouns be learned simultaneously? Do irregular present tense verbs really have to be introduced before the regular past tense? Although the systems-behavioral design has been applied primarily to learning morphology and syntax of language, Banathy and Lange (1972) have investigated other applications. Theoretically, the systems-behavioral design offers a means for classroom exploration of such areas as cultural patterns and information, stylistics, attitudes and feelings, and gestures. These applications of the systems-behavioral design, though, have not generally been put into practice.

The systems-behavioral design does have certain limitations in relation to the teaching of second languages. First, it is most easily adapted to the individual situation and therefore needs either to be carefully structured to include group activities, or supplemented by an approach more amenable to the group situation required for social language development. Second, the emphasis on analysis and on discrete item mastery may overshadow the resynthesis of these items into language used situationally for communication. Third, while the grammar of a language is easily incrementalized, the cultural content of a language course is inherently less suited to identification of discrete and ordered units. Even so, with an understanding of these limitations, teachers can successfully utilize a systems-behavioral design for a total course structure or for particular needs within a course.

Problem-Posing Education. The major proponent of problem-posing education is the Brazilian-born educator Paulo Freire (1970a, 1970b, 1973, 1978). Freire's educational position receives support from a group of curriculum theorists known as reconceptualists, among whom stand James Macdonald, Michael Apple, John Mann, Dwayne Huebner, Maxine Greene, Madeleine Grumet, William Pinar (1974, 1975), and George Willis (1978). The literature demonstrates concern for application of concepts included in problem-posing education to foreign language curricula (Bowers, 1980; Grittner, 1975; Grittner and Fearing, 1979; Holec, 1980; Jarvis, 1975; Lewis, 1976). Warriner (1974) and Lapan (1980) call attention specifically to the work of Paulo Freire. In contrast to the technological base of the systems-behavioral design, problem-posing education has its roots in the humanities, as evidenced in an instructional and evaluative methodology derived from existentialist and phenomenological philosophy (Denton, 1974).

From the existentialist emphasis, problem-posing education extracts a concern for the real-life situation of the learners as well as a perception of the student as decision maker. Problems faced by the learners in their daily living are the source of content for a problem-posing program. After a problem is identified, learners view it not by analytically dissecting it into its component parts, as in problem-solving education, but by synthetically relating it to other facets of their lives. For example, discussion of racial tensions felt in school may lead to consideration of housing patterns and the gerrymandering of school attendance areas. In the foreign language classroom, this discussion would extend to similar situations in the target culture, providing a basis for comparison of the two cultures. In and of itself, but particularly within the confines of second language education, this design is significantly cultural in orientation, with culture considered in terms of how people live and work. Thus, problem-posing education puts culture in the *central* position and understands language as a communicative tool expressive of that culture, a shift recently supported by Strasheim (1981a, 1981b).

With the course organized through the integration of language and culture, the language to be studied is defined in relation to a cultural theme, not a text or structural analysis of the language. This design assumes that language cannot be validly taught apart from its culture. Although problem-posing education enters the learning of language from the point of cultural issues, it does not neglect development of language skills. Throughout the problem-posing process, the learners play a decision-making role in the selection of the topic for study, the development and utilization of learning materials, and the determination of any action to be taken in relation to the topics of study.

The phenomenological aspect of problem-posing education appears in the emphasis on how the learners perceive their personal situation. This curriculum design, then, is purposefully subjective. Its respect for students' perceptions shifts the classroom orientation from teacher as dispenser of knowledge and students as recipients, to teachers and students as mutually reflecting on a cultural theme with both contributing valid insights. This shift in roles is expected to aid in developing the ability to think critically about the world. Language learning is structured into this framework.

Two central pedagogical concepts of this design are praxis and dialogue. Praxis is the method of problem-posing education and is defined as the unit of reflection and action. Instructional procedures must provide both an opportunity for reflection on the topic, so as to broaden perception of it, and an opportunity for taking action with regard to the topic, so as to improve the life situation with which it deals. Dialogue forms the educational context, the place where praxis occurs. The purpose of dialogue is to stimulate new ideas, opinions, and perceptions rather than simply to exchange them. The teacher participates in dialogue on an equal basis with the students. Since dialogue must take place in a group, it affirms learning as a social activity.

A brief example may clarify the previous discussion. The following description reports the application of problem-posing education at the college level (Johnson, 1980):

1. Identification of problem: Two students who have each recently experienced a death in the family voluntarily bring in to the class the bills from the funeral homes. They point out the high amount of the bills and the absence of detailed itemization of costs. The class decides to examine funeral practices and costs.
2. Praxis-Culture
   a. Reflection
      1. Native culture: Students visit funeral homes, and interview morticians and clergymen. The information and insights gained are shared in target language dialogue.
      2. Target culture: Students investigate funeral practices and costs in the target culture by reading relevant books, interviewing native speakers, viewing pictures, slides, and films, comparing city practices with rural or small town practices. This research is conducted in the target language. The information and insights gained are shared in target language dialogue.
      3. Native culture-target culture: In dialogue conducted in the target language, students compare the funeral practices and costs of the two cultures. As part of this process, they identify practices that they would like to change in their own culture, perhaps

incorporating influences from the target culture. In addition, students come to view the funeral home industry in its relations with political and economic systems; they also increase their awareness of cultural attitudes toward death.

b. Action: Students inform students in other classes of the information gained and the content of their dialogue through a newsletter that they write and publish in the target language. This stimulates responses printed in a "letters to the editor" column.

3. Praxis-Language Learning
a. Reflection
1. Students identify needed vocabulary.
2. Through the following student-initiated activities, teacher and students identify grammatical structures which must be learned, reviewed, or practiced for fluency:
    a. Listening to native speakers of the target language and to films
    b. Speaking to native speakers of the target language and to each other in the target language
    c. Reading books and the writings of other students in the target language
    d. Writing letters and newsletters in the target language, as well as keeping a daily journal recording personal reactions to the class.
b. Action
1. Students teach the needed vocabulary to each other, examine each other on accurate acquisition of the vocabulary, and use it in the above activities.
2. Students utilize available language learning resources in conjunction with the above activities in order to develop competence in the grammar of the language. This process is "personalized," as this term is used earlier in this chapter. Students or groups of students each focus on different grammatical structures. With the identification of a general weakness, the teacher sets

aside class periods for total group concentration on a single grammatical element using a variety of methodologies (e.g., oral drills, conversation practice, written exercises, and partner or group work) and is a combination of student-produced and commercially produced texts. The learned grammar is used in the cultural situation. Teacher and students both act as observers, checking for linguistic competence.

At the high school level, students in a problem-posing language class might initiate the topic of employment for teenagers. Students and teacher can reflect on this topic by interpreting a slide showing a student applying for a job, by gathering and discussing the implications of want ads directed toward teens, and by focusing on questions related to hours, wages, and the effect of work on social life, family life, and schoolwork. Students and teacher can extend this dialogue into reflection on similar materials from the target culture, leading to intercultural learning, comparison, and understanding. As a result, students might dress differently for a job interview, leave their friends behind when seeking employment, or present themselves more confidently. Vocabulary and grammatical structures related to this topic comprise the content for language learning. Students, for example, could generate conversations likely to occur in both a native culture and a target culture job interview. The teacher puts these conversations into the target language and identifies within them the vocabulary and structures that the students must learn. The teacher and students select and utilize appropriate language-learning techniques such as grammar explanations, charts, and the several types of written and oral drills. The cultural content of the student-generated conversations can in turn become the object of reflection.

Readers who find themselves sympathetic to problem-posing education or see a usefulness for it in their courses are referred to Crawford (1979), who details a problem-posing curriculum design for second language teaching, and Lange (1979), who applies a problem-posing curriculum process to cultural education and teacher training. Problem-posing education is process-oriented, aims at developing critical thinking, cultivates the ability to synthesize, takes a social posture toward learning, and centers on culture. The fact that language learning in a problem-posing design evolves out of an issue that is real to the students and is related to an imminent need to communicate in the target language forestalls motivational problems, centers language learning in a cultural base, and provides a purposefulness to the language-learning activities. Any application of this design should capitalize on these characteristics.

While problem-posing education holds promise for the teaching of second languages and cultures, certain cautions deserve attention. The design is as yet largely untried except in isolated instances (Bailey, 1977; Crawford, 1974; Ewert, 1978; Johnson, 1980; Lange, 1979; Pereira, 1978; Steckel, 1975), and therefore its effect on learning in general and language learning in particular has not been measured. The design lacks systematic materials, detailed goals, and prespecified objectives, thus requiring a large fund of resources as well as great flexibility and linguistic skill on the part of the teacher. The practical application of problem-posing education for the initial stages of language learning has not yet been sufficiently explored. The integration of language learning and cultural investigation requires careful treatment so that one supports, rather than overwhelms, the other.

Experimentation with problem-posing education in the foreign language classroom, however, could well begin by integrating it with the functional-notional syllabus and/or global education, both discussed later in this chapter. Problem-posing education holds the potential for providing the profession with an anthropological approach to the teaching of language. Currently, no well-developed anthropological model for the teaching of second languages exists, nor are teachers trained to pursue that direction. Research concentrated on such a model may 1) determine the feasibility of an anthropological approach to the teaching of languages, 2) reveal more about how language is learned, and 3) challenge some of the pedagogical tenets of the language teaching profession.

In theory, the systems-behavioral and problem-posing designs complement one another, each design accounting for the deficiencies of the other. However, in practice, the two designs are not compatible because they make different assumptions about how people learn. Problem-posing education argues that 1) the student must be actively involved in defining the content of learning, 2) language cannot be learned apart from its culture, 3) language learning does not have to follow a prespecified sequence, 4) language learning and evaluation do not have to proceed through discrete units, and 5) the development of critical thinking is the primary purpose of educational activity. The systems-behavioral design, on the other hand 1) defines the content for the learner, 2) accepts that language can be taught apart from its culture, 3) prespecifies objectives, and, generally, their sequence, 4) focuses on discrete item mastery and evaluation, and 5) acknowledges that the acquisition of knowledge can be the primary purpose of educational activity. Which of the two designs a teacher will employ depends partially on the teacher's personal beliefs about education and partially on the expectations of students, community, and supervisors.

Content Alternatives

The curriculum designs presented in the previous section supply a complete structure for the curriculum, including philosophy and assumptions through content definition and instructional strategies. On the other hand, the functional-notional syllabus as well as the interdisciplinary approaches discussed below are concerned mainly with the definition of content (i.e., what is to be studied) and with their own underlying philosophy and assumptions relating to that content.

Functional-Notional Syllabus. In contrast with the systems-behavioral and the problem-posing designs, the functional-notional syllabus defines the content for language study by consciously and formally combining the purposes to which language is put and grammatical analysis. Once the content is identified through this dual approach, it can conform to the instructional strategies of any chosen curriculum design.

Munby (1978) states that building this body of content requires acceptance of three assumptions. First, the selection of communicative units for inclusion in the content involves analysis at the level of human interaction (i.e., how language is used for different purposes). Second, rules of rhetoric and context deserve consideration equal to that traditionally accorded to rules of grammar and discrete vocabulary items. Third, if communicative competence is truly a goal, then the usual structure of syllabuses must be redefined to include that concern. Brumfit (1980) reminds those constructing communicative syllabuses that: "We are not teaching a limited set of behaviors, but a capacity to produce those behaviors: a capacity which cannot help enabling its user to behave in many ways other than those specified by a limited selection." Therefore, communicative syllabuses should provide learners with "strategies for interaction" rather than simply a list of rules or expected behaviors.

Applied linguists, especially those in Europe and England, have explored such communicative syllabuses, chiefly under the designation *functional-notional.* Van Ek (1977) comments

that this syllabus model dissects language behavior quite simply into performance (function) and expression or reference (notion). Function is a matter of purpose (i.e., what a person does by means of language: asking, commanding, persuading, greeting, etc.). Notion concerns the content of the purpose. For example, a person may ask (function) for a pen (notion), may command (function) another to stand (notion), may persuade (function) the customer to buy a dress (notion).

A functional-notional syllabus, then, identifies the purposes for which learners need the language and the notions they must handle with it. Munby (1978) proposes that these be determined by asking, "Who is communicating with whom, why, where, when, how, at what level, about what, and in what way?" Wilkins's (1976) answer to these questions produces a categorization of functions and notions in the form of a taxonomy and recognizes the need to integrate grammar in order to realize a complete syllabus. Munby (1978) also produces lists specifying functions and notions, but in addition develops a plan for integrating grammar, thus yielding a unified syllabus design. Brumfit (1980) would have grammar form the core of the syllabus with functions and notions treated in relation to grammatical concepts. He further suggests that the profession should be looking more for a communicative methodology than a communicative syllabus. Perhaps a functional-notional syllabus within a problem-posing curriculum design would shed light on such a methodology.

As this sampling of interpretations of the functional-notional syllabus indicates, the concept is still in the developmental and exploratory stages and is not sufficiently systematized for widespread classroom application. Although Guntermann (1979), McKay (1980), and Harlow, Smith, and Garfinkel (1980) have taken steps toward structuring communicative syllabuses for American schools, and Knop (1981) and Cross (1980) have offered suggestions for immediate classroom application of the functional-notional concept, no functional-notional syllabus has yet been published in the United States.

Indeed, problems of complexity may delay classroom utilization of the functional-notional syllabus for some time. The content of the functional-notional syllabus is itself complex. Functions and structures do not uniformly correspond to each other; one cannot be inferred from the other. Further, classroom incorporation of the functional-notional syllabus complicates the teacher's task by requiring consideration of the social purposes of language in addition to morphology, phonology, syntax, and lexicon (Valdman, 1978). And, as Wilkins (1976) points out, the social purposes to which second language students in general courses will put the target language are frequently nonexistent, unknown, or at best ill-defined.

Valdman and Warriner-Burke (1980) propose that, lacking specification of communicative purpose, communicative objectives serve to provide students with samples of verbal social interaction. Following on George's (1972) concept of a "little" language, they offer a reductionist approach to designing syllabuses aimed at developing communicative ability. This approach simplifies the vocabulary and structural elements introduced, provides for realistic speech patterns, and gives high priority to communicative goals. The amount of material that must be mastered is therefore reduced, allowing students to gain fluency within a limited corpus of language. Despite the complexity, the potential for the functional-notional syllabus is great, both in a pedagogical and a theoretical sense: pedagogical in that it could provide just the information needed to devise better career-oriented courses and courses for other specific purposes, and theoretical in that it appreciates language and the learning of language as a unit of purpose and structure.

Interdisciplinary Approaches. Interdisciplinary approaches bring to the language class topics not traditionally included in second language curricula. Language teachers are in an unusual and very flexible position if they consider language as a communicative tool. Herein lies the flexibility. The learners should communicate about something: it does not matter about what. Course topics are not restricted a priori; the only stricture is that the target language be used, and therefore developed, in addressing some topic.

Cross-disciplinary techniques have the advantage of involving the language students in work assigned to them in other classes, thus reinforcing other teachers' efforts and gaining their support. By *cross-disciplinary* is meant the incorporation into the language class of material being taught in other departments (Guntermann, 1981). For example, why not label the parts of a microscope in French, write a review in Spanish of a book read in English class, utilize worksheets from mathematics classes for the teaching of numbers in German, transcribe a recipe from cooking class into metric measurement, research child care in France for a report for a child development class, or follow the foreign language instructions on a pattern for a sewing class. On more than one occasion, language teachers have discovered that the teacher of the content area class had some background in the target language and offered to accept additional assignments from students in the foreign language.

Cross-disciplinary can also mean the expansion of a language class project to involve students and teachers of other classes (Crouse et al., 1979; Galloway, 1981). Discussion with one high school teacher (Ross, 1981) generated the following example. Language students could rewrite in storybook form a play they had written and performed earlier in the year. They would then work with art students to illustrate the text, being sure that the representations were culturally appropriate. Students from the graphics department could be invited to print and bind the storybook, which could be used with elementary-level students. A difficulty experienced in moving toward implementation of such an idea is suspicion on the part of the other teachers and/or students that they are being "used" by the foreign language department and asked to do "extra work." This negative feeling can be avoided by joint planning, which generates enthusiasm for the project on the part of all the teachers involved. Planning should occur well enough in advance of the project so that the non-foreign-language teachers can incorporate the project as an integral part of their courses rather than as an awkward add-on.

In the preceding example, students in each department use their skills for a productive purpose, thus suggesting career education. Career education is a primary thrust in contemporary education (Beckerman, 1980; Neill, 1977a, 1977b; Reinhart, 1979). It responds to a general concern that young people make vocational decisions wisely and with a broad base of information about themselves and the world of work. Ideally, career education involves a K–12 program moving through five stages: awareness, exploration, preparation, placement, and continuing education (McLure, 1975). Language teachers should have an additional interest in career education because student awareness of career uses for second languages will strengthen the language program as well as provide employers with people trained in language (Galt, 1980). Elling (1980) outlines a five-step process for language teachers committed to a comprehensive career education program. At a more general level, career education in second languages should 1) expose students to the variety of jobs that require language skills, and 2) provide training oriented toward entering a specific career. Foreign language departments could sponsor career days in conjunction with another department; these could be held in the evening so parents could participate (Foreign Language Education, 1981). If foreign language proficiency is indeed useful in securing positions in, for example, business or a trade area, perhaps

the respective departments could be convinced to include foreign language as a suggested course for students to follow in preparing for their careers (Business Education, n.d.). Cooperative work programs offer another exciting opportunity for students actually to be placed in positions requiring their use of a second language.

In addition to efforts in conjunction with other departments, second language teachers should review their own course offerings, beginning with course descriptions in the registration booklet. The typical language course description does not deviate too far from the following:

French (German, Spanish) I (II, III, IV)
All Year

At this level, you will develop the skills of listening, speaking, reading, and writing in [target language]. The course will explore the culture of [target language] through films and literature.

And then we wonder why students do not sign up for the course! What is there in the description to attract the student? Why must all language courses be identified solely by level? Why must they all be year-long courses? Why is it not the practice to include in course descriptions purposes for which the language might be used? Consider the following:

German for the Medical Professions: Intermediate Level
One semester

In this course you will participate in activities in which you play both the roles of medical professional and patient. These activities will include reading a medical chart, taking down a health history, and discussing symptoms. In addition, you will study medical professions as they are practiced in Germany and will investigate medical careers open to you in the United States.

French for Secretarial Careers: Advanced Level
One semester

This course will provide you with practice in skills necessary for a position as a bilingual secretary, French-English. You will learn the format of French business letters, practice typing in French, read and respond to French business correspondence, function as a receptionist in French, and use the telephone for business purposes in French. Opportunities for clerical and secretarial positions both in the United States and in French-speaking nations will be explored, and you will also learn about the life and work of a secretary in France.

It is conceivable that courses of these types, or parts of other courses, could be developed for even the beginning levels. Beginning level classes could collect want ads from both target and native language sources in order to compare them and to become exposed to the occupational advantages of knowing two languages. Units could concentrate vocabulary and dialogues on a particular job cluster. Through individual projects, students could investigate personal career choices, identify and learn vocabulary relevant to those choices, and compare their choice with its counterpart in the target culture.

Additional guidance for incorporating career education into the foreign language curriculum is contained in Busse (1978), who reviews several programs in progress and provides a list of career education resources. Hunter (1979), who compiled an annotated bibliography for career education within foreign language curricula, and DeLorenzo (n.d.), whose comprehensive packet supplies both a conceptual orientation to career education and practical suggestions for its implementation in the foreign language classroom. Inclusion of career education broadens the foreign language curriculum, thus strengthening its ability to attract and retain students.

Students are also entering a world where nation affects nation. The third interdisciplinary approach, global education, focuses on international understanding and on preparing students to deal with world problems and issues by developing their capacity to address questions of interdependence, conflict, communication, growth, and change. Educators have not yet agreed on a single definition for global educa-

tion (Bragaw, Loew, and Wooster, 1981), but Hanvey (1975) points teachers toward five goals: awareness of the current planetary situation, awareness of the choices people can and must make, understanding of the dynamics of international relationships, consciousness of and respect for different ways of viewing the world, and cross-cultural awareness. Although global education should pervade all disciplines at all levels (Strasheim, 1981), at present it generally comes under the auspices of social studies departments (Collins, n.d.).

There has recently been increasing cooperation among social studies and foreign language professional organizations (Bragaw, Loew, and Wooster, 1981; "Recommendations," 1979). In 1981 both the Northeast and the Central States Conferences took global education as their theme (Conner, 1981; Geno, 1981), and ACTFL projected a joint conference with the National Council for the Social Studies in 1983 (Lange, 1981). Social studies teachers recognize the affinity of modern languages for global studies but note that the effectiveness of language classes for global understanding is hampered if cultural studies are insufficiently pursued (Collins, n.d.). Strasheim (1979, 1981c) points out that language teachers cannot presume a role in global education simply on the basis of language study. A study by Barrows et al. (1981) reinforces this view. The researchers found no relationship between foreign language proficiency and knowledge of global affairs and only a moderate relationship between foreign language proficiency and affective responsiveness to global matters. Language-culture study, however, carries the potential for opening the student to new ways of viewing the world and to an understanding of how various languages and cultures interact (Strasheim, 1981).

This cultural understanding can be achieved by increasing implementation of culture-learning strategies such as culture assimilators, capsules, and clusters; coordinating with social studies teachers on topics; cultural concepts, and current events; and maintaining the attitude that language study is not just skill-learning but is also learning about the world (Elling, 1980; Seelye, 1974; Strasheim, 1979). Greater integration of global education into the foreign language classroom can be achieved by changing the content of instruction rather than by adding on to it. Bragaw et al. (1981) propose three change strategies, in increasing order of degree of change required. The most basic change involves evaluating currently used material for its potential in terms of global education. Based on the evaluation, a teacher would either use the material as is, adapt it more closely to global education, or reject it. The authors offer a criteria checklist for conducting this evaluation. A second change strategy proposed is that of organizing units around universal cultural topics such as education, recreation, or economic systems. This technique may be facilitated by the development of files into which teachers and students put any materials relevant to the topic. The third change suggests reorganizing course content around concepts such as nationalism. Vocabulary and grammatical structures would be taught in relation to the global issue under study. For example, a pattern drill on possessive pronouns could correspond to a study of personal possessions. Strasheim's (1980) idea of curricular complements furthers the interdisciplinary practice of global education. With this approach, teachers from various departments jointly decide on a global topic to which each discipline can contribute. In treating the topic of food, for example, Strasheim suggests that foreign language teachers can teach table manners, meals, and eating habits; home economics teachers can work with students to prepare foreign foods; and social studies teachers can deal with the food chain, food quality, and the specific foods people choose.

The three interdisciplinary approaches discussed above all demand that the language teacher take the initiative in talking to teachers in other departments. If the programs are presented as mutually beneficial, other teachers may be more eager to collaborate. In addition to being offered as individual courses, each of the approaches can be topically structured as units integrated into a basic course (Jorstad, 1979). This organization allows the teacher time to gather materials and sources for a full-length course. Logan (1973) suggests allowing students to follow a course of a certain difficulty level with another course of different content but the *same* difficulty level. Adapting this idea to the interdisciplinary approaches could relieve some of the tension felt in trying to retain student enrollment over three or four years. After finishing Level II, a student could leave the language department for a course in data processing and return a semester later, again at Level II but with an emphasis on business careers. Currently, such a student would probably be lost to the language department.

Besides supporting student enrollment in language classes, interdisciplinary approaches, although requiring time for preparation and collection of materials, can be professionally rewarding as teachers fulfill their responsibility of preparing students for life. This responsibility also means that language teachers must identify languages of importance and train people in them. World trends today indicate a growing need for languages beyond French, German, and Spanish, languages such as Japanese for commerce, Russian and Arabic for international relations, and Hmong, Vietnamese, Cambodian, and Chinese for work in social service organizations. Forward-looking teachers and prospective teachers would do well to become prepared in these languages so that the profession can offer them to students.

Instructional Alternatives

The broad purpose of this chapter is to identify for teachers a range of ways to alter the educational environment in order to meet student needs. Therefore, four instructional strategies are treated: suggestopedia, counseling-learning, the Silent Way, and cooperative learning, the first three of which are extensively reviewed by Stevick (1980). Recognizing that each of these strategies reaches beyond methodology into areas such as philosophy, sociology, and psychology of learning, I use the term *instructional strategy* because their primary impact is on the "how" of presenting material.

Suggestopedia. Lozanov (1978) is the originator of suggestopedia and Bancroft (1978), Racle (1979), and Schaefer (1980) have summarized the method for language teachers and reported on efforts to adapt it to North American education. According to the theory of suggestology, learning engages the unconscious as well as the conscious faculties. If the unconscious mind is tense or constricted by social norms that tell students they can learn only so much so fast, then learning is indeed hampered. However, if these psychic tensions can be removed and kept away, students can learn more in a shorter period of time. Suggestopedia accomplishes this by a combination of intensive time periods, a secure atmosphere, rhythmic breathing exercises, and baroque music.

The method is intensive and is designed for three- or four-hour sessions five to six days a week, ideally with a group of six males and six females. A secure atmosphere derives from confidence in the teacher and removal of personal risk to the student. The teacher, who preferably has special training in acting and psychology, assumes the role of benevolent dictator with unquestionable authority and unbeatable competence. Upon entering the classroom, the students leave behind their identities, and each one becomes a new person with a new name, history, and occupation. This new identity helps to reduce inhibitions and is frequently prestigious and/or interesting. Thus, students are proud of and engaged in learning about their new personality and role as well as those of the other students. The personal anonymity frees the students from concern over the self and provides a protective shield. The fault for linguistic errors can be shifted from the self to the character one plays in the classroom. A soft, pleasant, and cheerful room decor enhances the secure climate.

Suggestopedia's instructional procedure consists of three distinct parts. First is a review of the preceding day's work through conversations, games, skits, and so forth. Lozanov prefers these more active techniques and does not employ rote structure drills. During this review, the native language is kept to a minimum. Second, new material is introduced in a fairly traditional manner using dialogues centered on situations with which students are familiar. Several major grammatical features may be introduced along with perhaps two hundred new vocabulary items. Learning this quantity of material is made possible by the third stage, which is the unique one.

The séance, as the third stage is called, is divided into active and passive parts and aims at unconscious memorization of the new material. During the active part, the teacher reads the text with designated intonation in time with the students' defined breathing rhythm. The students assume a yoga posture and practice yoga breathing to the count of eight. They follow the printed dialogue, divided into groups of three lines, while the teacher reads each group aloud three times, first in a normal tone of voice, then in a persuasive whisper, finally in a loud, authoritative manner. The native-language translation is read in a matter-of-fact, unobtrusive manner. The passive section combines baroque music with an artistic rendering of the text. Baroque music is selected because of its steady, predictable rhythm and soothing continuo accompaniment. This passive or concert section consists of three parts. First, there is a brief baroque music introduction. Second, students breathe in rhythm with a slow baroque movement while the teacher interprets the dialogue emotionally and artistically. Third, brisk baroque music draws the students out of their relaxed state. This tapping of unconscious resources during the séance has been reported to accelerate the quantity of language learned, the quality of language use, and the long-term retention of what has been learned (Herr, 1979; Lozanov, 1978; Ostrander and Schroeder, 1970; Racle, 1977, 1979; Schaefer, 1980).

Despite the success of suggestopedia, the method may find only restricted classroom application. Suggestopedic teachers require dramatic ability and specialized training in the method and related disciplines. The Eastern yoga influence may not appeal to some Western students. Racle (1977) advises that suggestopedia be implemented only as a total method and that it not be modified. However, the intensive time structure makes its adoption within the traditional one-hour, five-days-a-week instructional setting impossible. Nevertheless, some of the principles of suggestopedia could be successfully adapted to the American classroom. Chief among these principles are the following: 1) the more competence a teacher exhibits, the more secure the students will be and thus the more they will learn and 2) the less tense students are and the more they are convinced of their own capacity for learning, the greater and the swifter will be their learning.

Counseling-Learning. Counseling-learning, like suggestopedia, aims at creating an atmosphere of security for the students, but it takes a different approach to that end. The psychologist Curran (1976) pioneered counseling-learning and its application to the teaching of second languages. *Understanding* is a key concept of counseling-learning. It is expressed by the teacher's 1) accepting the students without judgment or an effort to control, 2) believing that students are capable of integrating the self harmoniously, and 3) briefly sharing personal experiences and values when they relate to the classroom discussion. With this posture, the teacher-counselor-

knower structures a learning situation which Curran (1976) summarizes in the acronym SARD, representing the concepts security, aggressiveness/attention, reflection/retention, and discrimination.

The first word represented in the acronym is *security.* The more secure students feel, the more ready they are to risk new learning. Security is assured by the understanding atmosphere and progresses through five stages. These stages differ by source of security rather than degree of security. Initially, the knower, who possesses the sought-after knowledge, provides security to the learners. The teacher closely manages the amount of new material presented to the students, corrects errors with care not to upset the accepting and nonjudgmental quality of the classroom, and ensures that students grasp the language elements introduced. Gradually, the learners attempt new learning on their own, creating previously untried sentences, formulating grammar generalizations, transposing adjectives into adverbs into verbs. Throughout these intermediate stages of security, the students depend less and less on the teacher, needing only to be restrained from taking a wrong direction or to have major errors corrected. Finally, the learners become independent of the teacher for their security. They enter into a more mature and mutual relationship with the teacher and are free to become fluent in their new language skill.

Secure learners trust their own *aggressiveness* (*A* in the acronym), growing in courage to ask questions and make suggestions, thereby investing something of the self in the learning process. The assertive learner may not only explore the language, by for example, seeking new vocabulary to express ideas in a writing assignment or by wrestling with a new structure in discussion, but that learner may also suggest alternative teaching learning techniques to the teacher or reflect on the effectiveness of the techniques applied. Through such assertions, learners put a part of themselves into the language-learning task; they make an investment. Investment involves risk, but it also creates commitment. Therefore, *A* also stands for the *attention* students more willingly give to material in which they have some investment, a share of themselves.

R symbolizes *reflection,* which is of two types. First, accepting that feelings and learning are related, the teacher-counselor reflects back to the students their own feelings about the learning experience. In doing this, the teacher does not judge the feelings but merely states them as facts. Whether the feelings are those of frustration and anger or of satisfaction and pleasure, the teacher reports them back to the students in a supportive manner. Second, the students reflect on the content, examining it through different media or from different perspectives. Students might listen to an audiotape of their discussion or read their own written material. *Retention,* also an element of the *R,* is a result of reflection and signifies that the students can now retrieve and use the new material. As the students reflect on the content and view it from different perspectives, the network of associations grows and the new material becomes embedded in the mind of the learner. Thus, after students work with the formation of questions with *est-ce que* in French to the point of retention, this structure can be easily retrieved and applied in later discussion or when learning interrogatives such as *pourquoi, quand,* and *qui.* This example suggests the final letter, *D,* which stands for *discrimination.* Discrimination involves comparing new knowledge with prior knowledge in order to tell them apart. It also implies the appropriate integration of new knowledge with old knowledge, as in the preceding example of interrogative structure.

The principles of counseling-learning have been applied to second language education under a model called Community Language Learning, which utilizes a three-phase instructional process: investment, reflection, and discrimination. In this model, a secure environment for learning is established as students sit in a tight circle with the teacher outside. A student makes a statement in English, the teacher translates it into the target language, and the student repeats the target language version while recording it on tape. Through this procedure, students make a concrete contribution, which immediately results in a taped target-language dialogue of student-designated content in student voices. This initial investment phase is followed by teacher reflection on student reactions and by reflection on the content through techniques such as listening to the tape, writing out the dialogue, and silent thinking. The final discrimination phase is carried out through small-group discussion, construction of charts, and differentiation of word segments through color-coding. The principles of counseling-learning, however, with their conscious orientation toward the learner, are potentially adaptable beyond the Community Language Learning model to a variety of methodologies.

Counseling-learning shares some of the drawbacks of problem-posing education. Goals are stated only very generally: communication and the study of grammar. Clear, detailed, specific objectives are absent. Since the content is student-generated, there are no systematic materials; this places on the teacher the burden of checking for adequate exposure to grammar and vocabulary. The concept of security in counseling-learning also generates problems. First, although the intent is for steadily decreasing reliance on the teacher-counselor and increasing student independence, this situation is difficult to achieve in practice. If it were truly achieved, the teacher may feel threatened by the students' self-reliance and suffer from an "empty classroom syndrome" just as a mother might experience the "empty nest." Second, the concept of security contained in counseling-learning is a matter of maturity, a person's maturity depends of many influences in addition to those found in the classroom. In any case, maturity is gained slowly. The security desired by counseling-learning, therefore, could best be considered a goal of a total foreign language sequence or program rather than of a semester or year-long course.

The Silent Way. The teacher in the Silent Way assumes even a lower profile than does the teacher in counseling-learning. Gattegno (1972, 1976) has directed two books on the Silent Way to teachers of second language. These books are summarized by Stevick (1980) along with examples of the method's implementation. The Silent Way is built on a two-step learning theory. The first step is a conscious intellectual commitment to mental action. The second step, which may take place during the unconscious state of sleep, is that of retaining or assimilating the product of the conscious mental action. Meaningful practice improves fluency and secures its retention over a period of time. The goal of this sequence is for learners to internalize the knowledge so that it becomes an active and accessible resource to be drawn from within the learner. In order to achieve this goal, the teacher must perceive and promote in learners the qualities of independence, autonomy, and responsibility.

The Silent Way thus introduces a model of learning from which practitioners have derived instructional procedures commonly used in courses based on that model. Initially, instruction concentrates on pronunciation. The teacher might write on the board a target language word that speakers of English could be expected to pronounce correctly or nearly correctly (e.g., *dos* in Spanish). Or, the teacher could use two charts, one in English and one in the target language. Sounds that are the same in the two languages would be color-coded the same. Thus, the English *I* or *eye* and the *ei-* in the German *eins* might all appear in red. For sounds that are totally unfamiliar, the teacher would provide a single, clear example, requiring students to concentrate on the one model. Students would repeat the sound based on the one

model, thus providing each other with reinforcement of correct pronunciation.

Similar procedures are employed to introduce common words. Here, much use is made of a set of color rods of various lengths which can be manipulated to stimulate speech. For example, the teacher could place the orange rod next to other orange objects, give one example of the target language word for *orange* and lead students to produce the word for *orange*. Further manipulation could stimulate the students to combinations such as *one orange rod*. Likewise, the terms for spatial relationships (e.g., *over, under,* and *next to,* and adjectives such as *long, tall, short,* and *square*) can be easily communicated through manipulation of the rods. Just as color-coding can be used to represent sounds in the teaching of pronunciation, so can the rods symbolize grammatical features such as prefixes, suffixes, and endings. The teacher can then direct students to proper case endings in German or verb endings in French. However, it would seem necessary for a teacher to gain a good deal of training and skill in order to apply the Silent Way to the teaching of a total grammar in all its complexity, if such a broad application is, in fact, possible. The rods can also be used to symbolize other nouns. One rod could be designated *house* and another could be designated *car,* leading to produce "The car is in front of the house." The addition of other realia to the rods could enrich the noun vocabulary introduced as well as the methodology itself.

Throughout the instructional process, the teacher remains essentially silent, giving perhaps only an occasional model. In the Silent Way, students do the talking and the recombining of material. Under the skillful direction of the teacher, they provide each other with correct models and encourage each other's initiative. The Silent Way thus fosters interdependence and cooperation among students at the same time that it promotes independence from the teacher and reliance on what one knows to learn what one does not know.

Cooperative Learning. Interdependence and cooperation are also goals of cooperative learning. Cooperative learning has been promoted by Johnson and Johnson (1975) with accounts of its implementation in a second language classroom supplied by Gunderson (1978) and Gunderson and Johnson (1980). It accepts that learning grows primarily out of peer interaction rather than in the adult-child relationship of the traditional classroom (Johnson, 1980). The distinguishing element of this instructional approach is the concept of goal structure, of which there are three types. An individualized goal structure specifies that one student's achieving of a goal has no effect on and is not affected by other students' goal attainment. In a competitive goal structure, a student's chance of reaching a goal increases as other students fall farther from the goal, as when grading is done on a curve. Under a cooperative goal structure, a student's possibility of achieving a goal is increased as other students are successful at achieving the goal. Cooperation and intergroup competition may be combined to form a fourth goal structure (Johnson et al., 1981).

The crux of cooperative learning is the assignment of a group goal, such as a project or high group test performance, coupled to a reward for group achievement (Johnson and Johnson, 1981). This cooperative interrelatedness may be achieved through 1) physical reorganization of the classroom, 2) assignment of responsibilities to students, 3) devising joint learning activities, and 4) grading on a mutual basis. The cooperative classroom is organized into small groups of five to six students per group. Students are assigned to groups, which are arranged so that group members are close together while the groups are separated from each other. Each group carries a responsibility it must fulfill for the total class such as handing out or collecting materials, keeping track of classroom items, acting as receptionist to visitors, monitoring the tidiness of the room, and organizing class activities. Within groups, each individual has a task: taking attendance, recording information, cleaning up, and distributing materials and assignments.

Certain learning activities are done cooperatively. If the teacher has carefully specified the instructional objectives, appropriate materials can be supplied to the students and the group task or goal can be clearly explained. Students may help each other on worksheets, projects, conversation practice, and studying for tests. Gunderson (1978) integrates these cooperative activities with intergroup competitive activities and individual projects and tests. With evaluation based on a criterion-referenced system, a student's grade to a certain extent becomes dependent on other group members' success. One grade may be assigned for the total group performance and recorded for each group member. Alternatively, a particular grade may be an average of the student's individually earned grade and the average grade of all the students in the group. If a group has grades of A, C, B, A, and C, the average group grade is a B. When the individual and group grades are combined, the students would receive grades of B+, C+, B, B+, and C+, respectively.

The intent of mutual grading is to motivate students to achieve and to encourage them to help each other to study and learn the material. In reference to the example given, however, while the student whose grade went from a C to a C+ might have no complaints, the student, as well as the student's parents, whose grade changed from A to B+ may question the grading philosophy. This issue could be addressed by 1) reexplaining and reaffirming the cooperative plan, 2) introducing cooperative activities well ahead of cooperative grading, 3) using cooperative activities with a reward other than a grade, or 4) rewarding group activities with an individual grade as well as a group grade. In addition to traditional evaluation, students can participate in evaluating group progress by using checklist or discussion methods. The teacher gains insight into group progress by careful observation of students' interaction and reflecting on the instances when it becomes necessary to intervene to help a group solve a problem.

Although convinced that cooperative learning should predominate in the classroom, Johnson and Johnson (1975, 1978) advise the appropriate classroom use of competitive and individual as well as cooperative goal structures. Competitive drills and games conducted in an atmosphere of fun can stimulate students and provide variety in activities. Simple skills can be learned individually and later put to use in a cooperative setting. In the foreign language classroom, speaking skills can be practiced individually with a tape recorder and applied in a group conversation, skit, or program. As a social approach that fosters interaction among students, cooperative learning may be particularly adaptable to second language learning, in which the ultimate goal is interaction.

SUMMARY AND CONCLUSION

Every second language classroom contains a unique set of learners, available materials, physical structure, and teacher, all of which receive further definition by the total school and community surroundings. Furthermore, the classroom and its surroundings constantly change as events take place: a new principal favors innovative methods, a housing project is replaced by high-rise apartments that bring a new clientele, or the central office announces a cut in textbook purchasing. Accommodation of this individuality, complexity, and mutability requires the ability to adjust and combine alternatives to suit the particular learning situation.

Adjustment of an alternative is achieved by altering one or more of the structural variables as suggested above. With regard to combining alternatives, the alternatives should not be considered mutually exclusive. Rather, the teacher should select elements from them to produce the most advantageous and appropriate combination. This eclecticism could result in a cooperative, problem-posing design for global education, cross-disciplinary career education, or a systems-behavioral format for a functional-notational syllabus.

When making these selections and combinations, teachers, department heads, and supervisors must remember that each alternative grew as an answer to a certain set of questions. No one alternative is *the* answer. Each alternative promotes a unique instructional process, which reveals a belief about the learners and how they learn, and aims at a particular set of desired outcomes. The foreign-language coordinator who imposes the cooperative model on a districtwide basis may obtain disappointing results in the one school located in a community where parents foster highly competitive attitudes. A department head writing an experimental curriculum will find that problem-posing education cannot be combined with suggestopedia because the former advances an active, decision-making student role while the latter calls for a passive-receptive student posture. A teacher who is considering counseling-learning but is convinced that the teacher must retain a very directive role in the classroom and in the determination of content would achieve better results by acting on the latter beliefs. The teacher who holds cultural understanding as a high priority may well incorporate global education into the curriculum. Thus, the alternatives selected must be appropriate to the situation, the people involved in the situation, and the desired learning outcomes. For a combination of alternatives to be viable, the alternatives must be congruent and compatible.

The creative exercise and mixture of alternatives holds promise for addressing classroom problems. The content alternatives may attract and retain students with a broader range of interests. Problem posing and functional-notional approaches, with their union of culture and language, provide authenticity and relevance as well as a structure amenable to multilevel classes. Scheduling problems can receive relief from the flexibility offered by a systems-behavioral design. Through the instructional alternatives, the teacher can respond to the personality and mood of a class.

While the innovations of the late 1960s and early 1970s grew mainly out of the industrial model, the alternatives of the 1980s are tempered by a humanistic appeal. For language educators, this humanism involves an appreciation of language as more than a marvel of structure: language is interaction and communication. This communicative nature of language specifies a direction for future curriculum development: the union of grammatical, cultural, and functional syllabuses with a design that accommodates this holistic view of language.

REFERENCES

Altman, Howard B., and Robert L. Politzer, eds. *Individualizing Foreign Language Instruction.* The Proceedings of the Stanford Conference. Rowley, MA: Newbury House Publishers, 1971.

Bailey, Janet P. Consciousness raising groups for women: Implications of Paulo Freire's theory of critical consciousness for psychotherapy and education. *Dissertation Abstracts International* 38 (1977): 164–65A. [Ed.D. 1977, University of Massachusetts.]

Banathy, Bela H., and Dale L. Lange. *A Design for Foreign Language Curriculum.* Lexington, MA: D. C. Heath and Company, 1972.

Bancroft, W. Jane. The Lozanov method and its American adaptations. *Modern Language Journal* 62 (1978): 167–75.

Barrows, Thomas S. et al. *College Students' Knowledge and Beliefs: A Survey of Global Understanding.* New Rochelle, NY: Change Magazine Press, 1981.

Beckerman, Leon. Career education: More visibility. *NASSP Bulletin* 64, cdxxxv (1980): 120–23.

Bowers, Roger. The individual learner in the general class. In Howard B. Altman and C. Vaughan James, eds., *Foreign Language Teaching: Meeting Individual Needs.* Papers from the First Pergamon Institute of English Seminar, 66–80. New York: Pergamon Press, 1980.

Bragaw, Donald H., Helene Z. Loew, and Judith S. Wooster. Global responsibility: The role of the foreign language teacher, 47–89. In Thomas H. Geno, ed., *Foreign Language and International Studies: Toward Cooperation and Integration.* Report of the Northeast Conference on the Teaching of Foreign Languages. Middlebury, VT: Northeast Conference on the Teaching of Foreign Languages, 1981.

Brumfit, Christopher J. From defining to designing: Communicative specifications versus communicative methodology in foreign language teaching. *Studies in Second Language Acquisition* 3, i (1980): 1–9.

"Business Education." *Decisions for Your Future.* Secondary Vocational Education, Special Newsletter. Anoka, MN: Anoka-Hennepin School District Number 11, n.d.

Busse, Bonnie B. FLASK and career development: Retrospect and prospect. In Reid E. Baker, ed., *Teaching for Tomorrow in the Foreign Language Classroom.* Report of Central States Conference on Foreign Language Education, 66–79. Skokie, IL: National Textbook Co., 1978.

Charles, C. M. *Individualizing Instruction.* Saint Louis, MO: The C. V. Mosby Co., 1976.

Collins, H. Thomas. *Global Education and the States: Some Observations, Some Programs & Some Suggestions.* A Report to the Council of Chief State School Officers. New York: American Field Service, n.d.

Conner, Maurice W., ed. *A Global Approach to Foreign Language Education.* Report of Central States Conference on Foreign Language Education. Skokie, IL: National Textbook Co., 1981.

_____. New curricular connections. In June K. Phillips, ed, *The Language Connection: From the Classroom to the World.* The ACTFL Foreign Language Education Series, Volume 9, 95–121. Skokie, IL: National Textbook Co., 1977.

Crawford, Linda M. *French III and French IV.* Cardinal Cushing Central High School, South Boston, MA, 1974–75.

_____. Paulo Freire's philosophy: Derivation of curricular principles and their application to second language curriculum design. Ph.D. Dissertation. Minneapolis: University of Minnesota, 1978. [*Dissertation Abstracts International* 39 (1979): 7130A.]

Cross, David. Personalized language learning, 111–24. In Howard B. Altman and C. Vaughan James, eds., *Foreign Language Teaching: Meeting Individual Needs.* Papers from the First Pergamon Institute of English Seminar. New York: Pergamon Press, 1980.

Crouse, Gale, Krin Gabbard, Leanne Wierenga, and D. L. Schrader. Foreign languages and the total curriculum: Exploring alternative basics, 63–77. In David P. Benseler, ed., *Teaching the Basics in the Foreign Language Classroom: Options and Strategies.* Report of Central States Conference on Foreign Language Education. Skokie, IL: National Textbook Co., 1979.

Curran, Charles A. *Counseling-Learning in Second Languages.* Apple River, IL: Apple River Press, 1976.

DeLorenzo, William E. *The Foreign Language Career Education Sampler.* New York: ACTFL Materials Center, n.d.

Denton, David, ed. *Existentialism & Phenomenology in Education: Collected Essays.* New York: Teachers College Press, 1974.

Elling, Barbara. Special curricula for special needs. In June K. Phillips, ed., *The New Imperative: Expanding the Horizons of Foreign Language Education.* The ACTFL Foreign Language Education Series Volume 11, 83–115. Skokie, IL: National Textbook Co., 1980.

Ewert, David M. Freire's concept of critical consciousness and social structure in rural Zaire. *Dissertation Abstracts International* 38 (1978):5189–90A. [Ph.D. 1977, University of Wisconsin, Madison.]

Foreign Language Education-Business Education Joint Career Night. Anoka-Hennepin School District Number 11, 1981.

Freire, Paulo. *Cultural Action for Freedom.* Monograph Series Number 1. Cambridge, MA: *Harvard Educational Review* and Center for the Study of Development and Social Change, 1970a.

_____. *Pedagogy of the Oppressed.* Translated by Myra Bergman Ramos. New York: Herder and Herder, 1970b.

_____. *Education for Critical Consciousness.* New York: The Seabury Press, 1973.

_____. *Pedagogy in Process: The Letters to Guinea—Bissau.* Translated by Carman St. John Hunter. New York: The Seabury Press, 1978.

Galloway, Vicki B. Public relations: Making an impact. In June K. Phillips, ed., *Action for the '80s: A Political, Professional, and Public Program for Foreign Language Education.* The ACTFL Foreign Language Education Series Volume 12, 15–41. Skokie, IL: National Textbook Co., 1981.

Galt, Alan. Realizing the potential, broadening the base. In June K. Phillips, ed., *The New Imperative: Expanding the Horizons of Foreign Language Education.* The ACTFL Foreign Language Education Series Volume 11, 117–32. Skokie, IL: National Textbook Co., 1980.

Gattegno, Caleb. *The Common Sense of Teaching Foreign Languages.* New York: Educational Solutions, 1976.

_____. *Teaching Foreign Languages in Schools: The Silent Way.* New York: Educational Solutions, 1972.

Genesee, Fred. Acquisition of reading skills in immersion programs. *Foreign Language Annals* 12 (1979): 71–77.

Geno, Thomas H., ed. *Foreign Language and International Studies: Toward Cooperation and Integration.* Report of the Northeast Conference on the Teaching of Foreign Languages. Middlebury, VT: Northeast Conference on the Teaching of Foreign Languages, 1981.

George, H. V. *Common Errors in Language Learning: Insights from English.* Rowley, MA: Newbury House Publishers, 1972.

Gougher, Ronald L., ed. *Individualization of Instruction in Foreign Languages: A Practical Guide.* Language and the Teacher: A Series in Applied Linguistics, Volume 13. Philadelphia: The Center for Curriculum Development, 1972.

Grittner, Frank M. Democratization in the humanistic studies and academic excellence. *Modern Language Journal* 59 (1975): 225–34.

———, and Percy B. Fearing. Futurism in foreign language learning. In Jermaine D. Arendt, Dale L. Lange, and Pamela J. Myers, eds., *Foreign Language Learning, Today and Tomorrow: Essays in Honor of Emma M. Birkmaier,* 1–12. New York: Pergamon Press, 1979.

———, and Fred H. LaLeike. *Individualized Foreign Language Instruction.* Skokie, IL: National Textbook Co., 1973.

Gronlund, Norman E. *Stating Behavioral Objectives for Classroom Instruction.* New York: The Macmillan Company, 1970.

Gunderson, Barbara. Cooperative structures in the foreign language classroom, 37–52. In Reid E. Baker, ed., *Teaching for Tomorrow in the Foreign Language Classroom.* Report of Central States Conference on Foreign Language Education. Skokie, IL: National Textbook Co., 1978.

———, and David Johnson. Building positive attitudes by using cooperative learning groups. *Foreign Language Annals* 13 (1980): 39–43.

Guntermann, Gail. Learning outcomes in the language classroom. In June K. Phillips, ed., *Action for the '80s: A Political, Professional, and Public Program for Foreign Language Education.* The ACTFL Foreign Language Education Series Volume 12, 97–128. Skokie, IL: National Textbook Co., 1981.

———. Purposeful communication practice: Developing functional proficiency in a foreign language. *Foreign Language Annals* 12 (1979): 219–25.

Hanvey, Robert G. *An Attainable Global Perspective.* New York: Center for Global Perspectives, 1975.

Harlow, Linda L., W. Flint Smith, and Alan Garfinkel. Student-perceived communication needs: Infrastructure of the functional notional syllabus. *Foreign Language Annals* 13 (1980): 11–22.

Hawkins, Eric. *Modern Languages in the Curriculum.* New York: Cambridge University Press, 1981.

Herr, Kay U. Suggestive-accelerative learning and teaching in foreign languages." In David P. Benseler, ed., *Teaching the Basics in the Foreign Language Classroom: Options and Strategies.* Report of Central States Conference on Foreign Language Education, 31–41. Skokie, IL: National Textbook Co., 1979.

Holec, Henri. Learner training: Meeting needs in self-directed learning. In Howard B. Altman and C. Vaughan James. eds., *Foreign Language Teaching: Meeting Individual Needs.* Papers from the First Pergamon Institute of English Seminar, 30–45. New York: Pergamon Press, 1980.

Hornby, Peter A. Achieving second language fluency through immersion education. *Foreign Language Annals* 13 (1980): 107–13.

Hunter, H. Baird. *Incorporating the Career Education Concept in Foreign Language Curricula: A Selected, Annotated Bibliography.* New York: ACTFL Materials Center, 1979.

Jarvis, Gilbert A. Molecule by molecule: Building hope for man. *Modern Language Journal* 59 (1975): 221–24.

Johnson, David W. Group processes: Influences of student-student interaction on school outcomes. In James McMillan, ed., *The Social Psychology of School Learning,* 123–68. New York: Academic Press, 1980.

———, and Roger T. Johnson. Cooperative, competitive, and individualistic learning. *Journal of Research and Development in Education* 12 (1978): 3–15.

———, and Roger T. Johnson. *Learning Together and Alone: Cooperation, Competition, and Individualization.* Englewood Cliffs, NJ: Prentice-Hall, 1975.

———, Geoffrey Maruyama, Roger Johnson, Deborah Nelson, and Linda Skon. Effects of cooperative, competitive, and individualistic goal structures on achievement: A meta-analysis. *Psychological Bulletin* 89 (1981): 47–62.

Johnson, Mary E. *French Expression 70312.* Augsburg College, Minneapolis, MN, Spring, 1980.

Jorstad, Helen L. Objectives for new programs: A thematic approach in second language learning. In Jermaine D. Arendt, Dale L. Lange, and Pamela J. Myers, eds., *Foreign Language Learning, Today and Tomorrow: Essays in Honor of Emma M. Birkmaier,* 25–40. New York: Pergamon Press, 1979.

Knop, Constance K. Notional-functional syllabus: From theory to classroom applications. In Maurice W. Conner, ed., *A Global Approach to Foreign Language Education.* Report of Central States

Conference on Foreign Language Education, 105–21. Skokie, IL: National Textbook Co., 1981.

Lange, Dale L. Personal Communication, 1981.

———. Suggestions for the continuing development of pre- and in-service programs for teachers of second languages. In Jermaine D. Arendt, Dale L. Lange, and Pamela J. Myers, eds., *Foreign Language Learning, Today and Tomorrow: Essays in Honor of Emma M. Birkmaier,* 169–92. New York: Pergamon Press, 1979.

———. Testimony on H. R. 7580. *Foreign Language Annals* 13 (1980): 443–46.

Lapan, Maureen T. Acting on the realities in second-language education. In June K. Phillips, ed., *The New Imperative: Expanding the Horizons of Foreign Language Education.* The ACTFL Foreign Language Education Series Volume 11, 133–52. Skokie, IL: National Textbook Co., 1980.

Lewis, Paula Gilbert. An interdisciplinary approach to the teaching of foreign literature. *Modern Language Journal* 60 (1976): 251–53.

Logan, Gerald E. Individualized foreign language instruction: American patterns for accommodating learner differences in the classroom. In Howard B. Altman and C. Vaughan James. eds., *Foreign Language Teaching: Meeting Individual Needs.* Papers from the First Pergamon Institute of English Seminar, 94–110. New York: Pergamon Press, 1980.

———. *Individualized Foreign Language Learning: An Organic Process.* Rowley, MA: Newbury House Publishers, 1973.

Lozanov, Georgi. *Suggestology and Outlines of Suggestopedy.* Translated by Marjorie Hall-Pozharlieva and Krassimira Pashmakova. New York: Gordon and Breach Science Publishers, 1978.

Mager, Robert F. *Preparing Instructional Objectives.* Belmont, CA: Fearon Publishers, 1962.

McClure, Larry. *Career Education Survival Manual: A Guidebook for Career Educators and Their Friends.* Salt Lake City: Olympus Publishing Company, 1975.

McKay, Sandra Lee. On notional syllabuses. *Modern Language Journal* 64 (1980): 179–86.

Munby, John. *Communicative Syllabus Design: A Sociolinguistic Model for Defining the Content of Purpose-Specific Language Programmes.* New York: Cambridge University Press, 1978.

Neill, Shirley Boes. According to Hoyt. *American Education* 13, ii (1977a): 10–11.

———. Clearing the air in career education. *American Education* 13, ii (1977b): 6–9, 13.

Ostrander, Sheila, and Lynn Schroeder. *Psychic Discoveries Behind the Iron Curtain.* Introduction by Ivan T. Sanderson. Englewood Cliffs, NJ: Prentice-Hall, 1970.

Pereira, Carlos A. The implementation of Paulo Freire's educational philosophy in an American setting. *Dissertation Abstracts International* 38 (1978): 541A [Ed.D. 1977, Boston University School of Education.]

Pinar, William, ed. *Heightened Consciousness, Cultural Revolution, and Curriculum Theory: The Proceedings of the Rochester Conference.* Berkeley, CA: McCutchan Publishing Corporation, 1974.

———. *Curriculum Theorizing: The Reconceptualists.* Berkeley, CA: McCutchan Publishing Corporation, 1975.

Racle, Gabriel L. Can suggestopaedia revolutionize language teaching? *Foreign Language Annals* 12 (1979): 39–49.

———. *Practical Developments and Theoretical Concepts of Suggestopaedia in Language Teaching in Canada.* 1977. [EDRS: ED 152 064.]

Recommendations to the President's Commission on Foreign Language and International Studies. *Foreign Language Annals* 12 (1979): 383–86.

Reinhart, Bruce. *Career Education: From Concept to Reality.* With a chapter by James W. Altschuld. New York: McGraw-Hill, 1979.

Ross, Marvel. Personal Communication, 1981.

Saville, Anthony. *Instructional Programming: Issues and Innovations in School Scheduling.* Columbus, OH: Charles E. Merrill Publishing Company, 1973.

Saylor, J. Galen, William M. Alexander, and Arthur J. Lewis. *Curriculum Planning for Better Teaching and Learning.* Fourth Edition. New York: Holt, Rinehart and Winston, 1981.

Schaefer, Dolores A. My experiences with the Lozanov method. *Foreign Language Annals* 13 (1980): 273–78.

Schulz, Renate A., and David P. Benseler. *Intensive Foreign Language Courses.* Language in Education: Theory and Practice, Volume 2, Number 18.

Arlington, VA: Center for Applied Linguistics, 1979.

Seelye, H. Ned. *Teaching Culture: Strategies for Foreign Language Educators.* Skokie, IL: National Textbook Co., 1974.

Simon, Paul. *The Tongue-Tied American: Confronting the Foreign Language Crisis.* New York: The Continuum Publishing Corporation, 1980.

Skinner, B. F. *Beyond Freedom and Dignity.* New York: Knopf, 1971.

————. *Science and Human Behavior.* New York: The Free Press Division, The Macmillan Company, 1953.

————. The science of learning and the art of teaching. *Harvard Educational Review* 24 (1954): 86–97.

————. *The Technology of Teaching.* New York: Appleton-Century-Crofts, 1968.

Steckel, Richard A. The transferability of Paulo Freire's educational ideas to American society. *Dissertation Abstracts International* 36 (1975): 92A [Ed.D. 1975, Boston University School of Education.]

Stern, H. H., and Jim Cummins. Language teaching/learning research: A Canadian perspective on status and directions. In June K. Phillips, ed., *Action for the '80s: A Political, Professional, and Public Program for Foreign Language Education.* The ACTFL Foreign Language Education Series Volume 12, 195–248. Skokie, IL: National Textbook Co., 1981.

Stevick, Earl W. *Teaching Languages: A Way and Ways.* Rowley, MA: Newbury House Publishers, 1980.

Strasheim, Lorraine A. An issue on the horizon: The role of foreign languages in global education. *Foreign Language Annals* 12 (1979): 29–34.

————. Interdisciplinary cooperation: Will teachers in 'average' schools be left out? *Foreign Language Annals* 13 (1980): 59–61.

————. Establishing a professional agenda for integrating culture into K–12 foreign languages: An editorial. *Modern Language Journal* 65 (1981a): 67–69.

————. Language is the medium, culture is the message: Globalizing foreign languages. In Maurice W. Conner, ed., *A Global Approach to Foreign Language Education.* Report of Central States Conference on Foreign Language Educa-

tion, 1–16. Skokie, IL: National Textbook Co., 1981b.

————. Broadening the middle school curriculum through content: Globalizing foreign languages. In June K. Phillips, ed., *Action for the '80s: A Political, Professional, and Public Program for Foreign Language Education.* The ACTFL Foreign Language Education Series Volume 12, 129–45. Skokie, IL: National Textbook Company, 1981c.

Strength through Wisdom: A Critique of U.S. Capability, A Report to the President from the President's Commission on Foreign Language and International Studies. Washington, DC: US Government Printing Office, 1979. [Reprinted by the American Council on the Teaching of Foreign Languages.]

U.S. Congress. House. *A Bill to Provide for Per Capita Grants to Reimburse Elementary Schools and Institutions of Higher Education for Part of the Costs of Providing Foreign Language Instruction.* H.R. 7580, 96th Cong., 2d sess., 1980.

Valdman, Albert. Communicative use of language and syllabus design. *Foreign Language Annals* 11 (1978): 567–78.

————, and Helen P. Warriner-Burke. Major surgery due: Redesigning the syllabus and texts. *Foreign Language Annals* 13 (1980): 261–70.

van Ek, J. A. *The Threshold Level for Modern Language Learning in Schools.* With contributions by L. G. Alexander. London: Longman, 1977. [First published by the Council of Europe, Strasbourg, 1976.]

Warriner, Helen P. The teacher as quality control: Program options. In Frank M. Grittner, ed., *Student Motivation and the Foreign Language Teacher: A Guide for Building the Modern Curriculum.* Report of Central States Conference on Foreign Language Education, 30–44. IL: National Textbook Co., 1974.

Wattenmaker, Beverly. An intensive approach to high school foreign language learning. *Foreign Language Annals* 12 (1979): 65–70.

Wilkins, D. A. *Notional Syllabuses: A Taxonomy and Its Relevance to Foreign Language Curriculum Development.* New York: Oxford University Press, 1976.

Willis, George, ed. *Qualitative Evaluation: Concepts and Cases in Curriculum Criticism.* Berkeley, CA: McCutchan Publishing Corporation, 1978.

CHAPTER
11

Method: Approach, Design, and Procedure

Jack C. Richards
Ted Rodgers

A comparison of the state of the art in language teaching today with the field as it was some twenty years ago reveals some interesting differences. In the fifties and sixties language teaching represented a reasonably unified body of theory and practice. It was clearly linked in its theoretical foundations to linguistics and psychology, particularly as these disciplines were represented in North America. The methodology of language teaching was identified with the orthodoxy of audiolingualism. Language teachers in the eighties, however, have a considerable array of theories and methods to choose from. Contemporary language teaching draws on a number of areas which were unknown or unconsulted by the linguists and psychologists of the fifties and sixties. These include (following Candlin, 1976) studies in textual cohesion, language functions, speech act theory, sociolinguistic variation, presuppositional semantics, interaction analysis, ethnomethodology and face to face analysis, ethnography of speaking, process analysis, and discourse analysis. Methodologies unheard of in the sixties are now familiar, at least by name: Silent

Way, Total Physical Response, Communicative Language Teaching, Counseling Learning, Suggestopedia.

The practitioner is thus confronted with a somewhat bewildering set of options at the levels of both theory and practice. One conclusion might be that the field of language teaching has moved away from a generally accepted body of principles as a basis for the organization of language teaching. It is our belief, however, that current practices need not be seen as random or radical departures from the mainstream of applied linguistic thought and practice. Today's innovations in teaching practice represent variations on familiar themes, rather than radical departures or totally new practices. Given this point of view, we wish to outline a model for the systematic description and comparison of language teaching methods in the hope that such a model may make it easier to understand recent developments in methodology in terms of some general principles.

As a point of departure we use a three-part distinction made some twenty years ago by Edward Anthony when he proposed an analysis of language teaching practices using the terms *approach, method,* and *technique* (Anthony, 1963). But since we prefer *method* as an umbrella term for the specification and interrelation of theory and practice, we find it convenient to modify Anthony's terminology for the present purpose and speak of *approach, design,* and *procedure.*

These terms will be used to label three interrelated elements of organization upon which language teaching practices are founded. The first level, *approach,* defines those assumptions, beliefs, and theories about the nature of language and the nature of language learning which operate as axiomatic constructs or reference points and provide a theoretical foundation for what language teachers ultimately do with learners in classrooms. The second level in the system, *design,* specifies the relationship of theories of language and learning to both the form and function of instructional materials and activities in instructional settings. The third level, *procedure,* comprises the classroom techniques and practices which are consequences of particular approaches and designs.

These three levels of organization form an interdependent system. When faced with a plethora of new language teaching proposals, by focusing on the relationships between the levels of approach, design, and procedure, we can better understand the ways in which one method resembles or differs from another and hence more readily describe and evaluate the claims of different methods. We begin by defining the relevant elements of a teaching-learning system that form the basis for the description and com-

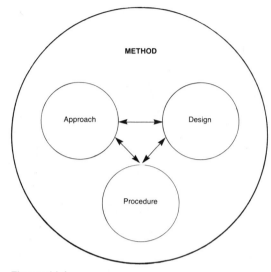

Figure 11.1

parison of methods. The system is illustrated in Figure 11.1.

We do not wish to imply that the ideal methodological development proceeds, rather neatly, from approach, to design, to procedure. It is not clear whether such a developmental formula is possible, and it certainly does not describe the typical case. Methodologies can develop out of any of the three categories (in our diagram, clockwise, counterclockwise, or both). One can, for example, stumble on or invent a teaching procedure that appears to be successful on some measure and then later develop (counterclockwise) a design and a theoretical approach which explain or justify the given procedures. Several currently popular methods appear, in fact, to have been developed from procedure to approach (see, for example, Scovel's 1979 review of Suggestopedia).

APPROACH

Approach encompasses both theories of language and language learning. All language teaching methods operate explicitly from a the-ory of language and beliefs or theories about how language is learned. Theories at the level of approach relate directly to the level of design since they provide the basis for determining the goals and content of a language syllabus. They also relate to the level of procedure since they provide the linguistic and psycholinguistic rationale for selection of particular teaching techniques and activities.

At least three different theoretical views of language explicitly or implicitly underlie currently popular language teaching methods. The first, and the most traditional of the three, is the structural view, the view that language is a system of structurally related elements for the coding of meaning. The target of language learning is seen to be the acquisition of the elements of this system, which are generally defined in terms of grammatical units (clause, phrase, sentence) and grammatical operations (adding, shifting, joining elements). The second view of language is the functional view—the view that language is a vehicle for the expression of meaning. This approach emphasizes the semantic rather than the grammatical potential of language and leads to a specification and organization of language teaching content by categories of function rather than by categories of form. A third view of language which informs some current methods of language teaching might be called the interactional view. It sees language as a vehicle for the realization of interpersonal relations and for the performance of social transactions between individuals. Areas of language inquiry which are being drawn on in the development of interactional language teaching include studies in interaction analysis, discourse analysis, ethnomethodology, and second language acquisition. Interactional theories focus on the patterns of moves, acts, and exchanges in communication. Language teaching content, according to this view, may be specified and organized by patterns of exchange or may be left unspecified—to be shaped by the inclination of the learners as interactors.

Structural, functional, or interactional models of language (or variations on them) provide the axioms and theoretical framework of support underlying particular methods of language teaching. But in themselves they are incomplete and need to be complemented by theories of language learning. There often appear to be natural affinities between certain theories of language and theories of language learning; however, one can imagine different pairings of language theory to learning theory which might have worked as well as those we observe. The linking of structuralism (a linguistic theory) to behaviorism (a learning theory) produced audiolingualism. That particular link was not inevitable, however. Cognitive-code proponents, for example, have attempted to link structuralism to a more mentalistic and less behavioristic brand of learning theory.

Halliday (1975) has developed a theory of language focusing on "meaning potential," and he has proposed an account of how the capacity to use and understand the meaning potential of language develops in children. We can imagine a parallel account which describes the developmental stages by which meaning potential and communicative fluency are acquired by adult learners of a second language. Such an account would represent a learning model which might be paired with a notional/functional view of language.

Studies relevant to interactional models of learning are fewer and less developed than those relevant to interactional models of language. However, some proto-theories of interactive language learning are available, and others are imaginable. Weeks (1979) offers evidence of what we might call a *compulsion to converse* (our term) which she feels directs the course of language acquisition of young children. Curran (1972, 1976) speaks of a relationship of *redemptive convalidation* which exists between knower and learner. It is a state of interdependence which enables them to reach self-fulfillment. Human beings seek such redemptive convalidation, and Curran's Counseling Learning identifies this as the driving force of language learning. Compulsion to converse or redemptive convalidation present proto-theories of interactive language learning which ultimately might support a theory of interactive linguistic organization as discussed above.

At the level of approach, we examine the theoretical principles underlying particular methods. With respect to language theory, we are concerned with a model of linguistic competence and an account of the basic features of linguistic organization. With respect to learning theory, we are concerned with an account of the central processes of language learning (e.g., memorization, inference, habit learning) and an account of the variables believed to promote successful language learning (e.g., frequency of stimulus, motivation, age, meaningfulness, type of learning, task, communality, activity).

DESIGN

We now consider how the views of language and learning identified in a particular approach are linked to a design for language teaching. Such a design includes specifications of 1) the content of instruction, i.e., the syllabus, 2) learner roles in the system, 3) teacher roles in the system, 4) instructional materials types and functions.[1] Different approaches to language teaching manifest themselves in different design elements in language teaching systems. Let us consider these elements, their relationship, and the outputs they determine.

Content Choice and Organization Within the Instructional System: The Syllabus

All methods of language teaching involve the use of the target language. All methods involve decisions concerning the selection of content that is to be used within the teaching program. Content concerns involve both subject matter and linguistic matter. In straightforward terms one makes decisions as to what to talk about (subject matter) and how to talk about it (linguistic matter). ESP and immersion courses, for example, are necessarily subject-matter focused. Structurally based courses are necessarily linguistically focused. Methods typically differ in what they see as the relevant language and subject matter around which language instruction should be organized and in the principles they make use of in structuring and sequencing content units within a course. These involve issues of selection and gradation that ultimately shape the syllabus adopted in a language course, as well as the instructional materials.

Within a design built on a structural theory of language, linguistic matter is identified with lexis and grammar, and the syllabus is an arrangement of linguistic units determined by such criteria as learnability, frequency of use, linguistic complexity, etc. Within a design built on a functional theory of language, linguistic content is organized conceptually. An explicit notional syllabus, for example, would contain a specification of the propositional, conceptual, and communicative content of a language course, a selection of the linguistic means by which these are realized, and an organization of the product of such an analysis in terms of pedagogic priorities. Designs built on interactional theories of language and of language learning ostensibly use affective and interactive goals as organizing principles for the selection and structuring of content. The progression within the course might be rationalized in terms of developing patterns of relationships between teachers and learners. An alternative solution for developing a syllabus within an interactional approach is illustrated by Community Language Learning (CLL). The emphasis in CLL is on having learners enter into a creative affiliation with other students and the teacher. To this end, CLL offers neither linguistic nor subject matter specification. Learners select content for themselves by choosing topics which they wish to talk about. These are then translated into the target language and used as the basis for interaction and second language practice and development.

Conceptions of syllabus thus range from code-based to relationship-based. These conceptions lead to different solutions to the question of how the content of a course or textbook is to be chosen and organized. The evaluation and testing procedures and teacher training proposals defined for a particular teaching method may also suggest the syllabus implicit in a particular method. A useful exercise which we use in teacher training is to have trainees examine textbooks, course designs, language learner protocols, and testing instruments in order to reconstruct the rationale for the selection and organization of content that has been followed. In the absence of these resources, trainees read what Asher, Curran, Gattegno, Candlin, and others have written about their own proposals for language teaching and then attempt to abstract specific principles for the selection and gradation of language content, that is, the actual criteria for syllabus design as specified or implied.

> With respect to the selection and organization of content, design is thus the level which is concerned with the general objectives of a method (e.g., choice of language skills to be taught), the specific objectives of the method (e.g., target vocabulary or level to be taught in a conversation method), the criteria for the selection, sequencing, and organization of linguistic and/or subject matter content (e.g., frequency, learnability, complexity, personal utility), the form in which that content is presented in the syllabus (e.g., grammatical structures, situations, topics, functions, exchanges).

Use of Content in the Instructional System: Learners, Teachers, and Materials

The syllabus is the first component of the level of design. The other components concern the use of the syllabus in the system by the learners and teachers as they interact with the instructional materials. Design considerations thus deal with assumptions about the content and the context for teaching and learning—with how learners are expected to learn in the system and with how teachers are expected to teach with respect to a particular set of instructional materials organized according to the criteria of a syllabus.

Language teaching methods differ in the weighting they give to these variables and in the assumptions they make about them. A notional syllabus, for example, is rightly termed a syllabus and not a method. Discussions of notional syllabuses (e.g., Wilkins, 1976) are directed to the organization of the linguistic content of language teaching. They say nothing about the roles of learners, teachers, or types of instructional materials. We might compare this to the Breen and Candlin discussion of communicative language teaching, for example, where they have tried to relate the syllabus to specific roles for learners, teachers, and materials (Breen and Candlin, 1980). We return to this below. Individualized approaches to language learning have also redefined the roles of learner and teacher. This has led to a reconsideration of the kinds and uses of instructional materials and, in turn, to new requirements for specification of linguistic content, that is, new kinds of syllabuses for use in individualized instruction.

We will discuss design considerations as they relate to learners, teachers, and materials in the next three sections.

Learner Roles. The majority of the world's population is bilingual, and formal classroom teaching has contributed only insignificantly to this statistic. Thus, it is easy to find successful language learning situations which formally possess neither syllabus, teachers, nor instructional materials. It is difficult to imagine a language learning situation without learners, however. Learners are the *sine qua non* of language learning.

> What roles do learners play in the design of formal instructional systems? Many of the newer methodologies reflect a rethinking of the learner's contribution to the learning process and acknowledgment that the design of an instructional system will be much influenced by the kinds of assumptions made about learners. Such assumptions reflect explicit or implicit responses to such issues as the types of learning tasks set for learners, the degree of control learners have over the content of learning, the patterns of learner groupings which are recommended or implied, the degree to which learners influence the learning of others, the view of the learner as a processor, performer, initiator, problem solver, etc.

Much of the criticism of audiolingualism came from the recognition of the very limited options available to learners in audiolingual methodology. Learners were seen as stimulus-response mechanisms whose learning was a direct product of repetitive practice. Newer methodologies customarily exhibit more concern for learner roles and variation among learners. Breen and Candlin describe the learner's role within a communicative methodology in the following terms. "The role of learner as negotiator —between the self, the learning process, and the object of learning—emerges from and interacts with the role of joint negotiator within the group and within the classroom procedures and activities which the group undertakes. The implication for the learner is that he should contribute as much as he gains, and thereby learn in an interdependent way" (Breen and Candlin, 1980:110).

Johnson and Paulston (1976:39–46) spell out learner roles in an individualized approach to language learning: a) The learner is planner of his or her own learning program and thus ultimately assumes responsibility for what he or she does in the classroom; b) The learner is monitor and evaluator of his or her own progress; c) The learner is a member of a group and learns by interacting with others; d) The learner is a tutor of other learners; e) The learner learns from the teacher, from other students, and from other teaching sources.

Counseling Learning views learners as having roles that change developmentally; indeed, Curran uses an ontogenetic metaphor to suggest this development. The developmental process is divided into five stages extending from total dependency of the learner in Stage 1 to total independence in Stage 5. These learner stages Curran sees as parallel to "the growth of a child from embryo to independent adulthood passing through childhood and adolescence" (Curran, 1980).

Teacher Roles. Clearly linked to the roles defined for the learner are the roles the teacher is expected to play in the instructional process. Teacher roles, too, must ultimately be related both to assumptions about content and, at the level of approach, to particular views of language and language learning. Some instructional systems are totally dependent on the teacher as the source of knowledge and direction; others see the teacher's role as catalyst, consultant, diagnostician, guide, and model for learning; still others try to teacher-proof the instructional system by limiting teacher initiative and building instructional content and direction into texts or lesson plans. Teacher and learner roles define the type of interaction characteristic of classrooms in which a particular method is being used.

Teacher roles in methods are related to the following issues: the types of functions teachers are expected to fulfill (e.g., practice director, counselor, model), the degree of control the teacher influences over learning, the degree to which the teacher is responsible for determining linguistic content, and the interactional patterns assumed between teachers and learners.

Typically methods turn most critically on teacher roles and their realization. In the classical audiolingual method the teacher is regarded as the source of language and learning. The teacher is the conductor of the orchestra, whose prime goal is to keep the players in tune and time, and without whom no music could be performed. Less teacher conducted learning, however, still may have very specific and sometimes more demanding roles for the teacher. Such roles often require thorough training and methodological initiation on the teacher's part. Only the teacher who is thoroughly sure of one's role, and of the concomitant learner's role, will risk departure from the security of traditional textbook-oriented learning.

For a functional/communicative method, the roles of the teacher have been described in the following terms:

The teacher has two main roles: the first role is to facilitate the communication process between all participants in the classroom, and between these participants and the various activities and texts. The second role is to act as an independent participant within the learning-teaching group. The latter role is closely related to the objectives of the first role and arises from it. These roles imply a set of secondary roles for the teacher; first, as an organizer of resources and as a resource himself, second as a guide within the classroom procedures and activities. . . . A third role for the teacher is that of researcher and learner, with much to contribute in terms of appropriate knowledge and abilities, actual and observed experience of the nature of learning, and organizational capacities. (Breen and Candlin, 1980:99)

Similarly, individualized approaches to learning define roles for the teacher which create specific patterns of interaction between the teachers and the learners in the classroom. These are designed to gradually shift responsibility for learning from the teacher to the learner (Johnson and Paulston, 1976).

CLL sees the teacher (knower) role as that of psychological counselor—the effectiveness of the teacher role being a measure of counseling skills and attributes: warmth, acceptance, and sensitivity. As these examples suggest, the potential role relationships of learner and teacher are many and varied. These include asymmetrical relationships such as those of conductor to orchestra member, therapist to patient, and coach to player. Some contemporary methodologies have sought to establish more symmetrical kinds of learner/teacher relationships: friend to friend, colleague to colleague, teammate to teammate, etc.

Role of Instructional Materials. The fourth design component is concerned with the role of instructional materials within the instructional system. What is specified with respect to content (the syllabus) and with respect to learner and teacher roles suggests the functions for materials within the system. The syllabus defines linguistic content in terms of language elements: structures, topics, notions, functions, exchanges, or whatever. It also specifies the selection and ordering of particular language items to be taught which represent the elements. Finally, it defines the goals for language learning. The instructional materials, in their turn, specify subject matter content (even where the syllabus may not). They also define or suggest the intensity of coverage for particular syllabus items: how much time, attention, and detail are devoted to specific language items. Finally, instructional materials define (or imply) the day-to-day learning objectives which (should) collectively constitute the goals of the syllabus. Materials designed on the assumption that learning is initiated and monitored by the teacher must meet quite different requirements from those materials designed for student self-instruction or for peer tutoring. Some methods require the instructional use of existing materials, found materials, and realia. Some assume teacher-proof materials that even poorly trained teachers with imperfect control of the target language can teach from. Some materials require specially trained teachers with near-native competence in the target language. Some are designed to enable learning to take place independently; that is, the materials are designed to replace the teacher. Some materials dictate various interactional patterns in the classroom; others inhibit classroom interaction; still others are noncommital as regards interaction between teacher and learner or learner and learner.

> The role of instructional materials within an instructional system will reflect decisions concerning the primary goal of materials (e.g., to present content, to practice content, to facilitate communication between learners, to enable the learners to practice content without the teacher, etc.), the form of materials (e.g., textbook, audiovisual, computer display, etc.), the relation materials hold to other sources of input (i.e., whether they serve as the major source of input, or only as a minor component of input), and the abilities of the teacher (e.g., competence in the language, degree of training, etc.).

A particular design for an instructional system may imply a particular set of roles for instructional materials in support of the syllabus and the teachers and learners. For example, the role of instructional materials within a func-

tional/communicative methodology might be specified in terms such as the following:

1. The materials will facilitate the communicative abilities of interpretation, expression, and negotiation.
2. Materials will focus on understandable and relevant communication rather than on grammatical form.
3. Materials will command the learners' interests and involve their intelligence and creativity.
4. Materials will involve different types of text, and different media, which the participants can use to develop their competence through a variety of different activities and tasks.

By comparison, the role of instructional materials within an individualized instructional system might include such specifications as these:

1. Materials will allow learners to progress at their own rates of learning.
2. Materials will cater for different styles of learning.
3. Materials will provide opportunities for independent study and use.
4. Materials will provide for student self-evaluation and progress in learning.

The content of CLL is assumed to be a product of the interests of the learners. In that sense it would appear that no linguistic content or materials are specified within the method. On the other hand, CLL acknowledges the need for learner mastery of certain linguistic mechanics such as the learning of vocabulary, appropriate pronunciation, and grammatical rules. CLL sees these issues as falling outside the teacher/knower's central role as counselor. Thus, CLL has proposed the use of teaching machines and other learning apparatus to support the learning of such mechanics so as to free the teacher to function increasingly as a learning counselor.

PROCEDURE

The last level of conceptualization and organization within an instructional system is what we refer to as procedure. Here the focus is on the actual moment-to-moment techniques, practices, and activities that operate in teaching and learning a language according to a particular method.

Many contemporary methods are characterized primarily by their techniques and practices. When we ask for impressions of these methods, we customarily get responses dealing with procedure rather than with approach or design. Free association to Silent Way elicits descriptions like "manipulating colored rods;" to Total Physical Response, "jumping up and down;" to Suggestopedia, "lying in a chaise lounge listening to soothing music;" to Counseling Learning, "sitting in a conversation circle," and so forth. All of these responses deal with the procedural element of particular methods.

Differences in approach and design are likely to manifest themselves at the level of procedure in different types of activities and exercise in materials and in the classroom and in different uses for particular exercise types. Types of exercises include drill, dialogue, dictation, cloze sentence completion, (guided, semi-guided, and free) composition and conversation, role-play games, simulation, etc. For a particular exercise type, procedure includes a specification of context of use and a description of precisely what is expected in terms of execution and outcome for each exercise type. For example, interactive games are often used in audiolingual methodology for motivation and change of pace from pattern practice drills. In contemporary communicative methodology, the same games may be used to introduce or provide practice for particular types of interaction exchanges.

Within a particular version of a functional/communicative methodology, the following requirements have been specified for exercise type and use. Exercises must be interactive, authentic, purposive, and contextualized (cf. Palmer and Rodgers, 1982). Thus the materials make use of dialogues as one exercise type, but within these the learner has to provide the content. The learner has to make decisions based on minimal clues rather than memorize prepackaged language since it is argued that purposeful communication involves encoding meaning.

Another example of practices recommended within a particular method is seen in the types of drills proposed in the individualized instructional system advocated by Johnson and Paulston. Drills are permitted only if they pass a test of "responsiveness."

> Practice is most effective when it is conducted in a responsive environment in which what is said by one learner matters to another or other learners, because they may in turn have to respond to what is said. . . . The most useful type of practice for developing communication skill is for the learner to say something and then have another learner respond entirely on the basis of what was said. It is apparent that in terms of responsiveness, the forms for practice easiest to provide in the classroom will be the request form and the question and answer form. A measure of effectiveness of practice will be the degree of responsiveness that a set of materials can incorporate into the practice of a sentence pattern. (Johnson and Paulston, 1976:31).

Procedure, then, is concerned with issues such as the following: the types of teaching and learning techniques, the types of exercises and practice activities, the resources—time, space, equipment—required to implement recommended practices.

We have now completed our discussion of the three elements and subelements which in their specification and interrelation constitute a statement of method. These elements and subelements are summarized in Figure 11.2. We conclude by suggesting several types of applications to which we think the model can usefully be put.

APPLICATIONS

The model just discussed represents an attempt to provide a framework which can be used to describe, evaluate, and compare methods in language teaching. It attempts to define elements which are common to all methods and to highlight alternative realizations of these for particular methods. It is hoped that the model permits localization of points of similarity and difference between methods as well as identification of areas wherein particular methods may not have been defined with sufficient precision or detail. We can see that communicative language teaching, for example, was described initially at the level of approach (see Wilkins, 1976; Breen and Candlin, 1980) and has only recently been more fully elaborated at the levels of design (see Munby, 1978) and procedure (Littlewood, 1980; Johnson, 1982).

We can overlay the grid (Figure 11.2) on a particular methodological statement to determine the degree of specificity and adequacy with which the method has been described. As an example, let us briefly consider Asher's Total Physical Response using this overlay technique. The method statement examined is that of Asher (1977).

guage is viewed as a vehicle for controlling the behavior of others, as a manipulative instrument.

Asher's learning theory is one based on the belief that language is learned through motor activity. In child language learning, "there is an intimate relationship between language and the child's body" (p. 4), and this is the model for adult learning. Orchestrating language production with bodily movement is thought to promote success in learning, and this is the key to the method. There is a belief in transfer across skills, and skills acquired in speaking are thought to transfer to writing and reading.

TPR at the Design Level

The general objectives of TPR are to teach the spoken language to beginning level students. Comprehension precedes production. Specific objectives are not elaborated. Due to the criteria for selection of language items, common conversational forms are not selected.

The syllabus is sentence-based, primarily lexical, and grammatical. Items are selected according to the ease with which they may be used in the imperative form to initiate actions. "Most of the grammatical structure of the target language and hundreds of vocabulary items can be learned from the skillful use of the imperative by the instructor" (p. 4). Vocabulary must be concrete and situational, and the verbs selected, action verbs. The progression of items is from concrete to abstract, and syllabus items are presented in sentence patterns.

Learners primarily perform actions from

TPR at the Approach Level

Asher's theory of language is implicit rather than explicit, but it appears to be based on a formalistic structural model of language focusing primarily on the form rather than the content of communication. It uses a surface-level concept of a grammatical system in which language is viewed as a code composed of structural elements which have to be mastered. Lan-

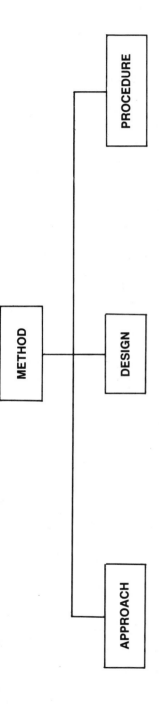

METHOD

APPROACH

a. *A Theory of the Nature of Language*
   - a model of linguistic competence
   - an account of the basic units of language structure
b. *A Theory of the Nature of Language Learning*
   - an account of the central processes of language learning
   - an account of what promotes success in language learning

DESIGN

a. *A Definition of Linguistic Content and Specifications for the Selection and Organization of Content*
   - the general objectives of the method
   - the specific objectives of the method
   - criteria for the selection and organization of linguistic and/or subject matter content
   - a syllabus model
   - the form in which content is presented in the syllabus
b. *A Specification of the Role of Learners*
   - the types of learning tasks set for learners
   - the degree of control learners have over the content of learning
   - the patterns of learner groupings which are recommended or implied
   - the degree to which learners influence the learning of others
   - the view of the learner as a processor, performer, initiator, problem solver
c. *A Specification of the Role of Teachers*
   - the types of functions teachers fulfill
   - the degree of control or teacher influence over learning
   - the degree to which the teacher determines linguistic content
   - the types of interaction between teachers and learners
d. *A Specification of the Role of Materials*
   - the primary goal of materials
   - the form materials take (e.g., textbook, audiovisual format, etc.)
   - the relation materials have to other sources of input
   - the assumptions the materials make about teachers and learners

PROCEDURE

Descriptions of Techniques and Practices in the Instructional System
   - the types of techniques and tactics used by teachers for presenting and practicing language content
   - the types of exercises and practice activities that are used in materials or suggested for teachers to follow
   - the resources in terms of time, space, and equipment used to implement recommended classroom practices

Figure 11.2

commands given by the teacher. The emphasis is primarily receptive, and the learners have no control over what is said. At a more advanced level, learners may also give commands to other students. Learners learn in groups, but pair work is also possible at later stages. Learners typically learn from the teacher, and they are viewed as responders.

The teacher is the initiator of activities and communication. The teacher has considerable freedom of choice over what language is taught, provided the command-based mode of selection and practice is followed. Interaction is primarily nonreciprocal. The teacher commands, and students react.

Teaching may proceed without materials. Materials play a primarily supplementary role (word charts, slides, pictures) and are teacher-produced.

TPR at the Procedure Level

The activities used are primarily command-based drills. Meaning is communicated via gesture, mime, and demonstration. Written and spoken forms are presented at the same time. Both individual and group work are used. Errors are allowed and are not corrected initially. Comprehension is emphasized before production.

A fuller description of the Total Physical Response method would take into account all the elements of the model. The model, however, can also be used to compare and contrast methods. As an example, let us consider two methods: Total Physical Response (TPR) and Community Language Learning (CLL).

Superficially the two methods seem quite antithetical. Comparing elements at the level of design, we find TPR typically has a written syllabus with paced introductions of structures and vocabulary. CLL has no syllabus and operates out of what learners feel they need to know. In TPR, the teacher role is one of drill master, director, and motivator. In CLL, the teacher/knower is counselor, supporter, and facilitator. TPR learners are physically active and mobile. CLL learners are sedentary and in a fixed configuration. TPR assumes that no particular relationship develops between learners and emphasizes the importance of individuals acting alone. CLL is rooted, as its title suggests, in a communal relationship between learners and teachers acting supportively and in concert. At the level of procedure, we find that TPR language practice is largely mechanical, with much emphasis on listening. CLL language practice is innovative, with emphasis on production.

However, there are elements of commonality which can easily be overlooked. In approach, both TPR and CLL see stress, defensiveness, and embarassment as the major blocks to successful language learning. They both see the learner's commitment, attention, and participation as group members as central to overcoming these barriers. They both view the stages of adult learning as recapitulations of the stages of childhood learning. Both CLL and TPR consider mediation, memory, and recall of linguistic elements as central issues and see physical activity as a way to facilitate these—CLL through manipulation of a button-operated, color-coded language item practice device, TPR through mimetic physical enactment. TPR holds with CLL that learning is multi-modal—that "more involvement must be provided the student than simply sitting in his seat and passively listening. He must be somatically or physiologically, as well as intellectually, engaged" (Curran, 1976:79). At the level of design, neither TPR nor CLL assumes method-specific materials, but both assume materials can be locally produced as needed.

CONCLUSIONS

The view of method outlined here relates theory to practice by focusing on assumptions and the programs and practices which relate to these assumptions. The model offered represents a claim as to what a descriptively adequate statement of method should comprise. It is also claimed that the reasonably fine-grained analysis which the present model directs can help provide insights into the internal adequacy of particular methods, as well as into the similarities and differences which exist between alternative methods.

NOTE

1. We acknowledge that some methods lack both teachers and teaching materials. A more general model of design would comprise: 1) knowledge considerations (content), 2) learner considerations, and 3) instructional considerations (presentation). However, since most current methods assume the existence of teachers and teaching materials, these are specified in the present model.

REFERENCES

Anthony, Edward M. 1963. Approach, method and technique. *English Language Teaching 17:*63–67.

Asher, James J. 1977. *Learning Another Language Through Actions: The Complete Teacher's Guidebook.* Los Gatos, CA: Sky Oaks Productions.

Breen, Michael P., and Christopher Candlin. 1980. The essentials of a communicative curriculum in language teaching. *Applied Linguistics 1,* 2:89–112.

Candlin, Christopher. 1976. Communicative language teaching and the debt to pragmatics. In C. Rameh (ed.), *Georgetown University Round Table on Languages and Linguistics.* Washington, D.C.: Georgetown University Press. 237–256.

Curran, Charles A. 1972. *Counseling-Learning: A Whole-Person Approach for Education.* Apple River, IL: Apple River Press.

Curran, Charles A. 1976. *Counseling-Learning in Second Language.* Apple River, IL: Apple River Press.

Gattegno, Caleb. 1976. *The Common Sense of Teaching Foreign Languages.* New York: Educational Solutions.

Halliday, M. A. K. 1975. *Learning How to Mean: Explorations in the Development of Language.* London: Edward Arnold.

Johnson, Francis, and Christina Bratt Paulston. 1976. *Individualizing in the Language Classroom.* Cambridge: Jacaranda.

Johnson, Keith. 1982. *Communicative Syllabus Design and Methodology.* Oxford: Pergamon.

Littlewood, W. 1980. *Communicative Language Teaching.* Cambridge: Cambridge University Press.

Munby, John. 1978. *Communicative Syllabus Design.* Cambridge: Cambridge University Press.

Palmer, A., and Ted Rodgers. 1982. Communicative and instructional considerations in language teaching. *Language Learning and Communication. 1,* 3:235–256. New York: Wiley.

Scovel, T. 1979. Review of Georgi Lozanov, *Suggestology and Outlines of Suggestopedy. TESOL Quarterly 13,* 2:255–266.

Weeks, T. E. 1979. *Born to Talk.* Rowley, MA: Newbury House Publishers.

Wilkins, D. 1976. *Notional Syllabuses.* Oxford: Oxford University Press.

Section Five

LISTENING

INTRODUCTION

Current approaches to the teaching of listening comprehension emphasize that two complementary processes appear to be involved in listening. One, sometimes referred to as "bottom-up processing," involves decoding the incoming utterance or message and making use of the linguistic signals actually transmitted. Bottom-up processing involves such things as identifying and distinguishing words, structures, grammar, and other features of the message. The other process, known as "top-down processing," involves the listener making use of previous knowledge and information, which is not transmitted in the message, and using this information as a basis for interpreting the message. Both aspects of listening comprehension and their implications for teaching are discussed in this section. Richards discusses a model of bottom-up processing that emphasizes the role of constituent identification in listening comprehension. He compares this with a top-down approach which involves scripts and schemata derived from the use of language in particular situations for specific purposes. He shows how an understanding of the processes involved in listening comprehension as well as consideration of the characteristics of authentic spoken discourse can lead to the identification of the particular listening skills which should be the focus of instructional materials and activities. The importance of developing relevant objectives for listening activities is stressed, and the applications of his approach are illustrated from an evaluation and adaptation of a listening text.

Porter and Roberts elaborate further features of authentic conversational discourse and note the difference between this and the kind of language typically contained in EFL/ESL materials. Such materials, because they fail to represent accurately the nature of real spoken discourse, cannot prepare learners for listening in the real world. They make a strong case for using authentic materials in the classroom and demonstrate how classroom activities can be prepared which make use of authentic listening "texts." As in the example in Richards' paper, learners are prepared for listening to authentic discourse by using pre-listening activities to provide them with the necessary scripts, schemata, and language. These, together with the use of appropriate listening tasks during listening, allow the learner to use selection, inferencing, and prediction strategies. They also involve an integrated approach to listening in which listening and speaking play complementary roles.

DISCUSSION QUESTIONS

1. Both papers suggest that the crucial work in teaching listening comprehension comes *before* students listen to an oral text, and they suggest that pre-listening activities are an important part of listening comprehension. Select a listening task (e.g., listening to a description of something or listening to a lecture) and show how pre-listening activities can be used to prepare listeners for the sort of listening they will have to do.

2. Analyze a particular listening task (e.g., listening to the telephone or listening to a news broadcast). Draw up a list of what Richards calls the *microskills* and what Porter and Roberts call the *listening processes* that the task requires. Choose only the most important ones. Suggest activities that could help develop these skills in ESL/EFL learners.

3. Select a listening comprehension text and examine one unit from it. Determine the objectives for the unit and the micro-skills or listening processes that it covers, and review the exercise types that are used. To what extent does the unit test or teach? If necessary, adapt the exercise, following the suggestions and procedures suggested by Richards.

4. How might the ability to guess and predict, stressed in both papers, be developed and practiced in classroom activities? Select a listening activity where this is important, and develop exercises to develop predicting and guessing strategies.

5. What sorts of authentic speech can be used in ESL/EFL classes? What are the advantages and disadvantages of using authentic speech in the classroom? Select a sample of authentic speech and show how it could be used for the teaching of an aspect of listening comprehension, following the procedures discussed by Porter and Roberts.

FURTHER READING

1. British Council. 1981. *The Teaching of Listening Comprehension.* ELT Documents. London: The British Council.
2. G. Brown. 1977. *Listening to Spoken English.* London: Longman.
3. D. McKeating. 1981. Comprehension and listening. In G. Abbot and P. Wingard (eds.), *The Teaching of English as an International Language.* London: Collins. 57–80.
4. P. Ur. 1984. *Teaching Listening Comprehension.* Cambridge: Cambridge University Press.
5. H. Winitz (ed). 1981. *The Comprehension Approach to Foreign Language Instruction.* Rowley, MA: Newbury House Publishers.

CHAPTER
12

Listening Comprehension:
Approach, Design, Procedure

Jack C. Richards

Not to let a word get in the way of its sentence
Nor to let a sentence get in the way of its
intention,
But to send your mind out to meet the intention as a guest;
THAT is understanding.
                Chinese proverb, fourth century B.C.

In this paper, three dimensions of conceptualization, planning, and performance involved in the teaching of listening comprehension are considered. These are referred to as *approach, design,* and *procedure* (Richards and Rodgers, 1982). Initially, an outline of some of what is known about the processes involved in listening is presented. This is the level of approach, where assumptions about how listeners proceed in decoding utterances to extract meanings are spelled out. The next level, that of design, is where an operationalization is made of the component micro-skills which constitute our competence as listeners. This in turn enables objectives to be defined for the teaching of listening comprehension. At the third level, that of procedure, questions concerning exercise types and teaching techniques are examined. These three levels illustrate the domain of *methodology* in language teaching.

APPROACH

Message Factors

Current understanding of the nature of listening comprehension draws on research in psycholinguistics, semantics, pragmatics, discourse analysis, and cognitive science (e.g., Clark and Clark, 1977; Leech, 1977; Schank and Abelson, 1977; Marslen-Wilson and Tyler, 1980; Dore and McDermott, 1982; Clark and Carlson, 1982). There is little direct research on second language listening comprehension, however, and what follows is an interpretation of relevant native language research. Three related levels of discourse processing appear to be involved in listening: propositional identification, interpretation of illocutionary force, and activation of real world knowledge. The central question from both a theoretical and pedagogical perspective concerns the nature of the units listeners make use of in understanding language. Do we listen for intonation, stress, words, grammar, sentences, or some other type of language unit?

Much of the linguistic and psycholinguistic literature on comprehension suggests that propositions are the basic units of meaning involved in comprehension and that the listener's ultimate goal is to determine the propositions which an utterance or speech event expresses (Clark and Clark, 1977; Foss and Hakes, 1978). But propositions are represented indirectly in the surface structure of utterances. Listeners make use of two kinds of knowledge to identify propositions: knowledge of the syntax of the target language, and real world knowledge. Syntactic knowledge enables the listener to *chunk* incoming discourse into segments or constituents. The sentence:

I am informed that your appointment has been terminated.

would have to be chunked as in (1) rather than (2) in order to identify its propositional meaning:

1. I am informed/that your appointment/ has been terminated.
2. I am/informed that your/appointment has/been terminated.

The ability to correctly identify chunks or constituents is a by-product of grammatical competence. Knowledge of the structure of noun phrases, verb phrases, and the grammatical devices used to express such relationships as complementation, relativization, and coordination in English allows us to segment discourse into the appropriate chunks as part of the process of propositional identification. Where segmentation is difficult, comprehension is also difficult.

But knowledge of the world is also used to help identify propositions, enabling listeners to sometimes bypass the constituent identification process. Hence, (1) below is understood as (2) because, in real life, this is a plausible recon-

struction of likely events involving cats and rats:

1. and rat cat it chased the ate the
2. The cat chased the rat and ate it.

The following processes therefore appear to be involved in comprehension:

1. The listener takes in raw speech and holds an image of it in short-term memory.
2. An attempt is made to organize what was heard into constitutents, identifying their content and function.
3. As constituents are identified, they are used to construct propositions, grouping the propositions together to form a coherent message.
4. Once the listener has identified and reconstructed the propositional meanings, these are held in long-term memory, and the form in which the message was originally received is deleted (Clark and Clark, 1977:49).

Permanent, or long-term, memory works with meaning, not with form. The propositional meaning of sentences is retained, not the actual words or grammatical devices that were used to express it. Thus, after hearing *Tom said that the car had been fixed and could be collected at 5,* a listener is likely only to remember the fact that the car is now ready to be picked up, and not whether the speaker said *the car is fixed* rather than *the car has been fixed,* or *could be collected* rather than *will be ready to be collected.* Memory works with propositions, not with sentences.

The above is a semantically based view of how a listener decides what a sentence means. Leech distinguishes this view of meaning from a pragmatic perspective, that is, one which focuses on what an utterance means to a person in a particular speech situation. "The semantic structure of a sentence specifies what that sentence means as a structure in a given language, in abstraction from speaker and addressee;

whereas pragmatics deals with that meaning as it is interpreted interactionally in a given situation" (Leech, 1977:1). Theories which describe how pragmatic meanings are understood derive from speech act theory, conversational analysis, and discourse analysis (Schmidt and Richards, 1980).

Speech act theory is concerned with the relationship between the form of utterances and their function in social interaction and rests on the distinction between propositional meaning and the illocutionary force of utterances. For example, the sentence *Helen likes chocolates* as a proposition attributes a certain quality to Helen, but does not tell us whether the sentence was uttered in order to offer an *explanation* of her obesity, a *suggestion* as to what to do with the chocolates, or a *denial* of a previous assertion. Speech act and other interactional approaches to meaning assume that when we use language for communication, the meanings that are communicated are a function of the interactions between speakers and hearers meeting in specific circumstances for the achievement of particular goals. In arriving at an interpretation of the illocutionary force of an utterance (that is, in determining the speaker's intention), listeners call upon their knowledge of the situation, the participants, their purposes, goals, rights, and duties, as well as the position of the utterance within the sequence of utterances preceding it. In an illuminating analysis of how the interpretation of talk is organized by context, Dore and McDermott observe that ". . . in the course of organizing sensible moments with each other, people use talk as a social tool, relying on the social work they are doing together to specify the meaning of utterances" (1982: 375).

Grice proposed that one source of knowledge listeners make use of is their understanding of the nature and goals of conversation. He stated this knowledge in the form of maxims of conversational behavior, each of which illustrates the "cooperative principle" that dictates the sort of contributions people make during conversational interaction:

1. Maxim of quantity: Make your contribution just as informative as required.
2. Maxim of quality: Make your contribution one that is true.
3. Maxim of relation: Be relevant.
4. Maxim of manner: Avoid obscurity, ambiguity, prolixity. Be orderly.
   (Quoted in Clark and Clark, 1977:122)

Conversationalists, hence, normally act on the assumption that remarks made during conversation will be relevant to the ongoing concerns of speaker and hearer. Thus, if I invite you to dinner, I assume that you will respond with a remark that is relevant to my purposes. I will try to interpret what you say as an acceptance or a refusal. But if you respond with *There's a white Cadillac on the corner of the street,* I will have great difficulty assigning this utterance to the category of reply I anticipated.

Interactional views of meaning stress the crucial role of inferencing and interpretation in listening comprehension and remind us of the active and creative dimensions of listening. Work in cognitive science reveals an added dimension of this inferential process.

Script and schema theory (Schank and Abelson, 1977) describe the role of prior knowledge in comprehension. For example, in understanding *I went to the dentist this morning. He gave me an injection and I didn't feel a thing,* the following prior knowledge is referred to:

1. We normally go to see a dentist when we need a check-up or when we have something wrong with our teeth.
2. Dentists typically check, drill, repair, or remove teeth.
3. This process is painful.
4. An injection can be given to relieve the pain.

This body of knowledge about a specific situation (at the dentist's), particular participants (the dentist, the assistant, the patient), goals of the situation (remedying a problem with the patient's teeth), and procedures (drilling a tooth, giving an injection) can be referred to as the *dentist's script.* Script or schema knowledge is what we know about particular situations, and the goals, participants, and procedures which are commonly associated with them. Much of our knowledge of the world is organized around *scripts,* that is, memory for typical episodes that occur in specific situations. Our knowledge of dentist's scripts, cinema scripts, library scripts, drugstore scripts, school scripts, meal scripts, and so on, enables us to interpret a great deal of the language of everyday life. The information needed to understand many utterances is therefore not explicitly present in the utterance but is provided by the listeners from their repertoire of scripts. This means that many of the connections between events need not be specified when we talk about them, since they are already known and can be inferred. But if we lack a relevant script, comprehension may be difficult. For example, we have no available script which can be used to understand this sequence of events: *I climbed onto an elephant. The piano was out of tune. The rabbit tasted delicious.*

We are able to understand many utterances from our general awareness of how people achieve goals and from our assumptions that most human behavior is purposeful and directed toward particular ends. Non-native speakers, however, may lack many culturally specific scripts; their individual scripts may differ in degree and content from target language scripts, and this poses additional problems for the non-native listener.

We are now able to expand the tentative model of the processes involved in comprehension:

1. The type of interactional act or speech event in which the listener is involved is determined (e.g., conversation, lecture, discussion, debate).

2. Scripts relevant to the particular situation are recalled.
3. The goals of the speaker are inferred through reference to the situation, the script, and the sequential position of the utterance.
4. The propositional meaning of the utterance is determined.
5. An illocutionary meaning is assigned to the message.
6. This information is retained and acted upon, and the form in which it was originally received is deleted.

Medium Factors

The preceding discussion has focused on how meanings are understood in listening. But listeners confront another dimension of comprehension when processing speech. The act of speaking imposes a particular form on utterances, and this considerably affects how messages are understood. We call factors which result from this *medium factors.* Medium factors vary according to the nature of the discourse (whether planned or unplanned), the speaker's attitude toward the message or the listeners, and the situation in which the act of communication takes place (e.g., classroom, lecture room, or informal setting). We will consider nine such factors here, each of which influences the work listeners must do to process speech.

Clausal Basis of Speech.   Whereas the unit of organization of written discourse is the sentence, spoken language is generally delivered one clause at a time (Pawley, undated). The unit of conversational discourse is not the full sentence but the clause, and longer utterances in conversation generally consist of several clauses coordinated. Most of the clauses used are simple conjuncts or adjuncts, and Pawley points out that cases of complex clauses in conversation are rare. Clauses appear to be a major constituent in both the planning and delivery of speech.

The frequent use of coordinating conjunctions is illustrated in this example from Stanley:

Um perhaps the most celebrated near miss was a twin reactor two reactors side by side in Tennessee in 1975, *and* that was due to a worker at the plant using a candle to test which way the air was flowing, underneath the control room, *and* it caught fire. *And* they had a very serious fire there for fourteen hours. They didn't know how to put it out . . . *And* it was only shut down in the end *and* a very you know, a major accident averted by an operator using a very unusual *and* quite clever way of shutting it down by hand (1980:78).

Reduced Forms.

In articulating clauses, speakers are guided by the need to express meanings efficiently. This means that words which play a less crucial role in the message may be slurred or dropped, and other words given more prominence (Brown, 1977). In addition, consonants and vowels within words are affected by the positions in which they occur. In speech there is not always time for the tongue to assume the ideal position required to articulate a sound. Consequently, patterns of assimilation are common, leading to the disappearance of word boundaries, to the omission of certain vowels and consonants, and to substitutions occurring for elements within words. Sentences also occur frequently in elliptical forms, with the deletion of such elements as subjects, auxiliaries, verbs, articles, and pronouns when context makes their presence redundant, as in *When will you be back? Tomorrow maybe* (instead of, *Maybe I'll be back tomorrow*).

Ungrammatical Forms.

Due to the effort speakers put into planning and organizing the content of their utterances in ongoing time, grammaticality is often less relevant than ideational coherence. Consequently, ungrammatical forms and constructions are frequent. For example:

Big companies can only really make lots of money out of high technology centralized systems . . . And because of that *it* is tending to go into high technology solutions.

(lack of agreement)

And after that we arrived in a little town that there was no hotel anywhere . . .

(faulty clause construction)

Pausing and Speech Errors.

An important component of human speech consists of the pauses, hesitations, false starts, and corrections which make up such a large portion of what we actually say. In natural speech, between 30% and 50% of speaking time may consist of pauses and hesitations, indicating some of the selection and planning processes speakers make use of. Pauses may be either silent pauses or filled pauses. Filled pauses contain items such as *uh, oh, hmm, ah, well, say, sort of, just, kind of, I mean, I think, I guess,* which indicate that the speaker is searching for a word, or has found the word or an approximation of it.

Rate of Delivery.

Pausing also affects our perception of the pace of speech. The impression of faster or slower speech generally results from the amount of intraclausal pausing that speakers use. If such pauses are eliminated, the impression of rapid speech is created. Fast and slow speakers are hence distinguished by the amount of pausing they make use of. Rivers cites the following figures:

Fast: above 220 wpm
Moderately fast: 190 → 220 wpm
Average: 160 → 220 wpm
Moderately slow: 130 → 160 wpm
Slow: below 130 wpm

(1981:173)

Rhythm and Stress.

The rhythmic pattern of spoken English is another of its distinctive features. In many languages, the length of time required to pronounce an utterance depends upon the number of syllables it contains, since syllables are of about equal length. English, however, is a stress-timed language. Within an utterance, only particular syllables are stressed, and the remaining syllables in the utterance, no matter how many there are, must accommodate to the rhythm established by the stressed syllables, which recur at more or less regular intervals. According to Woods (1979), there is a major stressed syllable on the average of every 0.6 seconds in English. This means that the following sentences would take about the same amount of time to articulate, even though the number of syllables contained in each sentence is very different:

The CAT is INTerested in proTECTing its KITTens.
LARGE   CARS   WASTE   GAS.

This adds yet another dimension to the listener's task, since listeners must be able to identify words according to the rhythmic structure within which they occur. They must be able to interpret words in both stressed, mildly stressed, and unstressed forms, and not merely in their ideal forms as listed in a dictionary.

Cohesive Devices.   Speech shares with written discourse the mechanisms for marking grammatical ties within and between sentences, but many function differently in spoken discourse. The referents of cohesive markers such as *this, these,* and *you* are sometimes not readily identifiable in speech. For example:

Well *you* know, there was *this* guy, and here *we* were talking about, you know, girls, and all *that* sort of thing . . . and *here's* what he says . . .

Information Content.   Since conversation involves both a speaker and a hearer, meanings are constructed cooperatively. A particular speaker does not say everything he or she wants to say in a single burst. Each speaker adds information a little at a time, often by repeating something of what has been said and then adding to it (Brown, 1977). For example:

A.   Are you pleased with the results?
B.   Yes, I'm very pleased with them. They are better than I expected.
A.   Is it impossible?
B.   No, it's not impossible, just difficult.

Proposition markers such as *of course* and *really* may indicate the attitude of the speaker to preceding or subsequent propositions, and discourse markers such as *well, anyway, actually, of course,* and *now* signal the continuity between one utterance and another.

This means that the concept of coherence, as applied to conversational discourse, is very different from the way coherence is created in written discourse. Written discourse is planned, tightly organized, and generally the product of a single person. Spoken discourse is not pre-planned, but is produced in ongoing time through mutual cooperation. Consequently, it presents meaning in a very different way from written discourse. Topics are developed gradually, and the conventions for topic development and topic shift are distinctive to the spoken register. Listeners must use cues such as *talking about that, reminds you of . . . , by the way, as far as that goes* to identify directions in topic development.

Interactive.   Conversation is interactive. The listener's presence is indicated by gestures, movement, gaze, and facial expressions. Both speaker and listener send a variety of verbal and non-verbal signals back and forth indicating attention, interest, understanding, or lack of it (Murphy and Candlin, 1979). The degree of formality or informality of the interaction may also be signaled by the presence or absence of idioms, humor, and colloquial expressions, or by the use of solidarity markers such as *you see* or *you know.*

DESIGN

The factors reviewed above indicate some of the central processes of listening comprehension and ways in which spoken discourse differs from written text. The application of such information to the teaching of listening comprehension is in the design component of methodology, and it enables the identification of component micro-skills which provide the focus for instructional activities. Design thus refers to the operationalization of information and theory into a form that will enable objectives to be formulated and learning experiences planned. The design phase in curriculum development consists of:

Assessment of learner needs
This refers to procedures aimed at identifying the type of listening skills the learner requires, according to situations and purposes the listener will encounter.

Isolation of micro-skills
From the information obtained from needs analysis and from an analysis of the features of the target language discourse that the learner will encounter (e.g., conversation, lectures), particular listening skills are isolated which correspond to the listening abilities the learner requires. The product of this operation is a skills taxonomy.

Diagnostic testing
From proficiency or diagnostic testing, a profile is established of the learner's present listening abilities. Particular micro-skills from the skills taxonomy are then selected.

Formulation of instructional objectives
Using information from diagnostic or proficiency testing, instructional objectives for a listening comprehension program can be developed.

The above procedures are essential before instructional activities can be selected or developed. Let us now consider each of these dimensions in turn.

Needs Assessment

Needs assessment focuses on the purposes for which the learners need listening skills and on an analysis of the situations, activities, and tasks in which the learners will be involved as second language learners. Listening purposes vary according to whether learners are involved in listening as a component of social interaction (e.g., conversational listening), listening for information, academic listening (e.g., lectures), listening for pleasure (e.g., radio, movies, television), or for some other reason. Needs assessment procedures may involve interviews with learners, participant observation, questionnaires, target discourse analysis, literature surveys of related research, and other measures designed to obtain a profile of learner needs and to establish priorities among them.

Taxonomy of Listening Skills

Taxonomies of micro-skills involved in different types of listening are developed from a variety of sources, including needs analysis, discourse analysis, and related research. The analysis of listening processes and features of spoken discourse which were discussed in the first section of this article suggests that micro-skills such as the following are required for conversational listening:

Micro-Skills: Conversational Listening
1. Ability to retain chunks of language of different lengths for short periods
2. Ability to discriminate among the distinctive sounds of the target language
3. Ability to recognize the stress patterns of words
4. Ability to recognize the rhythmic structure of English

5. Ability to recognize the functions of stress and intonation to signal the information structure of utterances
6. Ability to identify words in stressed and unstressed positions
7. Ability to recognize reduced forms of words
8. Ability to distinguish word boundaries
9. Ability to recognize typical word order patterns in the target language
10. Ability to recognize vocabulary used in core conversational topics
11. Ability to detect key words (i.e., those which identify topics and propositions)
12. Ability to guess the meanings of words from the contexts in which they occur
13. Ability to recognize grammatical word classes (parts of speech)
14. Ability to recognize major syntactic patterns and devices
15. Ability to recognize cohesive devices in spoken discourse
16. Ability to recognize elliptical forms of grammatical units and sentences
17. Ability to detect sentence constituents
18. Ability to distinguish between major and minor constituents
19. Ability to detect meanings expressed in differing grammatical forms/sentence types (i.e., that a particular meaning may be expressed in different ways)
20. Ability to recognize the communicative functions of utterances, according to situations, participants, goals
21. Ability to reconstruct or infer situations, goals, participants, procedures
22. Ability to use real world knowledge and experience to work out purposes, goals, settings, procedures
23. Ability to predict outcomes from events described
24. Ability to infer links and connections between events
25. Ability to deduce causes and effects from events
26. Ability to distinguish between literal and implied meanings
27. Ability to identify and reconstruct topics and coherent structure from ongoing discourse involving two or more speakers
28. Ability to recognize markers of coherence in discourse, and to detect such relations as main idea, supporting idea, given information, new information, generalization, exemplification
29. Ability to process speech at different rates
30. Ability to process speech containing pauses, errors, corrections
31. Ability to make use of facial, paralinguistic, and other clues to work out meanings
32. Ability to adjust listening strategies to different kinds of listener purposes or goals
33. Ability to signal comprehension or lack of comprehension, verbally and non-verbally

Diagnostic testing or detailed analysis of results of proficiency tests allows particular micro-skills to be further operationalized. Micro-skills relevant to academic listening include the following:

Micro-Skills: Academic Listening (Listening to Lectures)
1. Ability to identify purpose and scope of lecture
2. Ability to identify topic of lecture and follow topic development
3. Ability to identify relationships among units within discourse (e.g., major ideas, generalizations, hypotheses, supporting ideas, examples)
4. Ability to identify role of discourse markers in signaling structure of a lecture (e.g., conjunctions, adverbs, gambits, routines)
5. Ability to infer relationships (e.g., cause, effect, conclusion)
6. Ability to recognize key lexical items related to subject/topic
7. Ability to deduce meanings of words from context
8. Ability to recognize markers of cohesion

9. Ability to recognize function of intonation to signal information structure (e.g., pitch, volume, pace, key)
10. Ability to detect attitude of speaker toward subject matter
11. Ability to follow different modes of lecturing: spoken, audio, audio-visual
12. Ability to follow lecture despite differences in accent and speed
13. Familiarity with different styles of lecturing: formal, conversational, read, unplanned
14. Familiarity with different registers: written versus colloquial
15. Ability to recognize irrelevant matter: jokes, digressions, meanderings
16. Ability to recognize function of non-verbal cues as markers of emphasis and attitude
17. Knowledge of classroom conventions (e.g., turn taking, clarification requests)
18. Ability to recognize instructional/learner tasks (e.g., warnings, suggestions, recommendations, advice, instructions)

The above taxonomies are suggestive of the sort of information that curriculum developers should aim to obtain from tests and other sources.

Diagnostic Testing/Assessment

Diagnostic tests and assessment procedures give a detailed breakdown of how learners perform with respect to particular micro-skills. A good example of how detailed information on learner ability can be obtained from the use of a listening proficiency rating scale is provided by an instrument developed by Brindley (1982). By means of interviews, a profile of the student's learning ability is built up, and the learner is classified into one of eight levels ranging from minimal to native-speaker-like. Brindley describes characteristics of a learner at the second level on the scale in the following way:

Listening Comprehension
Able to understand enough to manage a very limited interchange about areas of immediate need. Can understand most predictable requests for basic personal and family information of the kind required by officials, though repetition often necessary if questions are not phrased in familiar form.

Can recognize a few basic intonation patterns (e.g., Yes/no questions).

Little understanding of syntax. Meaning deduced from juxtaposition of words and context. Still responds to isolated words in connected speech.

Can handle very short, simple, ritual social exchanges but rarely able to understand enough to keep conversation going of his/her own accord.

Can identify individual items in very short, simple recorded passages relevant to needs. May get global meaning but would need more than one hearing. However misunderstandings frequent when s/he cannot see person speaking.

When s/he does not understand, can usually ask very simply for repetition.

Characteristic Problems
Has great difficulty coping with subjects other than immediate priorities.

Finds longer utterances (especially those containing subordinate clauses) very hard to understand, owing to limitations on short-term memory load.

Often fails to understand questions which require other than a short, concrete answer (e.g., *why* or *how* questions).

Idiomatic expressions (even commonly used ones related to priority areas) normally not understood. Only understands when questions/statements are phrased in simplest, non-idiomatic form.

Has great difficulty using grammatical cues to extrapolate meaning. What seems clear to a native speaker would often be misinterpreted or seen as ambiguous by a listener at this level, owing to his/her inability to recognize the form and function of many syntactic structures.

May identify occasional words in a conversation between native speakers but could not identify topic.

Similar-sounding words/segments often confused, causing misunderstandings.

(Brindley, 1982:1)

Using information such as this together with a skills taxonomy, it is possible to identify the micro-skills which would be most crucial for a learner at this level. Among the micro-skills which this type of learner lacks, for example, are:

1. Ability to identify and reconstruct topics from ongoing discourse
2. Ability to recognize typical word order patterns in English
3. Ability to recognize major syntactic patterns in English

By systematically comparing information in the skills taxonomy with the learner profile, it is now possible to formulate objectives for the target group of learners.

Formulation of Objectives

Objectives translate the content identified in the skills selection process into a statement of what the student is expected to be able to do at the end of a course of instruction. Objectives defined this way are also known as *behavioral objectives* (Nicholls and Nicholls, 1972). They serve as goals toward which the teacher should be aiming in a course, and hence help determine the choice of appropriate methodology and classroom procedures. They also enable teachers to assess the extent to which learning has

been accomplished. Basically, what is required is a clearly set out group of statements identifying what is to be achieved—methodology and the syllabus identify the means; objectives specify the ends. Objectives thus break down the micro-skills into descriptions of behavior or performance in terms which can be taught and tested. Objectives for the hypothetical target group identified above, for example, might be stated in the following terms:

1. The student will have a listening vocabulary of approximately 800 words, including dates, time, and numbers up to 100.
2. The student can recognize the different intonation patterns used for questions, statements, instructions.
3. The student can understand *yes/no* questions and *wh*-questions on topics connected with home life, the family, school, free time, health, shopping, personal identification.
4. The student can understand common phrases used in short conversations and interviews on the above topics.
5. The student can identify the topics of conversations between native speakers on the above topics.
6. The student can understand utterances within an 800 word vocabulary in which the following grammatical constructions are used: *sub V comp, sub V obj, . . .*
7. The student can understand utterances within an 800 word vocabulary containing subordinate and coordinating clauses.

From the formulation of instructional objectives we are now able to consider the development of instructional procedures and activities which enable the objectives to be realized. These are questions of procedure, that is, of techniques and exercise types.

PROCEDURE

In teaching listening comprehension our aim is to provide opportunities for the learner to

acquire particular micro-skills, those individual listening abilities which we have identified and used in specifying particular teaching objectives. In teaching listening we can manipulate two variables, both of which serve to develop ability in particular skill areas. We can either manipulate the *input,* that is, the language which the learner hears, controlling for selected features such as grammatical complexity, topic, and rate of delivery, or we can manipulate the *tasks* we set for the learner. Manipulation of either (or both) is directed toward developing particular micro-skills.

In examining procedures for teaching listening comprehension, we will focus first on some general criteria that can be applied to the evaluation of exercises and classroom procedures and then look at techniques and procedures themselves.

Criteria for Evaluating Activities and Exercises

In teaching listening skills our aim is to provide comprehensible, focused input and purposeful listening tasks which develop competence in particular listening abilities. The following criteria serve as a checklist in developing listening tasks (British Council, 1981; McKeating, 1981; Porter and Roberts, 1981; Stanley, 1978; Maley and Moulding, 1981; Thomas, 1982):

Content validity
Does the activity practice listening comprehension or something else? How closely does the input or task relate to the micro-skills which listening comprehension involves? Many listening materials contain activities that depend more on reading or general intelligence than on listening skills. The question of content validity raises the issue of whether the activity adequately or actually makes use of skills and behavior that are part of listen-

ing in the real world. Two related factors have to do with memory and purposefulness.

Listening comprehension or memory
We saw above that a variety of processing activities in listening precede storage of information in long-term memory. Many listening activities focus on retrieval of information from long-term memory rather than on the processing activities themselves. An exercise involving listening to a passage and responding to true/false questions about the content of it typically focuses on memory rather than on comprehension.

Purposefulness and transferability
Does the activity reflect a purpose for listening that approximates authentic real life listening? Do the abilities which the exercise develops transfer to real-life listening purposes, or is the learner simply developing the ability to perform classroom exercises? An activity which makes use of news broadcasts as input, for example, should reflect the reasons why people typically listen to news broadcasts, such as listening for information about events. Cloze exercises requiring the learner to supply grammatical words on listening to the news item do not reflect the purposes for which people listen to news broadcasts. It is not a situation which corresponds to any real-life listening purpose, and hence involves a low degree of transfer.

Testing or teaching
Does the activity or set of procedures assume that a set of skills is already acquired and simply provide opportunities for the learner to practice them, or does it assume that the skills are not known and try to help the learner acquire them? A great many listening activities test, rather than teach. For example, a set of true/false questions following a passage on a tape might indicate how much of the material the learner can remember, but this kind of activity in no way helps the learner develop the ability to grasp main ideas or extract relevant details. The amount of preparation the learner is given prior to a listening task is often important in giving a teaching rather than a testing focus to an

activity. Pre-listening activities generally have this purpose. They activate the learner's script and set a purpose for listening. They may take the form of discussion, questions, or a short paragraph to read which creates the script, providing information about the situation, the characters, and the events. Activities which teach rather than test may require much more use of pre-listening tasks and tasks completed as the student listens, than post-listening tasks.

Authenticity

To what degree does the input resemble natural discourse? While much authentic discourse may be too disfluent or difficult to understand without contextual support, materials should aim for relative authenticity if they are to prepare listeners for real listening. Many current commercial listening materials are spoken at an artificially slow pace, in prestige dialects that are not typical of ordinary speech. They are often oral readings of written material articulated in a precise "acting" style, lacking the pauses and self-corrections of natural speech. Furthermore, the value of such materials must be examined in the light of Krashen's (1982) proposal that authentic learning experiences should provide an opportunity for *acquisition;* that is, they should provide comprehensible input which requires negotiation of meaning and which contains linguistic features a little beyond the learner's current level of competence.

Exercise Types

In developing classroom materials and activities we can manipulate the input or the tasks. Input, for example, may be in the form of dialogue or monologue. Dialogue may be scripted or unscripted, between native speakers, between native and non-native speakers, or between non-native speakers. Difficulty in both dialogue and monologue may vary according to the rate of delivery, level of vocabulary, topic, information content, fluency (amount of pausing, errors),

and coherence. Tasks may vary according to whether they require *global comprehension* (where the learner is required to attempt to understand the overall meaning) or *partial comprehension* (where only comprehension of specific items is required) (Blundell and Stokes, 1981). Tasks may also vary according to whether they require a *mechanical, meaningful,* or *communicative* response (Paulston, 1971). A task requiring a mechanical response, for example, would be a discrimination task where the learner is required to distinguish between two words or sounds and where comprehension is not required. A meaningful response would be one in which comprehension of the input is required, but no creative abilities are called into play as, for example, when a learner has to match one of two sentence to one which he or she hears. A communicative response is one in which the learner has to create a suitable response on the basis of what is understood, and where interpretation, adaptation, and the addition of new information is required. For example, the listener may hear a problem discussed and then have to suggest a solution. The criterion for selecting and evaluating tasks, however, is not their interest or ingenuity, but the degree to which they relate to teaching rather than testing objectives. Among common task types in materials are:

Matching or distinguishing   Choosing a response in written or pictorial form that corresponds with what was heard (e.g., placing pictures in a sequence which matches a story or set of events; choosing a picture to match a situation, such as listening to a radio advertisement and finding the product from a set of pictures).

Transferring   Exercises of this type involve receiving information in one form and transferring the information or parts of it into another form (e.g., listening to a discussion about a house and then sketching the house).

Transcribing   Listening, and then writing down what was heard. Dictation is the most common example of this activity.

Scanning   Exercises in which listeners must extract selected items by scanning the input in order to find a specific piece of information (e.g., listening to a news broadcast and identifying the name of the winning party in an election).

Extending   Exercises which involve going beyond what is provided, such as reconstructing a dialogue when alternate lines are missing or providing a conclusion to a story.

Condensing   Reducing what is heard to an outline of main points, such as is required in notetaking.

Answering   Answering questions from the input. Different sorts of questions will focus on different levels of listening (e.g., questions which require recall of details, those which require inferences and deductions, those which require evaluation or reactions).

Predicting   Guessing or predicting outcomes, causes, relationships, and so forth, based on information presented in a conversation or narrative.

APPLICATIONS

As an example of approach, design, and procedural elements of listening comprehension methodology, we will now show how a listening exercise which was presented to a materials development class at the University of Hawaii was adapted by the students in that class to give it a more relevant focus. This discussion also illustrates the sorts of activities which are useful in teaching workshops for teachers on developing materials for listening comprehension.

The text selected was *Have You Heard* (Underwood, 1979), which is described as providing

> listening comprehension practice for students of English as a foreign language who have had little opportunity to hear native English speakers. Each of the 20 units contains recorded extracts centered around a particular language function. The recordings are of spontaneous conversations in a range of accents and bring the students as close as possible to a real life situation (extract from jacket).

The task set for the teacher trainees who were in this course was first to examine the text and the exercises in terms of content validity, testing or teaching, and the other criteria discussed above. It was found that the existing exercises in the text mainly tested memory rather than listening comprehension, and many

were found to have little relation to listening. In considering alternate exercises, the materials were first examined to determine the types of listening tasks and micro-skills that the conversational samples involved. From these, objectives and exercises were developed.[1]

Unit 1 of the text, for example, focuses on "people talking about things they like." The unit contains three short conversations on the topic by different people. The first is entitled "Felix talks about his job as a school-master." The following pre-listening information is given:

> Felix shows his pleasure by mentioning the good things about his job. He begins by saying that he decided quite quickly about what he wanted to do as a job (9).

A few difficult vocabulary items are presented, then the teacher is instructed to play the tape. True/false exercises, vocabulary exercises, and a transcription/dictation task follow. The conversational listening extract is as follows:

> So there was no great lengthy process deciding what I was going to do—but I don't feel I've made a mistake—I enjoy it—I enjoy the company of other members of the staff in the staff room where they are colleagues of yours but

you're not in a structured system where they are your boss or you are theirs—everyone is in the same boat—everyone is in the same level and yet—you don't actually work with one another—you just work with the same boys— and therefore I think that unlike an office situation—you get to know the-the other members of the staff—as friends more than as work-mates—and also I enjoy—the difference in the job—it isn't the same thing every year—in a yearly situation—you can do things a different way the second year, the third year—and I enjoy the differences it brings—every day— different classes, different age groups, different attitudes . . . (transcribed from tape).

It was decided to replace all the exercises suggested in the text. In developing alternative exercises the trainees produced the following:

Objectives
Listen for general understanding of the gist of a conversation.

Identify the speaker's attitude toward a topic.

Micro-skills
Identify and follow the topic of a conversation.

Recognize vocabulary for expressing positive and negative attitudes.

Infer speaker's attitude from reasons given.

Infer meanings of words from context.

Pre-listening activities
Students work in groups and discuss what makes a job enjoyable or undesirable.

Students rank their findings.

Students discuss the advantages and disadvantages of school teaching.

(The goal of the pre-listening activities is to activate background knowledge or scripts and to prepare students for some of the vocabulary they will hear.)

Teaching procedure
1. On first listening, students are given a simple task. They are instructed to answer the following questions as they listen:
   a. What is Felix's job?
   b. How does he feel about his job? Does he like it or not?
   (By posing the task before the students listen to the tape, the listeners are given a purpose for listening which forces them to focus on selected information. They can also compare information they hear with information they obtained from their pre-listening group discussions.)
2. After listening to the tape and discussing their answers, the students are given a more specific task to be completed during a second listening: Which of the following does Felix say are important for him about his job?
   a. The salary
   b. The holidays
   c. Not having a boss
   d. Not having a fixed routine
   e. The power it gives
   f. His colleagues
3. During a third listening, students answer true/false questions:
   a. It took Felix a long time to choose a job.
   b. Felix believes he chose the right job.
   c. Felix says his job is like working in an office.
   d. Felix wants to change his job.
   e. Felix has to do the same thing every year.
4. A post-listening exercise involves deducing the meanings of words from the context in which they were used in the conversation. What do these expressions in the conversation mean?
   a. "To be in the same boat with other people"
   b. "To enjoy the company of other people"

The exercises suggested by the trainees thus involve primarily pre-listening and "complete while listening" tasks, rather than the usual battery of post-listening exercises. They prepare the students for listening before listening begins and focus on a level of comprehension relevant to conversational listening.

CONCLUSION

The teaching of listening comprehension, or of any language skill, involves considering the objectives we are teaching toward and the micro-skills our procedures cover. An educated response is dependent, in turn, on how much of an attempt we have made to appreciate the nature of the listening comprehension process itself. Any informed methodology or teaching program looks both at techniques and classroom routines, and beyond them, to the broader principles which serve as their justification.

NOTE

1. The exercises which will be presented here were prepared by Andrew Harper, Esther Soong, Philip Pinsent, Holly Uyeda, Joel Wiskin, Floria Abe, Tereseta Kawamoto, and Pi-chong Su.

REFERENCES

Blundell, Lesley, and Jackie Stokes. 1981. *Task Listening.* Cambridge: Cambridge University Press.

Brindley, Geoffrey P. 1982. *Listening Proficiency Descriptions.* Sydney: Adult Migrant Education Service.

British Council. 1981. *The Teaching of Listening Comprehension. ELT Documents.* London: The British Council.

Brown, Gillian. 1977. *Listening to Spoken English.* London: Longman.

Clark, Herbert H., and Eve V. Clark. 1977. *Psychology and Language.* New York: Harcourt Brace Jovanovich.

Clark, Herbert H., and Thomas Carlson. 1982. Hearers and speech acts. *Language* 58 (2):332–373.

Dore, John, and R. P. McDermott. 1982. Linguistic indeterminacy and social context in utterance interpretation. *Language* 58 (2): 374–398.

Foss, Donald J., and David T. Hakes. 1978. *Psycholinguistics: An Introduction to the Psychology of Language.* Englewood Cliffs, NJ: Prentice-Hall, Inc.

Krashen, Stephen D. 1982. *Principles and Practice in Second Language Acquisition.* Oxford: Pergamon.

Leech, Geoffrey N. 1977. *Language and Tact.* Treer: University of Treer.

Maley, Alan, and Sandra Moulding. 1981. *Learning to Listen.* Cambridge: Cambridge University Press.

Marslen-Wilson, W., and L. K. Tyler. 1980. The temporal structure of spoken language. *Cognition* 8:1–71.

McKeating, Douglas. 1981. Comprehension and listening. In *The Teaching of English as an International Language,* Gerry Abbot and Peter Wingard (eds.), 57–80. London: Collins.

Murphy, Dermot, and Christopher Candlin. 1979. Engineering lecture discourse and listening comprehension. *Practical Papers in English Language Education* (University of Lancaster) 2:1–79.

Nicholls, Audrey, and Howard Nicholls. 1972. *Developing a Curriculum: A Practical Guide.* London: George Allen and Unwin.

Paulston, Christina Bratt. 1971. The sequencing of structural pattern drills. *TESOL, Quarterly* 5: 197–208.

Pawley, Andrew K. Undated. Lecture notes on conversational analysis. University of Auckland.

Porter, Don, and Jon Roberts. 1981. Authentic listening activities. *ELT Journal* 36 (1):37–47.

Richards, Jack C., and Ted Rodgers. 1982. Method: Approach, design and procedure. *TESOL Quarterly* 16 (2):153–168.

Rivers, Wilga M. 1981. *Teaching Foreign Language Skills.* Second Edition. Chicago: University of Chicago Press.

Rixon, Shelagh. 1981. The design of materials to foster particular listening skills. In *The Teaching of Listening Comprehension. ELT Documents* 121: 68–106. London: The British Council.

Schank, Roger C., and Robert P. Abelson. 1977. Scripts, plans, and knowledge. In *Thinking: Readings in Cognitive Science,* P. N. Johnson-Laird and P. C. Wason (eds.), 421–432. Cambridge: Cambridge University Press.

Schmidt, Richard, and Jack C. Richards. 1980. Speech acts and second language learning. *Applied Linguistics* 1 (2):129–157.

Stanley, John A. 1980. Are listening materials just for listening to? *RELC Journal* 11 (1):78–88.

_____. 1978. Teaching listening comprehension. *TESOL Quarterly* 12 (3):285–296.

Thomas, Howard. 1982. Survey review: Recent materials for developing listening skill. *ELT Journal* 36 (3):192–199.

Underwood, Mary. 1979. *Have You Heard.* Oxford: Oxford University Press.

Woods, H.B. 1979. *Rhythm and Unstress.* Hull, Canada: Canadian Government Publishing Center.

13

Authentic Listening Activities[1]

Don Porter
Jon Roberts

AUTHENTIC LANGUAGE

Native speakers or teachers of English as a foreign language are able with little hesitation and considerable accuracy to distinguish between listening texts which have been specially prepared for ELT and "the real thing"—instances of spoken language which were *not* initiated for the purpose of teaching. We shall call this "real" language not intended for non-native learners *authentic.*

When asked to pinpoint what it is that "gives away" the ELT listening text, listeners mention a very wide range of linguistic features. We might note:

Intonation

There is a tendency for the intonation used in EFL listening materials to resemble that which indulgent mothers use to babies. It is marked by unusually wide and unusually frequent pitch-movement. Although intonation of this sort may be appropriate to young children, it is clearly inappropriate in most of the situations and uses occurring in ELT. At best, it causes amusement in learners; at worst, it is a source of irritation, of a tendency to reject the materials, and of general demotivation.

Received pronunciation (RP)

With a few recent exceptions, speakers on the majority of British ELT tapes and cassettes have an RP accent, or a very close approximation to it. What the learner listens to is thus quite unlike what he will normally hear in Britain, since only a tiny minority of British speakers have this accent.[2]

Enunciation

Speakers tend to enunciate words with excessive precision; assimilation and elision are minimal.

Structural repetition

A particular function or structure recurs with obtrusive frequency.

Complete sentences

Not only do ELT listening materials normally avoid the fragmentation of linguistic structures at various levels which characterizes most informal speech, but the speakers in such materials also typically express themselves in neat, simple, rather short, well-formed discrete sentences, rather than in more natural sequences of loosely connected clauses.[3]

Distinct turn-taking

Where there is a conversation, discussion or

other transaction involving more than one speaker, listeners in ELT texts wait for the person speaking to finish before themselves beginning; in authentic situations, they often do not.

Pace
The typical ELT listening text has a uniform pace—and it is slow. The uniformity may be inappropriate to the type of speech, and may prove boring; the slowness may irritate. The learner will moreover not have been familiarized with the relative rapidity and variability in pace of authentic discourse.

Quantity
In the typical ELT dialogue, both speakers say an approximately equal amount, and neither says very much. In real life, it is more often the case that one speaker dominates the interaction for some time, while the other plays a subsidiary role, until by tacit agreement or force majeure the roles are reversed.

Attention signals
ELT conversational exchanges are often rather uncanny because of the absence of normal attention signals. These "uhuh's" and "mm's" are important indicators that the listener is participating actively.

Formality
There is a tendency for materials to be biased toward standardized, quasi-literary language. Thus, syntax and lexis tend to be rather formal. Swear-words never occur, for example, while slang and other colloquial forms are rare.

Limited vocabulary
Vocabulary in ELT texts has almost always been "tidied up" and restricted in a variety of ways. There seems to be a general feeling that textual content should be "disengaged" from the particularities of everyday life or of specific incidents and times. In the authentic listening experience, these particularities constantly intrude. It is the specific references to "Woolworth's" or "the Co-op," to "parkas" and "music-centers," to "mortgage interest rates" and "the Ayatollah," which anchor language in reality. It is the general

absence of such references which renders many ELT texts anodyne.

Too much information
An intuitive grasp of the fact that shared knowledge is at a minimum between speakers in ELT materials and those who listen to them often leads the materials writer to include more explicit reference to objects, people and experiences than would normally be there in the authentic situation.

Mutilation
Listening texts are rarely marred by disturbing extraneous noise such as typewriters in the background, passing cars, other people talking, etc. Such "mutilation of the message" is, however, a natural and integral part of the authentic listening experience.

One could go on. But one thing that this list makes abundantly clear is that there is a massive *mismatch* between the characteristics of the discourse we normally listen to and those of the language which the student normally hears in the ELT classroom. There is, moreover, an unrealistic *match* between the characteristics of the language which the student listens to and that which he is taught to produce. This match between the language for production and reception is perhaps a major reason for the classic situation in which students do well in the classroom but are unable to transfer their skills to the world outside. They have, of course, never been allowed to come to grips with the language of the world outside. They produce their neatly constructed sentences in rather formal English, within the limitations of their vocabulary, in an approximation to an RP accent. They are, of course, understood. Then their interlocutors reply with loosely constructed strings of phrases and clauses, laced with colloquialism and references to what is wrongly assumed to be shared knowledge, the whole in a regional accent which is in any case not very clearly pronounced. The students understand little or nothing. They expect others to speak the way they themselves have been taught to speak; the sad fact is that practically no one does.

Why has it come about that the characteristics of production and reception have been confused in this way? In our opinion, almost entirely because listening, more than any other "skill," has been sold short: it has been made to play the role of handmaiden to all other aspects of language work. This role was made explicit in the ordering of language skills advocated in the audio-lingual approach: listen—speak—read—write. The purpose of listening practice was thus primarily to *model* structures for language production (Rivers, 1964: 103). Listening was the first step in a teaching strategy for production, and so had nothing to do with the handling of new information and unpredicted language with its diverse characteristics, which are the essence of authentic listening.

If we are to help learners cope with the authentic situation of *mismatch* between the language they produce and that which they hear, we must at least expose them to authentic language and, if possible, lead them to work out strategies for coming to terms with it. We would stress here that we are certainly not advocating exposing the learners solely—or even mainly—to recordings from life; the use of listening to provide models for production is legitimate and an important part of teaching. But we would also stress that we cannot expect learners to handle types of language they have never, or hardly ever, been exposed to.

AUTHENTIC LISTENING ACTIVITY

The need for and usefulness of authentic materials have been increasingly acknowledged in recent years. But should we stop there, with the linguistic characteristics of authenticity? It is our belief that there is much more involved in authentic listening, particularly concerning the type of activity, the kind of process to which the listener submits the language he hears, and the physical results of these processes. The richness and variety of activities, processes and resultant behavior has scarcely begun to be exploited in ELT materials. It is, of course, possible to exploit authentic texts in non-authentic ways, but we feel that to limit ourselves to such exploitation is to miss a great many opportunities: where it is possible to approach authenticity, why not do so? In our experience, the closer the learner comes to normal language use, the greater is his enthusiasm.

As an illustration, consider the times when you listen during the course of your normal day. Consider what is going on in your head as you listen (process) and how this is exhibited in external behavior (output). Here are some samples from a normal day:

Activity
Listening to the radio, e.g., weather, news, the "Today" program.
Process
1. "In one ear and out of the other." This is very superficial listening with little awareness of the content of what is being said. *Output:* Zero.
2. Evaluative listening and scanning for topics of interest to self or companion(s). This involves matching topics against one's own and/or companion's interests, and making mental notes. *Output:* Summarize and later retell to companion.
3. Focused listening for specific information, e.g., about the day's weather. *Output:* Selection of appropriate activities for the day, or of appropriate clothes to wear, etc.

Activity
Listening in face-to-face conversational interaction.

Process
1. Evaluation, mental commentary, and developing a line of thought. *Output:* Oral response.
2. Listening for conversational signals indicating the possibility of starting one's own turn. *Output:* Taking a turn at the appropriate moment.
3. Affective listening, i.e., not to what the speaker is saying but to how he or she is saying it (e.g., is he or she annoyed, pleased, taken aback, etc.). *Output:* Response to affective signals.
4. Listening for feedback. In this kind of listening the speaker monitors his or her own success in getting a message across. *Output:* Appropriate modification or repetition of utterance content.
5. Labelling. Whenever we listen to someone, we immediately begin to form impressions about them—where they come from, what sort of background they have, whether they are lively or quiet, or have a sense of humour, etc. *Output:* Varying degrees of modification in behavior toward the speaker, depending on how we see ourselves.

Activity
Listening to greetings.

Process
Confirming acceptance by other members of one's social group (i.e., failure to note greetings and to respond to them could well be resented by other members of one's social group). *Output:* Respond in kind.

Activity
Listening to administrative requirements *(face to face)* involving requests, suggestions or instructions.

Process
Determine necessary action. *Output:* Perform some physical activity, make a considered oral response, telephone someone and impart or solicit information, etc.

Activity
Listening on the telephone   This will include the same processes and outputs as, e.g., conversational interaction and listening to administrative requirements, but the absence of visual reinforcement places particular emphasis on listening for feedback, affective listening, and labelling.

Activity
Eavesdropping   Some may have moral scruples about listening in to other people's private conversations, but this activity holds great fascination for many foreign language learners. The reason is that they are listening to utterances which have in no way been doctored for their consumption—the essentially private nature of the communication underlines its authenticity. There is also the added attraction of a total absence of pressure on the learner to participate. Much ELT listening material implicitly casts the learner in the role of eavesdropper, but not authentically: he or she is expected to understand everything, whereas in authentic eavesdropping the listener catches snatches of conversation and has to piece them together. Thus the authentic eavesdropping situation reflects in miniature the learner-listener's permanent need to pick up bits and pieces of meaning and put them together in the way that makes best sense.

Process
Reconstruction of a meaningful message from fragments. *Output:* If the listener is alone, zero, with possible later retelling. If the listener is accompanied, there may be an exchange of information ('What did she say?'). A variant form of eavesdropping is listening to someone making a telephone call.

Process
Reconstruction of the unheard half of the dialogue in accordance with the structural, syntactic, semantic and phonological clues supplied in the half that is heard. *Output:* Zero, or the eavesdropper tries to confirm his or her guesses about the unheard half by questioning the person who made the call.

Activity
Watching T.V., seeing a film at the cinema, etc.

Process
Follow plot-development, logical argument, etc., with reference to visible speaker(s), or visual information about the content. *Output:* 1) laughter at the right moments; 2) later discussion of plot, motivation, acting; 3) re-telling—"I liked it when/My favorite bit was when Bond tore off Jaws' parachute in mid-air!"

Activity
Listening to recordings of songs.
Process
1. In one ear and out of the other.
2. Trying to catch the words. A favorite teenage occupation is trying to catch the words of the latest hit, often writing them down as part of the process *(Output)*.
3. Picking up the chorus and tune. *Output:* Singing along.

The activities, processes and outputs outlined here are not intended to constitute an exhaustive list: on the contrary, they represent only a small selection. A few moments' thought about your own daily life will certainly produce further examples. But just as the linguistic features of authentic language were shown earlier to be rich in variety, this short list of listening activities, processes, and outputs should suggest that there is a wealth of *ways* of listening. If the learner is to achieve any degree of real profi-

ciency in language use—as opposed to a rather abstract proficiency, which operates only under the strictly controlled, laboratory-like conditions of the classroom—then he or she must be given the chance to listen *in authentic ways*.

Of course, a certain amount of weighting and selecting must be done. Individual teachers and materials-constructors will feel that it is inappropriate in one case, or uneconomic in another, to introduce some of these activities into the classroom, while other activities should be given varying degrees of emphasis. Thus for example it might be felt that eavesdropping should not be encouraged, that listening and reacting appropriately to greetings should probably take up very little time in any course, but that listening for specific information through different degrees of mutilation, or following the logical development of an argument with televisual support, might be given considerable attention. Whatever the decision is, *some* opportunity to listen in a variety of authentic ways will always be desirable.

It is our argument that at least some provision should be made in ELT for the student to become involved in the listening processes demanded in authentic listening situations. The second part of this article will discuss specific listening activities, and provide examples.

AUTHENTIC LISTENING ACTIVITIES IN THE CLASSROOM

Active guessing

Multiple choice questions and wh questions are still widely used in the exploitation of listening materials, even when they consist of authentic speech. However, we suggest that the kind of processing of the text that these questions require might encourage learners to adopt counterproductive attitudes to their own experience of the target language. Teachers frequently note

that learners seem to believe: "unless I understand everything, I won't understand anything," and expect "total comprehension" of all texts as a prerequisite to interpreting worthwhile meaning. However, there are signs that good language learners have different attitudes. In the "Good Language Learner" study (Naimann et al., 1978) it is suggested that the learner at beginner level needs to be a "willing and active guesser" who makes full use of his own direct linguistic experiences. This implies that it is desirable to encourage learners to make the most of their "incomplete" comprehension and use every clue available to them as the basis for active guessing.

It seems to us that multiple choice exercises and many forms of questioning are liable to inhibit such desirable attitudes to text. They may induce teacher dependency and a fear of "incomplete" comprehension, that is, not being able to understand and recall large chunks of the text. These exercises, we feel, may lead to the assumption that the learner's comprehension goals are represented only in terms of the knowledge of the text that exists in the teacher's head, a knowledge which is "complete" and rich in fine discriminations, and so is only approachable with the teacher's mediation between text and learner. The learner will only be able to show that his "knowledge" of the text is approximating to that of the teacher through tests, reproduction, and answers to "higher inference" questions. Where the text does contain target knowledge, then such an approach is probably appropriate. However, we listen for many different reasons, and this "complete comprehension" represents only one. Through alternative exercises the learner can see that texts may be experienced other than as models of language.

A broader approach to comprehension recognizes that we understand a target language at different levels according to our ability to use linguistic clues and situational and paralinguistic information. Even native speakers do not impose a standard of total comprehension on themselves, and tolerate vagueness. For example, on the BBC weather forecasts for shipping, millions of listeners may hear that a wind is 'backing southeasterly." To a layman, "backing" will mean "moving" and he is quite content with that, though aware that there is probably a finer distinction contained in the term.[4] His comprehension is partial, but sufficient for his needs, and in proportion to his knowledge. This single example points to a general truth: we can, indeed must, tolerate degrees of vagueness in our comprehension of text. However, the language learner is trained to demand of him or herself complete comprehension in every experience of every kind of text. We would advocate a broader range of textual experiences, so that at certain stages learners would be encouraged to ignore the parts of a message which they do not need, and also to make "best guesses" about a text, in the recognition that such guesses entail partial comprehension. Learners can always get *something* from an English text. Below are examples of how "partial comprehension" may be realized, where text is used for message value, not as a model or source of knowledge.

AUTHENTIC TEXT, AUTHENTIC USE

Authentic texts for listening comprehension commit us to trying to replicate in class the roles the native speaker plays in the authentic situation. This is because authentic texts are structured according to their purpose. For instance, a radio commercial is brief and striking, designed to be heard many times, and relays a small quantity of information very dramatically. It is designed to attract attention and drive home a very limited message (a jingle, brand name), and is often supported by other media. The listener's role indicates how this text type might be exploited appropriately in class: recognition of brand names; noting down information (prices, phone numbers and addresses); voluntary recall. It would hardly conform with the nature of the text to attempt detailed questioning, or to require the sort of semantic discrimination commonly found in multiple choice items. It is clear that we should be wary of a form of exploitation that is not appropriate to the sample. It would be reasonable to use "information transfer" activities with a spoken itinerary, but not with a song. It would be suitable for learners to attempt highly selective "scan" listening with a weather forecast or a station announcement, but not with an expository monologue where there is great interdependence of the component parts of the text. This rather obvious point is in fact often overlooked in the exploitation of authentic texts.

We conclude that the use of text as a language model, presupposed in such exercise types as multiple choice, questioning, and language focus, does not allow the range of listening experiences encountered in the real world. The learner should experience this range in the classroom. There is also a stronger, if more speculative claim, namely that these conventional exercises may actually *inhibit* productive and desirable language learning strategies. We therefore think it worthwhile to parallel in classroom activities processes and outputs of the types specified above, while taking into account the conditions of learning of a given group. Ultimately, we are arguing for a kind of "listening role play."

Station Announcements

(The material we used was recorded on Reading Station. There is background noise, and distortion caused by the public address system.)

Aims

To provide experience of the features of a "mutilated message"; to encourage listening for a purpose, in which the learner develops expectancies which are later confirmed or rejected.

Procedure

1. Pre-listening phase: the teacher may encourage the learners to pool their "background

knowledge" and expectations of the announcement, and expose them to some key vocabulary before it occurs in the authentic text. The teacher may ask questions such as: "You are at the station. You are going to hear an announcement. Is the announcer going to be a man or a woman? What is he/she going to talk about? What is he/she going to tell us about the train that is arriving?" (Possible responses: the time, a delay, which train it is.) "What else will he/she tell us?" (Possible response: the platform.) Each learner's contribution is built on and developed. The teacher can then elicit suggestions about what the station announcer will actually say. For example, if the learners suggest there will be information about the arrival time, the teacher can ask what the announcer will say: 'Will he/she say "A train is coming at 11.02"?' (A visual aid of a station might help, as this phase might well reveal cultural differences and unfamiliarity with what a British station is like.) The length of time devoted to the pre-listening phase will vary according to the length of the announcement.

2. Listening phase: students listen to the message and comment on what was actually contained in it. This could be followed by further listening while reading a transcription. Alternatively, the teacher could give each learner a role card (see Figure 13.1).

The output of listening may be no more than a response to the questions or a development of the role play in which learners check if they are on the right train. The teacher may act as a traveller or a railway employee.

Weather Forecasts

(preferably very recent)

Aims

To practice focused listening for specific information without visual support; to promote a sense of involvement in the native speaker's envi-

You are going to Torquay from Paddington.
You are on the 11.12 to Cardiff and
it stops at Reading.

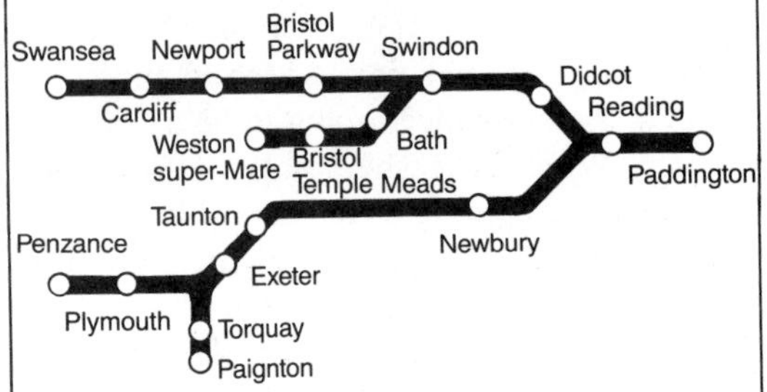

Listen to the announcement. Must you change?
If so, where? If you are not sure, ask someone.

Figure 13.1

ronment; use of shared knowledge to predict
form and content of the message; familiarization
with regional accents; and exposure to a text of
moderate length with a repetitious structure.

Procedure

The teacher elicits learners' knowledge of forecast structure and content. Learners adopt a
location on a map, either from free choice, or
according to a role card. They then listen and
note relevant weather details. Then learners
may:

1. Report regional weather details to the
   teacher;
2. Exchange information with others in
   small groups;
3. Select appropriate clothing;
4. Discuss and choose alternative activities
   for the day.

Two Radio Broadcasts

(Preferably very recent and separated by a
very short space of time, e.g., one hour)

Aims

Evaluative listening and scanning, without visual support; use of background knowledge to
predict content; exposure to texts of moderate
length with repetitious structure and delivered
at a moderate pace.

Procedure

The teacher elicits students' knowledge of news
content and organization.

1. Learners listen to the first broadcast for
items of interest to them, and compare items
they noted with those noted by others. They
then listen to the second broadcast for new information or other differences.

2. Learners predict the content of the first
broadcast. They then listen, check predictions,
and predict changes in the priority of items in
the second broadcast. Finally they listen to this
and check predictions.

3. Learners scan newspapers of the same
date, or pages from them, for the main topics,
and listen to the broadcast to see which do/do
not occur, and with what developments.[5]

Tape Recording of a Song

Aims

"In one ear and out of the other"; assimilation
of some knowledge of the language and culture.
Listening for precise words and phrases; use of
context, cultural knowledge, etc., to predict
form and content. Exposure to texts delivered at
a moderate-to-slow pace with strong internal
structure.

Procedure

1. Learners hear the song in the background.

2. Learners read an incomplete text, representing an intermediate stage in a learner's attempt to write down the words, and they then
predict the content and form of the incomplete
sections. They guess the meaning of unknown
words, and listen to the song repeatedly until

the text is complete, checking their predictions. Finally they can play the recording and "sing along."

Radio Advertisements

Aims

To encourage "minimal" comprehension; exposure to a text incorporating features of mutilation and variation. As for (1), but with some limited transfer of information.

Procedure

1. Show packages of four brands of a popular product (e.g. cereal). Learners then listen to several adverts., one of which promotes one of the four brands seen. Students identify the brand (and, optionally, indicate if they would buy it).

2. Learners are given role cards, e.g.,

It is November. You do not have a warm winter overcoat. You want to buy one, or
You are going to the cinema tonight with friends. You like westerns and horror films, or
You are a housewife. You want some new recipes for your children's meals. They like vegetables, fish, chicken, and eggs.

Learners hear a series of advertisements, including ones for a winter coat sale, a horror film, and eggs. In the latter, listeners are told to write for a free egg recipe. Learners note down the names, phone numbers, addresses, or titles mentioned which are relevant to them.

3. The teacher records a set of advertisements for entertainments, and also constructs a complementary "What's On" guide from newspaper clippings. Learners first consult the guide and select what they want to do. They then hear the tape and extract any further information needed, e.g. days of showing, times, cost, etc.[6]

4. Learners listen to advertisements with strong 'personality' voices, and try to match the voices with a set of pictures of people. They then attempt to explain their choices.

Extracts from Conversations

Aims

To encourage guessing: the listener must hold clues in his memory in order to form and then check "hypotheses."

Procedure

In the role of a guest at a party, the learner is asked to "eavesdrop" on a series of short overheard conversations. The level will determine the degree of detail required in comprehension: guessing the general topic will often be sufficient. A "starter" is given on a worksheet to help the learners tune in to new speech styles. The sample has features of pace and regional variation, and may be mutilated. Worksheet:

Eavesdropping

You are at a party given by the Director of Studies at your school. A lot of teachers and students are there. As you go around, you can hear pieces of conversation. Try to guess what the people are talking about. You hear four different conversations. Would you like to join any of them? You can write notes if you want:

Topic	Are you interested?
1	
2	
3	
4	

A transcript of the first few words of each is given.

Notes on Exploitation of Material

1. These types of activities work least well when offered as an isolated listening comprehension activity, unrelated to the rest of a

course. After all, authentic listening never happens in isolation. We feel that the listening should be integrated, for example by topic, or through its inclusion in a series of related experiences.

2. Students will find listening to authentic texts more difficult than listening to the usual idealized and standardized material. The degree to which they can perform the activities suggested will depend on what linguistic and paralinguistic clues are available and how able the learners are to make use of them. This sort of consideration will determine which texts are chosen. There is nevertheless a danger of rejecting many authentic texts in the interest of ensuring learner success; the teacher should guard against selecting texts which are so easy that no guessing or selective listening will go on, although it would have been an appropriate activity.

It is preferable in these activities not to use a transcript or frequent replays except where this is appropriate to the listener's normal role vis-à-vis a text. The decision not to use a transcript or rely on multiple replays does, however, imply using texts that are either very short in themselves, or have a clear, predictable and repetitive inner structure (such as news broadcasts), as a step towards experience of longer texts. Using short texts, or sequences of short episodes, avoids the risk of overload, of incomprehension of one element which may lead to incomprehension of the whole text.

3. Many learners find it extremely helpful in dealing with authentic speech simply to listen and to use a transcription. They may listen, then simultaneously listen and read, then listen again. This is very helpful in aiding segmentation of the stream of sound and recognition of weak forms or other features of reduction. We see this exploitation of authentic materials as a useful strand in developing listening competencies which are complementary to the activities we suggest.

4. A source of difficulty in the use of authentic samples is that in the real life setting, the listener is assisted in his interpretation of the oral language by features of the situation (the setting, the appearance and body language of speakers, etc.), and also by general knowledge of the world. Clearly the 'guessability' of an authentic text is greatly reduced if either situational information or culturally acquired knowledge is not available. If you know how news broadcasts are structured and what is likely to appear in them, your ability to extract meaning is greater. If, on the other hand, you have no experience of news broadcasts and do not know what is likely to be reported, your ability to understand is vastly reduced, and transcripts, replays, or even simultaneous translation may be of little help. Hence, the degree to which the student knows the text format or prerequisite information will suggest which texts to select, how to exploit them, and the nature of possible preparatory work. It is clear that acquiring knowledge of format and probable content is part of the cultural boundary-crossing entailed in target language learning.

CONCLUSION

We hope we have suggested not a replacement of conventional listening activities, but a valuable addition to them, one which will contribute to better preparation of learners for the experience of authentic listening.

NOTES

1. This article is based on a presentation made by the authors at International House, London, in November 1979.

2. Hughes and Trudgill (1979) estimate that 3% of the population of Britain speak RP.

3. See Crystal and Davy, 1969, p. 110.

4. "Backing" means "moving counter-sunwise."

5. Suggested by Brian Abbs.

6. Suggested by Brian Abbs.

REFERENCES

Crystal, D., and D. Davy. 1969. *Investigating English Style.* London: Longman.

Hughes, A., and P. Trudgill. 1979. *English Accents and Dialects.* London: Arnold.

Naimann, N., M. Frohlich, H. Stern, and A. Todesco. 1978. *The Good Language Learner.* Research in Education Series No. 7, Ontario Institute for Studies in Education.

Rivers, W. M. 1964. *The Psychologist and the Foreign Language Teacher.* Chicago: Chicago University Press.

SPEAKING

INTRODUCTION

Conversational competence is a complex set of abilities that involves many components, including pronunciation, listening, and grammar skills. The papers in Section Five reviewed some of the processes involved in conversational interaction and should be reviewed before reading the papers in this section, where implications for the teaching of speaking skills are considered.

In recent years methodologists of many persuasions have emphasized the limitations of traditional approaches to the teaching of conversation, where repetitive imitation, drills, and memorization of dialogs formed the primary focus of classroom activities. Such activities fail to address conversation as a process. They fail to teach learners how to initiate, develop, and terminate conversational encounters; how to use appropriate language; or how to negotiate and interact conversationally. Alternative classroom arrangements and activities are required which give learners the opportunity to practice conversational processes in the classroom, and hence to acquire conversational competence through doing "conversation work."

Carruthers offers an approach to the teaching of pronunciation, an important component of conversational competence. The techniques and procedures he discusses, although not in themselves communicative, could usefully form a follow-up to the kinds of communicative activities discussed in the two papers that follow. Bassano and Christison discuss ways of setting up conversation groups. Group work is an essential activity in a conversation course because the kind of conversational interaction produced in group activities has been shown to be quantitatively as well as qualitatively different from that which goes on in teacher-dominated lessons. In teacher-led classes, the teacher does most of the talking, and students often do little more than respond to Wh or Yes-No questions. In group work, students do all of the talking and have to take the responsibility for using conversational resources to complete a task. Students thus not only get more opportunities to speak, but they also have the chance to use and practice a greater variety of conversational strategies than they would in traditional class activities. This is illustrated in the paper by Scarcella, in which she reports on an activity she calls "socio-drama." From the analysis of the language that learners use when they take part in this kind of activity, she finds that socio-drama provides opportunities for development of vocabulary, grammatical proficiency, discourse strategies, strategies of social interaction, and awareness of cross-cultural differences.

DISCUSSION QUESTIONS

1. What do you think the goals of the teaching of pronunciation should be? To what extent is native-like pronunciation a reasonable or realistic goal for the teaching of pronunciation? What are the alternatives?

2. Record an interview or conversation with a low level or lower-intermediate ESL/EFL learner and analyze it to determine the learner's pronunciation problems. How serious are these relative to other difficulties the learner has? Talk to the learner and find out how important he or she considers pronunciation to be. Prepare a classroom activity to focus on one of the learner's pronunciation problems following the guidelines suggested by Carruthers.

3. Select one of the group activities discussed by Bassano and Christison. Complete the activity, but assign an observer to each group and have him or her tape-record the activity. Then have each group examine the activity in terms of its interactional and conversational features. Under interactional features, look for how the activity was completed. How much and what kind of participation did each group member have? Under conversational features, look in a general way at the kind of language that was used in completing the activity. What aspects of conversational competence is the activity good for?

4. Design a group activity for use with a class of ESL learners. Try out the activity and suggest what its main features are. Prepare guidelines for the use of the activity.

5. Prepare a socio-drama following the procedures discussed by Scarcella. Try it out in your class and evaluate the usefulness of the activity with ESL learners.

FURTHER READING

1. G. Brown, and G. Yule. 1983. *Teaching the Spoken Language.* Cambridge: Cambridge University Press.
2. F. Klippel. 1984. *Keep Talking: Communicative Fluency Activities for Language Teaching.* Cambridge: Cambridge University Press.
3. M. H. Long, and P. Porter. 1985. Group work, interlanguage talk and second language acquisition. *TESOL Quarterly* 19, 2, 207–228.
4. S. Sadow. 1982. *Idea Bank: Creative Activities for the Language Class.* Rowley, MA: Newbury House Publishers.
5. P. Ur. 1981. *Discussions that Work.* Cambridge: Cambridge University Press.

CHAPTER 14

Teaching Pronunciation

Rod Carruthers

QUESTIONS

1. Why do most people have such extreme difficulty in mastering pronunciation in a second language?
2. What is considered to be acceptable pronunciation? What goals should we set for the teaching of pronunciation?
3. What are the most common types of error that second language students make in pronunciation?
4. What is the value of using a phonemic script in the teaching of pronunciation?
5. When should pronunciation be taught?

6. What guidelines and techniques are useful in the teaching of pronunciation?

That good pronunciation is necessary for the mastery of a second language is accepted as axiomatic by teachers of ESL, yet exactly how this idea translates into the methodologies and techniques of the ESL classroom is a question which admits much less clarity and consensus. In addressing the questions posed above, this chapter will explore the subject of teaching pronunciation and suggest some approaches that the teacher might find effective.

PROBLEMS IN PRONUNCIATION

All languages use component sounds to express meaning and each language has its own set of distinctive sounds or *phonemes.* All normal people are physically equipped to produce the sounds of any human language and do, at a very early age, learn to speak at least one language. Why then is it usually so extraordinarily difficult for speakers of one language to learn the sounds of another? The first reason, of course, is that some sounds of the new or target language do not exist in the learner's native language. The phonemes /θ/ ((thin) and /ð/ (this) are found in English but in very few other lan-

guages. Students of English, confronted with these sounds, will generally substitute the closest sounds to these in their own languages, closeness being defined both by place and manner of articulation. Thus /θ/ may be replaced by /f/, by /t/, or by /s/. Similarly /ð/, the voiced counterpart of /θ/, may be replaced by any of /v/, /d/, or /z/, the voiced counterparts of the sounds mentioned above. The result is an English where /θ/ and one of /f/, /t/ and /s/ do not contrast and where *thin* /θɪn/ is confused with *fin* /fɪn/, *tin* /tɪn/, or *sin* /sɪn/.

The second reason for difficulty is that even

though a given sound may exist in both the native and the target language, the distribution may differ. A Polish woman, finding herself in Berlin in the autumn of 1939, learned flawless German in three months because survival was at stake. After the war she moved to Britain where now, almost forty years later, she still speaks English without /θ/. Why? Because in Polish /θ/ exists only as a mispronunciation of /s/. When she tries to use /θ/, a sound she can produce easily, she automatically substitutes it for /s/. Her solution is to speak English without /θ/, preferring to sound like a foreigner rather than a lisper. English speakers often encounter the same problem with Castilian Spanish where "soft" *c* is pronounced as /θ/ while *s* is pronounced as /s/. English speakers, equating the two, find themselves lisping. Thus in learning good pronunciation one must learn not only to form sounds correctly, but also to use them in the correct places.

ACCEPTABLE PRONUNCIATION

To attempt to correct every pronunciation error in a class would be an impossible task even for the most enterprising of teachers. The sheer volume of the work would prohibit its completion. A selection of problems must be made, based upon both frequency and seriousness of errors. The first consideration must be comprehension. Any pronunciation which causes the speaker to be misunderstood or not understood at all must be corrected. When the students are understood, it is probably best to spend very little more valuable class time concentrating on pronunciation drills. Still, there are degrees of acceptability. A truly acceptable pronunciation is one which allows the listener to understand the content of a message without being distracted by its form. Any pronunciation which repeatedly draws attention to itself probably merits further consideration. For this reason it is often useful to work individually with students whose accents, although easily comprehensible, irritate the listener and may cause the students embarrassment or ridicule.

Another question to consider is which of the many acceptable pronunciations of English should be used as a model for the class. For purely pragmatic reasons, since the students are living in North America, it seems wise to aim at a standard North American pronunciation.

Teachers who speak other dialects, however, need not feel embarrassed by the fact; nor should they distort their own speech into a strange and unnatural imitation of North American standard. In this country of immigrants, students must learn to recognize many different pronunciations as acceptable, though ideally they will learn to produce a standard North American speech. With tapes, films, records, and other native speakers available, the ESL teacher has many different models to draw on.

Is it possible or even desirable to eliminate all traces of a foreign accent? In rare cases adult learners do manage to acquire native speaker pronunciation. However, such a goal is unrealistic for most students since the time required would be much better spent learning structures and vocabulary. There are indeed times when near perfect pronunciation can be an embarrassing handicap. Native speakers may assume that a foreigner whose accent is good understands far more than is actually the case. An excellent pronunciation may get beginners or even fairly advanced students well over their heads in a hurry. If they are not perceived as foreigners when they fail to understand, they might be perceived as stupid. Which would you prefer?

The goal we should strive for then is a standard North American pronunciation which is easily understood and does not attract attention to itself at the expense of the message.

COMMON TYPES OF ERROR

We often assume that a major problem for ESL students is the substitution of one phoneme or sound for another, such as /t/ for /d/ or /r/ for /l/ and that this will lead to mortifying embarrassment when two words are confused. Fortunately for us all, this seldom happens except, perhaps, at the very beginning stages of instruction. We do not speak in isolated sounds, nor even in isolated words. Usually context, both linguistic and situational, will clarify meaning. In a classroom someone is far more likely to be looking for a *pen* than a *pan,* while a stranger winding a watch will probably be asking for the *time* rather than for a *dime.* Although texts listing minimal pairs (words differing in only one distinctive sound) are available[1] and useful for teaching isolated sounds, upon closer examination we see that few of the pairs are potentially confusing. Often the words are different parts of speech or differ so greatly in sphere of meaning that they would never cause problems. Can we honestly expect a misunderstanding of *dough* for *though? burgeon* for *virgin?* In reception classes it will be necessary to drill sounds in isolation using lists of minimal pairs. Later, although further drill may be necessary for individual students, other problems demand greater attention.

Studies have shown that ESL students are more frequently not understood than misunderstood[2] and that it is often the cumulative effect of a number of small but general phonetic errors which causes this breakdown in communication. For the teacher this means that dealing with one basic phonetic problem may have far-reaching effects on the general intelligibility of a student's speech. It is these general features of pronunciation which should be isolated and taught one at a time. For example, strong aspiration, a puff of air following the opening of the lips, is a characteristic feature of initial /p/ in English and serves, perhaps as much as voicing,[3] to distinguish it from /b/. Students taught to aspirate initial /p/ can be quickly shown to do the same to /t/ and /k/. In this way not only will /p/ be distinguished from /b/ but /t/ and /k/ will also be distinguished from /d/ and /g/. Teaching aspiration once is far easier than treating the pronunciation of /p/, /t/, and /k/ as three separate problems. Similarly, attention paid to the voicing of final consonants can be applied to eight different pairs of phonemes and will result in immediate improvement in the pronunciation of the *-s* and *-ed* suffixes. Other general features of pronunciation which can be handled in this way are intonation contours, even placement of stress in sentences, and the reduction of unstressed vowels to /ə/ as for example in the "uh" (a) sound of "can" when we say "He can come."

A PHONEMIC SCRIPT

The best way to learn to pronounce a second language is to imitate a native speaker. Nonetheless, for adults who are used to analyzing and explaining, mere imitation is often insufficient. Students like to have explanations of how to articulate sounds and of what to imitate.

To provide such explanations, a way to write sounds unambiguously is necessary. English spelling, although it attempts to represent the sound of words, is often inconsistent and unclear. There are more significantly different sounds in the language than letters in our alphabet to represent them. As a result, some sounds are spelled in several different ways, e.g., /k/ in *c*at, *k*itten, tech*nique;* and some symbols have several different pronunciations, e.g., the *ch* in *ch*urch /č/, *ch*emical /k/, and *ch*auffeur /š/. A phonemic alphabet is one which uses a different symbol for each significantly different or contrasting consonant, vowel or semi-vowel sound in the language. It is traditional to write phonemic symbols between slashes to distinguish them from the ordinary spelling of English words. Thus /p/ indicates the phoneme /p/ not the letter p. Stress marks may be written over or before stressed vowels.

Far from being an extra burden to impose upon the adult student, a phonemic script is a great aid to learning. It is consistent and reliable, a ready reference point to the sound system of the language. It is equally useful for teachers whenever they wish to refer to specific sounds or explain pronunciation. Because a phonemic script is analytical, it can draw students' attention to features disguised by the traditional spelling system (e.g., the three different pronunciations of the suffix *-ed*) and help them remember by giving them a visual as well as an aural pattern to recall. Finally, a phonemic script helps students to become independent quickly. With it they can use their dictionaries profitably to learn the pronunciation as well as the meaning of new words met in reading. They can also write down new words they have heard and recall them accurately later when they have the opportunity to consult native speakers about the correct spelling. Thus knowledge of a way to write the sounds of English liberates students from total dependence on the presence of a native speaker.

As any wide selection of dictionaries will prove, there are several different systems used to record English sounds. In this chapter a modified form of IPA (the International Phonetic Alphabet) is used, the same system used in the booklet *The Sound System of English* published by the Ontario Ministry of Citizenship and Culture. Other systems differ from IPA chiefly in the way they transcribe vowel sounds. Which system a teacher uses will depend upon many factors, the availability of texts, the other books students must consult, systems used by other teachers in the school, ease of typing, personal preference. Each has its merits; one should be chosen.[4]

Another system which is not strictly phonemic is commonly used in North American schools and in many dictionaries. This system marks stressed vowels either "long" (ā) or "short" (ă) and gives general rules to predict vowel quality from traditional spelling. Its two merits are that it is widely used and familiar to most native speakers of North American English and that it does show vowel quality without distorting the traditional spelling of most words. The numerous exceptions to rules and the fact that the terms *long* and *short* have little phonetic justification are drawbacks, but familiarity and widespread use may override these arguments. In chapters fifteen and sixteen of their *Manual of American English Pronunciation,* Prator and Robinett explain the relationship between traditional spelling and the pronunciation of words with reference to this analysis. The system, if carefully used, may be a great help to an ESL teacher and have the added advantage of integrating the ESL classroom into the main body of English classes in the school.

WHEN PRONUNCIATION SHOULD BE TAUGHT

Since the sound system is an integral and inseparable part of any language, the study of

pronunciation must form an important part of an ESL program, arising naturally from other lesson material. It certainly cannot be relegated to a hit and miss, come-by-chance position in the course of studies. Two important ways can be used to integrate the study of pronunciation into a lesson. The first is to anticipate problems or important considerations which will develop naturally from other material being discussed in a unit. For example, a discussion of voiced and voiceless sounds would fit well into lessons using the simple past tense, for the pronunciation of the *-ed* suffix is conditioned by the voiced or voiceless quality of the preceding phoneme. One could begin a lesson on verbs by grouping them into voiced and voiceless categories. Depending on the level and ability of the class, several different activities could be developed from this same basic idea.

The second way to develop a pronunciation lesson is to work from student errors, using them as a basis for the lesson. Teachers should develop the habit of listening carefully at all times for pronunciation problems, especially with more advanced students. Hear the accent, isolate the problem and build a lesson on the material provided by the class. Wherever possible look for general problems which affect many words or sentences, problems like voicing, aspiration, or sentence rhythm. Then a pronunciation drill can be built using vocabulary and sentences from the lesson material or student conversations. Often a few minutes at the end of a class can be used profitably in this way to work with correcting student errors. Care must be taken, of course, not to embarrass students by selecting their mistakes and difficulties as a focus of class discussion.

Though pronunciation work should flow naturally from other work in class, there are many times when it should not be done. Teachers must listen for problems. They should not interrupt the flow of a reading lesson or a conversation to teach a phonetic nicety. Communication is the goal of language. When it is happening in the classroom, don't break in. Occasionally teachers may feel the need to correct a word. They can do this by taking part in the conversation and using the problem word in a question or statement to provide a model without changing the topic of discussion. In a reading lesson they may read the next paragraph or ask a question about the story and so use the problem word without making it the focus of attention.

Some student errors require immediate attention. Mispronunciations which result in inadvertent obscenities are a case in point. The ESL teacher has a duty to protect students from potential embarrassment outside the classroom. Students making such errors should be taken aside after class or while other students are busy and the error explained. Often the potential embarrassment will be the extra push needed to overcome the problem. Students will be very thankful for the protection and concern. Knowing what not to say is an important and necessary part of language learning.

Thus the cardinal rules are: incorporate pronunciation practice into the lesson, anticipate problems, build on problems, handle emergencies with tact, and never interrupt real communication.

GUIDELINES AND TECHNIQUES

The following guidelines, implied in the discussion above, should be kept in mind for the planning of lessons in pronunciation:

1. Base your lessons on material collected by constant and careful observation of your students' pronunciation. Remember that you must teach your students to overcome their individual problems. Real data from real students will help you to make every lesson meaningful.

2. Correct only one thing at a time. If you

try to correct everything at once, students will become discouraged. Students concentrating on one specific problem, in and out of class for a week, will make real progress. For example, in many European languages /t/ and /d/ are pronounced with the tip of the tongue touching the teeth. Students taught to focus their attention on their alveolar ridge (the upper gum ridge), or just told to think "a little farther back" will find that in one week they have the feel of the English alveolar placement of these and other consonants.

3. The three main points of a pronunciation lesson are imitation, explanation, and drill. You may use yourself, recordings, or other speakers as the model to be imitated. Use diagrams, words and any other resources at hand to explain how sounds are made and contrasted with other sounds. Don't be afraid to exploit the sense of touch. Students should be encouraged to become familiar with the parts of their mouths and to feel the position of tongue and jaw. Adult students in particular will find that a clear explanation will help them not only to make a sound, but also to remember how to make it again. Drill puts theory into practice.

4. Always use real language in the classroom. Many teachers tend to overpronounce and to speak far too slowly with the result that students are seldom exposed to one of the most difficult features of English pronunciation, namely the reduction of unstressed vowels. Real language means normal speed. The question *What did you do?* more often sounds like /wʌǰə ˈdu/ than /ˈwʌtˈdɪd ˈyu ˈdu/. The latter would be heard only in the context of giving dictation in an office or perhaps to a telegraph company. Remember that you are teaching communicative competence. Take your vocabulary and structures from the students' world.

5. Move from the known to the unknown, using the students' abilities to help them over their difficulties. For example, most Chinese speakers have great difficulty with final voiced consonants in English. If they cannot hear the

voicing, use what they can hear to help them. Voiced consonants have a strong influence on the vowels that precede them. This is heard as a distinct lengthening often with a slight change in the pitch contour. Chinese students, speaking a tonal language, can hear this readily and improve both their listening and speaking skills almost immediately.

Finally, let us move from general guidelines to specific tools and techniques which have been found useful in the classroom for teaching pronunciation.

Minimal Pairs

Minimal pairs are useful for teaching individual phonemes and may be used to promote accurate listening and good oral production. To tune the ear to discriminate between two similar sounds, the most basic exercise is a monotony drill. One member of a minimal pair is repeated several times rapidly. Then, without warning or delay, the teacher switches to the other member of the pair. Students must note the change by raising their hands. After this has been done several times, students can be read pairs of words together and asked if they are the same or different. An alternative is to send students to the blackboard and have them point to the word the teacher pronounces or to pronounce the word the teacher points to. Try to pick useful words from the students' vocabulary.

Articulatory Charts and Hands

In explaining how to make individual sounds, a simple diagram of the speech organs is useful. Leave out the tongue and use your hand to represent it and you can show how the tongue moves for different sounds. A diagram like this hung at the front of the room can save much time, as you will not have to draw repeated diagrams on the blackboard. Often, though, there are times when you are working individually with a student and cannot easily go to the chart. Use your hands instead. With fingers slightly arched and palm down, one hand can represent the roof of the mouth. The tips of the fingers may point down to represent teeth or be clenched in to represent lips. The other hand represents the tongue. Your hands can then become a portable diagram, both for teaching how a sound is made and also for serving as a silent reminder for correcting errors as they occur.

Foreign Accent

Often students have a foreign accent even though everything they say is clear. How can you help them hear the difference between an English and a French /d/? One good way is to put the English sound in a French word where it will be out of place. Students who can mimic an English accent in their own language have learned how to pronounce English sounds. So you don't speak French? All the better. Let students try to teach you some words in their languages. They will quickly hear an English accent. There is an added bonus in this approach. Your own difficulty shows that you too are human and fallible, even if demanding. Students feel proud of their own abilities and you understand their problems better.

Tongue Twisters

Tongue twisters are a wonderful way to practice pronunciation and have fun at the same time. Because they are difficult, even for native speakers, no one feels dreadfully upset at making mistakes, yet there is a huge challenge to do well. Most tongue twisters contrast similar sounds. Longer ones can be used to practise sentence rhythm. A favorite for the /θ, s, f/ contrast is *Theophilus Thistledown, the successful thistle sifter, in sifting a sieve of unsifted thistles, thrust three thousand thistles through the thick of his thumb.* For the /s, š/ contrast there is *She sells seashells by the seashore.* Students can have fun writing their own tongue twisters using words which cause them difficulty. These can be shared with partners, small groups, or the whole class.

Rhythm and Rhyme

A feature of English which causes much difficulty to some students is the regular placement of stressed syllables in a sentence. English has a regular beat. Songs and poetry are very popular aids in establishing this. What is more regular than a limerick? Have students tap or clap the beat as a poem is read or as they read in chorus. Better still, have them walk, putting a foot down on each beat.

Not only poems and songs have rhythm; so do large numbers. Read large numbers and have students walk, putting a foot down each time you snap your fingers. Keep the speed fast and the beat regular. For example, read the following number, snapping your fingers on each underlined syllable: *Three hundred and seventy-five million, eight hundred and thirty-three thousand, two hundred and four.*

Songs and poems may be used to teach rhyme as well as rhythm. Here students must learn to match stressed vowels and following consonants in different words. Give students the lyrics to a song with the rhyming words omitted. Have them listen carefully for the missing words and say them for you.

Intonation

Since English sentences have distinctive intonation contours, distortion occurs when words are taken out of context for pronunciation practice. Two useful devices help to overcome this problem. First, whenever you have students repeat a list, make sure that the first member is repeated at the end or picked up to begin the next list so that it will be heard with both initial and final intonation. For example, when you teach the days of the week, have students drill: *Sunday, Monday, Tuesday; Tuesday, Wednesday, Thursday; Thursday, Friday, Saturday; Saturday, Sunday, Monday.*

The second method of retaining natural intonation contours is known as backwards buildup. This is used when a long sentence is broken up into parts for pronunciation drill. The sentence is built up from the end as follows:

bank
the bank
robbed the bank
bandits robbed the bank
The bandits robbed the bank.

This kind of drill, also known as a pyramid drill, gives students practice in pronouncing increasingly longer groups of words which always end with a natural final intonation contour. It also gives natural word groups so that articles will never be left at the end as they would if you built up from the beginning of a sentence. Choose sentences from your reading lessons or from student conversations to use in this way.

These few are only some of the many techniques which may be used in a pronunciation lesson. You will develop others on your own, usually as you need them. Be sure to jot them down, even if they seem obvious or simple, and to share them with your colleagues.

NOTES

1. An excellent example is Nilsen and Nilsen, *Pronunciation Contrasts in English.*

2. For a description of studies carried out at the University of California, Los Angeles, see Prator and Robinett, pp. xi–xiv.

3. Voicing-voiced/unvoiced. These terms refer to sounds made with the vocal cords open (unvoiced or voiceless) and with the vocal cords closed (voiced), e.g., f (voiceless)—v (voiced), p (voiceless)—b (voiced).

4. Recent technological advances have been of great assistance to ESL teachers and students. With the advent of the microcomputer and the dot matrix printer, any phonetic symbol is easily typed today. Charts and diagrams can be accurately and quickly drawn, rapidly and aesthetically printed, and then filed on disk for future use. Such word-processing programs as *Gutenberg Sr* provide type fonts that include not only phonetic symbols, but also most of the standard alphabetic scripts used today.

REFERENCES

Fox, James, ed. 1974. *Teaching English as a Second Language—A Methodology.* Newcomer Services Branch, Ontario Ministry of Citizenship and Culture. Unrevised Edition.

Gutenberg Sr: Gutenberg Software Limited, 47 Lewiston Road, Scarborough, Ontario, Canada M1P 1X8 © 1981, 1985.

Nilsen, Don L. F., and Alleen Pace Nilsen. 1973. *Pronunciation Contrasts in English.* New York: Regents Publishing Company.

Prator, Clifford H. Jr., and Betty Wallace Robinett. 1972. *Manual of American English Pronunciation.* New York: Holt, Rinehart and Winston, Inc. (3rd ed.).

Robinett, Betty Wallace. 1978. *Teaching English to Speakers of Other Languages.* Minneapolis: University of Minnesota Press.

The Sound System of English for Teachers of English as a Second Language. Newcomer Services Branch, Ministry of Citizenship and Culture.

RELATED READING

1. Bowen, Donald J. 1979. Contextualizing pronunciation practice in the ESOL classroom. In *Teaching English as a Second or Foreign Language,* Marianne Celce-Murcia and Lois McIntosh, (eds.). Rowley, MA: Newbury House Publishers, pp. 101–110.

2. Essig, Janet. 1978. Runningallourwordstogethernaturallyorflowingriverversusraindropspeech. *TESL talk 9.* I (Winter 1978): 21–27.

3. Hill, Clifford, and Leslie Beebe. 1980. Contraction and blending: The use of orthographic clues in teaching pronunciation. *TESOL Quarterly* XIV. 3: 299–323.

4. Neufeld, Gerald G. 1980. On the adult's ability to acquire phonology. *TESOL Quarterly* XIV. 3: 285–298.

5. Parish, Charles. 1980. A practical philosophy of pronunciation. In *Readings on English as a Second Language,* Kenneth Croft (ed.). Cambridge, MA: Winthrop Publishers (2nd ed.). pp. 258–264.

6. Stevick, Earl W. 1982. Building auditory images: Pronunciation. In *Teaching and Learning Languages.* Cambridge: Cambridge University Press.

APPENDIX

International Phonetic Alphabet (IPA) with some modification. Taken from *The Sound System of English for Teachers of English as a Second Language.* Newcomer Services Branch, Ministry of Citizenship and Culture.

Consonants

Modified IPA	English Word	Modified IPA	English Word
b	bat	s	sip
p	pat	m	mice
d	door	n	nice
t	tore	l	lip
g	good	r	rip
k	could, kind	h	house
v	van	y	yes
f	fan	w	window
z	zip		

Modified IPA	IPA	English Word
š	ʃ	ship
ž	ʒ	pleasure
tš (č)	tʃ	chat, catch
dž (ǰ)	dʒ	judge
ð		this
θ		thin
ŋ		singing

Vowels and Diphthongs

ə	but, about
i	beet, beat, be
ɪ	bit
ε	bet
æ	bat
α (a)	*cot, caught
o	bore, for
υ	good, could
u	food, soon
ey (εγ)	bait, bate
ay (αγ)	bide, side
oy	boy
aw (αw)	bound
ow	boat, go, slow

*Although for Ontario speakers these two words are homonyms, certain varieties of American English and British English employ different vowel sounds in the two words. The vowel sound used in the word "caught" is represented by the symbol /ɔ/ and is produced further back in the mouth than /a/.

15

Developing Successful Conversation Groups

Sharron Kay Bassano
Mary Ann Christison

Ask any student of English as a second language what it is that he or she wants from the language class experience and nine times out of ten the answer will be, "More conversation practice." We have thought about this request frequently and have wondered just what our students mean. If students are living and studying in the United States, don't they have plenty of opportunity to practice their English? Isn't the free conversation experience waiting for them daily just out of the classroom door?

We believe that students are, in fact, asking for more opportunity to become themselves in the new language. They want to become enthusiastically and authentically involved. They want to know that they are genuinely respected and treated as individuals by their teachers and classmates. It is so easy for our classes to become mechanistic and dull for the students. It is certainly easier to provide rote drills and endless pattern practice for them than it is to devise meaningful and relevant communication! We may be giving them ample opportunities to manipulate their new language, but too little time to become truly involved.

Outside of class, our students may have the chance to interact with the clerk in the market, the postmaster or the bus driver, but personal communication is often only available with friends from the same native language background. Many times real conversation with native speakers of English is severely limited.

Being aware of the input students receive both in and out of the classroom, we have often experimented with the free conversation session. Sometimes we succeed and we are able to touch our students in just the right spot and they "take off." Sometimes we see our great plans fall flat! It often seems like a case of good or bad luck—no guarantees. Many times we put our students in a circle, give them a topic for discussion that we think is particularly stimulating and we see them just sit and look at one another in an embarrassing silence, constrained, nervous, and tense. We end up bailing out the group and carrying the bulk of the dialogue ourselves! Often, too, there is one aggressive student who seems to feel a need to be the center of attention at all times, a student who shows little awareness of functional group interaction patterns, and even less self-discipline. Other times, we have one or two students who are either too shy to participate or who have such low self-esteem that they feel they have nothing of interest to offer the group. (What do *I* have to contribute? Who could possibly be interested in what *I* have to say?)

Another very real problem is that most of our foreign students come to us from an academic background that is typified by straight rows of desks, all eyes to the front on the teacher who is directing each classroom activity like a conductor leading an orchestra. They have had no experience in directing their own classroom use of language, and consequently fall apart when left to their own devices. Many subconsciously assume that learning is not possible without the teacher present.

We have come to believe that when conversation groups fail it is neither the fault of the activities presented, nor due to the lack of creativity or energy expended on the part of the teacher. Hours are spent conscientiously developing and designing activities and topics to cue exciting and effective conversation among the students. Our hearts are in the right place! Rather, the problem lies with unrealistic expectations. We put a room full of strangers into a circle, and we expect them to act as close friends before they even know or trust each other. We expect them to be well versed in the dynamics of group process such as turn talking, interrupting, active listening, etc. We expect them to know how to deal with the more vocal members and draw out the more timid or self-conscious ones. They are expected to know how to conduct themselves as a cohesive entity with no previous experience at self-direction in the classroom. Too often we give them topics that are too hot to handle—topics that require a great deal of personal disclosure.

What we propose as a solution to these problems is a progressive format or *sequencing* of strategies in the conversation class which carefully prepares students, that systematically breaks down student stereotypes of classroom procedure and allows them to begin interacting

democratically and independently. Through this approach, students learn step-by-step, functional interaction techniques at the same time the group spirit or trust is being built. By careful sequencing of strategies, plenty of attention can be given to the boisterous students in an acceptable manner and the quiet, retiring ones can be drawn into action in a painless procedure. All interpersonal activities should move from low-risk, non-personal content, such as games, information gathering, reporting, problem solving, etc., to activities which ask for the sharing of personal values, beliefs and feelings.

Through classroom experimentation, we have identified and worked with six activity categories or strategies.[1] We call them: restructuring, one-centered, unified group, dyads, small group, and large group. Each one of the hundred or so activities we introduce to our conversation classes fits into one of these strategies. The objectives and formats are as follows:

Restructuring

1. To break down expected classroom structures.
2. To create opportunities for supportive behavior.
3. To dispel fears and anxieties.
4. To relax both the student and the teacher.

Restructuring activities usually require the students to get up and out of their chairs, to interact physically as a group. There is minimal participation by the teacher. Often the communication is done non-verbally, through action, drawings, or quick-written statements, and is usually non-personal.

One-Centered

1. To provide each student with individual attention and acceptance from the entire group.
2. To increase the likelihood of contribu-

tions in the discussions which will follow later.

One-centered activities always put one student in the spotlight for a short time on a voluntary basis. Content can be either personal or non-personal, and, depending on the student's self-confidence, may entail maximum or minimum verbalization, from the front of the class or in his or her seat.

Unified Group

1. To develop co-operation among group members.
2. To emphasize each group member's value to the group.
3. To provide opportunities for group success.

Unified group activities require the participation of each group member. No one may bow out. Each person's contribution is essential to completion of the activity. The teacher is only minimally engaged in the activity, and content may be both personal or non-personal.

Dyads

1. To get students accustomed to dealing openly with their own feelings, sensitivities, and emotions.
2. To provide opportunity for simple interaction with only one other class member at a time.
3. To develop sincere interpersonal communication in the second language.

Paired activities include both personal and non-personal content. Time is usually given to gather thoughts individually before sharing with the partner. Often these activities are followed up with a short written assignment or journal entries.

Small Group

1. To develop in each individual a growing sense of commitment to the group.
2. To develop trust and co-operation among group members.
3. To develop group interaction techniques that facilitate fair interaction.

Group activities require patience and good listening patterns. They require attention sharing, turn-taking, and fair interruptions. The teacher is usually facilitator and participator.

Large Group

The objectives for large groups are the same as for small groups. The only difference is the inclusion of a wider range of individuals whom the student has learned to trust.

We include here 12 sample activities, two for each strategy, to illustrate how the objectives are met. As you read them, consider what activities you personally have done in your conversation classes that might fit into each category or strategy.

STRATEGY TYPE: RESTRUCTURING

Title: Everybody Votes

Hang large newsprint sheets around the room, each sheet having as a heading a conversation topic—politics, religion, family, fun and

recreation, work, love and romance, friendship, etc. Ask students to consider what their personal favorite conversation area is, and to signify their choice by going over and standing by the chart. After all have noticed the balance of interests, ask them to move and go stand by the chart that is their least favorite topic of conversation. After all have gotten a feeling for who is in the class and what some of their interests might be, give them all colored pens and ask them to mill about the room considering each chart and ask them to write some graffiti—a comment, a statement or a question they might personally have regarding each topic. Let this activity continue until all have had a chance to write something and to read what others have written.

To process or complete this restructuring activity, you might ask the group as a whole how they felt doing this exercise, what they noticed, what they heard. Or they might sit down in small groups and comment on what they were compelled to write or on something they read that they didn't agree with.

Title: Introductions

Give each student a piece of colored paper (12 × 18) and some colored pens. Ask them to do the following:

Make a picture of yourself that shows us how you feel today, something you have, something you like to do, something you need or want. Under the picture, write three words that end with *-ing* that tell us three things you do very well. Over the picture write your first name.

Allow five or six minutes for this activity, then have the students pin the drawing to the front of their shirts and have them mill about *silently* for a few minutes—ask them to get acquainted—to learn a little bit about each other only with their eyes. After they have done this, ask them to stop where they are and think about:

Did you see anything similar to your drawing?

Did you see something very different from your drawing?

What did you see that interested you?

Whom do you think you would like to talk with?

Was there anything you didn't understand?

Now, ask them to mill about again, this time asking questions or making comments or pointing out similarities of differences. After this activity, you might want to ask each student to choose a partner to sit down with and find out a little more about that person.

STRATEGY TYPE: ONE-CENTERED

Title: What Am I?

Prepare 20 three by five cards with the name of an animal or a thing written on each one. These items can range from easy ones like *tree, cat, dog, elephant,* and *book* to more complicated ones like *glue, coca-cola,* and *matches.* The teacher asks for a volunteer from the class to be the first participant. If you don't get a volunteer, pick one of the more aggressive students. The student is then asked to come to the front of the class and sit on a chair.

Instructions. Ask for a volunteer from the class. Have the student come forward and turn around with his or her back to the rest of the class. Now show the class one of the three by five cards with the name of an animal or thing written on it. Pin the card on the student's back. The student now becomes that thing or animal, i.e., *dog, cat, soap,* etc. The volunteer student does not know what he is, but the class does. The only way for the volunteer student to find out what he is, is to ask the class questions. Class members give only the information asked for. Each volunteer is allowed to ask 10 questions of 10 different class members. After five questions, the student may ask one of the class members for a hint. If the student does not get the correct answer after 10 questions, the class may give him hints until he or she finds the answer. Make certain all class members understand the rules before the activity begins.

Instructions. For the shyer, less verbal student, turn the activity around. Let the spotlighted person know what the card says, but not the rest of the class. The class members must ask the questions to find out what is on the card, the focus person only has to answer yes or no! This is, obviously, a very painless, low risk way to be the star of the show.

Title: In the Spotlight

Thought Gathering: Give each student a copy of a list of possible interview questions and allow them a few minutes of quiet reflection—a chance to think about how they might answer the questions.

Sharing. Ask a volunteer to come up to the front of the class and sit comfortably in a chair. Allow group members to ask questions from the list or their own original questions to the volunteer. The one being interviewed has the right to say "I pass," on any question that she or he can't or doesn't want to answer. She or he also has the opportunity after eight minutes of interviewing to ask back to members of the group any question that was posed to him or her. Be sure that the group understands that there is a time limit, a right to pass, and an opportunity to ask the three questions back.

STRATEGY TYPE: UNIFIED GROUP

Title: Line Ups

Ask your students to line up in the room according to a certain pattern (listed examples below). In order to form their lines, it will be necessary for them to speak with each other to determine their relative positions.

Use these ideas and invent your own!

1. Alphabetical order according to last names.
2. Alphabetical order according to native country name.
3. How long have you been in the United States?
4. How long have you studied English?
5. How many brothers and sisters do you have?
6. How many people do you know in this town that are from your native country?
7. What time did you get up this morning?
8. What time did you go to bed last night?
9. How old are you?
10. How tall are you?
11. How many different girlfriends/boyfriends have you had?
12. How long is your hair?
13. Who is wearing the brightest color clothing?
14. How much money do you have in your pocket right now?

Title: Strip Story

Find a short story or make up a story with a very simple plot. Divide the story into parts equal to the number of students in the class. Type each part on a separate piece of paper. Give each student a part of the story in random order. The task is for the class to put the story back together again. Students will have to understand what is contained in each part and will have to ask each other questions in order to discover where the part they have fits into the main plot of the story.

Instructions. You have just been given a slip of paper with a sentence on it. This sentence is part of a larger story. Each member of your group has one sentence from the story. You will now have 5 minutes to memorize the sentence on your paper. After you have memorized your sentence, give the paper to me.

Now give the students 20 minutes to put the story back together again from memory. After the students feel they have the correct order, have them tell the story to the rest of the class. Each individual in the group must remember his or her portion of the story in order for it to be successful.

STRATEGY TYPE: DYADS

Title: Where Do I Put It?

The following two activities involve one student giving directions to his or her partner. A screen of some sort is set up between the two students who sit facing each other so that they can see each other's face and hear each other clearly but *cannot* see each other's paper or materials. A manila file folder opened out and set on edge works fine for a screen or barrier.

Activity 1. One student has a blank sheet which he or she folds into nine squares and then opens out to use as a game board. The partner has a sheet that has nine squares with a small simple illustration in each square. The illustrations might be something like a cup and saucer, a cat, a tennis racket, an old car, a woman's shoe, a garbage can, a flag, a brush, and a flower. The student with the illustrated sheet must tell his partner what to draw and where to draw it with as much detail as possible. He or she may not use his or her hands and may not show the drawings to the partner. When they are finished, they should compare papers. You might have

them then switch roles, using another prepared sheet with different illustrations.

Activity 2. Give all students a piece of paper and have them fold it into nine squares and open it out to form a game board. Give both of the partners an identical set of nine picture cards. Tell the students they must place the pictures on the game board in exactly the same positions, but they must not look at each other's board or pieces. Have one student decide to be the speaker, the other, the listener. The speaker describes the pictures and tells the listener where to place them. When all the pieces are in place, have the students compare and then switch roles.

STRATEGY TYPE: SMALL GROUP

Title: Pictures! Pictures! Pictures!

Divide students into two or three groups with no more than five to a group. Each group will receive 20 pictures to pass around and look at. These should be a variety of pictures from magazines and should be mounted on 8½ × 11 colored construction paper.

Instructions. Your group has just been given 20 pictures to pass around and look at. It will be the responsibility of your group to find things that these pictures have in common and place them in groups. Use your imagination and creativity. For example, let's say I have a picture of a bear, a cat, a dog, and an elephant.

These pictures belong in the same group because they are all *animals*. This is something they all have in common. Appoint a secretary for the group. Have that individual write the number or letter of each picture which belongs in the group. Make certain that each picture belongs in a group.

After each group has finished, ask them to come up to the front of the class and display their pictures by groups. The class must see if they can guess what the pictures have in common.

Title: Word Search

Divide the class into groups of three to five. Write a polysyllabic English word on the board, e.g., *Encyclopedia* or *Translation*.

Instructions. I have just written the word _____ on the board. Your group will now have three minutes to make as many words as possible from the letters in this word. Possible words from *Encyclopedia,* for example, would be *can, an, loan,* and *pedal.* Words from *Translation* would be *train, sit, rat,* etc. (Write on board.) Your group will receive a score equal to the number of correct words. Each group should have a secretary. Only the secretary can write words within the group. If you think of a word, tell the group secretary and she or he will write it down. Your group may challenge any of the other groups or correct words. If you do not believe the word they have is correct, you say *challenge.* Look up the word in the dictionary. If you do *not* find the word, you get their point. If you find the word, they get the point. Make certain all class members understand the instructions before going on with the activity.

STRATEGY TYPE: LARGE GROUP

Title: Grab bag

Ask each student in the class to bring a small personal item to class. Tell them what they bring should be a secret. They should not let anyone else in the class know what they are bringing. It's a good idea to tell the students to bring items which are small and which will not break. Show them an average size grocery bag and tell them that all the items from the class must fit in the bag. After you have collected one item from every individual in the class, you are ready to start the activity. (Sometimes it takes several days to get *one* item from everyone, so plan ahead!) Have a volunteer student come up to the front of the class and pick out an object and show it to the class. The class will offer suggestions as to whose object it is and why they believe it is true. After one or two minutes of discussion the student who drew the item should find out if the class was correct.

NOTE

1. The six strategies were originally developed for a workshop entitled "A Structural Approach to the Conversation Class" for TESOL '80 in San Francisco, presented by Karl J. Krahnke, Mary Ann Christison, and Thomas Schroeder.

16

Socio-Drama for Social Interaction

Robin C. Scarcella

It is often recognized that greater emphasis should be placed on developing communication skills. Socio-drama can be used effectively to attain this goal. First, by participating in several enactments, students produce new sentences based on their own behavior or the spontaneous constructions produced by other students. Second, as in real life communication, socio-drama obliges students to restructure their language use according to the social context. Third, socio-drama promotes social-interaction, a prerequisite for communication.

Socio-drama has high student appeal. Its game structure allows students to try out new behaviors without fear of social penalty. It also encourages students to repair communication lapses occurring in both their own and in others' speech. This in turn enables the teacher to diagnose communication breakdowns for future lessons. Socio-drama creates a comfortable atmosphere which promotes cross-cultural understanding.

For many years, ESL educators have been aware of the need to develop students' conversation skills. At the same time, they have experienced the difficulty of creating class activities leading to the attainment of this goal. One activity which has been found to be a successful catalyst for social interaction and hence communication is socio-drama.

Socio-drama is a type of role-play involving a series of student enactments of solutions to a social problem. The problem takes the form of an open-ended story containing one clear, easily identifiable conflict which is of relevance to the students. (For a complete description refer to Shaftel and Shaftel, 1967, and Chesler and Fox, 1966.)

Another type of role-play which is frequently used in the ESL class is situation role-play. However, socio-drama differs from situation role-play in several important ways. First, the technique for using socio-drama is unique because it involves a series of specific steps. (See below.) Second, socio-drama is student- rather than teacher-oriented. Students frequently define their own roles and always determine their own course of action in the enactments. Only those students who seem to relate to the roles are selected to enact them. Also, socio-drama involves several enactments and therefore lasts much longer than situation role-play.

TECHNIQUE[1]

Steps in socio-drama may include:

1. Warm-up. The teacher introduces the socio-drama topic and stimulates student interest. During this time the teacher tries to create a relaxed atmosphere.
2. Presentation of new vocabulary. A minimal number of new vocabulary words and expressions are presented.
3. Presentation of dilemma. Good socio-drama stories are written with specific teaching objectives in mind. The story must be relevant to the students and contain a clearly identifiable problem and climax. The story stops at the dilemma point. The students are asked to focus their attention on the conflict in the socio-drama story as it is related to them by their teacher. (See Appendix for sample socio-drama story.)
4. Discussion of the situation and selection of roles. In this stage the problem and roles are discussed. The teacher selects students who relate to the roles and who have offered solutions to the problem to come to the front of the class to participate in the enactment.
5. Audience Preparation. Students in the class who are not selected to participate in the enactment become the audience. Members of the audience are given specific tasks. For example, they may be asked to determine why the conflict is or is not being resolved.

6. Enactment. The role-players enact the solutions which they have suggested. To help the students initiate the enactment, the teacher may repeat the last few lines of the socio-drama, give students a minute to gather their thoughts, as well as ask the students to reformulate their description of the roles and their intended course of action.
7. Discussion of the situation and selection of new role-players. Alternative ways of solving the problem are explored. New role-players are chosen.
8. Re-enactment. Students replay the problem situation and attempt to solve the socio-drama dilemma by using new strategies.

At this point steps 5, 6, and 7 may be repeated until many different possible solutions have been presented and discussed in terms of their consequences.

9. Summary. The teacher guides the students to summarize what was presented in the enactments and asks, when appropriate, if there are any final comments or generalizations about the problems and proposed solutions.
10. Follow-up. Follow-up activities may include: a writing exercise, extended discussion, an aural comprehension exercise, or a related reading exercise. Some teachers like to give a mini-lesson on a communication breakdown occurring in the session.

USES

Socio-drama may be used effectively to develop vocabulary, grammar, discourse strategies, strategies for social interaction, to promote cultural understanding, and to elicit oral production from all students.

Claims made here about the uses of socio-drama and the effectiveness of socio-drama as a technique are based on transcriptions of socio-drama sessions video-taped at the American Language Institute at the University of Southern California. Participants in the sessions included intermediate and advanced students of English as a second language and native English speakers.

One use of socio-drama is in the development of vocabulary. Socio-drama supplies contextual clues from which the students can induce the meanings of words. In addition to allowing the L2 acquirer to observe the vocabulary which is needed in various situations in order to carry on a conversation, socio-drama provides students with opportunities to try out the vocabulary. Participants in the socio-drama help each other communicate by supplying vocabulary items and expressions as the following examples demonstrate. R and J are advanced ESL students.

> R: We plan to have dinner at 7:00 but uh uh =
> J: = But we have a surprise for you.
> R: Yeah. A surprise.
> Native Why don't you want to eat?
> speaker: Are you on a diet?
> J: On a diet. Yeah. I'm on a diet.

Furthermore, because the enactments are often very similar, the input is frequently repeated. Repetition of this kind leads to better comprehension.

Grammar can be developed through socio-drama. It has been proposed that language acquisition evolves out of learning how to participate in conversation (Hatch, 1976), that the L2 student first learns communication strategies which facilitate conversation and then learns how to interact verbally. From this interaction arises the student's increasing ability to produce grammatical sentences. In socio-drama students can produce spontaneous constructions based on their own behavior or on the spontaneous constructions produced by other students as illustrated by the following example.

> J: Where ya gonna take me?
> K: Lovely restaurant. Lovely restaurant. I'm gonna take you to a lovely restaurant.

In this case, K, an intermediate student, appears to be copying the progressive verb form used by J, an advanced student.

Another use of socio-drama is in the development of discourse strategies. Strategies for attention-getting, topic initiation, and topic change may be developed through socio-drama. During the early enactments of socio-drama the students have difficulty initiating conversation and the teacher must help the students by setting the scene. However, as the socio-drama progresses the students become better at initiating conversation and no longer rely on the teacher. Students learn to initiate conversation by use of attention-getters such as "Excuse me," "Hello," "What's new," and "How are you." These expressions occurred frequently in the socio-drama transcriptions and were modeled after expressions used by the native English speakers as well as by fellow students. Also, as the socio-drama advances, the students spend less time groping for the appropriate words to initiate the topic. For example, in one socio-drama session, students hesitated 3 seconds before beginning the first topic, 2.4 seconds before beginning the second topic, and did not hesitate at all before beginning the third and fourth topics. Finally, socio-drama gives students practice in changing the topic. "By the way," "I've been thinking," and You know what else?" were some of the expressions which students in the transcribed socio-drama sessions used to change the topic. In order to encourage the development of these strategies, the teacher may choose to focus on them before introducing the socio-drama story.

Strategies for social interaction may also be developed through socio-drama. These strategies are essential for communication and language development. In fact, social interaction is often considered the first stage of L2 acquisition. Students must develop strategies for making and maintaining relationships in order to receive the necessary input. Socio-drama promotes the development of the social strategies suggested by L. Fillmore (1976). These include initiating interaction with others, establishing and maintaining relationships, providing others with encouragement, and counting on others for help.

Socio-drama can also be used to heighten awareness of cultural differences. Rivers (1972) has suggested that cultural patterns, values, attitudes, relationships, and taboos can be acquired through discourse. Since language is a part of culture, successful communication can arise only when the speaker can predict how the hearer will react and the hearer can predict the speaker's intentions. By participating in socio-drama, students become aware of discourse in relation to social expectations, formulas of politeness, social attitudes, and appropriateness of response to a cultural situation. For example, in a socio-drama story involving university professors, students get practice using politeness formulas. Any inappropriate behavior can be resolved during the discussions. Also, the socio-drama sessions which are most successful in promoting cultural understanding are those in which native speakers participate and serve as models.

Teachers may use socio-drama to elicit communication from all students, since socio-drama creates a relaxed atmosphere, one in which even shy students feel free to participate. The teacher endeavors to foster a comfortable environment by (1) calling on native speakers or the most verbal and socially accepted students to participate in early enactments; (2) not criticizing students; (3) not forcing students to participate against their will; (4) giving shy students passive roles at first to get them use to being in front of the class; (5) clearly dissociating the role-players from the parts which they enact. As a consequence of these procedures, students are given practice and security in performing before others.

RATIONALE

Many reasons explain the success of socio-drama in teaching ESL. Of primary significance is the fact that socio-drama serves to increase the students' "intake." Corder (1967) describes the small part of language which *is* processed as "intake." Wagner-Gough (1975) reports that an important ingredient for "intake" is attention. It follows then that good activities capture the students' attention.

Socio-drama is an activity which obliges students to attend to the verbal environment. First, it is relevant to the students' interests, utilizing both extrinsic motivation, which refers to the students' daily interests and cares, and intrinsic motivation, which refers to the students' internal feelings and attitudes (Stevick, 1971). Second, students pay attention because they expect to participate; even the audience is given an active role. Third, the participants are often friends. The importance of peers in language development is frequently noted. Furthermore, socio-drama is a problem-solving activity which stimulates real life situations and requires active student involvement.

Teaching experience tells us that different students acquire language in different ways. Some students make heavy use of learned rules while others rely more upon the language acquisition process (Krashen, 1976). A further advantage of socio-drama is that it combines both formal and informal learning environments and allows the students to benefit from both so that the rule-oriented student is free to search for rules, while the less rule-oriented student can use the intake provided by acquisition alone. In the vocabulary stage the teacher isolates vocabulary, and perhaps some grammatical structures and discourse strategies in a formal way and appeals to the students' conscious learning processes. However, in the enactment stage there is no overt teaching. Thus, the students are free to accept or reject language from the enactment discourse much as speakers do in everyday language situations (Rietmann, 1977).

Socio-drama cannot possibly be used to accomplish all of the goals of an ESL class. Its effectiveness as a technique has yet to be experimentally validated. Yet, on the basis of the transcriptions of video-taped socio-drama sessions, as well as my own and others' experience, socio-drama can be said to be a valuable supplementary activity. It can be used effectively to teach ESL, a subject in which social interaction is important.

NOTE

1. Adapted from Shaftel and Shaftel, 1967.

REFERENCES

Chesler, M., and R. Fox. 1966. *Role-Playing Methods in the Classroom.* Chicago: Science Research Associates, Inc.

Corder, S. P. 1967. The significance of the learner's errors. *IRAL 4,* 161–169.

Fillmore, L. 1976. Cognitive and social strategies in second language acquisition. Unpublished Ph.D. dissertation, University of California, Berkeley.

Hatch, E. 1976. Discourse analysis, speech acts, and second language acquisition. *Working Papers in TESOL 10,* 51–64, UCLA.

Krashen, S. 1976. The monitor model of second language performance. Paper presented at the 6th Annual California Linguistic Association Conference.

Rietmann, K. 1977. Error repair and discourse strategies in socio-drama and other formal and informal second language environments. Unpublished paper.

Rivers, W. 1972. *Speaking in Many Tongues.* Rowley, MA: Newbury House Publishers.

Shaftel, F., and G. Shaftel. 1967. *Role-Playing for Social Values.* Englewood Cliffs, NJ: Prentice-Hall.

Stevick, E. 1971. *Adapting and Writing Language Lessons.* Washington, D.C. Foreign Service Institute.

Wagner-Gough, J. 1975. Comparative studies in second language learning. Unpublished thesis, UCLA.

APPENDIX

The following is an example of a socio-drama story used in a university ESL class to teach Advanced Spoken English.

Mrs. Watson was very upset when Robert, her youngest son, decided to marry Kathy. Mrs. Watson did not think that any girl was good enough to marry her son. "Look, Robert," she said, "you're not old enough to get married and support a wife. You're only twenty-eight. Kathy won't make you happy. She can't cook like I can. Please don't get married and leave me alone. I'm a widow. I'll be so lonely without my only son."

Nevertheless, Kathy and Robert got married. When they returned from their honeymoon, Kathy received a phone call from Mrs. Watson. "How I've missed you!" Mrs. Watson said. "Why haven't you called me? This Friday is my birthday and I've been wondering if you plan to invite me to visit you. I hate to feel lonely on my birthday."

Kathy replied, "Of course I want you to come here this Friday. We don't want you to be alone on your birthday. I'd love to have you for dessert."

That Friday Kathy was very busy. She wanted to make sure that everything was perfect for her mother-in-law. Kathy spent the entire day cleaning the house. At first, everything went very well. Mrs. Watson arrived promptly at seven o'clock. Kathy served Mrs. Watson a drink and then left her to talk with Robert while she returned to the kitchen.

When Kathy went to take the cake she was baking out of the oven, she was shocked. The cake was completely burned! Kathy quickly shut the oven door so that the smoke would not escape. Then she brought Mrs. Watson another drink. "Here, Mom," Kathy said, "Would you like another drink?"

Mrs. Watson replied, "No thanks. I don't care for another drink right now. You invited me for dessert. When are we going to eat it?"

Kathy replied, ". . . ."

Section Seven

READING

INTRODUCTION

The articles in this section reflect insights from psycholinguistics into the processes involved in (chiefly first language) reading comprehension. Although only a small amount of the research by Goodman, Rumelhart, Smith, and others has been shown to apply to second language readers, some replication studies have been conducted, generally with supportive findings. In the absence of a fully articulated theory of second language reading, the first language work seems a viable basis for efforts by EFL and ESL teachers at present.

In the first article, Carrell and Eisterhold review theory and research on the role of background knowledge structures, or schemata, with which readers supplement their linguistic knowledge when interpreting meaning from written text. Reading for information appears to involve both data-driven (text stimulated) bottom-up processing and conceptually driven top-down processing, with both types of processing occurring at all levels simultaneously. Carrell and Eisterhold report some replication studies of the effect of background knowledge on reading conducted with second language populations, and they go on to suggest implications of the first and second language work for EFL and ESL teachers. They pay special attention to procedures for dealing with the fact that much background knowledge is culturally based, and thus a likely filter on accurate reading comprehension in a second language.

Clarke and Silberstein begin by reviewing insights from the work of Miller, Kolers, Goodman, Smith, and others. The picture of reading they provide is one in which readers project a series of hypotheses about what they will encounter in a text, and then they scan parts of ensuing sentences for broad semantic confirmation of their hypotheses, only returning for linguistic details when initial readings produce unexpected results—a sort of "psycholinguistic guessing-game." Clarke and Silberstein then outline a set of classroom procedures, together with a detailed lesson plan, which encourage the learner's active contribution to the reading process. They urge teachers to be quite clear about which reading *skills,* such as skimming, scanning, and critical reading, any particular exercise is focusing upon.

In the final article, Mackay describes a series of carefully designed exercise types, many derived from work with teaching EFL students to read academic prose, but suitable for reading programs with any EFL or ESL learner. As his title suggests, Mackay focuses on reading for information. His exercise types and formats attempt to provide students with an implicit knowledge of the discourse structure of written texts, with work on such critical features as textual cohesion and logical sentence connectors. Exercises of the kinds advocated by Mackay have been incorporated in several commercially published reading texts designed for EFL and ESL settings.

DISCUSSION QUESTIONS

1. What is meant by describing reading as "hypothesis-testing" and as a "psycholinguistic guessing-game"? Do such views of reading suggest that teachers should encourage students to pay more attention to morpho-syntactic detail or to semantic cues in texts?

2. Would you expect culturally based schemata to influence the reading of scientific discourse (e.g., a journal article reporting a physics or psychology experiment) or would it be reasonable to expect scientific writing to be culturally neutral?

3. Choose a commercially published set of materials for teaching EFL or ESL reading. Classify the exercises you find into exercise types, being careful to distinguish between different types as opposed to different formats within the same type. What generalizations can you make about the variety of types the writer(s) use, the consistency across units or chapters, the relationship between purpose and type, and so on? How could the materials be improved in these respects?

4. Many EFL/ESL reading texts are criticized for providing (a) too little reading material of any kind, and/or (b) inappropriate reading material. (For example, some texts supposedly designed to prepare college students to read academic prose use selections from fictional narratives, newspaper excerpts, restaurant menus, and the like.) Find two texts designed to teach reading to the same type of student and compare them for the quantity and appropriateness of the sample reading materials the authors chose to include.

5. Some experienced reading teachers claim that the best way to teach students to read is to have them read (a lot), i.e., that you cannot *teach* reading, only encourage students to learn to read. Do you agree? What evidence can you provide for or against this view? (How did *you* learn to read?)

6. A commonly made distinction is that between "intensive" and "extensive" reading. The first involves detailed in-class analysis, led by the teacher, of vocabulary and grammar points in a short passage. The second has students read large amounts of high-interest material, usually out of class, concentrating on meaning, "reading for gist," and skipping unknown words. What advantages and disadvantages does each procedure have? Would your answer differ depending on the type of student?

7. What is meant by "simplified" reading materials? In what ways are EFL/ESL readers simplified? What arguments can you think of for using (a) simplified, and (b) authentic reading materials? Would your answer vary with such factors as the age, proficiency level, or ultimate reading needs of the students concerned?

FURTHER READING

1. J. C. Alderson, and A. H. Urquhart (eds.). 1984. *Reading in a Foreign Language.* London: Longman.
2. M. A. Clarke. 1979. Reading in Spanish and English: Evidence from adult ESL students. *Language Learning* 29, 1, 121–150.
3. G. Cziko. 1980. Language competence and reading strategies: A comparison of first and second language oral reading errors. *Language Learning* 30, 1, 101–116.
4. F. Grellet. 1981. *Developing Reading Skills. A Practical Guide to Reading Comprehension Exercises.* Cambridge: Cambridge University Press.
5. C. Hosenfeld. 1981. Second language reading: A curricular sequence for teaching reading strategies. *Foreign Language Annals* 14, 5, 415–422.
6. R. Mackay, B. Barkman, and R. R. Jordan (eds.). 1979. *Reading in a Second Language.* Rowley, MA: Newbury House Publishers.
7. C. Nuttall. 1982. *Teaching Reading Skills in a Foreign Language.* London: Heinemann.
8. F. Smith (ed.) 1973. *Psycholinguistics and Reading.* New York: Holt, Rinehart and Winston.

CHAPTER 17

Schema Theory and ESL Reading Pedagogy

Patricia L. Carrell
Joan C. Eisterhold

Every act of comprehension involves one's knowledge of the world as well.

(Anderson, Reynolds, Schallert, and Goetz, 1977:369)

INTRODUCTION

The idea expressed by the above quote is certainly not new, but it is one worth reminding ourselves of when we consider comprehension in a second or foreign language, and specifically reading comprehension in EFL/ESL. If, as Immanuel Kant claimed as long ago as 1781, new information, new concepts, new ideas can have meaning only when they can be related to something the individual already knows (Kant, 1781/1963), this applies as much to second language comprehension as it does to comprehension in one's native language. Yet, traditionally in the study of second language comprehension (as much as, if not more so than, in the study of first language comprehension), the emphasis has been almost exclusively on the language to be comprehended and not on the comprehender (listener or reader). In this perspective, each

word, each well-formed sentence, and every well-formed text passage is said to "have" a meaning. Meaning is often conceived to be "in" the utterance or text, to have a separate, independent existence from both the speaker or writer and the listener or reader. Also in this view, failures to comprehend a non-defective communication are always attributed to language-specific deficits—perhaps a word was not in the reader's vocabulary, a rule of grammar was misapplied, an anaphoric cohesive tie was improperly coordinated, and so on.

Recent empirical research in the field which has come to be known as *schema theory* has demonstrated the truth of Kant's original observation and of the opening quote from Anderson et al. Schema theory research has shown the importance of background knowledge within a psycholinguistic model of reading. The purpose of this article is twofold. Our first goal is to give a brief overview of schema theory as part of a reader-centered, psycholinguistic processing model of EFL/ESL reading. This goal is addressed in the first part of this paper, in which we discuss how EFL/ESL reading comprehension involves background knowledge which goes far beyond linguistic knowledge. Our second purpose is to explore the relationship of culture-specific background knowledge and EFL/ESL reading methodology and is taken up in the second part of the article, where we review this relationship as it has been discussed in the extant methodology literature. We illustrate this discussion of the culturally based and culturally biased nature of background knowledge with sample reading passages which have actually caused comprehension problems for EFL/ESL students. Finally, we suggest a variety of techniques and classroom activities for accommodating this phenomenon in a reader-centered EFL/ESL reading program.

THE PSYCHOLINGUISTIC MODEL OF READING

During the past decade, EFL/ESL reading theory has come under the influence of psycholinguistics and Goodman's (1967, 1971, 1973a) psycholinguistic model of reading (see also Smith, 1971). Goodman has described reading as a "psycholinguistic guessing game" (1967) in which the "reader reconstructs, as best as he can, a message which has been encoded by a writer as a graphic display" (1971: 135). Goodman views this act of the construction of meaning as being an ongoing, cyclical process of sampling from the input text, predicting, testing and confirming or revising those predictions, and sampling further. In this model, the reader need not (and the efficient reader *does* not) use all of the textual cues. The better the reader is able to make correct predictions, the less confirming via the text is necessary, that is, the less visual perceptual information the reader requires:

> the reader does not use all the information available to him. Reading is a process in which the reader picks and chooses from the available information only enough to select and predict a language structure which is decodable. It is not in any sense a precise perceptual process. (Goodman, 1973b:164)

These views are by now generally well known and widely accepted in our field.

Coady (1979) has elaborated on this basic psycholinguistic model and has suggested a model in which the EFL/ESL reader's background knowledge interacts with conceptual abilities and process strategies, more or less successfully, to produce comprehension (see Figure 17.1).

By *conceptual ability,* Coady means general intellectual capacity. By *processing strategies,* Coady means various subcomponents of reading ability, including many which are also more general language processing skills which also apply to oral language (e.g., grapheme-morpho-phoneme correspondences, syllable-morpheme information, syntactic information [deep and surface], lexical meaning, and contextual meaning). Coady says little more about the role of

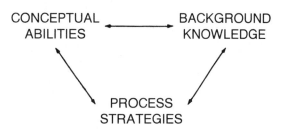

Figure 17.1 Coady's (1979) Model of the ESL Reader

background knowledge other than to observe that

> background knowledge becomes an important variable when we notice, as many have, that students with a Western background of some kind learn English faster, on the average, than those without such a background. (Coady, 1979:7)

Coady also suggests that background knowledge may be able to compensate for certain syntactic deficiencies:

> The subject of reading materials should be of high interest and relate well to the background of the reader, since strong semantic input can help compensate when syntactic control is weak. The interest and background knowledge will enable the student to comprehend at a reasonable rate and keep him involved in the material in spite of its syntactic difficulty. (Coady, 1979:12)

It is this third factor, background knowledge, that has been the most neglected in EFL/ ESL reading. Even though the psycholinguistic model of reading is seen as an interaction of factors, it has generally failed to give sufficient emphasis to the role of background knowledge. Recent research indicates that what the reader brings to the reading task is more pervasive and more powerful than the general psycholinguistic model suggests:

> More information is contributed by the reader than by the print on the page. That is, readers understand what they read because they are able to take the stimulus beyond its graphic representation and assign it membership to an appropriate group of concepts already stored in their memories. . . . The reader brings to the task a formidable amount of information and ideas, attitudes and beliefs. This knowledge, coupled with the ability to make linguistic predictions, determines the expectations the reader will develop as he reads. Skill in reading depends on the efficient interaction between linguistic knowledge and knowledge of the world. (Clarke and Silberstein, 1977:136–137)

THE SCHEMA THEORY MODEL

The role of background knowledge in language comprehension has been formalized as *schema theory* (Bartlett, 1932; Rumelhart and Ortony, 1977; Rumelhart, 1980), which has as one of its fundamental tenets that text, any text, either spoken or written, does not by itself carry meaning. Rather, according to schema theory, a text only provides directions for listeners or readers as to how they should retrieve or construct meaning from their own, previously acquired knowledge. This previously acquired knowledge is called the reader's *background knowledge,* and the previously acquired knowledge structures are called *schemata* (Bartlett, 1932; Adams and Collins, 1979, Rumelhart, 1980).[1] According to scheme theory, compre-

hending a text is an interactive process between the reader's background knowledge and the text. Efficient comprehension requires the ability to relate the textual material to one's own knowledge. Comprehending words, sentences, and entire texts involves more than just relying on one's linguistic knowledge. As the opening quote from Anderson et al. points out, "every act of comprehension involves one's knowledge of the world as well" (Anderson et al., 1977: 369).

According to schema theory, the process of interpretation is guided by the principle that every input is mapped against some existing schema and that all aspects of that schema must be compatible with the input information. This principle results in two basic modes of information processing, called *bottom-up* and *top-down* processing. Bottom-up processing is evoked by the incoming data; the features of the data enter the system through the best fitting, bottom-level schemata. Schemata are hierarchically organized, from most general at the top to most specific at the bottom. As these bottom-level schemata converge into higher level, more general schemata, these too become activated. Bottom-up processing is, therefore, called *data-driven*. Top-down processing, on the other hand, occurs as the system makes general predictions based on higher level, general schemata and then searches the input for information to fit into these partially satisfied, higher order schemata. Top-down processing is, therefore, called *conceptually driven*.

An important aspect of top-down and bottom-up processing is that both should be occurring at all levels simultaneously (Rumelhart, 1980). The data that are needed to *instantiate,* or fill out, the schemata become available through bottom-up processing; top-down processing facilitates their assimilation if they are anticipated by or consistent with the listener/reader's conceptual expectations. Bottom-up processing ensures that the listeners/readers will be sensitive to information that is novel or that does not fit their ongoing hypotheses about the content or structure of the text; top-down processing helps the listeners/readers to resolve ambiguities or to select between alternative possible interpretations of the incoming data.

To illustrate the effects of background knowledge, schematic interpretation, and the simultaneity of top-down and bottom-up processing, consider the following mini-text (originally from Collins and Quillian, 1972; discussed in Rumelhart, 1977:267):

The policeman held up his hand and stopped the car.

In the process of trying to understand this sentence, we try to relate it to something familiar, some schema which will account for the event described. There are many schemata possible, but perhaps the most likely is the one involving a traffic cop who is signaling to a driver of a car to stop. Notice that when we interpret this mini-text against that schema, a number of related concepts come to the fore which are not literally mentioned in the text. In particular, we imagine that the car has a driver and that the policeman got the car to stop through signaling to the driver, who then put on the brakes of the car, which, in turn, caused the car to stop. The proximal cause of the car's stopping is, in this interpretation, the operation of the car's brakes. Further, the significance of the policeman's holding up his hand is that of a signal to the driver to stop. This fact is neither stated in the sentence nor is it even in the direct visual perception of such a situation, but is rather a fact in our prior cultural knowledge about the way traffic police are known to communicate with automobile drivers. Notice how the interpretation of the text would change if the policeman were known to be Superman and the car were known to be without a driver. A completely different schema would be required to understand the text. Notice how the relationship of the policeman's holding up his hand and the car's stopping takes on an entirely different interpretation when the text is interpreted against the Superman schema. Now, holding up the hand is not interpreted as a signal at all, but rather the direct physical mechanism for stopping the car. In this interpretation, the hand actually comes into physical contact with the car and is the proximal physical cause of the car's halting. The brakes of the car do not come into play in this schema.

Notice how sets of inferential reading comprehension questions would receive diametrically opposed answers depending upon which of the two schemata was activated in the mind of the reader:

Question	Answer	
	Traffic cop schema	**Superman schema**
Did the policeman's hand touch the car?	No	Yes
Were the car's brakes applied?	Yes	No

Now let us consider a slightly longer text from Rumelhart:

> Mary heard the ice cream man coming down the street. She remembered her birthday money and rushed into the house. . . . (1977: 265)

Upon reading just these few lines, most readers are able to construct a rather complete interpretation of the text. Presumably, Mary is a little girl who heard the ice cream man coming and wanted to buy some ice cream from this ice cream man. Buying ice cream costs money, so she had to think quickly of a source of funds. She remembered some money which she had been given for her birthday and which, presumably, was in the house. So she hurried into the house to try to get the money before the ice cream man arrived. Of course, the text does not say all of this; we readers are inferring a lot of this in giving the text an interpretation. Other interpretations are also possible. Yet, most readers will probably give this text an interpretation quite similar to the one suggested here, and most readers will retain this interpretation unless some contradictory information is encountered. Notice what happens if the reader next encounters the phrase:

> . . . and locked the door.[2]

The reader is unable to fit this new piece of textual input information into the developing interpretation. The reader is forced to revise the interpretation in such a way as to make this new information compatible with the previous infor-

mation—to make the whole text cohere. If there were no such thing as schemata guiding the developing interpretation in a top-down processing mode, causing the reader to make conceptual predictions about the meaning of the text, then why would encountering the added phrase cause the reaction it does in the reader? What has happened, we claim, is that as long as the incoming information being processed through bottom-up processing and the conceptual predictions being made through top-down processing are compatible, we have a satisfactory interpretation of the text. When we encounter a mismatch between the top-down predictions and the bottom-up information, we are forced to revise the interpretation in such a way as to make the two compatible once again. In this example, we must revise our interpretation to accommodate the information about Mary's locking the door. Perhaps we infer that for some reason Mary is afraid that the ice cream man might steal her birthday money and that she locks the door to protect it and herself. We believe these two examples vividly demonstrate the existence and operation of schemata in the process of text interpretation.

Thus, it seems clear that readers activate an appropriate schema against which they try to give a text a consistent interpretation. To the extent that they are successful, we may say that they have comprehended the text. However, one potential source of reading difficulties may be that the reader has a consistent interpretation for the text, but it may not be the one intended by the author. Nonetheless, the basic point is that much of the meaning understood from a text is really not actually in the text, per se, but in the reader, in the background or schematic knowledge of the reader. What is understood from a text is a function of the particular schema that is activated at the time of processing (i.e., reading) the text.

In seeking to understand the role of background knowledge in reading comprehension, it is often useful to draw a distinction between *formal* schemata (background knowledge of the formal, rhetorical organizational structures of different types of texts) and *content* schemata (background knowledge of the content area of a text) (Carrell, 1983b). In other words, one type of schema which readers are said to possess is background knowledge about, and expectations of, differences among rhetorical structures, such as differences in genre, differences in the structure of fables, simple stories, scientific texts, newspaper articles, poetry, and so forth. Our schema for simple stories, for example, includes the information that the story should have, minimally, a setting, a beginning, a development, and an ending. Also for simple stories, Mandler (1978) distinguishes between schemata for causally connected and temporally connected stories. For expository texts, Meyer and her colleagues (Meyer, 1975, 1977, 1981; Meyer and Rice, 1982) recognize five different types of expository rhetorical organization: *collection*—list, *causation*—cause and effect, *response*—problem and solution, *comparison*—comparison and contrast, and *description*—attribution. Each of these types, they say, represents a different abstract schema of ways writers organize and readers understand topics.

In schema theory research, this type of *formal* schematic knowledge is usually contrasted with *content* schematic knowledge, which is claimed to be background knowledge about the content area of a text, such as a text about washing clothes, celebrating New Year's Eve in Hawaii or Halloween in Carbondale, or about the economy of Mexico, the history of Canada, problems of nuclear breeder reactors, and so forth.

A reader's failure to activate an appropriate schema (formal or content) during reading results in various degrees of non-comprehension. This failure to activate an appropriate schema may either be due to the writer's not having provided sufficient clues in the text for the reader to effectively utilize a bottom-up processing mode to activate schemata the reader may

already possess, or it may be due to the fact that the reader does not possess the appropriate schema anticipated by the author and thus fails to comprehend: In both instances there is a mismatch between what the writer anticipates the reader can do to extract meaning from the text and what the reader is actually able to do. The point is that the appropriate schemata must exist and must be activated during text processing.

One of the most obvious reasons why a particular content schema may fail to exist for a reader is that the schema is culturally specific and is not part of a particular reader's cultural background. Studies by Steffensen, Joag-dev, and Anderson (1979), Johnson (1981), and Carrell (1981a) have shown that the implicit cultural content knowledge presupposed by a text interacts with the reader's own cultural background knowledge of content to make texts whose content is based on one's own culture easier to read and understand than syntactically and rhetorically equivalent texts based on a less familiar, more distant culture.

Other research has shown general effects of content schemata on EFL/ESL reading comprehension. Johnson (1982) has shown that a text on a familiar topic is better recalled by ESL readers than a similar text on an unfamiliar topic. Hudson (1982) reports a study showing an interaction between overall linguistic proficiency in ESL and content-induced schematic effects in ESL reading comprehension. Specifically, that study demonstrates the facilitating effects on comprehension of explicitly inducing content schemata through pre-reading activities, especially at the beginning and intermediate proficiency levels, as compared to two other methods of inducing content schemata (through vocabulary activities and read-reread activities). Finally, Alderson and Urquhart (1983) have found a discipline-specific effect of content background knowledge in measuring reading comprehension in ESP/EST.

Several recent studies have shown the effects

of formal, rhetorical schemata in EFL/ESL. In a study by Carrell (1981b), two groups of university-bound, intermediate-level ESL subjects each read a different type of simple story—one type well structured according to a simple story schema structure and the other type deliberately violating the story schema structure. Results showed that when stories violating the story schema are processed by second language learners, both the quantity of recall and the temporal sequences of recall are affected. In other words, when the content is kept constant but the rhetorical structure is varied, second language reading comprehension is affected.

Studies done in the area of contrastive rhetoric (Kaplan, 1966) also demonstrate the effects of formal schemata on both the comprehension and production of written texts in a second language (Ostler and Kaplan, 1982). In particular, Hinds' research (1982, 1983) shows the contrasting effects on different groups of readers of typical Japanese rhetorical organization and typical English rhetorical organization. Burtoff (1983) has found differences among the typical rhetorical patterns of expository prose produced by writers with different formal schemata according to their native-language/native-culture backgrounds.

Thus, a growing body of empirical research attests to the role of both content and formal schemata in EFL/ESL reading comprehension and to the potential cultural specificity of both types of schemata. In the following sections, we focus on the implications of the cultural specificity of content schemata for EFL/ESL readers and EFL/ESL reading methodology.

IMPLICATIONS FOR EFL/ESL READERS

Given the role of content schemata in reading comprehension, there are obvious implications for the EFL/ESL reader. The background knowledge that second language readers bring to a text is often culture-specific. Hudson notes that

> the reading problems of the L_2 reader are not due to an absence of attempts at fitting and providing specific schemata . . . Rather, the problem lies in projecting appropriate schemata. (Hudson, 1982:9)

Second language readers attempt to provide schemata to make sense of texts, and they do so persistently. However, these efforts will fail if the reader cannot access the appropriate existing schemata, or if the reader does not possess the appropriate schemata necessary to understand a text.

Most commonly, accessing appropriate content schemata depends initially on textual cues; the graphic display must be somehow reconstructed by the reader as meaningful language. At this point, general language processing skills are most important. For second language readers, then, obviously *some* language proficiency is required to activate relevant schemata, and it is not surprising that failures to access appropriate schemata (i.e., comprehend) are often interpreted solely as deficiencies in language processing skills. Consequently, poor readers are encouraged to expand their vocabularies and to gain greater control over complex syntactic structures in order to improve reading comprehension. Indeed, some reading problems are related to such language skill deficiencies. However, as we have noted, reading comprehension depends crucially on the reader's being able to relate information from the text to already existing background knowledge.

In the EFL/ESL classroom, we must be particularly sensitive to reading problems that result from the implicit cultural knowledge presupposed by a text. A review of the literature in EFL/ESL methodology shows that the role of cultural knowledge as a factor in reading comprehension has been an issue for some time. Fries (1945, 1963) talked about meaning at the social-cultural level—that is, the meaning that transcends the language code and is related to the background knowledge of the native speakers of that code. Reading comprehension occurs when the total meaning of a passage is fitted into this network of information organized in ways meaningful to a society. The following passage from an ESL reading text[3] illustrates Fries' concept of social-cultural meaning:

By voting against mass transportation, voters have chosen to continue on a road to ruin. Our interstate highways, those much praised golden avenues built to whisk suburban travelers in and out of downtown have turned into the world's most expensive parking lots. That expense is not only economic—it is social. These highways have created great walls separating neighborhood from neighborhood, disrupting the complex social connections that help make a city livable. (Baudoin et al., 1977: 159)

In reading this passage, some ESL students fail to perceive the connection between mass transportation and highways. In the United States, where individual ownership of cars results in an overabundance of highways and a reduced need for mass transportation, this passage makes sense. Sometimes, however, students perceive that highways are built *for* mass transportation, which renders this passage (and especially the critical reading question which asks whether the author supports the idea of mass transportation) at best illogical, at worst incomprehensible.

The social-cultural meaning in this passage relates to the culture-specific schema of the cars/mass transportation opposition. Furthermore, comprehension can also be related to semantic associations available when a schema is accessed. The notion of interstate highways, here referred to narrowly as those in urban

areas, invites the semantic associations of crowding, congestion, and rush hour traffic. The meaning of the phrase *the world's most expensive parking lots* is associated with, and can only be understood with reference to, this specific *urban* highway subschema.

Elsewhere in the EFL/ESL methodology literature, Rivers (1968) recommends that the strong bond between culture and language must be maintained for the student to have a complete understanding of the meaning of language. She believes that differences in values and attitudes are one of the main sources of problems in foreign language learning. Culture-specific values can be a significant factor in comprehension if the values expressed by the text differ from the values held by the reader. Devout Muslim students, for example, tend to have problems with the following passage:

There is a question about the extent to which any one of us can be free of a prejudiced view in the area of religion. (Baudoin et al., 1977: 185)

While this sentence is excellent for developing critical reading skills, the mention of religion in this context does not coincide with Islamic values. A subsequent exercise requires the student to analyze the relation of the original text to the following sentence: *Because we can't be free of prejudice in the area of religion, we should not practice a religion.* One student refused to even consider the premise of this sentence; his only comment: "For me, it's false."

More recently, Rivers and Temperley (1978) have emphasized the importance of providing background information, explaining high-frequency but culturally loaded terms, and using illustrations with reading passages to provide additional meaning to texts. The important point is that problems with individual lexical items may not be as pervasive as problems related to the absence of appropriate generalized information assumed by the writer and possessed by a reader sharing that writer's cultural background.

The relevance of appropriate generalized, underlying information is illustrated by the following text:

> Although housewives still make up the majority of volunteer groups, male participation is reported on the rise nationwide as traditional distinctions between men's work and women's work begin to fade. (Baudoin et al., 1977:184).

The phrase *volunteer groups* requires appropriate underlying information before this sentence can be understood. Although the lexical items *volunteer* and *groups* were clearly understood by one student, the concept of *volunteer groups* (predominantly female, unpaid social workers) was clearly not understood since he wondered if these women had volunteered to be housewives.

Paulston and Bruder (1976) also discuss covert information and reading. Proficient readers, they say, must draw on their own experience in order to supply a semantic component to a message. They argue that texts with familiar settings and even specialized low-frequency vocabulary are appropriate (even though the texts may "feel" as if they are not appropriate) because they are relevant to the students' world (and are, thus, easier to read). Robinett (1978) agrees that covert cultural information is a factor in reading performance and suggests that the teacher facilitate reading by providing specific background experience.

When covert information is assumed by the writer, it must be supplied by the reader and is sometimes done so erroneously.

> I saw by the clock of the city jail that it was past eleven, so I decided to go to the newspaper immediately. (Baudoin et al., 1977:83)

After reading this sentence, one student was convinced that the writer had been in jail at the time because, as he said, "an outside clock is only on a church." He had concluded that the only place the writer could have seen *the clock of the city jail* was from inside the jail itself. If this sentence merely "sets the scene," then this misinterpretation is insignificant. However, if the misreading causes the reader to consider such a scene significant (when it is not), or to dismiss it as *in*significant (when it is not), then a serious comprehension problem has resulted.

Finally in the methodology literature, Marquardt's work (1967, 1969) is representative of the pedagogical approach that holds that reading should be in the literature of the target culture for the express purpose of teaching that culture to foreign students. Such literature, however, must be chosen carefully. Consider the following passage from *Cheaper by the Dozen:*

> Mother the psychologist and Dad the motion study man and general contractor decided to look into the new field of the psychology of management, and the old field of psychologically managing a houseful of children. They believed that what would work in the home would work in the factory, and what would work in the factory would work in the home.
>
> Dad put the theory to a test shortly after we moved to Montclair. The house was too big for Tom Grieves, the handyman, and Mrs. Cunningham, the cook, to keep in order. Dad decided we were going to have to help them, and he wanted us to offer the help willingly. He had found that the best way to get cooperation out of employees in a factory was set up a joint employer-employee board, which would make work assignments on a basis of personal choice and aptitude. He and Mother set up a Family Council, patterned after an employer-employee board. The Council met every Sunday afternoon, immediately after dinner. (Baudoin et al., 1977:91)

This text would require considerable background teaching before the text itself could teach anything (even if we considered what it has to teach to be culturally relevant). Using literature to teach *culture* may be the most direct way to teach culture, but it certainly implies thorough background preparation and may, in fact, not be the best way to teach *language.*

There is much in these methods that is of value, but in light of the broad message behind the schema-theoretic view of reading, are they sufficiently sensitive to cross-cultural interference at all levels of meaning? The factors noted above are important not just to "ground" words and phrases for the reader. Rather, notions such

as *social-cultural meaning, culture-specific values,* and *covert information* refer to different aspects of the same problem, and that is how to deal with reading difficulties caused by the mismatch of the background knowledge presupposed by the text and the background knowledge possessed by the reader. A schema-theoretic view of reading suggests the pervasive effects of such a mismatch and requires our being sensitive to these reading difficulties on a more global level.

CLASSROOM ACTIVITIES

Our immediate goal as EFL/ESL reading teachers is to minimize reading difficulties and to maximize comprehension by providing culturally relevant information. Goodman puts the issue into focus when he says that

> even highly effective readers are severely limited in comprehension of texts by what they already know before they read. The author may influence the comprehensibility of a text particularly for specific targeted audiences. But no author can completely compensate in writing for the range of differences among all potential readers of a given text. (Goodman, 1979:658)

Since no author can compensate for the individual variation among readers, especially readers from different cultural backgrounds, this is one of the roles of the teacher in the EFL/ESL reading classroom. As teachers we can approach this problem by manipulating either one of the two variables: the text and/or the reader.

Text

What can we do with texts to minimize cultural conflicts and interference and to maximize

comprehension? For the beginning reader, the Language Experience Approach (LEA) (Rigg, 1981) is an excellent way to control vocabulary, structure, and content. The basic LEA technique uses the students' ideas and the students' own words in the preparation of beginning reading materials. The students decide what they want to say and how to say it, and then dictate to the teacher, who acts as a scribe. LEA works when the students' beginning reading materials, developed by them with the teacher's help, have the students' ideas in their own words. LEA works because students tend to be able to read what they have just said. The students, in effect, write their own texts, neutralizing problems of unfamiliar content.

Another way to minimize interference from the text is to encourage narrow reading, as suggested by Krashen (1981). Narrow reading refers to reading that is confined to a single topic or to the texts of a single author. Krashen suggests that "narrow reading, and perhaps narrow input in general, is more efficient for second language acquisition" (Krashen, 1981:23). Reading teachers usually provide short and varied selections which never allow students to adjust to an author's style, to become familiar with the specialized vocabulary of the topic, or to develop enough context to facilitate comprehension. Rather, such selections force students to move from frustration to frustration.

However, students who read either a single topic or a single author find that the text becomes easier to comprehend after the first few pages. Readers adjust either to the repeated vocabulary of a particular topic or to the particular style of a writer. Furthermore, repetitions of vocabulary and structure mean that review is built into the reading. The significant advantage from the schema-theoretic point of view is that schemata are repeatedly accessed and further expanded and refined, resulting in increased comprehension.

The third possibility of text facilitation is to develop materials along the lines of those proposed by Paulston and Bruder (1976). As we have noted, they suggest using texts with local settings and specialized low-frequency vocabulary. These materials might be student or local newspapers, pamphlets, brochures, or booklets about local places of interest. English travel guides or *National Geographic*-type articles from the students' own countries are also good sources for the EFL/ESL reader.

Finally, Sustained Silent Reading (SSR) is an excellent activity for ESL readers. Through silent reading of texts, students become self-directed agents seeking meaning. To be effective, however, an SSR program must be based on student-selected texts so that the students will be interested in what they are reading. Students select their own reading texts with respect to content, level of difficulty, and length. What is important, from our point of view, is that readers tend to be interested in reading texts that are relevant to their own experiences. Students who choose their own texts are, in effect, also providing their own appropriate background knowledge for understanding the text.

Reader

Instead of, or in addition to, text control, we also need to consider what we can do with the readers themselves. Providing background information and previewing content for the reader seem to be the most obvious strategies for the language teacher. We want to avoid having students read material "cold." Asking students to manipulate both the linguistic and cultural codes (sometimes linguistically easy but culturally difficult, and vice versa) is asking too much.

Providing background information and previewing are particularly important for the less proficient language student (see the findings of Hudson, 1982). These readers are more word-bound, and meaning tends to break down at the word level. Thus, less proficient students tend to have vocabulary acquisition emphasized and, as such, are encouraged to do a lot of specific (and less efficient) word-by-word processing exclusively in a bottom-up processing mode. Readers who are more proficient in a language tend to receive content previews because they are no longer as susceptible to vocabulary and structure difficulties in reading. As a result, these more proficient students are encouraged to do more global, predictive (and more efficient) processing in the top-down processing mode. One thing we surely want to remind ourselves of, however, is that less proficient readers also need familiar content selections and/or content preview as much as, if not more than, more proficient readers. Illustrations may be particularly appropriate for students with minimal language skills. Providing the semantic content component for low-level readers will free them to focus on vocabulary and structure expressive of that content.

Previewing is an important activity in the reading classroom, but it is not necessarily a process of simply providing a preliminary outline of what is to be read. Sometimes, it involves teaching a key concept which is culturally loaded such as the one in the short story *The Lottery* (Baudoin et al., 1977:140–145). If one does not understand the process or purpose of a lottery, then this short story about one woman who "wins" and is then killed by her neighbors will be totally incomprehensible. In this case, a discussion of lotteries before assigning the reading would be absolutely necessary.

Previewing can also include presenting specialized vocabulary and structures that the teacher predicts will cause difficulties. In the mass transportation passage cited earlier, students who could not come up with the appropriate background information also had difficulty with the phrase *road to ruin (a road for ruining, as in an apple to eat?) and expensive parking lots (parking will be expensive?).* Even a sentence that supposedly contains within it enough experiential context to explain the word *mildew* is often incomprehensible to many students from arid regions: *What could John expect? He had left his wet swimming trunks in the dark closet for over a week. Of course they had begun to mildew* (Baudoin et al., 1977:5).

Finally, by carefully listening to what our students say about the texts they are asked to read, we can become further sensitized to their hidden comprehension problems. As teachers, we should not respond to what the reader does (right/wrong) as much as to what the reader is *trying* to do. Given that the reader is trying to make sense of the text (construct meaning), a teacher who listens carefully and responds to a student's efforts will become aware of both the background knowledge and the cultural problems that students themselves bring to the text. In any case, the most valuable information is in our students' perceptions and not our own. This is the type of information that is gleaned through asking open-ended questions, probing for inferences from the text, and asking students to justify answers to more direct questions (for example, "Why do you think so?"). In addition, having students provide oral or written summaries will help teachers to discern problem areas in comprehension.

CONCLUSION

Thus, in achieving our immediate goals in the EFL/ESL reading classroom, we must strive for an optimum balance between the background knowledge presupposed by the texts our students read and the background knowledge our students possess. As we have shown by means of the foregoing classroom activities and techniques, this balance may be achieved by manipulating either the text and/or the reader variable.

Of course, our long-range goal as reading teachers is to develop independent readers outside the EFL/ESL classroom, readers whose purpose in learning to read in English as a foreign or second language is to *learn* from the texts they read.[4] But there, too, as Anderson notes, "without some schema into which it can be assimilated, an experience is incomprehensible, and therefore, little can be *learned* from it" (Anderson, 1977:429; emphasis added).

What makes the classroom activities and other techniques we have described valid is their applicability to the "real" world beyond the EFL/ESL reading classroom. Every culture-specific interference problem dealt with in the classroom presents an opportunity to build new culture-specific schemata that will be available to the EFL/ESL student outside the classroom. In addition, however, and possibly more importantly, the process of identifying and dealing with cultural interference in reading should make our EFL/ESL students more sensitive to such interference when they read on their own. By using the classroom activities and techniques we have described, our EFL/ESL readers should become more aware that reading is a highly interactive process between themselves and their prior background knowledge, on the one hand, and the text itself, on the other.

NOTES

1. Other closely related concepts, which are technically distinct from *schemata* but which may be thought of as part of the same general, cognitive approach to text processing, are *scripts, plans,* and *goals* (Schank and Abelson, 1977), *frames* (Minsky, 1975; Fillmore, 1976; Tannen, 1979), *expectations* (Tannen, 1978), and *event chains* (Warren, Nicholas, and Trabasso, 1979). All of these terms emanate from basic research at the intersection of artificial intelligence, cognitive psychology, and linguistics in the new discipline called *cognitive science.* These terms are not identical or even interchangeable; however, they may all be broadly characterized as part of a schema-theoretical orientation to text processing.

Carrell (1983a) gives an extensive overview of schema theory and the relevant theoretical literature as well as the empirical research in first language processing (children and adults) and second language processing (adults).

2. This example was offered by Charles J. Fillmore in a class lecture at the University of California, Berkeley, in 1980.

3. The passages chosen to illustrate reading problems related to culture-specific background information are all drawn from *Reader's Choice* (Baudoin, Bober, Clarke, Dobson, and Silberstein, 1977), a widely used and widely respected ESL reading text. The difficulties noted with the passages from this text are in no way intended as a criticism of the book, which we consider an excellent text based on psycholinguistic principles. Rather, these passages were chosen because they caused actual classroom problems and because they illustrate often subtle or hidden problems which we, as EFL/ESL teachers, may find difficult to identify.

4. We use the phrase "reading to *learn* from texts" in the broadest sense, including reading for academic purposes, reading for survival purposes or for purposes of functioning in society at various levels, and even reading for recreation or entertainment.

REFERENCES

Adams, Marilyn J., and Allan Collins. 1979. A schema-theoretic view of reading. In *New Directions in Discourse Processing,* Roy O. Freedle (ed.) 1–22. Norwood, NJ: Ablex Publishing Corporation.

Alderson, J. Charles, and Alexander Urquhart. 1983. This test is unfair: I'm not an economist. Paper presented at the 17th Annual TESOL Convention Toronto, Canada, March, 1983.

Anderson, Richard C. 1977. The notion of schemata and the educational enterprise: General discussion of the conference. In *Schooling and the Acquisition of Knowledge,* Richard C. Anderson, Rand J. Spiro, and William E. Montague (eds.), 415-431. Hillsdale, NJ: Lawrence Erlbaum Associates.

Anderson, Richard C., Ralph E. Reynolds, Diane L. Schallert, and Ernest T. Goetz. 1977. Frameworks for comprehending discourse. *American Educational Research Journal* 14(4):367–381.

Bartlett, Frederic C. 1932. *Remembering: A Study in Experimental and Social Psychology.* Cambridge: Cambridge University Press.

Baudoin, E. Margaret, Ellen S. Bober Mark A. Clarke, Barbara K. Dobson, and Sandra Silberstein. 1977. *Reader's Choice: A Reading Skills Textbook for Students of English as a Second Language.* Ann Arbor: University of Michigan Press.

Burtoff, Michele. 1983. Organizational patterns of expository prose: A comparative study of native Arabic, Japanese and English speakers. Paper presented at the 17th Annual TESOL Convention, Toronto, Canada, March, 1983.

Carrell, Patricia L. 1981a. Culture-specific schemata

in L2 comprehension. In *Selected Papers from the Ninth Illinois TESOL/BE Annual Convention, the First Midwest TESOL Conference,* Richard Orem and John Haskell (eds.), 123–132. Chicago: Illinois TESOL/BE.

Carrell, Patricia L. 1981b. The role of schemata in L2 comprehension. Paper presented at the 15th Annual TESOL Convention, Detroit, Michigan, March, 1981.

Carrell, Patricia L. 1983a. Background knowledge in second language comprehension. *Language Learning and Communication* 2(1):25–34.

Carrell, Patricia L. 1983b. Some issues in studying the role of schemata, or background knowledge, in second language comprehension. Paper presented at the 17th Annual TESOL Convention, Toronto, Canada, March, 1983.

Clarke, Mark A., and Sandra Silberstein. 1977. Toward a realization of psycholinguistic principles in the ESL reading class. *Language Learning* 27(1): 135–154.

Coady, James. 1979. A psycholinguistic model of the ESL reader. In *Reading in a Second Language,* Ronald Mackay, Bruce Barkman, and R. R. Jordan (eds.), 5–12. Rowley, MA: Newbury House Publishers.

Collins, Allan M., and M. Ross Quillian. 1972. How to make a language user. In *Organization of Memory,* Endel Tulving and Wayne Donaldson (eds.), 310–351. New York: Academic Press.

Fillmore, Charles J. 1976. The need for a frame semantics within linguistics. In *Statistical Methods in Linguistics,* 5–29. Stockholm: Sprakforlaget Skriptor.

Fries, Charles C. 1945. *Teaching and Learning English as a Foreign Language.* Ann Arbor: University of Michigan Press.

Fries, Charles C. 1963. *Linguistics and Reading.* New York: Holt, Rinehart and Winston.

Goodman, Kenneth S. 1967. Reading: A psycholinguistic guessing game. *Journal of the Reading Specialist* 6(1):126–135.

Goodman, Kenneth S. 1971. Psycholinguistic universals in the reading process. In *The Psychology of Second Language Learning,* Paul Pimsleur and Terence Quinn (eds.), 135–142. Cambridge: Cambridge University Press.

Goodman, Kenneth S. 1973a. On the psycholinguistic method of teaching reading. In *Psycholinguis-*

tics and Reading, Frank Smith (ed.), 177–182. New York: Holt, Rinehart and Winston.

Goodman, Kenneth S. 1973b. Analysis of oral reading miscues: Applied psycholinguistics. In *Psycholinguistics and Reading,* Frank Smith (ed.), 158–176. New York: Holt, Rinehart and Winston.

Goodman, Kenneth S. 1979. The know-more and the know-nothing movements in reading: A personal response. *Language Arts* 55(6):657–663.

Hinds, John. 1982. Contrastive rhetoric: Japanese and English. Paper presented at the 16th Annual TESOL Convention, Honolulu, Hawaii, May, 1982.

Hinds, John. 1983. Retention of information using a Japanese style of presentation. Paper presented at the 17th Annual TESOL Convention, Toronto, Canada, March, 1983.

Hudson, Thom. 1982. The effects of induced schemata on the "short circuit" in L2 reading: Non-decoding factors in L2 reading performance. *Language Learning* 32(1):1–31.

Johnson, Patricia. 1981. Effects on reading comprehension of language complexity and cultural background of a text. *TESOL Quarterly* 15(2): 169–181.

Johnson, Patricia. 1982. Effects on reading comprehension of building background knowledge. *TESOL Quarterly* 16(4):503–516.

Kant, Immanuel. 1963. *Critique of Pure Reason.* (1st ed. 1781, 2nd ed. 1787, N. Kemp Smith, translator.) London: MacMillan Publishing Co.

Kaplan, Robert B. 1966. Cultural thought patterns in inter-cultural education. *Language Learning* 16(1–2):1–20.

Krashen, Stephen D. 1981. The case for narrow reading. *TESOL Newsletter* 15(6):23.

Mandler, Jean M. 1978. A code in the node: The use of a story schema in retrieval. *Discourse Processes* 1(1):14–35.

Marquardt, William F. 1967. Literature and cross-culture communication in the course in English for international students. *The Florida Foreign Language Reporter* 5(1):9–10.

Marquardt, William F. 1969. Creating empathy through literature between members of the mainstream culture and disadvantaged learners of the minority cultures. *The Florida Foreign Language Reporter* 7(1):133–141, 157.

Meyer, Bonnie J. F. 1975. *The Organization of Prose*

and its Effects on Memory. Amsterdam: North-Holland Publishing Co.

Meyer, Bonnie J. F. 1977. The structure of prose: Effects on learning and memory and implications for educational practice. In *Schooling and the Acquisition of Knowledge,* Richard C. Anderson, Rand J. Spiro, and William E. Montague (eds.), 179–208. Hillsdale, NJ: Lawrence Erlbaum Associates.

Meyer, Bonnie J. F. 1981. Basic research on prose comprehension: A critical review. In *Comprehension and the Competent Reader: Inter-Specialty Perspectives,* Dennis F. Fisher and Charles W. Peters (eds.), 8–35. New York: Praeger.

Meyer, Bonnie J. F., and G. Elizabeth Rice. 1982. The interaction of reader strategies and the organization of text. *Text* 2(1–3):155–192.

Minsky, Marvin. 1975. A framework for representing knowledge. In *The Psychology of Computer Vision,* Patrick Henry Winston (ed.), 211–277. New York: McGraw-Hill.

Ostler, Shirley E., and Robert B. Kaplan. 1982. Contrastive rhetoric revisited. Paper presented at the 16th Annual TESOL Convention, Honolulu, Hawaii, May, 1982.

Paulston, Christina Bratt, and Mary N. Bruder. 1976. *Teaching English as a Second Language: Techniques and Procedures.* Cambridge, MA: Winthrop.

Rigg, Pat. 1981. Beginning to read in English the LEA way. In *Reading English as a Second Language: Moving from Theory,* C. W. Twyford, William Diehl, and Karen Feathers (eds.), 81–90. *Monographs in Language and Reading Studies* 4. Bloomington, IN: Indiana University.

Rivers, Wilga M. 1968. *Teaching Foreign Language Skills.* Chicago: University of Chicago Press.

Rivers, Wilga M., and Mary S. Temperley. 1978. *A Practical Guide to the Teaching of English as a Second or Foreign Language.* New York: Oxford University Press.

Robinett, Betty Wallace. 1978. *Teaching English to Speakers of Other Languages.* New York: McGraw-Hill.

Rumelhart, David E. 1977. Understanding and summarizing brief stories. In *Basic Processes in Reading: Perception and Comprehension,* David LaBerge and S. Jay Samuels (eds.), 265–303. Hillsdale, NJ: Lawrence Erlbaum Associates.

Rumelhart, David E. 1980. Schemata: The building blocks of cognition. In *Theoretical Issues in Reading Comprehension,* Rand J. Spiro, Bertram C. Bruce, and William E. Brewer (eds.), 33–58. Hillsdale, NJ: Lawrence Erlbaum Associates.

Rumelhart, David E., and Andrew Ortony. 1977. The representation of knowledge in memory. In *Schooling and the Acquisition of Knowledge,* Richard C. Anderson, Rand J. Spiro, and William E. Montague (eds.), 99–135. Hillsdale, NJ: Lawrence Erlbaum Associates.

Schank, Roger C., and Robert P. Abelson. 1977. *Scripts, Plans, Goals and Understanding.* Hillsdale, NJ: Lawrence Erlbaum Associates.

Smith, Frank. 1971. *Understanding Reading: A Psycholinguistic Analysis of Reading and Learning to Read.* New York: Holt, Rinehart and Winston.

Steffensen, Margaret S., Chitra Joag-dev, and Richard C. Anderson. 1979. A cross-cultural perspective on reading comprehension. *Reading Research Quarterly* 15(1):10–29.

Tannen, Deborah. 1978. The effect of expectations on conversation. *Discourse Processes* 1(2):203–209.

Tannen, Deborah. 1979. What's in a frame? Surface evidence for underlying expectations. In *New Directions in Discourse Processing,* Roy O. Freedle (ed.), 137–181. Norwood, NJ: Ablex Publishing Corporation.

Warren, William H., David W. Nicholas, and Tom Trabasso. 1979. Event chains and inferences in understanding narratives. In *New Directions in Discourse Processing,* Roy O. Freedle (ed.), 23–52. Norwood, NJ: Ablex Publishing Corporation.

CHAPTER 18

Toward a Realization of Psycholinguistic Principles in the ESL Reading Class

Mark A. Clarke
Sandra Silberstein

This article is an attempt to utilize psycholinguistic research to develop a framework for the teaching of reading to second language (L2) learners. The first section highlights current psycholinguistic reading theory and develops goals for L2 reading teachers based on this theory. The proficient reader is viewed as an active, information-processing individual who uses a minimum number of clues to extract the author's message from the page. It becomes the responsibility of teachers to train students to determine their own goals and strategies for a particular reading, to give students practice and encouragement in using a minimum number of syntactic and semantic clues to obtain the maximum amount of information, and to encourage students to take risks, to guess, and to ignore their impulses to be always correct. In an attempt to translate theory into practice, the second section of the article explores the implications of a psycholinguistic perspective for the learning environment, teacher behavior, and the preparation and use of L2 reading materials. The optimum learning environment is viewed as one in which students and teachers work together: teacher intervention is minimized as students are encouraged to use their developing skills to solve reading problems on their own. Materials development is viewed as being composed of the development of reading skills exercises (scanning, skimming, reading for thorough comprehension, and critical reading) and the development of language skills exercises (vocabulary, structure, and discourse). The third section of the article discusses lesson planning within a psycholinguistic framework and presents a sample lesson plan in English as a second language which emphasizes a skills approach to reading. Lessons are planned for maximum flexibility, allowing the teacher to take advantage of students' interests and needs.

THEORETICAL PREMISES

There is no "psycholinguistic method" for teaching reading; the value of psycholinguistics lies in the insights it provides into the reading process (see, for example, Smith and Goodman, 1973). In the past the reader was viewed as working through a text in a rigid, word-by-word fashion, decoding information in a precise manner from print to speech to aural comprehension. Frank Smith (1973) emphasizes two important contributions of psycholinguistics which make such an interpretation impossible.

First, it has been established that there is a severe limit to the amount of information that we are able to receive, process and remember (Miller, 1967). The reader, therefore, does not use all the information on the page, but rather, must select the most productive language cues in determining the message of the writer. From this it follows that reading is necessarily a rapid process which could not proceed word by word.

Second, research has shown that reading is only incidentally visual (Kolers, 1969). More information is contributed by the reader than by the print on the page. That is, readers understand what they read because they are able to take the stimulus beyond its graphic representation and assign it membership to an appropriate group of concepts already stored in their memories.

Goodman (1970) summarizes the psycholinguistic perspective of reading:

> Reading is a selective process. It involves partial use of available minimal language cues selected from perceptual input on the basis of the reader's expectation. As this partial information is processed, tentative decisions are made to be confirmed, rejected or refined as reading progresses. (260)

From this paragraph, which describes the proficient native-language reader, inferences can be drawn which are important in the preparation and use of second language (L2) reading materials.

First, the definition assumes that reading is an active process. The reader forms a preliminary expectation about the material, then selects the fewest, most productive cues necessary to confirm or reject that expectation. This is a sampling process in which the reader takes advantage of his knowledge of vocabulary, syntax, discourse, and the "real world." Skill in reading, therefore, depends on precise coordination of a number of special skills. Providing students with practice in these skills and helping them to develop consistent "attack strategies" should be the focus of any reading program.

The second inference, closely tied to the first, is that reading must be viewed as a two-fold phenomenon involving process—comprehending—and product—comprehension. (For a discussion of this distinction see Goodman and Burke, 1973.) The process of working through a reading task, with the mistakes and false starts that this involves, is often as important as producing correct responses to *post facto* comprehension questions. Our responsibility as reading teachers, therefore, goes beyond presenting our students with passages followed by comprehension questions. We must construct reading tasks which reward students as much for trying as for getting the correct answer.

Third, reading involves, as Goodman (1970) stated, an interaction between thought and language. The reader brings to the task a formidable amount of information and ideas, attitudes and beliefs. This knowledge, coupled with the ability to make linguistic predictions, determines the expectations the reader will develop as he reads. Skill in reading depends on the efficient interaction between linguistic knowledge and knowledge of the world. Two things follow from this. Students must have "conceptual readiness" for each task: reading activities must either hook into the students' knowledge of the world, or the teacher must fill in the gaps *before* the task is begun. Furthermore, this perspective underscores the importance of individualized reading tasks since it is recognized that each student brings special strengths and weaknesses to every activity.

Fourth, psycholinguistic theory emphasizes the importance of using semantically complete readings. Research shows (see, for example Menosky, 1971; Goodman and Burke, 1973) that reading errors change significantly as the reader progresses into a passage, supporting the position that the reader builds on a previous store of knowledge by adding information from the reading. This finding suggests that successful reading lessons depend not only on the students' efficient use of strategies and knowledge, but also on the nature of the reading passage. The easiest passage is not necessarily the shortest, but rather the one which is conceptually complete.

Following directly from this perspective, our goals as reading teachers are: (a) to train our students to determine beforehand their goals and expectations for a given reading activity; (b) to teach our students to use reading strategies appropriate to the task at hand; (c) to encourage our students to take risks, to guess, to ignore their impulses to always be correct; and (d) to give our students practice and encouragement in using the minimum number of syntactic/semantic clues to obtain the maximum amount of information when reading.

In the confusion of preparing and presenting lessons to large, heterogeneous classes, it seems almost impossible to adhere to a productive theoretical framework. How do we build bridges between theory and practice? How do we introduce our students to effective reading strategies? How do we teach the group while assisting individuals? Most importantly, how do we build bridges between the classroom and the real world; how do we develop an independence in our students that allows them to leave our classrooms with a *modus operandi* which serves them well in new and more challenging environments? These issues are examined in the next section.

ACHIEVING GOALS

Learning Environment

Our ultimate goal is to foster independence in our students. An independent student not only uses various skills and strategies on cue, but is able to determine for himself his predictions for a reading, his goals, and appropriate reading strategies. The following learning environment encourages such independence.

We advocate a learning environment that involves all individuals—teachers as well as students—in a cooperative process of setting and achieving goals. Classroom activities should parallel the "real world" as closely as possible. Since language is a tool of communication, methods and materials should concentrate on the message, not the medium. In addition, the purposes of reading should be the same in class as they are in real life: 1) to obtain a specific fact, or piece of information (scanning), 2) to obtain the general idea of the author (skimming), 3) to obtain a comprehensive understanding of a reading, as in reading a textbook (thorough comprehension), or 4) to evaluate information in order to determine where it fits into one's own system of beliefs (critical reading). Our students should become as conscious as we are of the purpose for reading, so that they will be able to determine the proper approaches to a reading task.

Role of Teacher

Following the admonitions of Earl Stevick (for example, 1973a, b; 1974a, b; 1975), we utilize a paradigm of L2 classroom activity which minimizes teacher intervention, forcing the students to use and develop their new language skills. Within this paradigm we see three roles for the teacher: the teacher as teacher, the teacher as participant, and the teacher as facilitator.

The teacher as teacher is necessary only when the class is attempting to resolve a language problem, for it is only in this situation that the teacher is automatically presumed to possess more knowledge than the students. This role can be minimized if the students' attack strategies and reading skills have been effectively developed. If the task is realistic, and if the students have learned to adjust their reading strategies according to the task, there should be little need for teacher intervention.

The teacher is a participant in activities in which the knowledge and opinions of all persons in the class are of equal weight. Such activities would include discussions arising from reading activities, forming judgments about ideas encountered in readings, and activities which emphasize learning about a subject through the medium of the L2.

The teacher is a facilitator when creating an environment in which learning can take place, where linguistic expertise is required only in the event of communication breakdown. Often assignments can be discussed and corrected without teacher participation. Individualized assignments or small group sessions also require little direct teacher intervention.

This paradigm of the L2 classroom has two important advantages. First, it puts teachers in their place, emphasizing the individuality of students and reducing the compulsion we sometimes feel to control classroom activity. This relieves us of feelings of guilt and frustration occasioned by unsuccessful attempts at coercing

the students to keep together. Second, it puts the responsibility for learning squarely on the shoulders of the students, which is where it belongs.

Materials

The problem of materials is one faced by all teachers. While it may be true that a good teacher can make almost any set of reading materials work in class, it is obvious that properly conceived reading exercises free the teacher to work more efficiently with students to solve individual reading problems. As reading teachers we generally find ourselves in one of two situations: either we are trying to adapt a textbook to suit our needs, or we are trying to find readings and write our own exercises to fill gaps in our curriculum. The following sections discuss the evaluation, preparation and use of materials in the L2 reading class.

Evaluating Reading Selections. Whether we are looking for readings from the "real world" or deciding which selection to use from an assigned text, there are two factors that need to be considered before a reading is taken into the classroom.

Is the reading selection appropriate to both the proficiency level and the interest of the students? Both aspects of a reading, linguistic difficulty and semantic relevance, should be weighed before it is selected for use. There is evidence to suggest that relevance is a more important criterion than difficulty in selecting readings (Niles, 1970). A student with the requisite amount of knowledge and interest in a subject is more likely to force himself through a difficult passage than through a relatively easy selection in which he has no interest.

Can the selection be made to provide practice in the skills which you need to reinforce? Given the demands of day-to-day teaching it is easy to fall into the trap of using a particular type of exercise because it is easy and enjoyable. It is at this point, however, that we need to shift to a different type of task since ease of execution is one indication that students have mastered a particular skill. It is also important from the viewpoint of classroom dynamics to vary the focus of skill work in a realistic way, thereby emphasizing the fact that outside the classroom reading goals and tasks vary greatly from one type of material to the next. It is also true that a single reading might provide practice in a number of skills. A menu, for example, is usually scanned, but skimming for a general idea of the type of restaurant, and the range of prices, is also realistic. Poetry is often used in reading classes only to increase students' literary appreciation, but it is an excellent vehicle for working on vocabulary-from-context skills, getting the main idea, or drawing inference. An essay might be skimmed initially to determine the author's attitude toward an issue, followed by careful then critical reading to determine such things as who the intended audience is, if the author's presuppositions are valid, and ultimately whether or not the reader agrees with the author.

By varying the tasks students are expected to perform, we not only make classes interesting, but also show students that skills can be used with a wide range of materials and that the same reading might profitably be attacked several ways.

Preparing and Using Materials. Once we have decided to use a reading passage, we need to make a number of decisions concerning the tasks we ask our students to perform with the selection. First, the selection determines what we try to do with it. If we want students to practice determining the main idea of a passage, we must find readings which are well organized with topic sentences and supporting details. If a selection contains many facts and figures, it would probably work well in a scanning exercise. We should not force students to perform an unrealistic task with a reading merely because we have determined that it is time to work on a particular skill. If we want to work on skimming, for example, it is our responsibility to search until we find an appropriate reading.

Next, we must be careful to teach, then test. A common problem with reading texts is the tendency to ask students to produce a vocabulary item or to exhibit proficiency with a skill before they have been given adequate exposure and practice. Whether we are writing our own materials or adapting textbooks, we must make a consistent effort to introduce, model, reinforce, and review new learning tasks before we expect students to perform on their own. A good rule of thumb is to initially evaluate all exercises to determine exactly what is being required of the students, then to mentally review previous learning activities to make sure students can reasonably be expected to perform that task. Many cloze-type tests which pass for vocabulary review exercises actually require a firm grasp of syntax skills which may not have been explicitly taught. Students' failure to do well on such exercises may indicate weaknesses in knowledge of the structure of the L2, not in knowledge of vocabulary. In addition, cloze exercises require productive knowledge of vocabulary while students may not yet have been provided with the opportunity to develop productive control of these items.

Third, exercises should be written and used to provide maximum individualization. Reading involves an interaction between thought and language, a point of view which places great importance on the information and experiences that each reader brings to a task. Furthermore, we can assume that no two human beings learn languages at the same rate or in quite the same way. These two facts offer a strong case for individualizing instruction; while it is clearly impossible to prepare a separate lesson for each student, there are a number of things we can do to increase the individualization of our teaching. By producing a large number of exercises arranged hierarchically according to difficulty or by adding to the number of exercises or exercise items already in a text, we make it possible for each student to do as much as he is able to do. This gives all students ample practice. In addition, class time can be arranged so as to give teachers the opportunity to work with individuals and small groups. Of course, it may sometimes be necessary to find or produce exercises for individuals, to assign extra work to faster students or remedial work to slower students.

Finally, it is important that we develop flexibility in sequencing the use of exercises which accompany a reading. Typically, textbook exercises follow the reading selection. However, students can benefit by working with selected vocabulary and comprehension activities as well as discussion/composition topics before they begin to read. Students are more likely to experience success with a reading if they are familiar with selected vocabulary items before they begin reading. Likewise, attempting to answer comprehension questions before reading challenges students to read a passage to confirm or refute their guesses. If discussion/composition questions are discussed before the selection is read, students are given the opportunity to think the issues through in advance and thus are able to read far more critically.

Working through exercises before students attack a reading can be the single most effective tool in getting them to take the risk and read to the end. As long as we maintain a sound theoretical perspective of the work we ask our students to do, we should not feel obligated to follow the "accepted" textbook sequences of: reading, comprehension questions, vocabulary, discussion, and composition.

Developing Reading and Language Skills. At the intermediate and advanced levels we can assume that students possess a basic competence in English and that our primary task is to teach reading. Reading is, however, a language process, and reading teachers are inextricably bound up in the teaching of the second language itself. Although in practice it is impossible to separate reading instruction from general language instruction, for the purposes of discussion it is convenient to consider materials development as being composed of two tasks: the development of reading skill exercises (scanning, skimming, reading for thorough comprehension, and critical reading) and the development of language skill exercises (vocabulary, structure, discourse), both of which enable students to read more efficiently by using a minimum number of linguistic clues to obtain maximum information. First let us turn our attention to reading skills.

Reading Skills. *Skimming* is quick reading for the general drift of a passage. It is an activity which is appropriate when there is not time to read something carefully or when trying to decide if careful reading is merited. It is reading with a general question in mind: "Does this book treat generative semantics or merely transformational grammar?" or "Is this author for or against capital punishment?" Since we assume that students skim in their own languages, we see our task as helping them to transfer this skill to English. Although tips such as "Take advantage of chapter titles and subheadings," "Read first and last sentences in the paragraphs," and "Let your eyes travel quickly, catching adjectives and adverbs" are useful, the only way to improve this skill is to be forced to read more and more rapidly and to formulate appropriate questions before beginning. At first we must provide the skimming questions and coach students through passages; later students are expected to form appropriate questions and predictions and to push themselves to read quickly. (Many times textbook comprehension questions are general enough to be good pre-reading skimming questions.)

Scanning is similar to skimming in that the

reader is pushing himself through a selection at an initially uncomfortable rate, but the search is more focused since the information needed is very specific—usually a date, a number, or a place. Before scanning the reader forms preliminary questions such as: "When will the candidates debate the tax reform bill?" or "What was the final score of the rugby match?" In addition to teaching students to take advantage of textual clues, as they do in skimming, we should also make them aware of the graphic form the answer is likely to take: written number, numeral, capitalized word, or short phrase containing key words. As in skimming, students gradually become less dependent on our cues until they become self-sufficient. It is important to use selections which can be realistically scanned (that is, those containing specific information) and selections which are commonly scanned in "real life": for example, the sports page, menus, classified ads, and telephone books. (Many textbook questions meant for general comprehension are good scanning questions because they focus on minute points.)

Reading for thorough comprehension is reading in order to master the total message of the writer, both main points and supporting details. It is that stage of understanding at which the reader is able to paraphrase the author's ideas but has not yet made a critical evaluation of those ideas. This type of reading is the primary concern of most reading classes. In fact, the most common weakness of reading courses is that this style of reading—the careful word-by-word approach—is practiced exclusively, without recognition of the fact that it is not necessary for some tasks and insufficient for others. Of course, holding students accountable for what they have read is valid. However, when developing thorough comprehension questions, a number of pitfalls should be avoided. We must make sure the questions reflect the focus and direction of a passage and that the information demanded by a question is accessible to the students during a careful reading. A good rule of

thumb to follow when developing exercises is to read the passage and construct initial questions on the major points without looking back to the selection; we can hardly expect students to retain more after one reading than we have. Certain materials (such as research articles or textbooks) require careful reading and study, and we should expose students to a number of such readings. We do so, however, only after we are confident that they understand the situations in which such study is warranted.

Finally, *critical reading* requires us to push our students beyond the "thorough comprehension" stage of reading, to encourage them to react to readings with the same critical judgment they probably exercise when reading in their native languages. This critical reading ability is often suspended when students undertake reading tasks in a second language, perhaps because they feel a great sense of accomplishment merely at having deciphered the author's message. In order to build critical reading skills, we need to find readings which argue a point of view or which presume certain attitudes on the part of the readers. Examples of critical reading questions are: "For what purpose and for what audience is this intended?" "What knowledge and attitudes does the author presume of the audience?" "Are you convinced by the evidence presented by the author to support the claims made?" "Does your own experience support the conclusions reached by the author?" and "Do you share the author's point of view?" Such questions open up for students a completely new perspective of the selection, and lead to discussion in which they must use vocabulary and information from the passage to support their opinions. Many ESL reading texts for example, are guilty of hindering students' critical reading skills by taking the author's credentials for granted, by not asking students to critically evaluate the issues. (Critical reading demands a certain amount of class discussion time if students are to answer questions such as those posed above.)

Language Skills. Our students' efficiency in using reading skills is directly dependent upon their overall language proficiency—their general language skills. In addition to presenting exercises such as those mentioned above, we must also systematically treat specific language problems in the mode of reading. There are three areas of language skills work on which we focus: vocabulary, syntax, and discourse. At this point we turn specifically to *English* as the target language for consideration.

Vocabulary work is the easiest to devise and the easiest to abuse. Virtually all texts in English as a second language (ESL) work with vocabulary items, but it takes a teacher with a strong theoretical commitment to use such exercises effectively. A basic premise which should not be violated is: *work with real language contexts.* Words are vehicles of meaning and as such rarely occur in isolation. Three types of vocabulary attack strategies emphasized are: obtaining meaning from context, from morphological analysis, and from monolingual English dictionaries.

Guessing vocabulary from context is perhaps the most important of the vocabulary attack skills. Students must be made aware of the number of language clues available to them when they are stopped by an unfamiliar word. They should realize that they can usually continue reading and obtain a general understanding of the item. In context work, there are syntactic and semantic parameters of which we should make our students aware. We can emphasize the redundancy of language by demonstrating the types of contexts which can provide the meaning of an unfamiliar word:

Synonym in apposition: Our uncle was a *nomad,* an incurable wanderer who never could stay in one place.

Antonym: While the aunt loved Marty deeply, she absolutely *despised* his twin brother Smarty.

Cause and effect: By surrounding the protest-ers with armed policemen, and by arresting the leaders of the movement, the rebellion was effectively *quashed.*

Association between an object and its purpose or use: The scientist removed the *treatise* from the shelf and began to read.

Description: Tom received a new *roadster* for his birthday. It is a sports model, red with white interior and bucket seats, capable of reaching speeds of more than 150 mph.

Example: Mary can be quite *gauche;* yesterday she blew her nose on the new linen table-cloth.

Without burdening the student with linguistic jargon we can teach students to recognize the punctuation, syntax, and discourse clues which operate in each of the above examples. Most importantly, they must be taught to recognize situations in which the meaning of a word or phrase is not essential for adequate comprehension of the passage.

If context does not provide the meaning of an unfamiliar word, morphological analysis will often provide a clue. Many ESL texts provide lists of stems and affixes with accompanying exercises. These can be used to systematically introduce the most common stems and affixes. In subsequent reading tasks, students' familiarity with morphological items can be increased by continued practice in deciphering unfamiliar words.

Finally, if all else fails and if students feel they cannot continue without knowing the meaning of a word, the dictionary can be used. Students require a systematic introduction to dictionary work if they are to become efficient dictionary users. Practice in scanning for words, and in the use of syntactic and semantic clues to select the proper definition for a given context should be provided.

In using ESL reading textbooks, we become more effective if we are aware of a number of common weaknesses of the vocabulary exercises. Often the rationale for choosing the words to be glossed seems arbitrary; one doesn't know if the words are glossed because they are difficult or because they are useful. It is often unclear if students are expected to make these items part of their active vocabularies. What vocabulary "teaching" there is consists of lists of words in isolation or with definitions. Neither format successfully teaches vocabulary. Many vocabulary exercises test without any teaching and are often unrealistic in two ways. Either the task itself is unrealistic: ("Form a sentence with the word *dilemma*") or the presumed ability to do the task is unrealistic (asking students to produce vocabulary of which they have only a receptive command).

In such cases it is up to the teacher to determine how much vocabulary building should take place and then to provide contexts in which words can be introduced and subsequently reinforced. Introducing unfamiliar vocabulary in several sentences, each providing a clear context, has proved to be successful. (Of course, prereading vocabulary work should be restricted to only those items whose meaning is not accessible from the passage.) Assuring that vocabulary items appear again and again in comprehension and discussion activities serves as reinforcement. If a word appears in a technical context in a reading but would be of use to students in more generalized contexts, the teacher should provide such contexts for the learner. This can be done orally or in writing. Items which do not impede communication of the author's ideas and which will not prove useful later should be ignored. Items which impede understanding, but which are rarely used in English should be quickly glossed by the teacher and then ignored.

Syntax work in reading classes is conducted on a diagnostic basis: only when a syntactic structure causes a communication breakdown do we work with it. When encountered in a reading, structure problems should be pulled out and explained. If a particular structure persists in causing comprehension difficulties or if the whole class is troubled by it, relevant exercises from grammar texts or teacher-constructed drills should be presented for intensive work. It is important, however, to emphasize grammar work as a tool for improving reading skills and to constantly reinforce the tactic of analyzing difficult prose for recognizable grammatical elements. Likewise, grammar exercises in reading texts should be analyzed to determine if the syntactic elements studied actually cause reading problems. If they do, the teacher should make explicit their value to the students and should build the necessary bridges between the exercises and the reading. If the exercises treat grammar points which do not give our students trouble when they read, we should not hesitate to skip the exercises entirely.

Discourse analysis consists of making students conscious of the effect of organization on the message of a writer. Rough outlining can be of value in showing students how one idea leads to the next. Many times this kind of work can be tied into the students' writing classes, where they may be working with such organizational schemes as comparison and contrast, generalization and specifics, and chronological order. ESL students should be made aware of the strong tendency in English for linear argumentation. Unlike many other languages, contiguous English sentences often imply causation or chronological sequence of events. Therefore, it is necessary to emphasize the arrangement of ideas as an important clue in deciphering the overall meaning of a text. We must also take pains to point out the styles which generally accompany certain types of writing. Discourse work lacks the rigor of vocabulary and syntax because the system of organizing larger-than-sentence language units is not rigid and because writers are not always as careful in organizing their ideas as they are in checking their grammar and word usage. Although discourse work cannot be reduced to formulas as easily as our vocabulary and syntax lessons, it is nevertheless imperative to help students develop an awareness of the conceptual presuppositions that native-speaker writers and readers apply to the organization of a text. In addition to increasing the ability to make predictions based on syntax and semantics, students should be developing an ability to predict content on the basis of textual organization.

SAMPLE LESSON PLAN

In the preceding pages we have attempted to show how a psycholinguistic perspective of reading might affect the learning environment, teacher behavior, and the preparation of L2 reading materials. We will narrow the focus now to describe a week's sequence of events in an intermediate or advanced ESL reading class (see Sample Lesson Plan, pp. 245–247).

A few general comments apply to all lesson plan preparation. First, although lessons are planned painstakingly, we must also allow for maximum flexibility. On the one hand, we should plan carefully, establishing loose time limits for each task. On the other hand, it is assumed that teachers will take advantage of any situation which may arise, abandoning prepared tasks for activities which spark student interest. This does not mean that reinforcement in a particular skill will be forfeited; our constant efforts to systematically reinforce and recycle all skills work throughout the semester allow us flexibility on a day-to-day basis. Approximate time limits are established in advance for each activity so that the teacher realizes, for example, that a successful activity is being continued at the expense of another. This type of flexibility in the classroom—spontaneously extending the time allotted for one activity so that not enough time remains for a second planned activity—may leave teachers with time on their hands at the end of the hour. In an effort to avoid this problem more than enough work is planned for each day. If we have extra exercises ready to use, we are less likely to push forward with a task which is boring, too difficult, or too long.

Second, while we acknowledge the value of such non-reading activities as discussion, writing, and focused grammar or vocabulary work, we are committed to the view that one learns by doing: in a reading class, students should read. Furthermore, as much as possible, students should work with conceptually complete reading tasks. Focused work on words, sentences and paragraphs is tolerated because a teacher can thereby deal more effectively with specific language problems which have caused comprehension difficulties in longer readings.

Finally, because our ultimate goal is to make students independent of our guidance, we should allow for consistently greater student participation in determining the appropriate strategies for particular readings. As the semester progresses, it is hoped that the class will gradually develop into a group of people working together to increase their reading skills.

A few comments are necessary concerning the lesson plan presented here. The activities outlined would be appropriate for intermediate or advanced students who have worked together for several weeks. This is important for two reasons. First, we hope that a non-threatening atmosphere has been established in which people feel free to volunteer opinions and make guesses without fear of ridicule or censure. Second, we can assume that by now students recognize the importance of a skills-based reading program and that they are working with the teacher to improve those skills using a variety of readings and exercises. That is, they have been introduced to all of the skill exercise types and are working toward that ultimate goal of complete independence.

The lesson plan is meant only as an example

of how goals might be translated into practice. We do not imply that a particular presentation is the only one possible for a given reading activity nor that the exercises presented here are the only activities possible to achieve our goals.

These lessons, planned for 50-minute, ESL reading classes, are ambitious; we have chosen to provide more than enough work in the belief that it is better to err in the direction of too much rather than too little. Approximate time limits for each activity are indicated. Below each exercise heading appear possible sources of materials and a brief description of how the exercise type might be used.

A close examination of the sample lesson plan reveals several important characteristics to be found in any successful teaching situation. First, and most importantly, the plan represents a skills approach to the teaching of ESL reading. The students do more than merely read passages and answer questions; the type of reading that the students are asked to perform varies from task to task. They scan the train schedule and newspaper, skim the longer reading and read it and several other selections carefully. The vocabulary and syntax work is presented as a tool for comprehension, appropriate for helping students solve persistent reading problems.

Second, within a single week a great variety of activities is presented. In the course of any single lesson the tempo and task change several times. Monday, for example, begins with a scanning exercise, followed by paragraph work, concluding with a vocabulary and skimming introduction to the longer reading which will not be due until Wednesday. In the course of the week, virtually all language and reading skills are reinforced in a variety of contexts and with a variety of materials.

Of course, the classroom dynamics change to fit the task. The train schedule and poem are treated as a class activity, the teacher encouraging students to volunteer answers and opinions. The paragraph work on Monday, as well as the vocabulary and structure exercises on Tuesday

and Thursday, might be organized as workshop sessions, giving students the chance to work at their own pace and providing the teacher with the opportunity to assist individuals. For such lessons it is necessary to provide either a great number of exercise items or several worksheets, so that faster students are challenged either by the quantity or difficulty of the material. We have had great success having students discuss reading comprehension questions in small groups. Students choose a chairperson who is responsible for seeing that everyone talks, that all comprehension problems are resolved, and that consensus is reached on each exercise item. Students are forced to defend their choices with portions of the text. This process encourages student autonomy and responsibility and minimizes teacher intervention.

The role of the teacher also changes from activity to activity. During vocabulary and structure work, the teacher is a teacher, providing help and encouragement as students work to solve language problems. The teacher is a facilitator during the poetry and short passage readings, intervening only in the event that linguistic expertise is needed to keep discussion going. In the analysis of news events and discussions of how readings relate to the "real world," the teacher is primarily a participant on equal terms with the students in exploring a mutually interesting topic. Of course, the role and behavior of the teacher can change a number of times in the course of one session to suit the situation. It is hoped, however, that, as the semester progresses, the teacher as teacher will gradually be replaced by the teacher as facilitator and participant.

A third important feature of this lesson plan is the opportunity to encourage students to choose their own reading strategies and to apply the skills dictated by the strategy chosen. It should be noted that the longer reading is introduced by the teacher through vocabulary work and discussion, followed by skimming. It is often the case that students are discouraged by long readings and should therefore be given as much of this kind of support as necessary in attacking a long selection. It is hoped that the procedure used by the teacher will be repeated by the student when similar readings are attacked in the future. Later in the week, students are encouraged to choose their own strategies for attacking Thursday's short selection and to be able to defend their approaches. Often the teacher will want to simulate a "real life" situation, give the students a task, and ask them how they would approach it. One's approach to a newspaper editorial, for example, might be quite different depending on whether one is reading the selection for pleasure or for a university political science course.

Throughout the semester, students are taught to shift gears, to vary their reading strategies according to their goals for the selection at hand. As they become more proficient readers, we expect them to determine for themselves what they read, why they read it, and how they read it.

REFERENCES

Baudoin, E. M., E. S. Bober, M. A. Clarke, B. K. Dobson, and S. Silberstein. 1977. *Reader's Choice: A Reading Skills Textbook for Students of English as a Second Language.* Ann Arbor: University of Michigan Press.

Baumwoll, D., and R. L. Saitz. 1965. *Advanced Reading and Writing.* New York: Holt, Rinehart and Winston.

Goodman, K. S. 1970. Reading: A psycholinguistic guessing game. In H. Singer and R. B. Ruddell (eds.), *Theoretical Models and Processes of Reading,* 259–271. Newark, DE: International Reading Association.

Goodman, K. S., and C. Burke. 1973. *Theoretically Based Studies of Patterns of Miscues in Oral Reading Performance.* U. S. Department of Health, Education and Welfare, Office of Education.

Harris, D. P. 1966. *Reading Improvement Exercises for Students of English as a Second Language.* Englewood Cliffs, NJ: Prentice-Hall.

Hirasawa, L., and L. Markstein. 1974. *Developing Reading Skills: Advanced.* Rowley, MA: Newbury House Publishers.

Kolers, P. A. 1969. Reading is only incidentally visual. In K. S. Goodman and J. T. Fleming (eds.), *Psycholinguistics and the Teaching of Reading,* 8–16. Newark, DE: International Reading Association.

Menosky, D. M. 1971. A psycholinguistic description of oral reading miscues generated during the reading of varying portions of text by selected readers from grades two, four, six and eight. Unpublished doctoral dissertation. Wayne State University.

Miller, G. A. 1967. The magical number seven, plus or minus two: Some limits on our capacity for processing information. In G. A. Miller, *The Psychology of Communication,* 14–43. New York: Basic Books.

Niles, O. S. 1970. School programs: The necessary conditions. In K. S. Goodman and O. S. Niles (eds), *Reading: Process and Program,* 41–74. Urbana, IL: National Council of Teachers of English.

Praninskas, J. 1975. *Rapid Review of English Grammar,* (2nd ed.). Englewood Cliffs, NJ: Prentice-Hall.

Quirk, R., and S. Greenbaum. 1973. *A Concise Grammar of Contemporary English.* New York: Harcourt Brace Jovanovich, Inc.

Rutherford, W. E. 1968. *Modern English.* New York: Harcourt, Brace and World. Revised 1974.

Saitz, R. L., and D. Carr. 1972. Selected Readings in English. Cambridge, MA: Winthrop Publishers.

Smith, F. (ed.). 1973. *Psycholinguistics and Reading.* New York: Holt, Rinehart and Winston.

Smith, F., and K. S. Goodman. 1973. On the psycholinguistic method of teaching reading. In F. Smith (ed.), *Psycholinguistics and Reading,* 177–182. New York: Holt, Rinehart and Winston.

Science Research Associates. 1965. *Rate and Power Builders.* Chicago, Illinois.

Stevick, E. W. 1973a. Review of Curran's counseling-learning: A whole person model for education. *Language Learning* 23.259–271.

Stevick, E. W. 1973b. Before linguistics and beneath method. In *Georgetown University Roundtable,* 99–106. Washington, D. C.: Georgetown University Press.

Stevick, E. W. 1974a. Language teaching must do an about face. *Modern Language Journal* 58.379–383.

Stevick, E. W. 1974b. Review of Gattegno's teaching foreign languages in the schools: The silent way. *TESOL Quarterly* 8.305–314.

Stevick, E. W. 1975. One simple visual aid: A psychodynamic view. *Language Learning* 25.63–72.

Yorkey, R. C. 1970. *Study Skills for Students of English as a Second Language.* New York: McGraw Hill.

Sample Five-Day Lesson Plan

Day 1

1. Non-prose reading (15 min) (train schedule, menu, map, graph, etc.)
   a. Students are given teacher-prepared questions and told to scan to find the answers.
   b. The questions should reflect "real life" situations.
   c. The work is fast-paced and oral, students working individually or in small groups.

2. Paragraph work (20 min) (paragraphs from Baudoin et al., Harris, SRA, or teacher-prepared)
   a. As an introduction, a paragraph is read by the teacher, and the students are given time to answer the questions. Discussion follows, with students defending answers using vocabulary and syntax analysis. Students are then given the opportunity to work individually.
   b. Students read silently and answer questions.
   c. Discussion follows with the class as a whole, in small groups, or in pairs. Intensive work is done on determining the main idea, drawing inferences, as well as sentence and discourse work.
   d. If students aren't able to finish in the allotted time or if problems arise, the work can be continued as homework.

3. Introduction to longer reading (15 min) (ESL textbook reading of over 2000 words found, for example, in Baudoin et al., and Baumwoll and Saitz)
   a. Reading is introduced by a discussion relating the topic to students' experiences, followed by an introduction of potentially difficult vocabulary from the reading.
   b. The teacher reads the first few paragraphs orally to introduce the students to the reading. Discussion follows on the topic and on potential vocabulary and syntax problems.
   c. If time permits, students skim the selection to answer general questions posed by the teacher.

4. Assignment
   a. Read longer reading, answer comprehension questions for Day 3.
   b. Finish paragraph work, if necessary.

Day 2

1. Paragraph work (10 min)
   a. Finish paragraph work begun on Day 1.

2. *Vocabulary work* (15 min) (vocabulary from context, stem/affix, or dictionary: exercises taken from Baudoin et al., Harris, Yorkey, or other skills textbook or are teacher-prepared)

    a. Intensive oral skill work in which students are pushed at fast pace. Focus is on skills not on learning new vocabulary.

    b. Teacher-prepared exercises can be used to introduce vocabulary from the next reading selection.

3. *Short passage* (25 min) (ESL textbook such as Baudoin et al., Saitz and Carr, Hirasawa and Markstein, or teacher-prepared activity; reading of 500–1000 words)

    a. Students do intensive forced reading for a particular purpose. (The reading determines what you do with it.)

    b. The teacher reads the passage orally to the students while they read silently forcing them to read quickly, or sets a time limit for silent reading.

    c. The reading is followed by comprehension questions to be done orally, or in writing if true/false, multiple choice format is used.

    d. Discussion of questions can take place with the class as a whole, in small groups or in pairs.

4. *Assignment*

    a. Reminder from Day 1 to read longer reading and answer comprehension questions.

Day 3

1. *Longer reading* (50 min)

    a. Vocabulary exercises are answered orally and quickly.

    b. Comprehension questions are discussed, flipping back and forth from questions to passage to scan for answers when difficulties arise. This can be done by the class as a whole, in small groups or in pairs.

    c. Teacher pulls out sentences and vocabulary items for explanation and discussion as problems arise. Care is taken to build bridges between this and previous syntax and vocabulary skill work.

    d. The passage is discussed using text and teacher-prepared questions.

    e. Teacher can act as facilitator: keeping discussion moving, encouraging all students to contribute, or small groups can elect a chairperson from among the students. Discussion focuses on evaluations arising from critical reading.

    f. Teacher moves students through a variety of activities so that, although the content is the same for fifty minutes, the pace and focus keep everyone interested in the work.

2. *Assignment*

    a. Vocabulary review exercises or possibly a composition based on the reading passage. The assignment should allow students to capitalize on vocabulary and syntax work which accompanied the lesson.

Day 4

1. *Go over homework.*

2. *Structure work* (15 min) (worksheets from Quirk and Greenbaum, Rutherford, Praninskas, or teacher-prepared).

    a. Work should be done orally or, if in writing, in a workshop setting where the teacher moves from student to student. Discussion occurs with class as a whole, in small groups, or in pairs.

b. Teacher can provide work on structures which have caused reading comprehension problems in previous reading. This might include work on problems uncovered in Wednesday's work.

c. Extra work can be assigned as homework as needed.

3. *Short passage* (20 min) (ESL textbook or teacher-prepared reading of approximately 500 words with comprehension, vocabulary, and syntax exercises as appropriate)

a. Reading can be on a topic seen earlier, or a new content area can be introduced.

b. Students can be asked to determine the proper goals and strategies for the task. A time limit is agreed upon.

c. The passage is read and exercises are completed in class.

d. Discussion follows reading, guided by comprehension questions.

4. *Realia* (15 min)

a. Discussion of current news which students are likely to know about from TV or radio, and which the teacher can predict will appear in newspapers daily.

b. Teacher and students discuss topic; the teacher provides cultural, vocabulary information, as needed.

5. *Assignment*

a. Buy the same English language newspaper that evening and scan to find all articles on "realia" topic. Read the articles. Answer teacher-prepared questions, the preparation of which requires only a general knowledge of the kinds of information available daily on the "realia" topic e.g., "Who is Mr. X?" "What arguments are used by opponents of the proposed project?" Bring newspaper to class on Day 5.

Day 5

1. *Realia* (35 min)

a. Students discuss the articles which treat Thursday's "realia" topic. Teacher will have read the articles and prepared appropriate exercises.

b. Students do intensive oral work with the newspaper. Tasks are realistic: comparison shopping with classified ads, analysis of news reports, etc. Work can be done as a class, in small groups, or in pairs.

2. *Poetry* (15 min) (teacher-prepared exercises)

a. This kind of activity is done for a change of pace. Teacher should emphasize that poetry requires the same skills as other reading selections.

b. Poetry is especially good for reinforcing vocabulary from context skills, using syntax clues and for drawing inferences.

CHAPTER 19

Teaching the Information Gathering Skills

Ronald Mackay

In many parts of the world where English is not the mother tongue, students are expected to extract information from spoken or written texts in the English language as part of their postschool training.

From having studied English as a subject in the school syllabus, they are now required to use English as an instrument of learning. In many cases their efforts to do so meet with a decided lack of success which may have a prejudicial effect on their vocational or academic progress.

The purpose of this paper is to suggest that there are areas of linguistic knowledge which we have tended to neglect or even omit from our teaching in the intermediate and advanced comprehension class but which are essential for the successful comprehension of either spoken or written texts. The word *text* will be used throughout this paper to cover both spoken and written manifestations of the language.

While it is acknowledged that the skills of listening and reading are not identical, they may be discussed together under the term "information-gathering skills." Both are comprehension skills involving the perception and interpretation of all the linguistic signals which make up the text. Moreover, the use of magnetic tape in the classroom has eliminated one of the greatest differences between spoken discourse and written texts, namely, the ephemeral nature of the former. Thus a student presented with either listening or reading materials can take his own time over them in the sense that he can regress as often as he finds is necessary. He has no "author" present and therefore has to cope with an immutable permanent text. Neither does he have any source of extra- or paralinguistic clues, unless, of course, illustrations are provided to supplement the text. We will focus our discussion upon texts which do not incorporate illustrations or figures. After all, many lectures, tutorials, or discussions which students or trainees are required to listen to do not involve visual aids, nor do their textbooks include many illustrations. We are concerned, then, in this chapter with texts in which all the information is marked linguistically—either graphically on paper or orally on magnetic tape.

In discussing the information-gathering skills we must distinguish between the skills which can be exhibited as a result of comprehension and the linguistic knowledge which the learner is required to have in order to exhibit the comprehension skills. The distinction is an important one not only for materials development but also for syllabus planning and for testing.

A typical taxonomy of comprehension skills would include, for example, the ability to extract the literal meaning from the text, to identify the main ideas or facts supporting details and the relationships between ideas or facts, and to identify longer units of text which convey "thought units" or "units of information" essential to the development of the information. They are a description of successful comprehension in terms of the skills the student can demonstrate to have mastered. But they tell us nothing about the kind or amount of linguistic knowledge a student requires in order to master them. They are behavioral goals; as teachers and course planners we require additional information, namely, a clear specification of the language items we have to teach our students in order to develop each of these skills.

To ask a student to demonstrate a skill may indicate whether or not he has mastered it, but it may teach the student nothing. If our purpose is not to *test* comprehension but to teach it, then our materials should provide the student with linguistic information about how a text conveys meaning so that he can use that information in order to understand not only the text under scrutiny, but any text his studies may require him to cope with.

The successful demonstration of a comprehension skill implies knowledge of the language system in question and an operational knowledge of how that system is used to convey meaning. All information in a text is signaled linguistically. The successful demonstration of the skill must therefore depend upon a correct interpretation of the linguistic signals in the text.

In order to illustrate what is meant by "linguistic knowledge," consider the following example. Imagine you did not hear or see part of the last word of the following sentence (based on Smith, 1971, p. 20):

The captain ordered the sailors to haul up the an_____ .

What kinds of knowledge do we call upon to complete the sentence ourselves? "None" may initially appear to be an appropriate answer to some; the last word is "obviously" anchor. The most likely word is, of course, *anchor,* but how did we arrive at that decision? We have called upon one or several kinds of knowledge about the English language, although we may have done so unconsciously. We may have used:

1. *Knowledge of the spelling or phonological system of English.* If the word is an English word, it must correspond to the spelling or pronunciation rules of English and so cannot be continued using b, f, h, j, m, p, q, r, w, or z.

2. *Knowledge of the grammatical system of English.* The word is almost certain to be a noun. After "the" a pronoun or a verb cannot follow and, as the word completes the sentence, it cannot in this instance be an adjective or an adverb.

3. *Semantic knowledge.* While words like *anger, anchovy,* and *anarchist* satisfy the requirements of the system outlined in (1) and (2), our knowledge of the world tells us that they are either impossible or unlikely in the context. A verb like *haul up* must have a concrete object; thus an abstract noun like *anger* is unacceptable. Moreover the concrete object of *haul up* must also be heavy, and so, although *anchovy* has the right association in the context, it too must be ruled out. The word *anarchist* is merely unlikely in the context; it does not obviously collocate with *captain* and *sailors.* Only the context in which the entire sentence appears could provide the information necessary to accept or reject it. *Anchor* seems to be the most acceptable; it satisfies the requirements in (1) and (2), it is a heavy concrete object which would require to be *hauled up* by more than one man, and it collocates satisfactorily with *captain*

and *sailors* and fits into our understanding of the duties of the crew of a sailing ship.

Of course we did not *consciously* go through the procedures described in 1, 2, and 3 in deciding that the word was *anchor,* yet in solving the problem we made use of our knowledge of the graphological, phonological, and grammatical system of English. An inadequate competence would have resulted in an inadequate performance in the problem. In other words, we have used specified "linguistic knowledge" in order to solve a problem of comprehension.

The linguistic knowledge we drew upon in this example was knowledge of what makes a sentence a sentence. When we are dealing with the comprehension of longer stretches of language, we must make use not only of the linguistic knowledge of what makes a sentence a sentence, but also of what makes a text a text.

Consider the difference in the linguistic knowledge required in order to answer questions 1 and 2 below:

> Over the past century pollutants have been released into the air in mounting quantities. In recent years a good deal of attention has been given to the possibility that these may affect the climate of the earth as a whole.

Question 1:   What have been released into the air in mounting quantities over the past century?
Answer: Pollutants.
Question 2:   What may affect the climate of the earth?
Answer: (Mounting quantities of) pollutants.

To answer question 1 correctly requires a knowledge of sentence grammar only. The "What" of the question deletes the immediate constituent "pollutants" of the first sentence. To answer question 2 correctly requires a knowledge of one kind of intersentence cohesive tie. The "What" of the question deletes the word "these" in the second sentence whose referent is "pollutants" in the first sentence. The word

"these" is an anaphoric tie syntactically linking the two sentences to make a short text.

While adequate grammatical descriptions of sentence structure in English exist, there is correspondingly little in the way of descriptions of the syntactic features which contribute to the cohesion of text. Since most teaching materials are based on one or other of the various descriptions of sentence grammar, the materials we use for teaching comprehension at the higher stages tend to be linguistically uninformed. Our students lack *instruction* in the grammar of text, and the grammar of sentence structure is generally assumed to have been mastered at the more elementary level. What they do learn about textual cohesion is the by-product rather than the direct result of systematic teaching.

In teaching the information-gathering skills, we need to be able to identify those linguistic features of text which *hinder* comprehension, if they are unfamiliar and which *facilitate* comprehension, once their role is properly understood. Since the grammar book has traditionally been concerned with sentence grammar, the kind of linguistic information we need is often missing from traditional grammars. The recent volume, "A Grammar of Contemporary English" (Quirk et al. 1972), is a notable exception.

Let us examine a short sample text in order to try to identify some of the kinds of cohesive features of text we have in mind.

1 The dumping of massive and durable pieces of
2. junk, like the hulks of old vehicles and
3. abandoned kitchen equipment, has become a
4. nuisance. This debris is a menace to the farmer,
5. destroys amenities, and costs money to the
6. individuals or the local authorities who have to
7. clean it up. Hence this problem cannot be
8. allowed to expand in parallel with growth in the
9. number of vehicles in service or with the increase
10. in the total amount of household equipment
11. produced. Dumping of waste by people in this
12. way is already illegal and prosecutions are

13. brought from time to time. Moreover, all local
14. authorities have established and advertised the
15. existence of tips to which those who are not
16. prepared to incur the cost of a special collection
17. can bring bulky objects for disposal. Therefore,
18. the solution appears to be in the further
19. development of the current threefold approach of
20. legislative penalty, improved public services, and
21. increased public awareness.

We recognize "intuitively" that the above paragraph is a text and not just a collection of unrelated sentences; there are identifiable and describable linguistic relationships of various kinds set up between the sentences which contribute to the overall cohesion of the text. Let us consider these in more detail.

First there are *lexical relationships.* The phrase "massive and durable pieces of junk" (lines 1–2) is repeated as "debris" (line 4) and as "waste" (line 11). The relationship here is one of "inclusion" or hyponomy, which can be illustrated thus

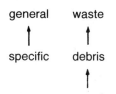

The introduction of a specific term which is later introduced as a more general term is characteristic of texts; e.g., *wolf* can be repeated later in the text as the more general *animal* or as the even more general *creature; Rolls Royce* can be repeated as *car* or as *vehicle.* Consider the unacceptability of working from the general term to the specific:

Last night a construction (1) was gutted by fire in the dock area of Singapore. Firemen fought the blaze for six hours but were unable to save the building (2). Early this morning what was left of the eight-story warehouse (3) was declared a public hazard and the authorities have granted permission for its demolition.

The most specific *eight-story warehouse* must be used at (1) and the hierarchically dominant, i.e., more general, term *construction* must be placed at (3).

There is also another kind of lexical relationship within the sample text—that of equivalence or synonymy. *Massive and durable pieces of junk* (lines 1–2) is repeated as the textual equivalent *bulky objects for disposal* (line 17); likewise *nuisance* (line 4), *menace* (line 4), and *problem* (line 7) are used as synonyms or near synonyms in the text.

It is clear then, that vocabulary difficulties are a matter of not just the meanings of unknown words, but also the relationships holding between lexical items in a given text. I believe that the responsibility for the solution of the difficulties encountered by unknown words at the advanced level lies with the learner rather than with the teacher. The student must make the same effort as the native speaker when faced with a new field involving a new vocabulary, that is, guess intelligently, use an appropriate dictionary, and develop the memory sufficiently to allow recognition of the word when it is met subsequently. However, the relationships of hyponomy and synonymy into which lexical items may fit and thereby provide textual cohesion can be usefully pointed out and practiced in the class. For example, consider an exercise like the following, where the student is required to fill in the blanks in the text from the words supplied:

Experience has proved that _____ are of great value in the protection of crops and livestock. Most _____ in use were developed in the past 30 years and demand for new _____ continues to grow.
   a. products
   b. ones
   c. pesticides
But it is well known that the good effects of _____ can be offset by dangers to the natural environment. An advisory committee on pesticides and other toxic chemicals made a thorough investigation of _____ such as _____ and _____

a. organochlorine insecticides
b. pesticides
c. dieldrin
d. DDT

The committee found that the persistence of these _____ may cause harm to beneficial _____ such as _____, to fish, birds, and other wild life.

a. substances
b. bees
c. insects

Once the student has been taught the nature of the lexical relationships to be found in text and has had experience of how they operate, he will be more capable of interpreting the value of the vocabulary items he meets in new texts. Of course, to some extent he will have to rely upon the knowledge of his subject to help determine the relationship between, for example, "organochlorine insecticides" and "pesticides," recognizing that the latter includes the former. It is relationships and how they contribute to textual cohesion that are being taught.

Second, there are *syntactic relationships* holding between sentences. The most obvious are those signaling anaphoric reference. Referring back to the sample text, the demonstrative "this" (line 4) refers back to "massive and durable pieces of junk" (lines 1–2). The demonstrative "this" (line 7) has a more general reference function referring back to the fact, presented in the first sentence, that dumping has become a nuisance; the phrase "in this way" (lines 11–12) likewise has no single word or phrase as its referent but refers to the dumping of waste in such a way that it has become a problem—the content of sentences 1, 2, and 3. The pronoun "it" (line 7), on the other hand, has a single word referent—"debris" in line 4 and "those" (line 15) refers back to people in line 11.

The use of pronominals and demonstratives are only two of the ways in which a text is made to cohere syntactically. Other syntactic devices of anaphoric reference follow.

Comparison

When we find expressions of similarity or difference, we may have to look back in the text in order to find the basis of the comparison, e.g.,

Aung scored 80% in the examination. Both Ting and Fong got the *same* mark but Chan scored more than 10% *less*.

In 1970 there were approximately 16 million motor vehicles in Great Britain. This was 3 million *more* than in 1965 and 6½ million *more* than in 1960. However, it is 4 million *fewer* than the estimate for 1975.

In order to answer the questions

1. How many motor vehicles were there in Great Britain in *(a)* 1965 *(b)* 1960?
2. What is the estimated figure for 1975?

the point of reference must be taken from the first sentence.

Nominal and Verbal Substitution

1. I'd like a vehicle which is self-propelled, has no running costs, does not depreciate, and travels at up to 50 mph.
2. I'd like *one* too.
3. *So* would I.

Summary Words

These are words which are used to summarize a stretch of text, e.g.,

First she boiled the water in a small pot. Then she added a lot of sugar and after that, the coffee. She let it almost boil over three times before she was satisfied that it was ready. The whole *process* took about 15 minutes.

Other common summary words are *case/affair/problem/idea/business*.

The student's attention can be directed to such syntactic features of cohesion by asking him to read or listen to a piece of text and asking a question which focuses upon the feature. For example:

Tape: And then finally, stage four, a true horse, with only one huge toe on each foot, an animal made to run really fast—as it had to, to keep alive, in a land of sabre-tooth tigers!

Workbook: as *it had* to
   a. To what does *it* refer?
      Answer: _____
   b. What did it have to do?
      Answer: _____

Tape: Well, now, back to our question. How? The horse didn't decide to change its toes and its legs and its teeth—but it did change. It did evolve. Well, this is how it happens.

Workbook: Well this is how *it* happens.
   a. To what does *it* here refer?
      Answer: It refers to _____

Tape: Almost every plant and animal is the result of the mating of a female with a male. She has the eggs or seed—he has the sperm or the pollen. The two come together and make a cell which will eventually grow into a new living thing.

Workbook: The *two* come together and make a cell.
   The *two* refers to:
   a. she and he
   b. the sperm and the pollen
   c. the egg and the sperm

The above examples are taken from a listening comprehension course (Morrison, 1974), which uses live discussions on tape as the teaching text. In the eight units, features of cohesion are focused upon where they occur naturally in the text. The set of texts were selected on the basis of the breadth of coverage it provided.

Third, there are *logical relationships* holding between sentences or stretches of text, marked by the use of logical connectors. In the sample text "Hence" (line 7) introduces a deduction which may be deducted logically from the information which precedes it. "Moreover" (line 13) introduces additional information reinforcing the information given in the previous sentence. "Therefore" (line 17) introduces the logical conclusion to be drawn from the information presented so far.

It is clear, at this point, that we are now dealing with a different kind of cohesion from the lexical and syntactic relations we discussed above. In considering the logical or meaningful relationships holding between sentences or larger units, we are not now primarily concerned with the linguistic properties of the excerpt as text but with "the communicative function of the sample as discourse" (Widdowson, 1974). That is, in addition to reacting to the formal devices used to combine sentences into continuous text, we are now reacting to the linguistic signals, or "discourse markers" (Wijasuriya, 1971), which tell us whether to interpret a stretch of text as an observation, a reinforcement, a conclusion, or some other act of communication.

These discourse markers, usually adverbs or prepositional phrases, can be grouped in notional or semantic categories as shown in Table 19.1.

The student's attention should be focused upon these discourse markers, and the meanings they introduce can be explained whenever they occur. Once they have been taught, multiple choice questions can be used to make the student focus on the meaning. For example:

Tape: The first thing that one has to realize about a robot is that man is

Table 19.1   TYPES OF DISCOURSE MARKERS

Notional category/meaning	Marker
1. *Enumerative.* Introduce the order in which points are to be made or the time sequence in which actions or processes took place.	first(ly), second(ly), third(ly), one, two, three / a, b, c, next, then, finally, last(ly), in the first / second place, for one thing / for another thing, to begin with, subsequently, eventually, finally, in the end, to conclude
2. *Additive*	
2.1 Reinforcing. Introduces a reinforcement or confirmation of what has preceded.	again, then again, also, moreover, furthermore, in addition, above all, what is more
2.2 Similarity. Introduces a statement of similarity with what has preceded.	equally, likewise, similarly, correspondingly, in the same way
2.3 Transition. Introduces a new stage in the sequence of presentation of information.	now, well, incidentally, by the way, O.K., fine
3. *Logical Sequence*	
3.1 Summative. Introduces a summary of what has preceded.	so, so far, altogether, overall, then, thus, therefore, in short, to sum up, to conclude, to summarize
3.2 Resultative. Introduces an expression of the result or consequence of what preceded (and includes inductive and deductive acts).	so, as a result, consequently, hence, now, therefore, thus, as a consequence, in consequence
4. *Explicative.* Introduces an explanation or reformulation of what preceded.	namely, in other words, that is to say, better, rather, by (this) we mean
5. *Illustrative.* Introduces an illustration or example of what preceded.	for example, for instance
6. *Contrastive*	
6.1 Replacive. Introduces an alternative to what preceded.	alternatively, (or) again, (or) rather, (but) then, on the other hand
6.2 Antithetic. Introduces information in opposition to what preceded.	conversely, instead, then, on the contrary, by contrast, on the other hand
6.3 Concessive. Introduces information which is unexpected in view of what preceded.	anyway, anyhow, however, nevertheless, nonetheless, notwithstanding, still, though, yet, for all that, in spite of (that), at the same time, all the same

God for the robot—he creates the robot. Therefore, its good qualities and its bad qualities are his fault, either way.

Workbook: The word *Therefore* here means:

a. Because this is the first thing one must realize about a robot.

b. Because man is the one who creates the robot.

Alternatively, suitable passages can be retyped omitting the discourse marker and the student asked to fill in the blanks from a list of alternatives. For example:

The digestibility and therefore the feeding value of grass falls rapidly after an emergence. _____ (1) silage made from overmature grass will reflect this reduced feeding value. _____ (2) cuts for silage, particularly first cuts, have to be made over a short period if uniformly good silage with a high feeding value is to result. _____ (3) efficient organization of labor and machinery is one of the most important aspects of good silage making. _____ (4) it will help to minimize the effect of unsettled weather if this occurs at the critical time.

In the blanks above, supply the most appropriate marker from the list:

1. For example, in spite of that, again, alternatively
2. Again, similarly, therefore, incidentally
3. Likewise, finally, hence, however
4. Nevertheless, moreover, for example, on the other hand

It is also a useful procedure to have the students formally recognize the kind of communicative acts being performed in the discourse. Once they have been made familiar with the notional categories into which acts can fall, they can be asked to reorder a given list of acts to conform to the pattern exhibited in the passage.

The above discussion has attempted to illustrate that the adequate comprehension of texts from which information has to be extracted requires the reader to make use of a different kind of linguistic knowledge than sentence grammar

provides. Of course, there is no suggestion whatsoever that "text grammar" is a *substitute* for sentence grammar; mastery of the former depends upon mastery of the latter.

The implication which can be drawn is that the features which make up the grammatical cohesion of text and the communicative cohesion of discourse (Allen and Widdowson, 1978) must be taught to the student at the intermediate and advanced stages in a systematic and purposeful way, just as sentence grammar was taught systematically in the elementary stage. Much of what passes for "advanced comprehension teaching" consists of little more than asking the student to perform a skill which he has not the competence to perform because he has never been formally taught the linguistic knowledge required for the performance of the skill.

CONCLUSION

In this paper features of continuous spoken and written language which are seldom systematically taught to the intermediate and advanced learner have been discussed. These features of lexical inclusion and equivalence, anaphoric reference and intersentential connection form part of the linguistic system of all texts, and since the information in a text is signaled linguistically, an inadequate mastery of these features must hinder comprehension. If the student knows only part of what he needs to know in order to understand a text, he will be a poor information gatherer, and where professional or vocational success depends upon gathering information from English texts he will fall below the required standards.

Successful teaching of the information-gathering skills depends upon:

1. The teacher being able to identify in linguistic (phonological, grammatical, or

lexical) terms the knowledge a student must possess in order to understand a given level or kind of text.
2. The teacher systematically teaching that knowledge to his students.
3. The teacher providing his students with the opportunities for practicing that knowledge.

Testing a student's comprehension only tells us if he possesses the necessary linguistic knowledge for comprehension; systematic teaching provides the necessary knowledge and exercises it. When "teaching comprehension" the teacher should always be able to answer the question "What kind of language knowledge does this text or this question on the text require?" Focusing on the appropriate language knowledge required for comprehension guarantees that we are indeed *teaching* comprehension, and not testing it.

REFERENCES

Allen, J. P. B. and H. G. Widdowson. 1978. Teaching the communicative use of English. In R. Mackay and A. Mountford (eds.), *English for Specific Purposes*. London: Longman, 56–77.

Morrison, J. W. 1974. *An Advanced Course in Listening Comprehension*. Newcastle Upon Tyne University, UK.

Quirk, R., S. Greenbaum, G. Leech, and J. Svartik. 1972. *A Grammar of Contemporary English*. London: Longman.

Smith, Frank 1971. *Understanding Reading: A Psycholinguistic Analysis of Reading and Learning to Read*. New York: Holt, Rinehart and Winston.

Widdowson, H. G. 1974. An approach to the teaching of scientific English discourse. *RELC Journal* 5, 1, 27–40.

Wijasuriya, B. S. 1971. The occurrence of discourse markers and inter-sentence connectives in university lectures and their place in the testing and teaching of listening comprehension in English as a foreign language. M.Ed. Thesis. University of Manchester, UK.

Section Eight

WRITING

INTRODUCTION

Although all writers are concerned to produce writing that is readable, coherent, and appropriate to their purposes, a concern with the overall form of the finished products of writing has tended to have an undue effect on the methodology of teaching writing in ESL/EFL. ESL/EFL writing texts hence typically deal with sentence-level writing and with copying and imitating paragraphs that have been especially written to illustrate different patterns of rhetorical organization. What has been missing is attention to the composing processes that efficient writers use.

White's paper exemplifies a primarily product-focus in teaching writing to low-level ESL learners. He discusses a variety of exercise types which can be used to teach aspects of basic sentence and paragraph organization. His approach starts by presenting learners with a model of the kind of text they will be expected to produce. Various items are then selected from the text and used as the basis for practice activities. White shows how this approach can be used across different levels of writing. As is typical in product-based approaches, a large amount of guidance and control is exercised over both the content and the form of what learners write, and an effort is made to avoid errors.

Zamel discusses the philosophy behind the "process-approach" to writing. Central to this approach is an attempt to let student writing activities reflect the natural composing processes made use of in writing. Writers do not usually start out with a clear idea of either what they are going to say or how they are going to say it. Rather, the process of writing generates its own forms and meanings. Zamel reviews some of the research that has led to this observation. Writers typically begin with activities that allow them to develop ideas about the topic they will write about (rehearsal activities), but then they let the ideas change and develop as a consequence of expressing them. The act of writing does not occur as a linear event, however. Writing involves successive cycles of rehearsing, drafting, and revising. An undue concern with the final product of writing is likely to retard the development of efficient writing strategies in ESL learners. The challenge for ESL teachers lies in how to develop activities and classroom exercises that allow students to produce good writing as well as develop good writing strategies. These activities should give learners the opportunity to approach the task of writing in a more natural way than exercises that involve merely sentence manipulation and copying.

DISCUSSION QUESTIONS

1. White observes that "in writing there are conventions which govern the form and style of virtually any text type, from the informal note to the formal report." Examine several examples of a given text type (e.g., a newspaper editorial, a personal letter, or a short piece of descriptive writing) and try to determine the rhetorical principles that govern its organization.

2. Central to activities that reflect a concern for the processes of writing are opportunities for learners to develop ideas to write about, draft sections of what they write, revise these based on feedback of different kinds, and to continue with the drafting and revising process until they complete the final version of their composition. Examine the kinds of low-level writing tasks that White discusses. Can these be approached by activities other than those which involve copying, substitution, and transformation?

3. What should the role of models be in the teaching of writing? When and how might it be appropriate for learners to examine good models of writing?

4. For your next writing assignment in any class, keep a diary of how you completed the assignment. Record in as much detail as possible how you accomplished your writing task. What difficulties did you encounter? How did you resolve them? When you have finished, write up your observations of what you have learned about your own writing processes.

5. At what stage in the teaching of writing is a concern with correct grammar and sentence organization appropriate in dealing with a written assignment? What kinds of options are available in giving feedback on the formal aspects of writing? Compare the advantages and disadvantages of peer feedback and teacher feedback on student writing.

FURTHER READING

1. P. Elbow. 1973. *Writing without Teachers.* London: Oxford University Press.
2. E. D. Hirsch. 1977. *The Philosophy of Composition.* Chicago: University of Chicago Press.
3. S. McKay (ed.). 1984. *Composing in a Second Language.* Rowley, MA: Newbury House Publishers.
4. D. Murray. 1984. *Write to Learn.* New York: Holt, Rinehart and Winston.
5. A. Raimes. 1983. *Techniques in Teaching Writing.* New York: Oxford University Press.
6. F. Smith. 1982. *Writing and the Writer.* New York: Holt, Rinehart and Winston.
7. R. V. White. 1980. *Teaching Written English.* London: George Allen and Unwin.

CHAPTER

20

Approaches to Writing[1]

Ronald V. White

WRITING: ITS PLACE IN THE SYLLABUS

As one of the four skills, writing has traditionally occupied a place in most English language syllabuses. Even so, arguments are sometimes put forward for not teaching students to write because it is felt that a command of the spoken language and of reading is more important. For many students, this may be true, but today, given the importance of English as an international language, more and more people need to learn to write in English for occupational or academic purposes. Thus, in terms of student needs, writing may be seen to occupy an equal role with the other language skills.

There are other reasons why writing merits a place in the language syllabus. To begin with, writing remains the commonest way of examining student performance in English. Virtually all public examinations include a composition, while even gap-filling tests require some competence in the written language. Consequently, ability to write remains a key to examination success. Furthermore, in the eyes of both parents and students, ability to write may be associated with evidence of having learned the language. Writing is tangible—parents and students can see what has been done and what has been achieved. So it has high 'face validity.'

In the classroom, writing may be used as one of a number of techniques to help add variety and interest to the lesson. In addition, writing lends itself to integration with other activities in the classroom; thus, a reading activity may lead into discussion from which a piece of writing evolves, while dictation is a well known example of integrating listening with writing. The teacher can also use writing to provide a break for himself or herself as it is difficult to maintain an unflagging pace through lesson after lesson in which both students and teacher are constantly active.

The teacher may also use writing as a testing device—not necessarily to grade the students, but rather to provide a feed-back on what the students have learned. A written exercise or a composition will be completed without the potential distraction and hidden prompting which can occur with spoken language practice, while the teacher also has the opportunity of reading and marking the work in relative tranquility. Student writing can provide useful evidence of successes and failures in learning, of confusions, and errors, and the teacher can diagnose individual as well as general problems on the basis of such written work.

Finally, writing requires thought, discipline, and concentration. Writing involves committing something to a relatively permanent form. It is a record by which we are judged by whoever reads what we have written. Quite apart from matters such as handwriting, spelling, and grammar, our reader will judge us by our style and the content and logic of what we have written. So writing demands care and thought. For this reason alone its merits a place in the syllabus.

WRITING: ITS CHARACTERISTICS

Writing is not a natural activity. All physically and mentally normal people learn to speak a language. Yet all people have to be taught how to write. This is a crucial difference between the spoken and written forms of language. There are other important differences as well. Writing, unlike speech is displaced in time. Indeed, this must be one reason why writing originally evolved since it makes possible the transmission of a message from one place to another and from one point of time to another. A written message can be received, stored and referred back to at any time. It is permanent in comparison with the ephemeral 'here one minute and gone the next' character of spoken language—even of spoken language that is recorded on tape or disc.

One consequence of the displacement of writing in space and time is that the writer and reader will be physically separated. Indeed, if both are present simultaneously when the message is being sent, there is no reason for writing, unless of course the message is to act as a reminder or an instruction which the receiver can carry away with him/her. The physical separation of writer and reader puts the writer in a very different position from that of face-to-face communication. In spoken interaction we can normally judge how our message is being received and comprehended by looking at how our audience is responding. In writing, this is impossible, except at a remove. Feedback from the reader will always be delayed, and it will be too late to change or improve the written message by then, anyway.

Fortunately, the writer has an advantage which the speaker doesn't normally enjoy. As writers write, they are able to monitor their own performance and to make corrections and improvements without the reader being aware of this process of self-correction. In speech, hesitations and corrections are obvious to the hearer, whereas in writing such features need never be revealed to the reader. So, the writer can spend a lot of time and effort producing a "perfect" message, and it is possible to be far more fluent and accurate in writing than in speaking.

Another important difference between speaking and writing concerns the explicitness of the message. Because the writer and reader are normally physically separated, it is important that the writer should be explicit and not take for granted shared knowledge with the reader. Different types of writing have developed conventions for making shared knowledge explicit; for instance, business correspondence will often open with such phrases as "With reference to . . ." in which the writer establishes a context and shared understanding of what he or she is writing about.

The final important difference between speaking and writing is in the use of expressive features. Whereas in speaking there are many ways of indicating shades of meaning—through stress, intonation, tone of voice—such features are absent in writing. Instead, there is a limited range of possibilities, such as underlining, the use of italics, bold, and upper and lowercase print. These, however, are a pale reflection of the range of expressive features available in speech. The claim that a famous actress could read aloud the telephone directory and make an audience weep indicates the difference in expressive features between speaking and writing.

TEXT TYPE

Writing, unlike speech, has a number of different forms or types of message, with associated conventions. Although there are, in speaking, some text types which have a conventionalized form (e.g., valedictory speeches, after dinner speeches, sermons, addresses of welcome, etc.) such text types tend to be associated with the domain of public speaking, and they do not form part of the conventional language syllabus. By contrast, in writing there are conventions which govern the form and style of virtually any text type, from the informal note to the formal report.

The next types may be classified into two main groups: personal and institutional. Personal text types include notes, telegrams, post cards, personal messages, diaries and letters. Institutional text types include advertisements, instructions, public notices, business letters, catalogues, forms, abstracts and summaries, reports, and essays. The teaching of writing will involve familiarizing students with the conventions of those text types which are appropriate to their needs.

LEVELS OF WRITING

Wilga Rivers suggests that there are four stages in writing, summarized in Table 20.1 (Rivers and Temperley, 1978:265).

Traditionally, Stages I and II—and especially Stage II—have formed an important part of teaching, since reinforcement in written form of language presented and practiced orally has been a much used type of writing activity. Even up-to-date textbooks make use of Stage II writing practice, and typically, the workbooks which have become a fashionable adjunct to main courses incorporate many such exercises.

Stage III writing corresponds to composition in which the learner produces short pieces of writing consisting of one or more paragraphs. Such writing tends to be controlled for content or language, and the student is writing for the teacher as part of learning the language. At its most advanced level, Stage III writing shades into Stage IV.

Expressive writing at Stage IV levels is a relatively advanced type of writing, and typically tends not to be practiced until the student has been learning English for several years. Some students never reach this stage—even, perhaps, in their native language. Essentially, it involves students in producing an original composition of their own for a real audience—possibly each other—rather than simply for the teacher. It will come closest to writing in the "real world" outside the classroom.

Table 20.1

Stage	Name	Goal
I	Writing down	Learning the conventions of the code
II	Writing in the language	Learning the potential of the code
III	Production	Practising the construction of fluent expressive sentences & paragraphs
IV	Expressive writing	Using the code for purposeful communication

TEACHING WRITING: A SEQUENCE

Writing which is concerned with more than sentence level manipulation or reinforcement will need to take instances of writing as a guide or model to the learner. Even when writing in our own language we often need to refer to a model for guidance. The model may be an actual instance of the type of writing we have to produce, or it may be a model in a manual. The use of a model is a natural, respectable, and sensible thing to do, and is even more essential when one is working in a foreign language.

So, then, the student is presented with a model, which may be used as a reading comprehension text. The teacher focuses the students' attention on parts of the text, and selects from it items for practice. The practice phrase may involve sentence level manipulation as a prelude to parallel writing, in which the student is provided with information (possibly in visual form) to be used as the content for writing a composition, paralleling the model.

The final step will involve the students using their own information to produce their own communication which, however, may parallel the original model. Something which is usually ignored at this stage, but which is important in order to help recreate the conditions under which real writing takes place, is to have the students write for an audience other than the teacher. To this end, pair work writing (rather like pair work spoken interaction) can be used so that the students are writing for each other, and are accountable to each other for what they write.

TYPES OF EXERCISES FOR DIFFERENT LEVELS

At Stages I and II, there are a number of variations which involve the creation of sentences from scrambled or muddled strings of words. Here are several examples:

1. The students use notes to write complete sentences, following a given model:

   model: the gun he carries is never loaded.

   lorry/drive/usually/overload

   piano/play/often/hire

2. Unscrambling muddled sentence elements. The pattern or specification of the sentence structure may be provided, e.g.,

   Pattern 1   second is the Fiji Islands island Vanua Levu of the
   Pattern 2   along of mountains run island middle the the

3. Unscrambling a muddle substitution table linked to visual cues or to a written or spoken text, e.g.,

Liz	came	down her ladder
	asked	Jillian and Martin to come in
	told	them about the painting

	went	to the kitchen to make tea
	told	Jillian not to paint the house herself
	telephoned	the painters

4. Controlled table filling, the parts of the sentences being indicated:

SEQUENCER	SUBJECT	VERB	OBJECT
First	he	hit	a Mercedes.
Then	he	bumped	a BMW.

5. The students rewrite sentences with a change of Subject, for instance, from *He* to *She,* from singular to plural, with accompanying changes as required.

6. Students select from alternatives, to write in the singular or plural. This involves matching verb form with the subject, complement with subject, and so on, e.g.,

   Cows/the cow is/are an animal/animals. They/It gives/give us milk. Etc., etc.

   Stage II writing will involve parallel writing activities in which students are provided with a cue or prompt. Using this cue they produce a text which parallels the model.

1. Students are given a model, possibly linked to a visual, such as a description of a place or object. They then have to rewrite the text, but in reverse order, e.g., How to go from A to B becomes How to go from B to A. This will involve changes in expressions of location and direction (for instance, *on the right* becomes *on the left*) as well as other alterations.

2. Minimal cues are given and the students have to create a text, using these cues, and following the example of the model text. For instance, a verb sequence can be given, the order of which must not be altered, and the students have to write a story using only these verbs in the given sequence.

3. Read this description of the port of Calcutta, and then write similar descriptions of the ports of Southampton, Marseilles, and New York. The necessary information is given below. (This example is from Spencer, 1967: 13.)

   Calcutta is a port in India. It is situated on the northeast coast, on the estuary of the River Hooghly, which flows into the Bay of Bengal. The population of the city is six million. The distance from New Delhi, the capital of the country is about one thousand miles.
   a. Southampton—Britain—south coast—River Itchen—English Channel—three hundred thousand—London—eighty miles.
   b. Marseilles—France—south coast—River Rhone—Mediterranean Sea—seven hundred thousand—Paris—four hundred miles.
   c. New York—the USA—east coast—River Hudson—Atlantic Ocean—eight million—Washington—two hundred and fifty miles.

4. Students are given a model text from which they transfer information to a visual, e.g., a description of the processing of rubber. Students complete a flow diagram summary of the process. Then they are given a flow diagram of another process (such as processing sugar), which they use to produce a written description.

Stage IV writing will be concerned not only with correctness of expression but also with the organization of ideas and the production of logically coherent prose. In fact, concern with logical organization is not something which should be left to an advanced level, since even at Stage II there must be some concern with this important aspect of writing. Stage III writing will involve such considerations to an even greater extent. For instance, the teaching of narrative writing will go hand in hand with attention to both the concept and expression of sequence, while an explanation of something will involve both the idea and expression of causality and reason. Likewise, at Stage III, the problem of how to introduce new information and how to relate new information to information already stated will be important.

Concern with the logical organization of a text is as much a reading as a writing problem, and initially there may be considerable overlap of the two activities. For instance, students and teachers can work together to create a text. The teacher may start by providing the first sentence and inviting students to conjecture as to what the next sentence could be. The next sentence can then be revealed, and further discussion and conjecture precedes the disclosure of the third sentence, and so on. Alternatively, the second and subsequent sentences can be produced by the students themselves, so that the text is a creation of the class. The important point is that each successive sentence must conform to the content and logical development of those which precede it.

Another way of focusing on the development of a paragraph is to provide a series of questions, the answers to which will form a coherent piece of prose. The answers can also be supplied, but in muddled order, so that the students have to match each answer to the appropriate question. Alternatively, the students can supply the answers themselves. An exercise of this type should not be confused with the hackneyed and rather dubious practice of linking factual questions to a reading comprehension text with a view to producing a rather clumsy summary or précis of the original. The text-as-dialogue kind of composition is best employed for a topic which is of a more explanatory nature.

Once students have grasped the idea of logical organization, they can be given exercises which involve them in reorganizing, adding and augmenting given paragraphs. Keith Johnson (1981: 21, 67) in *Communicate in Writing* uses a number of such activities, of which the following two are representative. (Note that for economy's sake the "passage" referred to has been omitted.)

1. If we wish to clarify something we have said, we can say it in another way, using the expression "in other words." Find an example of this expression in the passage. Notice where in the sentence the expression is put. Which points in the passage are the following clarifying? Where would you put them in the passage? Where would you write "in other words"?
    a. They are given no light at all.
    b. The environment is unimportant.
    c. Their circadian cycle should continue unchanged.
    d. He changed their environment completely.
2. Paragraph 2 of the passage on page 16 begins by talking about Hymenoptera, and finishes by talking about bees. Rewrite the paragraph so that it begins by talking about bees, and finishes by talking about Hymenoptera.

Make this your opening sentence: Bees are stinging insects, or aculeata.

The next step can involve expressing points of view and reservations. Again, Keith Johnson incorporates a number of activities in *Communicate in Writing* which focus on this aspect of writing. For instance, students are instructed to rewrite a given section so as to support a different viewpoint from the one given in the original. Or they are given the script of a discussion between two people of different viewpoints, and they have to write a paragraph in which they support one speaker's viewpoint while expressing the reservations of the other.

Finally, there is pair work writing, in which students exchange compositions and transfer the information to a table similar to one which was employed in an earlier parallel writing phase. Here are two examples:

1. Using maps 3 and 4[2] of an unnamed island, do the following:
    a. Use Map 3.
    b. Give the island a name.
    c. Add towns, villages, mountains and other features.
    d. Write a description of your island.
    e. Exchange descriptions with your partner.
    f. Use your partner's description to complete Map 4.
    g. Finally, compare your Map 4 with your partner's Map 3, and make any necessary changes or corrections.
2. Working in pairs, do the following:
    a. *You* write a paragraph mentioning similarities between polar climates, but emphasizing their differences: a contrast.
    b. *Your partner* writes a paragraph mentioning differences between polar climates, but emphasizing their similarities: a comparison.
    c. Then look at each other's paragraphs and notice the different ways you have written about the same facts.

One of the advantages of such pair work writing is that the students have a sense of audience because they are writing for each other rather than for a teacher. If they can't understand what their partner has written, they can then send the text back to the writer and ask for an explanation. The accountability of the writer to his reader is made obvious by such a procedure, and it serves to emphasize the need for clear, unambiguous, explicit and well organized writing in a way which the teacher's exhortations may fail to achieve.

CONCLUSION

This brief review of approaches to the teaching of writing may have served to show that there is a variety of techniques available to teach an important language skill which has unique characteristics of its own. Writing is not just speaking in written form. In order to teach writing as a form of communication, it is necessary to go beyond sentence level manipulation to the production of paragraphs and subsequently of multi-paragraph compositions. Once the students are involved in writing two or more interconnected sentences, they have to be trained in using both grammar and vocabulary as a means of linking sentences together. They also have to be trained in organizing ideas, and it is here that the integration of reading and writing can be exploited. There is now a range of materials available covering all these stages of writing. Even so, it is clear there is room for more work and more teaching material to deal with the demand for a wide variety of types of writing among students for whom English is an occupational and academic tool. The papers in this section will provide other ideas on how to deal with the teaching of writing at various levels.

NOTES

1. In writing this paper I have drawn on ideas found in Byrne (1979), Johnson (1981), and Rivers and Temperley (1978).

2. For economy's sake the maps referred to have been omitted.

REFERENCES

Byrne, Donn. 1979. *Teaching Writing Skills.* London: Longman.

Johnson, Keith. 1981. *Communicate in Writing.* London: Longman.

Rivers, Wilga, and Mary S. Temperley. 1978. *A Practical Guide to the Teaching of English as a Second or Foreign Language.* New York: Oxford University Press.

Spencer, D. H. 1967. *Guided Composition Exercises.* London: Longman.

ANNOTATED BIBLIOGRAPHY

1. Two useful books about writing, including suggestions on methodology and content are: Byrne, Donn. 1979. *Teaching Writing Skills.* London: Longman. Ronald V. White. 1980. *Teaching Written English.* London: Heinemann.

2. Writing is dealt with as part of a comprehensive review of methodology by: Rivers, Wilga, and Mary S. Temperley. 1978. *A Practical Guide to the Teaching of English as a Second or Foreign Language.* New York: Oxford University Press.

3. There is a wide range of materials available for teaching writing at virtually all levels. An extremely useful book, particularly as a source of supplementary writing exercises is:

Spencer, D. H. 1967. *Guided Composition Exercises.* London: Longman.

4. A recently published title aimed at the elementary level student is:

Jupp, T., and J. Milne. 1980. *Basic Writing Skills in English.* London: Heinemann.

5. At a higher, intermediate level, and covering a variety of types and styles of writing, there is:

Cullop, M. 1981. *Write it in English.* London: Nelson.

6. Letter writing is of obvious relevance to many learners and will constitute the main type of writing which many people have to perform. A very well organized book in this field is:

Hodlin, S., and T. Hodlin. 1979. *Writing Letters in English.* London: Oxford University Press.

7. For students who are concerned with writing compositions, particularly for upper secondary and university level studies in English medium, the following titles are suggested:

Arnold, J., and J. Harmer. 1978. *Advanced Writing Skills.* London: Longman.
Cooper, J. 1979. *Think and Link.* London: Arnold.
Johnson, K. 1981. *Communicate in Writing.* London: Longman.
Jordan, R. R. 1980. *Academic Writing Course.* London: Collins.
Raimes, A. 1978. *Focus on Composition.* New York: Oxford University Press.

CHAPTER 21

Writing: The Process of Discovering Meaning

Vivian Zamel

Until quite recently research on composition and the classroom practices that it influenced focused on the written products that students composed. Researchers and writing teachers, realizing that this focus on product did not take into account the act of writing itself, therefore began to investigate the process of composing. This research has both identified the complex nature of the composing process and raised questions about past approaches to the teaching of writing. A study of the composing processes of proficient ESL writers corroborates the findings of this research and likewise challenges ESL writing pedagogy.

Since writers do not seem to know beforehand what it is they will say, writing is a process through which meaning is created. This suggests composition instruction that recognizes the importance of generating, formulating, and refining one's ideas. It implies that revision should become the main component of this instruction, that writing teachers should intervene throughout the process, and that students should learn to view their writing as someone else's reading. Methods that emphasize form and correctness ignore how ideas get explored through writing and fail to teach students that writing is essentially a process of discovery.

Research on composition has traditionally been concerned with the written product. The studies reported by Braddock et al. (1963) reflect this concern since, by and large, researchers investigated the effects that certain teaching methodologies had on writing. In many cases these studies sought to prove the efficacy of one grammar over another, thus perpetuating the belief that a better pedagogical approach, particularly one that focused on usage, structure, or correct form, would improve writing.

Since this line of research depended upon the evaluation of compositions that students wrote after having received certain types of instruction, little attention was paid to other, more important considerations such as purpose, audience, and the process of composing itself. Questions dealing with why or for whom students were writing were not taken into account. The whole notion of how writers write—where ideas come from, how they are formulated and developed, what the various stages of composing entail—was ignored. And this state of the art was both influenced by and, in turn, influenced classroom practices and the textbooks that were written (Young, 1978: 31–2). Given the emphasis on the composed product, teachers adopted methods and materials they assumed would positively influence their students' writing.

Recently, however, the focus of research on composition has shifted. Rather than investigating what students write, teachers and researchers are beginning to study the composing process itself. They are now working under the assumption that before we know how to teach writing, we must first understand how we write. And what they are finding out about this process seriously challenges the ways in which composition has been taught in the past. The composing process seems to be an extremely complex undertaking, the nature of which "militate[s] against prescriptive approaches to the teaching of writing" (Witte and Faigley, 1981: 202); it involves much more than studying a particular grammar, analyzing and imitating rhetorical models, or outlining what it is one plans to say. The process involves not only the act of writing itself, but prewriting and rewriting, all of which are interdependent.

ESL teachers concerned with language acquisition and error analysis emphasize, even more than other writing teachers, correctness and form. Widdowson (1978) is particularly critical of ESL teaching practices because they focus upon usage rather than real communication. A cursory look at ESL composition texts indicates that, for the most part, writing assignments are made for the sole purpose of testing the mastery of specific grammatical structures and that few involve invention techniques or prewriting strategies. Furthermore, research on ESL composition is almost negligible. Those few studies that do exist are directed towards investigating the effects of certain types of writing practice on compositions, thereby still indicating a concern with product (see, for example, Konneker and Perkins, 1981). It is therefore important that ESL teachers of writing take into account the current findings in research on composition. While this point has been made before (Zamel, 1976), it is especially appropriate now, given the absence of our own research and our continuing emphasis on the surface features of writing.

RESEARCH ON THE COMPOSING PROCESS

Janet Emig's (1971) classic study represented one of the first attempts to investigate what writers do when they compose. Adopting a case-study approach, which in and of itself was a break from the more traditional experimental designs, she discovered how naive our past assumptions about composing had been. While composing, students seemed to exhibit a variety of behaviors, all of which indicated the nonlinear nature of writing. Emig therefore concluded that teachers of composition tend to "underconceptualize and oversimplify the process of composing" (1971: 98).

Perhaps one of Emig's most important findings was that writing involved a continuing attempt to discover what it is one wanted to say. It is this act of discovery that Murray (1978,

1980) has identified as the main feature of the writing process. While this process entails several stages, such as "rehearsing," "drafting," and "revising" (Murray, 1980: 4–5), these stages interact together and repeatedly in order to discover meaning. Writing viewed from this perspective is the process of exploring one's thoughts and learning from the act of writing itself what these thoughts are. Rather than being the development of some preconceived and well-formed idea, writing is "the record of an idea developing. [It] is a process whereby an initial idea gets extended and refined" (Shaughnessy, 1977: 234). As one writes and rewrites, thereby approximating more closely and more accurately one's intended meaning, the form with which to express this meaning suggests itself. Given this definition of composing, the short-comings of traditional approaches to teaching composition become obvious. Requiring students to formulate their ideas beforehand, to elaborate upon them by using some prescribed rhetorical framework and to submit these written products for grading purposes seems to ignore everything we have learned about the process.

Sondra Perl (1980a), again using the case-study approach of the current research paradigm, found that even unskilled writers employ consistent and stable composing strategies which represent their attempts to discover meaning. "Through the act of seeing their ideas on paper, students are enabled to reflect upon them and develop them further" (Perl, 1980a: 24). In this way, these unskilled writers, reexamining what they had already written in order to discover the direction of their thoughts, were using behaviors identified by other researchers:

> We [shape] the utterances as we write; and when the seam is 'played out' or we are interrupted, we get started again by reading what we have written. (Britton, 1978: 24)

Perl also found that writing was affected by the mode of discourse specified. Students wrote more and with greater fluency and satisfaction when their writing involved them personally, while they wrote with less facility when the writing was more objectified (1980a: 30–1). This is certainly an important finding, given that the purpose of most assigned writing seems to be the transmission of objectively described information for the teacher (Britton, 1978: 15).

Perl went on to study the writing strategies of more proficient writers and again observed the recursive nature of the writing process, that is, that writers go back in order to move forward. She reiterates the notion of writing as discovery:

When we are successful at this process, we end up with a product that teaches us something, that clarifies what we know (or what we know at one point only implicitly), and that lifts out or explicates or enlarges our experience. (Perl, 1980b: 368)

While Perl indicates that all writers, both skilled and unskilled, use what she calls retrospective structuring in order to discover, less skilled writers who view composing as more mechanical and formulaic are so inhibited by their concerns with correctness and form that they cannot get beyond the surface in order to anticipate the needs and expectations of their readers (1980b: 368). This ability to project oneself into the role of another reader, what she calls projective structuring, is a skill that most beginning writers lack and another important aspect of the composing process (see, for example, Barritt and Kroll, 1978; Brostoff and Beyer, 1980; Emig, 1978; Flower, 1979; Judy, 1980).

Sommers (1980), like Perl, studied the writing strategies of less experienced and more experienced writers. While she focused on revision, one should bear in mind that revision and writing were being viewed, as most researchers now view them, as interchangeable terms. She found that less skilled writers revised in the most limited way; they were basically concerned with lexicon and teacher-generated rules and rarely modified ideas that had already been written down. While the unskilled writers in Perl's study (1980a) seemed to understand that writing is a process that involves constant revision, it should be pointed out that they too were concerned almost constantly with form, usage, and grammar. Unlike these writers, the more experienced writers observed by Sommers viewed their writing from a more global perspective. In the process of discovering meaning, these experienced writers changed whole chunks of discourse, and each of these changes represented a reordering of the whole. Sommers concluded that "it is a sense of writing as discovery—a repeated process of beginning over again, starting out new—that the less experienced students failed to have" (1980: 387).

Perl and Sommers both suggest that inexperienced writers pay so much undue attention to form that the ongoing process of discovery is constantly interrupted. As Perl put it, "premature and rigid attempts to correct and edit their work truncate the flow of composing" (1980a: 22). Rose (1980) arrives at the same conclusion after investigating why certain writers experience writer's block. Like Perl's unskilled basic writers and Sommers' less experienced writers, Rose's "blockers" felt restricted by "writing rules or planning strategies that impeded rather than enhanced the composing process" (1980: 390). The "non-blockers," on the other hand, while operating according to certain rules and plans, were also aware that these rules and plans are subject to modification. It is this flexibility that allowed these writers to review what they had written and shift directions when necessary. Thus, when writing is experienced as the mechanical act of transcribing one's ideas, when the language itself rather than "the purpose for which the language is used" becomes the focus (Britton, 1978: 24), when production becomes more important than meaning (Barritt and Kroll, 1978: 52), when attention to form becomes the "dominant and absorbing activity" (Emig, 1978: 62), the act of writing as discovery cannot be explored. Halsted (1975: 82) comments, "The obsession with the final product . . . is what ultimately leads to serious writing block. More importantly, it is a sure way to close off avenues to discovering what it is you have to say."

THE COMPOSING PROCESS OF PROFICIENT ESL WRITERS

While the research thus far reported has taught us a great deal about the composing processes of both less proficient and more proficient writers, it became important to investigate to what extent the findings apply to ESL writers. Are ESL students experiencing writing as a creative act of discovery, or are they attending so much to language and correct form that writing is reduced to a mechanical exercise? How do these students generate their ideas? What happens after these ideas are written down? What does a record of their writing, (from the initial notes to the final draft), indicate about their writing experiences?

These are some of the questions I tried to answer. As in the other process studies, a case-study approach was adopted. Eight ESL students (one Japanese, one Hispanic, two Arabic, two Italian, and two Greek) were interviewed individually about their writing experiences and behaviors.[1] Different stages of their writing were also studied to determine whether their actual writing reflected the experiences that were reported. These ESL students were proficient to the extent that they were no longer enrolled in ESL writing courses and were successfully completing the writing assigned in university-level content area courses. While their writing still indicated some linguistic idiosyncracies, it was basically free of the kind of language-related errors that can obfuscate meaning and demonstrated almost total control of organizational skills. Proficient writers were used for this study not only in order to find out whether their writing experiences resemble those of other writers, but also because it is by studying the composing processes of skilled ESL writers that we can begin to evaluate whether our teaching methods and approaches promote and reinforce these processes or inhibit and undermine them.

An important dimension of the writing process involves the period before the actual writing begins, that is, how writers get and form ideas before putting pen to paper. All of the students talked about the importance of classroom discussion specifically related to a particular topic and how these discussions helped them delineate their ideas. Several mentioned the frustrations they felt, as beginning writers, when they were assigned a paper that was totally unrelated to what had been discussed in class or one that they had no interest in writing about. This raised another important issue, whether or not they had preferences for specific types of discourse. While they indicated that writing about what they knew was important when they first were learning to compose, they by and large now preferred more objective, informationally based assignments. One student, recalling some of his first ESL writing assignments, thought that personal matters were "none of my teacher's business," while another exclaimed, "My teacher is not a confessor, preacher, or psychologist!"

Since these students are now taking courses which require papers that may only be peripherally related to the lectures and discussions, they talked about the strategies they now use to generate their ideas. While at first they may just read and reread course materials until they experience what Perl (1980b) calls a "felt sense," what may happen at this point is quite intriguing. Several students reported having some sort of internal dialogue, "a conversation with an invisible person," as one student put it, in order to figure out how to proceed.

Once the actual writing begins, it may take the form of some sketchy notes or fully articulated sentences and paragraphs. Only one student reported using a formal outline and depending upon it in order to write. This student indicated a still-felt insecurity with English and didn't feel confident enough to compose without resorting to a fairly complex outline. While the use of this outline gave him a sense of control, he did admit that once the outline was completed, he found the actual

writing both boring and mechanical. One can not help but speculate, since his writing was fairly accomplished, as to whether he really needed the outline or whether he had learned his English teacher's lessons too well. One other student reported writing an outline, but not necessarily using it: "Very often the paper I wind up with is different from the outline. I don't see the missing pieces when I write the outline. I can't anticipate what's going to go wrong in my logic when I do the outline." The other students never wrote outlines, although two recalled courses in which they wrote outlines after they wrote the papers in order to comply with their teachers' assignments. One student asked, "How can I write an outline when my ideas are flying back and forth?," while another indicated that only "when the material falls together, I discover my outline."

These students talked about writing down ideas, rethinking them, and then writing some more, not exactly sure of what would next appear on the paper. They discussed the thinking they do about their writing even as they are involved in the most mundane activities, for example, washing the dishes or getting ready for bed. They mentioned needing a great deal of time not only to actually write, but also to leave their writing and come back to it again and again and reread it in order to go on. As one student put it, "The more days go by, the more ideas come. It's like fruit; it needs time to ripen." For some students the inner dialogue that began prior to the actual writing continues as they reread their papers. As one student indicated, "It's through the conversation with myself that I learn what I'm going to say." This dialogue also allows them to "hear" and thereby evaluate the clarity of their writing. One student resorts to using her hands while she reads her writing aloud, as if she were talking to somebody else. As they reread what they have written, they may experience a sense of dissatisfaction, at which point they may have to make partial changes or start anew. If, however, what they have written expresses what they intended to say, they continue writing, finding out in the process what they will say next. These activities do not take place in a series of stages, but rather are transactional and overlapping. Thus, new insights can occur at almost any time during the process, thereby creating the need for more time for the incubation of these ideas (Britton, 1978: 23). While the students talked about the pain involved in the act of writing, they also discussed the feeling of accomplishment they experience when they are satisfied with what they have written. This satisfaction derives not only from the accomplishment itself, but from the knowledge that another reader will be able to appreciate the product of all these efforts. As one student indicated: "When I write, I keep in mind the reader. The professor is not the reader because he has heard it a million times before. . . . My reader is an imaginary person who may not know something about which I write. You have to think that you are informing somebody even though this person never sees it."

An interesting discovery was made when the most proficient writer, a graduate student of English, admitted to writing first in her own native language and then translating into English. None of the other students used translation except when they were stuck, couldn't think of a particular word in English and, in order not to lose their thread of thought, put down the word or expression in their own language. Otherwise, they reacted negatively to the idea of translation. As one student hypothesized, "It would be like being pulled by two brains." This student in resorting to translation, however, did not in fact contradict any of the experiences reported by the other students; rather, it corroborated the fact that writing and creating seem to be simultaneous and reciprocal. She explained that for her writing had to be continuous. If she had to stop because she lacked a particular vocabulary word, she lost the flow of thought and

this made her anxious. "When I write in my own language, I feel great because I can express my writing as part of myself. It's like painting. It materializes on a piece of paper, and other people can share what I feel." Many of the students comments reflected the same idea, that writing provides a means for discovering, creating, and giving form to ones thoughts and ideas. The students themselves articulated it best: "I have in my mind some general ideas. I don't know where I'm going to end. By rereading, the direction, although shapeless, comes to my mind. . . ." And, "Writing helps me assess the clarity of my ideas. When I have a new idea, I try to write it as soon as possible because this is a way of checking if my ideas are clear or confused." Again, "When I go back to my writing, I often find that the order of ideas that I planned get reversed. As soon as you are writing and your ideas are coming, you realize that secondary arguments become primary. I don't know why this happens."

The following longer excerpt was written by one of the students who was so fascinated by the interview that she gave further serious thought to her composing experiences:

> Whenever I'm to write something, the material is an amorphous mass in my head; it seems a very scary and threatening task. How am I going to deal with that—to make sense out of this lump of information? I spend a lot of time thinking about that—when I drive, eat, before I go to sleep, and generally when I'm not engaged in any other intellectual activity.
>
> Progressively, by thinking about it, the amorphous mass channels itself in a very crude manner. Then, I take pen and paper and write down my thoughts; *seeing* them is very helpful; they are in a very raw stage, but nevertheless, it is a concrete start. Usually, I spare [sic] a lot of paper in writing just about everything that comes into mind; this way, the ideas flow without me realizing that I had them in the first place.
>
> At this point, I have to remove myself from my writing. I find it helpful, even for five minutes;

but I don't want to stay away too long for I won't be interested to continue working on it with the same zest. The most I can remove myself from it is a day. When I do return to it, I read it, and most of the time I do some more writing—add some things and/or cut others. From there, I start organizing, maybe develop an outline, which I don't find always necessary —a well organized summary will do it.

Before the final organization of the paper, I have to remove myself from it once more. When I resume my writing, it is in its final stages of completion. This is the time when I need a large 'chunk' of time uninterrupted because I want to have a total command for the material without leaving any possible holes. When I feel that there's nothing more I could do to make it more of a complete piece, I leave it again—to simmer.

When I return to it, I do it with a colored pen and read it very critically; at this point, I edit it—a process which may bring some changes but they are usually small; then, I type it.

After all this process is finished, I usually have a pretty decent paper. I need the time away from it because when I return, I see it with a clearer mind—the time away from it helps me discard the overfamiliarity with the subject and as a consequence, I have a more objective approach. Depending upon the subject I'm writing, the time *chunks,* and how often I have to remove myself from it varies a great deal— the shorter the paper, the shorter the time I need, and, of course, the simpler the subject, the shorter time I need to write it. Generally though, in order to write something and enjoy doing it by putting the best of my efforts, I have to identify with it—either oppose or support. In short, my writing seems to take the developmental process that of a fetus; it begins as an amorphous mass and slowly shapes itself. Eventually, it develops to what it supposes to be, my finished written work—my baby.

As this account indicates, writing about the process itself seems to have given her further insight into the process.

An examination of these students' written papers, which included all of their written attempts to deal with a particular course-related topic, from their first notes to the final copy, attested to the creative nature of the writing process as it was described during the interviews. All of the students wrote several drafts, indicating their struggle to discover and approximate meaning. Even the one student who adhered rigidly to his outline wrote two outlines and no less than three prose drafts. But while he made corrections in his drafts that were basically at the lexical and syntactic level, the other students made changes that were more radical. First drafts contained entire paragraphs that were deleted and rewritten. Paragraphs that appear on separate pieces of paper were added to pages that had already been completed. Some writers used their own symbols to indicate where information was missing. Other writers wrote themselves marginal comments. Second and even third drafts indicated changes of the same magnitude, but much fewer of them. More sentence-level and syntactic concerns seem to have been attended to, although these were addressed from the outset. Final parts of sentences were crossed out and reworded as if the authors realized in midstream that what they ended up expressing was not what they had intended. Some sentences were totally rewritten so that the relationship between the preceding sentence and the one that followed became more logical and clearer. As students got closer to the final product they were proofreading and polishing their texts. Changes in sentence structure were much more numerous. Vocabulary, tense, and punctuation were frequently focused on. Inflections were added where they had been omitted before. All in all, the different versions of their writing serve as a tangible record of how their ideas got generated, clarified, rearticulated, and refined.

IMPLICATIONS FOR TEACHING

It is quite clear that ESL writers who are ready to compose and express their ideas use strategies similar to those used by native speakers of English. Their writing behaviors suggest approaches to the teaching of composition that ESL teachers may have felt were only appropriate for native speakers but which, in fact, may be effective for teaching all levels of writing, including ESL composition.

Students first of all need ideas to explore and write about. While more skilled writers have established certain methods that allow them to proceed with this exploration, less proficient writers need to be taught how to make use of prewriting strategies or invention techniques. As Shaughnessy points out, "Instruction in writing must begin with the more fundamental processes whereby writers get their thoughts in the first place and then get them underway" (1977: 245). An instructional method based on the traditional read-analyze-write model of teaching composition ignores this crucial aspect of the composing process. It fails to take into account that students need the opportunity to "talk about, to expand and even to relearn or reexamine their experiences . . . prior to writing" (Judy, 1980: 39). Since students may lack systematic strategies necessary for finding a focus and beginning (Brostoff and Beyer, 1980: 39–40), they need to be taught how to explore topics, develop ideas, and discover relationships by making use of the kinds of invention techniques described by Koch and Brazil (1978: 25–63), Lauer (1980: 57–59), Maimon et al. (1981: 23–45), Wiener (1980: 90–92), and Young (1978: 35–39). While the ESL field is beginning to recognize the importance of these activities (see, for example Daubney-Davis, 1981; McKay, 1981; and Taylor, 1981), it still seems dominated by a concern with product, thus supporting the finding that school-sponsored writing provides little time for prewriting (Emig, 1971: 92).

Another important aspect of the composing process concerns the way writers feel about the topics they are asked to write about. Raimes is critical of the narrow range of topics ESL students are typically assigned (1979: 17–19), and Taylor claims that "Rarely is a writing assignment compelling enough to give students an opportunity to immerse themselves totally in the topic to the extent that they have something important to say" (1981: 9). Writing instruction that focuses on rhetorical forms and requires students to compose papers on artificial topics in order to demonstrate mastery of these forms fails to recognize that writers write both quantitatively more and qualitatively better when they are composing papers about topics that engage them (Perl, 1980a: 30–31). Students' writing thus should be motivated by their feelings about and responses to a topic with which they have had some experience (Judy, 1980: 39; Lauer, 1980: 56). This does not mean, however, that writing assignments need be entirely student generated or that they involve only personal accounts, but rather that even academic writing should allow students to become involved in a subject (Weiss, 1980: 146–146) or provide them with a way into the topic (Perl, 1980a: 31).

As far as writing about truly personal topics is concerned, it should be kept in mind that the ESL students that were interviewed expressed dissatisfaction with more personally oriented assigned writing, a finding that has been reported before (Kroll, 1979). Perhaps this dissatisfaction stems from the fact they are in the habit of using their own native language when writing about more private matters and therefore feel that the academic setting is inappropriate for this type of discourse. Or, perhaps because these assignments were collected, evaluated for error, and graded, these students were never given to understand the purpose of this type of writing, that it was meant to get them in touch with and value their felt thoughts and responses. Once students and their teachers recognize the function of expressive or reflective writing (Britton, 1978: 16; Emig, 1971: 91), they may begin to appreciate its importance. By keeping personal journals, for example, students may come to realize that writing is indeed a way to explore one's feelings and thoughts.

While students are rarely provided with pre-writing practice and may have little idea as to the reasons why they are asked to write particular types of discourse, it is the actual process of composing of which they may have the least understanding and with which they are probably given the least experience. Not knowing how writers behave and what the process involves, students "tend to think that the point of writing is to get everything right the first time and that the need to change things is the work of the amateur" (Shaughnessy, 1977: 79). They may have the misconception that, because of our attention to form, "writers know the form before they know the content" (Murray, 1980: 13). They may have the impression that writers "know exactly what they are going to say before they say it" (Murray, 1978: 100). But we know from the research findings that this is not the case, and this knowledge needs to be imparted to our students. We must allow them to experience the process of discovering what they want to say through writing. We must provide them with ample time to write and rewrite, to learn that several drafts may be needed before intention and expression become one. We need to show them our own attempts to write and the different transformations that this writing undergoes, for "one of the most important facts about the composing process that seems to get hidden from students is that the process that creates precision is itself messy" (Shaughnessy, 1977: 222). In this way they may come to appreciate that revising may mean deleting and adding paragraphs or even pages, not the editing or proofreading that revising has traditionally been synonymous with. They also need to be taught that since writers do not produce perfect essays in one sitting certain features of composing are focused upon before others. This helps reinforce the idea that content and organization are of primary importance and that editing, though to some extent inevitable throughout, is really the province of the last stage of composing. Furthermore this may keep students from experiencing a cognitive overload, a situation which results when too many factors, concerns, or problems are being attended to simultaneously (Maimon et al., 1981: 10; Hirsch, 1980: 159).

Rather than require students to prepare comprehensive outlines (Britton, 1978; Halsted, 1975; Taylor, 1981), we should encourage them to take more informal notes or jot down ideas and reassure them that they need not know from the outset what it is they are going to say. Otherwise, rather than struggling to make sense of their ideas, they may be struggling because "we have put writing in a framework that inhibits communication and/or expression" (Petty, 1978: 83). We may also need to reexamine our use of the prose models which we ask our students to imitate, a practice that seems to be pervasive in ESL, perhaps because of Kaplan's (1967) study of culture-specific rhetorical thought patterns. But this methodology can be misleading because it may give students the impression that the linear, straightforward writing they are supposed to imitate is the result of a process that was itself linear. It fails to show students that the thinking and writing that preceded these models may have been chaotic and disorganized and that their own attempts to write may involve this same disorder. The study of such models puts undue emphasis on the final and correct product and by doing so threatens students with the idea that they are expected to achieve the same level of competency and may render them incapable of even beginning (Eschholz, 1980: 23). Instead of asking students to match their writing to a particular model, we need to teach them that "form grows from content and is inseparable from it" (Judy, 1980: 41), that structuring and organizing one's ideas and thoughts only make sense with reference to the nature of those ideas and thoughts. Finally, because ESL students may still be in the process of acquiring language skills, it needs to be emphasized that grammar-based approaches to teaching writing serve neither as substitutes nor prerequisites for instruction in the process of composing (Lauer, 1980: 54). Extensive research has shown that grammar study may have little to do with composing (Zamel, 1976: 72–74), and it has been pointed out that even low-level students should be given the opportunity to explore this process (Taylor, 1976: 310–311; Raimes, 1979: 3).

Writing taught as a process of discovery implies that revision becomes the main focus of the course and that the teacher, who traditionally provides feedback after the fact, intervenes to guide students through the process. Teacher-student conferences need to be regularly held between drafts so that students learn, while they are creating, what areas need to be worked on. Some educators feel that individual conferences are so effective that they should take the place of all in-class instruction (Carnicelli, 1980). This, however, would deny the students the opportunity to share their writing with other students, an activity that forms the basis of much process-centered instruction (see, for example, Dowst, 1980; Judy, 1980; Lauer, 1980; Maimon, 1980; Murray, 1980; Wiener, 1980). This shared experience reinforces the fact that the teacher is truly not the only reader, a claim which we repeatedly make but fail to convince our students of, and that audience considerations therefore need to be taken into account. Moreover, this type of experience helps develop in students the crucial ability of reviewing their writing with the eyes of another. Most beginning students who are unable to adopt another's frame of reference, compose essays that are egocentric (Brostoff and Beyer, 1980: 44; Odell et al., 1978: 5). They may not be aware that their prose is writer-based rather than reader-based (Flower, 1979) and that as we write "our needs as readers become paramount" (Emig, 1978: 66). Peers who serve as a real and immediate audience can help establish these needs.

It should not be concluded from the foregoing discussion that engaging students in the process of composing eliminates our obligation to upgrade their linguistic competencies. Raimes (1979) talks about the numerous language skills that ESL composition teachers need to attend to. But what needs to be emphasized is that this obligation should not form the basis of our writing instruction. Syntax, vocabulary, and rhetorical form are important features of writing, but they need to be taught not as ends in and of themselves, but as the means with which to better express one's meaning. Otherwise, students may never understand why these features are important:

> Cut off from the impulse to say something, or from the sense that anything he might say is important to anyone else, he is automatically cut off from the grammatical intuitions that would serve him in a truly communicative situation. (Shaughnessy, 1977: 86)

If, however, students learn that writing is a process through which they can explore and discover their thoughts and ideas, then product is likely to improve as well.

NOTE

1. It should be noted that while self-reports are generally recognized as methodologically less rigorous than the "talk-aloud" or observation methods adopted by composing process researchers, interviews were used here as a preliminary attempt to gain insight into ESL

composing processes. In order to understand fully what these processes entail, therefore, studies similar to those reported earlier need to be undertaken.

REFERENCES

Barritt, Loren S., and Barry M. Kroll. 1978. Some implications of cognitive-developmental psychology for research in composing. In C. Cooper and L. Odell (eds.), *Research on Composing.* Urbana, IL: National Council of Teachers of English.

Braddock, Richard et al. 1963. *Research in Written Composition.* Champaign, IL: National Council of Teachers of English.

Britton, James. 1978. The composing process and the functions of writing. In C. Cooper and L. Odell (eds.), *Research on Composing.* Urbana, IL: National Council of Teachers of English.

Brostoff, Anita, and Barry K. Beyer. 1980. An approach to integrating writing into a history course. *Journal of Basic Writing 2,* 4:36–52.

Carnicelli, Thomas A. 1980. The writing conference: A one-to-one conversation. In T. R. Donovan and B. W. McClelland (eds.), *Eight Approaches to Teaching Composition.* Urbana, IL: National Council of Teachers of English.

Daubney-Davis, Ann E. 1981. Invention techniques: What we can learn from freshman composition. Paper presented at the Fifteenth Annual TESOL Convention, Detroit, Michigan, March 1981.

Dowst, Kenneth. 1980. The epistemic approach: Writing, knowing, and learning. In T. R. Donovan and B. W. McClelland (eds.), *Eight Approaches to Teaching Composition.* Urbana, IL: National Council of Teachers of English.

Emig, Janet. 1971. *The Composing Processes of Twelfth Graders.* Urbana, IL: National Council of Teachers of English.

Emig, Janet. 1978. Hand, eye, brain: Some "basics" in the writing process. In C. Cooper and L. Odell (eds.), *Research on Composing.* Urbana, IL: National Council of Teachers of English.

Eschholz, Paul E. 1980. The prose models approach: Using products in the process. In T. R. Donovan and B. W. McClelland (eds.), *Eight Approaches to Teaching Composition.* Urbana, IL: National Council of Teachers of English.

Flower, Linda. 1979. Writer-based prose: A cognitive basis for problems in writing. *College English 41:* 19–37.

Halsted, Isabella. 1975. Putting error in its place. *Journal of Basic Writing 1,* 1:72–86.

Hirsch, Donald E. 1980. Research in writing: The issues. In L. N. Kasden and D. R. Hoeber (eds.), *Basic Writing.* Urbana, IL: National Council of Teachers of English.

Judy, Stephen. 1980. The experiential approach: Inner world to outer worlds. In T. R. Donovan and B. W. McClelland (eds.), *Eight Approaches to Teaching Composition.* Urbana, IL: National Council of Teachers of English.

Kaplan, Robert B. 1967. Contrastive rhetoric and the teaching of composition. *TESOL Quarterly 1,* 3: 10–16.

Koch, Carl and James M. Brazil. 1978. *Strategies for Teaching the Composition Process.* Urbana, IL: National Council of Teachers of English.

Konneker, Beverly H., and Kyle Perkins. 1981. Testing the effectiveness of sentence-combining for ESL composition. Paper presented at the Fifteenth Annual TESOL Convention, Detroit, Michigan, March 1981.

Kroll, Barbara. 1979. A survey of writing needs of foreign and American college freshmen. *English Language Teaching Journal 33,* 3:219–226.

Lauer, Janice M. 1980. The rhetorical approach: Stages of writing and strategies for writers. In T. R. Donovan and B. W. McClelland (eds.), *Eight Approaches to Teaching Composition.* Urbana, IL: National Council of Teachers of English.

Maimon, Elaine P. 1980. Demythologizing writing across the curriculum. *Journal of Basic Writing 2,* 4:3–11.

Maimon, Elaine P. et al. 1981. *Writing in the Arts and Sciences.* Cambridge, MA: Winthrop Publishers.

McKay, Sandra L. 1981. Pre-writing activities. *TEC-FORS Newsletter 4,* 3:1–2.

Murray, Donald M. 1978. Internal revision: A process of discovery. In C. Cooper and L. Odell (eds.), *Research on Composing*. Urbana, IL: National Council of Teachers of English.

Murray, Donald M. 1980. Writing as process: How writing finds its own meaning. In T. R. Donovan and B. W. McClelland (eds.), *Eight Approaches to Teaching Composition*. Urbana, IL: National Council of Teachers of English.

Odell, Lee et al. 1978. Discourse theory: Implications for research on composing. In C. Cooper and L. Odell (eds.), *Research on Composing*. Urbana, IL: National Council of Teachers of English.

Perl, Sondra. 1980a. A look at basic writers in the process of composing. In L. N. Kasden and D. R. Hoeber (eds.), *Basic Writing*. Urbana, IL: National Council of Teachers of English.

Perl, Sondra. 1980b. Understanding composing. *College Composition and Communication 31*, 4:363–369.

Petty, Walter T. 1978. The writing of young children. In C. Cooper and L. Odell (eds.), *Research on Composing*. Urbana, IL: National Council of Teachers of English.

Raimes, Ann. 1979. Problems and teaching strategies in ESL composition. In *Language in Education: Theory and Practice 14*. Arlington, VA: Center for Applied Linguistics.

Rose, Mike. 1980. Rigid rules, inflexible plans, and the stifling of language: A cognitivist analysis of writer's block. *College Composition and Communication 31*, 4:389–401.

Shaughnessy, Mina P. 1977. *Errors and Expectations*. New York: Oxford University Press.

Sommers, Nancy. 1980. Revision strategies of student writers and experienced adult writers. *College Composition and Communication 31*, 4:378–388.

Taylor, Barry P. 1976. Teaching composition to low-level ESL students. *TESOL Quarterly 10*, 3:309–319.

Taylor, Barry P. 1981. Content and written form: A two-way street. *TESOL Quarterly 15*, 1:5–13.

Weiss, Robert H. 1980. Writing in the total curriculum: A program for cross-disciplinary cooperation. In T. R. Donovan and B. W. McClelland (eds.), *Eight Approaches to Teaching Composition*. Urbana, IL: National Council of Teachers of English.

Widdowson, H. G. 1978. *Teaching Language as Communication*. New York: Oxford University Press.

Wiener, Harvey S. 1980. First days' thoughts on process and detail. In T. R. Donovan and B. W. McClelland (eds.), *Eight Approaches to Teaching Composition*. Urbana, IL: National Council of Teachers of English.

Witte, Stephen P., and Lester Faigley. 1981. Coherence, cohesion and writing quality. *College Composition and Communication 32*, 2:189–204.

Young, Richard E. 1978. Paradigms and problems: Needed research in rhetorical invention. In C. Cooper and L. Odell (eds.), *Research on Composing*. Urbana, IL: National Council of Teachers of English.

Zamel, Vivian. 1976. Teaching composition in the ESL classroom: What we can learn from research in the teaching of English. *TESOL Quarterly 10*, 1:67–76.

Section Nine

GRAMMAR

INTRODUCTION

Grammar has traditionally had a central role in language teaching. Particular theories of grammar and theories of learning associated with them have provided justifications for approaches to syllabus design and methodology for many years (see Sections Two and Four). In this section we consider classroom approaches to the teaching of grammar. Although grammatical proficiency and language proficiency are now no longer considered to be one and the same thing, grammar plays a role in speaking, listening, reading, and writing skills. Hence, it cannot be ignored. Characteristic of current approaches to the teaching of grammar is, consequently, a tendency to treat grammar as a component of other skills, rather than as a separate skill in itself. This means that particular grammatical items are dealt with when they are needed for specific kinds of communicative tasks and functions.

Eisenstein focuses on how grammar can be taught, considers various factors affecting how grammatical explanations can be given, and then briefly examines the approach to the teaching of grammar found in a number of language teaching methods. Solutions adopted depend on the age of the learners, their learning experience, their cognitive style, the setting, and the kind of grammatical rule being taught. These may determine whether a deductive or inductive approach will be employed, whether grammatical terminology will be used, and what the medium of explanation will be.

Richards examines the teaching of the *perfect* and suggests that in teaching any area of grammar, particularly one belonging to the domain of tense or aspect, potential confusion between overlapping forms can be avoided by selecting functions for new forms that do not duplicate functions covered by already known forms. In this case, confusion between the perfect and the simple past can be minimized by first teaching those meanings and uses of the perfect that are distinct from the simple past form. Richards expresses this as a maxim: teach new functions for new forms rather than new forms for old functions.

White examines the passive and suggests another principle underlying an approach to the teaching of grammar: teach new grammatical items as ways of performing new discourse functions rather than as ways of producing more complex sentences. This is illustrated in a lesson plan for the teaching of the passive in which it is used in the context of describing processes. White also emphasizes the need to find content matter that can provide an authentic context for specific grammatical features. Grammar is thus not an end itself, but a means to an end—it serves to help develop proficiency in other skill areas.

DISCUSSION QUESTIONS

1. Eisenstein discusses a number of factors that can affect an approach to the teaching of grammar. For a given group of ESL/EFL learners with whom you are familiar, draw up a profile of the factors pertaining to that group which will determine the approach you would take to the teaching of grammar.

2. You need to teach the following items to a class of low-level intermediate ESL learners:

relative pronouns: who, whom (e.g., as in "She is the girl *who* lives next door. She is the woman *whose* husband drives a Volvo.")

Learners find difficulty with these forms because they have only encountered *Who* and *Whom* as interrogative pronouns (e.g., as in "Who did you meet?"). How will you present and practice this form? Will you give a grammatical explanation of the form? If so, how?

3. Two "maxims" as part of an approach to the teaching of grammar were noted in the introduction to this section. How many additional maxims would you want to add to this list and what are they?

4. Consider the distinction between the *simple present* and the *present progressive* or between any two potentially overlapping areas of grammar. What confusions are learners likely to have with these forms? Suggest how these might be minimized by attention to the maxim "teach new functions for new forms rather than new forms for old functions."

5. What approach do Richards and White take toward the explanation of the meanings of new grammatical forms?

6. Following White's functional approach to the teaching of grammar, develop a lesson plan for the teaching of the imperative.

FURTHER READING

1. M. Celce-Murcia, and D. Larsen-Freeman. 1983. *The Grammar Book.* Rowley, MA: Newbury House Publishers.
2. R. A. Close. 1962. *English as a Foreign Language: Grammar and Syntax for Advanced Students.* London: George Allen and Unwin.

3. T. Higgs, and R. Clifford. 1982. The push towards communication. In T. Higgs (ed.), *Curriculum, Competence, and the Foreign Language Teacher.* Skokie, IL: National Textbook Company, 57–80.
4. H. Hoy Schmidt. 1981. Using authentic discourse in teaching the conditional. *Cross Currents* 8, 1, 1–13.
5. J. C. Richards. 1985. The role of grammar in the language curriculum. In J. C. Richards, *The Context of Language Teaching.* New York: Cambridge University Press, 144–157.

CHAPTER 22

Grammatical Explanations in ESL: Teach the Student, Not the Method

Miriam R. Eisenstein

Many methods have been proposed for the teaching of foreign languages. Different approaches have fallen in and out of fashion along with associated psychological or linguistic theories as well as dynamic individuals representing the different points of view. An eclectic approach has also been suggested, but there has been no principled basis for a decision on which aspect of which method one should choose in a particular circumstance. These different methodologies for language teaching have met with varying degrees of success and failure. What is amazing is that there are some examples of successful language learners for different and even contradictory methods (Stevick, 1976), and the question of which overall method is superior remains to be answered.

One of the difficulties inherent in the question of which approach is best is that the different methods vary in many ways including inherent view of language learning, importance and extent of teacher modeling, types of practice (drills, situations, etc.), skills covered and their order of presentation, and evaluation of student

progress. The specific realization of the target language used for teaching may vary in formality, meaningfulness to students, and view of what constitutes acceptable speech. As a result of the many variables involved, empirical research which attempts to compare the effectiveness of the different methods does not often produce clear cut results.

Therefore, this paper will focus on a more narrow area of second language teaching; the role of the grammatical explanation. Currently, there are several points of view. Opinions differ not only with reference to whether grammatical explanations should be stated by the teacher or deduced by the student; the very need or desirability of the grammatical explanation in the second language lesson has been seriously challenged, together with the need to isolate grammatical structures at all. This paper will claim that the function and presentation of the grammar explanation is a complex issue, and no single approach will be satisfactory in all situations. The teacher's decision should be dependent upon the backgrounds and needs of the learners. The treatment of grammatical explanations by the major language teaching methodologies will be reviewed, and the variables relevant to differing student populations will be explored. Recommendations will be made in terms of matching the appropriate type of grammatical presentation to the student population. Suggestions will be made on the basis of the literature as well as the author's experience as a language teacher and researcher.

THE LEARNER IS AN INDIVIDUAL

We must begin by recognizing the uniqueness of each language learner. A problem underlying the different approaches to language teaching, and the treatment of grammatical explanations in this context, is the assumption that all people learn languages in the same manner, thus a single method will be right for everyone. But there is evidence that this is not the case. Recent research shows that different individuals have different cognitive styles (Hartnett, 1974) and employ different strategies in approaching the language learning task (Ramsey, 1977).

Friedlander (1965) warns that "different modes of thinking may be related to more or less stable personality dimensions . . . a teaching method keyed especially to one set of traits is likely to generate frustration, annoyance, and difficulties for students whose style of thinking is oriented in the other direction."

In addition to cognitive style and strategy, learner variables include age, sex, socio-cultural background, literacy, previous language learning experience, motivation, and language aptitude. Student attitudes vary toward foreign language and culture, teacher and method (Politzer, 1972).

VARIABLES IN THE GRAMMAR EXPLANATION

There are several possible ways in which a grammar explanation can be presented in a second language lesson (Krashen and Seliger, 1975). The following is a summary of some of the alternative aspects of presentation.

1. Isolation
   The lesson is constructed in such a way that the student focuses upon and manipulates one particular rule or structure at a time.
2. Conscious statement
   The grammar rule or structural pattern is consciously stated either in terms of structural description, function or both.
3. Deductive vs. inductive statement
   This refers to the point in the lesson where the grammatical explanation takes place.

   a. *deductive statement*—Grammar explanation is made at the beginning of the lesson, and practice is essentially concerned with the application of the rule or structure.
   b. *inductive statement*—The explanation follows practice with the rule or structure being studied. (Students "discover" the rule, or the teacher states it, or both, see #5.)
4. Language of explanation
   A grammar explanation may be presented in terms of specific examples, everyday language, some form of abstract grammatical terminology or metalanguage, or combination of these.
5. The explainer
   The explanation may be made by the

teacher, the students, book, chart, or some combination of these.

6. Medium of explanation

An explanation may be presented orally, written on the board and/or read from a book or chart.

GRAMMAR EXPLANATIONS AS USED IN ESL METHODS

I will briefly review the treatment of grammatical explanations by some of the major ESL methods that have been advocated in the United States now and in the recent past. This is not meant to be an exhaustive study of all available methods; rather it is an attempt to show the variety of ways in which different methods deal with grammar explanations and may help teachers in evaluating available materials.

1. *Grammar translation* (Koolhoven, 1961, is an example) is associated with formal rule statement. Learning proceeds, deductively, and the rule is generally stated by the teacher, in a textbook, or both. Traditional abstract grammatical terminology is used. Drills include translation into native language.

2. *The direct method* (discussed in Lado, 1964, and Simoes, 1976) is characterized by meaningful practice and exclusion of the mother tongue. This method has had many interpretations, some of which include an analysis of structure, but generally without the use of abstract grammatical terminology.

3. *The audio-lingual method* (Lado, 1964) stresses an inductive presentation with extensive pattern practice. Writing is discouraged in the early stages of learning a structure. Here again, there has been considerable variation in the realization of this approach. In some cases, no grammatical explanation of any kind is offered. In others, the teacher might focus on a particular structure by isolating an example on the board, or through contrast. When grammatical explanation is offered it is usually done at the end of the lesson as a summary of behavior (Politzer, 1965), or in later versions of this method the rule might be stated in the middle of the lesson and followed by additional drills.

4. *Situational reinforcement* (Hall, 1967) emphasizes learning language in terms of real situations. Several related structures are presented at once so that only partial isolation occurs. A written summary or chart of the structures covered is included in the text, but this method is essentially inductive and grammatical explanations as such are a minimal part of the language learning experience.

5. *Cognitive code* (Chastain, 1970) stresses the ability of the individual to use order and rules in language in a creative way. Rules are presented deductively.

6. *The silent way* (Gattegno, 1976) approaches language learning as a series of problem solving situations. It achieves great control over and isolation of structure through the use of rods which limit vocabulary in the early stages of language learning and allow students to focus on structure. Grammar explanations are not stated by the teacher (but will be accepted from students if volunteered).

7. *Counseling learning* (Curran, 1972) deals with the needs and feelings of the student by providing each student with an individual counselor who speaks both his native language and the target language. The learner decides what he wants to say and his "counselor" will tell him how to say it in the target language, as well as translate what has been said by others. Analysis of what has been said follows the oral portion of the lesson, but I do not believe this method limits the way in which grammar explanations should be made. The placement of this analysis in the lesson means that this is an "inductive" approach.

Table 22.1

	Conscious grammar explanation	Isolation of (rule of structure)	Deductive or inductive presentation	The "explainer"	Language type used for explanation	Oral or written explanation
Grammar-translation	yes	yes	deductive	book and/or teacher	abstract	written
Direct method	yes or no	yes	inductive (if at all)	teacher (when done)	non-abstract	oral-written
Audio-lingual	yes or no	yes	inductive	teacher	example or non-abstract	oral-written
Situational reinforcement	no (but summary chart and structure notes provided)	no (several structures presented together—not one at a time)	inductive	book	non-abstract	written
Cognitive code	yes	yes	deductive	teacher	abstract	oral-written
The silent way	no	yes	inductive	student (when done)	non-abstract	oral
Counseling-learning	yes	no	inductive	counselor and learner	not-specified	oral-written

Table 22.1 provides a summary of the methods discussed and their treatment of grammar explanations.

As was stated earlier, rather than a general eclectic approach, this paper will recommend certain types of grammatical presentations in terms of specific learner variables.

SHOULD THERE BE CONSCIOUS GRAMMATICAL EXPLANATIONS?

The age of the learner is crucial in determining whether or not grammatical explanations should be the subject of conscious focus. Lenneberg (1967) postulated a critical period for language acquisition. The child who is learning a second language appears to be learning differently from the post-adolescent learner. Hale and Budar (1970) and Dulay and Burt (1973) have found that children learn languages best in a natural environment, through interaction with speakers of the target language. Neither formal instruction nor conscious grammatical explanations have been shown to have any positive influence on children. At this point in time, the research indicates that formal second language instruction for children is advisable only when there is not enough contact of the children with speakers of the target language in natural settings. When formal language classes are provided, emphasis should be on natural-like language practice rather than on conscious grammatical explanations.

Unlike children, adults are likely to benefit from formal language instruction (Krashen and Seliger, 1975). With adult learners, conscious grammatical explanation should be considered.

In dealing with adult learners, we must take into account culture and previous education experiences. Most adults who enter the classroom have been educated in terms of a learning system that may differ greatly from our own. In fact, some adults bring with them a specific idea of how to go about learning foreign languages, based on their experience.

In Russia, for example, (Belyayev, 1964) language learning usually involves the conscious statement of grammatical rules. Lewis (1974) discusses the stress in Soviet pedagogy on the value of conscious learning. He quotes Vygotsky as representative of the Russian view of language teaching in terms of "conscious employment of linguistic rules and strategies." It is not surprising then that Russian adults experience frustration when confronted with a language learning class in which there are no consciously stated rules (Flynn-Corros, personal communication).

The type of grammar explanation presented in a specific situation should take advantage of the previous learning experience of the students —not try to undermine it. Where there is reason to introduce divergent learning approaches, this should be done with sensitivity and care, in a manner that does not penalize the student for how he has learned to learn.

IS THERE A NEED FOR RULE ISOLATION?

Krashen and Seliger (1975) hypothesize that one reason adults find formal language instruction helpful is that rule isolation is frequently a factor within the formal setting. They further suggest that adults who seem to pick up languages outside of the classroom have some means of approaching items in the target language one at a time.

Rule isolation is usually a factor in lessons that include consciously stated rules. But it is quite possible to have careful rule isolation in a lesson, yet never actually deal with a rule or structure in any abstract way. The silent way is just such an approach.

Stern (1973) points out that languages are complex and all elements of language are not easily quantifiable. "When the argument is raised about whether we should teach English as an experience or in graded structural progression, should we not remind ourselves that languages are sufficiently complex to require both approaches?" This is a sensible view not only in terms of the nature of language itself, but also in terms of the learner. Ramsay (1977) in a study of successful language learners, found that some learners acquire language in an intuitive way; that is "knowledge that one possesses but reaches on a non-conscious level through some kind of bypass mechanism." And Belyayev (1964) claims that language learning can be both conscious and intuitive.

Krashen (1978) has found that not everybody learns via conscious rules. He has postulated the Monitor theory which recognizes two separate kinds of language learning. The acquisition of language through natural processes and the learning of language involving the use of conscious rules. Krashen further states that only simple rules appear to be useful for most learners.

In view of the complexity of language, our limited understanding of how it functions, and learner differences, the second language lesson should not be limited to presentation of language phenomena that we can easily explain through the grammars available to us. Rather, classes should provide various kinds of language learning approaches: realistic experiences with language that are not constrained by statable rules, rule isolation for adults, and conscious statement of grammar rules and structures for those individuals who have had experience with this kind of language approach as well as those learners who find conscious statement helpful because of their style of learning.

SHOULD A GRAMMATICAL EXPLANATION BE INDUCTIVE OR DEDUCTIVE?

An inductive approach to language learning has much in its favor. Friedlander (1965) recognizes its positive aspects, "It capitalizes on the very strong reward value of bringing order, clarity and meaning to experiences that were previously disorderly . . . (and it) involves the student as an active participant in his own instruction."

A deductive presentation has the advantage that the student is in control during practice and has less fear of drawing an incorrect conclusion in terms of how the target language is functioning.

A study of different language learners (Hartnett, 1974) reveals that some learners are more successful in deductive language classes while others do better in more inductive classes. This difference in cognitive styles may be linked to "different neurological mechanisms in the learners." Hartnett also found that deductive learners are "better language learners in general." This would help to explain the results of an experiment, (Seliger, 1975) which compared the results of deductive vs. inductive rule presentation with adult ESL learners. Seliger found that although there was no significant difference in learner performance on a test administered one day after the lesson (recall test), a second test done three weeks later (retention test) showed that a majority of learners taught deductively performed significantly better as compared with their scores on the first test. If it is the case that individuals predisposed to deductive learning are better language learners in general, then it is not surprising that the deductive group would do better. Of course, another possible explanation is that deductive learning is generally more successful with adults (as Seliger concluded) and so Hartnett could have found that deductive learners do better just because they use a more effective learning strategy. In either case, it is clear that some learners perform inductively with reference to language learning, while others perform deductively. And while more deductive learners are successful, there are examples of inductive learners who are also successful in language learning. (In Seliger's study, 27% of those inductively taught improved their scores on the retention test as compared with the recall test.)

Furthermore, Hammerly (1975) has found that "certain structures are more amenable to a deductive approach, while others . . . can be learned very well by an inductive approach."

So both deductive and inductive presentation can be useful depending on the cognitive style of the learner and the structure to be presented. In an individualized situation, the teacher can try both approaches with a particular student and concentrate on the one which gives the student greater success and satisfaction. In the traditional classroom, some kind of combined presentation would be desirable. A compromise would be to first present a structure in context without grammatical explanation (to allow induction), then state the rule (or allow the students to do so) and finally allow a substantial amount of time for manipulation of the structure by the learners (deductive).

WHO SHOULD PROVIDE THE GRAMMATICAL EXPLANATION?

When a purely deductive approach is used, it is obviously the teacher (or a book) who provides the grammatical explanation. In an inductive approach, either the students or teacher may do so. It has been noted that discovering explanations is a rewarding experience for many students. And there are many occasions when it would be desirable to give the students an opportunity to analyze, synthesize, and state the grammar explanation for the structure under discussion. But it is not wise to insist that students give explanations under all circumstances. There may be times when a student should be encouraged to try; it makes no sense for a teacher to embarrass a learner or cause him to grope in the dark (Stern, 1973) by refusing to provide an explanation.

The culture of the student should also be considered (Fathman, 1976; Woods, 1956). It is difficult for some students to guess at a grammar explanation in front of the class when there is a good chance that they might be mistaken. This may be the case for many Asian students, upon whom there is a great stress to succeed. In Asian culture, low achievement in school brings shame not only on the individual but on the entire family, while success brings honor to all (Sue, 1971). If such a learner is reluctant to state a rule, do not force him to do so. It is possible that he may have postulated an explanation in his own mind which the teacher's statement will either confirm or disconfirm.

In a study of relative clause use showing differential learner behavior, (Schachter, 1974) it was found that a disproportionate number of Chinese students exhibited avoidance behavior with respect to an unfamiliar structure. That is, they did not wish to guess about a structure they were not sure of. Although Schachter explained this behavior on the basis of a contrastive analysis of native and target language, I feel that cultural differences must have contributed to an avoidance strategy on the part of the Chinese learners.

Research into the function of language in the Navajo classroom (John, 1972) shows that pressures on the Navajo children for oral performance may be unreasonable in view of the children's culture in which it is "actions (not words) that tend to bring special rewards and attention."

Individual differences in avoiding a new structure or willingness to take the risk of guessing were also observed in people from varying cultural backgrounds (Bailey et al., 1976; Madden et al., 1978).

While we as teachers should try to provide a sympathetic climate in which students are free to express themselves, we should not force them to behave the way we want them to. We must respect the differing values and personalities they bring to the classroom and we should allow them the freedom to be silent.

HOW SHOULD THE GRAMMATICAL EXPLANATION BE MADE?

One of the reactions against the grammar translation method was the virtual abandonment of the abstract metalanguage which was traditionally used to analyze language. It was argued that terms such as "gerund" or "infinitive" were unnecessary baggage that interfered with the language learning process. The audiolingual approach used examples or structural notes (Lado, 1964) to point out how a structure functioned. Grammatical terms were avoided. Some specialists accept the usefulness of an abstract metalanguage for grammatical explanations, but feel a new metalanguage must be devised.

While it is true that many facts about language can be stated without resorting to grammatical abstractions, some metalinguistic categories may be useful. For example, an understanding of "mass vs. count nouns" may help a learner control the English system of "determiners."

We must also remember that some learners have already had previous experience in approaching a second language through the application of grammatical terminology. Using the same terms in learning another language may help such students to control the similarities and differences between the target language and other languages they know.

Teachers should be flexible enough to use abstract terms when students are acquainted with them and request them, or when an abstract category will help them to understand and/or manipulate a particular rule or structure.

Where there is no principled reason for the use of abstract terminology, it may be dispensed with. Furthermore, whether grammatical terms are used or not, they are never a substitute for specific examples and manipulation of a structure in realistic language situations by the students.

With reference to whether explanations should be made in oral or written form, once again the choice will vary with the student population. Teaching approaches must be responsive to the literacy of the students. When students cannot yet write they must begin with concrete oral explanations. Rivers (1964) found that "making the student depend on aural signals alone in the early stages of learning a foreign language puts a much greater strain on the student than is generally realized." So different learning styles are relevant here.

Baecher (1976) found that different cognitive styles among language learners include "theoretical visual linguistics: the ability to find meaning from words you see," and "theoretical auditory linguistics: the ability to acquire meaning from hearing spoken words." Brown (1973) also found that some learners are more oriented towards auditory learning while others rely more on reading.

In a classroom situation, make grammatical explanations in both oral and written forms. This will take different learning styles into consideration and provide for extra reinforcement. For non-literate learners it may sometimes be possible to make explanations visual through the use of pictures or diagrams to illustrate what is said. And in some cases, the teacher may decide to allow students who don't know the alphabet of the target language to write a summary of the explanation for themselves in their respective native languages.

Of course, writing or stating a rule does not constitute learning it or even understanding it. But the oral or written presentation of the rule may be a useful step for many students in the language learning process.

SUMMARY OF THE VARIABLES DISCUSSED AND THEIR APPLICATIONS IN THE LESSON

1. *Conscious explanation*
   a. Children: No conscious explanation seems necessary.
   b. Adults: Conscious explanations may be useful, depending on literacy and previous education.
2. *Rule isolation*
   a. Children: No evidence this is helpful.
   b. Adults: Appears to be helpful along with natural language experiences.
3. *Inductive-deductive presentation*
   Presenting the explanation in the middle of the lesson allows both inductive and deductive experiences to the different types of learners.

4. *The explainer*
   Give the students a chance to state the rule when possible, but be willing to state the rule as the teacher. Consider whether the learner uses avoidance or guessing strategy due to culture or personality.
5. *Use of grammatical terms*
   Be willing to use grammatical terms when the student is familiar with them or to make a concept easier to explain and apply.
6. *Medium of explanation*
   Provide both oral and written explanations since different learners favor one or the other medium for language learning.

CONCLUSION

The research on language learners and language learning argues against a single "method" for teaching a second language. The needs and feelings of the language student and his success in acquiring the target language must be the primary considerations. The contribution that the teacher will make in guiding the learner, not only in terms of grammatical explanations, but in every aspect of language teaching, should be dependent upon the unique qualities of individual learners.

REFERENCES

Baecher, R. 1976. Bilingual children and education: Cognitive style analysis. In *The Bilingual Child,* Antonio Simoes (ed.). New York: Academic Press.

Bailey, Nathalie, Miriam Eisenstein, and Carolyn Madden. 1976. The development of the questions in adult second language learners. In *On TESOL, '76,* John F. Fanselow and Ruth H. Crymes (eds.). Washington, D.C.: TESOL.

Belyayev, B. V. 1964. *The Psychology of Teaching Foreign Languages.* New York: Macmillan.

Brown, H. Douglas. 1973. Affective variables in second language acquisition. *Language Learning* 23.2: 231–44.

Carrol, John B. 1964. *Language and Thought.* Englewood Cliffs, NJ: Prentice-Hall.

Chastain, K. 1970. A methodological study comparing the audiolingual habit theory and the cognitive code learning theory: continued. *Modern Language Journal* 54:257–66.

Curran, Charles. 1972. *Counseling Learning.* New York: Grune and Stratton.

Dulay, H., and M. Burt. 1973. Should we teach children syntax? *Language Learning* 33:235–252.

Fathman, Ann K. 1976. Variables affecting the successful learning of English as a Second Language. *TESOL Quarterly* 10.4:433–41.

Friedlander, Bernard. 1965. A psychologist's second thoughts on concepts and discovery in teaching and learning. *Harvard Educational Review* 35: 18–38.

Fries, Charles C. 1945. *Teaching and Learning English as a Foreign Language.* Ann Arbor: The University of Michigan Press.

Gattegno, Caleb. 1976. *The Common Sense of Teaching Foreign Languages.* New York: Educational Solutions.

Hale, Thomas M., and Eva C. Budar, 1970. Are TESOL classes the only answer? *Modern Language Journal* 54:487–92.

Hall, Eugene J. 1967. *Situational Reinforcement: Orientation in American English.* Washington, D.C.: Institute of Modern Languages, Inc.

Hammerly, Hector. 1975. The deduction induction controversy. *Modern Language Journal* 59:15–18.

Hartnett, Dayle. 1974. The relation of cognitive style and hemispheric preference to deductive and inductive second language learning. Paper presented at the conference on Human Brain Function, Neuropsychiatric Institute, September 27.

John, Vera P. 1972. Styles of learning, styles of teaching: Reflections on the education of Navajo children. In *Function of Language in the Classroom,* Courtney Cazden, Vera P. John and Dell Hymes (eds.). New York: Teachers College Press.

Koolhoven, H. 1961. *Teach Yourself Books: Dutch.* London: The English Universities Press.

Krashen, Stephen D. 1975. Additional dimensions of the deductive-inductive controversy. *Modern Language Journal.*

———. 1978. Individual variation in the use of the monitor. In *Principles of Second Language Learning,* William Ritchie (ed.). New York: Academic Press.

Krashen, Stephen and Herbert Seliger. 1975. The essential contributions of formal instruction in adult second language learning. *TESOL Quarterly* 9.5:173–84.

Lado, Robert. 1964. *Language Teaching: A Scientific Approach.* New York: McGraw-Hill.

Lenneberg, E. H. 1967. *Biological Foundations of Language.* New York: John Wiley and Sons.

Lewis, Glyn E. 1974. *Linguistics and Second Language Pedagogy: A Theoretical Study.* The Hague: MOUTON.

Madden, Carolyn, Nathalie Bailey, Miriam Eisenstein, and Lloyd Anderson. 1978. Beyond statistics in second language learning. In *Principles of Second Language Learning,* William Ritchie (ed.). New York: Academic Press.

Politzer, Robert. 1965. *Teaching French: An Introduction to Applied Linguistics,* New York: Blaisdell Publishing Co.

———. 1972. *Linguistics and Applied Linguistics: Aims and Methods.* Philadelphia: Center for Curriculum Development.

Ramsay, Ruth. 1977. Multilinguals and Successful Language Learners: Cognitive Strategies and Approach Styles in Adult Language Learners. City University of New York Graduate Center. Unpublished dissertation.

Rivers, Wilga. 1964. *The Psychologist and the Foreign Language Teacher.* University of Chicago Press.

Schachter, Jacquelyn. 1974. An error in error analysis. *Language Learning* 24:205–14.

Seliger, Herbert. 1975. Inductive method and deductive method in language teaching: a re-examination. *International Review of Applied Linguistics* 13, 1:1–18.

Simoes, Antonio. 1976. *The Bilingual Child.* New York: Academic Press.

Stern, H. H. 1973. Psycholinguistics and second language teaching. In *Focus on the Learner,* John W. Oller, Jr. and Jack C. Richards (eds.). Rowley, MA: Newbury House Publishers.

Stevick, Earl W. 1976. *Memory, Meaning and Method.* Rowley, MA: Newbury House Publishers.

Sue, Stanley and Derald W. Sue 1971. Chinese American personality and mental health. In *Roots: An Asian American Reader,* Amy Tachiki, Eddie Wong, Franklin Odo and Duck Wong (eds.). Los Angeles: Continental Graphics.

Woods, Sister Frances Jerome. 1956. *Cultural Values of American Ethnic Groups.* New York: Harper and Row.

CHAPTER
23

Introducing the Perfect:
An Exercise in Pedagogic Grammar

Jack C. Richards

The field of syllabus design and materials development for second language teaching has been revitalized in recent years through emergence of notional and functional approaches to language teaching. The question of the selection of items for the realization of notions and functions remains problematic, however, since basic decisions concerning the choice of grammatical and lexical items still need to be made, despite the particular approach adopted. In a notional syllabus, both concept categories and functions form the focus of the syllabus. Concept categories include semantico-grammatical categories such as concepts of time, motion, frequency, and duration. Functions include speech acts such as requesting, ordering, describing, and informing. The present paper is concerned with an area of grammar within the field of concept categories, namely the perfect, and examines the concept covered by the perfect in an introductory language syllabus.

The perfect is variously described in the literature as both a tense and an aspect. In an attempt to clarify grammatical terms and concepts, Comrie (1976) argues that the perfect belongs to the aspectual rather than to the tense system of English. The tense system involves

distinctions of time, and is grammaticalized to give only two tenses: past and present. The aspect system involves distinctions that are distinct from the time perspective. An event may be viewed for example as *complete* or *incomplete* via the aspectual contrast of *non-progressive* versus *progressive*. Thus in the contrast *He read : He was reading,* although both sentences are in the past tense, the first sentence involves non-progressive aspect and the second progressive aspect. The perfect evokes a retrospective view of an event; "it establishes a relation between a state at one time and a situation at an earlier time" (Comrie, 1976:64). Thus, in the contrast *He moved the chair : He has moved the chair,* the difference is not a difference of tense; it does not concern the *time* at which the moving of the chair took place, but a difference in the way the event described by the verb is viewed.

Grammarians typically identify four perspectives associated with the use of the perfect in English:

1. We regard an event as a state leading up to the present. *I have lived here for six years.* This view of events is common with

verbs that are often used statively, such as *live, exist, own, be.*

2. We regard an event as occurring at an unspecified time within a time period extending up to the present. *Have you ever eaten frogs' legs?* This is the so-called "indefinite past."

3. We regard events as repeated within a time period leading up to the present. *We have always taken lunch together on Fridays.*

4. We regard an event as having results which extend to the present. *I have broken my watch.* This is the "resultative perfect."
   See Leech (1971).

Where should we start when we attempt to incorporate the perfect into our grammatical syllabus? Let us look at one possible approach, which is used in a recent film on methodology. Here is a transcript from the film, which deals with the teaching of the question forms of the present perfect. The teacher contextualizes the form by asking the pupils to perform actions in front of the class, and then asks questions about the pupils' actions.

Teacher: (To a pupil) Come up here Lim.
(Pupil goes to the front of the class.)
Teacher: Move the chair.
(The pupil moves the teacher's chair.)
Teacher: Go back to your seat.
           She has moved the chair.
           She hasn't moved the desk.
           Has she moved the chair?
           Yes, she has.
           Has she moved the desk?
           No, she hasn't.
           Come here Foo.
           Touch the blackboard.
(The pupil touches the blackboard.)
           He has touched the blackboard.
           Has he touched the blackboard?
           Yes, he has.

Has he touched the table?
No, he hasn't.
He hasn't touched the table.

And so on. The teacher calls other pupils to the front of the class, and using different objects (a book, a pen, etc.) demonstrates some of the other sentence patterns in which the present perfect can be used. It is a good classroom lesson in the terms in which it is thought out. The new form is taught through its association with a context and the students are actively involved in using the language. But what rules for the perfect are the pupils likely to have formed?

The context for the lesson was a series of completed actions performed by the pupils, a recounting of those actions by the teacher, and a series of questions about them. What verb forms did the teacher make use of? Looking back to our classification of the functions of the perfect we see that the perfect was used in the lesson in its resultative meaning much of the time: *He has moved the chair.* The resultative meaning is: *Now the chair is in a different position.* The question form, however, *Has he touched the table?,* illustrates a different function for the perfect, namely, the so called indefinite past, which would be more common with *yet (Have you finished your homework yet)* or with *ever (Have you ever . . . ?).* But the resultative function of the perfect is the dominant impression we get from the lesson. The resultative perfect is used to describe an event in the past which has results extending to the present. While all uses of the perfect involve a retrospective view of events (cf. Hirtle, 1975)—a looking back to a period or event in the past and then returning to the point of orientation in time—the resultative perfect offers us a special way of looking at events whereby the results or consequences of an event are seen to extend up to the present moment. There is nothing unusual or extraordinary about the resultative perfect. It is quite a frequent use of the perfect, and is seen in sentences like these:

What has happened to you?

An American Ambassador to China has just been appointed.

Jill has found an apartment at last.

I have come to Boston to attend the TESOL convention.

The president has said something about this recently.

It is the resultative perfect which reminds us that the perfect is not a tense but an aspect, a way of viewing events distinct from their time orientation, because another characteristic of the resultative is that it is an optional alternative to the simple past. Thus:

Resultative Perfect	Simple Past
What has happened to you?	What happened to you?
An American Ambassador to China has just been appointed.	An American Ambassador to China was just appointed.
Jill has found an apartment at last.	Jill found an apartment at last.
I have come to Boston to attend the TESOL convention.	I came to Boston to attend the TESOL convention.
The president has said something about this.	The president said something about this.

The fact that the resultative perfect can readily be replaced by the simple past is perhaps the reason why its additional, resultative meaning is difficult to grasp for the beginning student. While the reporting or narrative function of the past tense is fairly easy to identify and is generally supported by time adverbs, the additional meaning conveyed by the resultative perfect is not easy to understand for a beginner. Thus it would be very difficult for the students in the class discussed above to understand anything but a reporting or narrative function for the perfect tense, as it was used by the teacher. In fact it would have been more natural perhaps to have used the past rather than the perfect throughout the lesson, were it not for the fact

that the lesson was supposed to be about the perfect! The teacher could have just as easily said:

Move the chair.
She moved the chair.
She didn't move the desk.
Did she move the chair?
Yes, she did.
Did she move the desk?
No, she didn't.
etc.

In selecting the resultative meaning for the perfect as an introduction to the perfect, we have not made a particularly helpful step toward establishing a function for the perfect in the learner's mind, nor in reinforcing our prior teaching of the past tense. What we have probably succeeded in doing is to establish a rule like the following: The perfect tense is another way of describing past events. This rule will in turn account for students producing sentences such as the following:

Yesterday there has been a fire in the library building.
When I have got home last night I have felt ill.

Part of the problem is related to the fact that the same context or situation, that of narrating or reporting past events, has been used for the perfect as would normally have been used for the past. The syllabus designer's task is to minimize such conflicts by arranging the gradation of teaching items in such a way that new items are seen to be related to new functions, rather than being seen as alternative ways of doing things the learner can already do. Since the simple past is presumably already available for narration and for the reporting of past events—it is in fact, one of the most statistically frequent verb forms for this function in discourse (Ota, 1963)—the perfect, when it is introduced should be linked with a function that is new to the students. Thus as we saw earlier, although the language allows us the option of describing the same event in different ways through viewing it from a different mental view, this is not a luxury we can allow ourselves within a pedagogic grammar of English. Here we are justified in widening potential contrasts within the grammatical system of the language and of teaching limited options for talking about time and events. This suggests that we work from the premise of *one form for one function* for as long as possible. This has the additional advantage of providing a justification for the introduction of new language items, namely, that they are required for functions that cannot be performed by language items presently at the learner's disposal.

In introducing the perfect we will thus look for contexts which are different from those where the past is used. This can be done through starting with the first two of the functions we listed above, namely: 1) Its use with verbs describing states leading up to the present; and 2) Its use with events occurring at unspecified times within time periods extending up to the present. Let us look at these two options in more detail.

1. *States leading up to the present.* The starting point is verbs like *live, be, like, know,* reinforcing the time span adverbially with *since, for,* or similar words.

> I have known John for six years.

Habitual or repeated events in this sense are also regarded as states:

> I have worn glasses all my life.
> I have studied French since 1975.

The distinction needed here is "continuation up to the present" with the perfect, and "non-continuation" with the past. Thus, past tense versions of the last two sentences above are not acceptable:

> I wore glasses all my life.
> I studied French since 1975.

It would also be possible to use the present perfect progressive in place of the perfect in these sentences:

> I have been wearing glasses all my life.
> I have been studying French since 1975.

However, following the principle of one form for one function, we would avoid this use of the present perfect progressive, reserving it for contexts where it is not an alternative for the perfect, namely, temporary events leading up to the present:

> How long have you been waiting?

2. *With indefinite events.* The perfect is next used with events occurring at unspecified times within a time period leading up to the present, reinforced adverbially with *ever, never, before, now,* etc.

> Have you ever been to Florida?
> I have never eaten frogs' legs.

Leech (1971) draws attention to the fact that there is an implicit indefinite/definite contrast involved in the way the perfect leads into the simple past, in much the same way as indefinite articles lead to definite articles, reflecting the fact that in spoken discourse, conversation *starts* indefinitely and *then* progresses to definite reference. Thus:

Have you ever been to Florida?
Yes I went there in 1975.
There are a number of letters on the table.
The top one is for you.

The basic contrast, however, is between actions described in a time period which excludes the present (Last month I *went* to the cinema only once) and events completed within a time period which includes the present (I *have been* to the cinema three times this month). Contexts for the past tense must be linked with completed time periods in the past, with events of either long or short duration:

> I woke up at five o'clock
> I lived there for five years.

The major function of the past tense will then be the reporting of events in sequence, i.e., narration:

We *got up* at six o'clock, *left* the house, and soon *arrived* at the railway station . . .

This provides later a link into the first introduction of the past perfect, which will be used for the description of events which are out of sequence:

When we got outside we realized we had forgotten to lock the door.

The resultative use of the perfect should be the last of its functions to be introduced, and this only when the regular meanings of the perfect and the past are firmly established. It will be initially taught for recognition, with direct explanation of its special, stylistic effect. Thus, to conclude with a maxim: teach new functions for new forms, rather than new forms for old functions.

REFERENCES

Comrie, Bernard. 1976. *Aspect.* Cambridge: Cambridge University Press.

Hirtle, W. H. 1975. *Time, Aspect and the Verb.* Quebec: Laval University Press.

Leech, Geoffrey N. 1971. *Meaning and the English Verb.* London: Longman.

Ota A. 1963. *Tense and Aspect of Present-Day American English.* Tokyo: Kenkyusha.

24

Teaching the Passive

Ronald V. White

INTRODUCTION

Teaching the use of the passive voice constitutes a problem area in many language courses. Often it is treated as a transformation exercise, the student being required to rewrite active statements as passive ones. The result can be a confusion of forms, with a combination of elements which are neither active nor passive. Furthermore, the actual function of the passive, as a means of describing a sequentially ordered process, may not be obvious to the student as a result of such practice exercises.

If we look at how the passive is actually used, we find that typically it is associated with descriptions of process. A process consists of the following elements:

In the process, a raw product is transformed into a finished product. Descriptions of process are very common in scientific and technological literature, although they also occur in everything from advertisements to primary school textbooks. A receptive and active command of the language used to describe a process is, therefore, an important part of the repertoire of a very wide range of students.

Since the passive voice is so commonly used to describe a process, it clearly makes sense to draw on such descriptions in presenting and practising the passive. What follows is an account of a series of lessons to introduce the use of the passive voice in the context of describing processes.

LESSON 1 (40 MINUTES)

Aims
(i) To identify the formal features of the passive voice.

(ii) To relate the use of the passive voice to describing a process.

(iii) To translate a verbal description to diagramatic form.

Materials
(i) A text to be read aloud.

(ii) Copies of a table to be filled in by the students.

(iii) A blackboard copy of a flow diagram to be completed with the students.

Tell the class that they are going to learn how milk is processed. Refer them to the table with which they have been issued. Tell them that they are to listen for all the verbs of the pattern *is produced* while you read the text to them. Note that some of the verbs are already written in the table to help them. (For reasons of economy, the table reproduced here is given in full, though in the lesson being described most of the table would be blank at the beginning of the class.)

After the introduction, read the text aloud to the class. Read at a steady pace, pausing between sentences. Do not use contracted forms (e.g., *It's cooled*) at this stage. Read the text a second time to allow students to check their work, then elicit the verbs from the students and complete a blackboard equivalent of their tables.

When the verbs are set out in the blackboard table, ask the students to identify the common features of the verbs. These are, first, that each verb item consists of two elements: *is* or *are* plus past participle, and second, that the past principle in this particular text is always the −*ed* form. As a mnemonic to help the student recall the formal features of the verb, I prefer to call the past participle the *base* + *ed* part of the verb.

Following the discussion of the verbal element of the description, continue with a third reading during which students are to complete the subject column of their table. Elicit these from the students at the end of the reading and complete the appropriate part of the blackboard table.

Next, give a fourth and final reading, and this time the students complete the remaining parts of the table. Elicit the items and complete the blackboard table, including the important punctuation column.

When the table is complete, draw attention to the overall organization of the text, viz. that each sentence describes a step in the process and that the steps are sequentially organized, the sequence being indicated by the sequencers which form the first sentenced element. Attention can also be drawn to *backward pointing the,* this being an important cohesive feature of the text. With the students contributing, ring and arrow the text, thus:

Milk is produced . . .

The milk . . .

Now refer to the blackboard flow diagram. One or two boxes should be completed by way of example. Ask the students to give completions for the other boxes to finish the diagram. Then discuss the form of the flow diagram, pointing out how it summarizes the sequential organization of the process, with each step constituting an input/process/output sequence, with the output from one step being the input for the next. Note also how by-products, such as cream, are indicated, while subsidiary inputs, such as heat, bottles and crates, are also shown by appropriate arrows.

Next, ask students to read aloud from the completed blackboard table (Table 24.1) of the text. Have each student read more than one sentence, since it is important that the interconnection of sentences is stressed and practiced. After two or three turns around the class, obliterate or obscure the completed table and instruct students to put their completed tables away. Then use the completed flow diagram (Fig. 24.1) as a cue for oral production. Finally, instruct the students to reconstitute the text in written form, using the flow diagram as a cue.

Table 24.1 HOW MILK IS PROCESSED

Sequencer	Subject	Verb	Adverbial	Full stop
	Milk	is produced	on dairy farms	.
	The milk	is delivered	to a factory by tanker	.
	The milk	is weighed		,
and then	it	is tested		.
Next,	the milk	is separated		.
After this	the milk	is pasteurized	at a temperature of 72°F	.
Then	it	is cooled		.
Next	it	is bottled		.
After this,	the bottles	are packed	into crates	.
Finally,	the milk	is delivered	to customers	.

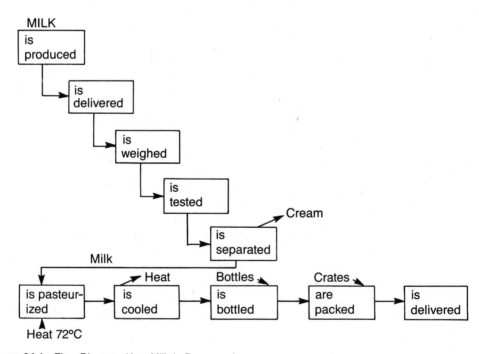

Figure 24.1 Flow Diagram: How Milk Is Processed

LESSON 2

Aims

To reconstitute a written description of process from a flow diagram.

To relate changes in the form of the finite verb to changes in number in the Subject of the sentence.

Begin by recapitulating the main points of the previous lesson, viz. the form of the passive verb group, the sequential organization of a description of process and the use of a flow diagram to summarize such a description.

Then refer to the initial element in the passive verb group, and take examples from the milk processing text. Focus on the following sentences:

> The milk *is* bottled.
> The bottles *are* packed into crates.

Elicit from the students the formal change from *is* to *are* and the change in number of the subject from singular *milk* to plural *bottles.*

Next, refer to the flow diagram of fish canning. Ask students to find a similar change in verb form from *is* to *are*. Then note the change in number of the subject, from singular *fish* (uncountable) to plural *cans* (countable).

After this elicit sentence completions for each step in the process. Complete a blackboard table of the description, as shown in Table 24.2.

When the blackboard table has been completed, elicit reading aloud of the sentences at random around the class. Again, have each student read more than one sentence in sequence so as to practice the production of more than one sentence at a time. After running through the description obliterate or obscure the blackboard table and ask students to complete a written description using only the flow diagram as a

Table 24.2   HOW FISH IS CANNED

Sequencer	Subject	Verb	Adverbial	Full stop
	Fish	is delivered	to a cannery	.
First,	the fish	is cleaned		,
and then	it	is washed		.
Next	it	is drained		,
and then	it	is soaked	in brine	.
After this	it	is washed	again	,
and then	it	is weighed		.
Next	cans	are filled	with fish	,
and then	liquid	is added	to the cans	.
Then	tops	are attached	to the cans	,
and	the cans	are sterilized		.
After this	the cans	are cooled		,
and then	they	are packed	into cartons	.
Finally,	the cartons	are stored	in a warehouse	.

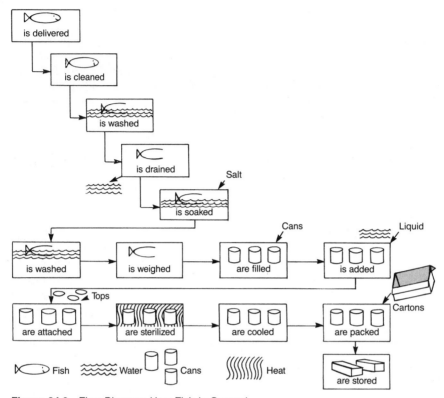

Figure 24.2 Flow Diagram: How Fish Is Canned

cue. Circulate around the class and check the work as it is being done.

It may be useful to draw attention to the punctuation patterns of the sequencers before the students begin to write. Put them up on the blackboard as follows:

_____. Then _____.
_____, and then _____.
_____. Next, _____.
_____. After this, _____.
_____. Finally, _____.

LESSON 3

This lesson can take one of two forms. First, students can be given a description of a process which they have to summarize in flow diagram form. A blank flow diagram with the requisite numbers of boxes to match the number of steps in the process can be issued as a worksheet. The completed worksheet can then become a cue sheet for written reconstruction of the text. Second, a completed flow diagram can be issued to act as a cue sheet for written production. The teacher will, of course, be the best judge as to the amount of prompting which the students may need in carrying out either task.

LESSON 4

Aims

Study the *to + base verb* adverbial of purpose.

Study the distinction between the active and passive voice.

The first of these items can be introduced in context, e.g., The milk is pasteurized at 72°F *to kill* harmful bacteria. Provide students with a text in which several such examples occur. Ask the students to identify them and then point out that such adverbials answer the question 'Why?'. In other words, they state a reason.

The distinction between active and passive can be made by contrasting such statements as:

Cows *produce* milk on dairy farms.
and Milk *is produced* on dairy farms.

Men *weigh* the milk.
and The milk *is weighed*.

Show how in a process the interest is on the product and the process rather than on the operators or the producers. In any case, in an industrial process the identity of the operatives in a process is usually irrelevant. The passive voice enables us to describe complex industrial processes without having to refer to the people involved in operating the machinery.

Finally, provide the students with a cue sheet from which they have to write a description of a process incorporating several instances of the *to + base verb* adverbial of reason.

FOLLOW-UP WORK

More exercises of the type described above can be used with variation of content and presentation technique. There is no shortage of suitable examples to draw on, since many school textbooks contain descriptions of process, as do such publications as *The Oxford Junior Encyclopaedia* and various titles in the *MacDonald Introduction to Technology* series. Manufacturing firms also publish descriptions of the processes involved in producing products as diverse as Kellogg's corn flakes and British Steel Corporation steel.

Students can be given a library assignment in which they have to locate a source, abstract a summary, and draw their own flow diagram. Factory visits also provide a splendid exemplification of a process in action, linking language work in the classroom with activity in the real world outside. Preparatory work for a factory visit can involve drawing a table or flow diagram in advance, the students having to fill in the table or diagram with the information they gather during their observation of the process at the factory. Such preparatory work is, in any case, essential since most manufacturing processes involve numerous stages and items of equipment so that unstructured observation—hindered, as often as not by the noise of moving machinery—can be very confusing. The impersonality of such industrial processes, a point covered in the contrast between active and passive, is well demonstrated by a visit to a factory.

Finally, although I have placed much stress on *industrialized* processes, there are processes in agricultural and pre-industrial cultures which can also be described using the passive voice. The cultivation of rice (in Asia) and the making of tapa cloth (Polynesia and Melanesia) are two examples which come to mind. In an English-medium situation, the work of the English and Geography teachers can be complementary in dealing with such topics from their respective viewpoints and can serve to demonstrate that the correct and appropriate use of English does not cease at the exit from the English language classroom.

VOCABULARY

INTRODUCTION

Vocabulary, like grammar, is an essential component of all uses of language. In ESL/EFL, it is generally dealt with in association with the teaching of reading, and in this section all three papers deal with vocabulary within the context of reading. Fox emphasizes the dimensions of the task involved. Although many ESL/EFL programs aim to teach a productive vocabulary of some 2000 words, this is inadequate as a basis for reading anything but simplified ESL readers. For wider reading purposes, a vocabulary of some 7000 to 10,000 words is needed. In fact, estimates of the recognition vocabulary of college students often place receptive vocabularies as high as 50,000 words. An ESL/EFL student who plans to read anything of substance in English thus needs to acquire as large a vocabulary as possible. How can this be achieved?

If an ESL/EFL program can only teach some 3000 words over three years, it is clearly impossible for the teacher to assume the responsibility of teaching students 7000 to 10,000 words in six months. What can be achieved, however, is to teach a set of strategies that can enable learners to acquire new vocabulary independently through reading. This is the position taken by all three papers in this section. Fox suggests a program of both extensive and intensive reading for students at the college level, in which students read at least seven books a semester. Kruse examines the skills needed to be able to guess the meanings of words from context, and discusses exercises that can be used to help students recognize prefixes, suffixes, and roots; read diagrams and charts which may provide clues to the meanings of new vocabulary items; recognize definitions; infer meanings of words from contexts; and use grammatical clues to infer word meanings. Honeyfield further examines the skill of inferring word meanings from context and shows how cloze exercises, words-in-context exercises, and context enrichment exercises can be used for this purpose.

DISCUSSION QUESTIONS

1. All of the papers in this section deal with vocabulary development within the context of reading. How important is vocabulary in other skill areas such as

speaking or writing? Should general vocabulary development be limited to its role within reading? What other options are available?

2. Working with a word list within the level of 2000 to 3000 words, take a passage of unsimplified English from a newspaper or magazine, and rewrite it using only words from the list. What strategies did you have to use in replacing words outside the list? Now look at the words that fell outside the list. How many of these could be guessed from context, or ignored because they didn't contribute anything significant to the passage?

3. Examine examples of unsimplified texts and see if you can find examples of the use of definition clues, as discussed by Kruse. Prepare exercises to give students practice in recognizing definition clues.

4. Examine examples of unsimplified texts for examples of inference clues, as discussed by Kruse, and prepare sample exercises aimed at developing inferencing skills.

5. Following Honeyfield, prepare cloze exercises, words-in-context exercises, and context enrichment exercises suitable for a specified group of ESL/EFL learners. Can you suggest other kinds of exercises that address the same goals?

FURTHER READING

1. J. A. Bright, and G. P. McGregor. 1970. Vocabulary. In J. A. Bright and G. P. McGregor, *Teaching English as a Second Language.* London: Longman, 14–51.
2. I. S. P. Nation. 1982. Beginning to learn foreign vocabulary: A review of the research. *RELC Journal* 13, 1, 14–36.
3. J. C. Richards. 1976. The role of vocabulary teaching. *TESOL Quarterly* 10, 78–89.
4. M. Wallace. 1982. *Teaching Vocabulary.* London, Heinemann.
5. W. M. Rivers. 1983. Apples of gold in pictures of silver: Where have all the words gone? In W. M. Rivers, *Communicating Naturally in a Second Language.* New York: Cambridge University Press, 114–132.

CHAPTER 25

On Acquiring an Adequate Second Language Vocabulary

Len Fox

It is my observation that many English as a second language programs are harming their students by dealing for too long only with simplified structures and simplified vocabulary. The result is that when the students leave our programs, they are actually far from being able to read unsimplified English which they are expected to read. The gap between the academic English they are now expected to understand and the simplified English they have been taught is too great.

For our ESL students, simplified English has been emphasized and vocabulary development neglected for some time. From the 1940s to the 1960s, linguists stressed the importance of structure. Vocabulary learning was described by Charles Hockett as the easiest phase of language learning, which "hardly requires formal instruction."[1] This emphasis on structure was appropriate earlier in the 20th century, when students had been learning foreign languages by a grammar-translation method which flooded them with new vocabulary items and grammatical structures, but did not allow them time to assimilate much. The emphasis on simplification and structure was an improvement. If we

simplify the language presented to our students, present language at a gradual rate, and give them sufficient practice to enable them to assimilate what they are learning, they can in fact learn to speak and write the simplified language pretty well. However, what happens to them if they are required to do unsimplified reading in English is illustrated by the following paragraph:

Many persons who "talk" with their hands are blunk. They have doubts about what they are saying, so they try to cover up by drolling a false parn of excitement and urgency. These same people are usually very gruk and may be overtalkative and speak too loudly. Hurbish feelings are belaved by the person who tries to keep all leeds to a monton; such a person is nep, porded, and lacking in self-ruck. Slussion is frequently trunded by a veeling wurd, zornish eye, and an inability to face other people directly. Blunkness and codision are shown in a number of leeds. A man may run his hand through his hair or over the top of his head if he is dork; a man or woman may frung the back of the neck. They are trying to tell themselves to galump. Jalup is kanted by a rantid loercion with one's modical abdurance. The woman or man who nardles with hair or keeps polluking clothing is arbushed and socially incrup. A woman may smooth out feluciary argles or blum at her skirt, and a man my blum at his tie or snickle his farn.[2]

The paragraph above contains a nonsense word for every word not included in Michael West's list of the 2000 most frequently used words in English. Now 2000 words is a lot of words. West published a "minimum adequate speech vocabulary" of only 1200 words, with which he claimed students could express practically any idea they would need to express.[3] The 2000 words in the West list would thus probably be a perfectly adequate *productive* vocabulary for a student to learn, but not an adequate *receptive* vocabulary (words which a student could understand in reading but which he doesn't necessarily use). The student who knows only 2000 words and attempts to read unsimplified English will have the same experience as the reader in reading the above paragraph: he will not understand about 20% of the words and will find the text practically incomprehensible.

Now, I do not wish to underemphasize the importance of an adequate productive vocabulary. ESL teachers must devote a good deal of time and effort to teaching one. In fact, it is extremely difficult for students to learn even one word in a foreign language. One reason for this is that one word usually has many meanings. Charles Fries estimated that, according to the *Oxford English Dictionary,* the 2000 words in the West frequency list have an average of 21 meanings per word.[4] Of course not all of these meanings would have to be learned by ESL students, but the current edition of the West list reports three to five common meanings for many of the words. Also, students must know in what idiomatic expressions and combinations a word can be used, what prepositions are required with certain words, what complements (infinitive, gerund, that-clause). Furthermore,

to truly understand a word, a student must know the meanings of a number of near-synonyms so that he knows exactly when and when not to use it.

Thus it is clearly appropriate for students to spend considerable time learning how to use a relatively small number of words correctly. It is of course not a new idea that students should concentrate on a small number of very common words in learning a language. As early as 1588, Timothy Bright published an "island vocabulary" of 559 English words which could be used to cover the meanings of 6000.[5] In this century, C. K. Ogden developed an 850 word list (Basic English) which he used to define 20,000 words in his *Basic English Dictionary;* West developed a "defining vocabulary" of 1500 words to define 30,000 in his *West Dictionary;* and Hornby used about 1500 to 2000 words to define 35,000 in his *Advanced Learner's Dictionary.* A student can obviously do quite a lot, and perhaps say or write almost whatever he wants to with a vocabulary of 2000 words. The importance of such a basic vocabulary is reflected in most ESL textbook series, which usually introduce 1500 to 2000 words in the first three years of English study.

Let us imagine then that our ESL or EFL students have acquired, after three years of study (or a shorter time in a more intensive course), a vocabulary of 2000 words. This is an important achievement, but I would remind the reader that the students at this point are far from having acquired an adequate receptive or reading vocabulary. We could say that they have successfully completed phase one of their language learning, and are now ready to go on to phase two, the *transition* from reading simplified to reading unsimplified English. Unfortunately, for many ESL students there never is a phase two. They are dumped from phase one directly into phase three (reading unsimplified English) and left to sink or swim. Many obviously sink.

If we are going to include a serious phase

two, or a *transition stage* in our ESL programs, we need to know what an adequate receptive vocabulary for reading unsimplified English would be. It is, of course, not necessary to know every word one will ever encounter in English. It is quite possible to fail to understand a word and still to understand the sentence or paragraph it is in, or even to deduce the meaning of an unknown word from its context. West suggests, however, that one should not encounter more than 25 unknown words per 1000 words of text (one word in 40, or one in every three or four lines of text), a guideline which J. A. Bright and G. P. McGregor (who have extensively taught ESL in Africa) say works in practice.[6]

In the reading text at the beginning of this paper, nonsense words were substituted for words not included in the 2000 word West list. If we use substitutes only for words not included in the most frequent 10,000 words of the Thorndike-Lorge list of 30,000 words, the passage comes out like this:

Many persons who "talk" with their hands are insecure. They have doubts about what they are saying, so they try to cover up by creating a false atmosphere of excitement and urgency. These same people are usually very emotional and may be overtalkative and speak too loudly. Hurbish feelings are revealed by the person who tries to keep all gestures to a minimum; such a person is shy, porded, and lacking in self-esteem. Depression is frequently indicated by a slumping posture, zornish eye, and an inability to face other people directly. Tenseness and apprehension are shown in a number of gestures. A man may run his hand through his hair or over the top of his head if he is bald; a man or woman may clasp the back of the neck. They are trying to tell themselves to relax. Distress is revealed by a constant loercion with one's physical appearance. The woman or man who fiddles with hair or keeps adjusting clothing is embarrassed and socially insecure. A woman may smooth out imaginary

wrinkles or tug at her skirt, and a man may tug at his tie or finger his farn.

In the above paragraph, there is one unknown word per 38 words of text, the readability ratio suggested by West. It is annoying when one encounters an unknown word, but the passage is clearly comprehensible. This suggests that about 10,000 words (not necessarily the first 10,000 on the Thorndike-Lorge list, which has been criticized for its literary bias and its neglect of spoken English) would be an adequate receptive vocabulary. In fact, since the 2000 words in the West list include more "lexical learning items" than the first 3000 words of the Thorndike-Lorge (T-L) list[7] (because the T-L list counts as separate items such related words as *abandon* and *abandoned*), perhaps 10,000 words on the T-L list really represent only about 7000 separate words. How then could a student acquire a receptive vocabulary of 7000 words?

One model is a program of instruction considered educationally sound by many secondary schools in Africa.[8] The students are expected to arrive at secondary school with a vocabulary of about 1500 to 2000 words (which they have acquired in perhaps three years of primary school English study).

In their first year of secondary school ("the plateau reading stage") the students read books at the 2000-word level. They are expected to read a total of 60 short books, 14 to be read by everyone in the class and an additional 46 to be chosen by each individual student and read in the library. The books would probably be about 100 pages long, two would be read each week in the 30-week school year, and book reports would be submitted on every book.

In their second year, the students make a "transition" from simplified to unsimplified reading, using short books with vocabulary in the 3000–7000-word range in the T-L list, of which they read 50, 14 read by everyone in the class and an additional 36 by each student in the library. Again book reports are submitted.

In their third year ("the free reading stage"), the students read eight or nine books which are written in unsimplified English. The books include such titles as *Animal Farm* by Orwell, *The Old Man and the Sea* by Hemingway, *Lord of the Flies* by Golding, but not "the classics."

At the end of three years of secondary school, or a total of six years of English language study, the students are supposed to be able to read unsimplified English. If they have acquired receptive knowledge of 100 words from each of the 50 books they have read in their second year of high school, they will have increased their vocabulary from 2000 to 7000 words, and if they have learned 330 words from each of the nine books of their third year (which means learning about two words per page in a 150-page book), they will now have a receptive vocabulary of 10,000 words.

What about our ESL programs in the United States? Do we do an adequate job of teaching vocabulary? I suspect not. In many ESL programs, students begin by taking low level courses for a few semesters in which very little emphasis is placed on reading. Perhaps they read a few simplified readers, but not enough to learn well a basic vocabulary of 1500 to 2000 words. In other words, they do not even successfully complete "phase one" of vocabulary learning. They then take a few intermediate/advanced courses in which they begin to concentrate on writing. They read a few intermediate or advanced readers at this stage, perhaps adding another 600 words to their vocabularies. Such a program is obviously inadequate for students who will have to read unsimplified English and be tested on their comprehension in American colleges.

How can ESL programs prepare students to read unsimplified English? First of all, reading should be introduced early and students should be given a good deal of reading at all levels. Developing vocabulary and reading skills takes time and extensive practice. Students can begin

with simplified readers at the under 2000-word frequency level. Collier-Macmillan, Longman, Oxford, and other publishers all have quite a few excellent books of this sort available.

Many ESL students, upon arriving at college (at least in the City University of New York), are unfortunately still at only a low intermediate level of English proficiency. Such students need to read a number of books (let us say seven— one every two weeks in a 15-week semester) at or below the 2000-word level to solidify their grasp of a basic English vocabulary. They then should work on reading at the intermediate/advanced level for two or three additional semesters, reading again about seven books each semester, and increasing their receptive vocabulary to about 8000 words. I am assuming that they will be doing discussion, writing, and vocabulary exercises to facilitate learning, and acquiring receptive knowledge of about 300 words from reading each book, which would mean in a 100-page book learning receptively three words per page; of course, it would be very helpful to have some good research done on rates of acquiring receptive vocabulary. At the intermediate/advanced level, students could read slightly simplified books, such as the Longman Bridge Series (which include words up to the 7000 frequency range on the Thorndike-Lorge list), or unsimplified readers with short reading selections (four or five pages) followed by reading and vocabulary exercises.

Exactly how reading is to be taught can vary from college to college. I would recommend having a sequence of three reading courses, separate from speaking-writing courses, in which students would read at least seven books a semester, perhaps working intensively on some books in class, and doing the others primarily at home or in a reading lab or library. The lowest level reading course should be only for ESL students, as native Americans do not have the same degree of difficulty with vocabulary. Perhaps in the intermediate/advanced courses, ESL students could be combined with remedial native American students.

Whether or not programs offer separate courses in reading, they should have reading labs or libraries where students should be required to read at least seven books a semester, handing in comprehension questions, exercises, summaries, etc., for each book. To set up a reading lab, Bright and McGregor recommend having for *low-level students* 20 books at the 1500-word level, 100 at the 2000-word level, and 20 at the over 2000-word level; for *"transitional students"* 20 books at the 2000-word level, 100 at the 3000–7000-word level (books with short unsimplified readings could be substituted for this type), and access to unsimplified books in a larger library; for the *"free reading stage"* plenty of light fiction, detective stories, historical novels, adventure stories, science fiction, and magazines and material related to other school subjects. It would be desirable to have several copies of each book and it would cost at least $2000, and perhaps $4000 to establish such a reading lab. If money were not available from schools, perhaps federal grants could be obtained for this purpose.

Although I feel that students should have separate reading classes, I nevertheless strongly feel that reading also has an important place in the "writing class." My own method of teaching writing is to read an essay or article, discuss it, noting the main idea and overall organization, and then discuss and write about ideas generated by the text. I am convinced that this method produces much better results than spending a great deal of time on grammar drills in class. In fact, reading and writing teachers are dealing with very similar skills and the lack of contact and communication between them in many programs is unfortunate.

In summary, we ESL teachers have been carefully nurturing our students' ability to produce language, but have been neglecting the receptive side of learning. We have been encouraged to do so by linguists who emphasize structure and by curricula which tell us that our students need read only one book a semester. Our students pay the price of this neglect when they graduate from our programs with an inadequate amount of English for functioning in the real world. It will not be easy to restructure our programs in order to teach reading and vocabulary effectively, but this is what must be done.

NOTES

1. Charles Hockett. 1958. *A Course in Linguistics.* New York: The Macmillan Company, p. 266.

2. Adapted from Jean Rosenbaum. 1976. Let's shake on that. In Lynn Quitman Troyka and Jerrold Nudelman, *Steps in Composition,* 2nd ed. Englewood Cliffs, NJ: Prentice-Hall, pp. 265–6.

3. In Michael West. 1960. *Teaching English in Difficult Circumstances.* London: Longman, Green, and Co., Ltd.

4. Charles C. Fries. 1950. *English Word Lists: A Study of Their Adaptability for Instruction.* Ann Arbor, MI: The George Wahr Publishing Co.

5. Fries, pp. 1–3.

6. J. A. Bright, and G. P. McGregor. 1970. *Teaching English as a Second Language.* London: Longman, p. 20.

7. *Ibid.,* p. 26.

8. *Ibid.,* pp. 61–63.

26

Vocabulary in Context

Anna Fisher Kruse

The teaching of reading is becoming increasingly important in TESL. In many areas of the world "Service English" programs are in use with goals specifically to teach reading rather than speaking, listening, or even writing. Skills in reading fall generally into four categories: mechanics, syntax, vocabulary, and comprehension. The mechanical, or physical, skills are important, but there is no proof that training in improving them has any great value for ESL readers (Macmillan, 1965).

Syntactical skills are of extreme importance. Foreign students especially have difficulties in garnering meaning from the often highly complex structures of written English (Eskey, 1971, p. 15). An example of a research project analyzing the syntactic structures used in various types of reading, and basing ESL textbooks on these analyses is reported by Cowan (1974).

Comprehension is a complex skill which involves combining all of the reading skills to get a message from the text. Reading-associated study skills often classed with comprehension, such as noting thought-organization, catching implications, and so on, are advanced skills often not attained by native speakers, let alone ESL students.

Of prime importance in reading is vocabulary skill. The reader must know the meanings of enough of the words in a sentence for it to make sense. He must also know how to combine individual word meanings within a sentence. Once the student is past the initial stages of reading, he spends a large percentage of his time encountering new vocabulary. This new vocabulary can be approached in a number of ways. The teacher can give the meaning for each new word, as is common in teaching reading to non-native students. Or, also common, the student may spend hours with a dictionary writing native-language glosses into his text. For the native speaker of English, the most common form of vocabulary building is guessing from context and/or word formations.

> Possessors of this skill in reading and listening are those who are somehow adjusted to encounter low frequency (often quite unfamiliar) vocabulary items and to somehow have a meaning for them in the context in which they are encountered . . . In short, the basic skill in vocabulary expansion is the habit of guessing from the context, using both grammatical and pragmatic clues. This habit appears to be normal in listening to and reading the native language, for those who really listen and read. It is not automatic in dealing with a foreign language. (Twaddell, 1972, p. 174)

In many of the language and cultural milieux in which we attempt to teach English there are high degrees of emphasis on rote memorization. In others, the approach to written materials is different in some other way from the approach that we, as native speakers of English, use. Cowan has stated that we cannot hope to depend on transfer of skills from the native language in vocabulary development (1972, p. 128).

Because vocabulary development skills are seldom specifically taught, the student is not aware of the skills or their benefits.

> The reader or listener encountering a 'new' word can panic. Especially if he has been trained to panic. Or he can have acquired the skill of inference from context. (Twaddell, 1972, p. 274.)

Most students have been trained to panic. Their first reaction on encountering a new word in a text is to stop and ask for a definition, even if the rest of the sentence defines it. The EFL student cannot begin to read with full comprehension until he has been taught to conquer the unknown word by using contextual aids. By this, I mean both the formation of the word itself and the environment in which it is found. Although in every publication dealing with the teaching of reading the desirability of this skill is touted, there is a dearth of suggestions as to methods of developing it.

Rivers (1968) suggests introducing vocabulary items in such a way as to allow the student to infer the meaning from the context and/or illustrations. She feels students should be encouraged to make intelligent guesses about word meanings and therefore readers should not contain glossaries. The new vocabulary should not co-occur with difficult structures and a certain amount of vagueness in guessing the meaning of words must be accepted. The teacher should not expect students to come up

with exact meanings while guessing in this manner.

Norris (1971) makes some of the few concrete suggestions for teaching vocabulary development skills that I have seen in TESL literature. He suggests exercises in word formation entailing work with prefixes and suffixes, in using the context to recognize which of several meanings a single word has in a given sentence, in recall of words from their definitions, in using words in sentences and in using context clues to identify a synonym or to construct a semantically equivalent phrase. The best source of material on this skill seems to be the literature on the teaching of reading to native speakers of English. The skill of vocabulary development has much greater stress here than in TESL literature, especially with regard to methods of dealing with unknown words encountered during reading.

By combining lists by various reading experts, we can develop a list of various types of contextual aids in vocabulary development particularly appropriate for EFL.

1. *Word elements such as prefixes, suffixes, and roots.* The ability to recognize component parts of words, word families, and so on is probably the single most important vocabulary skill a student of reading in EFL can have. It substantially reduces the number of completely new words he will encounter and increases his control of the English lexicon.
2. *Pictures, diagrams, and charts.* These clues, so obvious to the native speaker, must often be pointed out to the EFL student. He may not connect the illustration with the item that is giving him difficulty. He may also be unable to read charts and graphs in English.
3. *Clues of definition.* The student must be taught to notice the many types of highly useful definition clues. Among these are:
   a. Parentheses or footnotes, which are the most obvious definition clues. The student can be taught to recognize the physical characteristics of the clue.

b. Synonyms and antonyms usually occur along with other clues: *that is, is* clauses, explanations in parentheses, and so on.
   (1) *is* and *that is* (X is Y; X, that is Y) are easily recognizable signal words giving definition clues.
   (2) appositival clause constructions set off by commas, *which, or,* or dashes (X, Y, ; X—Y—; X, which is Y, ; X, or Y) are also physically recognizable clues.

4. *Inference clues from discourse,* which are usually not confined to one sentence:
   a. Example clues, where the meaning for the word can be inferred from an example, often use physical clues such as *i.e., e.g.,* and *for example.*
   b. Summary clues: from the sum of the information in a sentence or paragraph, the student can understand the word.
   c. Experience clues: the reader can get a meaning from a word by recalling a similar situation he has experienced and making the appropriate inference.

5. *General aids,* which usually do not help the student with specific meaning, narrow the possibilities. These include the function of the word in question, i.e., noun, adjective, etc.; and the subject being discussed.

The preceding breakdown relies largely, especially in its first items, on some kind of recognizable physical cue—a word, a part of a word, or punctuation. This is particularly important when dealing with non-native speakers. They do not have the ability to abstract semantically in the language that a native speaker does, and so, especially in the early stages, must be aided in using all the concrete clues available.

Norris understates: "Training in the use of context clues does not appear to have been developed in an organized way in texts presently available" (1971, p. 13). Although many texts take care to present vocabulary in context for at least a part of the time, there is no organization in the method of doing this. Word-building exercises are scarcely better; mostly groups of words are presented which form various parts of speech in various ways. But for ESL students, some kind of organization is absolutely necessary in order to increase both understanding of material and ability to retain and use it. I stress the necessity for not just a presentation of words in context, but the control of the type of context utilized to ensure the student's mastery of the various types of clues.

The generally accepted methods of teaching context-clue recognition, developed primarily for native speakers, are programmed learning, especially for word building (see DeVitis and Warner, 1966); and selection or production of a synonym following the reading of the sentence. This exercise has a variation in which the item selected is the word itself. Other approaches found are: recognition of words, errors, synonyms, and contextual variations in meanings; selection of homonyms, synonyms, and words from a group of semantically similar items; and correction of errors.

All of these approaches have validity, especially when used as aids to the native-speaking slow or defective readers they have been designed for. But they lack the systematic organization that would make them appropriate for ESL students.

I have conducted some experiments in my classes both overseas and in the United States during the past several years. These experiments have indicated that the teaching of context-clue recognition skills allows students with no previous knowledge of vocabulary items to equal or exceed the quiz performance of students who have been taught the vocabulary.

Considering the previous discussion, I would like to suggest the following program for teaching vocabulary development skills. The program is intended to be flexible enough to adapt to any service or other English program already extant or to serve as a core structure for the development of a new program. I have used it with a variety of reading texts and materials and found it highly productive.

A PROGRAM FOR TEACHING VOCABULARY DEVELOPMENT SKILLS

1. *Goals:*
   a. To improve the reading vocabulary skills of ESL students.
   b. To teach ESL students word-building skills.
   c. To teach ESL students to guess word meanings from context clues.
2. *General skills.* These skills should be practiced intensively in the beginning, and drill on them should continue throughout the term of instruction.
   a. Practice in recognizing word functions within sentences. This may be done using any grammar.
   b. Practice in the use of pictures, graphs, and charts.
3. *Word building*
   a. *Suffixes:* It may be a good idea simply to give a list of these to the student for memorization. Roots used for this section should be familiar.
      (1) Practice in suffix recognition, i.e., simple exercises in isolation of suffixes:

      good*ness* famili (ar) (ly)

      (2) Lesson and practice in noting grammatical changes effected by suffixes. Word tables might be very useful here.

      Adj. (good)+ness=N (goodness)
      Adj. (gloomy)+ly=Adv. (gloomily)

      (3) Practice in word *formation* through exercises in which the student adds and subtracts suffixes. Again the word table is useful. The student fills in the appropriate forms of a word by manipulating suffixes. It is of great importance to group words by the way they form variations so that all words being studied at one time add the same suffixes in the same manner

and regularity of change can be emphasized.
   b. *Prefixes:* These are more varied and less regular and therefore should not be presented until after suffixes have been mastered. A list of these can also be memorized.
      (1) Practice in prefix recognition.
      (2) Lesson and practice in meaning changes resulting from the use of prefixes, e.g., *in +formal =* not formal=casual. This is fairly difficult. The examples used should be straightforward in the early stages. Here again, the groupings must be of words that add the same prefixes in the same manner to achieve the same type of meaning. Groupings like UN in *untie* and UN in *unfair* must be avoided. As these are mastered, more difficult items requiring progressively higher degrees of interpretation may be introduced.
      (3) Practice in word formation:
         (a) Addition of prefixes. These exercises should progress in difficulty. E.g., Make a word meaning "not natural" (*unnatural*)
         (b) Addition of prefixes and suffixes.
   c. *Roots:* These are quite difficult, and should not be taught at all unless the student is fairly advanced and flexible in his approach to word forms. For a good list of Latin and Greek roots, refer to Dechant (1970, Ch. 12).
      (1) Recognizing roots. Isolation of root forms.
      (2) Effect of prefixes and suffixes on root forms.
4. *Definition clues*
   a. *Parentheses and footnotes:* X (Y); X*$*_y$
      (1) A lesson would first be given on these two types of clues stressing their physical structure and how to read them correctly.

(2) Practice in recognizing these clues. E.g. Draw a line under the words in parentheses: *The panther* (a large black animal related to a cat) *is very dangerous and deadly.*

(3) Practice in using the clue. Here exercises of the following sort are useful: *The principal* (main) *reason for wearing clothes is to keep warm.* What is the meaning of *principal* in the sentence?

b. *Synonyms and antonyms:* Most students have studied and enjoy learning words with similar and opposite meanings. The task is to get them to recognize the definitional role these often play.

(1) X *is* Y; X, *that is,* Y. Students can be taught that an unfamiliar word is often defined in a sentence using the copula *be* and a synonym.

(a) Clue recognitions, both of signal words and synonyms. E.g. Underline the signal word is, or, that is, : *A birthday party is an observance,* that is, *a remembrance of someone's day of birth.*

(b) Practice in using the clue. Again exercises in producing or recognizing a synonym are useful.

(2) X—Y—; X, *which* is Y; X, *or* Y; X, Y. Appositival constructions. This can be approached in essentially the same manner as the *is* and *that is* clues were.

5. *Inference clues*

These types of clues require a higher level of analytical skill and practice than previous types dealt with. They should be approached slowly, moving from obvious answers to increasingly vague exercises. The ESL student should never be expected to do the same kind of inferring that a native speaker could do, but should be encouraged to go as far as possible as long as the guessing is not allowed to become wild. For all three types of clues

(example, summary, and experience) the same method of practice in (i) recognition of clue elements and (ii) obtaining meaning from the elements, can be followed.

a. *Example:*

(1) Specific clues: X, *e.g.* Y; X, *i.e.* Y; X, *for example,* Y.
E.g. *Iran is trying to* restore *many of its ancient monuments. Persepolis, for example, is being partly rebuilt by a group of Italian experts.*

(2) No physical cue.
E.g. *Roberta Flack, Aretha Franklin, and Olivia Newton-John are popular female* vocalists.

b. *Summary:*

(1) Restatement.

(a) With a physical cue: . . . X. This Y . . .; . . . X. X is Y.
E.g. *Many products are sold to stop* perspiration. *This wetness that comes from your body whenever you are too warm, work very hard, or are afraid, usually doesn't smell very good.*

(b) Without physical cue.
Either: The same meaning. X, Y.
E.g. *He's a really good* athlete. *He plays sports well.*
Or: Opposite meaning. X. (neg) Y. E.g. *He's* bound *to win. He can't lose.*

(2) Information. E.g. *The* forsythia *was covered with the golden flowers that bloom early in the spring.*

c. *Experience:* The reader must decide from his own experiences what is probably meant by a word. E.g. *The old dog* snuffled *and* moped *as he slowly walked from the room.*

In summary, I have tried to give an indication of the lack of effective methods for teaching vocabulary in ESL reading programs. As a first step in filling the void, I have suggested a program for teaching vocabulary from context. The program is logical and extremely flexible and can, therefore, be effective. One hopes that new teaching strategies will appear in the future to cope still better with this great need.

REFERENCES

Cowan, J.R. 1972. Toward a comprehensive reading program for university students in Iran. *Proceedings of the Second Annual Seminar of the Assoc. of Professors of English in Iran.* Dept. of University Relations and Cooperation Ministry of Science and Higher Education and the Assoc. of Univ. Professors in Iran. Tehran, Iran.

Cowan, J.R. 1974. Lexical and syntactic research for the design of EFL reading materials. *TESOL Quarterly* 8, 4: 389–99.

Dechant, Emerald V. 1970. *Improving the Teaching of Reading.* Englewood Cliffs, NJ: Prentice-Hall.

DeVitis, A. A. and J. R. Warner. 1966. *Words in Context, A Vocabulary Builder,* 2nd ed. New York: Appleton-Century-Crofts.

Eskey, David E. 1971. Advanced reading: The Structural Problem. *English Teaching Forum,* IX, 5: 6–14.

Macmillan, M. 1965. *Efficiency in Reading,* ETIC Occasional Paper No. 6. The British Council English-Teaching Information Centre, London.

Norris, William E. 1971. Advanced reading: Goals, techniques, procedures. *English Teaching Forum,* IX, 5: 6–14.

Rivers, Wilga M. 1968. *Teaching Foreign-Language Skills.* Chicago: University of Chicago.

Twaddell, W. Freeman. 1972. Linguistics and language teachers. In *Readings on English as a Second Language,* Kenneth Croft (ed.) Cambridge, MA: Winthrop Publishers.

CHAPTER 27

Word Frequency and the Importance of Context in Vocabulary Learning

John G. Honeyfield

Today word frequency is still an important criterion of vocabulary selection for language teaching. In practice, other criteria which have been developed, for example, availability, familiarity, coverage, etc., tend to be used as supplementary to frequency, with frequency lists continuing to function as the reference or starting point. Perhaps the central consideration that helped to establish the importance of frequency was the idea that if a student knew a relatively small number of words (for English, about 3000) he would already know something like 80 or 90 percent of the words in almost any given text of the language (Bongers, 1947; see also Richards, 1974). This was an important discovery because it gave great impetus to the development of systematic vocabulary teaching and selection. A modern European language contains hundreds of thousands of words, yet classroom time is limited, and much time has to be devoted to topics other than vocabulary. Faced with such a situation, a teacher or textbook writer might simply despair. But if there is a relatively small number of words known to be highly useful, then systematic vocabulary selection and teaching would seem to be a realistic proposition.

The value of vocabulary selection using frequency and some other criteria largely continues to be accepted, but a further problem emerges when we realize that the unknown words in any page of text in the target language will still be quite numerous. Thus even a very diligent student who graduated from a course after learning all the 3000 selected words would find, on encountering an unsimplified text, that somewhere between 10 and 20 percent of the words are unknown to him. (The percentage could be even higher than 20 in certain types of material.) These would be not-so-frequent words in the language which had not been included in the 3000 words selected by the course designer. And even if the student's teachers had supplemented the vocabulary content of the course by teaching additional words, he might not be much better off, since the less frequently occurring words in a language are very numerous indeed. There are many of them, far more than the relatively small number of high-frequency words; individually they do not occur often, perhaps only once in a chapter or once in a book.

The problem we face, then, is simply this, that even with vocabulary selection according to the best principles, and good teaching, a school or university course cannot provide students with anywhere near the vocabulary they will need when encountering unsimplified reading materials in a second or foreign language. Students will have learned most of the frequent words, and some of the less-frequent words, but there will still be an enormous number of infrequent words which are unknown, and which may be met in reading at any time. We can never solve this problem by attempting to drastically increase the vocabulary content of courses. But what, then, can we do to help students with the vocabulary problems they will meet in reading?

Twaddell in an article about vocabulary statistics and their implications for language learning (Twaddell 1972) writes,

the reader or listener encountering a 'new word' can panic, especially if he has been trained to panic. Or he can have acquired the skill of inferring from context. In the latter case, he uses what is not unfamiliar in the context to convey a meaning (not necessarily complete, or precise) of the phrase or sentence. Whatever meaning he attributes to that phrase or to that sentence determines a meaning he can begin to have for that new word. (p. 274)

Twaddell's solution, then, is inferring unknown meanings from context. He thinks that other methods, such as memorizing lists of definitions, will be too time-consuming to provide students with the vocabulary resources they need.

Presumably the same could be said of looking up words in dictionaries (although this is not to say dictionaries play no part in vocabulary learning). A good dictionary can generally confirm or disconfirm a learner's inference. However, looking up words is extremely tedious and probably makes little contribution to vocabulary *learning*. Moreover, looking up breaks the reader's train of thought, the ongoing business of forming hypotheses about what the writer is saying, which is central to the reading process. It seems likely that refraining from looking up as much as possible may contribute more to learning, especially if it goes with attempting to infer. This is because the attempt to infer brings the unknown word into contact with an active searching and thinking process, involving consideration of possible meaning dimensions of the word (its denotation, field of application, syntactic behavior, connotations, etc.). In this way the word, through having tentative meaning dimensions assigned to it, is incorporated into a wider structure of thought. Trying to learn a new word by looking it up in a dictionary is akin to rote learning; on the other hand, attempting to infer the meaning of the word provides for meaningful learning which, according to contemporary cognitive theories of learning, is more efficient. (Brown 1972).

Twaddell suggests that "as the learner moves from the protection of a rigorously controlled vocabulary into something like a real use of the foreign language, the skill of sensible guessing becomes a major teaching objective" (1972: 275). However, about the only practical advice he gives is that teachers should be tolerant, not pouncing on students who make mistakes in guessing, and that guessing must "tolerate vagueness and the chance of misunderstanding." He is against prompt correction of every mistake (p. 275).

These suggestions are useful as far as they go. But I think we can go further than this in developing the skill of inferring from context. In the remainder of this article I want to discuss three kinds of exercises which are suitable for this purpose. The kinds of exercises discussed are *cloze exercises, words-in-context exercises* and what I call *context enrichment exercises*.

CLOZE EXERCISES

A cloze exercise is a passage of suitable length in which some words have been deleted.[1] Each deletion is indicated by a blank of standard length, say ten typewriter spaces. Here is the beginning of a cloze exercise of the suggested type. The first sentence has been left intact as a lead-in passage.[2]

A Cloze Exercise

Instructions: Some words have been taken out of this piece of English. Try to guess all the words and write them in the correct places. If you are not sure of a word, just guess.

Desert Plants

Many desert plants are able to turn their leaves to avoid the direct rays of the sun. Some leaves protect themselves from the great heat by not (1) _____ flat in their normal position but by curling up until the (2) _____ when it is cooler. Some plants have leaves that are covered with (3) _____ thin hairs that can draw moisture from the (4) _____. Others have hard or shiny surfaces that prevent loss of (5) _____.

Most cactus plants are covered with (6) _____ points known as 'thorns,' that protect them from being (7) _____. Other plants produce poison substances that (8) _____ hungry animals away.

(From Hollon, 1968:7)

One way of preparing cloze exercises is to delete every *n*th—often every fifth—word. The result of this procedure, however, is that we delete many functional words, e.g., prepositions and articles. While functional items may be inferred from context, such inferring is not very relevant when we wish to give practice in inferring the meanings of unknown vocabulary items (mainly content or lexical words). What we

must do, then, is to delete selected content words from a passage. There are various ways of doing this but the simplest is just to delete, say, every fifth content word.

In the approach suggested here, a cloze exercise is presented to test comprehension. Students are invited to fill in the missing words, but this can be preceded and/or followed by discussion, which should be guided by the following aims:

1. Avoid immediate correction of students' responses. If blanks are numbered, as they are in the sample passage above, we can write the numbers on the blackboard and then, beside each number, write all the responses offered by students. Through discussion the class can then eliminate most of the unacceptable responses. The teacher should draw out the *reasons* why various alternatives are acceptable or unacceptable. The teacher may also need to draw attention to one or two blanks which no one can fill, but even in these cases there will probably be limiting factors putting constraints on possible answers.

2. If any words not yet taught have been deleted, these will probably not be offered as responses. However, the teacher can supply some of the missing items, pointing out that students were able to guess acceptable alternatives, or at least were able to infer something of the meanings signified.

3. Perhaps the most important aim is to get students to discuss *the different kinds of information that are available from a passage,* and which point to, or at least put constraints on, the meanings of blanks. Encouraging this awareness is potentially much more valuable than successfully guessing particular missing items. This information, which can also be written on the blackboard, is of four kinds: syntactic, semantic, pragmatic, and factual.

Syntactic information is information about a missing word's position in a sentence and may indicate whether the word is a noun, verb, adjective, etc. Such information, of course, puts important constraints on what a word can mean. In *Desert Plants,* for example, item (1) is probably a verb since it occurs in the construction: *by not* ... + adjective. How do the leaves protect themselves from the heat? The answer could be, 'By not staying (or remaining or lying) flat'. The absence of a grammatical object also restricts the range of verbs here. Another example is blank (2) which follows *the,* and therefore probably represents a noun.

Semantic information is information about meanings; here we are concerned with the content of what is said in the passage. In the sample passage, blank (2) is preceded by *until* and followed by *when* as a relative adverb. These words suggest times of day, and the addition of *cooler* helps to narrow the answer to *evening, night or night-time.* A reader's ability to infer *sharp* for blank (6) will also depend on semantic information. Knowing the meanings of *point* and *thorn* will help—as will factual information about the way in which thorns could protect a plant from being eaten.

Pragmatic information is information concerning ways in which writers use the language in particular acts of communication, for instance, in explaining, describing, or presenting supporting information. Contrast is a device that is often used in clarifying, explaining and describing. It is used at several points in the sample passage. For example, in the second sentence we have the frame *by not* _____ *but*

by. ... The leaves protect themselves by not (1) _____ flat in their normal position but by curling up. Thus curling up is contrasted with some other, different action, presumably lying flat. In this way pragmatic information, too, helps us to infer meanings.

Finally, *factual information* from outside a passage itself can greatly assist inferring meanings within the passage. With the sample passage, some knowledge of how water can exist in the air and some experience of cactus or other desert plants would be helpful for understanding and inferring meanings. Factual information can be brought into the classroom discussion.

Before leaving this section I would like to explain how responding to a cloze exercise is similar to inferring the meanings of unknown words in reading. Superficially the two activities are different. In one case a student meets a blank space, while in the other case he meets a word he does not know. Yet actually there are important similarities. The main one is the inferring of meaning. The fact that the visible response to a cloze blank is a word, not a meaning, does tend to obscure the similarities. Yet while a student responds to a cloze blank with a word, he must find a meaning, and only then a word to fit the inferred meaning. The first stage, searching for meaning, is virtually identical with trying to infer the meaning of an unknown word in a reading passage. (The unknown word is, so to speak, a blank.)

WORDS-IN-CONTEXT EXERCISES

In its simplest form, a words-in-context exercise is a reading passage of suitable length containing some words which are probably not known by the class. These words can usually be identified by teachers on the basis of experience. Discussion should center on the information students can extract from the passage to help

them guess the unknown words. Needless to say, the aim is not always to guess a meaning exactly. That may be impossible. But at least students can become aware of the surrounding information in which a word is embedded, and which both influences and points to its meaning. Set questions can be used to get definite responses beforehand; these will help focus the discussion. The following is the beginning of a passage with sample questions. (The italicized words are assumed to be unknown.)

The Force of Circumstances

She was sitting on the verandah waiting for her husband to come in for luncheon. The Malay boy had *drawn* the *blinds* when the morning lost its freshness, but she had partly raised one of them so that she could look at the river. Under the *breathless* sun of midday it had the white *pallor* of death. A native was *paddling* along in a *dug-out* so small that it hardly showed above the surface of the water. The colours of the day were *ashy* and *wan*. They were *but* the various *tones* of the heat.

(From Maugham, 1969: 46)

Sample Exercises

1. Multiple choice questions, type 1
   In the story, a blind is
   a. a drawing;
   b. a set of double doors;
   c. a plant in a pot;
   d. a covering for a verandah.

2. Multiple choice questions, type 2
   Which of these pieces of information help you to guess the meaning of *pallor?*
   a. A native was paddling a dug-out in the river.
   b. It is midday.
   c. The colours of the day were ashy and wan.
   d. The river had pallor.
   e. Pallor is related to death.
   f. In the story, pallor is white.

3. Underlining relevant information
   Underline all the words and phrases which help you to guess the meaning of *pallor.*

4. Finding synonyms (or antonyms)
   Find words in the passage which mean about the same as
   a. had pulled down;
   b. without wind;
   c. paleness, especially of the face;
   d. pale.

Questions of any of these types could be starting points for discussion. Discussion should explore information of the four kinds mentioned under cloze exercises.[3]

CONTEXT ENRICHMENT EXERCISES

These exercises can help students to see how, by taking more and more context into account, they can have a much greater chance of guessing a meaning that is at first unknown. The following example is from a book by Yorkey (1970: 67; slightly adapted).

Instructions: This exercise will help to direct your attention to the kind of information that a context may give you. In the exercise there are three sentences, each one adding a little more information. Each sentence has three possible definitions of the italicized word. On the basis of information in the sentence, decide if the definition is *improbable, possible,* or *probable.* Write one of these words on the line for each definition.

1. We had a *whoosis.*
   a. a tropical fish _____
   b. an egg beater _____
   c. a leather suitcase _____
2. We had a *whoosis,* but the handle broke.
   a. a tropical fish _____
   b. an egg beater _____
   c. a leather suitcase _____
3. We had a *whoosis,* but the handle broke, so we had to beat the eggs with a fork.
   a. a tropical fish _____
   b. an egg beater _____
   c. a leather suitcase _____

Whoosis in context (a) cannot be guessed; the information is inadequate and all definitions are possible. In context (b), the extra information about a handle rules out tropical fish as the definition. Context enrichment in (c) makes an egg beater the only probable definition.

A teacher can construct more realistic context enrichment exercises by taking short sections from reading passages, and then successively expanding them to assist guessing of particular words.

CONCLUSION

There are, then, at least three types of exercises which can help develop the skill of inferring from context, and no doubt others could be developed. Besides presenting details of the particular exercises, I have attempted to outline a rationale for their use in terms of developing the skill of inferring from context. Inferring was presented as not only a partial alternative to dictionary use for coping with unknown words, but also as a practice which could contribute more to learning than looking up words in a dictionary, since the attempt to infer brings the unknown word into contact with an active searching and thinking process. The study of vocabulary statistics revealed that the number of unknown words encountered by a student would be large, and that a course could not teach more than a relatively small number of them. In this situation, the value of inferring seems obvious.

NOTES

1. There are two main types of deletion in cloze exercises, namely probabilistic (i.e. deleting every nth word) and judgmental (i.e., deleting selected words).

2. 250 words before deletion is often considered to be a suitable length for a cloze exercise. However, where classroom discussion is an important aim, slightly shorter passages may be more convenient. Cloze exercises can be used in many different ways. For surveys of these, see Riley (1973) and Robinson (1972).

3. Although these exercises may look similar to some conventional comprehension exercises, I prefer to call them words-in-context exercises because of the emphasis on vocabulary. Inferring words from context is an important comprehension skill, but not the only such skill.

REFERENCES

Bongers, Herman. 1947. *The History and Principles of Vocabulary Control.* Woerden: Wocopi.

Brown, H. Douglas. 1972. Cognitive pruning and second language acquisition. *The Modern Language Journal* 56:4, 218–227.

Hollon, W. Eugene. 1968. *The Great American Desert.* A *Ladder* book at the 200 word level. Adapted by C. Hotchkiss., New York: Washington Square Press.

Maugham, W. Somerset. 1969. *Maugham's Malaysian Stories.* Selected and introduced by Anthony Burgess. Kuala Lumpur: Heinemann Educational Books (Asia) Ltd.

Richards, Jack C. 1974. Word lists: Problems and prospects. *RELC Journal* 5:2, 69–84.

Riley, Pamela D. (comp.) 1973. *The Cloze Procedure.* A selected, annotated bibliography. Lae: Papua New Guinea University of Technology.

Robinson, Richard D. (comp.) 1972. *An Introduction to the Cloze Procedure.* An annotated bibliography. Newark, NJ: The International Reading Association.

Twaddell, W. Freeman. 1972. Linguistics and language teachers. In *Readings on English as a Second Language: For Teachers and Teacher-*

trainees, K. Croft. (ed.). Cambridge, MA: Winthrop.

Yorkey, Richard C. 1970. *Study Skills for Students of English as a Second Language.* New York: McGraw-Hill.

TEACHER-STUDENT INTERACTION

INTRODUCTION

Until recently, a great deal of thought in language teaching circles had gone into methods, syllabus design, and materials, but very little attention had ever been paid to what actually went on inside second language classrooms. Early investigations showed that many of the best intentioned changes in language teaching were not reaching students because the new ideas were being short-circuited by various features of teacher-student interaction. It turned out that there was often a great difference between what was supposed to happen and what actually happened, and also between what teachers thought they were doing and what they were actually doing. These differences were documented in detailed studies of classroom processes, especially of classroom conversation between teachers and students and among students at work in small groups.

In the first article in this section, Gaies describes three areas of classroom-centered research: teacher speech (linguistic input to the learner), teacher-student participation patterns, and teacher treatment of learner error. The data for investigating these phenomena in most studies have consisted of overt behavior: teacher and student talk. Although obviously closer to reality than broad prescriptive statements about methodology from *outside* classrooms, even this evidence, of course, ignores teachers' and students' thought processes during instruction. Hence, Gaies closes by suggesting that future research can produce richer findings by using various introspective procedures such as teacher and student diaries.

The second paper fleshes out one line of classroom process research, that on the role of native speaker/non-native speaker conversation inside and outside classrooms in providing learners with comprehensible input, probably a necessary (and Krashen would say sufficient) component of successful instruction. Long's paper emphasizes the importance of *two-way* tasks for obtaining comprehensible input, and also focuses on the rather narrow range of question types teachers tend to exploit, as shown in a study by Long and Sato. The findings on question patterns in ESL have since been replicated in other studies, including classrooms with students at more advanced levels of proficiency. In two studies, it has also been shown that (a) it is relatively easy for teachers to increase the frequency of (open and closed) *referential* questions, once they are made aware of this issue, and (b) this change in teachers' questioning patterns (i) improves the quantity and quality of student talk, and (ii) appears to be related to the amount of content learning that takes place where English is a medium of instruction.

Research has shown errors to be an inevitable, even healthy part of naturalistic or instructed second language learning. In some (non-literal) sense, they suggest hypothesis testing on the learners' part, and regularities in the errors and types of errors across speakers of different first languages reflect universal processes at work. Increases in error rate and new kinds of errors can often indicate progress as the learners attempt to restructure their interim second language grammars.

How, then, is the teacher to treat errors, given their new positive status? In the third article in this section, Hendrickson begins by providing a brief history of error treatment. The audiolingualist view was that any error that occurred meant the onset of a nasty new linguistic habit, which would become ingrained if allowed to multiply through practice, and so had to be swiftly "corrected" through more drill work. More recent cognitivist approaches to language teaching, which recognize the learner's active mental contribution to the learning process, *respect* errors in various ways, viewing them as signs of learning rather than as problems to be dealt with. However, although prescriptions abound, Hendrickson finds little agreement among current methodologists as to which errors should be corrected, how, or by whom.

DISCUSSION QUESTIONS

1. How would you respond to someone who says that it is unnecessary to examine classroom interaction because we can find out what teachers are doing by asking them which method they are using?

2. Tape-record yourself or (preferably) other teachers using two different methods. Transcribe as much of the tapes as you have time for. In what ways are the transcripts similar or different? You might look, for example, at the kinds of questions the teachers are asking, at the kinds of student participation that occurs, at what happens after students make errors, at how much of the language is drill-like and how much is genuinely communicative, or at any other aspects of the lessons you would *expect* to be different given the two methods (supposedly) involved.

3. Gaies reports on a series of topics investigated by classroom researchers and describes a variety of qualitative and quantitative methods they have used in their work. What additional aspects of teacher-student interaction do you think it would be important to study, and why? Which methods do you think it would be most appropriate to use to study them?

4. "Two-way" tasks are problem-solving activities in which each person,

teacher or student, starts with information that is unknown to the other people working on the task but needed by them all for the class or group to solve the problem. List three tasks that fit this description and three that do not, and say which features led you to classify each of them the way you did.

5. Does the fact that referential questions offer students qualitatively different speaking opportunities mean that display questions serve no useful purpose in the second language classroom? What value (if any) do you think they might have? How could you find out if display and referential questions actually have different effects on classroom SLA?

6. How much information (if any) of the kind obtained through classroom-centered research do you think it is useful for teachers to be aware of? In your view, is the information better suited for novice teachers, experienced teachers, neither or both?

7. Corder (1967) made a now well-known distinction between "errors," systematic deviations from target language rules which reflect a learner's underlying competence in the second language, and "mistakes," occasional slips which are the result of performance phenomena such as time pressure, nervousness, and tiredness and which are also made by native speakers. Do you think a teacher can or should usefully distinguish between errors and mistakes, as defined by Corder, in deciding whether or how to provide feedback? If so, how?

8. Hendrickson cites some classroom-centered research on teacher treatment of learner error at the end of his article. Tape-record yourself or another teacher, and study transcripts of the lesson(s) concerned to see how you or your colleague deals with errors. What are the main treatment strategies you observe? Do the learners appear to benefit from the treatments? What evidence is there of this? Do any particular strategies seem to help more than others?

9. Several researchers have reported that many adult EFL or ESL students say they like to be "corrected," and that some even wish their teachers would correct them more often. Does this "students'-eye" view affect your attitude toward error treatment? Would you give more feedback on error as a result?

10. Does feedback on error always need to be spoken or written, and always from the teacher? Could students learn that they are making errors through the design of ESL materials or the outcome of a communication game? Would there be any advantages or disadvantages to this manner of providing feedback or to peer feedback compared with teacher feedback on error?

11. Studies of ESL classrooms have revealed immediate repetition of the correct response to be by far the most frequent method of giving feedback on error, leading one researcher to recommend greater variety in the way teachers correct learners. Several studies have reported, however, that corrective feedback tends to be erratic, difficult for learners to perceive, and so of doubtful utility. Presumably, teachers will want to give *clear* feedback on aspects of the language that are *learnable* at the time and in ways that will not be threatening or inhibit the students' efforts to communicate in English. Do you think it is possible to reconcile all these factors in real time in an EFL or ESL lesson? Would your advice be the same to a teacher of adults as to a teacher of young children?

FURTHER READING

1. R. L. Allwright. 1975. Problems in the study of the language teacher's treatment of learner error. In M. K. Burt and H. C. Dulay (eds.), *On TESOL '75*. Washington, D.C.: TESOL, 96–109.

2. R. L. Allwright. 1983. Classroom-centered research on language teaching and learning: A brief historical overview. *TESOL Quarterly* 17, 2, 191–204.

3. R. L. Cathcart and J. W. B. Olsen. 1976. Teachers' and students' preferences for correction of classroom conversation errors. In J. H. Fanselow and R. H. Crymes (eds.), *On TESOL '76*. Washington, D.C.: TESOL, 41–53.

4. C. Chaudron. To appear. *Second Language Classrooms: Research on Teaching and Learning*. Cambridge: Cambridge University Press.

5. R. Ellis. 1984. *Classroom Second Language Development*. New York: Pergamon Press.

6. J. F. Fanselow. 1977. Beyond 'Rashomon': Conceptualizing and describing the teaching act. *TESOL Quarterly* 11, 1, 17–39.

7. M. H. Long. 1977. Teacher feedback on learner error: Mapping cognitions. In H. D. Brown, C. A. Yorio, and R. L. Crymes (eds.), *On TESOL '77*. Washington, D.C.: TESOL, 278–294.

8. M. H. Long. 1980. Inside the "black box": Methodological issues in classroom research on language learning. *Language Learning* 30, 1, 1–42.

9. M. H. Long, and G. Crookes. 1986. Intervention points in second language classroom processes. Paper presented at the RELC Regional Seminar, Singapore, 21-25 April.

10. J. C. Richards (ed.). 1974. *Error Analysis*. London: Longman.

11. J. Schachter. 1981. The hand signal system. *TESOL Quarterly* 15, 2, 125–138.

12. H. W. Seliger, and M. H. Long. 1983. *Classroom-Oriented Research in Second Language Acquisition*. Rowley, MA: Newbury House Publishers.

CHAPTER 28

The Investigation of Language Classroom Processes

Stephen J. Gaies

The second language classroom has long been a center of research interest. In the last several years, attempts to examine the second language classroom—to clarify how the language classroom experience differs from what is available outside the classroom and how language classrooms differ among themselves—have been increasingly guided by a shared set of goals and premises. *Classroom process research* is based on the priority of direct observation of second language classroom activity and is directed primarily at identifying the numerous factors which shape the second language instructional experience. The result has been a marked departure from earlier research on the nature and effects of classroom instruction in a second language.

Selected studies in three areas are reviewed: the linguistic environment of second language instruction, patterns of participation in the language classroom, and error treatment. Also reviewed are recent applications of introspective (mentalistic) research to the problem of describing the second language classroom experience.

The purpose of this paper is to examine recent attempts to characterize the second language instructional experience. The research to

be summarized all too briefly and selectively here has aimed at describing the linguistic and instructional environment which second language learners encounter in the classroom and how that environment might differ from what is available outside the classroom. The goals of such research have been both to specify what, if anything, is common to second language instruction and to identify the factors which cause classroom activities to vary from one setting to another.

The research in question, which will be referred to collectively as *classroom process research,* is at first glance highly diverse. One is struck by the enormous differences among settings investigated—foreign language classrooms, ESL programs, immersion programs, bilingual classrooms in a variety of cultural contexts, involving learners of all ages representing a variety of ethnic and educational backgrounds—and by the diversity of the investigative approaches employed. Indeed, it might sometimes appear that the only common feature of such research is that data are collected in language classrooms. In fact, however, classroom process research is based on several shared premises, which it might be well to summarize at the outset:

1. As Allwright (1983) has observed there has been a perceptible trend away from global categorizations of second language classroom instruction. We have largely rejected the notion that classrooms differ simply along a single variable such as *method.* The failure of experimental research to demonstrate the clear-cut superiority of any one method has undoubtedly been a factor in this, as has been the sheer difficulty of conducting such research. Classroom process research rejects as simplistic any univariate classification of the second language instructional experience.

2. The second premise underlying classroom process research is to some degree a corollary of the first one. The emphasis is on describing as fully as possible the complexity of the second language instructional environment. The key term here is *description.* The immediate goal of classroom process research is, as has often been stated (Long, 1980a; Gaies, 1981; Bailey, 1986), to identify variables of second language instruction and in so doing to generate hypotheses rather than to test hypotheses. This premise explains in large part the avowedly non-prescriptive nature of classroom process research. Classroom process research does not lead directly to empirically validated applications; rather, it is directed more at clarifying those factors which must ultimately be taken into account in any attempt to examine the effects of particular classroom treatments.

3. Another premise which unifies classroom process research is the priority of direct observation of classroom activity. All of the research summarized in this article is based on data collected wholly or substantially through the observation and measurement of second language classroom activity. Classroom process research seeks to inform our understanding of how teachers and learners "accomplish classroom lessons," to borrow a phrase from Mehan (1974); this can be done, it is argued, only through direct examination of the process.

To provide an overview of classroom process research, selected studies in three areas will be summarized. These areas are second language classroom language (classroom input), patterns of classroom participation, and error treatment. Toward the end of this paper, recent attempts to investigate individual or psychological process variables will be briefly discussed.

THE LINGUISTIC ENVIRONMENT

The first area of language classroom research to be reviewed here is the nature of the linguistic input available to learners in the classroom setting. One of the obvious differences between instructional and non-instructional settings, at least as far as language acquisition is concerned, is that while outside the classroom access to and opportunities for interaction with native speakers may be limited by a number of factors, the language classroom has, as a primary feature, a native (or at least a relatively proficient) speaker delegated to interact with learners. This delegated speaker—the teacher—thus provides, in many cases, an important source of linguistic input. Early studies of teachers' classroom language focused on the linguistic characteristics of teacher input. Many of these studies were intended to determine how teachers' classroom language differs from normal speech—that is, speech between native speakers. Specifically, researchers sought to determine whether second language teachers make linguistic accommodations on behalf of learners similar to the modifications present in caretaker speech to children acquiring their first language. Indeed, it was hypothesized that teachers' classroom language constituted a simple code which would facilitate the second language acquisition process.

An investigation by Gaies (1977) of the syntactic features of ESL teachers' classroom speech reflects the assumptions and goals of this line of research. A comparison of the language used by eight ESL teachers in the classroom and out of the classroom revealed that the subjects' classroom speech was syntactically less complex on a number of variables. Of considerable importance was the finding that the complexity of the subjects' classroom language was remarkably fine-tuned to their learners' level of proficiency. Along with similar data from a study (Chaudron, 1979) of teachers' speech in ESL classes, the Gaies study lends empirical support to the notion that classroom input, like caretaker speech, may facilitate acquisition.

A more recent study by Hamayan and Tucker (1980) extends research in language classroom input considerably by examining the effect of classroom input on learners' production. Hamayan and Tucker examined the speech and teaching behaviors at the third and fifth grade levels of three teachers in two French immersion schools and three teachers from regular French schools in Montreal. One aspect of the study was the tabulation of the frequency of occurrence in the teachers' classroom speech of nine structures in French, among which were indirect questions, contractions, reflexives, and subjunctives. The investigators found a strong correlation in the frequency with which these structures occurred at the two grade levels and in the two school systems. Furthermore, they found that the frequency of occurrence of these nine structures in teachers' speech correlated significantly with the frequency with which these structures were produced by the learners in a story-retelling task. Thus, the researchers found evidence to support an earlier claim by Larsen-Freeman (1976) that production of particular features by second language learners is related to the frequency with which those features occur in linguistic input.

The Hamayan and Tucker study is a logical extension of earlier work to describe the linguistic environment of the second language classroom. As is the case for all correlational studies, however, the results do not automatically indicate a cause-and-effect relationship. Indeed, for the present, our ability to test for such a relationship under adequately controlled conditions is highly doubtful.

PATTERNS OF CLASSROOM INTERACTION

More recently, attention has shifted from the nature of input to the nature of interaction between native speakers and second language acquirers. While modified input, such as can be observed both in and outside the classroom, is frequently available to second language acquirers, it is the interactional adjustments which native speakers make consistently in speech with non-native speakers that is now considered to be most crucial to second language attainment. Most notably, Krashen (1978, 1980) has argued that, through interaction, second language acquirers obtain "optimal input"—that is, input which is likely to lead to further acquisition. Long (1980b) has claimed that the modified interaction available through speech between native speakers and second language acquirers is the necessary and sufficient condition for second language acquisition to take place. This theoretical reorientation has caused the focus of research in teachers' classroom language to shift from the examination of the linguistic features of teachers' speech to the study of interactional patterns in the second language classroom, patterns which may indicate how learners internalize in- and out-of-classroom input.

A research study which reflects this change in focus is Long and Sato's (1983) examination of the forms and functions of ESL teachers' classroom questions. These were compared with previously established patterns of native speaker questioning behavior in native speaker/non-native speaker conversations outside classrooms. Long and Sato hypothesized that questions in and outside the classroom tend to serve different interactional functions; specifically, ESL teachers' classroom questions typically aim at having learners display knowledge of material covered in class rather than at eliciting referential or expressive information unknown to the teacher. The findings of Long and Sato confirmed this prediction. In the six ESL classrooms investigated, *display* questions (for example, "What's the opposite of *up* in English?"), which are intended to elicit information already known to the questioner, constituted more than half of all questions: furthermore, they outnumbered *referential* questions by almost four-to-one. In contrast, referential questions were the predominant question type in native/non-native speaker interaction outside the classroom; even more striking was the almost total absence of display questions. The fundamental feature of display questions is that they do not generally invite learners to respond at length and, even less, to initiate new topics and thus sustain interaction. Therefore, the predominance of display questions is seen by Long and Sato to diminish the value of second language classroom interaction as a source for learners to obtain optimal input.

Long and Sato's study does not concern itself with the actual patterns of verbal participation that took place in the classrooms they observed. This, however, has been a central focus of classroom process research; furthermore, it reflects, even more than other areas, the influence of general educational research on the study of language classroom phenomena. Roughly at the time when language classroom process research began on a large scale, *interaction analysis* (e.g., Flanders, 1970) predominated in educational research. The large issues addressed were: who talked in classrooms? how much? and with what

effect on the classroom verbal performance of others? Seliger's (1977) study of ESL classes lent empirical support to the notion that learners' participation in classroom activity is highly variable. Seliger identified, on the basis of a numerical count of classroom participations, two broad categories of learners: *high input generators* and *low input generators.* He found a correlation between membership in either of these groups and performance on a measure of field dependence; high input generators, who were more active in classroom interaction, tended to be more field independent. There was also evidence that they generated more input, or at least were likely to do so, in out-of-class contact with native speakers than did the low input generators. For Seliger, the distinction between high and low input generators is an important one, since it suggests that the experience of second language instruction is far from uniform; while some may exploit the classroom for extensive practice opportunities, others may be far more passive in this respect and may in fact require a different instructional experience altogether.

Sato's (1981) study of turn-taking in university-level ESL classes is an excellent illustration of how classroom process research may serve to refine our understanding of patterns of participation. Sato explored the relationship between ethnicity and the distribution of interactional turns in two intermediate ESL classrooms. Her comparison of nineteen Asian and twelve non-Asian learners showed that the Asian students initiated significantly fewer turns than did the non-Asians; furthermore, the Asian learners were called upon by their teachers significantly less often. Sato has thus added important evidence for ethnicity as a variable in the second language instructional process. She suggests that the relatively greater reticence of Asian students to participate may have caused their teachers to perceive them as "unwilling" to participate; thus, the teachers were led to call upon them less often. Learners, then, who do not avail themselves of the opportunity for taking turns in class and who rely on teacher-allocated turns may end up losing even this opportunity for classroom participation.

Schinke (1981) has examined patterns of participation in all-English content classes. Whereas Seliger's and Sato's studies were concerned with ESL classes, Schinke investigated the experience of limited English proficiency (LEP) students who had been mainstreamed and examined the linguistic and interactional environment available to learners in non-ESL classrooms. Schinke's study revealed findings about that environment that may, if confirmed by subsequent research, significantly alter the argument made on behalf of mainstreaming. She found that LEP learners have significantly fewer interactions with their teachers than do their native speaker counterparts—91% of the LEP students received six or fewer turns per hour. In addition, when interactions between teachers and LEP students do occur, they are functionally quite different from those between teachers and native speaker students; teacher-LEP student interactions tend to involve classroom and lesson management much more than genuinely instructional goals. Schinke argued that her findings have implications for the LEP students' acquisition, development of content skills, and self-esteem. These findings, of course, do not in themselves lead to suggestions for pedagogical reform; as has already been mentioned, classroom process research has been, and must be, at least for the present, decidedly non-prescriptive. These studies of patterns of participation by Seliger, Sato, and Schinke nonetheless point out how the direct examination of classroom processes may prevent the spread of misconceptions about the actual nature of the second language experience for groups of learners and for individual learners.[1]

ERROR TREATMENT

One aspect of second language classroom patterns of participation which has received special attention for several years is the way in which learner errors are treated. The emphasis which classroom researchers have given to corrective feedback is easy to understand. Second language research has come to attach great significance to the role of errors in acquisition. In the last fifteen years, errors have been viewed as windows to the language acquisition process; errors are seen as overt reflections of a learner's internalized knowledge of the language. They are furthermore regarded as an inevitable part of acquiring a second language; indeed, for some, errors are the best evidence that acquisition is taking place. In turn, methodologists have abandoned an "all-out" or global approach to error correction in the classroom and have sought a basis on which errors might be selectively treated.

Research to date in error treatment can only serve to encourage the search for classroom practices which promote a selective treatment of errors, since one of the consistent findings of such research is that errors are not treated in the second language classroom as universally as might be supposed. Fanselow's (1977) study of error treatment by eleven teachers using the same lesson plans and materials for a class in oral drillwork was one of the first quantitative accounts of error treatment. Fanselow found that fully 22% of the errors made by students received no treatment; either the teachers did not perceive the errors, or they chose to ignore them. Nystrom's (1983) study of four public school teachers of Spanish-dominant children also showed that a sizeable proportion of learner errors go untreated. Nystrom's data are even more striking, since the identification of errors in her study was made by teachers reviewing videotapes of their classes. Thus, as Nystrom points out, her data only include errors which her teachers identified either in class or on videotapes.

A second major focus in research on corrective feedback has been the kind of treatment which is provided. An important finding is that when teachers treat errors in the second language classroom, they do not necessarily provide overt corrections. Indeed, explicit correction of an error—that is, where the major thrust of a teacher's response to a learner utterance is to provide the correct form—often occurs less frequently than indirect or implicit feedback. Furthermore, teachers have available, and exploit to varying degrees, a wide variety of implicit corrective treatments. Several researchers (Allwright, 1975; Chaudron, 1977; Long, 1977) have offered taxonomies or models of error treatment options and the decision-making process which governs choices.

An especially interesting investigation of the variety of error treatment procedures available to teachers was conducted by Cathcart and Olsen (1976). In this study, twenty-one teachers of adult and university ESL classes responded to a questionnaire concerning their use of and preferences among twelve error treatment types. The twelve error treatments had been compiled from an analysis of videotapes of classes which these same teachers had taught. Cathcart and Olsen found that, in general, the teachers used those correcting moves in class which they preferred and which they reported using. They found also that the preferences expressed by these teachers' students on the same questionnaire corresponded fairly closely to the treatments which the teachers used in class. The only striking discrepancy between the teachers' and students' preferences was the students' wish to be corrected much more frequently than their teachers tended to.

Research in error treatment has also identified some of the specific variables which influence the nature of error treatment. Several studies (Fanselow, 1977; Cathcart and Olsen, 1976; Ramirez and Stromquist, 1979; Nystrom; 1983)

have demonstrated empirically that linguistic errors are treated differentially, depending on whether they are phonological, lexical, or syntactic in nature.[2] The type of classroom activity during which an error occurs also plays a role in the error treatment decisions made by a teacher. So, too, does the level of instruction. Hamayan and Tucker (1980) found that the third grade learners in a French immersion program received more explicit corrective feedback than did native speaker third graders; in contrast, the learners in a fifth grade immersion class received explicit correction less frequently than did the fifth grade native speaker learners. Nystrom's (1983) study provides forceful evidence of the importance of individual teacher styles as a variable in error treatment; one of her teachers treated 87% of all errors, two corrected 24% of all errors, and the other corrected no errors at all.

Several researchers have noted that error treatment in language classrooms is often inconsistent and ambiguous (Allwright, 1975; Fanselow, 1977; Long, 1977). It has even been suggested (Long, 1977) that in view of such inconsistency, error treatment may not make as vital a contribution to language classroom instruction as has generally been supposed (e.g., Krashen and Seliger, 1975). Others have stressed that greater consistency and clarity in error treatment may be extremely difficult to achieve, but that the way in which teachers treat errors is indeed central to teaching effectiveness. Allwright, for example, argues that "teachers need to be aware of the potential they have for creating confusion in the minds of learners" (1975:99), yet recognizes that the task of the teacher is "to sum up the whole situation on the spot, and then to react appropriately, in public, conscious of the need to treat the problems of the individual without misleading or confusing the other learners" (103).

The complexity of the task of error treatment is compounded in other ways. Chaudron (1977) has pointed out that error treatment usually consists not of a single teacher response, but rather of an exchange or cycle of verbal moves; thus, as Salica's (1981) empirical investigation of error treatment suggests, the treatment of errors often involves not a response, but a series of responses which follow each other in rapid succession. Furthermore, much research needs to be done to determine how error treatment choices reflect teachers' awareness of the need to find the proper balance, both for individual students and for classes as a whole, between feedback which focuses attention on an error *(negative cognitive feedback)* and feedback which encourages the learner to make further attempts at communication *(positive affective channel feedback)* (Vigil and Oller, 1976).

Indeed, one of the most consistent results of research in error treatment in particular and language classroom processes in general has been to underscore the enormous complexity of the language classroom teaching and learning process. We should not underestimate how greatly such research has heightened our awareness of the demands that classroom activity places on teachers' decision making. Again and again, the point of view expressed by Mehan that "the teacher's attention is demanded in too many places to make rationally calculated, statistically valid decisions during the flow of [classroom] conversation" (1974:113) has been persuasively confirmed by current classroom research.

Much of this greater sensitivity to the complexity of language classroom processes is of course the result of having made direct observation a key component of classroom research. The language classroom is no longer a "black box" (Long, 1980a) whose complexity we can conveniently choose to ignore, and it is the intensive observation, description, and analysis of classroom activity that makes current research so promising as a prelude to controlled investigation of the variables of second language teaching and learning. Recently, however, alternative —or perhaps better, complementary—approaches to the investigation of language classroom processes have been promoted, and some mention must be made of research which, in the view of many, can lead to an even fuller understanding of the nature of second language teaching and learning.

ALTERNATIVE RESEARCH APPROACHES

These alternative approaches are known by a variety of headings, among which are *anthropological, qualitative,* and *mentalistic* research. These are certainly not new approaches in any way, as Ochsner (1979) has pointed out. Indeed, their recent use in our field has resulted largely from the influence of related fields such as anthropology and sociology, in which such methodological approaches have a long tradition of use. With regard to classroom process research, these alternative research approaches are perhaps best known through the learner and (in a few cases) teacher diary studies (in which a participant observes his or her own classroom activity as well as that of other participants) and through other types of introspective and retrospective research studies which have been recently summarized by Cohen and Hosenfeld (1981).

The chief virtue of such research, its advocates claim, is that it allows for the investigation of aspects of classroom language learning which more conventional external observation cannot get at. Indeed, several advantages of non-quantitative research can be argued for on the basis of the limitations of conventional external observation:

1. Conventional classroom observation, in emphasizing the verbal dimension of classroom activity, provides insufficient accounting of

learners who are reluctant to participate orally in class.

2. Direct external observation and analysis of classroom activity cannot provide accurate insights into learners' conscious thought processes and thus does not allow for any direct examination of the means by which input is taken in.

3. Quantitative research requires the preselection of variables to be observed and measured, and it is thus not fully appropriate for a field in which it is assumed that many variables remain to be discovered or rediscovered. Thus, for a field of inquiry in which interest is, at present, primarily in generating hypotheses (as opposed to testing hypotheses), research methodologies which allow the investigator wide latitude in exploring classroom processes may be especially welcome.

Perhaps the most fully developed application of qualitative research to the study of language classroom processes is represented by the learner diary studies of recent years. Schumann and Schumann (1977) have argued that diaries can identify individual or psychological variables of the classroom experience. A similar argument was advanced by Bailey (1980), whose diary of her experience in learning French focuses on the role of anxiety and competitiveness in language learning. More recently, Bailey (1983) has compared her own diary to those of others in an attempt to discover to what extent her observations were idiosyncratic and to what degree they were shared by other learners.

It would be an exaggeration to say that alternative research approaches have been widely accepted for use in second language classroom process research. We might expect the debate over the relative strengths and limitations of quantitative and qualitative research to continue. However, even those who remain skeptical of the reliability of learner intuitions recognize that quantitative research is to some degree shaped by research intuitions and biases; and those who criticize the small sample sizes of anthropological studies recognize that most conventional research in language classroom processes is often based on relatively small samples also. Thus, it may be hoped that several research methodologies will be used with the rigor and care which each demands and that they will be viewed as complementing each other, and that in this way the enormous complexity of language classroom processes may be clarified from a number of perspectives.

As mentioned at the outset, a brief and selective review such as this is bound to be frustrating; one can only begin to explore the diversity of work in understanding language classroom processes. By way of conclusion, we might emphasize what may be for now the two most important dimensions of such activity. First, in revealing previously unexplored or underexplored aspects of classroom processes in which teachers and learners are involved, researchers have developed a greater awareness of and respect for the enormous complexity of language classroom activity. One immediate result of this that we might hope for is that practitioners will become more receptive to research efforts that recognize the complexity which confronts them daily in their classroom work. The other outstanding dimension of current classroom process research is that it may ultimately enable us to develop and test hypotheses about second language teaching and learning which reflect better than has been done in the past the complex activity which we seek to understand.

NOTES

1. The Schinke study is also important in suggesting that native speakers (in this case, the teachers in her study) may choose avoidance as a strategy for dealing with non-native

speakers (the LEP students in this study). Schinke's data put into better perspective some of the data collected in quasi-experimental investigations of native speaker, non-native speaker interaction, in which subjects have been, in effect, forced to communicate during a period of time. Indeed, one of the merits of classroom-based research is that it draws data from a "natural" participant group: for this reason, it should be viewed as an extremely useful complement to quasi-experimental approaches to research in language use.

2. The Ramirez and Stromquist study investigates the relationship between selected teaching behaviors and pupil achievement. Thus, unlike most of the studies on error treatment, it is correlational, rather than purely descriptive, in design. Ramirez and Stromquist found that while overt correction of grammatical errors correlated with pupil achievement (to a significant degree in the case of comprehension ability), correction of pronunciation errors was counterproductive to learner achievement.

REFERENCES

Allwright, Richard L. 1975. Problems in the study of teachers' treatment of learner error. In *On TESOL '75,* Marina K. Burt and Heidi C. Dulay (eds.), 96–109. Washington D.C.: TESOL.

———. 1983. Classroom-centered research on language teaching and learning: A brief historical overview. *TESOL Quarterly* 17(2): 191–204.

Bailey, Kathleen M. 1980. An introspective analysis of an individual's language learning experience. In *Research in Second Language Acquisition: Selected Papers of the Los Angeles Second Language Research Forum,* Stephen D. Krashen and Robin Scarcella (eds.), 58–65. Rowley, MA: Newbury House Publishers.

———. 1983 Competitiveness and anxiety in adult second language learning: Looking *at* and *through* diary studies. In *Classroom Oriented Research in Language Learning,* Herbert W. Seliger and Michael H. Long (eds.). Rowley, MA: Newbury House Publishers.

———. 1986. Classroom-centered research on language teaching and learning. In *Essays for Language Teachers,* Marianne Celce-Murcia (ed.). Rowley, MA: Newbury House Publishers.

Cathcart, Ruth L., and Judy E. W. B. Olsen. 1976. Teachers' and students' preferences for correction of classroom conversation errors. In *On TESOL '76,* John F. Fanselow and Ruth H. Crymes (eds.), 41–53. Washington, D.C.: TESOL.

Chaudron, Craig. 1977. A descriptive model of discourse in the corrective treatment of learners' errors. *Language Learning* 27(1): 29–46.

———. 1979. Complexity of teacher speech and vocabulary explanation/elaboration. Paper presented at the 13th Annual TESOL Convention, Boston, Massachusetts, February 27–March 4.

Cohen, Andrew D., and Carol Hosenfeld. 1981. Some uses of mentalistic data in second language research. *Language Learning* 31(2):285–313.

Fanselow, John. 1977. The treatment of error in oral work. *Foreign Language Annals* 10(6):583–593.

Flanders, Ned A. 1970. *Analyzing Teaching Behavior.* Reading, MA: Addison-Wesley.

Gaies, Stephen J. 1977. The nature of linguistic input in formal second language learning: Linguistic and communicative strategies in ESL teachers' classroom language. In *On TESOL '77,* H. Douglas Brown, Carlos Yorio, and Ruth Crymes (eds.), 204–212. Washington, D.C.: TESOL.

———. 1981. Experimental vs. non-experimental research on classroom second language learning. *Bilingual Education Paper Series* 5(4). Los Angeles, CA: Evaluation, Dissemination and Assessment Center, California State University, Los Angeles.

Hamayan, Else V., and G. Richard Tucker. 1980. Language input in the bilingual classroom and its relationship to second language achievement. *TESOL Quarterly* 14(4): 453–468.

Krashen, Stephen D. 1978. The monitor model for second-language acquisition. In *Second-Language*

Acquisition and Foreign Language Teaching, Rosario C. Gingras (ed.), 1–26. Washington, D.C.: Center for Applied Linguistics.

———. 1980. The theoretical and practical relevance of simple codes in second language acquisition. In *Research in Second Language Acquisition: Selected Papers of the Los Angeles Second Language Research Forum,* Stephen D. Krashen and Robin Scarcella (eds.), 7–18. Rowley, MA: Newbury House Publishers.

———, and Herbert W. Seliger. 1975. The essential contributions of formal instruction in adult second language learning. *TESOL Quarterly* 9(2): 173–183.

Larsen-Freeman, Diane. 1976. An explanation for the morpheme acquisition order of second language learners. *Language Learning* 26(1):125–134.

Long, Michael H. 1977. Teacher feedback on learner error: Mapping cognitions. In *On TESOL '77,* H. Douglas Brown, Carlos Yorio, and Ruth Crymes (eds.), 278–294. Washington, D.C.: TESOL.

———. 1980a. Inside the "black box": Methodological issues in classroom research on language learning. *Language Learning* 30(1): 1–42.

———. 1980b. Input, interaction, and second language acquisition. Ph.D. dissertation, University of California, Los Angeles.

———, and Charlene Sato. 1983. Classroom foreigner talk discourse: Forms and functions of teachers' questions. In *Classroom Oriented Research in Language Learning,* Herbert W. Seliger and Michael H. Long (eds.). Rowley, MA: Newbury House Publishers.

Mehan, Hugh. 1974. Accomplishing classroom lessons. In *Language Use and School Performance,* Aaron V. Cicourel et al. (eds.), 76–142. New York: Academic Press.

Nystrom, Nancy J. 1983. Teacher-student interaction in bilingual classrooms: Three approaches to error feedback. In *Classroom Oriented Research on Language Learning,* Herbert W. Seliger and Michael H. Long (eds.). Rowley, MA: Newbury House Publishers.

Ochsner, Robert. 1979. A poetics of second language acquisition. *Language Learning* 29(1): 53–80.

Ramirez, Arnulfo G., and Nelly P. Stromquist. 1979. ESL methodology and student language learning in bilingual elementary schools. *TESOL Quarterly* 13(2): 145–158.

Salica, Christine. 1981. Testing a model of corrective discourse. M.A. thesis, University of California, Los Angeles.

Sato, Charlene. 1981. Ethnic styles in classroom discourse. In *On TESOL '81,* Mary Hines and William Rutherford (eds.), 11–24. Washington, D.C.: TESOL.

Schinke, Linda. 1981. English foreigner talk in content classrooms. Ph.D. dissertation, Northwestern University.

Seliger, Herbert W. 1977. Does practice make perfect? A study of interaction patterns and L2 competence. *Language Learning* 27(2): 263–78.

Schumann, Francine M., and John H. Schumann. 1977. Diary of a language learner: An introspective study of second language learning. In *On TESOL '77,* H. Douglas Brown, Carlos Yorio, and Ruth Crymes (eds.), 241–249. Washington, D.C.: TESOL.

Vigil, Neddy A., and John W. Oller. 1976. Rule fossilization: A tentative model. *Language Learning* 26(2): 281–295.

CHAPTER
29
<hr>

Native Speaker/Non-Native Speaker Conversation in the Second Language Classroom

Michael H. Long

INTRODUCTION

Several recent studies of second language acquisition (SLA) and use have focused on native speaker/non-native speaker (NS-NNS) conversation and its role in the acquisition process. Much of that work has been concerned with ways in which samples of the target language are made comprehensible to the learner. This interest has been motivated by claims that it is primarily comprehensible input which feeds the acquisition process, language heard but not understood generally being thought to be of little or no use for this purpose. Other similarly motivated research has been conducted on talk by teachers and students. More recently, some explicit comparisons have been made of NS-NNS conversation inside and outside the SL classroom.

The purpose of this paper is briefly to review what has been learned by the research so far, and to suggest implications for SL teaching. The paper is in five sections. First, I summarize the evidence in support of what has become known as "the input hypothesis." Second, I describe ways in which input is made comprehensible to the SL learner. Third, I present some research findings which suggest a crucial characteristic of NS-NNS conversation whose product for the learner is comprehensible input. Fourth, I report some work on ESL teaching which looks at how successful classroom discourse is at providing learners with comprehensible input. Fifth, and last, I suggest some ways in which teaching might be improved in this respect.

THE INPUT HYPOTHESIS

To paraphrase Krashen (1980), the fundamental question for SLA research is how a learner at some stage, "i" of interlanguage development moves to the next stage, "i + 1." In other words, how does he or she acquire? Part of Krashen's answer is as follows:

> a necessary condition to move from stage i to stage i + 1 is that the acquirer understand input that contains i + 1, where 'understand' means that the acquirer is focused on the meaning and not the form of the utterance. (Krashen, 1980)

Krashen goes on to claim that this seemingly impossible task is achieved through use of the learner's current grammar, that which underlies "i," plus use of context, or extralinguistic information, i.e., knowledge of the world. The task is seemingly impossible because the learner by definition does not know language at "i + 1." Interlanguage development is achieved, in other words, through obtaining input which contains the structures of "i + 1" and yet is comprehensible. Understanding precedes growth. In support of his version of the input hypothesis, Krashen offers four pieces of evidence, which, for the sake of brevity, I merely summarize here (for details, see Krashen, 1977, 1980).

1. Caretaker speech is modified, not in a deliberate attempt to teach young children the language, but in order to aid comprehension. Further, and crucially, it is only *roughly* tuned to the child's current linguistic capabilities. It therefore contains structures below, at and *a little beyond* the child's level. Its frequent focus on the "here and now" is one way the new structures are made comprehensible.

2. Speech by NSs is modified for use with NNS in much the same way as caretaker speech. It, too, is only roughly tuned, more advanced learners getting more complex input, with the focus again on communication rather than on teaching the language per se. The modified code, "foreigner talk," also contains structures below, at, and a little beyond the learner's current proficiency level, with the same potential advantages to the acquirer (built-in "review" and opportunities for further development).

3. The "silent period" observed in some young children is due to the SL acquirer building up competence via listening, by understanding language, prior to speaking. Denial of the option of a silent period to the learner, e.g., through the pressure to speak (performance without competence) on most adults and formally instructed learners, is what leads to their having to fall back on the L1, resulting in first language transfer.

4. Research on the relative effectiveness of teaching methods suggests that there is little difference among various methods which provide learners with insufficient comprehensible input. On the other hand, methods which do provide such input, such as TPR and the Natural Approach, tend to do well when compared with those in the former group.

While the evidence Krashen adduces is indeed consistent with his claim, it is not very strong evidence. The data on caretaker speech and foreigner talk, as he is aware, merely show co-occurring phenomena. The silent period is by no means always found, even in child acquirers, and is open to various other interpretations (e.g., personality differences, language shock, culture shock). The "comparative methods" studies have often suffered from lack of control over potentially confounding variables (see Long, 1980a). There is, however, additional evidence for the input hypothesis. The following is again only a brief summary (for further details, see Long, 1981a).

5. While few direct comparisons are available, studies have generally found immersion programs superior to foreign or second language programs (for review, see Genesee, 1979; Swain, 1974; Tucker, 1980). Indeed, so successful is immersion that comparison groups are typically monolingual speakers of the immersion language, something nearly unthinkable for most foreign or SL program eval-

uation. While clearly not a monolithic concept, immersion may fairly be characterized, according to one authority (Swain, 1981a), as focusing initially on the development of target language comprehension rather than production skills, content rather than form, and as attempting to teach content through the SL in language the children can understand. Modern language teaching, on the other hand, generally focuses on formal accuracy, is structurally graded and sentence-bound, and demands early (even immediate) production of nearly all material presented to the learner.

6. For students in immersion programs, additional exposure to the target language outside the school does not seem to facilitate acquisition. Swain (1981b) found no difference in the French skills of French immersion students in Canadian towns where little or no French was spoken and those in towns where, as in the case of Montreal, as much as 65% of language on the street was French. This is presumably because the French of native speakers of French in the wider environment was not addressed to non-native speakers but to other native speakers, and was, therefore, incomprehensible to the immersion children.

7. Lastly, and the strongest evidence to date, acquisition is either severely delayed or does not occur at all if comprehensible input is *un*available. This is true for first and second language acquisition by both adults and children. Thus, hearing children of deaf adults have been severely language delayed when their only input was adult-adult speech on television, yet have caught up with other children when normal adult-child conversation was made available to them (Bard and Sachs, 1977; Jones and Quigley, 1979; Sachs, Bard, and Johnson, 1981; Sachs and Johnson, 1976). The hearing children of deaf adults who made normal progress, as reported by Schiff (1979), are not counter-examples since each child in that study had between 10 and 25 hours per week of conversation with hearing adults. Analo-

gous cases exist in the SLA literature. Thus, young Dutch children who watched German television programs have been noted not to acquire German through so doing (Snow, Arlman-Rupp, Hassing, Jobse, Joosten, and Vorster, 1976). Three motivated English-speaking adults, two of whom were linguistically sophisticated, were found to have acquired no more than some 50 stock vocabulary items and a few conversational formulae in Mandarin and Cantonese after seven months in a Chinese-speaking environment (see Long, 1981a, for further details). A single counter-example, reported by Larsen-Freeman (1979), of a German adult who claimed to have acquired Dutch only by listening to Dutch radio broadcasts can be explained by the similarities between the two languages allowing native fluency in one to serve as basic competence in the other.

In general, therefore, it seems that all the available evidence is consistent with the idea that a *beginning* learner, at least, must have comprehensible input if he or she is to acquire either a first or a second language:

1. Access to comprehensible input is a characteristic of all cases of successful acquisition, first and second (cases 1, 2, 3, and 5, above.).
2. Greater quantities of comprehensible input seem to result in better (or at least faster) acquisition (case 4).
3. And crucially, lack of access to comprehensible input (as distinct from *in*-comprehensible, not any, input) results in little or no acquisition (cases 6 and 7).

Like any genuine hypothesis, the input hypothesis has not been proven. There has been no direct test of it to date. Currently, however, it is sustained because the predictions it makes are consistent with the available data. It has yet to be disconfirmed.

HOW INPUT IS MADE COMPREHENSIBLE

Having established a *prima facie* case for the important role of comprehensible input in all forms of language acquisition, including SLA, the next question that arises is how input becomes comprehensible. It is widely believed that one way is through the hundred and one speech modifications NSs are supposed to make when talking to foreigners, e.g., use of shorter, syntactically less complex utterances, high frequency vocabulary and low type-token ratios (for review, see Hatch, 1979; Long, 1980b, 1981a). In other words, NSs are supposed to make input to NNSs comprehensible by modifying the input itself. There are, however, several problems with this position.

First, many of the input modifications often claimed to characterize foreigner talk have no empirical basis. They are the product of assertions by researchers after examining *only* speech by NSs to non-natives. For example, an impressionistic judgment is made that an NS is using short utterances or high frequency lexical items, and it is then claimed that foreigner talk is characterized by shorter utterances and higher frequency lexical items than speech to other NSs. For such a claim to be justified, *comparison* of speech to non-natives and natives is required. Further, when comparisons are made, the two corpora must be based on equivalent (preferably identical) speech situations, or else any differences observed may be due to differences in task, age, familiarity of speakers, etc. rather than or as well as the status of the interlocutor as a native or non-native speaker. A review of the foreigner talk literature (Long, 1980b, 1981b) found many studies to have used no NS baseline data at all, and almost none of those that had to have used data comparable in these ways. Further, findings had frequently not been quantified, and when quantified, often not tested for statistical significance of the claimed differences. Findings both within and across studies had also been very variable.

Second, there seems to be no evidence that input modifications made by NSs for the supposed benefit of NNSs actually have this effect. One study (Chaudron, 1983) explicitly deals with this issue in the area of lexical changes, and concludes that many modifications may actually cause the learner greater problems of comprehension. "Simplification" is an interactional phenomenon. As Meisel (1977) and Larsen-Freeman (1979) have pointed out, what may be easier to produce from the speaker's perspective may be more difficult to decode from the perspective of the hearer. A shorter utterance, for example, will usually exhibit less redundancy.

Third, there is a logical problem with the idea that changing the input will aid *acquisition.* If removal from the input of structures and lexical items the learner does not understand is what is involved in making speech comprehensible, how does the learner ever advance? Where is the input at i + 1 that is to appear in the learner's competence at the next stage of development?

Clearly, there must be other ways in which input is made comprehensible than modifying the input itself. One way, as Krashen, Hatch, and others have argued, is by use of the linguistic and extralinguistic context to fill in the gaps, just as NSs have been shown to do when the incoming speech signal is inadequate (Warren and Warren, 1970). Another way, as in caretaker speech, is through orienting even adult-adult NS-NNS conversation to the "here and now" (Gaies, 1981; Long, 1980b, 1981c). A third, more consistently used method is modifying not the input itself, but the *interactional structure of conversation* through such devices as self- and other-repetition, confirmation and comprehension checks and clarification requests (Long, 1980b, 1981a, 1982).

Two pieces of evidence suggest that this third way of making input comprehensible is the most important and most widely used of all. First, all

Table 29.1 DIFFERENCES BETWEEN NS-NS
AND NS-NNS CONVERSATION
ACROSS SIX TASKS[a]

In NS-NNS conversation, there was/were:	p level
INPUT	
1. shorter average length of T-units	.005
2. lower number of S-nodes per T-unit	NS
3. lower type-token ratio	NS
4. higher average lexical frequency of nouns and verbs	NS
5. higher proportion of copulas in total verbs	NS
INTERACTION	
6. more present (versus non-present) temporal marking of verbs	.001
7. different distribution of questions, statements, and imperatives in T-units (more questions)	.001
8. different distribution of question-types in T-units (more Wh questions)	.001
9. more conversational frames	NS
10. more confirmation checks	.005
11. more comprehension checks	.005
12. more clarification requests	.005
13. more self-repetitions	.005
14. more other-repetitions	.005
15. more expansions	.005
16. more of 9 through 15 combined	.005

[a]Data from Long (1980b).

studies which have looked at this dimension of NS-NNS conversation have found statistically significant modifications from NS-NS norms. Interactional modifications, in other words, are pervasive. Second, interactional modifications are found in NS-NNS conversation even when input modifications are not or are few and

minor. Thus, in one study (Long, 1980b), the structure of NS-NNS conversation in 16 dyads on six different tasks was significantly different from that of conversation in 16 NS-NS control dyads on the same tasks on 10 out of 11 measures (see Table 29.1). There were no statistically significant differences, on the other hand, on four out of five measures of input modification in the same conversations (see Table 29.1). Similar results have been obtained in several other studies (e.g., Gaies, 1981; Sperry, 1981; Yorinks, 1981; Weinberger, 1981).

In summary, there are probably several ways in which input is made comprehensible. (1) Use of structures and lexis with which the interlocutor is already familiar is certainly one way, but this kind of modification of the input itself may not be as widespread or as great as is often assumed. It can, in any case, serve only the immediate needs of communication, not the future interlanguage development of the learner, for by definition it denies him or her access to new linguistic material. (2) A "here and now" orientation in conversation and the use of linguistic and extralinguistic (contextual) information and general knowledge also play a role. So, more importantly, does (3) modification of the interactional structure of the conversation, i.e., change at the level of discourse. While all three methods may aid communication, (2) and (3) are those likely to aid acquisition, for each allows communication to proceed while exposing the learner to linguistic material which he or she cannot yet handle without their help. (2) and (3) serve to make that *unfamiliar* linguistic input comprehensible.

INFORMATION EXCHANGE AND COMPREHENSIBLE INPUT

As indicated above, the results reported in Table 29.1 were for performance by the 32 dyads across all six tasks in the study. One of the

general research hypotheses, however, was that there would be *differential* performance on the tasks. Specifically, it was predicted that modifications of both kinds (of input and of the interactional structure of conversation) in NS-NNS conversation would be greater on those tasks whose completion required a two-way exchange of information.

Work in both first and second language research has suggested that it is in part verbal feedback from the language learner that enables the caretaker or NS to adjust his or her speech to the interlocutor, child or adult (Berko Gleason, 1977; Gaies, 1983). Thus, Snow (1972) found that mothers, who were already familiar with their young children's linguistic abilities, nevertheless made few adjustments in their speech when preparing tape-recordings for them in their absence. The same mothers modified their speech significantly in face-to-face conversation with the children. Similarly, Stayaert (1977) found no statistically significant modifications in the speech of NSs telling stories to ESL classes, a result which could be explained by the lack of feedback in the story-telling task.

In both these studies, the tasks which did not produce significant changes in the competent speakers' speech involved participants with information communicating it to others who lacked it, hereafter "one-way" tasks. Tasks of this type in the Long (1980b) study were (in the order of their presentation): (2) vicarious narrative, (3) giving instructions, and (6) discussing the supposed purpose of the research (i.e., expressing an opinion). Three other tasks in that study were "two-way," in that each member of a dyad started with information which the other lacked but needed if the task were to be completed. These tasks were: (1) conversation, (4) and (5) playing two communication games, e.g., with visual contact prevented by a screen, finding differences between two nearly identical pictures. The tasks were performed by all dyads in the order indicated above.

The results are presented in Table 29.2. Performance by the NS-NNS dyads was statistically significantly different from that by NS-NS dyads on three tasks requiring a two-way information exchange for their completion, but not so on the three one-way tasks, those not requiring this exchange.

The model that is suggested by the findings reported above, together with the literature reviewed in the two previous sections of this paper, is shown in Figure 29.1. The need to

Table 29.2   RELATIONSHIP BETWEEN TASK-TYPE AND NS-NS AND NS-NNS CONVERSATION[a]

The degree of difference between NS-NS and NS-NNS conversation in performance on:	Tasks 1, 4 & 5 (+ information exchange)	Tasks 2, 3 & 6 (− information exchange)
INPUT		
1. average length of T-units	$p < .025$ (NS)	$p > .025$ (NS)
2. number of S-nodes per T-unit	$p < .01$ (NS)	$p < .025$ (NS)
INTERACTION		
3. distribution of questions, statements and imperatives in T-units	$p < .001$	$p < .005$
4. number of conversational frames	$p > .025$ (NS)	$p > .025$ (NS)
5. number of confirmation checks	$p < .005$	$p < .01$ (NS)
6. number of comprehension checks	$p < .005$	$p > .025$ (NS)
7. number of clarification requests	$p < .005$	$p < .005$
8. number of self-repetitions	$p < .005$	$p > .025$ (NS)
9. number of other-repetitions	$p < .005$	— (NS)[b]
10. number of expansions	$p < .005$	$p > .025$ (NS)
11. number of 4 through 10 combined	$p < .005$	$p > .025$ (NS)

[a]Data from Long (1980b).
[b]There were no instances of expansions on these tasks

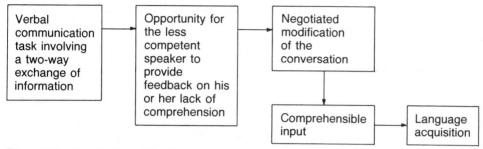

Figure 29.1   Model of the relationship between type of conversational task and language acquisition

obtain information from (not simply transmit information to) the less competent speaker means that the competent speaker cannot press ahead (in largely unmodified speech) without attending to the feedback (verbal and non-verbal) he or she is receiving. The option to provide feedback allows the less competent speaker to negotiate the conversation, to force the competent speaker to adjust his or her performance, via modifications of the kinds discussed earlier, until what he or she is saying is comprehensible. Comprehensible input, it has already been argued, feeds acquisition.

The model is presumably applicable to all conversations between those who control a code to a higher degree of proficiency than those with whom they are attempting to communicate, including NSs in conversation with NNSs, caretakers with young children, and normal adults and children with the mentally retarded. The model predicts, among other things, that communication involving a two-way exchange of information will provide more comprehensible input than communication which does not. Two-way communication tasks should also promote acquisition better than one-way tasks, for one-way tasks cannot guarantee the kinds of modifications needed to make input comprehensible.

CLASSROOM NS-NNS CONVERSATION

The data and discussion thus far have centered around NS-NNS conversation outside the classroom setting. This section reviews some recent empirical work on the same issues in classroom English as a second language (ESL).

Many traditional analyses of classroom discourse have emphasized its instructional purpose. The focus has been the language of participants in the roles of "teacher" and "student" rather than the conversation of native and non-native speakers. Thus, descriptive categories have included such items as "lecturing," "praising," "correction," "drill," "teacher question," and "student response," "presentation," and "practice," where the pedagogic function of classroom language is clearly uppermost in the researcher's mind. Direct reference to target language skills or subject matter has also been frequent, as shown by the use of such behavioral categories as "speaking," "reading," "oral reading," "writing," "grammar," and "vocabulary."

Research of this kind has also emphasized language *use* in the classroom rather than language *acquisition*. Comparisons are made between two or more "methods" of instruction (e.g., audio-lingual and grammar translation) or two or more types of instruction (e.g., SL teaching and immersion education). If non-instructional language is introduced as baseline data, it tends to be NS-NS conversation, e.g., that in a specialized occupational setting for which the learners are supposedly being prepared by their language instruction. The agenda for such research involves an effort to make classroom discourse (either spoken or written) approximate target language *use* for these situations.

It is not my intention to criticize such work in any way. It is obviously extremely valuable for a variety of concerns in applied linguistics, such as syllabus design, materials development, teacher education, and the improvement of classroom instruction. I wish to suggest, however, that when the focus is SL *acquisition* in a classroom setting, both the categories and the baseline data need to change.

Assuming that some version of the input hypothesis is correct, indeed to test that hypothesis, the analysis will need to include the same kinds of categories as the work on NS-NNS conversation outside classrooms. NS-NNS (not NS-NS) conversation will also become a source of baseline data. NS-NNS conversation, after all, is the context known to be capable of producing fluent sequential bilinguals. Witness its success in this regard in many multilingual societies where indigenous languages, in which no instruction is available, are routinely acquired with near native proficiency by large groups of people, often illiterate or poorly educated.[1]

These considerations motivated a recent study of talk in ESL classrooms, and a comparison of this discourse with NS-NNS conversation in an informal, non-instructional setting. The findings from this research permit some initial generalizations to be made concerning the success of SL instruction in providing classroom learners with comprehensible input.

Long and Sato (1983) compared the classroom conversations of six ESL teachers and their elementary level students with 36 informal NS-NNS conversations outside classrooms in which the NNSs were at the same (elementary) level of ESL proficiency. The six ESL teachers were all professionally experienced. They were audio-taped teaching their regular students, mostly young adults, from a variety of first language backgrounds, a lesson of ap-

proximately 50 minutes not especially prepared for the research, the purpose of which was unknown to teachers or students. There was an average of about 20 students per class. The researchers were not present in the classroom during the recordings in order to make the data collection as unobtrusive as possible. The six lessons, two in Honolulu, three in Los Angeles, and one in Philadelphia, varied in the type of material covered, but were all predominantly oral-aural and teacher-fronted. Impressionistically, they seemed to the researchers typical of much adult ESL teaching in the United States. None of the teachers adhered to any of the recent unconventional language teaching methods, such as Silent Way or Counseling-Learning. They based most of their oral work on textbook exercises, prepared dialogs and other teacher-made material of the sort common in audio-lingual, audio-visual, and structural-situational classrooms.

The conversational data outside classrooms were obtained from an earlier study (Long, 1981c). The 36 NS subjects consisted of three groups, 12 experienced ESL teachers, 12 teachers of other subjects (literature, linguistics, music, etc.) and 12 NSs who were not teachers of any kind (university administrators, lawyers, counselors, etc.). All were college educated speakers of a standard variety of American English. The 36 NNSs were all young Japanese adults enrolled in the elementary level of a special ESL program at UCLA in the summer of 1979. Controlling for sex of speaker and interlocutor and for the years of prior foreigner talk experience of the NSs, dyads were formed by random assignment such that there were an equal number of same-sex and cross-sex pairings. All subjects were meeting for the first time for the purpose of the study, which was unknown to them. Conversations took place in the researcher's office on the UCLA campus. Subjects were introduced by first name and asked to have a conversation of five minutes about anything they liked. The investigator then left the room. Subjects knew that their conversations were being tape-recorded.

Long and Sato (1983) coded transcripts of the ESL lessons and the 36 informal NS-NNS conversations for nine measures of input and interaction modifications. They then compared these results for statistically significant differences between the two corpora. For the purposes of this paper, measures were also obtained on three additional features of conversational structure: comprehension checks, clarification requests, and confirmation checks. All statistical analyses for these 12 measures were performed using simple or contingency chi-square tests, with Yates' correction for a two-way chi-square design with one degree of freedom where needed, with the exception of those for the morphology data, for which Spearman rank order correlation coefficients were calculated (oc = .05 in all cases). For reasons of space, the results are merely summarized here. (For further details, see Long 1981c and Long and Sato 1983.)

As had been predicted in the original study, NS speech and the interactional structure of NS-NNS conversation in the two corpora differed greatly.

1. ESL teachers used significantly more display than referential questions ($\chi^2 = 199.35$, p < .0005).
2. ESL teachers used significantly more display questions than did NSs addressing NNSs outside classrooms ($\chi^2 = 1,859,131.70$, p < .0005). In fact, display questions were virtually unknown in the informal NS-NNS conversations (2 out of a total of 1567 questions in T-units).
3. ESL teachers used significantly fewer referential questions than did NSs addressing NNSs outside classrooms ($\chi^2 = 844.01$, p < .0005).
4. In T-units in the two corpora, the frequencies of questions, statements and imperatives differed significantly ($\chi^2 = 308.10$, p < .0005), with ESL teachers

using fewer questions than the NSs outside classrooms (35% compared with 66%), more statements (54% compared with 33%) and more imperatives (11% compared with 1%).

5. ESL teachers' speech was significantly more oriented to the "here and now", as measured by the relative frequencies of verbs marked temporally for present and non-present reference ($\chi^2 = 4,109.87$, p < .0005).
6. ESL teachers' speech was significantly more oriented to the "here and now" than was the speech of the NSs in the informal NS-NNS conversations ($\chi^2 = 25.58$, p < .001).
7. The rank order of nine grammatical morphemes in the six ESL teachers' speech correlated positively with the order of the same items in the speech of the 36 NSs addressing NNSs outside classrooms (rho = .77, p < .005).
8. The rank order of the nine morphemes in teachers' speech was not significantly related to Krashen's (1977) "average order" for the accurate appearance of those items in the speech of ESL acquirers (rho = .46, p > .05, NS).
9. The relationship between the orders for the nine morphemes in the ESL teachers' speech and Krashen's "average order" for accurate production (.46) was weaker than the relationship between the orders for the nine morphemes in the NS speech to NNSs outside classrooms and Krashen's order (.77).
10. ESL teachers used a significantly greater number of comprehension checks than did NSs addressing NNSs outside classrooms ($\chi^2 = 102.88$, p < .001).
11. ESL teachers used fewer clarification requests than did NSs addressing NNSs outside classrooms, but the difference was not statistically significant ($\chi^2 = 0.89$, p > .50, NS).
12. ESL teachers used significantly fewer confirmation checks than did NSs addressing NNSs outside classrooms ($\chi^2 = 27.79$, p < .001).

Much could be said about these results, but again for reasons of space, I will confine myself to a few general points. (The interested reader is referred to Long and Sato, 1983, for more detailed discussion.)

Perhaps the most obvious conclusion to be drawn from the findings from this study is that, insofar as they are representative of at least *elementary* level ESL instruction, the SL classroom offers very little opportunity to the learner to communicate in the target language or to hear it used for communicative purposes by others. In these ESL lessons, at least, the main source of communicative language use for the students was the teachers' use of 224 imperatives, chiefly for classroom management, e.g.,

T: Give me the present perfect

and for disciplinary matters, e.g.,

T: Sit down, Maria

As the other results show, most of what the teachers said was, in Paulston's (1973) terms, "meaningful," i.e., contextually relevant, but not "communicative", i.e., bearing information unknown to the hearer.

Display, or what Mehan (1979) calls "known information" questions, predominate. Thus, the six teachers asked 476 questions of the following kind:

T: Are you a student?

and

T: Is the clock on the wall?

Only 128 questions were referential, i.e., asked the student to provide unknown information, e.g.,

T: What's the matter?

or

T: Why didn't she come to class?

In NS-NNS conversation outside the classroom, on the other hand, there were only two in-

stances of display questions, both uttered by one NS at the beginning of an encounter when she wished to be sure the NNS had heard her name correctly when the investigator had introduced them. In contrast, there were 999 referential questions.

Display questions are a good indication that we are dealing with what Barnes (1976) calls the "transmission model" of education, in which a "knower" imparts knowledge to those who do not know. The students are asked to display knowledge that the teacher already possesses, and often remarkably trivial knowledge at that. In other words, there is little two-way exchange of information.

The data on comprehension checks and confirmation checks tell the same story. A speaker uses a comprehension check to find out if the *interlocutor* understands something, e.g.,

T: Do you understand?

Confirmation checks, on the other hand, are used to ascertain whether the *speaker* has heard or understood something the interlocutor has said, e.g.,

S: I went/ny/
T: You went to New York?

or

S: I wan one job
T: You're looking for work?

Comprehension checks, therefore, will be more frequent when the major flow of information is from teacher to student, from NS to NNS; confirmation checks will be more frequent when information is also passing in the other direction. In this study, the six ESL teachers used significantly more comprehension checks and significantly fewer confirmation checks than the NSs in informal NS-NNS conversations.

The data on clarification requests show the same general pattern. Clarification requests are used when the speaker (teacher or NS) wants help in understanding something the *interlocutor* (student or NNS) has said, e.g.,

T: What do you mean?

Since ESL students, as has been shown, are seldom telling the teacher something unknown to him or her, we would expect there to be fewer clarification requests in the ESL corpus. This is indeed what was found, although the difference was not statistically significant. The lack of a statistically significant difference is presumably due to the fact that confirmation checks were preferred when the need arose to remove ambiguity from the NNSs' speech, both inside and outside the classroom. As noted earlier, teachers did use significantly fewer of these than the NSs in the informal NS-NNS conversations.

The examples of typical display questions given earlier *(Are you a student?* and *Is the clock on the wall?)* reflect another feature of ESL classroom discourse in this study, namely, its "here and now" orientation. Long (1980b) found the 16 NS-NNS dyads to employ significantly more verbs marked temporally for present and significantly fewer for non-present during informal conversation than the 16 NS-NS dyads ($\chi^2 = 11.58$, p $<$ .001), a finding confirmed by Gaies (1981) in a replication of the Long (1981c) study. In Long (1981c), which provided the informal NS-NNS corpus being considered here, the 36 NS-NNS conversations were found to be more oriented to the here and now, again as measured by present and non-present tense marking, than the baseline NS-NS conversational data. The difference on that occasion, however, just failed to make the required

level of significance ($\chi^2 = 3.33$, p $>$ .05, NS). Now, in the study by Long and Sato (1983), the six ESL lessons were found to be even more present-oriented than the 36 NS-NNS conversations ($\chi^2 = 25.58$, p $<$ n.001). The here and now orientation of the teachers' classroom speech, therefore, is far greater than that in informal NS-NS conversation.

Teachers appear to rely on this here and now orientation as an important way in which to make their speech comprehensible to classroom learners. The relatively high frequencies of present tense morphology (third person *s*) and low frequencies of past tense morphology (regular and irregular past) that this brings was the main cause of the disturbed input frequency order for the nine grammatical morphemes in Krashen's (1977) "average order," and, hence, for the non-significant correlation between the two orders.

In summary, despite the lip service paid to the importance of communication in the classroom by much recent writing in the "methods" literature, to the extent that these lessons are typical at least of teaching at the elementary level, little seems to have changed. The data suggest that the emphasis is still on usage, not use (Widdowson, 1972), and that, in Paulston's (1973) terms, "meaningful," not "communicative" use of the target language is the norm. As shown, among other ways, by the data on display and referential questions, ESL classroom discourse in this study reflected something approaching a pure transmission model of education. Within quite tightly controlled structural limits, the focus is on the accuracy of students' speech rather than its truth value.

SOME IMPLICATIONS FOR CLASSROOM TEACHING

Contrary to claims made by some researchers (e.g., Hale and Budar, 1970), there is a considerable amount of evidence to the effect that ESL instruction makes a positive contribution to SLA, both quantitatively and qualitatively.

(For review, see Long, 1983, and Pica, 1982.) As argued in the early sections of this article, however, there is also an increasing amount of evidence consistent with the input hypothesis. This stresses the importance for SLA of target language input made comprehensible to the learner chiefly through the negotiation for meaning involved in its use for communicative purposes. A concern arising from the data on NS-NNS conversation inside and outside classrooms must be that, at least at the elementary level, instruction in the SL per se is proceeding at the expense of SL communication and the provision of comprehensible input.

Now it might be argued that most of what the learners in these classes heard *was* comprehensible, as shown by their ability to respond appropriately. This was indeed the case. However, that the teachers' speech was comprehensible was due largely to the fact that the input itself was "impoverished" in various ways. In qualitative terms, what the ESL students heard consisted primarily of predigested sentences, structurally and lexically controlled, repetitious in the extreme, and with little or no communicative value. Input was comprehensible, in other words, mainly because it contained few linguistic surprises. Yet, it has been argued, it is these surprises that must occur if acquisition of new structures is to proceed. The input was limited quantitatively, too, in that relatively little was said. The drill-like nature of much of the instruction meant that short exchanges of a routine kind were repeated at the expense of extended discourse ranging over a wide variety of topics, as was found in the non-instructional conversations. As has been documented in a number of classroom studies, a common pattern consists of a teacher question *(Where's the clock?)*, a student response *(It's on the wall)*, and a teacher reaction/evaluation, often in the form of a repetition of the correct response *(The clock is on the wall)*. The *same* exchange is then repeated, with minor variations, as the sentence patterns are "drilled" with other students. These three sentences are the total input for the class while this procedure is carried out.

Once again, it should be stressed that I am *not* advocating that we abandon our attempts to *teach* the language, including grammatical ac-

curacy. Rather, it is a question of the relative emphasis given to accuracy over communicative effect that is at issue. I hope to have made a case for more attention and more class time being devoted to the latter, and close with a few suggestions for implementing such a change for those with the inclination to do so.

One basic difference between NS-NNS conversation in and out of classrooms indicated by the studies reported here is that classroom discourse is rarely motivated by a two-way exchange of information. However "phatic" much of the non-instructional conversation may be when the NNSs are beginners, NSs do not know the answer to questions like *Where are you from?* or *Where do you live?* when they ask them. And they ask each question only once. The same is not true of questions like *Are you a student?* or *Is the clock on the wall?*, especially at the fifth time of asking. An easy way to remedy this is by ensuring that students enter classroom exchanges as *informational equals*. This can be achieved by use of tasks whose solution requires that students convey information that only they possess when the conversation begins.

A wide variety of such tasks exists in published form, although they are more often to be found in books not originally intended for language teaching (Plaister, 1982). Materials designed to improve the reader's IQ and/or problem-solving skills are a particularly rich source, as are many games whose sole purpose is entertainment. Many of these can easily be altered by a teacher to suit the age, cultural background and interests of specific groups of learners, and often give rise to ideas for new versions. Some care must be taken in their selection, however. It is not enough that one person has information the other lacks. Rather, both must have information that is unknown to be needed by the other. Thus, while both are simple and useful, there is a difference between having one person describe a picture so that a second (or a whole class) can reproduce it, on the one hand, and, on the other, having two people discover differences between two versions of a nearly identical picture that each has when each version contains features the other version lacks.

Changes in the kind of tasks carried out, such as these, basically the introduction of "two-way" tasks, but also, e.g., having students describe personal photographs rather than pictures in textbooks (suggested by Charlene Sato), can lead to changes in the quality of classroom discourse. Principally, the need to convey and obtain unknown information will result in the negotiation for meaning characterized by modifications in the interactional structure of conversation as participants seek to make incoming speech comprehensible. That is, tasks of these kinds can bring about qualitative changes in classroom discourse.

Another concern expressed earlier was that the quantity of input needed to increase, too. Here, two suggestions can be made. First, teachers might like to consider using a wider variety of tasks rather than more frequent use of the same tasks, thus promoting a wider range of input. Second, having the tasks carried out by the students in small groups will multiply the amount of talk each student engages in individually. While the partial reduction in NS speech (or more native-like speech by a NNS teacher) this brings may yet turn out to be a problem, it is conceivable that this loss may be offset by the fact that what language the student hears is at least being negotiated (through his or her active participation in the small group conversation) to the appropriate level for his or her current SL competence. This is often not the case in "lockstep" conversation between teacher and whole class, where what the teacher says may be too easy for some, right for some, and too difficult for others. The use of potentially "communicative" language teaching materials in a lockstep (teacher to whole class) format may also be less guaranteed to achieve the qualitative changes of interest than their use in small groups of students. In one study, the number and variety of rhetorical acts, pedagogic moves and social skills engaged in by students using such materials was found to be greater for students working in pairs than in a larger group with the teacher, (Long, Adams, McLean, and Castaños, 1976).

SUMMARY

This paper began with a brief review of empirical evidence consistent with the input hypothesis, which states that progress in SLA involves *understanding* linguistic input containing lexis and structures not in the acquirer's current repetoire. Various ways in which this understanding is achieved were then outlined, with special importance being attributed to the modification, not of the input per se, but of the interactional structure of conversation between NSs and NNSs. Research findings were then presented which suggest that modifications of this kind are only assured when the conversation involves a two-way exchange of information.

An explicit comparison of NS-NNS conversation in ESL instruction and in informal, non-instructional talk then isolated several basic differences between them. Greatest significance was attributed to the relative lack of modification of the interactional structure of conversation in classroom discourse, with a concomitant poverty, both quantitative and qualitative, in the input available to students. The use of "two-way" tasks in small group work was suggested as one way of introducing more communicative language use in the SL classroom, and in this way, more comprehensible input. While preserving the benefits to be obtained from a focus on formal accuracy in some phases of teaching, these changes are designed to make other phases approximate NS-NNS conversation outside classrooms, and thereby, if the input hypothesis is correct, to facilitate SLA in a classroom setting.

NOTE

1. Such high levels of success are not guaranteed. A simple diet of conversation with NSs can also result in the development of "pidginized" speech, as happened with Alberto (Schumann, 1978), or in fluent but deviant SL performance, as in the case of Wes (Schmidt, 1981). Nevertheless, given modifications of the kind outlined earlier in this paper, NS-NNS conversation is known at least to facilitate SLA. It is, therefore, a relevant source of baseline data with which to compare discourse in SL classrooms. NS-NS conversation is relevant when target language use is at issue, but less so when the focus is acquisition.

REFERENCES

Andersen, R. W. (ed.) 1981. *New Dimensions in Second Language Acquisition Research.* Rowley, MA: Newbury House Publishers.

Bard, B., and J. Sachs. 1977. Language acquisition in two normal children of deaf parents. Paper presented to the Second Annual Boston Conference on Language Development. (ERIC #150 868)

Barnes, D. 1976. *From Communication to Curriculum.* Harmondsworth: Penguin Books.

Berko Gleason, J. 1977. Talking to children: Some notes on feedback. In C. E. Snow and C. A. Ferguson (eds.), *Talking to Children: Language Input and Acquisition.* Cambridge: Cambridge University Press.

Chaudron, C. 1983. Foreigner talk: An aid to learning? In H. W. Seliger and M. H. Long (eds.), *Classroom-Oriented Research on Second Language Acquistion.* Rowley, MA: Newbury House Publishers.

Gaies, S. J. 1981. Native speaker-nonnative speaker interaction among academic peers. Paper presented at the 56th Annual Meeting of the Linguistic Society of America, New York, NY, December 28–30.

Gaies, S. J. 1983. Learner feedback: An exploratory study of its role in the second language classroom. In H. W. Seliger and M. H. Long (eds.), *Classroom-Oriented Research on Second Language Acquisition.* Rowley, MA: Newbury House Publishers.

quisition.* Rowley, MA: Newbury House Publishers.

Genesee, F. 1979. Scholastic effects of French immersion: An overview after ten years. *Interchange* 9, 20–29.

Hale, T. M., and E. C. Budar. 1970. Are TESOL classes the only answer? *Modern Language Journal* 54, 487–92.

Hatch, E. M. 1979. Simplified input and second language acquisition. Paper presented at the Linguistic Society of America winter meeting, Los Angeles, CA, December.

Jones, M., and S. Quigley. 1979. The acquisition of question formation in spoken Spanish and American sign language by two hearing children of deaf parents. *Journal of Speech and Hearing Disorders* 44, 196–208.

Krashen, S. D. 1977. Some issues relating to the monitor model. In H. D. Brown, C. A. Yorio, and R. Crymes (eds.), *On TESOL '77. Teaching and Learning English as a Second Language: Trends in Research and Practice.* Washington, D. C.: TESOL.

_____. 1980. The input hypothesis. In J. E. Alatis (ed.), *Current Issues in Bilingual Education.* Washington, D. C.: Georgetown University Press.

Larsen-Freeman, D. 1979. The importance of input in second language acquisition. Paper presented at the Linguistic Society of America winter meeting, Los Angeles, CA, December.

Long, M. H. 1980a. Inside the "black box": Methodological issues in classroom research on language learning. *Language Learning* 30, 1, 1–42.

———. 1980b. Input, interaction, and second language acquisition. Unpublished Ph.D. dissertation, University of California, Los Angeles.

———. 1981a. Input, interaction, and second language acquisition. In H. Winitz (ed.), *Native Language and Foreign Language Acquisition. Annals of the New York Academy of Sciences* 379, 259–278.

———. 1981b. Variation in linguistic input for second language acquisition. Paper presented at the European-North American Workshop on Cross-Linguistic Second Language Acquisition Research, Lake Arrowhead, CA, September 7–14.

———. 1981c. Questions in foreigner talk discourse. *Language Learning* 31, 1, 135–157.

———. 1982. Native speaker/non-native speaker conversation and the negotiation of comprehensible input. Paper (in German translation) in special issue on second language acquisition of *Zeitschrift für Literaturwissenschaft und Linguistik,* W. Klein and J. Weissenborn (eds.) 1982, and in *Applied Linguistics* 4, 1983, 126–161.

———. 1983. Does second language instruction make a difference? A review of research. *TESOL Quarterly* 17, 3, 359–382.

———, L. Adams, M. McLean, and F. Castaños. 1976. Doing things with words: Verbal interaction in lockstep and small group classroom situations. In J. Fanselow and R. Crymes (eds.), *On TESOL '76.* Washington, D.C.: TESOL.

——— and C. J. Sato. 1983. Classroom foreigner talk discourse: Forms and functions of teachers' questions. In H. W. Seliger and M. H. Long (eds.), *Classroom-Oriented Research on Second Language Acquistion,* 268–285.

Mehan, H. 1979. "What time is it, Denise?" Asking known information questions in classroom discourse. *Theory into Practice* 18, 4, 285–294.

Meisel, J. M. 1977. Linguistic simplification: A study of immigrant workers' speech and foreigner talk. In S. P. Corder and E. Roulet (eds.), *The Notions of Simplification, Interlanguages and Pidgins and their Relation to Second Language Pedagogy.*

Actes du 5ème colloque de linguistique appliquée de Neuchâtel, 20–22 Mai. Genéve: Librairie Droz.

Paulston, C. B. 1973. From linguistic competence to communicative competence. *TESOL Quarterly* 7, 1.

Pica, T. 1982. An investigation of adult second language acquisition in three language contexts. Ph.D. dissertation, Philadelphia, University of Pennsylvania.

Plaister, T. 1982. The world is the ESL teacher's curricular oyster. Paper presented at the TESOL Conference, Honolulu, Hawaii, May.

Sachs, J., B. Bard, and M. L. Johnson. 1981. Language learning with restricted input. *Applied Psycholinguistics* 2, 1, 33–54.

———, and M. L. Johnson. 1976. Language development in a hearing child of deaf parents. In W. von Raffler-Engel and Y. Lebrun (eds.), *Baby Talk and Infant Speech.* Lisse, Netherlands: Swets and Zeitlinger.

Schiff, N. 1979. The influence of deviant maternal input on the development of language during the preschool years. *Journal of Speech and Hearing Research* 22, 581–603.

Schmidt, R. W. 1981. Interaction, acculturation and the acquisition of communicative competence: A case study of an adult. *University of Hawaii Workingpapers in Linguistics*, 13, 3, 29–77.

Schumann, J. H. 1978. *The Pidginization Process: A Model for Second Language Acquisition.* Rowley, MA: Newbury House Publishers.

Seliger, H. W., and M. H. Long (eds.) 1983. *Classroom-Oriented Research on Second Language Acquisition.* Rowley, MA: Newbury House Publishers.

Snow, C. E. 1972. Mothers' speech to children learning language. *Child Development* 43, 549–565.

———, A. Arlman-Rupp, Y. Hassing, J. Jobse, J. Joosten, and J. Vorster. 1976. Mothers' speech in three social classes. *Journal of Psycholinguistic Research* 5, 1–20.

Sperry, L. L. 1981. Some preliminary findings concerning child foreigner talk discourse. Unpublished term paper, Ed. 676, University of Pennsylvania.

Stayaert, M. 1977. A comparison of the speech of ESL teachers to native and non-native speakers of English. Paper presented to the winter meeting of the Linguistic Society of America, Chicago, IL.

Swain, M. 1974. French immersion programs across Canada: Research findings. *The Canadian Modern Language Review* 31, 117–129.

———. 1981a. Target language use in the wider environment as a factor in its acquisition. In R. W. Andersen (ed.), *New Dimensions in Second Language Acquisition Research.* Rowley, MA: Newbury House Publishers.

———. 1981b. Immersion education: Applicability for nonvernacular teaching to vernacular speakers. *Studies in Second Language Acquisition* 4, 1, 1–17.

Tucker, G. R. 1980. Implications for U.S. bilingual education: Evidence from Canadian research. *NCBE Focus* 2.

Warren, R. M., and R. P. Warren, 1970. Auditory illusions and confusions. *Scientific American* 223, 30–36.

Weinberger, P. 1981. Modified interaction in adult grammatical foreigner talk. Unpublished term paper, Ed. 676, University of Pennsylvania.

Widdowson, H. G. 1972. The teaching of English as communication. *English Language Teaching* 27, 1, 15–19.

Yorinks, M. 1981. Native-speaking child and native-speaking adult: Modifications in interaction with a non-native speaking child. Unpublished term paper, Ed. 676, University of Pennsylvania.

CHAPTER 30

Error Correction in Foreign Language Teaching: Recent Theory, Research, and Practice

James M. Hendrickson

AN HISTORICAL PERSPECTIVE OF LEARNER ERRORS[1]

Audiolingualism and Error Prevention

Throughout the 1950s and well into the 1960s, the audiolingual approach to teaching foreign languages was in full swing. Language students were supposed to spend many hours memorizing dialogs, manipulating pattern drills, and studying all sorts of grammatical generalizations. The assumed or explicit aim of this teaching method could be called "practice makes perfect," and presumably some day, when students needed to use a foreign language to communicate with native speakers, they would do so fluently and accurately.

We now realize that this was not what in most cases occurred. Some highly motivated students from audiolingual classrooms managed to become fairly proficient in a foreign language, but only after they had used the language in communicative situations. Predictably, most students who could not or did not take the effort to transfer audiolingual training to com-municative use soon forgot the dialog lines, the pattern drills, and the grammatical generalizations that they had studied or practiced in school. Put simply, the students had learned what they were taught—and soon forgot most of it.

Not only did many supporters of audiolingualism overestimate learning outcomes for most language students, but some of them regarded second language errors from a somewhat puritanical perspective. For example, in his book, *Language and Language Learning,* which became a manifesto of the language teaching profession of the 1960s, Nelson Brooks (1960) considered error to have a relationship to learning resembling that of sin to virtue: "Like sin, error is to be avoided and its influence overcome, but its presence is to be expected" (p. 58). Brooks suggested an instructional procedure that would, ostensibly, help language students produce error-free utterances: "The principal method of *avoiding* error in language learning is to observe and practice the right model a sufficient number of times; the principal way of *overcoming* it is to shorten the time lapse between the incorrect response and the presentation once more of the correct model" (p. 58). If students continued to produce errors using this stimulus-response method, inadequate teaching techniques or unsequenced instructional materials were to blame (Corder, 1967, p. 163). Appearing one year later in 1961, *The Teacher's Manual for German, Level One,* prepared by the Modern Language Materials Development Center (1961), provided specific guidelines for correction of student errors. The *Manual* states that teachers should correct all errors immediately (pp. 3, 17, 21, 26), and that students should be neither required nor permitted to discover and correct their own mistakes (pp. 28, 32).

Many foreign language educators never questioned the validity of this mechanistic approach to error prevention and error correction. In fact, well into the 1970s some of them continued to endorse it. The following statement, for example, is found in the introduction to an elementary English course published in 1970: "One of the teacher's aims should be to prevent mistakes from occurring. In the early stages while the pupils are wholly dependent on the teacher for what they learn, it should be possible to achieve this aim" (Lee, 1970). Similar advice was given to teachers in a first-year Spanish textbook, published four years later. Under the rubric "Suggestions for classroom procedure," the authors list suggestion No. 5: "Whenever a mistake is made, the teacher should correct it at once and then repeat the correct pattern or question for the benefit of the entire class" (Hansen and Wilkins, 1974, p. xvii).

Structural linguists introduced another mechanism for helping language teachers deal with students' errors. This mechanism, called contrastive analysis, assumed that interference from students' first language caused errors to occur in their target language speech. Many linguists believed that once a teacher had a systematic knowledge of the differences between the two languages, he or she could begin developing appropriate instructional techniques and materials that would help students avoid producing errors. However, considerable empirical evidence indicates that although interference from students' native language is the major source of *phonological* errors, interference errors are only one of many types of errors found in the lexicon, syntax, morphology, and orthography of students' utterances in the target language (Wolfe, 1967; Falk, 1968; Wilkins, 1968; Dušková, 1969; Selinker, 1969; Buteau, 1970; Ervin-Tripp, 1970; Grauberg, 1971; Hussein, 1971; George, 1972; Politzer and Ramirez, 1973; Richards, 1973a, 1973b; Burt, 1975; Hanzeli, 1975; and Hendrickson, 1977b).

Communicative Competence and the Value of Errors

Since the late 1960s studies in transformational-generative grammar, first language acquisition, and especially cognitive psychology have contributed to a trend away from audiolingualism and toward making language teaching more humanistic and less mechanistic. Foreign language teachers have begun to respond to this attitudinal change by examining the learning styles of their students and by stressing the use of language for communication. These new directions in language teaching are gradually changing the focus of foreign language learning objectives, instructional materials, and pedagogical strategies. Instead of expecting students to produce flawless sentences in a foreign language, for example, many of today's students are encouraged to *communicate* in the target language about things that matter to *them.* As Chastain wrote in 1971, "More important than error-free speech is the creation of an atmosphere in which the students want to talk" (p. 249).

This positive perspective toward second language errors is based partly upon analogy to the fact that children everywhere produce numerous errors while acquiring their first language—errors that their parents expect and accept as a natural and necessary part of child development. Many language educators propose that foreign language teachers also should expect many errors from their students, and should accept those errors as a natural phenomenon integral to the process of learning a second language. When teachers tolerate *some* student errors, students often feel more confident about using the target language than if *all* their errors are corrected. Teachers are reminded that people make mistakes when learning any new skill, but that people learn from their mistakes when they receive periodic, supportive feedback.

Not only do all language learners necessarily produce errors when they communicate, but systematic analyses of errors can provide useful insights into the processes of language acquisition. Because errors are signals that actual learning is taking place, they can indicate students' progress and success in language learning (Corder, 1967; Zydatiss, 1974; Lange, 1977; and Lantolf, 1977). Studying students' errors also has immediate practical applications for foreign language teachers (Corder, 1973, p. 265):

> Errors provide feedback, they tell the teacher something about the effectiveness of his teaching materials and his teaching techniques, and show him what parts of the syllabus he has been following have been inadequately learned or taught and need further attention. They enable him to decide whether he must devote more time to the item he has been working on. This is the day-to-day value of errors. But in terms of broader planning and with a new group of learners they provide the information for designing a remedial syllabus or a programme of reteaching.

To summarize, over the past three decades there has been a significant change in foreign language methodologies and materials. There has also been a shift in pedagogical focus from preventing errors to learning from errors—a fact that is reflected in George's (1972) statement that, "It is noteworthy that at the beginning of the sixties the word 'error' was associated with *correction*, at the end with *learning*" (p. 189). Education is becoming increasingly oriented toward meeting the needs and interests of individual learners. Many foreign language teachers already have responded to their students' needs by implementing innovative methods and materials that encourage creative self-expression and by not insisting on error-free communication. Furthermore, the results of many studies in first and second language acquisition have important implications for teaching foreign languages efficiently and for developing effective instructional materials.

A REVIEW OF THE LITERATURE ON ERROR CORRECTION

A review of the literature on error correction in foreign language teaching reveals that (a) no current standards exist on whether, when, which, or how student errors should be corrected or who should correct them (Burt, 1975, p. 53), (b) there are few widely accepted linguistic criteria of grammatical and lexical correction in foreign language teaching (Robinson, 1971, p. 261), and (c) much of what has been published on error correction is speculative, and needs to be validated by a great deal of empirical experimentation (Hendrickson, 1977b, p. 17). Despite these limitations, a sufficient body of literature on error correction exists to merit a systematic review. The information reported herein addresses five fundamental questions:

1. Should learner errors be corrected?
2. If so, when should learner errors be corrected?
3. Which learner errors should be corrected?
4. How should learner errors be corrected?
5. Who should correct learner errors?

Should Learner Errors Be Corrected?

Before correcting student errors, teachers need to consider whether the errors should be corrected at all, and, if so, why (Gorbet, 1974; p. 55). When students are not able to recognize their own errors, they need the assistance of someone more proficient in the language than they are (Corder, 1967; George, 1972; and Allwright, 1975). A recent survey on college students' attitudes toward error correction reveals that the students not only want to be corrected, but also they wish to be corrected more than teachers feel they should be (Cathcart and Olsen, 1976)! All teachers probably provide some means of correcting oral and written errors, just as parents correct their childrens' errors in a natural language learning environment. Correcting learners' errors helps them discover the functions and limitations of the syntactical and lexical forms of the target language (Kennedy, 1973). Error correction is especially useful to *adult* second language learners because it helps them learn the exact environment in which to apply rules and discover the precise semantic range of lexical items (Krashen and Seliger, 1975).

When Should Learner Errors Be Corrected?

Perhaps the most difficult challenge of language teaching is determining when to correct and when to ignore student errors (Gorbet, 1974, p. 19). The literature on error correction reveals clearly that many foreign language educators have rejected the obsessive concern with error avoidance that generally characterizes audiolingually-oriented language instruction (Corder, 1967; Grittner, 1969; Chastain, 1971; Holley and King, 1971; George, 1972; Dresdner, 1973; Dulay, 1974; Gorbet, 1974; Burt, 1975; Krashen and Seliger, 1975; Valdman, 1975; Hendrickson, 1977b; Lange, 1977; Lantolf, 1977; Terrell, 1977). These educators hold that producing errors is a natural and necessary phenomenon in language learning, and they recommend that teachers accept a wide margin of deviance from so-called "standard" forms and structures of the target language.

There appears to be affective as well as cognitive justification for tolerating some errors produced by language learners. Foreign language educators generally agree that tolerating some oral and written errors helps learners communicate more confidently in a foreign language. Because language learners take many risks in producing incorrect utterances when communicating, teachers need to consider whether or not their corrective techniques instill a feeling of success in students. Perhaps teachers should reserve error correction for manipulative grammar practice, and should tolerate more errors during communicative practice (Birckbichler, 1977). A fairly recent survey of 1,200 university students of foreign language was conducted partly to determine their reactions to having their errors corrected by their teachers. It was found that the "students prefer not to be marked down for each minor speaking and writing error because this practice destroys their confidence and forces them to expend so much effort on details that they lose the overall ability to use language" (Walker, 1973, p. 103). In other words, the students who were surveyed believed that it was more important to communicate *successfully* in a foreign language rather than to try to communicate *perfectly* in it. Stressing the need to consider the "economics of intervention," George (1972) recommends that teachers initially determine how likely it is that correcting learners' errors will improve their speech or written work, and how strongly the learners will sense their achievement. George suggests that drawing students' attention to every error they produce on their written compositions not only wastes time, but also it provides no guarantee that they will learn from their mistakes, as evidenced by similar errors that may reappear on their subsequent written work.

There has been little empirical evidence to suggest when to correct second language errors. More descriptive research is needed to determine the attitudes of students and teachers toward producing and correcting errors in the classroom. Experimental research should focus on the cognitive effects of error correction based on different levels of language proficiency and relevant personality factors such as willingness to take risks. For the present, teachers can consider which student errors should be corrected first and which ones should be allowed to remain uncorrected.

Which Learner Errors Should Be Corrected?

An increasing number of foreign language educators suggest that errors that impede the intelligibility of a message should receive top priority for correction. Powell (1975b) analyzed speech samples collected in individual oral interviews of 223 American high school students at the end of their second year of French. She found that the greatest number of errors resulted from reduction, especially in tense markers. In sentences that were to be marked for tense or mood, students reduced the marker to the present indicative in at least 55 percent of the cases. According to Powell, "the fact that reductions seemed to be influenced by the need to communicate, suggests that correcting student errors in terms of their comprehensibility to a native speaker might result in a more advanced grammar" (p. 38). Elsewhere, she notes

that "if error correction by the teacher results in a more adult grammar, it is possible that correction in terms of communication requirements might be more fruitful than any other kind, since this seems to be important to students" (Powell, 1973, p. 91). She further suggests that error in word order is perhaps the most serious threat to the communication of a message in French (Powell, 1975a, p. 12).

Hanzeli (1975) agrees that errors that interfere with the meaning of a message should be corrected more promptly and systematically than any other. He adds, however, that teachers who are native speakers of the target language would have difficulty establishing standard criteria for distinguishing communicative errors from non-communicative errors, because these teachers often have learned to interpret their own students' "Pidgin" (p. 431). The problem of correcting student errors consistently according to their effect on the comprehensibility of students' messages, would be an even greater dilemma for teachers who are nonnative speakers of the target language (Powell, 1973, p. 92). George (1972) observes that learners will anticipate or correct their errors according to the response they expect from the person who is listening to them or who is reading their work. Although he endorses the priority of correcting communicative errors, George believes that teachers often overestimate the degree to which such errors impair communication. He hypothesizes that native speakers would be able to understand the majority of students' deviant sentences. Indeed, there is some empirical evidence to support this assumption. An experiment was conducted to determine which deviations in passive voice sentences produced by 240 adolescent Swedish learners would most likely be misinterpreted by native Englishmen. It was found that the Englishmen understood nearly 70 percent of the 1000 utterances, and that generally, semantic errors blocked communication more than syntactic ones (Olsson, 1972).

An attempt has been made to distinguish

communicative errors from non-communicative errors. Burt and Kiparsky (1972) classify students' second language errors into two distinct categories: those errors that cause a listener or reader to misunderstand a message or to consider a sentence incomprehensible (global errors), and those errors that do not significantly hinder communication of a sentence's message (local errors). On the basis of how errors affect the comprehensibility of whole sentences, one could build a local-to-global hierarchy of errors that would potentially guide teachers to correct students' mistakes (Burt, 1971; Burt and Kiparsky, 1972; Valdman, 1975). In an investigation on the effects of error correction treatments upon students' writing proficiency, this writer modified Burt and Kiparsky's global/local error distinction. He defined a *global* error as a communicative error that causes a proficient speaker of a foreign language either to misinterpret an oral or written message or to consider the message incomprehensible with the textual content of the error. On the other hand, a *local* error is a linguistic error that makes a form or structure in a sentence appear awkward but, nevertheless, causes a proficient speaker of a foreign language little or no difficulty in understanding the intended meaning of a sentence, given its contextual framework. It was found that most global errors included in compositions written by intermediate students of English as a second language resulted from inadequate lexical knowledge, misuse of prepositions and pronouns, and seriously misspelled lexical items. Most local errors were caused by misuse and omission of prepositions, lack of subject-verb agreement, misspelled words, and faulty lexical choice (Hendrickson, 1977b). Burt (1975) argues persuasively that the global/local distinction is the most pervasive criterion for determining the communicative importance of errors (p. 58). She claims that the correction of one global error in a sentence clarifies the intended message more than the correction of several local errors in the same sentence (p. 62). Furthermore, she states that limiting correction to communicative errors allows students to increase their motivation and self-confidence toward learning the target language. Burt suggests that only when their production in the foreign language begins to become relatively free of communicative errors, should learners begin to concentrate on correcting local errors, if the learners are to approach near-native fluency (p. 58).

A number of language educators suggest that errors that stigmatize the learner from the perspective of native speakers should be among the first corrected (Johansson, 1973; Richards, 1973a; Sternglass, 1974; Corder, 1975; Hanzeli, 1975; Birckbichler, 1977). Undoubtedly, attitudes toward language influence human behavior. As Richards (1973a) points out, for example, "deviancy from grammatical or phonological norms of a speech community elicits evaluational reactions that may classify a person unfavorably" (p. 131). This hypothesis has been substantiated by a great deal of research on stereotyped judgments made on various features of Black English (Labov, 1972a, 1972b; Williams and Whitehead, 1973). Furthermore, sociolinguistic research in first language acquisition indicates that grammatical features tend to elicit more unfavorable reactions than phonological variables (Wolfram, 1973). This writer found several recent studies that relate to native speakers' reactions toward the errors of *second* language learners. In Guntermann's study (1977) thirty native speakers of Spanish listened to a tape recording of 43 sentences containing errors that American students most frequently produced on an oral test. The native informants were asked to interpret each sentence according to what they thought the speaker had meant to say. Of the 1290 interpretations given, 22 percent were inaccurate. The least comprehensible sentences were those containing multiple errors (32 percent misinterpreted), especially sentences that contained multiple errors of the *same* subtype. It was found that among the highest frequency errors produced by American students of Spanish, errors in article omissions were more acceptable to native speakers than errors in article agreement. The results also revealed that person errors were generally less acceptable by native speakers than the other two categories, and tense errors were generally preferred. Another recent study on the acceptability of second language utterances was conducted by Ervin (1977) who investigated how proficient speakers of Russian would accept (i.e., comprehend) language communication strategies used by American students based on their oral narrations of picture stories. Although there were no statistically significant differences in the informants' rankings of the students, there were systematic differences in the judges' numerical evaluations: The non-teacher native speakers of Russian were most accepting of the narrations of the mid- and high-proficiency students; the teachers of Russian who were native speakers of English were most accepting of the narrations of low proficiency students; and the teachers of Russian who were native speakers of Russian were the least accepting of the narrations overall.

There are excellent social motivations for teachers' drawing their students' attention to errors that appear to have become a permanent rather than a transitional feature of nonnatives' speech and writing (Richards, 1973a; Valdman, 1975). These so-called "fossilized" errors should be corrected based on their degree of incomprehensibility and unacceptability as judged by native speakers. Clearly, a great deal of research is needed in these two important areas of sociolinguistics. Researchers need to investigate the degree of stigma that native speakers attach to lexically, grammatically, phonologically, and orthographically deviant forms and structures that nonnative learners produce frequently in their speech or writing. Moreover, it would be worthwhile to determine whether or not the degree of stigma would differ depending on the social status of native speakers.

Several additional criteria have been suggested by language educators for establishing priorities of error correction. It has been suggested that high-frequency errors should be among the first errors that teachers should correct in students' oral and written communication (Holley and King, 1971; George, 1972, Dresdner, 1973; Bhatia, 1974; Allwright, 1975). Research is needed to determine which errors occur most frequently at various stages of second language learning among learners of varying native languages. The results of this research could serve as a basis for building hierarchies of language learning features; these hierarchies would have multiple applications including the establishment of priorities for correcting errors selectively and systematically. It has also been suggested that errors relevant to a specific pedagogic focus deserve to be corrected before other less important errors (Cohen, 1975), and that errors involving general grammatical rules are more deserving of attention than errors involving lexical exceptions (Johansson, 1973). Interestingly, language learners appear to have differing priorities of error correction than do language educators and teachers. Recently, a group of 188 college students was asked which errors they thought were the most important to correct. Students at all levels of proficiency agreed that pronunciation and grammar errors ranked highest, with pronunciation slightly higher than grammar errors (Cathcart and Olsen, 1976).

To sum up, there appears to be a consensus among many language educators that correcting three types of errors can be quite useful to second language learners: errors that impair communication significantly; errors that have highly stigmatizing effects on the listener or reader; and errors that occur frequently in students' speech and writing. A great deal more research needs to be conducted to determine the degree to which errors actually impede communication, which errors carry more social stigma than others, and which ones students produce often.

How Should Learner Errors Be Corrected?

Teachers need to be keenly aware of how they correct student errors and to avoid using correction strategies that might embarrass or frustrate students (Holley and King, 1971). However, most teacher training programs fail to prepare teachers to handle the variety of errors that occur inevitably in students' speech and writing (Burt, 1975). Nevertheless, the literature on error correction does contain some information on recent theory, research, and practical suggestions for correcting students' errors.

Fanselow (1977) attempted to determine how experienced teachers of English as a second language actually treated spoken errors in their regular classes. After videotaping eleven teachers who presented the same lesson to their students, transcripts containing both verbal and nonverbal behaviors were made. The analysis of the tapes showed similarities among the teachers both in the types of errors treated and in the treatment used; specifically, the teachers seemed less concerned with errors of grammar than with incorrect meaning, and giving the right answer was the most popular treatment. The process of analysis led Fanselow to develop four alternative treatments to correcting students' spoken errors for the purpose of reducing students' uncertainty about how language works. Fanselow concludes that time spent on doing these kinds of feedback tasks in class "is probably at least as well spent as time spent giving answers alone," and that "errors are part of learning—mistaken hypotheses and wrong connections are normal" (p. 591). Chaudron (1977) developed a structural model for observing and describing the effectiveness of teachers' corrections of linguistic errors. The model enables teachers to analyze their own corrective

techniques and decide which of these are most effective in their classrooms. Robbins (1977) investigated the effectiveness of eliciting explanations of incorrect verb forms produced by students of English as a second language (ESL). Eight intermediate adult ESL learners were randomly placed into a control group or an experimental group. For one trisemester the experimental subjects were given weekly error explanation sessions during which they attempted to locate their errors, correct them, and then were asked to provide an explanation for each error; the control group received other kinds of feedback on their errors. Robbins found that the experimental technique was ineffective in reducing the frequency of students' verb errors. She concluded that the technique appears to be dependent on external variables, such as a learner's attitude and motivation, personality, and past language learning history.

Many language teachers provide students with the correct form or structure of their written errors. Some foreign language educators assert, however, that this procedure is ineffective when helping students learn from their mistakes (Corder, 1967; Gorbet, 1974; Valdman, 1975). They propose that a *discovery* approach to error correction might help students to make inferences and formulate concepts about the target language, and to help them fix this information in their long-term memories. This writer conducted an experiment to determine what effects direct teacher correction would have upon foreign students' communicative and linguistic proficiency in English. He found that supplying the correct lexical forms and grammatical structures of students' errors had no statistically significant effect upon the writing proficiency of either high or low communicative groups of students (Hendrickson, 1976, 1977b).

There is some controversy on whether or not student errors should be corrected in some sort of systematic manner. Many teachers correct students' written work, for example, so imprecisely and inconsistently that it is often difficult for students to distinguish their major errors from their minor ones (Allwright, 1975). Indeed, recent research indicates that a major reason that the correction of students' compositions has no significant effect on reducing errors, is that teachers correct compositions inconsistently. It was hypothesized, therefore, that a systematic approach to error correction would be more effective than random correction (Cohen and Robbins, 1976). Dulay and Burt (1977) see, however, no reason to expect significantly different results with systematic correction techniques. They propose that "more *selective* feedback, tailored to the learner's internal level of linguistic development, may be more effective" than systematic feedback (p. 108).[2]

Several scholars recommend that teachers record their students' errors on diagnostic charts in order to reveal the linguistic features that are causing students learning problems (Lee, 1957; Corder, 1973; Cohen, 1975; Cohen and Robbins, 1976). Recently, this writer used Burt and Kiparsky's global/local error distinction as a basis for developing an error taxonomy for classifying, coding, and charting students' oral and written errors systematically. The following error chart reveals one student's major problem areas based on the coding and tallying of his composition errors (Hendrickson, 1977a):[3]

	Lexicon	Syntax	Morphology	Orthography	Total
Global Errors	4			2	6
Local Errors	8	5	8	17	38
Problem Area(s)	Nouns 9	Prepositions 4	Plural markers 5	Omitted letters 8	

Error charts are useful not only for diagnostic purposes, but also for developing individualized instructional materials, for building a hierarchy of error correction priorities, and for learning more about the process of second language acquisition.

Recent literature in foreign language methodology contains several specific suggestions for correcting students' oral errors. At the University of South Carolina pre-service teachers are given a partially self-instructional program designed to sensitize them to different types of oral errors and to involve them in dealing with these errors effectively. The error correction techniques "resemble the tactics of a parent who is trying to help a child express his ideas or those of one who is helping a foreigner communicate in a language which he knows imperfectly" (Joiner, 1975, p. 194). When the teacher cannot decipher a student's message it has been suggested that he "either reword the answer in an acceptable fashion, in such a manner as adults do with children, or at the end of the activity he may summarize and review the most common mistakes" (Chastain, 1971, p. 250). Another oral error correction method is to make tape recordings of student conversations; then each student edits his own tape for errors. If he does not recognize his mistakes, it may indicate that he has improperly learned the linguistic concepts at issue, and the teacher will then be responsible for formulating an appropriate corrective technique (Lantolf, 1977). Several suggestions have been given for teachers who use "The Silent Way" method developed by Gattegno. Silent teachers may respond to students' oral errors in many ways, preferably those that conform to two principles: "(1) Remain silent if at all possible. (2) Give only as much help as absolutely necessary" (Stevick, 1976, p. 143).

The literature also contains some specific suggestions for correcting students' *written* errors. One suggestion is to first identify and record the error types that each learner produces frequently. Then, the student reads his or her written work to search out and correct all high-frequency errors, one such error type at a time. For example, if a learner's composition customarily lacks subject-verb agreement, the student is asked to read the composition in order to identify the subject of the first sentence. He then puts the index finger of his left hand on the subject, and moves the index finger of his right hand until he has identified the verb, and checks for concord. After the student proceeds through the entire composition in this way, he reads it once again to check for other error types that he produces often. It is claimed that correcting errors in this way is a highly effective technique requiring relatively little time or effort on the part of the student (George, 1972, pp. 76–77). Another suggestion for correcting composition errors is to use different color inks for distinguishing more important errors from less important ones (Burt and Kipansky, 1977, p. 4). It has also been recommended that the teacher discuss each student's composition errors on cassette tapes, as a means of assuring that students will remember the comments (Farnsworth, 1974).

Currently, this writer uses a combination of various direct and indirect techniques to correct picture story compositions written by intermediate learners of Spanish. Some indirect techniques are underlining all misspelled words and omitted or superfluous affixes; placing a question mark above a confusing phrase or structure; and inserting an arrow (↑) to indicate a missing article or preposition. Generally, these indirect methods are used whenever it is assumed that students can correct their own errors using a good dictionary or grammar book. More direct correction techniques include underlining a word and providing a verbal tip such as "use subjunctive"; crossing out superfluous words; and supplying the correct form or structure—the most direct and least used technique. When students receive their corrected compositions, they rewrite them and turn them in at the next class session. The few errors that appear on the rewritten compositions are then corrected by supplying the correct form because it is assumed that students are not able to correct these errors by themselves. Thus far, these correction procedures have significantly improved students' expression of thought as well as their grammatical accuracy in Spanish. The procedures have also contributed to a considerable

increase of word output from the beginning to the end of each term.[4]

Finally, Wingfield (1975) points out that the teacher should choose corrective techniques that are most appropriate and most effective for individual students. He lists five techniques for correcting written errors (p. 311):

1. The teacher gives sufficient clues to enable self-correction to be made;
2. The teacher corrects the script;
3. The teacher deals with errors through marginal comments and footnotes;
4. The teacher explains orally to individual students;
5. The teacher uses the error as an illustration for a class explanation.

One educator concludes that any error correction process includes some of the following general features: indication that an error was committed, identification of the type of error, location of the error, mention of who made the error, selection of a remedy, provision of a correct model, the furnishing of an opportunity for a new attempt, indication of improvement (if applicable), and the offering of praise (Allwright, 1975).

Very few of the error correction theories and methods described above have been tested to determine their effect on facilitating second language proficiency. Clearly, there is a great need to conduct research that deals with this issue. It would be worthwhile, for example, to determine what native speakers do to facilitate communication with foreign learners in various types of free-learning situations, compared to what language teachers do in a classroom environment. Many other questions remain unanswered: What effects do correction in natural versus artificial settings have upon learners' language proficiency? Do native-speaking and nonnative-speaking teachers evaluate deviant speech and writing differently? If so, how do they correct students' errors, and how do students react to the different correction approaches?

Who Should Correct Learner Errors?

Most classroom teachers probably assume the responsibility for correcting their students' errors. The teacher is expected to be a source of information about the target language and to react to errors whenever it seems appropriate to do so (Allwright, 1975). One educator believes that the teacher's function in error correction is "to provide data and examples, and where necessary to offer explanations and descriptions and, more importantly, verification of the learner's hypothesis (i.e., correction)" about the target language (Corder, 1973, p. 336).

While few language educators would deny the teacher an active role in correcting errors, it has been suggested that he or she should not *dominate* the correction procedures. One alternative approach to correcting *written* work is to ask students to correct one another's papers. Peer correction would especially help students recognize more grammatical errors than lexical errors; this process would be reversed when students correct each other's spoken errors (Cohen, 1975, p. 419). In other words, students would tend to focus on linguistic forms of sentences when correcting each other's compositions; but when they would correct one another's spoken utterances, the students would concentrate on function words such as nouns, verbs, adjectives, and adverbs. Students would also tend to correct each other's spelling and pronunciation, depending on the modality of communication. Several scholars agree that in a heterogenous class, one student will be able to recognize another's error, especially when the corrector has himself just overcome some gram-

matical or lexical problems (Burt and Kiparsky, 1972; Corder, 1975; Valdman, 1975). Recently Witbeck (1976) experimented with four peer correction strategies, including whole class correction, immediate feedback and rewriting, problem-solving, and correction of modified and duplicated essays. He concludes that peer correction results in a "greater concern for achieving accuracy in written expression in individual students and creates a better classroom atmosphere for teaching the correctional aspects of composition" (p. 325).

Several language specialists propose that once students are made aware of their errors, they may learn more from correcting their own errors than by having their teacher correct them (George, 1972; Corder, 1973; and Ravem, 1973). Self-correction would probably be effective with grammatical errors but would be relatively ineffective with lexical errors (Wingfield, 1975).

It is apparent that the effects of these different approaches to who should correct learners' errors are based more on intuition than experimental research. The effects of the various methodologies of error correction discussed above need to be substantiated or refuted by conducting a series of carefully controlled experiments before correction strategies can be recommended or rejected as being effective for dealing with students' written or oral errors. It may well be that the specific effects on a learner's language proficiency in terms of *who* corrects his errors will depend upon *when* they are corrected, *which* ones are corrected, and especially *how* they are brought to the learner's attention.

SUMMARY

The literature on the correction of second language errors is quite speculative and relatively scant. Nevertheless, some general and specific implications for error correction can be drawn from the information reported herein.

The following implications respond directly to questions concerning whether, when, which, how, and by whom the student errors should be corrected.

1. It appears that correcting oral and written

errors produced by second language learners improves their proficiency in a foreign language more so than if their errors would remain uncorrected.

2. There appears to be no general consensus among language methodologists or teachers on when to correct student errors. Many language educators recognize, however, that correcting every error is counter-productive to learning a foreign language. Therefore, teachers need to create a supportive classroom environment in which their students can feel confident about expressing their ideas and feelings freely without suffering the threat or embarrassment of having each one of their oral or written errors corrected.

3. The question of when to correct student errors is closely related to which errors to correct. Many educators propose that some errors have higher priorities for correction than other errors, such as errors that seriously impair communication, errors that have stigmatizing effects upon the listener or reader, and errors that students produce frequently. Procedures for classifying and coding specific error types are being developed for purposes of building a hierarchy of error correction; one error taxonomy has already been developed to classify errors in communicative terms.

4. The literature reveals a wide variety of techniques that teachers currently use to correct their students' oral and written errors. Although there is no experimental evidence to substantiate whether any of these methods reduces student errors significantly, some empirical research indicates that *direct* types of corrective procedures have proven to be ineffective. Some very recent research has focused on how teachers actually correct student errors in their classrooms. It appears that continued research in this new area will contribute to the development of additional practical methods for correcting errors effectively and efficiently.

5. Although teacher correction of learner errors is helpful to many students, it may not necessarily be an effective instructional strategy for every student or in all language classrooms. Peer correction or self-correction with teacher guidance may be a more worthwhile investment of time and effort for some teachers and learners. However, no empirical research was found to substantiate these hypotheses.

NOTES

1. The definition of an "error," a word derived from Latin *errare* meaning "to wander, roam or stray," depends on its use for a particular purpose or objective. For the purpose of a discussion on error correction in foreign language teaching, this writer defines an error as an utterance, form, or structure that a particular language teacher deems unacceptable because of its inappropriate use or its absence in real-life discourse.

2. Interestingly, several researchers have found that second language errors appear to occur systematically in students' written work. Dušková (1969), for example, found that 75.1 percent of the errors in the written assignments of Czech university students studying English as foreign language were systematic. More recently, Ghadessy (1976) discovered that 77.3 percent of the writings of 370 Iranian university freshmen learning English contained systematic errors most of which were caused by the lack of reducing sentences by either conjunction or embedding (p. 80). Ghadessy concludes that because the majority of student written errors occur in systematic patterns, these patterns could serve as a basis for developing instructional materials for individual learners (p. 81). Although written errors produced by second language learners may occur systematically, there is no experimental evidence to suggest that they should be *corrected* systematically.

3. The writer has recently modified this taxonomy so that teachers can evaluate the

quantity and quality of information in students' communication samples using an error analysis approach.

4. An unexpected finding in a study conducted by the author was the substantial increase (30 percent) in the number of words that students wrote on their composition pretests compared to the number of words they wrote on identical composition post-tests after six weeks of practice describing picture stories in writing (Hendrickson, 1977b). It may be that writing practice, improvement in writing proficiency, self confidence in one's own writing ability, and total word output are closely related variables.

REFERENCES

Allwright, Richard L. 1975. Problems in the study of the language teacher's treatment of learner error. In Marina K. Burt and Heidi C. Dulay (eds.), *New Directions in Second Language Learning, Teaching, and Bilingual Education.* Washington, D.C.: TESOL, pp. 96–109.

Bhatia, Aban Tavadia. 1974. An error analysis of students' compositions. *International Review of Applied Linguistics* 12: 337–350.

Birckbichler, Diane W. 1977. Communication and beyond. In June K. Phillips (ed.), *The Language Connection: From the Classroom to the World.* Skokie, IL: National Textbook Company, 53–94.

Brooks, Nelson. 1960. *Language and Language Learning.* 2nd ed. New York: Harcourt, Brace and World.

Burt, Marina K. 1971. Goof analysis in English as a second language. (Paper presented at Harvard University, October.) EDRS ED 061 838.

_____. 1975. Error analysis in the adult EFL classroom. *TESOL Quarterly* 9: 53–63.

_____, and Carol Kiparsky. 1972. *The Gooficon: A Repair Manual for English.* Rowley, MA: Newbury House Publishers.

Buteau, M. F. 1970. Students' errors and the learning of French as a second language: A pilot study. *International Review of Applied Linguistics* 8: 133–145.

Cathcart, Ruth L., and Judy E. W. B. Olsen. 1976. Teachers' and students' preferences for correction of classroom conversation errors. In John F. Fanselow and Ruth H. Crymes (eds.), *On TESOL '76,* Washington, D.C.: TESOL.

Chastain, Kenneth. 1971. *The Development of Modern Language Skills: Theory to Practice.* Philadelphia: Center for Curriculum Development, Inc.

Chaudron, Craig. 1977. A descriptive model of discourse in the corrective treatment of learners' errors. *Language Learning* 27: 29–46.

Cohen, Andrew D. 1975. Error correction and the training of language teachers. *The Modern Language Journal* 59: 414–422.

_____ and Margaret Robbins. 1976. Toward assessing interlanguage performance: The relationship between selected errors, learners' characteristics, and learners' explanations. *Language Learning* 26: 45–66.

Corder, S. Pit. 1967. The significance of learner's errors. *International Review of Applied Linguistics* 5: 161–170.

_____. 1973. *Introducing Applied Linguistics.* Harmondsworth, Great Britain: Penguin.

_____. 1975. "The language of second-language learners: The broader issues." *The Modern Language Journal* 59: 409–413.

Dresdner, Mauricio P. 1973. Your students' errors can help you. *English Language Journal* 1: 5–8.

Dulay, Heidi C., and Marina K. Burt. 1974. Errors and strategies in child second language acquisition. *TESOL Quarterly* 8: 129–134.

_____. 1977. Remarks on creativity in language acquisition. In Marina Burt, Heidi Dulay, and Mary Finocchiaro, (eds.), *Viewpoints on English as a Second Language.* New York: Regents Publishing Company, 95–126.

Dušková, L. 1969. On sources of errors in foreign language learning. *International Review of Applied Linguistics* 7:11–36.

Ervin, Gerard Lewis. 1977. A study of the use and acceptability of target language communication strategies employed by American students of Russian. Unpublished Ph.D. dissertation. The Ohio State University.

Ervin-Tripp, Susan. 1970. Structure and process in language acquisition. In James Alatis (ed.), *21st Annual Georgetown Roundtable on Language and Linguistics.* Washington, D.C.: Georgetown University Press.

Falk, J. 1968. Nominalizations in Spanish. In *Studies in Linguistics and Language Learning.* V. Seattle: University of Washington Press.

Fanselow, John F. 1977. The treatment of error in oral work. *Foreign Language Annals* 10: 583–593.

Farnsworth, Maryruth B. 1974. The cassette recorder: A bonus or a bother in ESL composition correction? *TESOL Quarterly* 8: 285–291.

George, H. V. 1972. *Common Errors in Language Learning.* Rowley, MA: Newbury House Publishers.

Ghadessy, Mohsen. 1976. An error analysis of the writings of Iranian freshmen students learning English—A pilot study. *International Review of Applied Linguistics* 14: 71–81.

Gorbet, Frances. 1974. Error analysis: What the teacher can do: A new perspective. Ottawa: Research Division, Public Service Commission of Canada. November, EDRS: ED 100 193.

Grauberg, W. 1971. An error analysis in German of first-year university students. In Perren and Trim (eds.), *Applications of Linguistics.* Papers from the Second International Congress of Applied Linguistics. Cambridge, England: Cambridge University Press.

Grittner, Frank M. 1969. *Teaching Foreign Languages.* New York: Harper & Row.

Guntermann, Charlotte Gail. 1977. An investigation of the frequency, comprehensibility, and evaluational effects of errors in Spanish made by English-speaking learners in El Salvador. Unpublished Ph.D. dissertation. The Ohio State University.

Hansen, Terrence L., and Ernest J. Wilkins. 1974. *Español a lo vivo,* Level 1, 3rd Edition. New York: John Wiley and Sons.

Hanzeli, Victor E. 1975. "Learner's language: Implications of recent research for foreign language instruction. *The Modern Language Journal* 59: 426–432.

Hendrickson, James M. 1976. The effects of error correction treatments upon adequate and accurate communication in the written compositions of adult learners of English as a second language. Unpublished Ph.D. dissertation. The Ohio State University.

———. 1977a. Goof analysis for ESL teachers. ERIC: Center for Applied Linguistics. Arlington, VA. EDRS: ED 135 259.

———. 1977b. Error analysis and selective correction in the adult ESL classroom: An experiment. ERIC: Center for Applied Linguistics, Arlington, VA. EDRS: ED 135 260.

Holley, Freda M., and Janet K. King. 1971. Imitation and correction in foreign language learning. *The Modern Language Journal* 55: 494–498.

Hussein, A. I. 1971. Remedial English for speakers of Arabic: A psycholinguistic approach. Unpublished Ph.D. dissertation. University of Texas at Austin.

Johansson, Stig. 1973. The identification and evaluation of errors in foreign languages: A functional approach. In J. Svartik, (ed.), *Errata: Papers in Error Analysis.* Lund, Sweden: CWK Gleerup, 102–114.

Joiner, Elizabeth G. 1975. Training prospective teachers in the correction of student errors. *The French Review* 193–197.

Kennedy, Graeme. 1973. Conditions for language learning. In John W. Oller, Jr. and Jack C. Richards (eds.), *Focus on the Learner: Pragmatic Perspectives for the Language Teacher.* Rowley, MA: Newbury House Publishers, 66–82.

Krashen, Stephen D., and Herbert W. Seliger. 1975. The essential contributions of formal instruction in adult second language learning. *TESOL Quarterly* 9: 173–183.

Labov, William. 1972a. *Language in the Inner City.* Philadelphia: University of Pennsylvania Press.

———. 1972b. *Sociolinguistic Patterns.* Philadelphia: University of Pennsylvania Press.

Lange, Dale L. 1977. Report on Lange's Keynote address: Thoughts from Europe about learning a second language in the classroom. In *The Modern Language Journal* 265–267.

Lantolf, James P. 1977. Aspects of change in foreign language study. *The Modern Language Journal:* 242–251.

Lee, W. R. 1957. The linguistic context of language teaching. *English Language Teaching Journal* 11: 77–85.

_____. 1970. *The Dolphin English Course; Teacher's Companion.* London: Oxford University Press.

Modern Language Materials Development Center. 1961. *Teacher's Manual for German, Level One.* New York: Harcourt, Brace and World.

Olsson, Margareta. 1972. Intelligibility: A study of errors and their importance. Research Bulletin No. 12, Department of Educational Research, Gothenburg School of Education, Gothenburg, Sweden. EDRS: ED 072 681.

Politzer, Robert, and A. Ramirez. 1973. An error analysis of the spoken English of Mexican-American pupils in a bilingual school and a monolingual school. *Language Learning* 23: 1.

Powell, Patricia B. 1973. An investigation of selected syntactical and morphological structures in the conversation of secondary students after two years' study of French. Unpublished Ph.D. dissertation. The Ohio State University.

_____. 1975a. Error analysis in the classroom. ERIC Clearinghouse on Languages and Linguistics. Arlington, VA: Center for Applied Linguistics. EDRS: ED 104 161.

_____. 1975b. Moi Tarzan, Vous Jane?: A study of communicative competence. *Foreign Language Annals* 8: 38–42.

Ravem, Roar. 1973. Language acquisition in a second language environment. In John W. Oller, Jr. and Jack C. Richards (eds.), *Focus on the Learner: Pragmatic Perspectives for the Language Teacher.* Rowley, MA: Newbury House Publishers, 136–144.

Richards, Jack C. 1973a. Error analysis and second language strategies. In John W. Oller, Jr. and Jack C. Richards (eds.), *Focus on the Learner: Pragmatic Perspectives for the Language Teacher.* Rowley, MA: Newbury House Publishers, 114–135.

_____. 1973b. A non-contrastive approach to error analysis. In John W. Oller, Jr. and Jack C. Richards (eds.), *Focus on the Learner: Pragmatic Perspectives for the Language Teacher.* Rowley, MA: Newbury House Publishers, 96–113.

Robbins, Margaret. 1977. Error explanations: A procedure for examining written interlanguage performance. M.A. Thesis. University of California-Los Angeles.

Robinson, Peter. 1971. Oral Expression Tests: 2. *English Language Teaching Journal* 25: 260–266.

Selinker, Larry. 1969. Language transfer. *General Linguistics* 9: 67–92.

Sternglass, Marilyn S. 1974. Close similarities in dialect features of black and white college students in remedial composition classes. *TESOL Quarterly* 8: 271–283.

Stevick, Earl W. 1976. *Memory, Meaning and Method: Some Psychological Perspectives on Language Learning.* Rowley, MA: Newbury House Publishers.

Terrell, Tracy D. 1977. A natural approach to second language acquisition and learning. *The Modern Language Journal* 325–337.

Valdman, Albert. 1975. Learner systems and error analysis. In Gilbert A. Jarvis (ed.), *Perspective: A New Freedom.* Skokie, IL: National Textbook Company, 219–258.

Walker, John L. 1973. Opinions of university students about language teaching. *Foreign Language Annals* 7: 102–105.

Williams, Frederick, and Jack L. Whitehead. 1973. Language in the classroom: Studies of the Pygmalion effect. In Johanna S. DeStefano (ed.), *Language Society and Education: A Profile of Black English.* Worthington, OH: Charles A. Jones Publishing Company 169–176.

Wilkins, D. A. 1968. Review of *Trends in Language Teaching,* A. Valdman (ed.), *International Review of Applied Linguistics* 6: 99–107.

Wingfield, R. J. 1975. Five ways of dealing with errors in written compositions. *English Language Teaching Journal* 29: 311–313.

Witbeck, Michael C. 1976. Peer correction procedures for intermediate and advanced ESL composition lessons. *TESOL Quarterly* 10: 321–326.

Wolfe, D. L. 1967. Some theoretical aspects of language learning and language teaching. *Language Learning* 17: 173–188.

Wolfram, Walt. 1973. Sociolinguistic implications for educational sequencing. In Johanna S. DeStefano (ed.), *Language, Society and Education: A Profile of Black English.* Worthington, OH: Charles A. Jones Publishing Company, 251–262.

Zydatiss, Wolfgang. 1974. A 'kiss of life' for the notion of error. *International Review of Applied Linguistics* 12: 231–237.

Section Twelve

TESTING

INTRODUCTION

In one sense, articles on language testing have no place in a collection of papers on language teaching and learning. In another sense, however, their role is central, for as every experienced teacher knows, tests have a profound influence on what is taught and how it is taught, and so are directly related to methodology —a point made forcefully by all three writers here.

In the first paper, Wesche provides a very full and detailed overview of most of the major issues in language testing—types of test (proficiency, diagnostic, achievement), test characteristics (reliability, validity, feasibility), norm-referencing and criterion-referencing, discrete point, integrative and pragmatic tests, direct and indirect tests, and so on. Her main concern, however, is with the move to *communicative testing,* reflecting the current emphasis on communicative language teaching that has been noted in previous sections. Wesche provides thumbnail sketches of several existing communicative tests being used in Europe and North America. She notes the shift among test developers from an overriding concern with the psychometric qualities of a test to greater stress on validity and the relevance of a test to students' real-life communicative needs in English, and suspects that this change will have a highly beneficial "washback" effect on both EFL/ESL curricula and student motivation.

The second paper, by Keitges, concentrates exclusively on the interview as a test of students' proficiency in spoken English. Keitges first describes what has become perhaps the best-known such test, the U.S. Foreign Service Institute's Oral Interview procedure, noting some of its limitations and six modifications that have been made to it. He then provides a set of practical guidelines for designing, administering, and rating other language proficiency interviews that teachers may wish to use in evaluating their students' oral abilities in English.

Finally, Hinofotis provides an overview and evaluation of cloze testing. She considers cloze tests to be relatively easy to construct, administer, and score, and to have been shown to correlate well with larger, more complex tests, such as the

371

TOEFL, as well as with oral interview and composition tests. Hinofotis also reports work suggesting that cloze tests are usable with quite young children, not just adults, and that they also have a role to play as a teaching device.

DISCUSSION QUESTIONS

1. What is meant by reliability and validity? Can a test have one without the other?

2. What is the difference between norm-referenced and criterion-referenced tests? In what kinds of language testing situations might one kind or the other be more useful?

3. If given a copy of a new test, what features would you look at to determine if it was "communicative" in Wesche's sense? Take any test with which you are familiar and explain why you would or would not classify it as communicative.

4. What is the relationship between language teaching and language testing, according to Wesche, Keitges, and Hinofotis? Under what circumstances might a language test have a negative effect on the way English is taught?

5. If cloze tests are easy to construct, administer, and score, and they give similar results to oral proficiency measures, it might seem sensible to do away with the more complex and time-consuming measures such as the oral interviews. What differences among types of students and reasons for testing justify different types of tests?

6. What variable aspects of interviewer behavior, both verbal and non-verbal, could influence the outcome of an oral interview testing procedure? Could some kinds of oral proficiency tests be translated into an audiotaped format in order to deal with this problem?

FURTHER READING

1. L. F. Bachman. 1985. Performance on cloze tests with fixed-ratio and rational deletions. *TESOL Quarterly* 19, 3, 535–556.
2. G. Brindley and K. Singh. 1982. The use of second language learning research in ESL proficiency assessment. *Australian Review of Applied Linguistics* 5, 1, 84–111.
3. J. D. Brown. 1983. A closer look at cloze: Validity and reliability. In J. W. Oller, Jr. (ed.), *Issues in Language Testing Research.* Rowley, MA: Newbury House Publishers, 237–250.
4. J. B. Heaton. 1975. *Writing English Language Tests.* London: Longman.
5. T. Hudson, and B. Lynch. 1985. A criterion-referenced measurement approach to ESL achievement testing. *Language Testing* 2, 1, 171–201.
6. D. E. Ingram. 1985. Assessing proficiency: An overview on some aspects of testing. In K. Hyltenstam and M. Pienemann (eds.), *Modelling and Assessing Second Language Acquisition.* Clevedon, Avon: Multilingual Matters, 215–276.
7. J. W. Oller, Jr. 1979. *Language Tests at School: A Pragmatic Approach.* London: Longman.

CHAPTER 31

Communicative Testing
in a Second Language*

Marjorie Bingham Wesche

In the past decade or so, linguistic science has paid increasing attention to the communicative use of language, complementing an earlier almost exclusive emphasis on linguistic forms and the ways in which they could be combined to form grammatical sentences. The accompanying shift in our understanding of what it is that native speakers of a language "know" and "can do" has led to widespread rethinking about what the content and organization of second language courses should be. More recently, attention has increasingly been given to how the communicative ability of second language speakers can be tested. Some excellent discussions of this question now exist in the literature.[1] This article is an attempt to synthesize for the informed reader some of the main principles as well as some of the unresolved issues that have emerged from investigations of communicative aspects of language in a second language context, and to describe several promising approaches to the development of "communicative" tests.

WHAT IT IS TO "KNOW" A LANGUAGE: LINGUISTIC AND COMMUNICATIVE COMPETENCE

Chomsky's early hypotheses about the nature of language knowledge were influential in focusing the interests of linguists on the formulation of the linguistic rules which could describe or "generate" grammatical sentences. The goal was to characterize the native speaker's internalized grammar or the "competence" underlying language use. Since competence cannot be directly observed, its imperfect realization in concrete situations, or "performance," although of secondary interest to linguists, was important for the information it could provide about competence. Subsequent

*An earlier version of this essay was selected by the editorial board of the *Canadian Modern Language Review* (Anthony S. Mollica, Editor) as the best article to appear in that publication in 1981. Under the terms of an exchange agreement between *CMLR* and *The Modern Language Review* it was reprinted in the MLR in 1983 in an effort to enhance cooperation between language scholars in both countries.

work in sociolinguistics, pragmatics, and discourse analysis has convincingly demonstrated that the native speaker has, in addition to such a linguistic code grammar, other higher order internalized rule systems which are also important in determining his or her language behavior.[2] These include constraints and explicit organizational devices at the discourse level which clarify propositional content (reflected in what Widdowson calls the "cohesion" of the discourse).[3] They also include underlying regularities in the sequencing of the language functions expressed in discourse, which are themselves partially determined by constraints such as topic, speaker intention, the roles of participants, and other contextual features. Regularities in the illocutionary development of discourse comprise what Widdowson calls its "coherence," and represent one interface between the linguistic code and real-world phenomena. In addition to these discourse phenomena, further extralinguistic constraints on the linguistic forms of verbal behavior are apparent. For example, considerations of appropriateness may determine the actual choice and ordering of linguistic forms beyond considerations of propositional and illocutionary meaning. Canale and Swain have referred to these regularities in the pragmatic relationships between the linguistic code and the extralinguistic context as "rule-governed, universal and creative aspects of sociolinguistic competence."[4] Non-verbal communicative behavior is also intimately linked to verbal behavior, and thus to the particular forms of the linguistic codes that are used.

Thus there are multiple levels of verbal behavior at which one may speak of probabilities and constraints, or internalized rule-systems. These include, at least, grammatical, discourse, and sociolinguistic levels. All of these levels of competence are involved in the structuring of communication and contribute to the propositional and social meanings of utterances. Their psychological representation, as an integrated, internalized system for making partial predictions about what will come next in a verbal exchange, has been characterized by Oller as a "pragmatic grammar of expectancy."[5] The existence of this grammar of expectancy becomes apparent when our expectations about what will happen are violated. We will react with surprise or may even not understand what is said to us if its form or content is somehow unexpected. On the other hand, we often do not even notice mistakes made by a speaker when we are attending to meaning.[6] Meaning, then, does not exist ready-made in the linguistic code, but is rather a function of the relationships between language forms, functions, and context, including the intentions of the speaker and the expectations of the hearer.[7]

In this perspective, language competence may be viewed as a complex system of rule sets which operate simultaneously at many levels to determine the choice and organization of grammatical forms for the fulfillment of communicative and other language functions. Language competence is not "additive," or the sum of discrete sets of syntactic, phonological, morphological, semantic, and discourse-level items and organizational systems. Communicative competence (which includes linguistic competence) refers rather to an integrated system of knowledge, whose functioning depends at least as much on the redundancy between the different levels of organization as on any particular stock of items and patterns.[8]

Language testing that does not take into account propositional and illocutionary development beyond the sentence level, as well as the interaction between language behavior (verbal and non-verbal) and real-world phenomena, is at best getting at only a part of communicative competence. Small wonder that we often find that a student's success at second language classroom exercises and tests appears to bear little relationship to his or her ability to use the language effectively in a real-world situation.

LANGUAGE IN COMMUNICATION

Morrow has identified a number of features of language as it is used in communication which have been generally ignored in the teaching and testing of second languages.[9] Language in communication is, for example, *interaction-based* (occurs between participants in a speech act, each of whom dynamically influences the linguistic behavior of the other in a multitude of ways). It is to some extent *unpredictable* (although it has norms) so that participants must process new information under time constraints. It is always *purposive* (is intended to fulfill some communicative function such as persuading, conveying information, or accepting), is *authentic* (represents a particular dialect, level of formality, etc.), and *is related to the behavior* of the participants and others. It always occurs in both a verbal and extralinguistic *context.*

The implications of the psycholinguistic model of language competence and of our understanding of the nature of language in use, as described above, are profound. If we aim to evaluate the communicative abilities of second language learners and speakers, we need to test many levels of competence simultaneously. In other words, we need to engage the examinee's language processing system or grammar of expectancy. And to do this, the language and the tasks that we use in our tests must have the characteristics of "real" language in use.

ACQUIRING COMMUNICATIVE COMPETENCE

Similar considerations hold for second language acquisition. Researchers from several perspectives have found evidence that second languages are most efficiently acquired through use in meaningful, naturalistic situations, i.e., when language is used for communicative purposes, when realistic extralinguistic as well as verbal contexts are present or implied, and when various levels of the learner's language processing system are activated.[10] As Oller has expressed it, the brain does not store phonemes and morphemes according to their category of linguistic analysis, but rather mapped onto contexts. Human information processing abilities appear to function in this way, so that the higher the level at which language is contextualized (i.e., speech sounds contextualized in words, or words in sentences, versus utterances contextualized in discourse), the more effective language perception, processing, and acquisition will be.[11]

Information processing theory would at least partially attribute this phenomenon to the multiple associations that are simultaneously made with new linguistic material when it is contextualized at all possible levels. Associations made both within the linguistic system and with extralinguistic phenomena will reinforce each other and will lead to better retention and to multiple access channels in long-term memory. When second language learners interact with native speakers and use authentic written language materials, these associations will better represent native speaker probability rules for the relationships among forms in an utterance, among utterances in discourse, and for the communicative functions likely to be expressed in a given context. (Stevick would, of course, also emphasize the personal meaningfulness or "depth" of learner involvement in the communicative act in enhancing memory processes. Such involvement ensures learner response and more elaborated or "deeper" processing of the stimulus. It thus leads to better long-term retention and a greater likelihood of access to the new knowledge when a subsequent context offers appropriate cues.)[12]

It would thus appear that second languages are best acquired as well as tested through their naturalistic use in context.

CHARACTERISTICS OF LANGUAGE TESTS

Much work is currently in progress in the area of communicative syllabus design. In testing, however, in spite of recognition of the need for communicative tests, recent advances in procedures for developing such tests, and widespread experimentation with communicative tests for specific purposes, the field of testing communicative competence can at best be said to be at an embryonic stage.[13]

Communicative tests share a number of characteristics with other kinds of language tests. They tend to have one of three categories of purpose: evaluation of language *proficiency* (for placement in language courses, admission to programs, certification, etc.), *diagnosis* of particular areas of strength or weakness in language proficiency, and evaluation of *achievement* relevant to a particular instructional unit or program. Tests of all types can also serve to motivate students in their language learning endeavor (or the contrary) and may be used in the evaluation of instructional programs.

All tests are *samples* of behavior, intended to reflect whether the examinee possesses certain knowledge, or to predict whether he or she can perform certain acts. Tests generally consist of a number of items, each composed of *stimulus material* and a related *task* which requires a *response* on the part of the examiner. Responses are then scored according to certain *criteria.*

Other important characteristics of a test include its *validity* (does the test measure what it is intended to measure?), *reliability* (will it function in the same way, i.e., will the score gained approach the "true score" of the examinee each time it is given, and in a consistent way with different examinees?), and *feasibility* (is it too expensive and time-consuming with respect to development, administration, or scoring?). Feasibility is a relative concept based on the time and resources available, balanced against the criticality of the decisions to be made based on test results. It is a consideration that too often causes compromises with respect to validity and reliability. Tests should also be interesting and should not provoke undue anxiety (in the interest of validity and reliability, so that the examinee's best performance will be measured).

Davies has discussed three continua along which tests may be categorized which illuminate several current issues in communicative testing. These are: *discrete point* versus *integrative, indirect* versus *direct,* and *norm referenced* versus *criterion referenced.*[14] The first refers to the degree to which a test emphasizes isolated bits of language knowledge versus more global abilities. "Discrete point" has traditionally referred to tests of grammar in which single sentences are the maximum stimulus unit presented or response required. Such tests also use separate tasks or subtests to assess the "four skills." (Some current writers use the term for all tests in which one element at a time is emphasized, thus including tests of isolated communicative functions.[15] However, such an extension of meaning undermines the usefulness of the distinction between discrete point and integrative tests, since test tasks could conceivably be both at the same time.) The essential point is that discrete point tests select particular levels of language code organization (e.g., phonology, syntax) to test specific bits of knowledge (e.g., speech sound discrimination, correct choice of prepositions), while generally dealing with only one "skill" (reading, writing, listening, or speaking). Test stimuli and/or responses can be discrete point. The higher the level of language organization used in a test, the more "integrative" it is. Tests at the integrative end of the scale present language in discourse (rather than at the sentence, or word, or syllable level), and activate the expectancy grammar. Examples include auditory and written cloze, dictation, interviews, written essays, and reading and listening passages in which questions require global comprehension.

Oller distinguishes that subset of integrative tests which also take into account appropriate extralinguistic context as "pragmatic" tests and maintains that only with such tests can we validly measure language proficiency (i.e., communicative competence reflected in performance).[16] Some authors argue that discrete point tests (in the old sense) have a place when the purpose of the test is diagnostic,[17] but Oller and others maintain that, even for this purpose, integrative (or pragmatic) tasks are best; that analysis of the examinee's errors on a pragmatic task can tell more about his or her specific language problems than any highly artificial discrete point task. The implications for communicative testing would seem clear; our test tasks should be as high on the integrative scale as possible; the tests should be pragmatic. At the same time, in our analysis of examinee responses we can look at very specific aspects of performance if that fits our objectives (i.e., "discrete point" *scoring*).[18]

The indirect versus direct continuum refers to the degree to which a test task approaches the actual criterion performance. A direct (or "performance-based") test at the extreme end of the scale would involve actually performing the criterion behavior in a real-life situation (e.g., a university student demonstrating second language mastery by successfully functioning in a course of study in the host country; a public servant efficiently taking an office telephone message in the second language). Something short of direct testing is needed to predict how the examinee will function in the real-life situation. The tests that we devise for this purpose are always a simulation of some kind, but there is a range of artificiality or authenticity possible in a testing situation. Indirect testing involves using a sample of relatively unrelated behavior to predict the examinee's performance in the eventual target situation. The Test of English as a Foreign Language (TOEFL) is an example of a relatively indirect measure for prospective university students.[19] A written essay or true-false grammar test used to qualify tour guides or an oral interview used to certify graduate students as being able to do library research in their second language are at the extreme indirect end of the scale with respect to their objectives. Likewise, a written cloze test used to measure speaking proficiency is an indirect measure. Indirect measures are often favored for reasons of practicality. There may be some cases where results of indirect tests correlate quite highly with more direct measures of criterion performance. However, in any given case, this must be demonstrated. In communicative testing, it would seem that our tests should be as direct as possible, and that any indirect measures must be shown to reliably predict the criterion performance in real-life language use or at least to have concurrent validity with more direct measures.

The issue of norm referencing versus criterion referencing refers to the degree to which an examinee's performance on a test is judged in terms of the performance of others (as in standardized tests which yield percentile rankings), versus the degree to which it is a measure of his or her progress toward a specific objective and level of performance (as in a driving test, where a minimum score must be achieved regardless of the performance of others). Obviously, criterion referencing is only possible where specific objectives exist. The levels required may also be based on norm referencing, as an indication of what degree of proficiency may be reasonably expected. In communicative testing, norm referencing is probably appropriate when the purpose is to determine placement in a multilevel instructional program. But it would seem that achievement tests in instructional programs where learners need to reach a certain level of performance for given objectives or where different learners are working toward different objectives (as often happens at advanced levels) should give both students and instructors feedback on how far the students have advanced toward each objective. Test tasks should then ideally be designed to give not only a "yes" or "no" answer as to whether the examinee can "do" a task, but should indicate how well he or she can do it relative to how well he or she needs to do it. In some programs it may be appropriate to use both criterion referencing and norm referencing; in others, one or the other may be most appropriate. Because communicative testing presumes adequate definition of objectives, based on learner needs, criterion referencing is a possibility.

SPECIFYING OBJECTIVES FOR COMMUNICATIVE LANGUAGE TESTS

The format, content, and scoring criteria of any test should reflect its *objectives.* In the case of a communicative second language test, these objectives should be expressed in terms of what the examinee will be able to "do" in the target language in a naturalistic situation; i.e., whether he or she will be able to use the language effectively for a given communicative purpose. We are thus *not* talking about "behavioral objectives" in the sense that they have sometimes been understood in second language programs (e.g., "after hearing a sentence with two adverbial phrases, using the present continuous or simple present of 'to be' and most frequent verbs, . . . choose the best answer among four choices").[20]

Objectives are more easily formulated when the language is being learned for a specific purpose by persons with certain characteristics (e.g., businessmen for routine travel needs in a particular country, university students for a course of study in the second language, or immigrant children for integration into a new educational and cultural milieu), but it is also important to formulate such objectives for general purpose courses and examinations. These objectives will then serve as the basis for syllabus and test design.

The first step in determining such objectives is to describe the learner/examinee's second language needs. Such needs may be formulated in terms of the circumstances in which the target language will be used, if possible in terms of communicative acts (e.g., "read the sports pages of the newspaper"; "take an office telephone message"). The problem then is to specify the nature of these acts as precisely as possible, and to break them into teachable/testable units. As B. J. Carroll writes, "the needs of any individual aspiring user of a language derive from, and are specific to, the communicative encounters he is likely to experience. These needs are to be described in the first instance in non-language terms."[21]

Linguistics has yet to adequately explain how language is systematically related to experience, so we are not always certain which variables in communicative acts are the important ones. Still, it would seem that at least the following information should be clarified for each communicative act in the objectives: the *purpose* of the interaction (including which topics will be treated, related notions, and the language functions that the learner will need), *situational* aspects which will influence language behavior (including the social and psychological roles and relationships of the participants and the settings in which communicative interaction will take place), and the *types of discourse* which will be appropriate (genre, variety, visual, or auditory channel, etc.). It is also important to determine the *degree of skill* expected of the learner or examinee. Such definition of objectives will make it possible to determine the *language forms* (e.g., structures, words) needed by the second language speaker, or at least to specify the *kinds of authentic materials and instructions with native speakers* which would expose the learner or examinee to appropriate forms.

Several detailed models now exist for specifying learner needs and objectives in the second language, notably those of Richterich, Munby, and, more recently, a model by Carroll for language testing which draws on both of these.[22] These models are helpful in that they indicate the range of variables that might be considered in describing specific communicative needs. However, they have certain practical shortcomings. Munby's model, in particular, is extremely complex. It may exceed in its level of detail what it is possible (or even useful) to know about a learner's or examinee's future second language needs. Its implementation in needs specification is long and laborious as well. Because the models do not (and cannot) specify which variables are most important in determining language behavior, they may in fact lead to a distorted description of the "naturalistic" language use which is to be taught or tested. There is also the problem of native-speaker norms versus what might be expected of a second language speaker. Communication theory suggests that as much but only as much information need be included in a communicative interaction as is essential to make the message clear. Clearly, native speaker norms, based on shared cultural knowledge and expectations as well as on high-level mastery of the verbal and other communicative systems, will not be entirely appropriate even for fluently bilingual second language speakers and will be far beyond the reach of most second language speakers. At the same time, native speakers adjust their speech and expectations when communicating with non-

native speakers, simplifying and slowing their speech, repeating and pausing, and accepting poor accents and social faux pas. Thus the objectives should ideally reflect consideration of the level at which the given non-native learners can reasonably be expected to function in the second language setting, as well as of compensatory communicative strategies (such as inferring from context, paraphrasing, asking for repetition, and using gestures) which would usefully form part of their second language communication skills.[23] The important role of such strategies for non-proficient speakers interacting with native speakers is detailed by Stern in his description of Ontario-Quebec bilingual exchange visits for secondary school students.[24] Since such strategies can help language learners to communicate in spite of gaps in grammatical discourse or sociolinguistic knowledge, they should be included among the objectives of basic level language programs with a communicative orientation.[25] The measurement of such strategies must also be a consideration in communicative language testing. (This is not, however, to say that communicative strategies should have the same importance in a theoretical characterization of mature *native-speaker* communicative competence as they would in a characterization of a minimal second language "communicative competence" as a goal of instruction. The term is used with both meanings in the literature, often without clarification.)

The Council of Europe's "threshold level" and B. J. Carroll's specifications for different levels of learner proficiency represent attempts to clarify differences between native-speaker competencies and appropriate goals for second language programs and tests. Neither, however, takes into account the native speaker's adjustment of his or her language behavior when interacting with non-natives, nor do they specify communicative strategies needed by non-proficient second language users. Canale and Swain's "domain description" for Ontario's core French program is notable for its inclusion of specific communicative strategies among instructional goals.[26]

The alternative to reliance on needs-analysis models is an intuitive analysis of learner needs and objectives by someone familiar both with the target situations in which learners will have to use the second language and with the local requirements of language teaching and testing. Such an intuitive analysis can, of course, be informed by the existing theoretical models.

Once the communicative acts of interest are specified, the use of authentic target language materials appropriate to the learner's objectives, and his or her interaction with native speakers in situations similar to those specified, can

shortcut much of the need to describe every aspect of each communicative act to be taught or tested. To the extent that the classroom can provide experiences of naturalistic language use (at the learner's level), the learner will be exposed to vocabulary, syntax, functions, discourse characteristics, and pragmatic relations which are appropriate to the relevant communicative acts. To the extent that a test presents authentic language and communication tasks, with both a verbal (discourse level) and an extralinguistic context, it will be evoking communicative performance, and thus approach as nearly as possible the evaluation of communicative competence.

ISSUES IN COMMUNICATIVE TESTING

Several problems arise in communicative approaches to language testing. One has to do with the extent to which performance in one situation is generalizable to another situation. Does the learner's ability to ask for information at the train station tell us anything about his or her ability to participate in a social gathering or to read a newspaper? The more specific and limited the second language objectives are, the more precise and complete can be the performance evaluation. But where communicative tasks are used to measure global proficiency in courses with general objectives, it is essential that the underlying communicative rule systems rather than specific learned routines appropriate to a given context be tapped. It has been suggested that the ability to use the linguistic code is the most context-free and thus the most generalizable of communicative abilities—a possible justification of greater attention to this component in general-purpose courses. It may also be possible to define "enabling" or "subsidiary skills" which underlie many different communicative acts as the appropriate focus for general-purpose communicative testing.[27]

The generalizability of test results is related to the larger problem of establishing appropriate and reliable scoring criteria and procedures for communicative tests. Tests to determine whether the learner can function in given target language situations may require a global evaluation of whether he or she can "do" certain things in the second language. Alternatively, particular components of language behavior may be emphasized in the test tasks and scoring criteria, depending on the needs and backgrounds of the examinees. For example, high-level mastery of grammatical, discourse, and sociolinguistic components will be required for would-be translators and interpreters. These language components along with communication strategies will be important for foreign students preparing to study in the second language. Immigrants entering jobs that require relatively little interaction with native speakers might reasonably be evaluated more on their communication strategies, certain sociolinguistic elements, and specific vocabulary knowledge. If the purpose of testing is diagnostic or to evaluate progress in a language training program, detailed scoring grids might be in order, whereas global native-speaker judgments of whether or not the learner has the requisite second language communication skills might be more appropriate for placement or entrance requirements. In a second language training program in a bilingual area, such as Ottawa, much sociolinguistic knowledge would already be shared by the second language learners, so that evaluation grids (as well as instructional procedures) would emphasize the linguistic components of communicative competence. Foreign students, on the other hand, might be evaluated on the sociolinguistic appropriateness of their performance as well. Thus, the initial specification of test objectives, based on a consideration of both the previous knowledge and the language needs of the learner, will largely determine the format and content of testing. It will also suggest the criteria by which examinee performance is to be judged. The construction of scoring grids to reflect these criteria, and the training of raters to reliably and accurately judge performance, present other sticky problems in communicative test construction.

CHARACTERISTICS OF COMMUNICATIVE TESTS

How, then, should we test communicative ability in the second language?

1. We want to tap communicative and not only grammatical competence. Therefore our tests, to be *valid,* must activate the internalized rule systems by which discourse is meaningfully processed, including those by which sociolinguistic variables influence language behavior. Such tests should be *pragmatic,* involving the use of naturalistic language in both a verbal and situational context. Since we wish to test grammatical and discourse-level competence as part of communicative competence, we may wish to look explicitly at the *usage* characteristics of language (the correctness of grammatical forms and their organization) as demonstrated through language in *use.* Such evaluation, however, will center on the way the examinee's responses are scored, rather than on the nature of the tasks presented. The test tasks and scoring criteria should also allow evaluation of the *appropriateness* of the examinee's responses in terms of illocutionary development and the sociolinguistic variables present. At the least, they should evaluate whether the examinee can recognize appropriate (versus inappropriate) responses.[28]

2. We want to test the examinee's ability to meet specific target language needs in given situations, as defined in the objectives of the test. We want to know whether the learner can "do" something in the second language with an acceptable degree of efficiency, including such considerations as speed of processing and correctness as well as appropriateness to the situation. Ideally, then, our tests should be as *direct* or performance-based as possible. Role-playing, listening to or reading authentic second language material, and carrying out realistic tasks in the language are ways of simulating criterion situations.

3. We wish to test examinees in a range of situations that reflect our objectives. Thus, in most cases, we will wish to require manipulation of a *variety* of *language functions.* While oral interview tests of speaking proficiency may admirably evaluate performance of the functions of narration and information-giving in a formal, stranger/stranger, unequal-status communicative situation, and may also give us information about the quality of the examinee's language usage, they may tell us relatively little about his or her ability to "do" other kinds of things in the target language. The range and distribution of situations covered by our test items, then, should—at least until we have an

adequate theory of the generalizability of communicative enabling skills—correspond to the range and distribution of our objectives.

4. We want to know how well or how badly the examinee can meet particular objectives. Therefore we will ideally use *criterion referencing* in our tests, so that the performance of each examinee is compared with a definition of adequate performance on each task rather than with the performance of other examinees.

5. We want our tests to be *reliable*. This test characteristic is particularly problematic with respect to scoring criteria and procedures. Communicative tests of global productive skills (e.g., free composition, oral interview) will probably require a scoring method that uses global judgments by native speakers. High levels of inter- and intra-rater reliability can be achieved in such cases, but generally only through the careful training of raters and long experience with a particular test format and scoring grid (i.e., at considerable expense).[29] We must carefully experiment with and analyze the results of our new testing approaches to improve reliability.

6. We want our tests to be *feasible*. Therefore they obviously cannot have all of the above desirable characteristics all of the time. However, by taking into consideration these characteristics we can at least strive to make our tests better measures of communicative competence.

EXAMPLES OF COMMUNICATIVE TESTS

This section presents three tests which aim to evaluate second language communication skills. The first two, developed in Holland and in the United States, are based on van Ek's specifications of threshold second language objectives for European school children and adults.[30] The third, developed in Britain, exemplifies B. J. Carroll's system for test development and reflects Munby's work on the specification of language needs.

CITO Functional Dialogue Language Tests

Language tests recently developed for Dutch secondary school students by CITO (The National Institute for Educational Measurement) illustrate the utilization of Council of Europe second language objectives in measures of oral proficiency.[31] A brief description follows.

Format. A cross-indexed set of situational, thematic, and social skills "modules" in the form of written guidelines for dialogues and accompanying illustrations. A manual is also available.

Purpose. To test oral communicative ability in the performance of speech acts in the second language (French, German, English). Usable both as classroom exercises and for proficiency assessment.

Clientele. Secondary school students with approximately four years of study in the language (three periods per week).

Specifications. Test objectives conform to overall objectives in the language courses concerned. Three types of target language behavior have been selected, based on *situations, themes,* and stereotyped *social speech acts*. Selection was based on a consideration of what students might need to be able to do in the target language during travel abroad or in encounters with foreign tourists in Holland. Appropriate levels of difficulty were established through pretesting in the schools.

1. *Situations:* Fifteen situations and subcomponents were specified, along with the roles of participants, the language functions to be performed, and the specific notions needed. For example,

Situation: camping (Others include: "in a train compartment," "shopping," "at the police station.")

Sub-component: reception desk

Roles: receptionist, guest

Language functions: asking for information, persuading, etc.

Specific notions: site for a tent, equipment, departure time, etc.

2. *Themes:* Twelve themes, with sub-themes and language functions were specified. For example,

Theme: personal data (Others include: "daily life," "holidays," and various social and political problems.)

Sub-theme: name, address, age, etc.

Language functions: identifying, qualifying, etc.

3. *Social speech acts:* Seven social speech acts were specified. These include greeting, introducing oneself, thanking, taking leave, etc.

Procedures. Draft items were developed by CITO personnel, then pretested in the schools and revised.

Test Description. Each test consists of guidelines for a dialogue. One role is played by the examiner (teacher) and the other by the examinee. Each dialogue presents ten sequential tasks. For example,

T: "Le soir, vous arrivez à la réception du camping. Là il y a une vieille dame. Saluez la dame."

E: ("Bonsoir Madame")

T: "La dame dit "bonsoir." Puis vous demandez une place à la dame."

E: ("Je veux/voudrais camper ici," "une place pour ma tente," etc.)

Scoring. Scoring is done by the examiner. After considerable experimentation with varying formats and development of training materials for teacher raters, a rating system with adequate inter-rater reliability has been achieved.[32]

Comments. These tests conform to many of the principles of communicative testing outlined previously. They are based on a theoretical model of communicative competence and on specific learner objectives deriving from it. They are interaction-based, pragmatic tests (if properly administered), with verbal and situational context. The authenticity of the stimulus language might be disputed, along with the way in which language is used, since the examiner not only plays a dialogue participant role but continually instructs the learner on how to respond. Again, authenticity of the task will vary with administration procedures and with the degree to which both participants are able to role-play. The tests are relatively direct in terms of their purpose (to evaluate oral interaction skills and "doing" something in the language). Unpredictable responses are allowed. Appropriateness of responses is not taken into account in the original scoring system, however, it easily could be. The tests present varied situations and require a variety of language functions. They also provide the possibility of criterion referencing. Reliability of scoring is adequate when the training procedures have been used. The concurrent and predictive validity of the tests is uncertain, but both content and face validity would appear high. With respect to feasibility, the development of these tests required a considerable investment of time and expertise. In terms of administration and wide applicability, they are, however, very practical. They also provide a model which can be used by teachers in developing their own tests.

Functional Test for English as a Second Language Students at UCLA

Farhady has recently demonstrated a new approach to communicative test development, based on the van Ek threshold specifications for adults.[33]

Format. A 64-item multiple choice written test based on common university situations involving foreign students. A situation involving several participants is described. Examinees choose the one response of four which is both grammatically correct and socially appropriate.

Purpose. To test "functional competence" (defined by Farhady as of linguistic and sociocultural competence) in oral communication. Scores are to be used in the placement of incoming foreign students in ESL courses.

Specifications for Test Items. Two language functions, each with four subfunctions relevant to an academic environment, were selected from van Ek's taxonomy (e.g., "finding out and expressing intellectual attitudes," "getting things done"). The social relations of friend and stranger and equal or unequal status are reflected in terms representing all possible combinations of these variables for each subfunction.

Procedures. Situations were composed based on each subfunction. The test was then tried out in open-ended response form with both native and non-native speakers. Their responses provided the correct multiple choice responses (the preferred native speaker response) and three distractors for each item (chosen from non-native speaker incorrect responses). In each set of responses, one distractor was linguistically correct but socially inappropriate, one was linguistically incorrect but socially appropriate, and one was both incorrect and inappropriate. For example,

> *Interlocutors:* student and professor (unequal status, friend/friend)
>
> *Function:* getting things done
>
> *Subfunction:* requesting others to do something
>
> *Setting:* academic environment
>
> *Stimulus:* You are applying to a university and need a letter of recommendation. You go

to a professor, who is also your friend, and say:

1. "I'd appreciate it if you could write a letter of recommendation for me." ("functional," or correct and appropriate response)
2. "I want to ask you to write a letter of recommendation for me." (linguistically correct response)
3. "I wonder if you could write a letter recommending to me." (socially appropriate response)
4. "Hey, give me a recommendation letter." (distractor)

Extensive pretesting was done, first to elicit responses, then to verify native-speaker versus non-native-speaker performance on the multiple choice format.

Scoring. For each item the correct and appropriate "functional" response is worth two points, a response that is either correct or appropriate is worth one point, and the response that is neither appropriate nor correct receives no points.

Comments. This test has certain strong qualities, notably its testing of both linguistic accuracy and sociolinguistic appropriateness based on an explicit model of communicative competence. It also uses authentic (native-speaker) responses among the possible answers, and examinees are required to distinguish these from actually occurring non-native responses. It was constructed in accordance with specific communicative objectives. It presents varied situations requiring a variety of language functions. Statistical properties, including concurrent validity and, particularly, reliability, are high. It is not a direct test, however, of what the speaker would say, but rather an indirect test of his or her ability to recognize what should be said, based on the choices given. Since only sentence-level responses are required for a situation specified in a brief description, it is doubtful that discourse-level competence is tapped, although the test does not have some pragmatic qualities in the sense that contextual constraints on language behavior are important. The test is only indirectly "interaction based" nor does it require the examinee to deal with unpredictability. Scoring is objective, which makes high reliability possible. The test is very practical in administration and scoring, although the development process was laborious. Where large numbers of students must be tested on a regular basis this represents a feasible approach to evaluating certain aspects of communicative competence.

Royal Society of Arts Examinations in the Communicative Use of English as a Foreign Language

A series of innovative tests based on recent developments in the communicative teaching of foreign languages has been developed by the Royal Society of Arts Examinations Board.[34] The tests are grouped by modes (reading, writing, listening, and oral interaction) and by difficulty to provide examinations at three proficiency levels (basic, intermediate, and advanced). Advanced examinations use some of the basic and intermediate material plus additional tasks. Examinees who wish to establish their second language credentials may take tests representing different combinations of modes and levels, leading to a "profile" of scores.

The tests are based on detailed specifications of foreign students' language needs in Britain and represent naturalistic language tasks as well as texts.

Format. Reading tests include authentic texts (e.g., pamphlets, excerpts from books and magazines) from which examinees must extract various kinds of useful information. Listening tests provide tape-recorded texts. The writing tests include tasks such as filling out personal information forms, addressing envelopes, answering letters, and leaving brief messages. The oral tests require the participation of two native speakers, one to participate in a conversation with the examinee, given a simulated situation, and the other to evaluate the examinee's performance. Tasks include such functions as asking and giving information, requesting help, and giving advice.

Purpose. To determine the degree to which foreign students in Britain have the requisite English skills to "operate independently."

Clientele. Individuals over age sixteen, for whom English is a second language, who wish to study in Britain.

Specifications[35].

1. *General content areas:*

   Social interaction with native and non-native speakers of English.

   Dealing with official and semi-official bodies.

   Shopping and using services.

   Visiting places of interest and entertainment.

   Travelling and arranging for travel.

   Using media for information and entertainment.

   Medical attention and health.

   Studying for academic/occupational/social purposes.

Detailed specifications exist for the degree of skill to be expected in each mode at each level.

2. *Criteria:* Questions set in the tests of reading skills will take into account the following criteria in determining the degree of skill expected of the candidate.

   Size of the text which the candidate can handle.

   Complexity of the text which the candidate can handle.

   Range of language forms which the candidate can handle and comprehension skills which he can use.

Speed at which texts can be processed and questions answered.

Flexibility in adopting suitable reading strategies for the task set and adapting to developments in the text.

Independence from sources of reference.

3. *Examples for reading:*

Search through text to locate specific information.

Study text to decide upon an appropriate action.

Procedures.   Initial tests were developed and pilot tested in schools and colleges over a period of several years. The preparation of new versions is carried out on a continuing basis. Examinations are administered in a number of testing centers each spring.

Test Description.   Test tasks are quite varied. Several items from specimen papers for reading and writing are reproduced below.[36]

1. *Basic level reading:* You wrote to the Tourist Information Office at Stratford last week, and they have sent this letter, as well as the official guide:

Dear Sir/Madam,
Thank you for your recent letter enquiring about tourist facilities in the Stratford-upon-Avon area, and asking us to make a hotel reservation for you.

The letter contains five additional paragraphs, on which a number of questions are based. A sample question is as follows:

What does the letter tell you?

   A. They cannot reserve accommodation for you.

   B. They have reserved accommodation for you.

   C. You must pay 55p to reserve accommodation.

Put a cross (x) through the right answer on your
   answer sheet.

2. *Intermediate level writing:* You have to go away tomorrow evening for two days, but you unexpectedly receive this telegram from your friend.

POST OFFICE TELEGRAM
5TXZ/9.56/83 LON
YES THANKS STOP ARRIVING
TOMORROW EVENING

Write a short note to your friend to pin on the door. Explain why you are not there and where the keys are.

Scoring.   No published information is available on the scoring procedures used with these examinations. Clearly, many of the tasks would require global judgments by trained raters. The criteria used in scoring writing and oral performance include *accuracy* in the use of the forms and the *range* of language used by the examinee. *Complexity* is also a criterion for writing, and *flexibility* and *size* are criteria for oral performance (see preceding descriptions).

Comments.   These tests conform well to the communicative testing principles discussed in this paper. They set interaction-based, pragmatic language tasks. The language presented is naturalistic, with both verbal and extralinguistic context appropriate to the given task. Both the texts presented and the tasks set appear to be authentic, representing ways in which people use language in everyday life. The tests are thus high on the direct scale. From the limited information available, scoring procedures appear to take into account grammatical, sociolinguistic, and strategic components of the ability to use language. Face and construct validity appear to be very high; concurrent and predictive validity quotients are, however, unknown, as is the reliability of the tests (although information on these aspects of the examinations is currently being gathered). The tests represent a range of situations and language functions; they conform to specific objectives and thus would allow criterion referencing, although results are given in terms of levels. The lengthy procedures involved in development of these tests are hardly feasible for organizations other than those for whom test development is a major business. Nonetheless the types of tasks and texts used in the test are highly suggestive for persons involved in language testing in any capacity, including classroom teachers.

OTHER COMMUNICATIVE TESTS

Several, large-scale current communicative testing projects in Canada and Britain should be mentioned.[37] The Ontario Assessment Instrument Pool for French as a Second Language, developed at OISE for the Ministry of Education of Ontario, involved the collection or preparation of hundreds of testing instruments, classified according to Ministry objectives and the Canale and Swain model of communicative competence. The instruments are available to provincial school French programs. The Test, Measurement and Evaluation Service of the Canadian government's Language Training Branch has developed an integrated achievement evaluation system in response to the communicative orientations of the new language teaching curriculum for public servants. The system offers instruments and procedures to measure all aspects of student achievement, including role-play techniques to evaluate speaking and writing proficiency in work-related situations. Scoring criteria include, in addition to grammatical correctness, sociolinguistic and strategic components, the global ability to convey the message, and criteria specific to the skill being measured (e.g., fluency, for oral communication, and ordering of content, for writing proficiency).

A large-scale project with international implications which deserves mention involves the revised British Council ESL testing system (ELTS) for potential visa students to Britain at the university level. The tests, administered in over one hundred countries, are based on performance tasks in reading and writing authentic texts and oral interaction which simulate the kinds of language use skills required of university students in Britain. The tests include both a general academic English component and six alternate discipline-related components. In a similar vein, the Associated Examining Board has produced a performance-based ESL test, The Test of English for Educational Purposes (TEEP) for candidates for admission to universities in Britain. Test specifications were based on C. Weir's comprehensive study of the language needs of foreign students in Britain. A general academic English component combined with one of two alternate components for science versus non-science candidates are a feature of this test. A current project to develop a post-admissions ESL test for Ontario shares some of the features of ELTS and TEEP and goes further toward the direct or performance end of the scale in that the discipline-related modules are integrated by theme. Thus examinees read an academic text, listen to and take notes on a related lecture, read a second related text, and, in addition to answering comprehension questions, write a brief exam-type essay based on the foregoing subject matter. The theme material is again taken up in the OTESL oral interaction test which follows the written test.

OTHER CURRENT WORK IN COMMUNICATIVE TESTING

The preceding tests all represent large-scale investments of time and expertise, and envisage a fairly large clientele. A vital component in their development is the specification of objectives based on detailed models of language needs. Where a test is being prepared for a restricted clientele with very specific second language needs, a more intuitive description of needs and objectives may be both appropriate and more feasible. Hinofotis, Bailey, and Stern developed such a test at UCLA to evaluate the English oral communicative ability of foreign students employed as teaching assistants.[38] In this test, examinees are video-taped as they carry on a simulated teaching task in English. Trained raters subsequently view the tapes, giving both global and detailed diagnostic scores for aspects of linguistic proficiency, non-verbal behavior, and the effectiveness with which information is communicated. Acceptable reliability coefficients have been achieved through the careful training of raters, and the test appears to serve well as a measure of whether the assistants have the requisite English skills for various kinds of teaching assignments.

A number of second language tests for specific groups in a bilingual university setting have been prepared at the Centre for Second Language Learning of the University of Ottawa. These include French and English reading tests for graduate students in history, which utilize texts selected by history professors from current academic journals, and similar tests in human and physical geography.[39] Multiple choice written comprehension questions require examinees to extract information at various levels of detail, to infer meaning both from the selections presented and from their knowledge of the structure of historical argument or of geographical conventions, and to distinguish between such aspects of the message as objective facts and the author's point of view.

Another communicative test recently developed at the Centre is used to evaluate the functional second language skills in French (or English) of members of the Social Sciences Faculty.[40] Test content and tasks are based precisely on the faculty's second language requirements for professors, which stipulate that they must have the requisite language skills to participate receptively in administrative meetings where business is conducted in French (or English), be able to read administrative documents in French (or English) as well as academic texts in their area of specialization, and be able to answer students' questions on administrative matters in their second language. The subtests thus include oral questions to be answered in the second language, listening-comprehension questions based on a tape-recorded excerpt from a Faculty Council meeting (which examinees may answer in their first language), and a reading comprehension exercise based on a university memorandum. One subtest, individualized for each examinee, presents a one-page excerpt from a scholarly text in his or her area of specialization (e.g., subfields of pharmacology, criminology, or political science) to be summarized in the first language. Candidates' oral responses are tape-recorded. The scoring criteria vary for the different subtests, but, for example, in the oral interaction test, equal weight is given by raters to understanding the question, getting across an appropriate answer, and the linguistic correctness of the response. Performance is rated by a team of experienced language teachers, while the final (criterion-referenced) judgment about whether examinee performance reflects the second language skills needed on the job rests with the personnel committee and Dean of the Faculty.

The Centre has also developed second language tests of French and English for employees at the National Arts Centre.[41] After a needs analysis which included study of the organization and its job descriptions; discussions with administrators, personnel officers, and employees; and observation of employees at work in situations requiring use of the second language, two test formats were developed. One features oral interaction tasks for different job groups with restricted and specific requirements to use the second language with the public (e.g., ticket salespersons, parking attendants, or restaurant personnel). The other test, for administrative employees who have wide-ranging and higher level proficiency requirements, places more emphasis on accurate knowledge of the second language in written form. Tasks and texts in both tests reflect the relevant Arts Centre work contexts.

MAKING TESTS "MORE" COMMUNICATIVE

The preceding discussion and references provide a number of suggestions about how to develop tests which to some extent tap features of communicative competence. These suggestions also have relevance where new tests will not be developed, but where items or subtests may be replaced or changed. In situations where for practical reasons one is "hooked into" traditional test formats (e.g., where rapid mass testing is involved, communicative needs of examinees are heterogeneous or unknown, resources are not available to develop innovative tests, or instruction is grammar-based), so that "ideal" communication tests will not be developed in the foreseeable future, it is at least possible to give *some* importance to communicative aspects of language. This can be done by including in existing test formats some subtests or items clearly based on a communicative view of language competence. One can seek to use authentic, longer (discourse-level), contextualized language texts as stimulus material. (Reading passages, recorded dialogues, and cloze tests all lend themselves to this possibility.) One can ask listening and reading comprehension questions based on a global understanding of the meaning conveyed through language use in context, rather than pinpointing discrete grammatical points.[42] One can ask questions about the appropriateness of contextualized language behaviors, or about situational aspects of an exchange (e.g., the roles, relationships, attitudes, and intended meanings of participants). Scoring of oral and written performance tasks can take into account getting the message across, different ways of expressing ideas, and appropriateness—as well as grammatical aspects. Correct multiple choice responses and acceptable cloze answers can be based on native speaker responses, and multiple choice distractors can be generated from unacceptable non-native speaker responses.

CONCLUSION

An examination of the theoretical constructs, issues, and practical work done so far in communicative testing would appear to have relevance for anyone involved in second language testing. This work reflects a new emphasis on the validity of our measures, and their effect on instruction, redressing the overriding concerns with reliability and practicality of administration and scoring of the past several decades. While it is important to incorporate the psychometric lessons of recent years into these new approaches, their emphasis on careful specification of content, and on naturalistic language use in context, may lead to better tests. If we can make our tests more reflective of the kinds of discourse, situations, and purposes for which second language speakers will need their skills, we should be better able to evaluate how well they will be able to function using the target language in "real life." Such testing is also likely to have dramatic effects on the format and content of second language curricula, and to improve student motivation through its increased relevance. In fact, this "washback" effect may be one of the most compelling reasons to alter existing procedures.

NOTES

1. These include Morrow, (1979); B. J. Carroll (1978a, 1980, 1985); Canale and Swain (1980); Howard (1980); Jones (1985); Royal Society of Arts Examinations Board (1980).

2. See, for example, Hymes (1967, 1972); Campbell and Wales (1970); Oller (1973); Widdowson (1978). C. N. Candlin (1976) provides a helpful summary of theoretical work in this area through the mid-1970s.

3. See Widdowson (1978).

4. See Canale and Swain (1979).

5. See Oller (1973). A lengthier description of the operation of this grammar of expectancy, and its implications for language testing, may be found in Oller (1979).

6. H. H. Stern has often discussed the tendency of the listener to pay maximum attention to meaning in an interchange and minimal attention to form, in the context of implications of this aspect of psycholinguistic processing for language teaching and learning. See, for example, Stern (1981) and Oller (1978).

7. See discussion in Widdowson (1978).

8. See discussion in Krowitz and Garcia-Zamor (1978). Also see Spolsky (1978).

9. See Morrow (1979).

10. See, for example, Newmark, (1971); Macnamara (1973); Oller (1973); J. B. Carroll (1974); Stevick (1976); Terrell, (1977); Krashen (1978); Stern (1978a and 1978b).

11. See Oller (1973).

12. See J. B. Carroll (1974) for a model of information processing theory for language teachers, and Stevick (1976) for a review of research on memory and verbal learning interpreted in terms of its implications for language teaching. M. B. Wesche (1979) interprets results of a study of good language learners in an intensive training program according to an information processing model.

13. See references cited in note 1, as well as the tests described in the last part of this article.

14. See A. Davies (1979).

15. For example, Morrow (1979) and Howard (1980) use the term in this way.

16. See Oller (1973).

17. See, for example, Clark (1978) and Ingram (1978).

18. See Morrow (1979) and Howard (1980).

19. See Educational Testing Service (1981) and published versions of the TOEFL.

20. See Commission Scolaire Régionale de l'Outaouais (1978).

21. See B. J. Carroll (1978b).

22. See Richterich (1975); Munby (1978); and Carroll (1980).

23. H. H. Stern (1975, 1980) and S. Savignon (1977) have both made frequent reference to such strategies in their discussions of the learner's role in second language acquisition. Canale and Swain (1980) have recognized the importance of such strategies for second language learners in their theoretical framework for the components of communicative competence.

24. See Stern (1975, 1980).

25. Canale and Swain (1980) have defined the role of communicative strategies in this way.

26. See Canale and Swain (1979).

27. B. J. Carroll (1980) provides a tentative definition of such generalizable skills.

28. See Widdowson (1978) for a lucid discussion of language *usage* and *use,* and *illocutionary* versus *propositional* meaning.

29. See Clark (1978).

30. See van Ek (1975, 1976).

31. See van Ek (1975, 1976); Roos-Wygh (1978); and CITO (1984).

32. The development of the current rating scales is described in Noyons (1985).

33. See Farhady (1979) and van Ek (1975, 1976).

34. See Royal Society of Arts Examinations Board (1980).

35. The specification categories are quoted from the Royal Society of Arts Examinations Board (1980).

36. See Royal Society of Arts Examinations Board (1980) pp. 17 and 42.

37. Most of these tests, together with others, are described in Hauptman, LeBlanc, and Wesche (1985). In particular, see the articles by R. Proulx-Dubé and her colleagues, "Ateliers sur divers aspects de l'évaluation de la performance linguistique"; Allan Emmett, "The Associated Examining Board's Test in English for Educational Purposes (TEEP)"; Brendan J. Carroll, "Second Language Performance Testing for University and Professional Contexts"; and Ian Seaton, "Issues in the Validation of the English Language Testing Service (ELTS)," 1976–1983. Innovative performance-based tests of ESL survival skills for refugees to the United States and of academic French skills are also described in this book (Hauptman, LeBlanc, and Wesche, 1985) in articles by J. L. D. Clark and A. G. Grognet, "Development and validation of a performance-based test of ESL survival skills," and D. Z. Green, "Developing measures of communicative proficiency: a test for French immersion students in grades 9 and 10." The OTESL Project is described in Cray and Wesche (1984). The *Ontario Assessment Instrument Pool for French as a Second Language* (M. Canale, M. Swain, and N. Villaroel) may be purchased from the Ontario Institute for Studies in Education.

38. See Hinofotis, Bailey, and Stern (1979) and Bailey (1985).

39. See DesBrisay, Wesche, Taylor, and Feldberg (1980) and Godbout (1980).

40. See Krupka (1985).

41. See Tréville (1985).

42. See discussions in DesBrisay (1979, 1982).

43. I wish to thank M. DesBrisay, A. Todesco, M. Fröhlich, B. J. Carroll, J. Oller, B. Courchêne, and R. Godbout for their critical reading of earlier versions of this paper and for a very helpful ongoing exchange of ideas about communicative testing.

REFERENCES

Bailey, K. M. 1985. If I had known then what I know now: Performance testing of foreign teaching assistants. In P. Hauptman, R. LeBlanc, and M. Wesche (eds.), *Second Language Performance Testing/L'Evaluation de la "Performance" en Langue Seconde.* Ottawa: University of Ottawa Press.

Campbell, R., and R. Wales. 1970. The study of language acquisition. In J. Lyons (ed.), *New Horizons.* Harmondsworth: Penguin.

Canale, M., and M. Swain. 1979. *A Domain Description for Core FSL: Communication Skills.* Report for the Ministry of Education, Toronto, Ontario.

_____. 1980. Theoretical bases of communicative approaches to second language teaching and testing. *Applied Linguistics,* 1:1–47.

_____, and N. Villaroel. 1979. *The Ontario Assessment Instrument Pool: French as a Second Language, Junior and Intermediate Divisions.* Toronto: Ontario Ministry of Education.

Candlin, C. N. 1976. Communicative language teaching and the debt to pragmatics. In C. Rameh (ed.), *Semantics: Theory and Application.* Washington: Georgetown University Press.

Carroll, B. J. 1978a. *Guidelines for the Development of Communicative Tests.* London: Royal Society of Arts.

_____. 1978b. *The Assessment of Communicative Performance.* London: Royal Society of Arts.

_____. 1980. *Testing Communicative Performance.* Oxford: Pergamon.

_____. 1981. Specifications for an English Language Testing Service. In J. C. Alderson and A. Hughes (eds.), *Issues in Language Testing.* ELT Documents 111, London: The British Council.

_____. 1985. Second language performance testing for university and professional contexts. In P. Hauptman, R. LeBlanc, and M. Wesche (eds.), *Second Language Performance Testing/L'Evaluation de la "Performance" en Langue Seconde.* Ottawa: University of Ottawa Press.

Carroll, J. B. 1974. Learning theory for the classroom teacher. In G. Jarvis, *The Challenge of Communication.* Skokie, IL: National Textbook Co.

CITO (Dutch National Institute for Educational Measurement). 1984. *Spreek-toetsen* (Speaking Test Manual). Arnhem, The Netherlands: CITO.

Clark, J. L. D. 1978. Interview testing research at Educational Testing Service. In J. L. D. Clark (ed.), *Direct Testing of Speaking Proficiency: Theory and Application.* Princeton: Educational Testing Service.

_____, and A. G. Grognet. 1985. Development and validation of a performance-based test of ESL "survival skills." In P. Hauptman, R. LeBlanc and M. Wesche (eds.), *Second Language Performance Testing/L'Evaluation de la "Performance" en Langue Seconde.* Ottawa: University of Ottawa Press.

Commission Scolaire Régionale de l'Outaouais. 1978. *Program cadre: Programme par objectifs niveau 1, Module 1–4.* Service a l'Enseignement, Département des Langues Secondes.

Cray, E., and M. Wesche. 1984. The Ontario test of English as a second language (OTESL): A progress report. *TESL Talk,* 15, 3.

Davies, A. 1979. Continuum categories for language tests. Paper presented at the 13th annual TESOL Convention, Boston.

DesBrisay, M. 1979. A report on the English proficiency test. *Centre for Second Language Learning/Institut de Langues Vivantes Journal,* 20, 99–104.

_____. 1982. A feasibility study of large-scale communicative testing. *Journal of Applied Language Study,* 1, 1, 77–86.

_____, M. Wesche, D. Taylor, and W. Feldberg. 1980. Report on the Test of English Proficiency for graduate students in history. *Centre for Second Language Learning/Institute de Langues Vivantes Journal,* 22, 52–58.

Educational Testing Service. 1981. *TOEFL Test and Score Manual.* Princeton, NJ: Educational Testing Service.

Emmett, A. 1985. The Associated Examining Board's Test in English for Educational Purposes (TEEP). In P. Hauptman, R. LeBlanc, and M. Wesche (eds.), *Second Language Performance Testing/L'Évaluation de la "Performance" en Langue Seconde.* Ottawa: University of Ottawa Press.

Farhady, H. 1979. *New directions for ESL proficiency*

testing. Manuscript. TESL Program. University of Southern California, Los Angeles.

Godbout, R. 1980. Un problème spécifique d'évaluation: La compréhension de l'écrit aux études supérieures en histoire. *Centre for Second Language Learning/Institut de Langues Vivantes Journal,* 22, 46–51.

Green, Dana Z. 1985. Developing measures of communicative proficiency: A test for French immersion students in Grades 9 and 10. In P. Hauptman, R. LeBlanc, and M. Wesche (eds.), *Second Language Performance Testing/L'Evaluation de la "Performance" en Langue Seconde.* Ottawa: University of Ottawa Press.

Hauptman, P., R. LeBlanc, and M. Wesche. (eds.). 1985. *Second Language Performance Testing/ L'Évaluation de la "Performance" en Langue Seconde.* Ottawa: University of Ottawa Press.

Hinofotis, F. B., K. M. Bailey, and S. L. Stern. 1979. Assessing improvement in oral communication: Raters' perception of change. *UCLA Workpapers in Teaching English as a Second Language,* 13.

Howard, F. 1980. Testing communicative proficiency in French as a second language: A search for procedures. *Canadian Modern Language Review,* 36, 272–289.

Hymes, D. 1967. Models of the interaction of language and social setting. *Problems of Bilingualism: Journal of Social Issues,* 23, 8–28.

———. 1972. On communicative competence. In J. B. Pride and J. Holmes (eds.), *Sociolinguistics.* Harmondsworth: Penguin.

Ingram, E. 1978. The psycholinguistic basis. In B. Spolsky (ed.), *Approaches to Language Testing.* Arlington, VA: Center for Applied Linguistics.

Jones, R. L. 1985. Second language performance testing: An overview. In P. Hauptman, R. LeBlanc, and M. Wesche (eds.), *Second Language Performance Testing/L'Evaluation de la "Performance" en Langue Seconde.* Ottawa: University of Ottawa Press.

Krashen, S. D. 1978. Adult second language acquisition and learning: A review of theory and practice. Presentation at the Language Training Branch, Public Service Commission of Canada, Ottawa.

———. 1981. The "Fundamental Pedagogical Principle" in second language teaching. *Studia Linguistica,* 35, 1–2, 50–70.

———. 1982. *Principles and Practice in Second Language Acquisition.* Oxford: Pergamon Press.

Krowitz, M. J., and M. Garcia-Zamor. 1978. Towards measuring functional language proficiency. In G. Nickel (ed.), *Applied Linguistics: Language Testing.* Stuttgart: Hochschulverlag.

Krupka, L. 1985. Evaluation de la performance linguistique de professeurs d'université. In P. Hauptman, R. LeBlanc, and M. Wesche (eds.), *Second Language Performance Testing/L'Évaluation de la "Performance" en Langue Seconde.* Ottawa: University of Ottawa Press.

LeBlanc, R. 1985. Le testing de performance en langue seconde: Perspective canadienne (avec la collaboration de Renée Proulx-Dubé, Mireille Voyer, Diane Pruneau, Pascal-André Charlebois et Marjorie B. Wesche). In P. Hauptman, R. Le-Blanc, and M. Wesche (eds.), *Second Language Performance Testing/L'Évaluation de la "Performance" en Langue Seconde.* Ottawa: University of Ottawa Press.

Macnamara, J. 1973. Nurseries, streets and classrooms: Some comparisons and deductions. *Modern Language Journal,* 57, 250–254.

Morrow, K. R. 1979. Communicative language testing: Revolution or evolution? In C. Brumfit and K. Johnson (eds.), *The Communicative Approach to Language Teaching.* London: Oxford University Press.

Munby, J. 1978. *Communicative Syllabus Design.* Cambridge: Cambridge University Press.

Newmark, L.D. 1971. A minimal language teaching program. In P. Pimsleur and A. Quinn (eds.), *The Psychology of Second Language Learning.* Cambridge: Cambridge University Press.

Noyons, J. 1985. The standardized testing of oral proficiency in the Netherlands. In P. Hauptman, R. LeBlanc, and M. Wesche (eds.), *Second Language Performance Testing/L'Évaluation de la "Performance" en Langue Seconde.* Ottawa: University of Ottawa Press.

Oller, J. 1973. Pragmatic language testing. *Language Sciences,* 28, 7–12.

———. 1978. Application of pragmatic theory to language teaching and testing. Presentation at the Language Training Branch, Public Service Commission of Canada, Ottawa.

———. 1979. *Language Tests at School.* London: Longman.

Proulx-Dubé, R. 1985. Ateliers sur divers aspects de l'évaluation de la performance linguistique des candidats inscrits aux programmes de formation linguistique de la fonction publique canadienne. In P. Hauptman, R. LeBlanc, and M. Wesche (eds.), *Second Language Performance Testing/ L'Évaluation de la "Performance" en Langue Seconde.* Ottawa: University of Ottawa Press.

Richterich, R. 1975. L'analyse des besoins langagiers: Illusion, prétexte, nécessité. *Education et Culture,* 28, 9–14.

Roos-Wygh, I. 1978. Research and development projects in language proficiency interviewing. In J. L. D. Clark (ed.), *Direct Testing of Speaking Proficiency: Theory and Application.* Princeton, NJ: Educational Testing Service.

Royal Society of Arts Examinations Board. 1980. *Examinations in the Communicative Use of English as a Foreign Language.* London: Royal Society of Arts.

Savignon, S. J. 1977. Communicative competence: Theory and classroom practice. *Revue de la Société pour la Promotion de l'Anglais au Québec,* 1.

Seaton, I. 1985. Issues in the validation of the English Language Testing Service (ELTS). 1976–1983. In P. Hauptman, R. LeBlanc, and M. Wesche (eds.), *Second Language Performance Testing/L'Évaluation de la "Performance" en Langue Seconde.* Ottawa: University of Ottawa Press.

Spolsky, B. 1978. What does it mean to know a language? In *Educational Linguistics: An Introduction.* Rowley, MA: Newbury House Publishers.

Stern, H. H. 1975. What can we learn from the good language learner? *Canadian Modern Language Review,* 31, 304–318.

_____. 1978a. Bilingual schooling and foreign language education: Some implications of Canadian experiments in French immersion. In J. E. Alatis (ed.), *International Dimensions of Bilingual Education.* Washington: Georgetown University Press.

_____. 1978b. French immersion in Canada: Achievement and directions. *Canadian Modern Language Review,* 34, 836–854.

_____. 1980. Language learning on the spot, some thoughts on the language aspect of student exchange programs. *Canadian Modern Language Review,* 36, 659–669.

_____. 1981. Communicative language teaching and learning: Toward a synthesis. In H. B. Altman and P. M. Alatis (eds.), *The Second Language Classroom: Directions for the 1980's.* New York: Oxford University Press.

Stevick, E. 1976. *Memory, Meaning and Method.* Rowley, MA: Newbury House Publishers.

Swain, M. 1982. Large scale communicative language testing: A case study. Paper presented at the International Symposium on Language Testing, University of Hong Kong.

Terrell, T. D. 1977. A natural approach to second language acquisition and learning. *Modern Language Journal,* 61, 325–339.

Tréville, M. C. 1985. Deux tests faits sur mesure. In P. Hauptman, R. LeBlanc, and M. Wesche (eds.), *Second Language Performance Testing/L'Évaluation de la "Performance" en Langue Seconde,* Ottawa: University of Ottawa Press.

van Ek, J. A. 1975. *The Threshold Level in a European Unit/Credit System for Modern Language Learning by Adults.* Strasbourg: Council of Europe.

_____. 1976. *The Threshold Level in Modern Language Learning in Schools.* Strasbourg: Council of Europe.

Wesche, M. B. 1984. Performance testing at the University of Ottawa. *Centre for Second Language Learning/Institut de Langues Vivantes Journal,* 29, 156–166.

_____. 1979. Learning behaviors of successful adult students on intensive language training. *Canadian Modern Language Review.* 35, 415–430.

_____. 1985. Introduction. In P. Hauptman, R. LeBlanc, and M. Wesche (eds.), *Second Language Performance Testing/L'Évaluation de la "Performance" en Langue Seconde.* Ottawa: University of Ottawa Press.

Widdowson, H. G. 1978. *Teaching Language as Communication.* London: Oxford University Press.

CHAPTER 32

Language Proficency Interview Testing: An Overview

David J. Keitges

I. INTRODUCTION

"Language as communication" is a familiar theme found in journal articles, textbook prefaces, and in discussions among teachers and students of English in Japan today. By relating the two, writers and discussants are typically trying to redefine what language teaching—and language learning—must be concerned with—the acquisition of communicative competence in social settings. Learning another language as a communicative tool is hastened by a variety of factors, including academic use, commercial and technological uses in international trade, and touristic and other needs. Learning foreign languages in Japan has also become related to notions of "internationalism" and "intercultural communication." Language learning, then, has widened in scope and become a more practical endeavor than ever before.

Viewing language learning in such practical terms has focused critical attention on language education and its aspects: needs assessment, program design, methodology, evaluation. Increasingly, questions about language learning phrased by students, teachers, and others, relate to the authenticity and practicality of the language taught and the efficiency of the methods employed. Students want to know how they can learn "real" English, and teachers are attempting to bring "the real English-speaking world" into the classroom itself. Research has become preoccupied with the tasks of defining and describing needs, mounting courses, and evaluating progress.

Further, viewing language as a communicative tool requires increased sophistication in this evaluation. Assessing only a student's ability to manipulate discrete, separate elements of language on paper gives the teacher and administrator information of dubious value. A practical ability in speaking a second/foreign language demands evaluative procedures that can certify progress, diagnose weakness, and predict performance. Proficiency testing, therefore, is an essential part of any course or program which claims to teach language for use.

This paper will explore and discuss the usefulness and limitations of language proficiency interview testing, or, more specifically, the direct testing of speaking proficiency in the interview setting. Readers in mind are those of the English language teaching community, both native and non-native speakers, who teach language for communicative use. Also included are those who assess speaking proficiency on a more formal basis in company-wide, governmental, and other programs in which a higher proficiency rating can lead to promotion, an overseas post, a certificate for employment, and other career-related opportunities. After definitions of terms and anecdotes of recent experience, a model of language proficiency interviewing will be described and critiqued in Section II. Its limitations will be discussed in Section III and modifications of the model will be surveyed. Section IV will provide guidelines and suggestions for designing, administering, rating, and improving language proficiency interview tests.

Clark (1979, p. 36) distinguishes between direct, semi-direct, and indirect measures of speaking ability. Direct measures include all those procedures in which the "examinee is asked to engage in a face-to-face communicative exchange with one or more human interlocutors." Indirect measures require no active speech production by the examinee but depend on paper-and-pencil varieties of cloze tests and other such "productive" techniques. Semi-direct measures of speaking ability elicit active speech but by means of tape recordings, printed test booklets and other "nonhuman" elicitation procedures. Only direct measures involve actual oral exchanges and contain what Carroll (1980, p. 54) calls oral interaction: "constructive interplay with unpredictable stimuli."

Further, for our purposes, the evaluation of an individual's language proficiency must be distinguished from that same individual's language achievement. Proficiency refers to overall or global competence in a language, regardless of how that competence was acquired. Achievement evaluation, on the other hand, measures an individual's acquisition of specific linguistic features of the language that have been presented in, for example, a particular language course (Clark, 1979, p. 39). Therefore, we can define such language proficiency interviews as described above as evaluative sessions in which one or more persons perform communicative tasks elicited or assigned by one or more examiners who subsequently observe and rate the resultant speaking performance to determine speaking proficiency.

Anecdotal comments relayed from examining partner to partner and from colleague to colleague frequently pose rather significant questions about the usefulness and limitations of language proficiency interview testing. Some examiners complain that judging speaking proficiency is so subjective that the results of such tests are all too suspect; others reject such interview testing on the grounds that the "real" elements of language (grammar, vocabulary, etc.) cannot be fairly tested in this manner. A second category of difficulty relates to interview procedure. Examiners sometimes aren't sure how they are to elicit speech samples and exactly what they are to evaluate: the whole, the parts, the overall impression, what. And examiners working together who do not discuss criteria of evaluation beforehand often rate the proficiency of the same individual in very different ways. And even when checklist scales are used during interviews, some examiners question if "dismembering the discourse" is an appropriate way to judge the communicative proficiency of the interviewee. These concerns and numerous variations are frequently expressed. How, then, are we to regard the element of subjectivity in language proficiency interview testing? And what procedures can aid us in eliciting appropriate speech samples and evaluating them efficiently? These and other questions will be discussed in Sections II, III, and IV.

II. A TESTING MODEL: DESCRIPTION AND CRITIQUE

In the minds of many, the direct testing of speaking proficiency by interview is nearly synonymous with the procedure developed by the U.S. Foreign Service Institute (FSI). Most teachers and testers have at least a passing familiarity with this procedure as it has been widely though incompletely described in major teaching methods and testing texts (Valette, 1977, pp. 157–51; Rivers, 1981, pp. 368, 497–99). As much of the research and many of the modifications discussed in the literature are related to this particular testing model, perhaps it is wise to explore it briefly to distinguish its specific purpose, target population, and procedures.

Wilds (1975, pp. 29–44) has provided the most comprehensive description of the FSI interview test. The procedure, first adopted in 1956 and somewhat revised since then, was devised to assess the foreign language speaking abilities of U.S. Government personnel, especially diplomatic, military and aid officials, and, later, Peace Corps volunteers. The evaluation takes place in an interview conducted by two examiners for a sole interviewee. The trained examiners engaged the interviewee in a conversation to determine his speaking proficiency level as defined by the functionally based FSI Proficiency Ratings (Appendix A). In FSI usage, the team of examiners consists of a senior member, a native-speaking certified language examiner or a linguist thoroughly familiar with the target language, and a native-speaking junior member who elicits the samples of speech to be evaluated. The senior member, though an interested participant, usually refrains from actual elicitation. The speech samples of the interviewee are judged to range from elementary proficiency through limited working proficiency, minimum professional proficiency, and full professional proficiency, to native or bilingual proficiency. These five proficiency levels, which are further divided with plus (+) nota-

tions to indicate half-level proficiencies, were devised in response to the specific needs of the testing population.

The taped interview begins with simple social formulae which, if handled badly, leads the examiner to put a ceiling on the difficulty of subsequent questions (and thus the rating level) of the interviewee. If the initial queries are dealt with satisfactorily, the examiner will go on to more difficult topics of an autobiographical or professional nature. Informal oral interpretation between examiners is sometimes assigned to elicit certain desired grammatical or lexical items unused by the interviewee. The interview ranges from fifteen to less than thirty minutes in length. Final rating occurs either during the interview or directly after its conclusion. The examiners may (but are not required to) use a "Checklist of Performance Factors" (accent, grammar, vocabulary, fluency, comprehension) and a weighted conversion table (Appendix B) to reach their conclusions. The examiners may also report specific weaknesses to the interviewee at the interview's end or fill in a "Factors in Speaking Ability" chart designed for the same purpose (Clark, 1979, p. 40).

In terms of validity, reliability and practicality, the three imperatives of test design and administration, the FSI oral interview appears to be an excellent measure of the speaking proficiency of the target population. Consisting of an interview in which oral interaction occurs, it holds both *face* and reasonable *content* validity as it "measures what it is supposed to measure" —the ability of the person to speak the language (Clark, 1979, p. 37). It has also demonstrated high statistical reliability (Oller, 1979, p. 392; Hendricks et al., 1980, p. 78). The interview is also practical, at least for the FSI, as it can be administered, rated and interpreted with ease (Wilds, 1975, p. 29–30).

There are a number of practical factors, however, which underlie the validity and reliability of this procedure. Oller (1979, p. 326) states that interview validity (and hence reliability) depends on three factors: (1) how the speech acts are elicited; (2) what the rating scale(s) are referenced against (the criteria chosen for deciding proficiency); and (3) who is a qualified rater. It is in these practical aspects, the details of the procedure, that the reasons for its success can best be viewed.

The *Manual for Peace Corps Language Testers* (1970, p. 11) defines the purpose of the language proficiency interview in this way: "It is *not* simply a friendly conversation on whatever topics come to mind . . . It is rather a specialized procedure which efficiently uses the relatively brief testing period to explore many different aspects of the student's language competence in order to place him into one of the categories described." This definition emphasizes the importance of the elicitation of speech samples, the grading of them in reference to the predetermined proficiency criteria and ratings, and, further, implies the necessary training of the human administrators who must elicit and rate skillfully and reliably. These procedural requirements are fulfilled in various ways at the FSI. Wilds (1975, p. 34) reports that, for languages that are tested often (more than 60 languages are tested), there are libraries of tapes of previous tests of all levels for the training rater to use. In addition, there is a "substantial amount of written material aimed at clarifying standards and suggesting appropriate techniques." A much experienced staff also helps guide others in the achievement and maintenance of testing competence. But, it may be asked, does this training and the accumulated experience of the examiners, though impressive, fully explain the success of the FSI interview? What, if anything, underlies these aspects of interview test success?

The element of subjectivity, that of the examiner's personal judgement, present in judging oral performances has long been pinpointed by some as a major disadvantage, and one that inhibits its more extensive use. Without doubt, the examiner's personal judgment is present in the eliciting and rating of speech samples. It is obvious that the examiner must inject himself into the test by deciding which questions to ask and how to phrase them, and how the multitude of possible responses are to be rated in accordance with the still loosely defined criteria. But how shall this subjectivity be regarded? As a disadvantage, even an obstacle? Or as a benign or even beneficial component of the process?

Much has been done at the FSI to limit the influence of subjective judgment on testing: the Proficiency Ratings, based on functional use, have been devised; examiners have learned techniques of elicitation that furnish speech samples considered valid and appropriate for rating; raters are carefully trained to differentiate good, fair, and poor performances reliably according to defined criteria. Subjectivity, then, or at least its more negative influences, has been limited. Rivers (1981, p. 69) observes that oral evaluation is essentially subjective but notes that raters can be trained—as they are at the FSI—to reach basically comparable results. Oller (1979, p. 328) defines oral evaluation as judging "subjectively according to loosely stated criteria." Further, Oller (p. 48) notes that objective procedures in evaluating oral performance are not necessarily more reliable than subjective ones. "Certain aspects of language performances may simply lend themselves more to subjective judgement than they do to quantification by formula." Clark (1979, p. 41) agrees by noting studies that demonstrate that subjective rating of oral performances should not be regarded as "intrinsically unreliable." In addition, it may be unreasonable and unwise to ask that rating of oral performances be accomplished in a more "objective" manner. For, considering the paucity of our present knowledge and understanding of oral interaction, how and in what form would objective rating take place? In fact, instead of asking if the element of subjectivity is appropriate or not in proficiency rating, it may be more reasonable and useful to ask to what extent subjectivity, granted an informed variant, is necessary to the process. For this reason, it may be concluded that the FSI interview test is successful not only because of its established criteria and rating system and the careful training of its examiners, but also precisely because of the controlled or informed subjectivity exercised by those examiners during the interview process.

III. LIMITATIONS AND MODIFICATIONS

Up to this point, the design, procedure and rating system of the FSI interview test has been briefly reviewed. Its usefulness in assessing speaking proficiency has been outlined. Also, the reasons for its success have been explored. From now on, attention will be shifted to the limitations of language proficiency interviewing, and the FSI model in particular. Also, modifications of the model will be surveyed to demonstrate how teachers and researchers have dealt with these recognized limits of use.

Language proficiency interviewing leaves much to be desired. The described FSI procedure, although efficient with the specific group for which it was designed, has a number of limitations in its general applicability. Chief among these is its absolute scaling of performances. Absolute scaling requires reliable, consistent judgments by different examiners over time. Individuals tested today must have their performances rated under the same conditions as those rated previously, and those who will be rated in the future. The essence of absolute scaling, then, is consistency. Relative or normative scaling, on the other hand, seeks only to differentiate among members of a particular group at a particular time. There is no specific, absolute need for consistency over time. Relative scaling, in the classroom and at the employment agency, is the normal method, while absolute scaling is only for rare, special situations. The difficulty of the matter becomes apparent when one considers the training of the examiners charged with the rating responsibility. The need to maintain reliability over time further burdens, and strictly formalizes, the training of FSI examiners. Other, relative raters need not be so burdened. In addition, while the increased amount of this examiner-training and lengthy interview sessions may not be prohibitive for the FSI and other select groups, these requirements are burdensome for other testers. And, though the basic 5-level Proficiency Ratings discriminate abilities well enough for the FSI, these same ratings do not distinguish abilities well enough for secondary school and college learners with more limited proficiency (Reschke, 1978, pp. 80–1). Finally, the inclusion of listening comprehension as a checklist performance factor by the FSI is seen by many as undesirable as examiners, no matter how skillful, are exposed to so little evidence of comprehension that it is unlikely a fair and complete assessment of this important skill can be made in an interview alone. Therefore, although the FSI model is suitable for its designed purpose, it cannot be freely transferred to dissimilar testing situations. The implicit (and sometimes explicit) recommendations for its unmodified use by some writers need to be softened and qualified.

Other sorts of limitations of the FSI model have been indicated by "integrative" and "pragmatic" testers. This approach, backed by Carroll (1980), Cohen (1980), and Oller (1979), among others, differs most significantly from the FSI model in the scoring and rating of speech samples. Oller (p. 305) believes that scoring techniques used in interviews should relate not only to morphology and syntax as now, but also to the overall meanings contained in utterances. Thus, he calls for a wider array of criteria for judging speech beyond the traditional FSI set (accent, grammar, vocabulary, etc.). Other researchers (Callaway, 1980, p. 111; Hendricks et al., 1980, p. 85; Mullen, 1980, p. 101) have statistically examined the present FSI scoring techniques and found them wanting. This research suggests that using integrated or unitary scaling for scoring interviews, rather than the FSI multiple checklist scales, is preferable because there is not adequate evidence to prove that the FSI checklist scales actually measure different things. Mullen, in particular, noted that an overall scale of proficiency appeared to represent a composite of the four other scales in her research and was, statistically, more reliable —thus preferable. Qualified findings on unitary/multiple scaling have been reported by Bachman and Palmer (1981, p. 67). Callaway, in researching raters, found that the overall comprehensibility of speech behavior is what motivates examiner's evaluations of proficiency, thus further supporting arguments for unitary scaling in interview scoring techniques. In addition, these "pragmatic" critics also encourage the use of other criteria (naturalness, clarity, suitability) in the rating of speech (Cohen, 1980, pp. 20–23). Rating an individual's performance by such criteria as these, they argue, is pedagogically more useful and communicatively more accurate. An extended 9-level interview assessment scale of this type, designed by Carroll (1980, p. 135) is included as Appendix C.

Finally, in a general way, interview testing has important limitations that every tester must be aware of. Although interviews are planned to replicate as closely as possible everyday communication, in several ways they are atypical. Clark (1979, p. 38) has observed that "talking to the examiner isn't the same as speaking to a waiter, taxi driver or friend." The psychological and affectional components of communication present in the interview also differ from ordinary communication (Jones, 1979, p. 14). In addition, the usefulness of interview-based evaluations may be lessened by differences in communication style transferred from another language and culture by the interviewee to the target language. Richards (1981, pp. 7–26) details some of the problems that occur in conversations as a result of this communication style transference. These recognized limitations, however, do not invalidate interview tests as measures of speaking proficiency. They merely require that such interviews be designed and conducted with the utmost care and flexibility necessary.

Modification of a model is a natural consequence of recognized inadequacy. And, as the FSI model is limited in a number of practical ways, changes in its design and use have readily been made. These changes, briefly surveyed, come in six areas. The first, the use of a sole examiner instead of two at the FSI, is unavoidable for most teachers and testers due to the number of interviewees and the burden of other work. Further, examiner self-training (through reading, experience, heightened awareness) is a related accommodation to practical circumstances. The third common change, a shortening of interview-time, is also an obvious accommodation. Though the FSI can extend interviews to nearly half an hour, few teachers or testers can possibly do so. This has inevitably resulted in interviews being conducted in between five and ten minutes per interviewee. It is important to note here that the Educational Testing Service (Clark, 1978, p. 227–8) has determined that interviews in the five-to-seven minute range are adequate for valid and reliable rating by trained examiners. The fourth common change is to increase the efficiency of the interview by testing groups instead of individuals. Reschke (1978, p. 82) has suggested testing from three to five persons at each session. The present writer has much successful experience with groups of three. The fifth general modification concerns the checklist and rating scales. Clark (in Valette, 1977, p. 161) has simplified and shortened the FSI checklist scales to make them more useful in the classroom. Schulz and Bartz have developed "pragmatic" scales that score the level of communication present in the interviewee's speech sample. The Schulz Communicative Competence Scale (in Valette, 1977, p. 161) rates "fluency," "comprehensibility," "amount of communication," and "quality of communication." Bartz' scale (in Valette, 1977, pp. 150–1) mirrors Schulz' except that "effort to communicate" is interchanged with "comprehensibility" (Appendix D). The sixth and final major area of change from the FSI model is the specific use of the interview for other purposes. Although the majority of these other uses will be outlined in Section IV, the use of the interview for strictly diagnostic purposes has been discussed by Graham (1978, pp. 33–9).

These modifications demonstrate that the general format of the FSI oral interview is adequate as a model for the design of language proficiency interviews. Though the FSI model is strictly appropriate for only the specific purpose for which it was designed, it can be modified to serve wider testing requirements. Properly understood, the FSI interview model can aid both classroom teachers and more formal testers in their design, administration, and rating of proficiency interview tests.

IV. A PRACTICAL PRIMER: GUIDELINES AND SUGGESTIONS

The purpose of this section, plainly, is to provide some guidelines and practical suggestions for the designing, administering, and rating of language proficiency interviews. The three former sections presented a rationale for this kind of testing, described and critiqued the most prominent model, and surveyed limitations and modifications. This section is to be a practical conclusion. But, before launching into practicality, I would like to extend the discussion to include the many practical uses of proficiency interviews. These popular uses went largely unmentioned before in order to avoid unnecessary confusion during the description and critique of the FSI model. Now it aids in the effort to recognize these other purposes: the language proficiency interview (LPI) as a part of a formal or informal course or program needs assessment study; the use of the LPI in ability-grouping and as a motivational and self- and peer-grading technique; the LPI as a diagnostic evaluation instrument and as a practical means of establishing and maintaining classroom and program goals of communicative language use; and the use of the LPI to maintain certain course or program proficiency requirements or standards (foreign-language teacher certification, etc.).

These common uses demonstrate that interviewing can also be an instrumental means to various practical teaching and administrative ends.

The design of an appropriate LPI procedure implies more than the mere adoption of a recommended rating scale. In fact, proper design requires the employment of a process that can ensure a valid, reliable and practical test instrument. The FSI model, itself, is the successful product of just such a design process— a process others can use to create proficiency interview tests suited to their particular circumstances. This process of design is the main subject of discussion below.

Ryan and Frederiksen (1951), cited and discussed by Jones (1979, pp. 52–3), developed a process for the preparation of performance tests which are valid, reliable and practical. Though intended as a general process for a wide variety of testing needs, it can be adapted to the more specific needs of language proficiency interviewing. Ryan and Frederiksen listed seven steps in performance test design: (1) make a job analysis; (2) select tasks to represent the job; (3) develop a rating form; (4) survey the practical limitations; (5) develop a tentative operating plan; (6) try out the test and revise it; and (7) prepare directions for administration and use of the test.

This general process can be adapted to serve LPI testing. By rewording and grouping some of the steps, the process can be reduced to five easily remembered stages: (1) analyze the needs; (2) select representative tasks; (3) develop a rating form; (4) accommodate the limitations; and (5) train the examiner. By following these steps carefully, the test designer can devise an instrument for the specific group of learners which takes into account all of the variables of their language needs and use, as the FSI instrument does for those of its target population. These stages of test development are discussed separately below.

Analyze the Communicative Needs of the Interviewee(s)

For what reason is the interviewee being tested? To decide if his speaking proficiency is adequate or not for a certain job? To rank his ability in relation to his fellow learners? Questions of this type are critically important at this first stage. Before it is possible to decide *how* to conduct the interview, the need for which the interview is being held must be specified. Needs range from the communicatively narrow (taking customers' orders in a restaurant) to the very broad and complex (negotiating contracts for the purchase of computer components). Needs can also be teacher-derived (diagnosis) and program-centered (certification requirements). Once this need is specified clearly, the process of designing the interview test can proceed smoothly; without its description, the testing will be a hard and likely fruitless task.

Practically speaking, this need should be written down as the purpose statement of the test, for the designer's later reference when he is planning how to elicit and rate the speech samples. This written description should also include information relating to the target communicative settings (formal/informal business meetings, academic seminars, touristic exchanges, etc.), needs for expert knowledge (scientific, commercial, etc.), other special requirements (speech-making, for instance), and the tolerance of error allowable in the interactions. Further, the statement should list at least some of the functional uses of language that will be required. Most teachers and testers are familiar with the writings of D. A. Wilkins (1976) and J. A. van Ek (1976) on the notional and functional uses of language in communication. Van Ek (pp. 45–49) proposes a list of functions (accepting an offer or invitation, expressing capability or incapability, expressing disappointment, etc.) that can aid in this need specification of the interviewee. John Munby (1978, pp. 123–131) also provides a taxonomy of language skills which can be consulted for this purpose.

Select Representative Communication Tasks for Testing

At this stage, a representative sample of the communication tasks of the targeted need must be selected. Obviously, the interviewee cannot be tested for all of the needs that have been identified. Therefore, a small but appropriate sample must be chosen for the brief testing period. Sampling should range from the easy to the more difficult functional tasks (greeting, apologizing, explaining, defending, etc.) and deal with the specific areas and topics of discourse that have been pinpointed. Therefore, when interviewing electrical engineers, for example, some of the tasks must relate to true-to-life engineering topics, possibly the individual's special field or research. Asking only social/general questions of an individual being tested for engineering-specific speaking proficiency results in inadequate knowledge of his true proficiency and a wasted interview.

The second challenge of interview test design, then, is deciding what questions to ask and how to ask them. In a conversational format, two strategies for efficient questioning can be recommended. The first is the use of carefully prepared "ceiling questions" which are designed to test the interviewee's proficiency at the top of each level of the proficiency rating scale. Appropriate greetings and such opening formalities may convince the examiner that the interviewee possesses sufficient proficiency to be tested on the next higher level. Responses to subsequent "ceiling questions" may suggest that a certain level should be further explored for difficulty. When this tentative rating level has been found, the second strategy, that of asking several related questions of increasing difficulty on a specific topic, may be used. The purpose of this strategy is to make certain the rating level and explore the breadth of the interviewee's vocabulary and his general ability to engage in topical discussion. It has been noted by Morrow (in Carroll, 1980, p. 12) that language is essentially interactive, unpredictable, purposeful and contextualized. Therefore, the greatest care should be taken to ensure that the communicative exchanges initiated by the examiner replicate as closely as possible genuine language use. Both types of questions, in sufficient quantities, should be prepared ahead of time and written down for instant reference.

Direct interview testing, as defined in Section I, also includes the use of role-play, informal oral interpretation, reversal of roles, situational problems, group discussions on prepared to... and other techniques. These techn... cannot be discussed with accuracy and in suffi- cient detail. Vocabulary and grammar, likewise, be- pecially useful when more th... available for each int... interviews are he... viewing" groups... pre-planned disc... minutes is both... assess speaking...

Speeches, ... pared, howev... ciency evalu...

form, though oral, lacks the essentially *interactive* nature of genuine oral communication.

As long as the questions asked and the tasks assigned are directly related to the needs of the interviewees and are not so contrived as to tax the imagination unduly, these approaches to eliciting speech samples will be successful.

Develop a Rating Scale

Much has already been written about checklist and rating scales, and examples have been placed in the appendix for the review. Jones notes in his discussion (19?) that "the key to achieving objectivity in... ance test is the checklist and rating form." While this may be true of non-language... have seen that clear objectivity in interview... cannot be achieved completely due to the ... ety and complexity of oral communica... Nonetheless, predetermined rating criteria ... be used to "channel" the examiner's attention toward those factors considered most important in this communication. Criteria chosen for general consideration should include not only the traditional set (accent, grammar, comprehension, fluency, and, to the degree... sion) but also the so...ce, it is best to place communicative ... value the extent to which an ... explain the conclusions ... communicate his desires clearly ... pronunciation, in fact, should only ... a factor when it detracts from the ... e's communicative ability in a specific ... when the specified topics raised ... In attempting to judge communicative effec-

and how to ask them. In a conversational format, two strategies for efficient questioning can be recommended. The first is the use of carefully prepared "ceiling questions" which are designed to test the interviewee's proficiency at the top of each level of the proficiency rating scale. Appropriate greetings and such opening formalities may convince the examiner that the interviewee possesses sufficient proficiency to be tested on the next higher level. Responses to subsequent "ceiling questions" may suggest that a certain level should be further explored for difficulty. When this tentative rating level has been found, the second strategy, that of asking several related questions of increasing difficulty on a specific topic, may be used. The purpose of this strategy is to make certain the rating level and explore the breadth of the interviewee's vocabulary and his general ability to engage in topical discussion. It has been noted by Morrow (in Carroll, 1980, p. 12) that language is essentially interactive, unpredictable, purposeful and contextualized. Therefore, the greatest care should be taken to ensure that the communicative exchanges initiated by the examiner replicate as closely as possible genuine language use. Both types of questions, in sufficient quantities, should be prepared ahead of time and written down for instant reference.

Direct interview testing, as defined in Section I, also includes the use of role-play, informal oral interpretation, reversal of roles, situational problems, group discussions on prepared topics, and other techniques. These techniques are especially useful when more than ten minutes is available for each interview, and when group interviews are held. I have found that "interviewing" groups of three students engaged in a pre-planned discussion without notes for thirty minutes is both a useful and enjoyable way to assess speaking proficiency.

Speeches, both extemporaneous and prepared, however, should not be assigned as proficiency evaluation tasks. This communication form, though oral, lacks the essentially interactive nature of genuine oral communication.

As long as the questions asked and the tasks assigned are directly related to the needs of the interviewees and are not so contrived as to tax the imagination unduly, these approaches to eliciting speech samples will be successful.

Develop a Rating Scale

Much has already been written about checklist and rating scales, and examples have been placed in the appendix for the reader's review. Jones notes in his discussion (1979, p. 53) that "the key to achieving objectivity in a performance test is the checklist and rating scale." While this may be true of non-language tests, we have seen that clear objectivity in interview tests cannot be achieved completely due to the variety and complexity of oral communication. Nonetheless, predetermined rating criteria must be used to "channel" the examiner's attention toward those factors considered most important in this communication. Criteria chosen for general consideration should include not only the traditional set (accent, grammar, vocabulary, fluency, and, to the degree possible, comprehension) but also the so-called criteria of communication: quality and amount of communication, effort to communicate, and communicative effectiveness. In my experience, it is best to place emphasis on the latter group and allow the former set to qualify or explain the conclusions reached. Thus, I value the extent to which an individual can communicate his desires clearly in the language more than his excellence in pronunciation. Pronunciation, in fact, should only be considered a factor when it detracts from the interviewee's communicative ability in a specific setting. Vocabulary and grammar, likewise, become significant when the specified topics raised cannot be discussed with accuracy and in sufficient detail.

In attempting to judge communicative effectiveness, it is useful to qualify one's overall impression with the interviewee's use of rhetorical behaviors. These behaviors come into play as the proficiency of the individual increases. Einhorn (1981, pp. 217–228) has isolated six such behaviors (identification with interviewer, argument support, organization, style, delivery, and images conveyed) that determined success or failure for applicants in job interviews. Such behaviors are also significant factors in the effectiveness of interpersonal oral communication.

How one uses these chosen (and weighted) criteria in arriving at rating decisions is much in dispute. While the formal FSI model suggests that final rating is decided by the computation of five separately scored factors, in fact FSI examiners rarely use this procedure. Apparently, they are so familiar with the characteristics that differentiate one rating level from another that they can easily categorize performances. Whether they even analyze performance in terms of the five factors specifically is uncertain. Callaway (1980, p. 111) states that dividing oral performance into components is superfluous as raters make holistic unidimensional judgments. My experience suggests that it is unnecessary to compute separate scores but that intimate knowledge of the rating levels is necessary so that the rater can transfer his essentially subjective judgments to that scale efficiently. Criteria, written down as reference, are essential to maintain the examiner's approach to performance rating for all interviewees. Practical knowledge of the rating scale grounds the criteria in function.

With the foregoing in mind, a rating scale must be developed that relates directly to the interviewees. The FSI scale, gross in units (only five) and stretching from intermediate speaking ability to more advanced, may be appropriate for few testing situations. More detailed is the business-oriented Daiei scale (Appendix E) and Carroll's scale. The latter seems good for general academic use, and language school courses. In any case, as proficiency rating charts are ex-

tremely difficult to construct, especially when several levels of proficiency must be differentiated, it is recommended that already available scales be adapted for specific purposes. With adequate experience and special need, custommade proficiency ratings can be devised.

Accommodate the Limitations

Accommodating the limitations is the subprocess of fitting the interview test to the circumstances. At this stage of design and preparation, the test has already been shaped in a variety of ways, perhaps subconsciously, by the limits of time, ability level, urgency or importance of purpose, etc. The designer has likely already decided the length of each interview, whether individuals or groups will be tested, the amount of preparation required of the examiner, and other factors. It is useful, nonetheless, to review the form of the interview and its operating schedule to see if any improvements can be made or if anything has been forgotten. One factor that seems to be often neglected is examiner-fatigue. This is a malady which invariably attacks examiners about half way through planned interview schedules. To lessen its effects, a regular rest break should be taken during each hour of interviewing.

The Training of the Examiner

What remains to be accomplished is the training of the examiner and the pilot-testing of the planned interview test—two requirements that complement one another rather well. Just as the interviewees must have prepared themselves over their learning period to perform successfully, so must the individual examiner prepare himself to elicit and rate well. This preparation takes two forms, general and specific. General preparation involves the examiner's intellectual understanding of the interview as a forum of communication and as a testing vehicle. This form of preparation requires study in the disciplines of testing, discourse analysis, and related areas. It also requires an increased sensitivity toward language use and a keen ability to differentiate genuine and effective oral performances. Specific training is best accomplished in the interview process itself. As noted before, the FSI uses tapes of previous tests and anecdotal materials prepared by experienced examiners in the training of new raters. Few, if any, ordinary testers have an opportunity for such a careful training. Novice testers, however, can ask to join in interviews conducted by colleagues, or do "mock" interviews during class time to gain experience. Further, the novice can "test" the English of native-speakers and fluent non-native speakers as

means of setting appropriate expectations of performance for later interviews. There are many daily opportunities to evaluate speech, and these can be used for training purposes. In fact, the design of the interview test includes "training" in needs assessment, task selection, criteria choice, and measurement scale design. In the final stage of examiner training, the planned interview test can be pilot-tested with an unrelated group of individuals to test its actual practicality and the ability of the examiner to elicit and rate efficiently. These pilot-testings can be cassette-recorded and reviewed later. Thus, in any number of ways, examiners can prepare themselves for the difficult tasks involved in interview testing of speaking proficiency.

CONCLUSION

In Japan, perhaps more than elsewhere, testing defines learning. Learners readily identify the nature and worth of the experience by the form and difficulty of the test. Therefore, in language classes where the guiding aim has been shifted to communicative use, proficiency interview testing has a special role to play.

This proficiency interviewing has much to recommend it. In the classroom, it dramatically demonstrates the goal of the activities. Learners soon realize, at the time of the diagnostic group-interview, that it is their speaking proficiency, not their memorization skills, that is important

and "framing" a course with a beginning diagnostic interview and an ending proficiency evaluation is a powerful encouragement for taking all of the classroom communication activities seriously. Oral performances, characteristically both open and personal, force learners to monitor their own progress more carefully.

Valid and reliable proficiency interviewing is within the grasp of all teachers and testers. The process of test design and examiner training, though time-consuming initially, opens up new ways of thinking about language use—and language teaching and learning.

REFERENCES

Bachman, L. R., and A. S. Palmer. 1981. The construct validation of the FSI oral interview. *Language Learning*. 31, 1, 67–86.

Callaway, Donn R. 1980. Accent and the evaluation of ESL oral proficiency. In *Research in Language Testing*. J. W. Oller, Jr. and K. Perkins. Rowley, MA: Newbury House Publishers, 102–115.

Carroll, Brendan C. 1980. *Testing Communicative*

Performance: An Interim Study. London: Pergamon Press.

Clark, John L. D. 1978. Interview test research at educational testing and service. In *Direct Testing of Speaking Proficiency: Theory and Application*. John L. D. Clark (ed.). Princeton, NJ: Education and Testing Service, 211–228.

———. 1979. Direct vs. semi-direct tests of speaking

ability. In *Concepts in Language Testing: Some Recent Studies.* E. J. Brière and F. B. Hinofotis (eds.). Washington, D.C.: Teachers of English to Speakers of Other Languages, 35–49.

Cohen, Andrew D. 1980. *Testing Language Ability in the Classroom.* Rowley, MA: Newbury House Publishers.

Daiei's English Proficiency Level Breakdown. 1981. The Daiei Language Development Program.

Einhorn, Lois J. 1981. An inner view of the job interview: An investigation of successful communicative behaviors. *Communication Education.* 30, 217–228.

Graham, Stephen L. 1978. Using the FSI interview as a diagnostic evaluation instrument. In *Direct Testing of Speaking Proficiency: Theory and Application,* 31–40.

Hendricks, D. et al. 1980. Oral proficiency testing in an intensive English program. In *Research in Language Testing,* 77–90.

Jones, Randall L. 1979. Performance testing of second language proficiency. In *Concepts in Language Testing: Some Recent Studies,* 50–57.

Lado, Robert. 1978. Scope and limitations of interview-based language testing: Are we asking too much of the interview? In *Direct Testing of Speaking Proficiency: Theory and Application,* 113–128.

Manual for Peace Corps Language Testers. 1970. Princeton, NJ: Educational Testing Service, 11. In *Language Tests at School: A Pragmatic Approach.* J. W. Oller, Jr. London: Longman Group Limited, 324.

Mullen, Karen A. 1980. Rater reliability and oral proficiency evaluations. In *Research in Language Testing,* 91–101.

Munby, John. 1978. *Communicative Syllabus Design.* Cambridge: Cambridge University Press.

Oller, John W. Jr. 1979. *Language Tests at School: A Pragmatic Approach.* London: Longman Group Limited.

Reschke, Claus. 1978. Adaptation of the FSI interview scale for secondary schools and colleges. In *Direct Testing of Speaking Proficiency: Theory and Application.* 3, 7–26.

Richards, Jack C. 1981. Talking across cultures. *Canadian Modern Language Review,* 37, 3, 572–582.

Rivers, Wilga M. 1981. *Teaching Foreign Language Skills.* 2nd ed. Chicago: The University of Chicago Press, 184–258.

Ryan, D. G., and N. Frederiksen. 1951. Performance tests of educational achievement. In *Educational Measurement.* E. F. Lindquist (ed.). Washington, D.C.: American Council on Education, 483–92.

Sollenberger, Howard E. Development and current use of the FSI oral interview test. In *Direct Testing of Speaking Proficiency: Theory and Application.*

Valette, Rebecca M. 1977. *Modern Language Testing.* 2nd ed. New York: Harcourt Brace Jovanovich, Inc., 119–163.

van Ek, J. A. 1976. The oral interview test. In *Testing Language Proficiency.* R. L. Jones and B. Spolsky (eds.). Arlington, VA: Center for Applied Linguistics. 29–44.

Wilds, Claudia P. 1975. The oral interview test. In R. L. Jones and B. Spolsky (eds.) *Testing Language Proficiency.* Arlington, VA: Center for Applied Linguistics.

Wilkins, D. A. 1976. *Notional Syllabuses.* Oxford: Oxford University Press.

APPENDIX A

The FSI Proficiency Ratings

Level 1: *Able to satisfy routine travel needs and minimum courtesy requirements.* Can ask and answer questions on topics very familiar to him or her; within the scope of his or her very limited language experience can understand simple questions and statements, allowing for slowed speech, repetition or paraphrase; speaking vocabulary inadequate to express anything but the most elementary needs; errors in pronunciation and grammar are frequent, but can be understood by a native speaker used to dealing with foreigners attempting to speak his or her language. While elementary needs vary considerably from individual to individual, any person at level 1 should be able to order a simple meal, ask for shelter or lodging, ask and give simple directions, make purchases, and tell time.

Level 2: *Able to satisfy routine social demands and limited work requirements.* Can handle with confidence but not with facility most social situations including introductions and casual conversations about current events, as well as work, family, and autobiographical information; can handle limited work requirements, needing help in handling any complications or difficulties; can get the gist of most conversations on nontechnical subjects (i.e., topics that require no specialized knowledge) and has a speaking vocabulary sufficient to express himself or herself simply with some circumlocutions; accent, though often quite faulty, is intelligible; can usually handle elementary constructions quite accurately but does not have thorough or confident control of the grammar.

Level 3: *Able to speak the language with sufficient structural accuracy and vocabulary to participate effectively in most formal and informal conversations on practical, social, and professional topics.* Can discuss particular interests and special fields of competence with reasonable ease; comprehension is quite complete for a normal rate of speech; vocabulary is broad enough that he or she rarely has to grope for a word; accent may be obviously foreign; control of grammar good; errors never interfere with understanding and rarely disturb the native speaker.

Level 4: *Able to use the language fluently and accurately on all levels normally pertinent to professional needs.* Can understand and participate in any conversation within the range of his or her experience with a high degree of fluency and precision of vocabulary; would rarely be taken for a native speaker, but can respond appropriately even in unfamiliar situations; errors of pronunciation and grammar quite rare; can handle informal interpreting from and into the language.

Level 5: *Speaking proficiency equivalent to that of an educated native speaker.* Has complete fluency in the language such that his or her speech on all levels is fully accepted by educated native speakers in all of its features, including breadth of vocabulary and idiom, colloquialisms, and pertinent cultural references.

APPENDIX B

The FSI Checklist of Performance Factors and Descriptions

Accent
1. Pronunciation frequently unintelligible.
2. Frequent gross errors and a very heavy accent make understanding difficult, require frequent repetition.
3. "Foreign accent" requires concentrated listening and mispronunciations lead to occasional misunderstanding and apparent errors in grammar or vocabulary.
4. Marked "foreign accent" and occasional mispronunciations that do not interfere with understanding.
5. No conspicuous mispronunciations, but would not be taken for a native speaker.
6. Native pronunciation, with no trace of "foreign accent."

Grammar

1. Grammar almost entirely inaccurate except in stock phases.
2. Constant errors showing control of very few major patterns and frequently preventing communication.
3. Frequent errors showing some major patterns uncontrolled and causing occasional irritation and misunderstanding.
4. Occasional errors showing imperfect control of some patterns but no weakness that causes misunderstanding.
5. Few errors, with no patterns of failure.
6. No more than two errors during the interview.

Vocabulary

1. Vocabulary inadequate for even the simplest conversation.
2. Vocabulary limited to basic personal and survival areas (time, food, transportation, family, etc.).
3. Choice of words sometimes inaccurate, limitations of vocabulary prevent discussion of some common professional and social topics.
4. Professional vocabulary adequate to discuss special interests; general vocabulary permits discussion of any nontechnical subject with some circumlocutions.
5. Professional vocabulary broad and precise; general vocabulary adequate to cope with complex practical problems and varied social situations.
6. Vocabulary apparently as accurate and extensive as that of an educated native speaker.

Fluency

1. Speech is so halting and fragmentary that conversation is virtually impossible.
2. Speech is very slow and uneven except for short or routine sentences.
3. Speech is frequently hesitant and jerky; sentences may be left uncompleted.
4. Speech is occasionally hesitant, with some unevenness caused by rephrasing and groping for words.
5. Speech is effortless and smooth, but perceptibly non-native in speed and evenness.
6. Speech on all professional and general topics as effortless and smooth as a native speaker's.

Comprehension

1. Understands too little for the simplest type of conversation.
2. Understands only slow, very simple speech on common social and touristic topics; requires constant repetition and rephrasing.
3. Understands careful, somewhat simplified speech directed to him or her, with considerable repetition and rephrasing.
4. Understands quite well normal educated speech directed to him or her, but requires occasional repetition or rephrasing.
5. Understands everything in normal educated conversation except for very colloquial or low-frequency items or exceptionally rapid or slurred speech.
6. Understands everything in both formal and colloquial speech to be expected of an educated native speaker.

THE FSI WEIGHTING AND CONVERSION TABLES

FSI WEIGHTING TABLE

Proficiency Description →	1	2	3	4	5	6	
Accent	0	1	2	2	3	4	_____
Grammar	6	12	18	24	30	36	_____
Vocabulary	4	8	12	16	20	24	_____
Fluency	2	4	6	8	10	12	_____
Comprehension	4	8	12	15	19	23	_____
						Total:	_____

FSI CONVERSION TABLE

Total Score	Level	Total Score	Level	Total Score	Level
16–25	0+	43–52	2	73–82	3+
26–32	1	53–62	2+	83–92	4
33–42	1+	63–72	3	93–99	4+

APPENDIX C

CONVERSION TABLES

Band	
9	Expert speaker. Speaks with authority on a variety of topics. Can initiate, expand, and develop a theme.
8	Very good non-native speaker. Maintains effectively his own part of a discussion. Initiates, maintains, and elaborates as necessary. Reveals humor where needed and responds to attitudinal tones.
7	Good speaker. Presents case clearly and logically and can develop the dialogue coherently and constructively. Rather less flexible and fluent than Band 8 performer but can respond to main changes of tone or topic. Some hesitation and repetition due to a measure of language restriction but interacts effectively.
6	Competent speaker. Is able to maintain theme of dialogue, to follow topic switches, and to use and appreciate main attitude markers. Stumbles and hesitates at times but is reasonably fluent otherwise. Some errors and inappropriate language but these will not impede exchange of views. Shows some independence in discussion with ability to initiate.
5	Modest speaker. Although gist of dialogue is relevant and can be basically understood, there are noticeable deficiencies in mastery of language patterns and style. Needs to ask for repetition or clarification and similarly to be asked for them. Lacks flexibility and initiative. The interviewer often has to speak rather deliberately. Copes but not with great style or interest.
4	Marginal speaker. Can maintain dialogue but in a rather passive manner, rarely taking initiative or guiding the discussion. Has difficulty in following English at normal speed; lacks fluency and probably accuracy in speaking. The dialogue is therefore neither easy nor flowing. Nevertheless, gives the impression that he is in touch with the gist of the dialogue even if not wholly master of it. Marked L1 accent.
3	Extremely limited speaker. Dialogue is a drawn-out affair punctuated with hesitations and misunderstandings. Only catches part of normal speech and unable to produce continuous and accurate discourse. Basic merit is just hanging on to discussion gist, without making major contribution to it.
2	Intermittent speaker. No working facility; occasional, sporadic communication.
1/0	Non-speaker. Not able to understand and/or speak.

APPENDIX D

Bartz' Rating Scale

A. Fluency	1	2	3	4	5	6
B. Quality of Communication	1	2	3	4	5	6
C. Amount of Communication	1	2	3	4	5	6
D. Effort to Communicate	1	2	3	4	5	6

The levels of the scales are defined as follows:

A. *Fluency* (similar to the Foreign Service Institute scale)

B. *Quality of Communication*
   1. Speech consists *mostly* of inappropriate isolated words and/or incomplete sentences with just a *few* very short complete sentences.
   2. Speech consists of *many* inappropriate isolated words and/or incomplete sentences with *some* very short complete sentences.
   3. Speech consists of *some* inappropriate isolated words and/or incomplete sentences with *many* very short complete sentences.
   4. Speech consists of *hardly any* isolated words and/or incomplete sentences with *mostly* complete sentences.
   5. Speech consists of isolated words only if appropriate and *almost always* complete sentences.
   6. Speech consists of isolated words only if appropriate, otherwise *always* "native-like" appropriate complete sentences.

C. *Amount of Communication*
   1. *Virtually no* relevant information was conveyed by the student.
   2. *Very little* relevant information was conveyed by the student.
   3. *Some* relevant information was conveyed by the student.
   4. *A fair amount* of relevant information was conveyed by the student.
   5. *Most* relevant information was conveyed by the student.
   6. *All* relevant information was conveyed by the student.

D. *Effort to Communicate*
   1. Student withdraws into long periods of silence, without any apparent effort to complete the task.
   2. Student makes *little* effort to communicate, what he does do is "half-hearted," without any enthusiasm.
   3. Student makes *some* effort to communicate, but still shows a rather "disinterested" attitude.
   4. Student makes an effort to communicate but does not use any non-verbal resources, such as gestures.
   5. Student makes a real effort to communicate and uses some non-verbal resources such as gestures.
   6. Student makes a special (unusually high) effort to communicate and uses all possible resources, verbal and non-verbal, to express himself or herself.

APPENDIX E

The Daiei's English Proficiency Level Breakdown (slightly revised)

(A) Level—International Executive Level

Fluent both in daily conversation and in specific situations, he can be precise in many fields. His high-level command of the language enables him to participate effectively, intelligently, and logically in international conferences, to manage the overseas branch of a company, can conduct reliable negotiations, with perceptive understanding of Western thinking. Can fully comprehend Western speech and can convey the finer nuances as well as colloquial speech. May be competent enough to occasionally act as interpreter in social or formal situation. Can cope with study abroad, alone, e.g., post-graduate work, etc.

(B) Level—International Business Level

Competent and fluent enough to participate actively in conversations with Westerners, can discuss business without too many difficulties. May make some grammatical errors, minor or otherwise, but no serious problems in vocabulary, sentence structures, patterns, pronunciation, etc., in communicating. Can express himself relatively well and can be considered for job abroad. Though some lack of self-confidence may be shown, he should be able to handle most unexpected problems social or job-wise, without due stress. His fluency may not be on the par of the Westerners', but his comprehension and perception is almost up-to-par. Can be considered and is willing for long-term study or job abroad.

(C) Level—Basic Business Level

Can handle uncomplicated business related conversations, capable of most daily conversations on a social level, but fluency is not up-to-par with comprehension. Can express himself, though with some difficulty. Responses may be a little slow due to his concern regarding his English ability, and may be slightly ill-at-ease with Western speech and/or Westerners. Can fulfill overseas job, but may not handle it alone, easily, on a long-term basis. May be able to handle himself linguistically working as a trainee at an overseas branch. May be capable of auditing undergraduate work in an overseas university.

(D) Level—Basic Fluency Level

As he has already acquired basic vocabulary, sentence structures and patterns, he can generally understand daily conversation. Understands and is able to communicate only in very specific situations: meeting or assisting customers or guests, check-in and out of hotels, able to deal with people on a basic level, but not ready for more complicated discussions. Cannot convey complicated opinions and/or information. In a business conversation, can handle only on limited basis. May be able to fulfill his overseas duties if in a group on a short-term basis. Whether he is ready for working overseas may be questionable, and up to the discretion of his employer.

(E) Level—Basic Social Level

Can conduct simple social, basic conversation, greetings, etc. Can comprehend partially what the speaker says, but has difficulty in responding and expressing himself. His practical knowledge of advanced structures or vocabulary is lacking. If a lack of self-confidence is evident, in both himself, his job, etc., and his English, one can anticipate many problems, particularly if sent abroad alone only to be aggravated further by his too limited English.

(F) Level—Elementary Level

If the subjects are limited to simple, daily matters, he can converse, somewhat, though in a highly unskilled way and with frequent pauses, and sometimes or often responds incorrectly. There are still deficiencies in fundamental sentence structures, vocabulary, etc. Can understand to some extent if spoken to slowly, repetitively, and using simple words.

(G) Level—Introductory

Very basic level in English conversation. Can understand simple phrases and sentences only, and if spoken to slowly and clearly. Though restricted to the above level, he can respond, though his response may be long overdue and in a one or two word answer. Exchange of opinions and/or ideas almost impossible. Acquisition of further, intensive study of basic English is a necessity. Real conversation ability at this level is almost nil.

33

Cloze Testing: An Overview

Frances Butler Hinofotis

INTRODUCTION

When this paper was written in 1979, there was growing interest and enthusiasm for the cloze procedure as a measure of ESL proficiency. Many of us who were interested in language testing had begun to look more closely at the cloze procedure and, in doing so, had begun to ask basic questions about the efficacy of using cloze tests to evaluate second language proficiency. The scope of these questions has expanded dramatically over the past few years. For example, focus on establishing the concurrent validity of cloze tests has shifted to the present emphasis on questions regarding construct validity. Concern for establishing the reliability of cloze tests has generated interesting discussion, and continued interest in the multiple choice cloze format prompted a current study at the Educational Testing Service which examines the role of cloze items in the TOEFL.

These and other issues have led to research which is helping us better understand how and why cloze tests seem to function well as language proficiency measures. Many unanswered questions remain, but the acceptance of the cloze procedure by both classroom teachers and language testers suggests that cloze tests are now an established and viable option for language assessment.

THE CLOZE PROCEDURE

The cloze procedure is one of a variety of test formats frequently used today to assess the language proficiency of foreign students studying in the United States. It has received considerable attention since the early seventies when John Oller and his students at UCLA began investigating its potential as an ESL proficiency measure. This paper presents an overview of some of the work that has been done to date with cloze testing in ESL and then suggests how the procedure can be used as a teaching, as well as a testing, tool.

The cloze procedure, devised in 1953 by Wilson Taylor, was originally used for determining the difficulty level of prose passages for native English speakers; the average score of a large group of subjects provided a readability index of passage difficulty level.

The method involves systematically deleting every *n*th word from a prose passage and asking the person tested to supply the missing words in the blanks. The term "cloze" comes from the notion of clozure in Gestalt Psychology and refers to the human psychological tendency to fill in gaps in patterns. The cloze procedure is justified on the assumption that a person who is either a native speaker of the language tested or a reasonably proficient non-native speaker should be able to anticipate what words belong in the blanks given the contextual clues of the passage.

Once a passage is selected, a cloze test is easy to construct, requires a small amount of time to administer, and is relatively easy to score. (Scoring options will be discussed later.) A typical cloze test contains fifty blanks and usually has several sentences intact at the beginning of the passage to provide context. The size of the blanks is kept uniform throughout. Test directions suggest that the person taking the test read the entire passage at least once before beginning to fill in the blanks since the end of the passage may provide clues to blanks at the beginning.

As early as 1959, a small number of ESL teachers began investigating the use of cloze testing procedures as a measure of second language proficiency. But it has only been during the last decade that writers have advocated the use of the cloze technique as an ESL testing measure. Much of the impetus behind cloze testing has been the desire of testers to streamline the evaluation process whenever possible. Multiple choice tests like the TOEFL and other placement and proficiency examinations used at language centers and universities require considerable administration time. The tests are usually composed of a number of subtests, each one attempting to assess a different facet of language ability. In general, the composite score on such an examination is taken as an indicator of the examinee's overall language proficiency. Occasionally, more direct tests such as oral interviews and composition writing are included as part of the examination. But the direct tests also require considerable administration time and skilled evaluators as well.

Support for cloze testing has grown out of studies in which student performance on a cloze test was compared to student performance on a variety of established ESL test types. The major research consideration has been to see how well a cloze test functions in comparison to other more complex tests of second language proficiency. If results obtained on a cloze test are comparable for placement purposes to results on complex examinations, then perhaps the testing process could be simplified. Several studies have suggested that cloze may be a satisfactory substitute for the TOEFL (Pike, 1973), for the oral interview (Pike, 1973; Hinofotis, 1976) and for the composition writing task (Pike, 1973).

The studies addressing this issue have revealed two main trends. The first is that cloze tests correlate highly (.70 or better) with overall criterion measures such as the TOEFL and total placement examinations at such universities as UCLA, USC, and Southern Illinois University (SIU). The second trend is that, in terms of the criterion subtests, cloze tests tend to correlate most highly with those subtests that require high-level integrative skills such as dictation and listening comprehension rather than with discrete items of grammar or vocabulary. Thus, the evidence seems to indicate that a cloze test score may be more representative of general language ability than of single skills.

SCORING METHODS

The topic of preferred scoring method for cloze tests is one that has received considerable attention in the literature. Four major methods have been developed. The two primary methods of scoring are the *exact-word* and the *acceptable-word* scoring methods. Exact-word scoring allows for counting as correct only the exact words which have been deleted from the passage. This method is simple and objective. Acceptable-word scoring, on the other hand, allows for counting as correct any grammatically and contextually appropriate response. Judgment problems that may arise with the acceptable-word scoring procedure can be reduced through careful pretesting with native speakers. From the native speaker response, a list of acceptable answers can be established for use in scoring the tests given to non-native speakers. In addition to providing a list of acceptable answers, pretesting provides a mechanism for catching ineffective items. Occasionally, due to the random deletion process, a blank may be too difficult for even native speakers to fill in accurately. When this occurs during the pretesting stage, the sentence should be modified. If an item is too difficult for anyone to complete correctly, then it provides no information about the students' relative proficiency levels.

A third method for scoring cloze tests was developed in 1968 by Darnell and modified in 1971 by Reilly. It is referred to as the clozentrophy scoring method and provides "a measure of compatibility of a foreign student's language patterns with those of his native English speaking peers" (Darnell, 1968:52). This method is a complex mathematical procedure which involves weighing the non-native speaker responses with native speaker responses. Though results of studies using clozentrophy are impressive, the complexity of the procedure makes it impractical for use in most testing situations.

The fourth scoring method is multiple choice scoring. This procedure involves a slight format change because a *choice* of words is provided for each blank from which the student must select the appropriate response. The distractors (in-

correct word choices which are nevertheless plausible) included with the correct answers are typically obtained by first administering the open-ended version of the test to non-native speakers and then using the most frequent incorrect responses as distractors. The primary advantage of the multiple choice procedure is that tests can be computer-scored or quickly hand-scored with a key.

Of the four methods just described, which one is the best overall scoring method? Several studies have compared exact-word and acceptable-word results to results on criterion measures and the findings have varied. Oller (1972) and Hinofotis (1976) suggest that the acceptable-word scoring method yields more reliable scores and provides more accurate information about ESL proficiency levels. However, Stubbs and Tucker (1974) and Oller et al. (1974) indicate that there seems to be very little difference when the exact-word method is substituted for the acceptable-word method. So the choice between these two scoring methods is not obvious.

In a recent study, Brown (1978) compared all four of the scoring methods described above against the same criterion measure, the UCLA placement examination. The methods were analyzed in terms of the five qualities of a good test—validity, reliability, item facility, item discrimination, and usability. For each of the five qualities, the four scoring methods were ranked on the basis of statistical data. Brown concluded that the decision about which method to use would vary with the testing situation. For example, if usability is the sole concern of a tester, the exact-word method appears preferable. If, however, the best overall cloze test of productive second language skills is desirable, the acceptable-word method seems to be most appropriate. Brown provides a useful table that can serve as a guide for helping teachers and testers decide which method of scoring to use at a given time.

CLOZE TESTING WITH CHILDREN

An emerging area for research in the cloze testing domain involves the use of cloze tests to measure second language proficiency in children. Almost all of the research to date with the cloze procedure has been with adults. However, a few studies, mostly in Canada (Swain et al. 1976; Lapkin and Swain, 1977), have reported promising results in using cloze tests with children. In the Canadian studies, cloze tests were developed in English and French. Galvan and Hinofotis (1979) have been exploring the possibility of using cloze tests to assess the language proficiency gains in English and Spanish of monolingual English-speaking youngsters who are receiving their primary school education entirely in Spanish in Culver City, California. The preliminary results suggest that the cloze procedure is an effective language proficiency measure with children as well as with adults.

CLOZE AS A TEACHING DEVICE

In addition to being a reliable and powerful testing procedure, the cloze format can also be an effective teaching device. In the skill areas of reading and oral communication, the ability to anticipate is part of the natural communication process regardless of mode, and ESL teachers should encourage students to anticipate what is coming and to make educated guesses. The cloze procedure can be an effective means for developing the ability to anticipate because it requires the student to guess.

There are a number of variations in the standard cloze format that are especially well suited for classroom use. Three of these are discussed briefly below to suggest possibilities for modification; however, individual teachers might vary the cloze format to suit the needs of their students.

The first technique (Hisama, 1976) involves having the students listen to a recording of a given passage twice without looking at the same written cloze passage. Then, upon completion of the oral presentation, the students may look at the cloze passage and begin filling in the blanks. This procedure makes a difficult task less threatening by providing the complete passage first. The passage can be tape-recorded or the teacher can read it to the students. If the procedure is being used as a test, the passage should be tape-recorded to assure that the two readings will be identical. This modified cloze is a good exercise in listening comprehension; the results are similar to those involving the standard cloze.

In a teaching-learning situation, it is desirable to increase the amount of information available to the student in order to increase his chances of guessing correctly. One way of doing this with the cloze procedure involves using a dash for each letter of the deleted word and indicating what the first letter is if the letter is a consonant. With this approach, the teacher minimizes the testing aspects and maximizes the teaching ones. Attention is focused on spelling because if, for example, a student omits a double letter from a word that has one, he will have a blank space.

A third modification of the standard cloze procedure simply involves the deletion of specific classes of words such as articles, prepositions, verbs, etc., rather than following a random deletion pattern. This technique can provide a useful review exercise at the end of a grammatical unit. It can also provide diagnostic information at the beginning of a unit.

CONCLUSION

Whether in the future the close procedure will be as widely accepted as other testing formats, remains to be seen. However, cloze tests have proven thus far to be very powerful testing instruments partly because they tap the testees' language proficiency in much the same way natural language situations do. For the same reason, the cloze format deserves continued and increased consideration as a teaching device.

REFERENCES

Alderson, J. C. 1979. The cloze procedure and proficiency in English as a foreign language. *TESOL Quarterly* 13, 2, 219–227. Reprinted in J. W. Oller, Jr. (ed.), *Issues in Language Testing Research.* Rowley, MA: Newbury House.

Alderson, J. C. 1980. Native and non-native speaker performance on cloze tests. *Language Learning* 30, 1, 59–76.

Bachman, L. 1982. The trait structure of cloze test scores. *TESOL Quarterly* 16, 1, 61–71.

———. In progress. Performance of different item types in cloze tests using fixed-ratio and rational deletion procedures.

Bensoussan, M. and R. Ramraz. 1984. Testing ESL reading comprehension using a multiple-choice rational cloze. *Modern Language Journal* 68, 3, 230–239.

Briere, E. J. and F. B. Hinofotis. 1979. Cloze test cutoff points for placing students in ESL classes. In E. J. Briere and F. B. Hinofotis (eds.), *Concepts in Language Testing: Some Recent Studies.* Washington D.C.: Teachers of English to Speakers of Other Languages.

Brown, J. D. 1978. Correlational study of four methods for scoring cloze tests. Master's thesis, University of California, Los Angeles.

———. 1980. Relative merits of four methods for scoring cloze tests. *Modern Language Journal* 64, 3, 311–317.

———. 1983. A closer look at cloze: Validity and reliability. In J. W. Oller, Jr. (ed.), *Issues in Language Testing Research.* Rowley, MA: Newbury House.

Chihara, T., J. W. Oller, K. Weaver, and M. Chavez-Oller. 1977. Are cloze items sensitive to constraints across sentences? *Language Learning* 27, 1, 63–73.

Darnell, D. K. 1968. The development of an English language proficiency test of foreign students using a clozentrophy procedure. Final Report. University of Colorado, Boulder. *ERIC ED 024039.*

Farhady, H. 1983. New directions for ESL proficiency testing. In J. W. Oller, Jr. (ed.), *Issues in Language Testing Research.* Rowley, MA: Newbury House.

Galvan, J. and F. B. Hinofotis. 1979. Development of cloze tests for assessing second language proficiency and reading in children. Paper presented at the Research Colloquium on Bias in Standardized Testing. TESOL Conference, Boston.

Hale, G. A., C. S. Stansfield, J. W. Oller, Jr., and F. B. Hinofotis. In progress. The role of cloze items in the TOEFL. Princeton, NJ: Educational Testing Service.

Hinofotis, F. B. 1976. *An Investigation of the Concurrent Validity of Cloze Testing as a Measure of Overall Proficiency in English as a Second Language.* Doctoral dissertation, Southern Illinois University.

——— and B. G. Snow. 1980. An alternative cloze testing procedure: Multiple-choice format. In J. W. Oller, Jr. and K. Perkins (eds.), *Research in Language Testing.* Rowley, MA: Newbury House.

Hisama, K. 1976. *Design and Empirical Validation of the Cloze Procedure for Measuring Language Proficiency of Non-native Speakers.* Doctoral dissertation, Southern Illinois University.

Lapkins, S. and M. Swain. 1977. The use of English and French cloze tests in a bilingual education program evaluation: Validity and error analysis. *Language Learning* 27, 2, 279–314.

Lynch, B. K. 1982. The effect of content familiarity on cloze test scores in an EFL/ESP context. Master's thesis, University of California, Los Angeles.

Oller, J. W., Jr. 1972. Scoring methods and difficulty levels for cloze tests of proficiency in English as a second language. *Modern Language Journal* 56, 3, 151–157.

———, P. Irvine, and P. Atai. 1974. Cloze, dictation, and the test of English as a foreign language. *Language Learning* 24, 2, 245–252.

Pike, L. W. 1973. An evaluation of present and alternative item formats for use in the test of English as a foreign language. Unpublished manuscript. Princeton, NJ: Educational Testing Service.

Reilly, R. R. 1971. A note on clozentrophy: A procedure for testing English language proficiency of foreign students. *Speech Monographs* 38, 350–353.

Stansfield, C. and J. Hansen. 1983. Field dependence-independence as a variable in second language cloze test performance. *TESOL Quarterly* 17, 1, 29–38.

Stubbs, J. B. and G. R. Tucker. 1974. The cloze test as a measure of English proficiency. *Modern Language Journal* 58, 239–241.

Swain, M., S. Lapkin, and H. C. Barik. 1976. The cloze test as a measure of second language proficiency for young children. *Working Papers on Bilingualism* 11, 32–42.

Taylor, W. L. 1953. Cloze procedure: A new tool for measuring readability. *Journalism Quarterly* 30, 414–438.

Index

940